Personality and Individual Differences

SECOND EDITION

TOMAS CHAMORRO-PREMUZIC

The British Psychological Society | **BPS BLACKWELL**

This edition first published 2011 by the British Psychological Society and Blackwell Publishing Ltd.

Copyright © 2011 the British Psychological Society and Blackwell Publishing Ltd.

BPS Blackwell is an imprint of Blackwell Publishing, which was acquired by John Wiley & Sons Ltd in February 2007.

Registered office
John Wiley & Sons Ltd, The Atrium, Southern Gate, Chichester, West Sussex, PO19 8SQ, United Kingdom. For details of our global editorial offices, for customer services and for information about how to apply for permission to reuse the copyright material in this book please see our website at www.wiley.com.

The right of Tomas Chamorro-Premuzic to be identified as the author of this work has been asserted in accordance with the UK Copyright, Designs and Patents Act 1988.

Library of Congress Cataloging-in-Publication Data

Chamorro-Premuzic, Tomas.
    Personality and individual differences / Thomas Chamorro-Premuzic. — 2nd ed.
        p.   cm.
    Includes bibliographical references and index.
    ISBN 978-1-4051-9927-8 (pbk.)
        1. Personality.   I. Title.
    BF698.C5111 2011
    155.2'2—dc22

                                                            2011002184

A catalogue record for this book is available from the British Library.

Set in 11/12.5pt Dante MT by MPS Limited, a Macmillan Company, Chennai, India
Printed in Great Britain by Bell & Bain Ltd, Glasgow

The British Psychological Society's free Research Digest e-mail service rounds up the latest research and relates it to your syllabus in a user-friendly way. To subscribe go to www.researchdigest.org.uk or send a blank e-mail to subscribe-rd@lists.bps.org.uk

Commissioning Editor: Andrew McAleer
Assistant Editor: Georgia King
Marketing Managers: Fran Hunt and Jo Underwood
Project Editors: Nicole Burnett and Juliet Booker

1006222578

This book is dedicated to the Henry Ford of
of individual differences: Adrian Furnham

Brief Contents

Contents

Preface to Second Edition

Human behavior is complex. Unlike fish or squirrels, we have a big repertoire of behavioral choices at any time. This makes behavior hard to predict. However, the science of individual differences has enabled us to understand how and why people differ, and why these differences matter. Moreover, individual-differences research has produced valid theories to help us predict and understand human behavior. In this book, I have tried to summarize the main accomplishments (and failures) of this research. My hope is that this book will make you a passionate and skilled observer of human behavior, and that this is reflected in your course grade, too.

TCP, London

Preface to First Edition

Although most people would endorse the belief that every individual is unique, explanations of human behavior, whether by psychologists, biologists, economists, sociologists, or anthropologists, tend to assume, often explicitly, that "human nature" is a universal phenomenon.

In fact, only a relatively small number of scientists, even amongst psychologists, have actually devoted their lives to explaining exactly *how* and *why* people are different, whether and how we can *measure* these differences, and what the implications of such differences are.

Some progress has certainly been made, however. In the past 100 years, differential psychologists have developed powerful theories of personality and intelligence, using sophisticated statistical methods to identify the major psychological sources underlying differences in learning, reasoning, emotionality, motivation, and creativity (among other things) between one person and another.

Explanations of what causes these differences remain controversial, particularly when biological factors (i.e., genetic) rather than environmental ones (e.g., education, upbringing, experience) are highlighted. Indeed, politicians, journalists, and educational and religious authorities alike seem more inclined (at least in public) to embrace the belief that "we are all the same," although if this really were apparent, it would probably not be necessary to repeat it so often.

The fact is that individual differences coexist with the ubiquitous human desire to compete with others, which, in turn, is protected by the need to feel superior to others. Thus, saying that two people are different somehow suggests that one is somehow superior (e.g., morally, intellectually, physically) to the other. In the end, judgment matters more than truth. Yet, ignoring the truth has rarely been the best remedy for irrationality.

Finally, this book has been written with specific learning features to enhance its content and make it fully accessible. Each chapter is organized around a series of key ideas, listed in the Chapter Outline at the start of each chapter. From chapter 2, key terms are highlighted in bold on their first significant occurrence in the text, accompanied by a short definition in the margin. Each chapter's key terms are listed at the start of the chapter, and all key terms and definitions are included in the Glossary at the end of the book. At the end of each chapter, the Summary and Conclusions section provides a clear list of bullet points reviewing the chapter's important themes. As well as a consolidated Bibliography at the end of the book, each chapter provides a short list of Key Readings for pursuing a particular area in more detail.

TCP, London

Acknowledgments

Thanks are due to Adrian Furnham, for introducing me to individual differences and being always so inspirational; Jane Powell, for keeping me in the country and rescuing me from bureaucratic exile; Mylene Spence, for her love and support, and, most importantly, her contributions to chapter 5 (clearly a sign of high g); Linda Pring, for sharing my enthusiasm and making academic life more exciting every day she comes to work; to Ian Spence, for his careful assistance proofreading the final manuscript; and to Zdenka Premuzic and Enrique Chamorro, for reasons too obvious and numerous to mention.

I am grateful for Julia Hawkins for her help with the 2nd edition of this textbook.

About the Author

Doctor Tomas Chamorro-Premuzic is a rising star of psychology and a worldwide expert in personality, intelligence, human performance, and psychometrics. He is a Reader at Goldsmiths, Research Fellow at UCL, and Visiting Professor at NYU, and has previously taught at the London School of Economics and the University of Bath. Doctor Tomas has published more than 100 scientific articles and five books, covering a wide range of social and applied topics, such as interpersonal relationships and love, human intelligence and genius, consumer and media preferences, educational achievement, musical preferences, creativity, and leadership, and frequently appears in the media to provide psychological expertise to a wide audience. Doctor Tomas has been the resident psychologist in the past four seasons of *Big Brother* and held regular columns on the show. He is also an active consultant and has worked with the BBC, MTV, Yahoo Music, Sky, Unilever, HSBC, Endemol, and the British Army, and is an associate at Pulse-check and mi-id ltd. Doctor Tomas is a regular keynote speaker for the Institute of Economic Affairs and Intelligence Squared. He has lived in London for the past 10 years.

1 Introducing Individual Differences – From Everyday to Psychological Questions

LEARNING OUTCOMES

BY THE END OF THIS CHAPTER, YOU SHOULD BE ABLE TO ANSWER THE FOLLOWING FIVE KEY QUESTIONS:

1. What are the major topics in individual differences research?
2. How is individual differences research different from other areas of psychology?
3. What are the main goals of individual differences research?
4. What are the main areas of application of individual differences research?
5. What topics of controversy or public debate will be covered in this book?

KEY WORDS

Behavioral Genetics ● Consistent Patterns of Behavior ● Differential Psychology ● Fluency ● Heritability ● Intelligence ● Intelligence Theory ● Longitudinal Data ● Originality ● Taxonomy ● Trait

CHAPTER OUTLINE

1.1 INTRODUCTION

The study of individual differences is part of a well-established tradition in psychology that dates back more than a century. It encompasses several nonobservable or "latent" constructs, such as intelligence and personality, which represent major sources of variation in behavior. This makes individual differences a unique area in psychology. Whereas most psychological theories pretty much assume that everybody is the same and hence attempt to identify the universal aspects of human behavior, individual difference theories are concerned with *differences* between people, or what makes everyone unique.

For example, cognitive psychologists may try to explain the processes underlying short-term memory, whereas intelligence researchers may explain why some people have better short-term memory than others (Deary, 2001). Social psychologists may explain obedience to authority (Milgram, 1963), while personality theories may tell us why some people are more obedient than others (Adorno *et al.*, 1950). Educational psychologists may assess the impact of anxiety on learning (Darke, 1988), whereas personality researchers may assess an individual's likelihood of experiencing anxiety (Zeidner, 1998). Neuropsychologists may test whether recreational drugs, such as Ecstasy, have long-term effects on individuals' level of aggressiveness, whereas differential psychologists may investigate which individuals are more likely to use recreational drugs and why (Zuckerman, 1994).

PHOTO 1.1 *How and why do people differ? That is the key question in individual differences research.*
© PCL/Alamy

The goal of individual difference researchers, then, is to identify the most general aspects underlying individuality and conceptualize a theoretical classification for predicting differences and similarities in human thought, emotionality, and behavior. Simply put, individual difference researchers are concerned with explaining *how* and *why* people are different from one another, and aim to achieve a wide understanding of the psychological processes that determine such differences.

Throughout this chapter, I introduce the topic of individual differences from the perspective of real-life problems. In other words, I use a commonsense approach to explore the longstanding psychological questions that gave rise to the academic area of individual differences that is known as differential psychology. Although the boundaries of differential psychology are yet to be established, the label "individual differences" is normally used to refer to personality and intelligence. Accordingly, half of this book is, in one way or another, dedicated to these variables (see Chapters 2, 3, 5, 6, 7, and 8). However, personality and intelligence are not sufficient to explain differences between individuals, and the study of individual differences involves more than personality and intelligence theories. Thus, this book also covers psychopathology or abnormal behavior (Chapter 4), motivation and mood states (Chapter 9), creativity (Chapter 10), leadership (Chapter 11), and interests (Chapter 12). An overview and basic description of the chapters is presented in Figure 1.1.

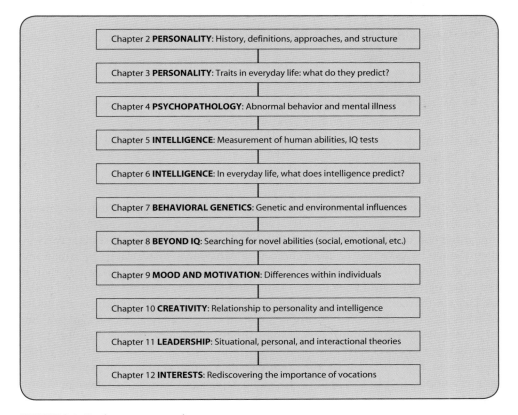

FIGURE 1.1 *Book contents at a glance*

1.2   PERSONALITY: A COMMONSENSE IDEA

Differential psychology aims to explain observable differences between individuals in terms of underlying psychological determinants. This implies that certain psychological differences, in the way people feel or think, lead to manifest differences in the way they act. To this end, differential psychologists collect enormous amounts of information on how people behave, paying particular attention to their consistent behavioral patterns, and establish comparisons between different people. This enables them to predict an individual's likelihood of behaving in one way or another. Take, for instance, the following examples.

> **differential psychology** the academic study of observable differences between individuals in terms of their underlying psychological determinants.

- Chloe is 21 and loves partying. She has many friends and an active social life. She prefers the company of others to studying or reading, and is easily bored staying at home.
- Laura, also 21, spends most weekends at home, reading and writing. She hates loud parties and dislikes talking to strangers. She enjoys spending time with her family and a few close friends, but makes no effort to meet other people.

Now, considering the information you have about Chloe and Laura, try to answer the following questions:

a)   Are you more similar to Chloe or Laura?

b)   What about your friends? Are they more similar to Chloe or Laura?

c)   How would you describe Chloe and Laura?

d)   What else would you need to know about Chloe and Laura to know what they are like?

e)   Why are Chloe and Laura different?

There are several assumptions underlying the above examples. First, we can see that individuals, even of the same age and gender, have different interests (e.g., reading, going out, meeting new people). Second, these interests may determine the way they usually behave; that is, their choices of behavior across a range of situations. Thus, if Chloe loves going to parties, she will be more likely to go partying than if she hated parties (as in Laura's case). Third, and following on from the second point, we can see that an idea implicit in the above examples is that individuals are aware of what they like and dislike. Not only are actors (e.g., Chloe and Laura) aware, but so too are observers (whoever is describing others' behavior). We are therefore faced with two perspectives for assessing differences in behavior; namely, self- and other-observation. Last but not least, the examples suggest that people tend to act in a consistent manner; that is, that there are specific patterns of behavior that are common or frequent in some individuals, but strange or infrequent in others.

In brief, the above examples suggest that:

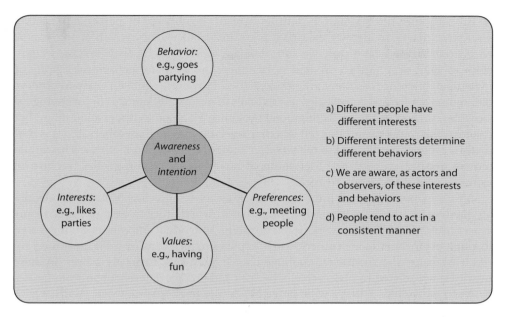

FIGURE 1.2 *Traits as dispositions to act according to interests, values, and preferences*

- Different people may have different interests, values, and preferences.
- People's interests, values, and preferences are reflected in their behaviors.
- We are aware, as actors and observers, of these interests, values, and preferences.
- People tend to act in a somewhat consistent manner across space and time (see Figure 1.2 for a graphical representation of these assumptions).

All of these assumptions are at the center of individual difference research, in particular theories of personality traits, which are the focus of Chapters 2 and 3.

1.3 **DESCRIBING INDIVIDUALS**

Theories of personality conceptualize behavioral differences in terms of wide psychological characteristics or **traits** (see Chapter 2), which are partly inherited and remain relatively stable throughout the lifespan, especially after adulthood. In the same way that we can describe individuals according to their physical characteristics (e.g., tall, blond, slim, fat, pale), personality theorists have attempted to develop a classification or **taxonomy** of individuals in terms of their psychological characteristics (e.g., extraverted, conscientious, agreeable, shy).

trait an internal psychological disposition that remains largely unchanged throughout the lifespan and determines differences between individuals. Examples of traits are extraversion, neuroticism, and agreeableness.

taxonomy a system of classification; in differential psychology, taxonomies identify the major personality or ability factors by which people differ.

In that sense, the first aim in putting forward the concept of personality traits is *descriptive*; that is, to identify the major patterns of behavior by which people can be compared. In physical terms, we can compare individuals by their height, weight, color of hair, skin, and so on, and in fact there are as many behavioral aspects of individual differences as there are physical ones. However, while it is easy to observe differences in physical complexity, it is difficult to observe differences in psychological variables, such as behavior, feelings, and thoughts, let alone to understand them. For instance, we can in most cases tell whether a person is *taller* than others, but it is normally far more complicated to tell whether someone is *shyer* than others. This would require not only systematic observation of how much a person speaks, but also an estimate of their intention to speak.

Another important issue is the *usefulness* of establishing a classification of individuals' tendencies to behave in specific ways; that is, whether it can help us improve any aspect of our lives, such as work or relationships. Individual differences are measured through psychometric instruments such as performance tests or self-report inventories, consisting of standardized multiple-choice questions. Crucially, scores on these measures are related to observable behaviors and predict differences and similarities between individuals across a wide range of settings (e.g., school, work, sports, everyday life). To the extent that such differences can be objectively assessed and related to real-life indicators or behavioral outcomes, they will help us to understand why and how individuals differ. There are several applied implications of theories aimed at providing a broad classification of human behavior, thoughts, and emotionality. Below, and in Figure 1.3, I consider a handful, but there are many others (this is something you may want to think about yourself!).

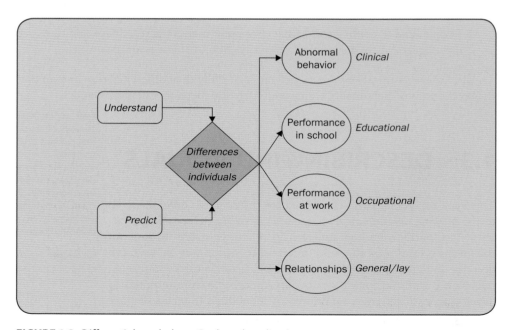

FIGURE 1.3 *Differential psychology: Goals and applications*

Teachers would benefit from knowing whether students have learning difficulties, or whether they are capable of learning so fast that they may become bored with the conventional curricula (see Photo 1.2). Employers would benefit if they could identify the applicants who would be best suited for a job, especially when previous work experience is of little importance. Sports managers would find it useful to know which psychological aspects of their athletes' personality determine whether they perform well at crucial stages of a competition. Army officers would find it useful to predict which recruits are best suited to take the lead in particular missions (assuming, of course, that war is necessary). Police authorities may like to have an accurate understanding of the motives underlying criminal offenders. People in general may want to know which men or women are compatible with them for establishing friendships and business or romantic relationships. Furthermore, knowing what others like and dislike may help us relate to others, and knowing what others are like may lead us to act in specific ways.

As can be seen, there are several avenues by which individual difference research can make an important contribution to our understanding of everyday life problems. No matter how abstract theories of individual differences may seem, the goal is always twofold; namely, theoretical *and* applied. To the extent that differential psychology aims to predict and understand human behavior in a general sense, this area

PHOTO 1.2 *Understanding individual differences is useful beyond theoretical reasons. For instance, teachers may benefit from understanding the causes of individual differences in learning and educational achievement.*
Image courtesy of Nadia Bettega, reproduced with permission.

of research is psychological par excellence. Furthermore, clinical psychology, one of the major areas of psychology concerned with the study and treatment of psychopathology (see Chapter 4), would be virtually undeveloped without the use of personality theories and assessment methods, as these play a vital role in diagnosis and therapeutic strategies.

1.4   ABNORMALITY

Most individual difference constructs are developed from real, everyday settings and refer to normal behavior. In clinical contexts (e.g., hospitals and psychiatric institutions), psychologists were able to develop theories of abnormal behavior and establish the criteria for judging "psychological health," which is the politically correct term for normality. The theoretical foundations of personality research can be traced back to the beginnings of clinical observation (from Emil Kraepelin to Sigmund Freud and Hans Eysenck), while the psychometric foundations of individual difference assessment originated in educational settings, specifically through attempts to identify the major determinants of school success (Alfred Binet in France and Charles Spearman in England). Insofar as individual differences are expressed in terms of both normal and abnormal behaviors, psychopathology and personality are so closely related that the former may be thought of as a subclass of the latter (see Figure 1.4).

Individual difference research has often been criticized for its political and social implications, and psychopathology's notion of "normality" is no exception (Szasz, 1958). Yet any explanation of human behavior will inevitably lead to generalizations involving a more or less explicit notion of typical and deviant behaviors. Just as medical doctors use predefined classifications to judge, for example, whether the

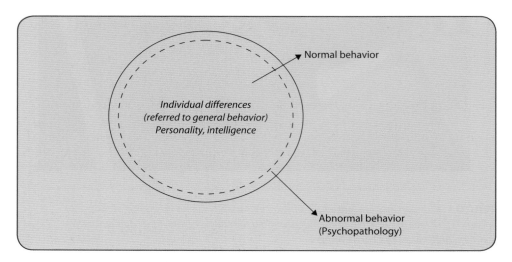

FIGURE 1.4 *Normality and abnormality in differential psychology and psychopathology*

malfunctioning of an organ may have caused painful symptoms, clinical psychologists need to establish whether a certain psychological complexity may be the cause of problematic behaviors in their patients (see Chapter 4). This can only be done by *measuring* levels of a given dimension and *comparing* these scores with predefined, normative levels. For example, whether someone is obese or not will depend on their weight, and whether someone is depressed or not will depend on whatever measure of depression we use. In both cases, though, it is necessary to identify the parameters of normality to determine the signs of pathology.

Unfortunately, the term "normality" is often abused and, what is worse, distorted by prejudiced individuals who may need to confirm their beliefs of self-superiority or normality. This alone, however, should not be a reason to abandon any comparative criteria. Few people would claim that, because fat or slim people experience prejudice, doctors should abandon their criteria for assessing obesity, or stop considering obesity as a health-related variable. The same can be said about psychological measures such as intellectual ability. Just because some individuals make fun of those they consider less bright, psychologists should not refrain from classifying people in terms of their intellectual abilities. It is a mistake to judge the usefulness of anything by the consequences of its misuse. We do not judge the usefulness of cars by the number of road accidents or drink-and-drive cases; we do not judge the usefulness of e-mail by the number of "spam" messages received; and we should not judge the usefulness of personality and intelligence theories by the incapacity (or unwillingness) of certain individuals to understand the meaning of individual differences. Indeed, scientific knowledge can help combat prejudiced and irrational beliefs about others, though much more is needed to succeed in this task. Moreover, individual difference theories should also be able to explain why some people are more likely to be prejudiced than others, and whether this type of behavior can be prevented (Adorno *et al.*, 1950).

1.5 INTELLIGENCE, COMPETITION, AND ADAPTATION

Normality does not always represent the most "desirable" classification. In fact, there are several situations in which you may be better off *distancing* yourself from the norm. For instance, most people have dental caries, but every dentist will tell you that it is healthier and better for your teeth not to have them (indeed, that is one of the reasons many people choose not to go to the dentist). Likewise, most university students in the UK (apologies for bringing this up!) are in debt, but surely those who are would be happier being part of the minority of "abnormal," debt-less students.

Even in psychological terms, it is not always better to be categorized within the majority. One clear example is **intelligence**, or the ability to solve mental problems that are related to performance in school, work,

intelligence the ability to solve mental problems that are related to performance in school, work, and most real-life settings.

and most real-life settings. Both logically and statistically, most people are of average intelligence, though most of us would prefer to be considered among the brightest people in the world; in fact, it is this desire that may largely explain people's negative attitudes toward IQ tests! Even being more intelligent than most people in a country, city, neighborhood, or school would be regarded as a very desirable form of abnormality.

Individual differences in intelligence refer to an individual's ability to solve problems that contribute toward their successful adaptation to the real world. Problems can range from very ordinary, everyday tasks to complex mathematical tests. This ability, which can be broken down into more specific abilities, is measured through a series of standardized tasks where individuals compete for the highest possible scores, pretty much as they compete in real-life settings. Unlike other areas of differential psychology, such as personality, intelligence is not assessed via self- or other-reports but through performance tests. This has made IQ tests a powerful and widely used tool for classifying and selecting individuals in educational and occupational settings (Furnham, 2005; see Table 1.1). But can we truly know whether certain individuals are more intelligent than others, and what does it mean to be more intelligent?

Although these questions will be addressed in depth elsewhere (notably in Chapters 5, 6, and, less directly, 7 and 8), consider the following example:

> On the first day of school, a teacher asks his pupils (about 6 years of age) a number of questions, such as "What time is it now?," "How much do 4 + 7 make?," "What is a zebra?," and "Why is it dark at night?" Some answer all questions correctly, while others do not. Furthermore, some pupils know the answer to some but not other questions, and even among those who get all the answers right, some are able to respond quicker than others, and some provide a more advanced explanation.

We may ask two simple questions: Why are some pupils better at solving the problems, and what are the *implications* of being better or worse at this, apparently very school-like, exercise? Unfortunately, the answers are far from simple and many differential psychologists (and even more laypeople) argue about these issues. While this book should enable you to develop an informed opinion on the validity of IQ tests, most of the controversies surrounding intelligence research are staged at more advanced levels and will only be introduced here.

Returning briefly to the example of the classroom, the question of why some pupils are better at solving the problems may have different answers. One possibility

Table 1.1 *Intelligence: Individual differences in competition and adaptation*

- *Intelligence*, also known as intellectual ability, IQ, cognitive ability, or "*g*" (for general intelligence).
- Measures an individual's ability to *adapt* and *solve problems*.
- Problems can range from *complex* mathematical tests to simple reaction time (RT) and even *practical* tasks.
- Intelligence can be broken down into minor skills or *abilities*.
- It is measured through *standardized* multiple-choice *tests*.
- Individual's *performance* is compared to the *norm* (that of others).
- IQ is a *powerful* and widely used *tool* for classificaton and selection of individuals.
- In educational and occupational settings, it has proven very *effective*.

is that previously acquired knowledge (taught by their parents) may determine pupils' capacity to solve problems. Another possibility is that children differ in their intellectual curiosity, which may lead some but not others to search for the solutions to these problems. On the other hand, one could argue that the ability to tackle these and other similar mental problems successfully is largely dependent on the level of functioning of the brain, implying that most underlying mental processes and operations required to solve such problems may be more genetically than educationally determined.

At the same time, we need to address the question of whether it *matters* that one is better at this kind of problem solving. Looking at the above example, can we really claim that those children who answer more questions are more intelligent than others? This is an important question, in particular considering the extent to which laypeople and experts agree or disagree about what intelligence really is and what intelligence tests really measure.

Regardless of the specific types of ability test we employ, the answer is simple: problems that (a) require mental operations and (b) are related to indicators of competence in real-life settings may be considered a measure of intelligence (see again Table 1.1). By definition, then, intelligence measures are important because they allow us to make predictions about individuals' level of future achievement (i.e., scoring high on mental problem solving will indicate a high potential for success, and vice versa), and compare their performance based on objective problems rather than subjective or biased opinions.

1.6   PREDICTING SUCCESS

It follows from our discussion in Section 1.5 that the central and immediate goal of intelligence research is highly pragmatic; namely, to predict future success and failure. Thus the essence of **intelligence theory** is *to describe, understand, and predict individual differences related to competition and adaptation*. There may be different abilities and individuals may be trained to develop different skills. However, there will always be observable individual differences in performance, and those attributed to differences in mental efficiency, use of verbal and nonverbal information, and knowledge acquisition and retrieval are believed to be the cause of performance differences across a wide range of settings.

> **intelligence theory** describes, understands, and predicts individual differences related to competition and adaptation.

Critics of differential psychology, specifically those opposed to intelligence theory and research, have often argued that classifying individuals in terms of their abilities or level of skills is over-simplistic and detrimental for both the individual and society, and that IQ tests may be used to discriminate against people, particularly economically disadvantaged individuals. It is, however, clear that such "discrimination" would be based on an empirical and rational evaluation of individuals' attributes, which in a sense is the opposite of discrimination. As it is normally understood, discrimination refers to prejudgmental beliefs ("prejudice") and negative attitudes toward an individual on the basis of their membership of a group and disregard for their individual qualities (Aronson, Wilson, & Akert, 2004), not their actual abilities.

Besides, the implications of acknowledging differences in intelligence are not necessarily negative. First, this may help us recruit the best people for each job, resulting in an economic gain for society (or would you rather recruit those less capable of doing the job?). Second, the individual would benefit from a more accurate and unbiased identification of their intellectual strengths and weaknesses, as teaching methods – and education in general – could be tailored to suit those who need it most and ultimately compensate for lower levels of intelligence. In fact, schools around the world tend currently to group children according to their age, assuming that age is the universal marker for intellectual development. Yet not all children from the same age group are equally able to learn and acquire knowledge. Third, it would be impossible to understand the processes underlying individual differences in cognitive ability if we did not have a way of measuring these differences in the first place; or could you, for instance, think of a way of understanding global warming without measuring temperature? Last but not least, differential psychology, as any other science, should be concerned with understanding its object of study rather than the consequences of its findings, whatever these are.

Another issue is that, although even the most enthusiastic IQ researchers accept that intelligence tests are not perfect, they are far superior to most alternatives, such as self-reports, interviews, biodata (a formalized, scored application form), or references (i.e., letters of recommendation). When the first IQ test was developed in France about a century ago (see Chapter 5, Section 5.3.3), the aim was to create an objective and effective tool to distinguish between fast and slow learners, with the intention of helping rather than punishing the latter (for instance by providing them with additional teaching and tutoring). More importantly, it was clear at this stage that *teachers'* judgments of pupils' abilities were rather inaccurate, mostly because they were biased against children with disciplinary rather than intellectual problems.

Today, we could think of similar examples in the workplace and educational settings. When it comes to recruiting new staff or students, it is better to focus on what individuals can actually do than on who they may know (e.g., references, recommendations, networking), what they "may" have done in the past (CVs typically exaggerate previous achievements), and which groups (e.g., gender, race, religion) they belong to. Moreover, critics of IQ testing would probably accept that relying on a subjective interview (especially if it is unstructured) is by no means a better alternative to IQ tests. Figure 1.5 depicts some of the most widely used predictors of performance in occupational and educational settings.

Thus, the present book will deal, among other things, with the measurement of those individual differences identified as determinants of future success. Such differences are at the heart of intelligence theories and measurement, and will be the focus of Chapters 5 and 6.

1.7   BORN DIFFERENT?

If the first and most spontaneous observation we make about ourselves is that we differ from one another, the hypothesis that these differences may be inherited rather than acquired or "learned" must come very close to third. Thus the second, albeit often implicit, assumption is that we resemble our own parents much more than

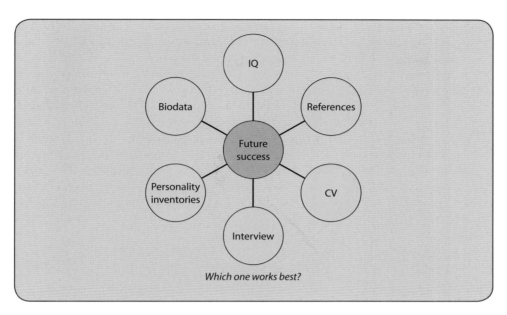

FIGURE 1.5 *Different predictors of future success (including IQ)*

those of others. This assumption is arguably enhanced by the fact that individuals tend to be *physically* more alike if they are from the same family, though, as noted, physical similarities tend to be more noticeable than psychological ones. For example, it is more difficult to know whether a person is brighter than others than whether a person is darker than others.

While it is apparent that physical traits, such as ginger hair or prominent cheekbones, may be the result of inherited genetic information, psychological similarities may also arise from environmental influences, such as parental rearing, formal education, and relationships with friends. We are thus faced with a dual problem, namely:

- Identifying psychological similarities between members of the same family (for instance in personality and intelligence).
- Figuring out whether these similarities are the result of genes or mere exposure to the same environment.

Thanks to a combination of technological advances and the meticulous efforts of gathering **longitudinal data** (i.e., multiple measures of the same group of individuals, termed a cohort, across extended periods), in particular from twins, recent years have seen unprecedented progress in the study of the biological basis of individual differences, an area known as **behavioral genetics**. These findings are examined more closely in Chapter 7. As will be seen, there is compelling evidence for the idea that both personality and intelligence are influenced by genes; that is, that large aspects of our

longitudinal data
multiple measures of the same group of individuals, termed a cohort, across extended periods.

behavioral genetics the study of the biological basis of individual differences.

PHOTO 1.3 *The nature versus nurture debate has been a central part of individual differences research for many decades. In particular, differential psychologists have attempted to assess the heritability of main personality traits and intelligence.*
Image courtesy of Tomas Chamorro-Premuzic.

personalities and abilities are inherited (via genes) from our parents and previous ancestors (grandparents, great-grandparents, and so on).

On the one hand, the resemblance between biological parents and their children is striking enough to be noticeable even for laypeople. Thus it is often pointed out that someone is more similar (psychologically as well as physically) to their mother or father. This is not merely a descriptive observation but also a causal inference attempting to explain an individual's behavior. However, even if there *is* a similarity between parents and children, it would be difficult to prove that the underlying processes leading to this causal relationship are purely related to genetic factors. The question, then, is whether we are like our parents because of shared genes or because they *taught* us to be like them (see Figure 1.6).

Brothers and sisters are not always alike, are they? Likewise, some people seem to be completely different from their parents. Furthermore, some individuals are similar, but genetically unrelated, which makes it quite unreasonable to argue that the basis of individual differences is solely genetic. For example, adoptive children may be similar to their adoptive parents despite not sharing any genetic information.

Although the implications of a biologically based theory of personality and intelligence are problematic, particularly with regard to educational settings, serious

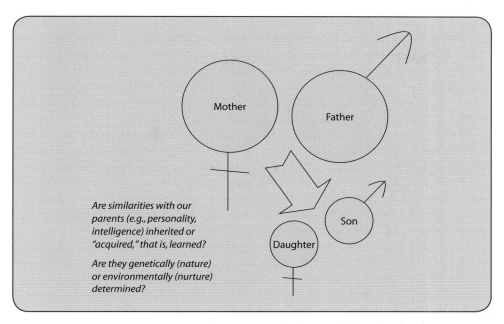

Are similarities with our parents (e.g., personality, intelligence) inherited or "acquired," that is, learned?

Are they genetically (nature) or environmentally (nurture) determined?

FIGURE 1.6 *Genetic and environmental determinants of individual differences*

research is needed to address the extent to which individual differences are inherited. If the first step of differential psychology is to *identify* the major aspects by which people differ, the second must be to understand the *causes* of these differences; that is, where they arise. Indeed, the question of whether differences are inherited (through nature) or acquired (through nurture) may represent the fundamental step toward an understanding of individual differences.

Unfortunately, findings on the **heritability** (the extent to which differences are due to genetic factors) of individual differences, particularly intelligence, have not always been reported in an objective, unbiased manner. Rather, the biological basis of individual differences has often been exploited to justify discriminatory claims – typically, of one group's superiority over another – or, in other cases, refuted by the equally ideological claims of those attempting to persuade the public that "we are all the same," at least when born. The truth, as we know it, is that people *are* different and nobody, not even identical twins, is born the same as

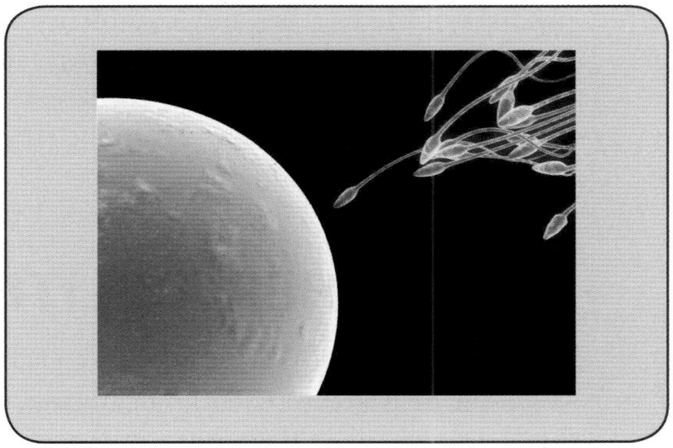

PHOTO 1.4 *Genetics play a role in determining individual differences.*

© Sebastian Kaulitzki/Shutterstock.com.

heritability the extent to which differences between individuals are due to genetic factors.

anyone else. More importantly, it should be noted (and this will become clear in Chapter 7) that even if there is robust statistical evidence for the heritability of individual differences, this does not imply that the environment (i.e., education, learning, rearing, nurture) has no influence on our personality or intelligence. On the contrary, identifying the degree to which traits are biologically influenced has helped us understand the degree to which nurture may influence individual differences. In short, then, both views are not incompatible but complementary.

In the same way that athletes may inherit a favorable condition for sports from their ancestors (such that a previous history of exercise, good nutrition, and a healthy lifestyle in general may lead to preliminary advantages), individuals may also inherit a specific physiological complexion that may predispose them to behave in certain ways more than others. Even if these processes were clearly outlined, however, it does not imply that factors other than genes may not play a role in shaping these general behavioral tendencies, preferences, and abilities.

Just as no person would ever become a professional athlete if they remained locked in a room all their life ("waiting for the genes to do the work"), no person would ever be capable of solving mathematical problems if they had never been taught mathematics, even if their parents were geniuses in that discipline. Likewise, no one would be able to play the piano if they had never seen a piano in his life, even if their father were Johann Sebastian Bach (1685–1750), who counted five accomplished musicians among his children (and many who were not). To paraphrase a basic information technology metaphor, you may have the fastest computer processor but few data stored on the hard drive, or, conversely, you may have a slow processor but invest the necessary time to store and load plenty of information on the hard drive. The question of nature versus nurture thus does not demand an "all-or-nothing," "either/or" type of response, but a probabilistic estimate of the impact of one of a number of factors, as well as interactions among them.

1.8 OTHER ABILITIES

Whether or not the psychological causes of everyday behavior are inherited is certainly important, but another relevant question is what *kind* of abilities should be considered essential. As will be seen in Chapters 5, 6, and 7, differential psychologists have tended to focus on abilities associated with school or university performance, such as verbal, mathematical, and logical abilities. Although one of psychology's most compelling findings is that these apparently abstract and decontextualized abilities tend to predict performance on a wide range of tasks, in the last 20 years psychologists have devoted much attention to the identification of other, less academic, and more practical abilities.

Those who support the cause for the identification of novel intelligences tend to be critical of the meaning and usefulness of traditional ability measures such as IQ tests. Famous psychologists, such as Gardner (1983), Goleman (1995), and Sternberg (1997), have all authored bestselling books against IQ tests, putting forward alternative "abilities" instead (in fact, their fame is largely a result of this enterprise). Although evidence for the predictive power of IQ tests is irrefutable (see Chapters 5 and 6), the idea that *not only* academically able individuals have the potential to succeed in everyday settings seems to reflect the opinion of an increasing number of differential psychologists, and even more laypeople. A typical example representing these "anti-IQ" views is that of "geeks" (see Photo 1.5) or "nutty professors," who are obviously intelligent in the traditional or academic sense of the word but appear to lack the necessary social or emotional skills for behaving "intelligently" in everyday life (e.g., interacting with others, being on time, catching the right bus).

On the other hand, most people seem capable of quickly citing several examples proving that low-IQ individuals or those who did badly at school can be extremely successful in their professions or occupations. Sadly, these examples are often used to "console" individuals who have done poorly in school and carry implicit messages such as "don't worry if your grades are terrible because *something else* is necessary to succeed in life." While nobody would claim that IQ scores are the only indicator of a person's potential for future achievement, the literature has shown that they *do* work rather well, suggesting that intelligence *does* matter.

Whether other abilities – such as the abilities to relate to people, manage emotions, control impulses, and make practical decisions – are more important is a challenging question. Unlike traditional abilities, which refer to problems that are well defined and have single correct answers (for instance,

PHOTO 1.5 *Are you really smart or just a geek? Is there a difference between the two? How intelligent are high IQ scorers? These questions are discussed in Chapter 8.*

Image courtesy of Nadia Bettega, reproduced with permission.

the capital of England is London and *only* London; the next number in the series 200, 400, 800 can *only* be 1600), novel abilities seem more reliant on subjective judgments and refer to ill-defined problems (see Table 1.2).

Table 1.2 *A Comparison between traditional and novel conceptions of intelligence*

Traditional intelligence (IQ)	Novel intelligences (Beyond IQ)
Good at: • Solving mathematical problems • Solving logical problems • Spatial ability tests • Expressing ideas verbally • School and university exams	*Good at:* • Relating to others (social) • Managing emotions (emotional) • Knowing oneself (intrapersonal) • Everday life problems (practical) • Gaining recognition (successful)

For example, "What should I do to make my boss like me?" is a question for which no correct answer can be identified, at least not for all possible scenarios. Thus, even if the ability to influence others is as important as the ability to solve mathematical problems, the question is how we can *measure* this ability and, having done so, whether it contributes to the prediction of performance *beyond* established IQ tests. These issues are discussed throughout Chapter 8.

1.9 VARIABILITY AND CHANGE: MOTIVATION AND MOOD STATES

consistent patterns of behavior those aspects of the individual that characterize the way they usually behave and make them different from others.

Although differential psychology is largely based on the study of **consistent patterns of behavior** – that is, those aspects of the individual that characterize the way they usually behave and make them different from others – it would be foolish to believe that people always behave in the same manner.

We are not robots or programmed computers who simply behave according to rigid, predetermined tendencies, and our responses to situations and the way we react to different environmental stimuli (e.g., death of a friend, winning the lottery, listening to a "moving" song) may vary from time to time. Furthermore, even in the absence of salient events, our mood and motivation fluctuate, leading us to act in very different ways. Let us examine the following examples:

- You wake up with a hangover after a late (and expensive!) night out. You have a headache and plan to sleep late because it is your day off, but . . . your mother knocks on your door early in the morning to get you out of bed. Even if you are usually a kind, calm, and stable person, it is likely that you will behave in an aggressive and rude manner.

- You are usually talkative and friendly and enjoy meeting others . . . but your boyfriend has just told you he has been sleeping with your best friend. Although you feel upset and annoyed, it is your birthday party and you have to make an effort to be a good host. Will you be looking forward to chatting to friends and meeting new people?

- At school, the arts teacher shows pupils how to paint in the impressionist style; although none of the students has previously been trained in this technique, some may be more talented than others and pick up the method more rapidly. On the other hand, some students are also more enthusiastic than others, and seem to try harder, discontented with their performance until they match the high standards set by the teacher. Why are some pupils more enthusiastic than others, and does their motivation vary from time to time?

The above examples suggest that behavior can be affected by a number of factors other than psychological traits or abilities. While it is important that differential psychology clarify the major issues underlying differences *between* individuals, we must also consider variations *within* individuals, which will cause stable traits, and even abilities, to be poor predictors of behavior.

Thus you may be a pretty relaxed and friendly person but still lose your temper when annoyed or in a bad mood. Traits such as agreeableness and psychoticism (see Chapter 2) may inform us of a person's typical level of aggressiveness but say little of their likelihood of reacting aggressively in a specific situation. Likewise, a person's level of intelligence or ability to think logically may be a poor predictor of performance if that person's motivation or level of effort is low. Figure 1.7 represents the relationship between stable traits and motivational and mood states as predictors of behavior. Whereas motivation and mood are influenced by trait variables, they are also affected by situational factors. Thus behavior is a consequence not only of internal disposition as personality characteristics, but also of situational factors.

In brief, personality traits are aggregated measures of behavioral tendencies and refer to "typical" performance, whereas ability tests measure "maximal" performance and thus indicate the best an individual can do (Cronbach, 1990/1949). Yet neither traits nor ability tests take into consideration the situational variables that affect an individual's behavior. Even when you are taking an IQ test or a university exam, your performance may not reflect your "true" ability because you may be worried, anxious, or

PHOTO 1.6 *A creative illustration of creativity*
Source: Greg Schurman MPA, www.blootung.com

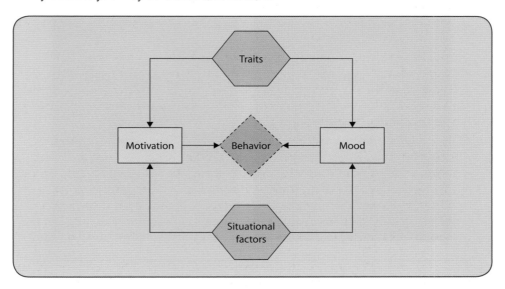

FIGURE 1.7 *Traits, motivation, mood, and situational factors*

distracted by other thoughts. Likewise, the aggregated score represented by most personality traits will not explain and fully predict an individual's behavior. It is therefore important to consider contextual factors when interpreting behavior, even if we are generally accurate at predicting people's behavior.

The effects of situational factors will be dealt with in Chapter 9, which is dedicated to the study of mood and motivation. Theories of motives, drive, and affect posit that, even though personality and intelligence are helpful in predicting individual difference outcomes, it is often necessary to interpret behavior at the state rather than trait level. Thus not every expression of behavior should be interpreted as a manifestation of a trait. Some behaviors are representative of traits while others are not, and personality is a general, not an absolute, disposition to act in specific ways.

1.10   CREATIVITY

The final chapters of this book deal with three constructs that have remained relatively unexplored in the history of individual differences, particularly in comparison with personality and abilities. These concepts are creativity, leadership, and interests and have a longstanding tradition in psychology, although they have also been considered to be outside individual difference research. Below, I anticipate some of the salient issues concerning individual differences in creativity.

It has often been suggested that creativity plays an important role in determining cultural and social landmarks. Why individuals feel the need to create and how they

PHOTO 1.7 *What does it take to compose like Mozart (left) or paint like Van Gogh (right)?*
© The Gallery Collection/Corbis.

are able to do so are largely unaddressed questions. Thus differential psychologists have tried to understand:

- Why some individuals are more creative than others.
- How we can measure these differences.
- Whether it is possible to predict creative achievement.

Two assumptions are generally made regarding individual differences in creativity. The first is that creativity is different from intelligence, implying that people may be bright but not creative, or creative but not bright. The second is that creativity involves certain personality characteristics, such as nonconformity or eccentricity, and even psychopathological traits, such as schizotypic thinking (see Chapter 4). Thus it has often been pointed out that artists and geniuses tend to be psychologically disturbed in one way or another.

Methodologically, the measurement of individual differences in creativity has posed an ongoing problem for psychometricians. Given that creativity is defined primarily in terms of novel and original ideas, it is difficult to predetermine which responses are better than others, not least because of individual differences in ratings of creative products. When critics told Mozart that one of his piano sonatas had "too many notes," the composer replied that it had "as many notes as it should." While Mozart enjoyed some fame in his lifetime, the artist Vincent van Gogh lived a poor, anonymous, and unsuccessful life, tortured by insanity and unable to deal with his contemporaries. Yet nobody today would think of telling Van Gogh that he should have added more water to his paint.

The examples of Mozart and Van Gogh – and there are many more, of course – show that creative outcomes, particularly within the arts, cannot be *objectively assessed* in the same way as cognitive performance or knowledge. On the other hand, personality alone is not sufficient to explain creative achievements. The fact that several leading creators lived eccentric lives and behaved in unusual or abnormal ways does not explain the quality of their work. Even if creative talent and "lunacy" may coexist, psychopathology does not cause exceptional creations. Besides, creativity should not be thought of merely as an artistic concept, but may also be related to scientific discoveries as well as everyday problem solving.

The relationship of personality and intelligence with creativity is complex. Leaving this relationship aside for a moment, and assuming that creativity is predominantly independent of other established individual difference constructs, the two salient approaches that have marked the scientific approach to creativity are **fluency** and **originality**. Fluency refers to the quantity of ideas or occurrences, while originality refers to the uniqueness of an idea or response compared to the responses of a larger group or norm. When combined, both concepts can be expected to give a fairly good indicator of creativity, as inventive or creative individuals tend to have *many* as well as *novel* ideas. A common test of creativity requires individuals to "name all the things they can do with" an object (e.g., a chair, stick, or pen) and computes both the total number of responses and the number of unique or original responses (see Figure 1.8 for an example).

fluency the ability to produce a large quantity of creative ideas.

originality whether an idea or response is unique.

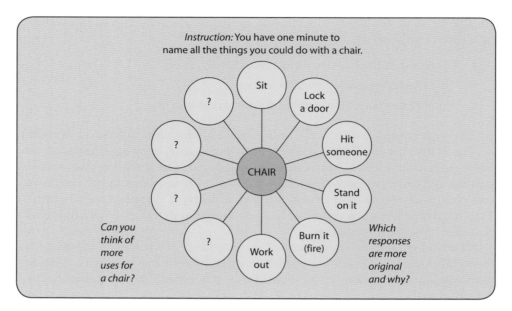

FIGURE 1.8 *Fluency and originality as indicators of creativity or creative responses*

To the extent that fluency and originality are related, we can hypothesize that having many ideas is a requirement for having new ideas. Thus, creative individuals are not suddenly surprised or inspired by the odd occasional idea but are permanently producing, examining, and applying ideas, and it is within the context of this "ideational storm" that great and original ideas are created. An apple falling on the head of Isaac Newton (1642–1727) may have inspired him to conceptualize the theory of gravity, but would only have caused a bump on most people's heads.

1.11   LEADING THE WAY

Another topic that has been historically associated with individual differences is *leadership*, although leaders have been studied more frequently in social rather than in differential psychology, as well as in other social sciences such as politics, history, and economics. In recent years, differential psychologists seem to have rediscovered the construct of leadership and a variety of novel theories have emerged (see Figure 1.9).

Individual differences in leadership have been examined primarily in terms of leadership "emergence" (i.e., who becomes a leader and why) and "effectiveness" (i.e., who leads successfully and who does not). Because of its applied implications – leadership plays a role in economic, organizational, educational, and political contexts – there has been widespread historical interest in predicting the emergence and effectiveness of leaders. This begs the question of whether leadership is more dependent on personal than on situational variables; in other words, are leaders born or made? For example, some people may have leadership qualities within them but "miss" the historical opportunities or situational events to become leaders.

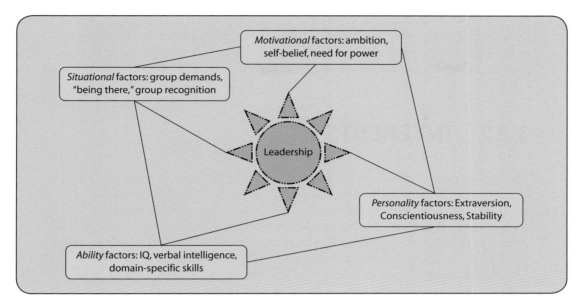

FIGURE 1.9 *What explains leadership?*

Another question is whether leadership may be dependent on specific domains, such that leaders may only be suitable to guide others in some activities (e.g., football tournament, peace march, achieving economic stability) but not others (e.g., scientific theory, political reform, artistic movement). On the other hand, some theorists have preferred to regard leadership as a *process of influence* and thus posit that there are no stable dispositions that are constitutive of leadership, but rather that there are simple relational paths between the leader and a group in a given situation.

Traditional approaches to leadership have supported the historical view of leaders as *great men* (see Section 11.2.2 in Chapter 11), regarding them as individuals who stand out from the crowd because of their atypical personality attributes, beliefs, or skills. In that sense, leadership may be an outcome of other individual difference constructs. Whether individual difference research is able to predict leadership is questionable, as most studies consist of retrospective examinations of leadership in relation to other personality or ability measures. However, some longitudinal studies shed light on the importance of various psychological factors as determinants of leadership. As with many other areas of differential psychology, recent conceptualizations of leadership have attempted to bridge

PHOTO 1.8 *President Barack Obama, a modern icon of leadership.*
Olivier Douliery/ABACA USA/PA

the gap between situational and personal factors in order to account for interactions between traits and contextual variables. In Chapter 11, a comprehensive review of leadership is presented, with the goal of addressing these and other central questions about leaders' personality, influence methods, and abilities.

1.12   INTERESTS

The final chapter of this book deals with individual differences in *interests*. This area of research attempts to explain vocational and career choices, often through a combination of ability and personality variables. Some have regarded interests as an essential aspect of individuals' personality because interests affect individuals' motivation, skills, and knowledge acquisition. Measures of interests are thus important to predict real-life outcomes, such as educational or occupation performance.

One fundamental question concerns the stability of interests throughout the lifespan. Whereas an individual's level of interest seems to fluctuate from time to time (as explained by mood and motivation research), their type of interests remains relatively stable throughout the life course. Thus some people have scientific interests, such as math, chemistry, or biology, whereas others have humanistic interests, such as literature, fine arts, and music. Classifying interests is almost as complex as classifying personalities, and much psychometric research has attempted to identify the major categories underlying individual differences in interests (see Figure 1.10). Just as with leadership, recent theories of interests seem particularly promising with regard to integrating different areas of individual differences and putting them in context. Thus they provide a comprehensive and detailed picture of how situational and personal variables may converge to explain some of the most important aspects of individuality.

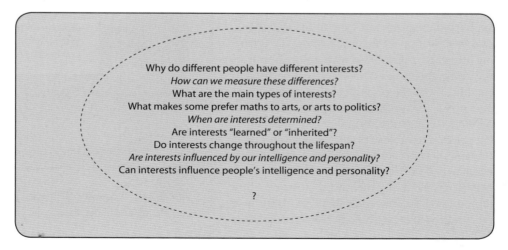

Why do different people have different interests?
How can we measure these differences?
What are the main types of interests?
What makes some prefer maths to arts, or arts to politics?
When are interests determined?
Are interests "learned" or "inherited"?
Do interests change throughout the lifespan?
Are interests influenced by our intelligence and personality?
Can interests influence people's intelligence and personality?

?

FIGURE 1.10 *Some questions regarding individual differences in interests*

2 Personality, Part I

LEARNING OUTCOMES

BY THE END OF THIS CHAPTER, YOU SHOULD BE ABLE TO ANSWER THE FOLLOWING FIVE KEY QUESTIONS:

1. What are the common definitions of personality traits?
2. What is the difference between personality traits and types?
3. How are individual differences in personality commonly assessed?
4. What are the major personality taxonomies?
5. What is the Big Five model of personality?

KEY WORDS

Biopsychological • Correlation • Dispositional Approach • Factor Analysis • Five Factor Model • Gigantic Three • Idiographic Paradigm • Lexical Hypothesis • Meta-analysis • Neuropsychology • Nomothetic Paradigm • Psychometrics • Reliability • Situational Approach • Taxonomy • Trait • Validity

CHAPTER OUTLINE

2.1   INTRODUCTION

As with many topics in psychology, definitions of personality are more complex than everyday uses of the term. Psychologists are often faced with the difficult and seemingly unnecessary task of providing theoretical definitions for words that appear not to need one. And yet it would be difficult to investigate any concept with rigorous scrutiny without first defining the variable properly. Moreover, in psychology it is important to "define away" personality from lay connotations of the concept. Accordingly, a scientific approach to the study of individual differences should begin by giving a clear definition of personality, beyond the discrepancies of pre-scientific knowledge and the lay uses and misuses of what is usually understood by the term.

The Latin root of the word "personality" is *persona*, which means "mask" and is also the origin of the word "person" in several languages, such as English, Spanish, and German. Thus the classic connotation of personality is associated with the "discovery" of the real causes of individuals' feelings and thoughts, expressed or projected through the mask of behavior.

In plain English, "personality" is used to refer to several different but often overlapping ideas. Consider, for instance, the following examples:

(a) Martin is a good friend of mine, but we have very different *personalities*.

(b) I don't find Jade very attractive, but she has an amazing *personality*.

(c) If there is one thing I can't stand in people, it's their lack of *personality*.

(d) Zoe and Sarah have such different *personalities*, I sometimes wonder whether they really are sisters.

(e) Joe has such a difficult *personality*, I don't understand how you get along with him.

Now consider the following examples, which, despite not mentioning the word "personality," seem to be referring, albeit implicitly, to similar concepts:

(f) Jennifer and Paul are very different, and yet they seem so compatible.

(g) I would like you to accept me as I am.

(h) Clever people always get along with each other.

(i) Mrs. Jones is a very reliable customer. I'm very surprised she forgot to send us the check.

As can be seen, personality seems to have various connotations, some more interchangeable than others. In the first set of examples, the term is used to emphasize: (a) general styles and preferences; (b) positive internal attributes; (c) passiveness or lack of initiative – i.e., conforming to the norm; (d) genetically influenced psychological similarities; and (e) bad temper – i.e., not getting along with others.

In the second set of examples, where personality is only implicitly referred to, we can see how (f) individuals are compared on the basis of apparent preferences and styles (they can be similar or not); (g) people use implicit autobiographical descriptions – i.e., "as I am" (self-descriptors that include the word "I" are typically representative of personality characteristics; Schultz & Schultz, 1994, p. 8); (h) people can be rated as clever or not; and (i) we are surprised when people act in an unexpected or different than usual manner. But how do these uses compare with the psychological definitions of personality?

2.2   OVERVIEW AND APPROACHES

In psychology, "personality" has been used to refer to different and often opposite ideas. Indeed, some definitions seem to question the very idea that personality exists. Let us examine a few examples of approaches to the conceptualization of personality.

One major distinction is that between nomothetic and idiographic paradigms. The **nomothetic paradigm** assumes that individual differences can be described, explained, and predicted in terms of predefined criteria or attributes. Accordingly, each individual's personality can be represented in terms of different levels of the same "vectors," just as every city in the world can be geographically located by using the same coordinates of latitude and longitude. Conversely, the **idiographic paradigm** assumes that every individual is unique, to the extent that we cannot describe two different people by means of the same concepts or terms. Instead, different "vectors" or coordinates would be needed to account for each person's individuality. Idiographic approaches are at the heart of psychodynamic theories, such as psychoanalysis (see Chapter 4), and emphasize the unique nature of individuals' life experiences. In this book, they will be mentioned only briefly.

Another distinction is that between **dispositional** and **situational approaches**, which differ on the basis of whether they conceptualize personality in terms of largely invariable and consistent *dispositions* to act, think, and feel in similar ways relatively independently of the context or, rather, in terms of a series of largely unrelated *states* that are predominantly a function of situational factors. Strictly speaking, the notion of personality as it refers to the essential and unchanging characteristics of an individual (what makes us who we are) is encompassed only by the dispositional approach to personality, whereas situational approaches are pretty much in conflict with the idea of a continuity or "essence" describing every individual. Instead, situational approaches argue that individuals behave differently in different contexts, making it impossible to capture the "core" psychological attributes of a person. (The antithesis between situational and dispositional approaches is further discussed in Section 2.5.)

Dispositional approaches are nomothetic in nature (i.e., they describe different people using the same terms), and can be further divided into *traits* and *types* according to whether they assess personality dimensions in an ordinal (traits) or categorical

nomothetic paradigm assumes that individual differences can be described, explained, and predicted in terms of predefined attributes.

idiographic paradigm assumes that individuals are unique and that two different people cannot be described using the same concepts or terms.

dispositional approach views personality in terms of consistent and unchanging dispositions to act, think, and feel, regardless of context.

situational approach views personality in terms of unrelated states or behaviors determined by situational factors.

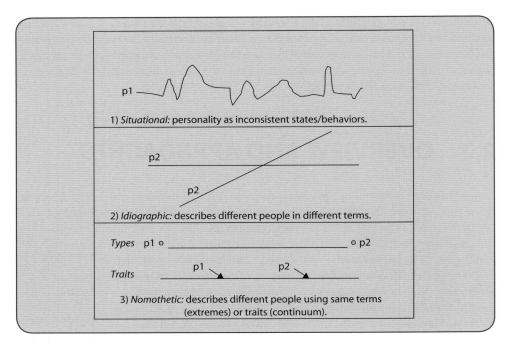

FIGURE 2.1 *Situational (states), idiographic, and nomothetic (types and traits) approaches to the study of personality (p = person)*

(types) fashion. For example, saying that someone is introverted or extraverted is a *categorical* distinction, whereas saying that someone's Extraversion score is 49 is an *ordinal* or *quantitative* distinction. Figure 2.1 presents a graphical depiction of the different approaches to the conceptualization of personality, which are further discussed in Chapter 3.

In this chapter I shall focus on the dispositional approaches to personality, which have represented the state-of-the-art approach to the study of individual differences for the past 50 years (Hogan, Johnson, & Briggs, 1997; Matthews & Deary, 1998; Pervin, 1996). It should also be noted that in published studies researchers do not always adhere to the technical distinctions explained above, although the term "personality" is increasingly employed to refer to personality traits.

2.3   DEFINITION OF PERSONALITY TRAITS

Personality **traits** have been defined as a "dynamic organization, inside the person, of psychophysical systems that create a person's characteristic patterns of behavior, thoughts, and feelings" (Carver & Scheier, 2000, p. 5). Another widely quoted definition is that of "an individual's characteristic pattern of thought, emotion, and behavior, together with the psychological mechanisms – hidden or not – behind those patterns" (Funder, 1997, pp. 1–2). These comprehensive and up-to-date definitions refer to internal and causal processes that account for an individual's typical manifestations of behavior, emotion, and thought in everyday life.

> **trait** an internal psychological disposition that remains largely unchanged throughout the lifespan and determines differences between individuals. Examples of traits are extraversion, neuroticism, and agreeableness.

In simple terms, then, we could define personality as that which makes a person different or similar to others. As Carver and Scheier (2000, p. 5) note,

> there are certain universal characteristics of the human race and particular features of individuals. We all for example experience stress, and the elevated cortisol that goes with it, and we all suffer the immune suppressive effects thereof. But each of us is unique too.

That means that some of us may be particularly likely to experience stress during university exams, while others may do so when meeting new people or traveling by plane. Furthermore, some of us may perform best under pressure, while others may only do well under relaxed conditions. What makes you anxious?

Research on personality traits deals with the fundamental differences and similarities between individuals. Beginning with a general classification or **taxonomy** of the stable and observable patterns of behavior, it goes on to assess the extent to which individuals differ on these variables or traits. Its goal is to predict differences in a wide range of outcomes, from simple reaction time to academic performance, stress, health, salary, and even happiness! Thus personality traits refer to an individual's description in general and provide a universal framework to compare individuals and account for everybody's individuality at the same time.

> **taxonomy** a system of classification; in differential psychology, taxonomies identify the major personality or ability factors by which people differ.

From the very first known attempts to identify major individual differences and elaborate a taxonomy of personality (usually attributed to the ancient Greek classification of temperaments discussed in Section 2.4) to the current differential and behavior-genetic approaches, personality theorists have attempted to do the same thing; namely, to identify, assess, explain, and predict systematic differences and similarities between individuals, looking for the fundamental and general causes of human behavior.

Personality psychologists have aimed to identify the main dimensions by which people differ, test that these dimensions remain relatively stable over time, and explain the etiological basis or causes of these differences between individuals (Cooper, 2002). In that sense, all they have attempted to do is to prove that personality, as defined by the stable and general attributes that explain an individual's predisposition to act in one way or another, exists (see Table 2.1).

However, rather than asking whether personality exists or not, it is important to determine whether the concept of personality traits is useful; that is, whether it will help us predict and understand human behavior and provide any scientific knowledge about the individual. This is the aim of this chapter.

Table 2.1 *Personality traits as psychological determinants of consistent behaviors*

WHAT ARE PERSONALITY TRAITS?
- *General* descriptions of individuals.
- *Internal* characteristics of the individual.
- *Causal* determinants of repetitive behaviors.
- Explain and predict systematic *deferences* as well as *similarities* between individuals.

3 EXAMPLES
A) *Pete is a selfish guy.*
B) *Lea is a happy girl.*
C) *Seven is incredibly obsessive.*

2.4   HISTORY OF PERSONALITY

Like most sciences, the history of personality dates back to ancient Greece. It is generally accepted that the first theory of personality derived from Hippocrates (460–370 BC), a Greek philosopher who is also credited with the invention of medicine. However, it was another Greek physician, Galen (130–200 AD), who documented – and probably further developed – this theory, which is thus referred to as the Hippocrates / Galen personality or temperament theory.

The Hippocrates / Galen theory was based on a classification of the major types of temperament as a function of both psychological and biological differences. As seen in Section 2.2, traits and types represent the dispositional approach for classifying and describing individuals' patterns of behavior, thought, and emotionality. While traits conceptualize personality variables in terms of a continuum, types refer to an "all-or-nothing" distinction between two opposite extremes of a bipolar variable (see Figure 2.2). In terms of types, then, you are either extraverted or introverted, pretty much in the same way as you are either pregnant or not.

The Greek classification of personality types assumed that biological differences (in physiological complexion) would cause behavioral differences (in psychological complexion), an idea that many centuries later would set the foundations of scientific psychology. In the late 19th century, William James (1842–1910), one of the founders of modern psychology, referred to this physio-psychological interaction as one of the major principles of psychology.

The four different types of temperament in Hippocrates / Galen's theory described biological differences in the level of specific fluids of the human body, or "humors," which would, in turn, determine individual differences in everyday behavior (see Photo 2.1 and Figure 2.3).

The *sanguine* temperament described enthusiastic, optimistic, and cheerful individuals, satisfied with life and generally enjoying good physical and mental health. This type of temperament was believed to be related to high levels of blood supply or the "strength" of the blood itself (*sanguis* is the Latin word for blood). Sanguine

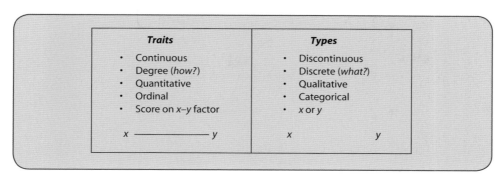

Traits	*Types*
• Continuous	• Discontinuous
• Degree (*how?*)	• Discrete (*what?*)
• Quantitative	• Qualitative
• Ordinal	• Categorical
• Score on *x–y* factor	• *x* or *y*
x ——————— *y*	*x* *y*

FIGURE 2.2 *Dispositional approaches to personality: traits and types*

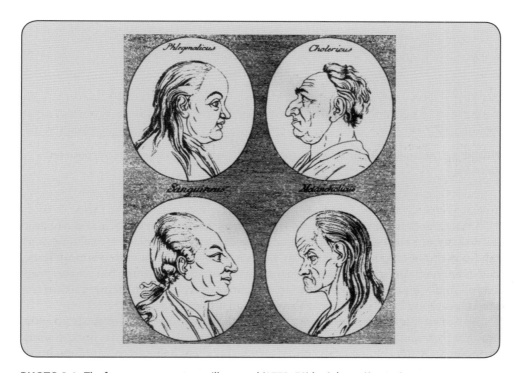

PHOTO 2.1 *The four temperaments as illustrated (1775–78) by Johann Kaspar Lavater.*

Source: http://en.wikipedia.org/wiki/Four_humors

people, then, are usually in a good mood, tend to be happy, and are also fun to be with (I wish I were more sanguine sometimes!).

A second type of temperament, the *choleric* type, referred to aggressive, volatile, and temperamental individuals. This type of temperament was believed to be caused by high levels of "yellow bile," a chemical released by the gall bladder during digestion. Although this hypothesis no longer stands, the description of irritable, emotional, bad-tempered individuals can still be applied to many people (including myself!).

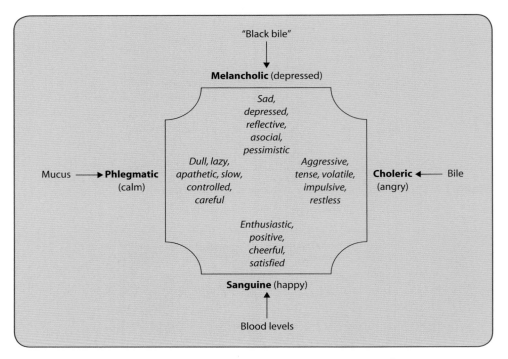

FIGURE 2.3 *Ancient Greek classification of humors and temperament types (after Hippocrates and Galen)*

A third temperament, the *phlegmatic* type, described calm, relaxed, and slow-paced individuals and was originally attributed to the "phlegm" or mucus of the lungs typical during flu or lung infections. Again, nobody today would think that boring, static, and unenergetic people have larger quantities of mucus in the lungs, but we can probably all think of people who may be representative of a phlegmatic temperament (for obvious reasons, I will not mention any particular cases here).

The fourth type of temperament, the *melancholic* type, as you may guess from the everyday connotation of the term, described sad, depressed, reflective, and pessimistic individuals. The biological origin of melancholy was believed to be the malfunctioning of an organ called "black bile," but this idea was probably abandoned after the Middle Ages. As will be seen in Chapter 4, melancholia is nowadays associated with abnormal rather than normal personality (see Section 4.7.2 for a modern psychopathological approach to depression). It is also important to note that, while we may all feel sad or "melancholic" at times – especially after experiencing upsetting events like a relative's or friend's death – melancholic individuals tend to feel sad or empty most of the time.

Despite the pre-scientific nature of the ancient Greek theory of temperament, several aspects of Hippocrates/Galen's classification had a significant impact on eminent intellectual figures of the modern era, notably the German philosopher Immanuel Kant (1724–1804). Influenced by the Greek theory of temperament, Kant published

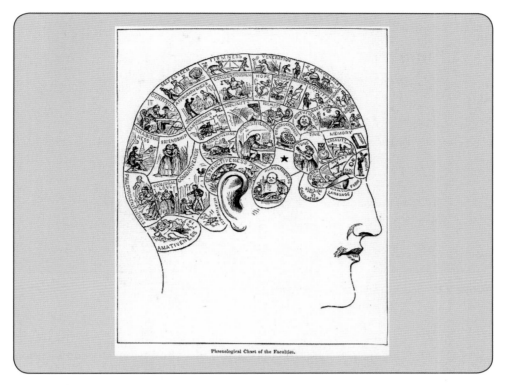

Phrenological Chart of the Faculties.

PHOTO 2.2: *Phrenologists believed that the shape of our skulls can reveal our personality and abilities*

Source: From People's Cyclopedia of Universal Knowledge (1883); http://en.wikipedia.org/wiki/Phrenologyy.

his *Anthropology from the Pragmatic Viewpoint* (1796), echoing the classification of the four types of temperament as an accurate description of individuality.

In the early 1800s, an entire discipline that attempted to link physical and psychological traits was developed by Franz Joseph Gall (1758–1828). This discipline was called *phrenology* and studied the shape of human physical parts such as the skull (see Photo 2.2). Phrenologists even modulated children's heads in an attempt to raise their intellectual capabilities! As obscure and unethical as this technique may seem today, phrenology was a highly fashionable science in 1830s England, where there were almost 30 societies dedicated to it. Although phrenology no longer constitutes a respectable scientific discipline, modern psychophysiological research provided evidence for established links between most brain regions and specific psychological processes.

The most notable psychologist to be influenced by the Greek classification of humors was Hans Eysenck (1916–97), who developed a biologically based personality theory for the assessment of temperament dimensions that were quite similar to those proposed by Hippocrates / Galen. These dimensions are *Neuroticism* and *Extraversion*, and still persist in most personality models today, though sometimes under different labels. Figure 2.4 represents the theoretical overlap between Eysenck's two early dimensions of temperament and the ancient classification of Hippocrates / Galen.

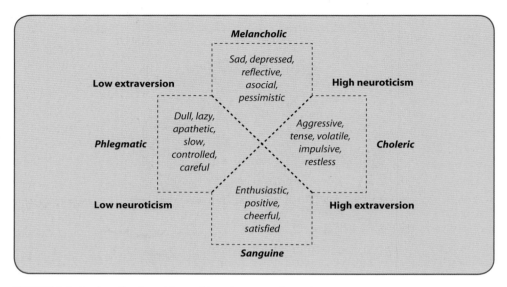

FIGURE 2.4 *Ancient Greek and Eysenck's early personality traits*

As shown in Figure 2.4, Eysenck conceptualized Extraversion as a combination of choleric and sanguine temperaments (now I feel relieved, as this trait also represents some of the more positive aspects of my personality!), while Introversion would represent both phlegmatic and melancholic types. The other major trait in Eysenck's theory was Neuroticism/Emotional Stability, which could be represented by a combination of melancholic and choleric types, while Emotional Stability would represent a mix of sanguine and phlegmatic types.

Other dispositional approaches conceptualizing personality in terms of types have included William Sheldon's (1899–1977) somatotype theory, Carl Jung's (1875–1961) psychoanalytical types, the Type A and Type B personality theory, and Block's (1971) personality types. Because of their relatively minor importance with regard to established trait taxonomies and wider personality theories, these alternative typologies will be discussed only briefly.

Sheldon's *somatotype theory* associated psychological dispositions and patterns of behavior with external – that is, physical – features. According to Sheldon's theory, there were three major personality types; namely, *endomorph*, *mesomorph*, and *ectomorph*. Endomorphic individuals tend to be sociable, peaceful, tolerant, and are generally overweight. Mesomorphic individuals are assertive, proactive, vigorous, and muscular. Ectomorphic people, on the other hand, are usually insecure, sensitive, and quiet; they are delicate and have weak muscles too. Although there has been much speculation about the causal processes by which psychological features may be influenced by physical traits and vice versa, Sheldon's typology remains largely anecdotic and is commonly regarded as a late exponent of early phrenological paradigms. Furthermore, independent researchers have failed to replicate Sheldon's typology, suggesting that his evidence was largely flawed.

A more influential theory of personality types is that of Carl Jung, a psychoanalyst and famous student of Sigmund Freud. Combining philosophical and mythological theories, Jung developed a complex psychoanalytical paradigm – second only in impact to that of Freud – to explain the personal process of individuation by which the historical events of upbringing interact with universal psychological determinants, often subconscious forces. Although Jung's theory, as did Freud's (see Section 4.4.1 in Chapter 4), remained mostly untested and was rarely supported by empirical evidence beyond case studies or mythological allegories, its personality taxonomy is represented by the *Myers–Briggs Type Indicator* (MBTI), a questionnaire that assesses extraversion–introversion, intuition–sensing, thinking–feeling, and judgment–perception as the four major functions of temperament.

PHOTO 2.3 *Carl Jung (1875–1961)*

© Mary Evans Picture Library/Alamy.

Extraversion–introversion, a trait that will be discussed as part of several systems throughout this book, refers to the extent to which individuals seek external (i.e., people) or internal (i.e., inner space / own thoughts) stimulation, respectively. *Intuition–sensing* describes the degree to which people rely on their inner judgment or empirical observation, respectively. *Thinking* refers to rational decision making, while *feeling* characterizes individuals who are driven by their emotions rather than by rational thought. Finally, *judgment* refers to a premeditated, organized lifestyle (planning ahead), while *perception* best describes individuals who avoid planning in advance, preferring spontaneity and improvisation. The MBTI has been widely used in occupational settings, notably personnel selection.

Personality types have also been conceptualized in terms of *Type A* and *Type B* personalities. Individuals classified as Type A tend to be proactive, driven, achievement oriented, and very impatient. They are usually "workaholics" and are at greater risk of suffering coronary diseases such as heart attacks. Conversely, people with Type B personalities tend to be relaxed, calm, and easygoing; they live a slow-paced life and are rarely at risk of coronary illness. As may be noted, this classification of personality may only refer to certain aspects of the individual, but has nonetheless proven important in clinical settings and health-related domains.

Finally, Block's (1971) *personality types* assess the extent to which individuals are well adjusted (e.g., flexible and adaptable in interpersonal interactions) or maladjusted. In turn, maladjusted types can be further divided into over-controlling (uptight people who are difficult to deal with) or under-controlling (impulsive, risk-taking, and aggressive individuals who tend to lack awareness and respect for social norms). Although critics have pointed out that Block's personality types are useful only for classifying a relatively small section of the population, notably bright and educated white males from upper-middle-class backgrounds, in recent years there has been a renewed interest in Block's typology (particularly in the *European Journal of Personality*).

Despite their limitations and over-simplistic nature, typological theories are still useful to identify major aspects of individual differences and establish general comparisons between individuals. Furthermore, as will be seen in forthcoming sections, several of the dominant personality trait theories are compatible with the typological taxonomies discussed above, and the apparent discrepancies between categorical and ordinal variables are often merely an artifact of statistical assessment methods.

2.5 PERSONALITY TRAITS AND STATES: DISPOSITIONAL VS. SITUATIONAL APPROACHES

Before concerning ourselves with the salient taxonomies of personality traits, it is important to understand the rationale underlying the trait approach to personality. One way of doing this is to look at the distinction between situational and dispositional models in more detail. Traits represent implicit associations between observable behaviors and internal dispositions or preferences to act. These associations are indicative of an individual's consistent patterns of behavior and determine differences between rather than within individuals; that is, why different people feel, think, and behave in different ways. On the other hand, differences within individuals – that is, why the same person may feel, think, and act differently in different situations – have been conceptualized in terms of states or situational approaches. States refer to sporadic or ephemeral acts or behaviors lasting perhaps no longer than a few hours, or even occasional moods such as joy or anger.

PHOTO 2.4 *People adjust their behavior to the situation, such that the same person will seem to have quite different personalities in different contexts (e.g., work and holidays).*

Images courtesy of Tomas Chamorro-Premuzic.

Some personality theorists, like Raymond Cattell (1957), argued that biological instincts, such as hunger, sex drive, and aggression, should also be considered part of an individual's personality, because they motivate or cause behavior. Although the study of motivation and mood states has constituted a separate area of research in psychology, these factors are important determinants of individuals' behavior and are thus discussed in Chapter 9. Furthermore, because individuals do not always behave in the same manner, it is often essential to understand the causes of behavior in terms of states rather than traits.

For example:

(a) If you had been wandering in the heat of the Sahara desert for three days without water, it would be irrelevant to know whether you are extra-verted or introverted to predict whether you would be likely to ask the first stranger you encounter if he or she had any water.

(b) The happiness you may express after being informed that you have won the lottery may not reflect the fact that you may be a melancholic or neurotic person.

(c) If you are a football fan and go to the stadium to support your team, you may have noticed that your behavior is not the same in that situation as it is, say, when you are being interviewed for a job!

In these three cases, traits, which reflect how you generally act, may not really predict states, which determine how you will behave "there and then." Moreover, traits are only predictive of behaviors to the extent that they can influence psycho-logical states and predispose an individual to action. As such, traits and states are not incompatible interpretations of personality but two different conceptual levels of explanation. For many years, however, psychologists were at odds over this concep-tual distinction.

The debate between dispositional and situational theories peaked in the late 1960s, notably after the publication of a **meta-analysis** (analysis of previous studies) by Mischel (1968), which reported an aggregated **correlation** of $r = .30$ between traits and behavior, though this value was later revised and increased to $r = .40$ (Funder, 2001). Accordingly, personality traits would on average account for as little as 16 percent of the variance in behavior (this value is calculated by squaring the correlation between two variables). If, however, we consider the 50 percent likelihood of predicting behavior by chance (e.g., will p do x, yes [50 percent] or no [50 percent]?), the 16 percent of *additional* variance accounted for by traits provides useful infor-mation for predicting behavior in a given situation. Traits may also determine the choice of a situation and are expressed across different behavioral patterns, constituting better predictors of general than specific behaviors. For example, measures of trait anxiety will be more accurate to predict whether an individual will experience stress during the next five years than during a specific exam.

meta-analysis a review of previous research that involves statistical analyses combining the results of many studies.

correlation the extent to which two variables, e.g., traits and behavior, are related; a correlation of +1 indicates a perfect positive association, a correlation of −1 a per-fect negative association.

Although the debate between situational and dispositional theories represents an important phase in the development of personality theory, it has been pointed out

psychometrics literally, measurement of the mind; the theory and measurement of psychological variables such as IQ (intelligence quotient) and personality via tests or questionnaires.

that such a debate "can at least be declared 98 percent over" (Funder, 2001). Thus, rather than further emphasizing this point, let us briefly examine how states and traits are associated in the **psychometric** assessment of personality traits. For those interested in the dispositional vs. situational debate, I recommend Brody's (1988) review of the topic.

Focus Point 2.1 is an example of a personality questionnaire. Figure 2.5 graphically represents the trait of Extraversion as derived from a set of observable and correlated states; that is, *smile, touch, move,* and *talk.* These states can be observed across different situations and interpreted as a consequence of Extraversion, which is the common underlying or latent factor. Accordingly, traits are conceptualized or inferred from a series of related states.

validity (psychometric) the extent to which a test measures what it claims to measure.

reliability the extent to which a given finding will be consistently reproduced on other occasions.

Although trait models have been questioned on the basis of the poor **validity** and **reliability** of specific questionnaires (Block, 1971), studies with reliable instruments provide sufficient evidence for the invariance of major personality traits across the adult lifespan. These studies have examined not only self- but also other-reports of personality traits and concluded that there is little change in the major

FOCUS POINT 2.1   AN EXAMPLE OF A PERSONALITY QUESTIONNAIRE: THE TEN-ITEM PERSONALITY INVENTORY (TIPI)

Instructions: Here are a number of personality traits that may or may not apply to you. Please write a number next to each statement to indicate the extent to which *you agree or disagree with that statement.* You should rate the extent to which the pair of traits applies to you, even if one characteristic applies more strongly than the other.

1 = Disagree strongly
2 = Disagree moderately
3 = Disagree a little
4 = Neither agree nor disagree
5 = Agree a little
6 = Agree moderately
7 = Agree strongly

I see myself as:

1. _____ Extraverted, enthusiastic.
2. _____ Critical, quarrelsome.
3. _____ Dependable, self-disciplined.
4. _____ Anxious, easily upset.
5. _____ Open to new experiences, complex.
6. _____ Reserved, quiet.
7. _____ Sympathetic, warm.
8. _____ Disorganized, careless.
9. _____ Calm, emotionally stable.
10. _____ Conventional, uncreative.

For information on this scale visit Sam Gosling's website: http://homepage.psy.utexas.edu/HomePage/Faculty/Gosling/scales_we.htm

Source: Gosling, S.D., Rentfrow, P.J., & Swann, W.B., Jr. (2003). A very brief measure of the big five personality domains. *Journal of Research in Personality, 37,* 504–28.

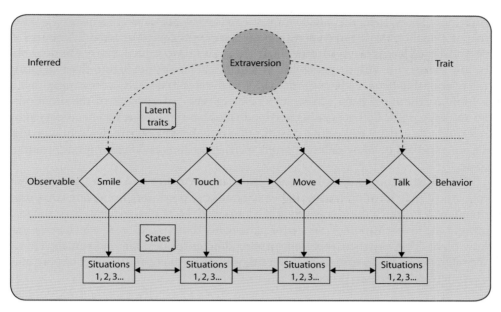

FIGURE 2.5 *Traits and states psychometrically and conceptually represented*

personality dimensions throughout an individual's life, particularly after the age of 30. For example, Costa, McCrae, and Arenberg (1980) report correlations for males of $r > .70$ over a 6- to 12-year period (notably for Neuroticism and Extraversion), and similar correlations have been reported for female samples, though it has also been noted that, in late adulthood, women tend to become more confident, dominant, and independent (Helson & Moane, 1987). Overall, personality traits show little change throughout the lifespan, which means that at the age of 80 (if we ever get there) we are still essentially the same person we were at the age of, say, 22 . . . just a lot older.

Further evidence for the stability of traits has been provided by behavior-genetic studies (see Chapter 7), which suggest that there is a substantial genetic influence on personality traits. This influence persists even in adulthood and undermines the importance of environmental factors, which only seem to play a minor role in personality development (Cooper, 2002). Thus Costa and McCrae (1988, p. 861) have argued:

> Many individuals will have undergone radical changes in their life structure. They may have married, divorced, remarried. They have probably moved their residence several times. Job changes, layoffs, promotions, and retirement are all likely to have occurred for many people. Close friends and confidants will have died or moved away or become alienated. Children will have been born, grown up, married, begun a family of their own. The individual will have aged biologically, with changes in appearances, health, vigor, memory, and sensory abilities. Internationally, wars, depressions, and social movements will have come and gone. Most subjects will have read dozens of books, seen hundreds of movies, watched thousands of hours of television. And yet, most people will not have changed appreciably in any of the personality dispositions measured by these tests.

After decades of theoretical debate on the nature of personality structure, psychometric evidence has led most researchers to conceptualize individual differences in personality in terms of traits rather than states. As I have argued above, this does not by any means rule out the possibility of situational factors mediating or moderating the relationship between latent traits and actual states. It does, however, mean that it is more useful to predict a wider range of behaviors – irrespective of the situation – by assessing traits. Differences between individuals can therefore be encompassed by referring to a general descriptive classification of behaviors, where different individuals are expected to show different levels of traits as well as different predispositions to act.

As will be seen, the idea that latent traits are the major and most general determinants of individual differences in behavior has not produced immediate consensus on the way in which these traits should be assessed. Most of the debate has centered around the identification of the major personality dimensions (e.g., which ones, and how many) that may best represent general differences between individuals. Hence the reference to three, sixteen, or five traits, though virtually any number of personality dimensions has been proposed.

2.6   EYSENCK'S GIGANTIC THREE AND THE BIOLOGICAL BASIS OF PERSONALITY TRAITS

Eysenck was born in Berlin, Germany, on 4 March 1916. In the 1930s he moved to England because of his strong opposition to the Nazi party. He went on to become a prominent psychologist by developing a biological theory of personality.

Gigantic Three theory derived from Eysenck's investigations on personality and individual differences, which posits three major personality dimensions – Neuroticism, Extraversion, and Psychoticism – for classifying individuals.

The **Gigantic Three** derives from Eysenck's systematic empirical investigations on personality and individual differences (Eysenck, 1947, 1957, 1967, 1991) and is one of the major theories and instruments for assessing personality traits. This theory posits that there are three major dimensions according to which every individual can be classified, namely *Neuroticism*, *Extraversion*, and *Psychoticism* (the latter only added to the taxonomy in 1976).

Eysenck provided several psychometric instruments to assess the Gigantic Three, including the original *Maudsley Medical Questionnaire* (MMQ), the *Eysenck Personality Inventory* (EPI), and the more recent *Revised Eysenck Personality Questionnaire* (EPQ-R) (Eysenck & Eysenck, 1985) and *Eysenck Personality Profiler* (EPP) (Jackson *et al.*, 2000), which also include a Lie scale to detect extreme responses or "faking good." Eysenck's inventories are self-report questionnaires comprising items about typical behavior (preferences and dispositions), which are answered on a two-point Likert-type scale (yes/no). Thus people report whether they agree or not with a variety of statements, indicating whether these are representative of the way they usually behave.

FOCUS POINT 2.2   HANS EYSENCK

In 1947, he conceptualized a two-dimensional model of personality based on Neuroticism and Extroversion. A third dimension, Psychoticism, was added to his theory in the late 1970s (based on the work he conducted with his wife, Sybil).

One of the major strengths of Eysenck's theory was that it provided a detailed account of the biological causes of personality. For example, he proposed that Extroversion was caused by variability in cortical arousal: Introverts are more cortically aroused, or naturally "stimulated" than Extroverts, such that they will seek to avoid external stimuli compared to Extroverts. Conversely, extroverts will seek out more stimulating activities as their arousal is low.

The major alternative to Eysenck's three-dimensional model of personality is the Big Five model (Costa & McCrae, 1985), which makes use of the following five broad traits: Openness to experience, Conscientiousness, Extraversion, Agreeableness, and Neuroticism. Although in recent years this theory has received more support than Eysenck's, the models are compatible, because Eysenck's P dimension can be broken down into low Aggression and Conscientiousness and high Openness.

Eysenck was the founding editor of the journal *Personality and Individual Differences*, and

PHOTO 2.5: *Hans Eysenck (1916–1997)*

authored over 50 books and over 900 academic articles. He was one of the most industrious scholars in individual differences and worked until his final days. Eysenck died in London on 4 September 1997, of a brain tumor.

Source: http://en.wikipedia.org/wiki/Hans_Eysenck

Theoretically, the three dimensions assessed by the EPQ-R are *orthogonal* or independent. This means that high scores on, say, Neuroticism do not provide any information about scores on the other two traits, and vice versa. Thus, you can be stable and extraverted, or stable and introverted, and so on. Accordingly, the description of an individual would not be fulfilled unless all three personality traits are assessed. At the same time, the Gigantic Three model implies that no more than these traits are needed to describe individuals, though an increasing number of researchers have argued otherwise (see Sections 2.10 and 2.11). A brief description of high and low scorers on each trait is presented in Table 2.2.

Neuroticism refers to an individual's level of emotionality and tendency to worry, be moody, touchy, and anxious. Thus the Neuroticism/Emotional Stability trait is a

Table 2.2 *Eysenck's Gigantic Three (characteristics of high and low scorers)*

	Neuroticism	**Extraversion**	**Psychoticism**
High	Anxious, moody, depressed, pessimistic, tense, shy, low self-esteem	Energetic, sociable, lively, active, assertive, confident, dominant	Unempathetic, creative, sensation seeking, aggressive, cold
Low	Stable, positive, calm, optimistic, confident, relaxed	Asociable, passive, slow, reflective, introspective, unconfident	Altruistic, rational, patient, conformist, organized, down-to-earth, empathic

Source: Based on Eysenck & Eysenck (1991).

continuum of upset and distress. People high on Neuroticism are generally anxious, stressed, pessimistic, and fearful and tend to have lower self-esteem. Conversely, people low on Neuroticism are emotionally stable, calm, and optimistic.

Extraversion assesses the degree to which individuals show a tendency to be talkative, outgoing, and energetic. Thus the Extraversion/Introversion factor represents a continuum of sociability, liveliness, and dominance. Extraverts tend to enjoy the company of others and express their feelings and emotions; they are energetic and optimistic, outgoing and confident. Conversely, introverts (low Extraversion scorers) are resilient to interpersonal contact, reserved, and quiet; they tend to be shy and lack confidence.

Psychoticism refers to an individual's level of conformity, aggressiveness, and feelings for others. High Psychoticism describes emotionally cruel, risk-taking, impulsive, and sensation-seeking individuals. They are *sociopathic*, which means that they show little respect for social norms, and are psychologically unattached to others. Conversely, low Psychoticism (known as tender-mindedness) describes caring, responsible, and socially driven individuals who are more likely to conform to given rules than to defy them.

It is important to understand that Table 2.2 describes *extreme* levels of each trait. Personality traits, like intelligence (discussed throughout Chapters 5 and 6), are normally distributed in the population. This means there are only about 10 percent of individuals who would fall into the extreme levels of scores. On the contrary, most individuals would score in the middle 50 percent of scores, implying that the majority of people are neither extremely neurotic nor extremely stable, and so forth. However, extreme cases, like case studies, are often helpful to grasp the meaning of concepts and, in this case, what personality traits represent. Let us therefore spend a few minutes on Activity Box 2.1.

Do you have any friends who are prototypically high or low on any of the three personality dimensions? How about famous people/celebrities? Actors? Musicians? Can you think of any profession that is representative of extreme scores on any of these traits (e.g., salespeople may be typically extraverted, artists may tend to be more psychotic, academics seem more introverted or neurotic). Finally, do you think there are any important aspects of personality not included in the Gigantic Three classification? If so, which ones?

2.7   SELF-REPORT INVENTORIES

The logic underlying the assessment of individual differences in personality traits follows an approach that blends common sense with probabilistic inference. The first two assumptions are:

- We know ourselves relatively well (certainly better than we know others and, consequently, better than others know us).
- Different people behave in different ways.

These are commonsense assumptions, though psychoanalysts, for instance, have long claimed that the major determinants of individuals' behavior are unconscious or unknown.

Instead of asking people direct questions about themselves, such as whether they are neurotic, extraverted, or psychotic, self-report inventories comprise indirect questions; namely, items about different preferences, tendencies, and behaviors (see Table 2.3).

Self-report items such as those in the EPQ-R refer to preferences or behaviors that individuals can evaluate straightforwardly, without much analysis of the motives or theories underlying their personalities. Once sufficient statements are answered, the data are analyzed or "reduced" through a statistical technique called **factor analysis**. This technique, which nowadays can be applied in seconds using computer software packages such as SPSS, determines which questions tend to be answered in similar ways. Factor analysis requires a large number of respondents to answer a large number of questions. There are in fact predefined rules of thumb that determine the number of participants per question needed, usually about five, though samples should always exceed $N = 100$. Let us exemplify this technique through a simple scenario.

factor analysis data-reduction technique where relationships between a large number of variables can be reduced to a relationship among fewer underlying factors.

Table 2.3 *Sample items for the Gigantic Three Personality traits (EPQ-R)*

Trait	Sample items
Neuroticism	"Does your mood often go up and down?" "Are you often troubled about feelings of guilt?" "Are you a worrier?"
Extraversion	"Do you tend to keep in the background on social occasions?" "Can you usually let yourself go and enjoy yourself at a lively party?" "Do you enjoy meeting new people?"
Psychoticism	"Would you take drugs which may have strange or dangerous effects?" "Do you enjoy hurting people you love?" "Have you ever taken advantage of someone?"

Source: Based on Eysenck & Eysenck (1985).

Suppose you want to find out whether someone likes classical music. There are several ways you could do this, for instance:

(a)   You could ask the person whether she likes classical music.

(b)   You could ask the person how much she likes classical music.

(c)   You could ask friends or relatives of the person whether she likes classical music.

(d)   You could hide in the person's house and observe how often she listens to classical music.

(e)   You could phone the person's credit card company to ask for a balance showing how much she spends on CDs and opera tickets.

(f)   You could test how much the person knows about classical music.

We can rapidly spot complications with each of the assessment techniques proposed above. Asking the person whether she likes classical music would be problematic if she decides to lie, and in certain circumstances there may be motives for her to lie – for instance if the question is being asked by a potential employer who happens to love classical music! Asking how much the person loves classical music would not only expose the same problem (faking/lying), but also different levels of subjective interpretation by which different people assess their preferences: "a lot" may represent more to some individuals than to others. Asking friends and relatives may overcome the problems of impression management, faking, and lying, though equally there is no reason to suppose that the person's friends and relatives are more likely to tell the truth, particularly if she has managed to "fool" them. Hiding in the person's house to observe how often she listens to classical music may be more effective, but also illegal. Phoning the person's bank to enquire about her spending would also require legal authorization, and even so the bank or credit card company is unlikely to have details about the products she purchased. Testing the person's knowledge of classical music may only be an indirect measure of how much she likes classical music: she could be extensively trained in classical music, but prefer to listen to R&B, pop, or jazz.

Another more practical and reliable option can be found in the psychometric approach, which consists of asking the person or anyone who knows her well different, supposedly related questions. In the case of preference for classical music, we could, for instance, ask the following questions:

(a) Do you like Bach?

(b) Do you often listen to Beethoven?

(c) Do you regularly buy classical music CDs?

(d) Would you find it difficult to spend more than a week without listening to classical music?

(e) Do you usually go to the opera?

(f) Do you think young people should spend more time listening to Chopin than Eminem?

Once these questions have been answered (and I should emphasize that the choice of questions is entirely subjective in this case), not by one but by, say, 100 individuals, factor analytical techniques such as principal components analysis can be used to determine whether these questions have something in common. If they do, we should be able to identify an underlying factor or component, which explains general patterns of responses. Depending on the meaning of the questions, we can then label the factor accordingly. In this case "preference for classical music" seems to be an obvious choice, though labeling will always remain more or less subjective.

Despite relying on self-reported information, the psychometric method "produces" more variability between individuals' levels of preferences. On the other hand, the use of multiple items allows us to assess different aspects of preference for classical music through simple and specific questions.

Thus, the statistical technique of data reduction provides a robust indicator of whether the different behaviors or preferences we enquire about are related to a common underlying dimension. If so, it is also possible to ask others to rate the person and calculate an overall score for each individual to represent their level of preference for classical music. That score can be compared with other information, for example number of classical CDs owned, amount of money spent on opera tickets, and knowledge of classical music. Personality inventories (see Figure 2.6) follow essentially the same principles as in our music example.

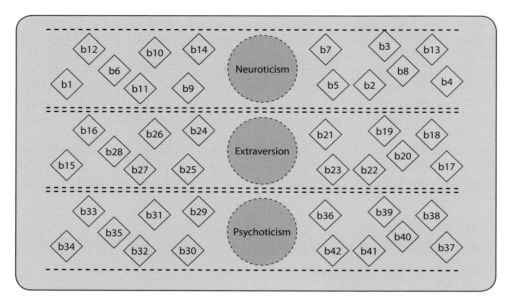

FIGURE 2.6 *Eysenck's Gigantic Three psychometrically assessed*

Note: Each of the diamonds b1 . . . b42 represents self-reported behaviors or preferences (e.g., "do you enjoy loud parties?"). Correlated behaviors are located within the same psychometric space (i.e., Neuroticism, Extraversion, or Psychoticism, the three independent/orthogonal traits).

2.8   THE BIOLOGICAL BASIS OF PERSONALITY

Another central element in Eysenck's theory is that it explains individual differences in personality in *biological* terms. Thus, different levels of Neuroticism, Extraversion, and Psychoticism are thought to be caused by genetic factors, which explains why personality remains largely unchanged throughout the lifespan (see Chapter 7). In particular, differences in temperament would be a consequence of individuals' level of cerebral arousability or the extent to which their brain is sensitive to stimulation.

According to Eysenck (1967; Eysenck & Eysenck, 1985), there are two major systems accounting for physiological and psychological differences between individuals; namely, the *reticulo-cortical*, located in the brain-stem reticular formation, and *reticulo-limbic*, situated in the visceral area, composed of the amygdala, hippocampus, septum, cingulum, and hypothalamus (see Figure 2.7). Whereas the former is in charge of controlling the cortical arousal produced by each incoming stimulus, the latter regulates responses to emotional stimuli.

Eysenck argued that Extraversion is the psychological consequence of physiological differences in the reticulo-cortical system, which determines levels of motivation, emotion, and conditioning according to either inhibitions or excitations of the cerebral cortex. These consistent patterns of arousability would also determine the extent

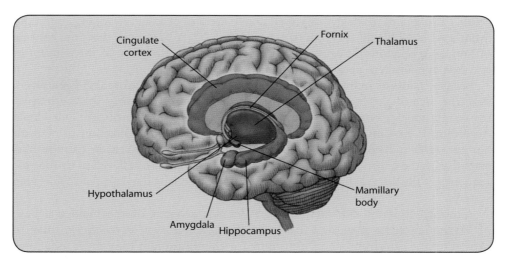

FIGURE 2.7 *Reticular activating system*

Source: H. Gleitman, A. J. Fridlund, & D. Reisburg, *Psychology, Fifth Edition* (New York: W. W. Norton, 1999), p. 27, Fig. 2.13.

to which an individual is extraverted or introverted; specifically, introverts would have a greater tendency to be cortically aroused than their extraverted counterparts, and vice versa. Thus, under equal conditions of external stimulation (i.e., in exactly the same situation), introverts will generate greater arousal than extraverts (Gale, 1973).

It follows that introverts need more time and effort to adapt to external stimuli and benefit from quiet environments. Conversely, extraverts, who have a greater need to compensate for their lower levels of arousal, tend to seek external stimulation and are more comfortable and able to deal with distracting environments or arousing activities. Studies on sensory deprivation, where extraverts seem to compensate for the lack of stimulation by moving around the room, appear to illustrate the interplay of physiological and psychological processes with external stimuli (Eysenck & Eysenck, 1985). Thus introverts' and extraverts' arousability levels would lead the former to avoid stimulus intensity and the latter to seek it. This search or avoidance would in turn enhance or reduce extraverts' and introverts' innate levels of habituation to stimuli, resulting in **biopsychological** feedback.

biopsychological interaction between biological factors and psychological factors.

On the other hand, Eysenck explained individual differences in Neuroticism in terms of the arousability of the limbic system, which generates activation that is perceived as arousal. Levels of arousability are induced by emotional stimuli, and the arousing activities in the brain of neurotic individuals can be translated into a predisposition to experience intense emotions, notably anxiety. Thus Neuroticism is explained by the relationship between an individual's level of excitability and emotional responsiveness, reflected in the autonomic activation of the neurotic system. Just as differences in Extraversion/Introversion are more evident in stimulus-intense environments, differences in autonomic activation leading to

Neuroticism are more clearly observed under stressful or anxiety-evoking conditions (Matthews & Gilliland, 1999). In fact, Eysenck (1967, p. 3) noticed that "the concept of fatigue in relation to extraversion–introversion takes the place of the concept of emotion in relation to neuroticism–stability."

Because neurotic individuals are characterized by a hyper-arousable visceral system (the area of the brain involved in emotional regulation), they are more sensitive to reproducing emotional reactions than are stable/low Neuroticism individuals. Accordingly, the same event may elicit an intense emotional reaction in neurotic but not stable individuals, and observable indicators such as sweat or galvanic skin response, as the experience of intense negative emotions, are believed to be the consequence of the visceral-brain activation and its consequent activation of the nervous system.

Although Eysenck did not provide a detailed account of the biological basis of Psychoticism, he suggested that individual differences in Psychoticism may be caused by the dopamine neurotransmitter, a chemical brain messenger associated with the experience and regulation of emotionality. Despite the wide replication of Neuroticism and Extraversion as major dimensions of personality, Psychoticism remained the focus of a largely unresolved psychometric dispute that opened the field to other important taxonomies (see Sections 2.10 and 2.11).

Other problems with Eysenck's psychobiological theory were its complexity, the physiological interdependence of the processes underlying the two supposedly unrelated traits of Neuroticism and Extraversion, and the lack of sufficient technological instruments – especially at the time – to test his hypotheses. Because of fast-paced technological advances in **neuropsychology**, several of the concepts underlying Eysenck's theory now seem as outdated as those used by Hippocrates and Galen at the time of Eysenck's preliminary theoretical developments. Some interesting research in this line is still being conducted, and there are some, notably Robinson (1996), who are concerned with reinterpreting and reexamining Eysenck's biological theory of temperament with state-of-the-art neuropsychological equipment. Yet the physiological part of Eysenck's theory is by and large disconfirmed, and most personality research has since been based on questionnaire rather than biological models.

> **neuropsychology** the area of psychology that studies how the brain relates to specific psychological processes.

2.9 GRAY'S PERSONALITY THEORY

Another influential personality theory, largely based on Eysenck's theory though pioneering in many aspects, was developed by Jeffrey Gray (1934–2004) and is known as the *behavioral activation system (BAS)/behavioral inhibition system (BIS)* personality theory. Gray's model was initially put forward as a variation of the Gigantic Three (see Sections 2.6 and 2.8), though once developed the theory was soon regarded as an alternative to Eysenck's. Because the BAS/BIS theory is also useful for understanding motivation and emotion, it will also be discussed in Chapter 9.

Gray developed his model on the basis of animal experiments – notably rats – though it applies largely to individuals. Like other animals, humans may respond to threatening stimuli in an active or passive way; in other words, by (actively) fighting or (passively) flying or running away. This system of response was conceptualized at three biological levels, each corresponding to parts of the brain; namely, the amygdala, the ventromedial hypothalamus, and the central gray of the midbrain. Table 2.4 summarizes the characteristics of the BAS and the BIS.

Gray's (1981) personality theory is based on the behavioral principles of *conditioning* – that is, reward and punishment – and their long-term effects on the brain. Like Eysenck, then, Gray developed a biologically based personality theory, though Gray emphasized the developmental effects of conditioning and focused mainly on anxiety. Thus the personality theories of Eysenck and Gray often work at different explanatory levels of the same phenomena, with Gray's model offering a more fine-grained description of the neuropsychological processes underlying individual differences in personality.

According to Gray (1982), the BAS motivates behavior toward obtaining a reward by making the individual aware of the reward and giving the "go-ahead" signal that triggers behavior. Whether the target is a box of chocolates, a pack of cigarettes, or a beautiful woman is theoretically indifferent, as the BAS causes the person to desire and act in the direction of the target. The BIS, on the other hand, is an anxiety system that inhibits behaviors associated with potential punishment or lack of reward. Thus the BIS encourages an individual to stop a particular behavior by increasing their level of awareness of the negative outcomes of a given behavior. A classic example is fear of a snake, followed by the inhibition against touching it and, in turn, the act of running away. BIS activity is psychologically expressed in terms of neurotic anxiety and depression (Gray, 1987).

Gray argued that individuals are biologically compelled to increase activity in the rewarding system, prompted by the BAS. Any rewarded behavior feeds back positively onto the BAS. On the other hand, individuals are also "programmed" to reduce

Table 2.4 *Gray's BAS/BIS personality theory*

BAS (Behavioral activation system)	BIS (Behavioral inhibition system)
Activates	**Inhibits**
Reward seeking	Punishment avoiding
Positive emotions (e.g., hope, joy)	Negative emotions (e.g., fear, anxiety)
Anticipation of positive event	Anticipation of negative event
High = impulsivity (sociopathy)	High = trait anxiety (anxiety disorders)
Low = low impulsivity	Low = emotional stability
Under-sensitive = depression	Over-sensitive = depression

activity in the BIS, which is achieved through stopping behaviors that may lead to punishment or fail to be rewarded (leading to frustration). Failure to inhibit these behaviors will increase the activity of the BIS. Both BIS and BAS are related through the mechanism of arousal, located in the reticular formation, conceived by Gray in terms of the dorsal noradrenergic bundle and as a separate system.

The most significant implication of Gray's theory with regard to personality taxonomy is the differentiation between the two distinct dimensions of *anxiety* and *impulsivity*, comparable – yet not equivalent – to Neuroticism and Extraversion, respectively. Interestingly, correlations between Gray's and Eysenck's models indicate that anxiety is negatively, albeit modestly, associated with both Extraversion and Psychoticism, suggesting that:

- There is a conceptual overlap between Extraversion and Psychoticism, namely impulsivity (both extravert and psychotic individuals tend to be impulsive).
- Psychoticism is characterized by risk taking, while Neuroticism, at the opposite end of the scale, may be characterized by risk avoiding (Gray, 1987). This idea is in line with a longstanding tradition in psychiatry that distinguishes between neuroses and psychoses, echoed, for instance, by Freud's psychoanalytic theory.

At the same time, Gray was generally in agreement with Eysenck about the inclusion of Psychoticism as a third major personality trait, and hypothesized this trait to be associated with the fight/flight system (Gray, 1991).

Despite the influence of Gray's theory, particularly in providing an empirically based theoretical framework for experimental research into the processes accounting for individual differences in major personality dimensions, dispositional approaches to personality have tended to focus on other taxonomies. However, Gray's theory has, perhaps like no other personality model, encouraged psychologists to combine psychometric/correlational with cognitive/experimental designs to explore the unaccounted processes underlying trait differences, a combination that has progressively undermined conceptual differences between state and trait approaches to personality. Hence the advantage of Gray's model, which works at both dispositional and situational levels.

2.10   CATTELL'S 16PF AND THE LEXICAL HYPOTHESIS

Another salient personality model is that developed by Raymond Cattell (1905–98), who argued that there are 16 major dimensions of personality (Cattell, Eber, & Tatsuoka, 1970). Cattell's personality model derived from an exhaustive and systematic analysis of the English language and was based on the assumption that every

FOCUS POINT 2.3   BIS/BAS PERSONALITY CONSTRUCTS AND COLLEGE STUDENTS' SUBSTANCE USE

INTRODUCTION

College students' substance abuse is a significant public health concern, and much previous research has found that substance use among this population is dependent on genetics, environmental factors, the presence of psychopathology, and various established individual differences.

Individual differences associated with drink and drug use behaviors generally include sensation seeking, novelty seeking, and impulsivity. Although Neuroticism has also been linked with substance abuse, its role is less clear.

Gray's (1991) two-dimensional personality model is one that may be particularly relevant to substance use as it represents approach and avoidance sensitivity. According to Gray's theory, there are two neurological systems that control behavior and emotions. These are the Behavioral Inhibition System (BIS) and the Behavioral Approach System (BAS).

The BIS is responsive to conditioned stimuli associated with punishment or signals of nonreward. The personality dimension associated with the BIS is the degree to which individuals' responses are triggered by stimuli that signal punitive measures or loss of reward. The BAS, on the other hand, is responsive to rewarding or nonpunishing stimuli, resulting in behavioral approach and arousal. The assumption in this theory is that individual differences in personality traits reflect the variation in sensitivity of BIS and BAS.

It is well known that all substances of abuse have rewarding properties. So it is stemming from this that Franken and Muris (2005) hypothesized that people with high levels of BAS should be more engaged in alcohol and drug use than their lower-BAS counterparts.

METHOD

In all, 276 undergraduate psychology students from Holland participated in the study. They were asked to complete three questionnaires. The first was the BIS/BAS Scale, which assesses individual differences in sensitivity of two motivational systems: the appetitive (BAS) and the aversive (BIS). Next, they completed a questionnaire measuring their drinking history over the past six months. Finally, they completed a "yes/no" (forced-choice) questionnaire asking them if they had consumed various illicit drugs in their lifetime, including cocaine, opiates, and cannabis.

RESULTS

Overall, 53 percent of the sample reported that they never consumed any drugs. For the remaining sample, men had used more illegal substances than women. The median frequency of drinking days a month was 6–8 days for men, compared to 4–5 days for women. The median quantity of drinks consumed was 4–5 per occasion for men, 3 for women.

There was a large sex difference in the amount of binge drinking: men's median reported bingeing was 1–3 times *per month*, whereas women's reported median was 1–2 times in *the past six months*.

An interesting finding was that BIS was somewhat significantly negatively correlated to drinking frequency ($r = -.14, p < .05$) and binge drinking ($r = -.16, p < .05$).

As for the main hypothesis, the BAS measure was divided into three categories, BAS Drive, BAS Fun Seeking, and BAS Reward. A positive correlation was found between BAS Drive and BAS Fun Seeking and number of illegal substances consumed ($r = .18$, p $< .01$; $r = .35$, p$< .001$ respectively). A test for comparing correlation coefficients found that BAS Fun Seeking was more strongly associated with drug use than BAS Drive, thus was a better predictor of such behavior ($z = 2.5$, p $< .05$). BAS Fun Seeking was also significantly positively correlated with drinking quantity ($r = .24$, p $< .001$) and binge drinking ($r = .25$, p $< .005$).

DISCUSSION

In this study Franken and Muris were able to demonstrate that college students' drug and alcohol use is related to their BIS/BAS personality characteristics.

More specifically, BAS Fun Seeking is positively correlated with the number of illegal substances one had used, the quantity of alcohol consumed per occasion, and the frequency of binge drinking. BAS Drive is also positively correlated to

substance use; however, BAS Fun Seeking is a stronger predictor. BAS Reward Responsiveness, on the other hand, is not at all related to college students' alcohol and drug consumption.

The BIS scale was found to be negatively correlated – albeit weakly – to alcohol quantity and binge drinking, but not to drinking frequency. This finding makes sense, as it may well be that individuals high in BIS want to avoid hangovers and other punishing/negative effects of drinking.

This study demonstrates that Gray's two-dimensional personality factors may be useful to study individual differences in substance use. As seen, some personality traits may be more useful than others when it comes to explaining certain outcomes.

Source: Franken, I. & Muris, P. (2005) BIS/BAS personality constructs and college students' substance use, *Personality and Individual Differences*, 40, 1497–503. With permission from Elsevier.

lexical hypothesis the idea that the major dimensions of personality can be derived from the total number of descriptors in any language system.

aspect of an individual's personality can be described by existing words. This assumption is known as the **lexical hypothesis**.

The first documented lexical study was conducted by Allport and Odbert (1936), who found as many as 17 953 words to describe psychological aspects by which individuals may be compared. These words may be thought of as personality adjectives, for instance "happy," "shy," "quiet," "stupid," "aggressive," and so on. Because there are often different words to describe the same trait or aspect of personality, the total number of descriptors can be reduced substantially. Starting from a list of 4500 words, Cattell obtained 180, then between 42 and 46, and eventually 16 personality traits. Factors from Cattell's taxonomy, the 16PF, are presented in Table 2.5.

Despite the wide range of behaviors covered by Cattell's 16 factors, moderate and high intercorrelations between several of these dimensions make it possible to reduce the taxonomy to fewer, higher-order factors; namely, QI, QII, and QVIII. This can be achieved through *oblique rotation*, a technique championed by Cattell that allows different factors to be correlated. Despite the technical jargon, the idea underlying oblique rotation is rather simple. Many variables that refer to everyday events happen to be oblique or related. For instance, alcohol and drug consumption in adolescents refer to different but related behaviors; another example is religious and political views.

QI (exvia-vs.-invia) and QII (adjustment-vs.-anxiety) are comparable to Extraversion and Neuroticism, respectively, while QVIII (superego) seems to overlap with Eysenck's Psychoticism trait, referring to levels of ego strengths, discipline, and self-concepts. However, several researchers – including Cattell himself – failed to

Table 2.5 *Factors in Cattell's 16PF*

No.	Factor
1	Factor A Warmth (Reserved vs. Warm)
2	Factor B Reasoning (Concrete vs. Abstract)
3	Factor C Emotional Stability (Reactive vs. Emotionally Stable)
4	Factor E Dominance (Deferential vs. Dominant)
5	Factor F Liveliness (Serious vs. Lively)
6	Factor G Rule-Consciousness (Expedient vs. Rule-Conscious)
7	Factor H Social Boldness (Shy vs. Socially Bold)
8	Factor I Sensitivity (Utilitarian vs. Sensitive)
9	Factor L Vigilance (Trusting vs. Vigilant)
10	Factor M Abstractedness (Grounded/Practical vs. Abstracted/Imaginative)
11	Factor N Privateness (Forthright vs. Private)
12	Factor O Apprehension (Self-Assured vs. Apprehensive)
13	Factor Q1 Openness to Change (Traditional vs. Open to Change)
14	Factor Q2 Self-Reliance (Group-Oriented vs. Self-Reliant)
15	Factor Q3 Perfectionism (Tolerates Disorder vs. Perfectionistic)
16	Factor Q4 Tension (Relaxed vs. Tense)

Source: Cattell, Eber, & Tatsuoka (1970).

replicate both the primary and secondary traits of the 16PF. Besides, Cattell argued that intelligence should be conceptualized as part of personality and assessed through self-report inventories, though most intelligence theories demand that abilities are measured through objective performance tests (see Chapters 5 and 6).

2.11 THE FIVE FACTOR MODEL (BIG FIVE)

If personality psychology were to advance from a preliminary classification of traits to the prediction of real-life outcomes and other psychological constructs, it would be essential to establish a consensus concerning the number and nature of traits that are necessary to describe the basic psychological differences between individuals. The system that appears to have won the vote of most differential psychologists (including mine and, I hope, yours by the time you finish reading this book) is the **Five Factor Model**, also referred to as the **Big Five** personality traits.

Five Factor Model a trait theory of personality positing that there are five major and universal factors of personality; namely, Neuroticism, Extraversion, Openness, Agreeableness, and Conscientiousness (also known as the **Big Five**).

FOCUS POINT 2.4   RAYMOND CATTELL

Raymond Bernard Cattell was born in Hilltop, a small English town near Birmingham, on 20 March 1905. At the age of 7 he moved to Devon with his family, where he quickly developed a passion for sailing and science. In 1921, Raymond was the first of his family to go to university, opting to study chemistry at the University of London. He was an excellent student, receiving a *magna cum laude* (Latin for "with great honour," which is the equivalent of a high first in England) BSc at the age of 19.

After seeing much destruction in the First World War, Cattell decided to do a PhD in psychology in order to apply some of the tools of science to understanding and solving some of the suffering and problems of humans around him.

In 1937, Cattell was invited by Edward Thorndike to work at Columbia University. In 1938, Thorndike recommended him for the prestigious G. Stanley Hall professorship at Clark University, where he was appointed at the age of 34.

Due to his chemistry background, Cattell was rigorously devoted to the scientific method in psychology. Thus, he developed factor analytical methods for exploring the basic dimensions of personality, rather than using what he called "verbal theorizing" (qualitative methods). One of the most important results of Cattell's factor analytic explorations was his 16 factor theory of human personality (see Table 2.5 for an example of some of these traits and associated questions).

In 1941, Cattell was invited by Gordon Allport to join Harvard University. There, he conducted the foundations of much of his later work, such as his work on intelligence, which includes a distinction between fluid and crystallized intelligence. The former is the ability to find meaning in confusion and solve new problems independently of acquired knowledge; the latter is the ability to use skills, knowledge, and experience based on previous experience or education. From this, Cattell developed the investment model of ability, arguing that crystallized ability emerged out of the investment of fluid ability in a topic of knowledge.

PHOTO 2.6: *Raymond Cattell (1905–98)*

Table 2.6 *Four of the 16 personality factors from Cattell's model, and examples of positively (+ive keyed Q) and negatively (−ive keyed Q) keyed questions for each*

	Warmth
+**ive keyed Q**	I enjoy bringing people together
−**ive keyed Q**	I don't like to get involved in other people's problems
	Reasoning
+**ive keyed Q**	I tend to analyze things
−**ive keyed Q**	I get confused easily
	Emotional Stability
+**ive keyed Q**	I am not easily frustrated
−**ive keyed Q**	I have frequent mood swings
	Vigilance
+**ive keyed Q**	I suspect hidden motives in others
−**ive keyed Q**	I believe that others have good intentions

Cattell died peacefully in his Honolulu home on 2 February 1998, just one month short of his 93rd birthday. In his will, Cattell left his remaining funds to build a school for underprivileged children in Cambodia.

Source: http://en.wikipedia.org/wiki/Raymond_Cattell

Like Cattell's 16PF, the Big Five personality framework originated from the lexical hypothesis; that is, the assumption that the major dimensions of individual differences can be derived from the total number of descriptors in any language system. After Cattell's initial version of a lexical-based personality model, Norman (1967) – based on Tupes and Christal (1961 / 1992) – identified 1431 major descriptors, which could be collapsed into a more fundamental list of 75 adjectives. Thus the Big Five model of personality is the result of statistical rather than theoretical or experimental research, and offers a descriptive rather than causal classification of individual differences, although in recent years behavior-genetic studies have provided evidence for the biological influences of the Big Five personality dimensions (discussed in Chapter 7).

Despite the lack of theoretical rationale for the etiology or origin of traits identified by the Five Factor model, and some isolated but persistent opposition (notably Block, 1995, 2001), there has been a good deal of consensus and empirical evidence to support the identification of the Big Five as the major dimensions of personality (Funder, 2001). Differential psychologists have also seemed to agree on the psychometrical advantages of the Big Five taxonomy proposed by Costa and McCrae (1985, 1992), often concluding that the Five Factor Model is "universal."

According to the Five Factor taxonomy, there are five major personality traits or factors; namely, Neuroticism, Extraversion (as we have seen, these two dimensions are also present in Eysenck's, Gray's, and Cattell's systems), Openness to Experience (added by Costa & McCrae, 1978), Agreeableness, and Conscientiousness. Hence the widely used abbreviations of NEOAC or OCEAN. Table 2.7 presents the complete supertraits and primary traits (facets) of the Revised NEO Personality Inventory (NEO-PI-R; Costa & McCrae, 1992) with their respective checklist. Sample items for each primary facet are presented in Table 2.8.

The first major personality trait is Neuroticism and can be described as the tendency to experience negative emotions, notably anxiety, depression, and anger. Neurotic individuals can be characterized by their tendency to experience anxiety, as opposed to the typically calm, relaxed personalities of low Neuroticism or emotionally stable individuals. The primary facets of Neuroticism are *anxiety*, *angry hostility*, *depression*, *self-consciousness*, *impulsiveness*, and *vulnerability*. Are you more stable or neurotic?

The second major personality dimension is Extraversion and refers to high activity, the experience of positive emotions, impulsiveness, assertiveness, and a tendency toward social behavior. Conversely, low Extraversion or Introversion is characterized by rather quiet, restrained, and withdrawn behavioral patterns. The primary facets of Extraversion are *warmth*, *gregariousness*, *assertiveness*, *activity*, *excitement-seeking*, and *positive emotions*. Are you more extraverted or introverted?

A third dimension, Openness to Experience, is derived from the ideas of Coan (1974) and represents the tendency to engage in intellectual activities and experience new sensations and ideas. This factor is also referred to as Creativity (see Chapter 10), Intellect, and Culture (Goldberg, 1993). It comprises the primary facets of *fantasy*, *aesthetics*, *feelings*, *actions*, *ideas*, and *values*. In a general sense, Openness to Experience is associated with intellectual curiosity, aesthetic sensitivity, vivid imagination, behavioral flexibility, and unconventional attitudes. People high on Openness to Experience tend to be dreamy, imaginative, inventive, and nonconservative in their thoughts and opinions. Poets and artists (and, to some extent, psychologists and psychology students too!) may be regarded as typical examples of high Openness scorers.

Table 2.7 *NEO-PI-R supertraits and primary traits (facets) with checklist items*

Traits (facets)	Checklist items
N1: anxiety	anxious, fearful, worrying, tense, nervous, – confident, – optimistic
N2: angry hostility	anxious, irritable, impatient, excitable, moody, – gentle, tense
N3: depression	worrying, – contented, – confident, – self-confident, pessimistic, moody, anxious
N4: self-consciousness	shy, – self-confident, timid, – confident, defensive, inhibited, anxious
N5: impulsiveness	moody, irritable, sarcastic, self-centered, loud, hasty, excitable
N6: vulnerability	clear-thinking, – self-confident, – confident, anxious, – efficient, – alert, careless
E1: warmth	friendly, warm, sociable, cheerful, – aloof, affectionate, outgoing
E2: gregariousness	sociable, outgoing, pleasure-seeking, – aloof, talkative, spontaneous, – withdrawn
E3: assertiveness	aggressive, – shy, assertive, self-confident, forceful, enthusiastic, confident
E4: activity	energetic, hurried, quick, determined, enthusiastic, aggressive, active
E5: excitement-seeking	pleasure-seeking, daring, adventurous, charming, handsome, spunky, clever
E6: positive emotions	enthusiastic, humorous, praising, spontaneous, pleasure-seeking, optimistic, jolly
O1: fantasy	dreamy, imaginative, humorous, mischievous, idealistic, artistic, complicated
O2: aesthetics	imaginative, artistic, original, enthusiastic, inventive, idealistic, versatile
O3: feelings	excitable, spontaneous, insightful, imaginative, affectionate, talkative, outgoing
O4: actions	interests wide, imaginative, adventurous, optimistic, – mild, talkative, versatile
O5: ideas	idealistic, interests wide, inventive, curious, original, imaginative, insightful
O6: values	conservative, unconventional, – cautious, flirtatious

A1: trust	forgiving, trusting, – suspicious, – wary, pessimistic, peaceable, – hard-hearted
A2: straightforwardness	complicated, – demanding, – clever, – flirtatious, – charming, – shrewd, – autocratic
A3: altruism	warm, soft-hearted, gentle, generous, kind, tolerant, – selfish
A4: compliance	stubborn, – demanding, – headstrong, – impatient, – intolerant, – outspoken, – hard-hearted
A5: modesty	show-off, – clever, – assertive, – argumentative, – self-confident, – aggressive, – idealistic
A6: tender-mindedness	friendly, warm, sympathetic, soft-hearted, gentle, – unstable, kind
C1: competence	efficient, self-confident, thorough, resourceful, confident, – confused, intelligent
C2: order	organized, thorough, efficient, precise, methodological, – absent-minded, – careless
C3: dutifulness	defensive, – distractible, – careless, – lazy, thorough, – absent-minded, – fault-finding
C4: achievement-striving	thorough, ambitious, industrious, enterprising, determined, confident, persistent
C5: self-discipline	organized, – lazy, efficient, – absent-minded, energetic, thorough, industrious
C6: deliberation	hasty, – impulsive, – careless, – impatient, – immature, thorough, – moody

Key: N = Neuroticism, E = Extraversion, O = Openness, A = Agreeableness, C = Conscientiousness.
Source: Adapted from Costa & McCrae (1992).

A fourth factor, Agreeableness (also known as Sociability), refers to friendly, considerate, and modest behavior. Thus Agreeableness is associated with a tendency toward friendliness and nurturance and comprises the primary facets of *trust*, *straightforwardness*, *altruism*, *compliance*, *modesty*, and *tender-mindedness*. Agreeable people can thus be described as caring, friendly, warm, and tolerant, and have a general predisposition to prosocial behavior.

Finally, Conscientiousness is associated with proactivity, responsibility, and self-discipline (does this apply to you? If you're reading this textbook just before your exam, perhaps not!). This factor includes the primary facets of *competence*, *order*, *dutifulness*, *achievement-striving*, *self-discipline*, and *deliberation*. Conscientious individuals are best identified for their efficiency, organization, determination, and productivity. No wonder,

Table 2.8 *NEO-PI-R primary traits (facets) with sample items*

Primary traits (facets)	Sample items
N1: anxiety	"I am not a worrier."
N2: angry hostility	"I often get angry at the way people treat me."
N3: depression	"I rarely feel lonely or blue."
N4: self-consciousness	"In dealing with other people, I always dread making a social blunder."
N5: impulsiveness	"I rarely overindulge in anything."
N6: vulnerability	"I often feel helpless and want someone else to solve my problems."
E1: warmth	"I really like most people I meet."
E2: gregariousness	"I shy away from crowds of people."
E3: assertiveness	"I am dominant, forceful, and assertive."
E4: activity	"I have a leisurely style in work and play."
E5: excitement-seeking	"I often crave excitement."
E6: positive emotions	"I have never literally jumped for joy."
O1: fantasy	"I have a very active imagination."
O2: aesthetics	"Aesthetic and artistic concerns aren't very important to me."
O3: feelings	"Without strong emotions, life would be uninteresting to me."
O4: actions	"I'm pretty set in my ways."
O5: ideas	"I often enjoy playing with theories or abstract ideas."
O6: values	"I believe letting students hear controversial speakers can only confuse and mislead them."
A1: trust	"I tend to be cynical and skeptical of others' intentions."
A2: straightforwardness	"I am not crafty or sly."
A3: altruism	"Some people think I am selfish and egotistical."
A4: compliance	"I would rather cooperate with others than compete with them."
A5: modesty	"I don't mind bragging about my talents and accomplishments."
A6: tender-mindedness	"I think political leaders need to be more aware of the human side of their policies."

C1: competence	"I am known for my prudence and common sense."
C2: order	"I would rather keep my options open than plan everything in advance."
C3: dutifulness	"I try to perform all the tasks assigned to me conscientiously."
C4: achievement-striving	"I am easy-going and lackadaisical."
C5: self-discipline	"I am pretty good about pacing myself so as to get things done on time."
C6: deliberation	"Over the years I have done some pretty stupid things."

Key: N = Neuroticism, E = Extraversion, O = Openness, A = Agreeableness, C = Conscientiousness.
Source: Adapted from Costa & McCrae (1992).

Table 2.9 *Correlations between the Gigantic Three and Big Five personality traits*

	Neuroticism	**Extraversion**	**Psychoticism**
Neuroticism	.75	−.05	.25
Extraversion	−.18	.69	−.04
Openness	.01	.15	.05
Agreeableness	−.18	.04	−.45
Conscientiousness	−.21	−.03	−.31

Source: Based on Costa & McCrae (1985).

then, that this personality dimension has been reported to be significantly associated with various types of performance (Chamorro-Premuzic & Furnham, 2005).

Thus there are three novel personality traits identified and included in the Big Five taxonomy that are not present – although they are arguably represented – in the Eysenckian model. Specifically, Eysenck's idea of Psychoticism would be conceptualized in terms of low Agreeableness, high Openness to Experience, and low Conscientiousness (Digman & Inouye, 1986; Goldberg, 1982; McCrae, 1987), but Eysenck considered Openness as an indicator of intelligence or the cognitive aspect of personality rather than of temperament. On the other hand, Eysenck and Eysenck (1985) conceptualized Agreeableness as a combination of low Psychoticism, low Neuroticism, and high Extraversion rather than as a personality dimension in its own right.

Table 2.9 reports a psychometric comparison between the Gigantic Three and Five Factor taxonomies. As shown, Neuroticism and Extraversion are overlapping dimensions in both systems, suggesting that the Big Five and Gigantic Three are assessing two pairs of almost identical traits. However, Agreeableness and Conscientiousness are only moderately correlated with Psychoticism ($r = -.45$ and $r = -.31$, respectively), and Openness is uncorrelated with Psychoticism ($r = .05$). Thus both systems seem to differ in their assessment of traits other than Neuroticism and Extraversion.

As mentioned, the Five Factor Model has been criticized for its lack of theoretical explanations for the development and nature of the processes underlying some of its personality factors, in particular Openness, Agreeableness, and Conscientiousness (see Matthews & Deary, 1998, for a detailed discussion on this topic). This means that, even if the Big Five factors represent an accurate description of individuals, it is not known from where differences in these traits arise.

Another more recent criticism regards the relationship among the Big Five traits. Although the five factors are meant to be orthogonal or unrelated, when Neuroticism is reversed and scored in terms of Emotional Stability several studies reported all five traits to be positively and significantly intercorrelated. Although these intercorrelations are usually modest, they may suggest that personality could be further simplified to more "basic" underlying traits, perhaps even one general factor. On the other hand, differential psychologists (such as Digman, 1997) have speculated on the possibility that these positive intercorrelations among the Big Five factors may be a reflection of sociably agreeable responding (or "faking good"), as high scores on the Big Five, at least in the United States and western European countries, are more "desirable" than low scores (remember, this rule only applies when Neuroticism is reversed).

However, the Five Factor Model has shown good validity and reliability, leading most researchers to agree on the existence of five major personality dimensions as well as the advantages of assessing these dimensions through the NEO-PI-R (Costa & McCrae, 1985, 1992). Perhaps the most obvious advantage of this consensus is the agreement itself, which allows researchers to compare and replicate studies on personality and other variables, providing a shared or common instrument to assess personality. Thus the Big Five are the "latitude and longitude" (Ozer & Reise, 1994, p. 361) along which any behavioral aspects can be consensually mapped.

In that sense, the choice of a unique instrument to assess individual differences in personality may be compared to that of a single and universal currency, software, or language, which provides a common ground for the trading and decoding of goods, information, or knowledge. Besides, the advantage of the NEO-PI-R Five Factor Model is that it accounts not only for a lay taxonomy of personality (based on the lexical hypothesis), but also for other established systems, which can be somehow "translated" into the Five Factor system. Thus findings on other scales may be interpreted in terms of the Big Five personality traits, just as other currencies can be converted into dollars or euros according to a given exchange rate. For example, self-monitoring, or the extent to which an individual evaluates their behavior and the way in which this may be perceived by others (Snyder, 1987), could be largely explained in terms of high Agreeableness, Extraversion, and Neuroticism. On the other hand, authoritarianism (Adorno *et al.*, 1950) may be partly understood as a combination of low Openness and Agreeableness.

2.12   SUMMARY AND CONCLUSIONS

In this chapter I have introduced the concept of personality, reviewing definitions, historical roots, and dominant classifications of personality types and traits. As noted:

(a)   The idea that there are consistent patterns of thought, emotion, and behavior that may be ascribed to latent variables or traits is as old as medicine, though modern psychology has provided reliable and empirical methods to investigate such variables in a scientific manner.

(b)   Although some personality theorists have questioned the very idea of internal traits, this concept represents the essence of personality research and differential psychology, as a robust empirical discipline is grounded on it. Furthermore, without the notion of traits it would be difficult to understand and predict human behavior across a variety of contexts. Thus Funder (2001, p. 213) has noted, "Someday a comprehensive history will be written of the permanent damage to the infrastructure of personality psychology wreaked by the person–situation debate of the 1970s and 1980s."

(c)   Debate on the number of personality traits that are needed to classify individual differences has dominated research since the early days of Eysenck and Cattell, two major figures in the field whose contributions to personality theory and research are unmatched. Eysenck's biological theory of personality comprised three main dimensions – Neuroticism, Extraversion, and Psychoticism – and is still widely used in differential research, although the biological aspects of the theory seem outdated and the conceptualization of Psychoticism remains contested. Cattell's approach, based on the lexical hypothesis (the assumption that all aspects of personality can be mapped onto existing words and language), was abandoned on psychometric grounds, but gave birth to the current reigning taxonomy, the Five Factor or Big Five model.

(d)   Despite the lack of explanatory power of the Big Five framework (in particular compared to Eysenck's more causal theory), the robust psychometric properties of self-report inventories such as the NEO-PI-R (Costa & McCrae, 1985, 1992) have persuaded most differential psychologists to conceptualize personality in terms of five supertraits – Neuroticism, Extraversion, Openness to Experience, Agreeableness, and Conscientiousness – as well as their underlying primary facets.

However, are personality traits useful for predicting and explaining different psychologically relevant constructs such as cognitive performance, health, and happiness? Chapter 3 will attempt to answer this question.

TEXTS FOR FURTHER READING

Block, J. (1995). A contrarian view of the five-factor approach to personality description. *Psychological Bulletin,* 117, 187–215.

Costa, P.T., Jr. & McCrae, R.R. (1988). Personality in adulthood: A six-year longitudinal study of self-reports and spouse ratings on the NEO Personality Inventory. *Journal of Personality and Social Psychology,* 54, 853–63.

Eysenck, H.J. (1991). Dimensions of personality: 16, 5, or 3? Criteria for a taxonomic paradigm. *Personality and Individual Differences,* 12, 773–90.

Funder, D.C. (2001). Personality. *Annual Review of Psychology,* 52, 197–221.

3 Personality, Part II – Validating Personality Traits

LEARNING OUTCOMES

BY THE END OF THIS CHAPTER, YOU SHOULD BE ABLE TO ANSWER THE FOLLOWING FIVE KEY QUESTIONS:

1. How are personality tests validated?
2. What information do correlation and regression tests provide?
3. How can mediation be used to infer causation?
4. What real-world outcomes does personality predict?
5. What are the major paradigms of personality outside the trait approach?

KEY WORDS

Behaviorism ● Central Tendency ● Cognitive Psychology ● Mean ● Mediation ● Moderation ● Pearson Correlation ● Phenomenology ● Positive Psychology ● Psychoanalysis ● Psychodynamic Theories ● Psychogenic ● Regression Analysis ● Schema ● Self-Efficacy ● Somatogenic ● Standard Deviation

CHAPTER OUTLINE

3.1   INTRODUCTION

The previous chapter was concerned with the key theoretical and methodological issues underlying the scientific approach to the study of personality. From a methodological point of view, the focus of Chapter 2 was largely *psychometric*, as this approach represents the state-of-the-art technique for assessing latent individual differences. The theoretical focus, on the other hand, was on the notion of personality *traits* as dispositional tendencies defining major differences between individuals' consistent patterns of thoughts, emotionality, and behavior. Thus, Chapter 2 was largely devoted to explaining how self-report inventories have been used to identify the major dimensions by which people differ.

After a longstanding debate on whether individual differences in personality should be conceptualized in terms of three, five, or sixteen major traits, most differential psychologists agree on the advantages of utilizing a Five Factor or Big Five framework, which posits Neuroticism, Extraversion, Openness to Experience, Agreeableness, and Conscientiousness as the basic dimensions of personality (Costa & McCrae, 1992). Today, the Big Five model represents the common currency or universal language of personality research, enabling researchers to interpret, compare, and integrate findings in an orderly and reliable manner.

Does personality matter? Consensus on which taxonomy and instrument should be used is necessary but not sufficient to answer this question. Rather, individual differences in personality need to be compared with other outcomes if one wishes to test whether personality measures are useful to predict different behaviors and real-life outcomes. To this end, this chapter will examine the relationship of personality with other constructs, such as educational attainment (Chamorro-Premuzic & Furnham, 2003a, 2003b), job performance (Ones, Viswesvaran, & Schmidt, 1993), antisocial behavior (Krueger, Caspi, & Moffitt, 2000), interpersonal relations (Caughlin, Huston, & Houts, 2000), and happiness (Furnham & Cheng, 1997, 1999). Ozer and Benet-Martinez's (2006) review of the "consequential outcomes of personality" provides a fresh perspective on the variety of real-life implications of personality traits and is testimony to the unprecedented interest that exists in personality correlates.

It would be impossible to understand the relationship between personality and any other construct without having at least a basic idea of the statistical analyses used. Thus, before looking at the different consequences of personality traits, I will briefly examine the rationale underlying correlational designs, including historical antecedents of such surveys and the problem of causality.

This chapter concludes by looking at nondispositional approaches to personality and assesses the current status of some of the "grand theories" of personality that dominated the field during most of the 20th century.

3.2   TESTING PERSONALITY THEORIES

The beginnings of personality research were characterized by the use of precarious methods of data collection, such that personality theories were often derived from *introspection*, *observations*, and *case studies* (see Focus Point 3.1). However, modern

FOCUS POINT 3.1   NON-CORRELATIONAL RESEARCH METHODS IN PSYCHOLOGY

Introspection is one of the oldest methodological tools of psychology and consists of thinking about one's own experience in order to understand a phenomenon such as memory or personality. For example:

> Imagine a researcher is attempting to study memory, which he defines as the capacity to retain and recall information. In order to test this capacity, he takes one hour to memorize a poem. During this time he reads the poem over and over again and tries to remember as many details about it as he can. After that, he closes the book and starts writing what he remembers. At the same time, however, he tries to identify and describe the processes that are occurring in his mind.

In the above example there is no distinction between the experimenter and his object of study. Thus, object and subject of knowledge are the same and as variations in one take place, variations in the other take place too. Memory is affecting the experimenter's capacity not only to remember the poem but also to recall the events that took place while he was studying the poem. Although contemporary studies are often based on the premise of introspection (for instance, in vision experiments the experimenter is often the only subject of the study), they meet objective and reliable criteria by combining established technological instruments with mathematical algorithms. But the beginnings of scientific psychology were based on a more rudimentary notion of introspection, particularly when examining latent variables such as personality.

One alternative to introspection has been the *observational* method, whereby experimenters observe *others* rather than themselves. Although observational designs overcome the epistemological problem of including the experimenter within the object of study, they do not solve the problem of subjectivity. First, it is diffi-cult to observe any social event without being at least tacitly part of that situation. Anthropologists have long been aware of this difficulty and have thus preferred the term "participant observation" to refer to observational designs. Indeed, there have been extensive epistemological accounts, such as that by Bachelard (1938/1996), of the scientific bias underlying participant observation, which turns subjectivity into an "epistemological obstacle." Second, experimenters may often establish comparisons (even if implicitly) between themselves and the participants, which brings us back to the problem of self-observation. Last but not least, individuals may behave in a different way if they know that they are being observed. Although this last point has long been addressed by different means that ensure the "absence" of the experimenter (e.g., confederates, one-way mirrors, hidden video cameras), most observations take place in laboratory conditions that differ quite drastically from individuals' natural settings.

A third method, *case studies*, attempts to provide a parsimonious and detailed picture of individual cases. No wonder, then, that case studies have constituted the primary tool of psychodynamic theories such as psychoanalysis. In their basic form, case studies may simply consist of repeated observations and are thus observational in nature. More sophisticated versions, however, may incorporate different techniques, such as unstructured interviews and even standardized tests. In psychology, most case studies are drawn from clinical sessions and rely on the therapist's observations. The major weakness of case studies is that, by definition, they are unlikely to be representative of the wider population. As such they are most useful to highlight aspects of theories that may not be as clearly manifested in the overall population. To the extent that theorists are "selective" when reporting case studies – by focusing on those cases that are most supportive of their theories – case studies may be exceptions rather than examples and their underlying theories may not be supported by larger, more representative sets of data.

Most if not all methodological drawbacks discussed above can be overcome by using *experimental designs*, which enable the experimenter to manipulate conditions or independent variables to test their effects on outcomes or dependent variables. Thus experimental designs are particularly robust for testing direct causational paths. This, however, requires the experimenter to "control" for irrelevant factors, which can be achieved through randomization and standardization of laboratory conditions.

Although experimental designs represent the state-of-the-art methodology in most areas of psychology, they are not straightforwardly applied to personality studies. One problem is that it is not possible to manipulate personality traits, which represent latent behavioral dispositions. Indeed, the study of personality would lose much of its appeal if we artificially changed people's habitual way of behaving, thinking, and feeling. This still leaves us with the possibility of manipulating variables that may moderate the relationship between personality and behavior; that is, have a joint impact with personality on behavioral outcomes. For example, a study may test whether caffeine moderates the relationship between Extraversion and arousal, or whether pressure moderates the effects of Neuroticism on test anxiety. This, however, requires measures of personality – which cannot be obtained through experimental means.

approaches to personality can be distinguished from other more theoretical or speculative approaches in terms of their systematic gathering and analyses of empirical data. As seen in Chapter 2, dispositional theories depend on large datasets, which are generated by self-report inventories. After these have been collected, the relationship between different variables can be examined through diverse statistical tests, notably Pearson's correlation coefficients (see below). Effectively, this process enables researchers to validate or test personality theories.

3.2.1 Correlation

The statistical test of correlation is widely employed to assess the extent to which two variables are related to each other. It is important to summarize the essential idea underlying this test before we examine the relationship between personality traits and other constructs.

Pearson correlation
commonly used name for the Pearson Product-Moment Correlation Coefficient, represented by *r*, indicating the degree to which two variables are related.

The most widely used correlational test is the *Pearson Product-Moment Correlation Coefficient*, simply known as the **Pearson correlation**. This coefficient is represented by the lower-case letter *r* and takes its name from Karl Pearson (1857–1936), a famous British statistician. Pearson entered university at the age of 9 and studied a variety of subjects, including medieval and German literature, before founding the world's first university statistics department at University College London. Pearson's statistical tests were an attempt at providing robust scientific instruments for the study of individual differences, in particular Galton's theory of hereditary genius (see Section 5.3.1 in Chapter 5).

In simple terms, the Pearson correlation is a measure of the extent to which two variables (e.g., *x* and *y*) are interrelated or vary with each other. This relationship is represented in a *linear* manner, so that, when graphically depicted, we can trace a straight line through all the data points plotted along the *x* and *y* coordinates of a scattergraph (see Figure 3.1).

In each panel, 1000 pairs of normally distributed numbers are plotted against one another (bottom left), and the corresponding correlation coefficient is shown (top right). Along the diagonal, each set of numbers is plotted against itself, defining a straight line with correlation +1. Five sets of numbers were used, resulting in 15 pairwise plots.

For example, let variable *x* = smoking (measured by number of cigarettes per day) and variable *y* = Neuroticism (measured by a self-report scale with a 0–60 range). Both *x* and *y* are measurable, quantitative variables. To calculate the correlation between *x* and *y*, the following formula can be used:

PHOTO 3.1 *Karl Pearson, 1857–1936*

Image courtesy of http://en.wikipedia.org/wiki/Karl_Pearson

$$r = \frac{\sum_{i-1}^{n}(x_i - x)(y_i - y)}{(n-1)S_x S_y}$$

Although few people today would calculate correlations by hand, it is useful to understand this formula. As stated, *x* and *y* represent our variables, respectively smoking and Neuroticism. The bar above these letters symbolizes the *average* or arithmetic **mean**, which is obtained by adding up all scores and dividing them by the number of cases. *S* stands for **standard deviation** (another measure developed by Pearson) and is an indicator of the average distance between the mean and other cases in the sample (see also Section 5.3.3 in Chapter 5). Thus the standard deviation tells us what the **central tendency** is or how widely spread the scores are. For instance, a sample with a mean of 10 (cigarettes smoked per day) and a standard deviation of 1 would indicate that most participants smoke between 9 and 11 cigarettes, whereas a sample with a mean of 10 and a standard deviation of 5 would indicate that most participants smoke between 5 and 15 cigarettes. Finally, *n* refers to the sample size (number of participants).

Let us assume that our sample is composed of 50 participants (*n* = 50) and that the average number of cigarettes smoked per day is 8. Let us also suppose that the average score on Neuroticism is 13. If a participant smokes more than 8 cigarettes per day and has a Neuroticism score higher than 13, the multiplication in the upper part of

mean the average value, obtained by adding up all scores and dividing them by the number of cases.

standard deviation a comparative indicator of a person's score against the general population.

central tendency measures of the "average," which indicates what constitutes a typical value.

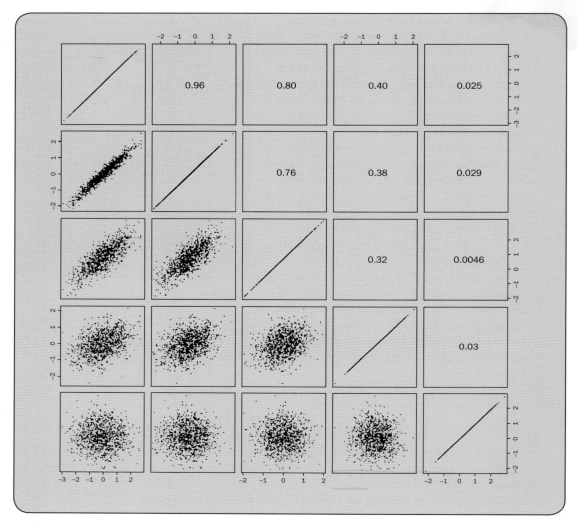

FIGURE 3.1 *Simple example of linear correlation*

the formula will result in a positive number. The same would happen if both values were below average (for instance, if a participant smoked 7 cigarettes per day and had a stress score of 10), because the product between two negative numbers is always positive. Thus a positive *r* value refers to a pattern in the data where large values of one variable are associated with large values of the other variable, and vice versa. Conversely, if the general tendency was that larger values of one variable are associated with smaller values of the other variable, the correlation would be negative. In order to arrive not just at the sign – positive or negative – but also at the *value* of the correlation, we need to include information about the standard deviation.

The value of *r* can range from −1.00 (a perfect negative relationship between two variables) to +1.00 (a perfect positive relationship between two variables), with an intermediate value of 0 (no association at all between two variables). Such values, however, are rarely found in psychological research. More frequently we find *r* values close to 0, indicating weak or no association between two variables. Then there are all the values in between. The general consensus in psychology (it would be very different if we were doing research in the natural sciences) is to consider *r* > .70 and < −.70 as indicating a "strong" or "high" relationship, while *r* values ranging from .30 to .70 and −.30 to −.70 are typically regarded as "moderate," and *r* values ranging from .00 to .30 and .00 to −.30 are usually taken as indicators of a "weak" or "modest" relationship. However, it is always difficult to interpret the *causal* direction underlying a correlation; that is, which variable, if any, influences which (see Focus Point 3.2).

FOCUS POINT 3.2   CORRELATION AND CAUSATION

The problem of *causality* has concerned philosophers and scientists alike for centuries. Causality is also a central issue in psychology. Given the large number of correlational designs employed in differential psychology, it is important to dedicate a few paragraphs – and hopefully much more time – to thinking about this issue.

PHOTO 3.2 *Bertrand Russell (1872–1970)*

Image courtesy of http://en.wikipedia.org/wiki/Bertrand_Russell

The British philosopher Bertrand Russell (1872–1970) argued that a series of events may be called a "causal line if, given some of them, we can infer something about the others without having to know anything about the environment" (Russell, 1948, p. 333). How does this philosophical notion apply to psychological research designs?

Correlational designs indicate the relationship between different variables and can be interpreted according to both size (e.g., modest, moderate, large) and direction (i.e., negative or positive). However, interpretational problems arise when we attempt to understand the underlying causal paths to correlations, as correlation does not mean causation. Statistically, there is no scientific solution to this problem: causational tests seem to exceed the explanatory scope of correlational designs.

For example, knowing that smoking and Neuroticism are positively correlated does not really tell us whether one variable truly *affects* the other, and, if so, which one affects which. In Figure 3.2 you can see a graphical depiction of the hypothetical causational paths that may underlie the correlation between smoking and Neuroticism, and in fact the correlation between any two variables.

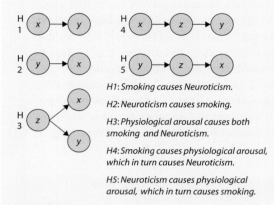

H1: Smoking causes Neuroticism.

H2: Neuroticism causes smoking.

H3: Physiological arousal causes both smoking and Neuroticism.

H4: Smoking causes physiological arousal, which in turn causes Neuroticism.

H5: Neuroticism causes physiological arousal, which in turn causes smoking.

FIGURE 3.2 *Correlation and causation: Five hypothetical paths*

Accordingly, the correlation between Neuroticism and smoking may indicate that

(H1) smoking causes Neuroticism (i.e., the more you smoke, the more anxious you will be); (H2) Neuroticism causes smoking (i.e., the more anxious you are, the more you will smoke); (H3) a third variable (e.g., physiological arousal) may simultaneously affect both smoking and Neuroticism; (H4) a third variable (e.g., physiological arousal) may mediate the effects of smoking on Neuroticism; and (H5) a third variable (e.g., physiological arousal) may mediate the effects of Neuroticism on smoking.

More sophisticated designs, such as longitudinal studies, can provide "chronological" data that may help us interpret the causational paths underlying correlations.

3.2.2   Regression Analysis

regression analysis a statistical technique that enables one variable (the criterion) to be predicted by another set of variables (the predictors).

If you understood the basic idea underlying correlations, you should have no trouble understanding **regression analysis**, which follows very similar principles and was also introduced by Pearson. Indeed, when there are only two variables, there is no difference between correlational and regression analyses. When more variables are considered, however, the statistical method of regression enables us to *predict* one variable (the criterion) by another set of variables (the predictors). Although there are several types of regressions, such as logistic, poisson, and supervised, here I shall focus on *linear* regression analysis, which, like Pearson's correlation, involves fitting a line through the data.

Typical examples of regressions in differential psychology are the dependence of overall school grades on students' IQ and study habits (e.g., number of hours revised), or the dependence of job satisfaction on personality and motivation. This dependence is called the *regression* of Y (e.g., school grades, job satisfaction) on X (e.g., IQ, motivation). In fact, regression applies to a great part of this chapter as it deals with the predictive validity of personality with regard to different outcomes, such as social and antisocial behavior, educational and job performance, romantic relationships, and health.

If we plot a line in a bidimensional space (corresponding to two variables), the linear regression can be defined in terms of $Y = a + b \times X$, which simply means that, in order to calculate the value of factor Y, we need a constant value or *intercept* (a), plus the product between the inclination or *slope* (also known as the "regression coefficient") (*b*) and the value of factor *X*. For instance, if we wanted to estimate a student's final marks or grade point average (GPA) as a function of her intelligence score (IQ), we could apply the following values to the formula: Y (GPA) $= 1 + .02 \times X$ (IQ). Accordingly, a student with an IQ of 98 would be expected to have a GPA of 2.96, whereas a student with an IQ of 140 would be expected to have a GPA of 3.80.

Although predictions are never as accurate in psychology, that is no excuse for abandoning regression. On the contrary, regressions are important because they provide information on how accurate the prediction can be, or, in more technical terms, *how much variance is accounted for*. This information is provided by the *R* coefficient (not to be confused with the lower-case *r* for correlation). *R* indicates the extent to which the predictors (*X* variables) are related to the criterion (*Y* variable). The value of *R* may range from 0 to 1, and the higher this value the more accurate the prediction or the more the variance is explained.

On the other hand, the relationship between each predictor and the criterion variables is represented by the β coefficient, which, like the *r* coefficient in correlations, indicates the degree and direction of the relationship between two variables. β values have an absolute value that may range from 0 to 1, and the sign indicates whether variables move in the same (positive) or opposite (negative) direction. In addition, regression analysis indicates the degree to which a predictor and a criterion are related when controlling for other predictors. This information is provided by the standardized β coefficient. When the predictors are significantly intercorrelated, standardized βs will differ quite drastically from normal βs. For instance, IQ and educational level may successfully predict future job salary (i.e., how much a person will earn) and have moderate β values. Yet, since these two predictors are likely to show a substantial degree of overlap, the standardized βs for one may be higher than for the other. Thus standardized βs tell us which is the strongest predictor in the model when all predictors are considered simultaneously.

3.2.3 Mediation, Moderation, and Structural Equation Modeling

Structural equation modeling (SEM) is a statistical tool that enables researchers to test causal models. In essence SEM is a form of regression, although it allows for more sophisticated analyses to be conducted. For example, regression analyses distinguish clearly between a set of predictors and a criterion, whereas SEM can treat a variable as predictor and criterion at the same time. Thus with SEM we may test a *causal chain*, or whether some *x* affects *y* and *y* affects *z* at the same time. Furthermore, SEM allows us to test whether the relationship between *x* and *z* is merely a function of *y*. This type of association is called **mediation** (Baron & Kenny, 1986) and is graphically represented and exemplified in Figure 3.3.

mediation a correlation between two variables (e.g., gender and stress) that is caused by a third or latent variable (e.g., smoking).

Although mediational tests do not completely solve the problem of causality (i.e., they are still based on correlational or similar statistical indicators), they represent a step forward from correlations and regressions because they reveal information about

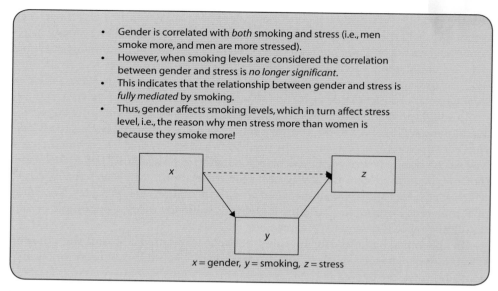

- Gender is correlated with *both* smoking and stress (i.e., men smoke more, and men are more stressed).
- However, when smoking levels are considered the correlation between gender and stress is *no longer significant*.
- This indicates that the relationship between gender and stress is *fully mediated* by smoking.
- Thus, gender affects smoking levels, which in turn affect stress level, i.e., the reason why men stress more than women is because they smoke more!

x = gender, y = smoking, z = stress

FIGURE 3.3 *Mediation*

latent effects. For example, in Figure 3.3 variable y would be identified as the third or latent factor causing variables x and z to correlate, because when y is eliminated from the model, x and z are significantly correlated, but when y is included they no longer correlate significantly. It is also noteworthy that the model shown in Figure 3.3 represents a *full* mediation between the variables. Yet, there are cases whereby third variables *partially* mediate others. In a partial mediation, the correlation between x and z would decrease, but still be significant, when y is considered.

A different causal path can be tested through *moderational* models (Baron & Kenny, 1986), which consist in independent effects of two or more variables on another (see Figure 3.4). Unlike mediation, **moderation** has uncorrelated predictors. For example, let us assume that gender (x) and smoking (y) are *not* significantly related (i.e., number of cigarettes smoked is not a function of whether individuals are male or female), but that both variables are related to stress (z). In that case, the effects of gender on stress may be *moderated* by the number of cigarettes smoked: men will stress more if they are smokers, and so will women, whereas smokers will stress more if they are men, and so will nonsmokers.

moderation the independent effects of two or more variables on another variable.

In Figure 3.4, both predictors are related to the outcome (although the connector from y has been pointed toward the $x \rightarrow z$ path to emphasize the moderation). However, third variables can moderate a relation even if they do not exert a main effect on the outcome. In fact, it is often the case that the effects of the moderating variable go in the *opposite* direction than the other predictor. For example, exercise may moderate the relationship between smoking and health, such that nonsmokers who do not exercise may be as unhealthy as smokers who exercise, and vice versa.

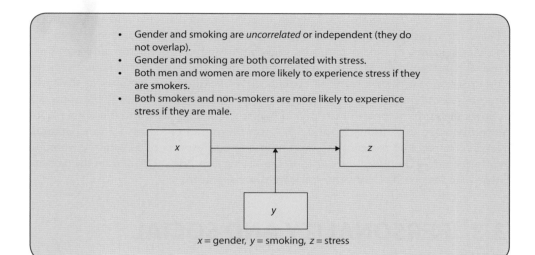

- Gender and smoking are *uncorrelated* or independent (they do not overlap).
- Gender and smoking are both correlated with stress.
- Both men and women are more likely to experience stress if they are smokers.
- Both smokers and non-smokers are more likely to experience stress if they are male.

x = gender, y = smoking, z = stress

FIGURE 3.4 *Moderation*

PHOTO 3.3 *A smoking ban sign for Japanese pedestrians. Tokyo has some of the highest stress and smoking levels in the world, but which causes which? Proper statistics could answer this question.*

Image courtesy of Tomas Chamorro-Premuzic.

Although SEM provides ideal access to tests for mediational and moderational effects, these can also be tested through regressions (i.e., by entering each predictor in different steps or blocks first, and then regressing one predictor onto another). Unlike regressions, SEM can simultaneously treat the same variable as predictor and criterion. Furthermore, SEM enables us to include *latent variables* at the same time by identifying factors underlying a set of measured variables. This approach follows the same rationale illustrated in Figure 2.5 in Chapter 2 and the sequence of steps discussed in Sections 2.7 and 5.5 – also illustrated in Figure 5.2 in Chapter 5. Needless to say, the technicalities and mathematical aspects of SEM are covered in relevant sources (Bentler, 1995, 2002; Bollen, 1989; Jöreskog, 1978) and on the website http://ssc.utexas.edu/software/software-tutorials#amos.

3.3   PERSONALITY AND SOCIAL BEHAVIOR

Although almost every form of behavior has social implications, psychologists have used the terms *prosocial* and *antisocial* to refer to a relatively specific set of behavioral outcomes. Prosocial behaviors include altruism, volunteerism, community involvement, and social services, whereas antisocial behaviors include crime, substance abuse, and truancy. Predictably, there has been wider interest in antisocial than in prosocial behavior, though recent years have seen an upsurge in studies examining the positive social correlates of personality (Ozer & Benet-Martinez, 2006).

The most important personality correlates of prosocial behavior are Extraversion and Agreeableness (Carlo *et al.*, 2005). Studies suggest that extraverted and agreeable individuals have a general tendency to help others and are more motivated to engage in altruistic behaviors, such as volunteering and charity work. Penner *et al.* (1995) identified two salient components underlying prosocial behavior, namely *empathy* and *helpfulness*, and found the former to be strongly correlated with Agreeableness and the latter with Extraversion (see also Penner, 2002).

On the other hand, studies on the personality correlates of antisocial behavior have identified low Conscientiousness and low Neuroticism as the major predictors. The fact that antisocial behavior was more related to these traits than to Extraversion emphasizes the idea that prosocial and antisocial behavior are not two opposite extremes of the same dimension but, rather, two different factors (though negative correlations would be expected; Krueger, Hicks, & McGue, 2001). The effects of Conscientiousness on antisocial behavior seem widespread. Low Conscientiousness predicts adolescent conflicts (Ge & Conger, 1999), substance abuse (Walton & Roberts, 2004), criminal acts (Wiebe, 2004), and even suicide attempts (Verona, Patrick, & Joiner, 2001). These findings are consistent with the interpretation of Conscientiousness as a negative correlate of Psychoticism (Eysenck & Eysenck, 1985; Eysenck, 1992) and highlight the fact that conscientious individuals have a higher sense of morality and self-control, which is the tendency to suppress impulsive, risk-taking, and physical behaviors (see Figure 3.5).

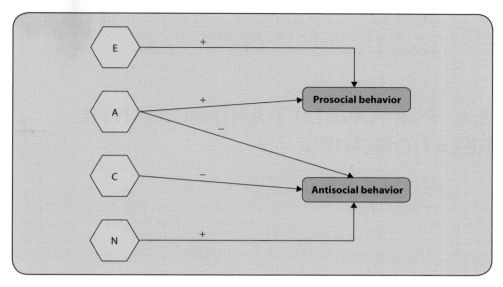

FIGURE 3.5 *Personality and social behavior*

Key: E = Extraversion, A = Agreeableness, C = Conscientiousness, N = Neuroticism.

The Big Five personality traits have also been examined with regard to political attitudes, which are undoubtedly important predictors of social behavior. The strongest personality correlate of political attitudes is Openness to Experience, which is negatively associated with *conservatism* and *authoritarianism* (a construct put forward by Adorno *et al.*, 1950).

For instance, Riemann *et al.* (1993) and Van Hiel and Mervielde (1996) report correlations in the order of $r = -.57$ and $-.42$, respectively, between Openness and conservatism in European samples. Similar results have been reported for larger US samples. For example, McCrae (1996) reported a correlation of $r = -.35$ between Openness and authoritarianism, while Trapnell (1996) reported more variable correlations of Openness with conservatism (from $r = -.18$ to $r = -.64$) on the one hand, and authoritarianism ($r = -.29$ to $r = -.63$) on the other. Some predicted a quadratic relationship between Openness and political ideology, such that extreme attitudes (both left and right) are associated with lower Openness scores (Greenberg & Jonas, 2003; Wilson, 1973). Thus higher Openness would be associated with moderate political views and more critical attitudes toward authority: "questioning authority is a natural extension of an open individual's curiosity" (McCrae & Costa, 1997, p. 837). However, Stone and Smith (1993, p. 154) argue that political psychologists tend to "base their case on intuitive evidence . . . concerning apparent similarities between regimes of the far left and far right, rather than on a system review of the empirical data on any personality and ideology."

There is also evidence for a negative relationship between Openness and prejudice, including racial discrimination. Thus, having an open mind would predispose people to be more tolerant toward other groups and perceive them as equal. Such findings are interesting because racial attitudes and prejudice have always been explained in terms of general social processes, such as in-group versus out-group membership. However, strong individual difference factors seem to operate.

3.4 PERSONALITY AND ROMANTIC RELATIONSHIPS

Although the study of personality and romantic relationships represents a relatively small area within individual differences, it is growing steadily and in the past 10 years an increasing number of studies have provided evidence for the idea that personality traits have longstanding effects on our love life, affecting choice, compatibility, congeniality, and level of romantic attachment. Reviewers have noted that "attraction of a suitable partner, propensity to establish a relationship intended to be permanent, and maintenance of that relationship may have related aetiologies and that these

PHOTO 3.4 *Can personality determine romantic compatibility?*

Longitudinal studies have tried to answer this question. One of the interesting issues is whether people are more compatible if they have similar or different personalities. Because personality is relatively stable from adolescence, it is possible to use early measures of personality to predict future relationship outcomes, including marriage.

aetiologies may have their roots in personality" (Johnson *et al.*, 2004, p. 285). On the other hand, it has been argued that "satisfying close relationships constitute the very best thing in life" (Berscheid, 1999, p. 260) and have implications for both mental and physical health (Gottman, 1998). Hence the importance of examining whether personality variables improve or impair romantic relationships, which ones are involved, and to what extent.

The best evidence for the effects of personality traits on romantic relationships derives from longitudinal studies. For example, Newman *et al.* (1997) found that temperament measures at the age of 3 predict relationship quality at the age of 21. Likewise, Robins, Caspi, and Moffitt (2002) showed that positive emotionality measured at age 18 predicted quality of relationship at age 26. Despite these impressive findings, the literature is small and few longitudinal designs examined the role of all Big Five personality dimensions, with most studies comparing between positive and negative emotionality (see Section 9.6 in Chapter 9).

One important aspect of interpersonal relationships is marriage. Although the connotation of marriage differs widely across eras, religions, and cultures, its positive implications seem to be ubiquitous. Married individuals tend to live safer (Bachman *et al.*, 1997), healthier (Horwitz, White, & Howell-White, 1996), wealthier (Gray, 1997), and longer (Hu & Goldman, 1990) lives. As with many other correlates of personality traits (see Chapter 7), these aspects of interpersonal relationships seem to have a large genetic component. For instance, McGue and Lykken (1992) found that divorce rates tend to be similar across generations and can therefore be explained in terms of inherited differences.

At the same time, developmental studies highlight the importance of upbringing, in particular implicit observation and imitation of parental relationships (Amato & Booth, 2001), as a constituent of romantic relationships. Along these lines, Conger *et al.* (2000) reported that supportive upbringing during childhood predicted less hostile relationships in adulthood. In fact, a study (Donnellan, Larsen-Rife, & Conger, 2005) has shown that parenting styles can predict romantic relationships even when the personality (of the child) is taken into account. But which personality traits predict marital satisfaction and stability?

The most consistent predictor of romantic relationships is undoubtedly Neuroticism, which is negatively correlated with marital satisfaction and a number of similar indicators. Whereas this correlation has often been interpreted as a mere artifact of neurotics' negative self-bias (neurotics are more pessimistic and thus generally more likely to report negative ratings of anything), there is wide consensus on the fact that Neuroticism is actually detrimental for relationships (Bouchard, Lussier, & Sabourin, 1999). Furthermore, some have defined competence in romantic relationships as "the set of behaviors that enable an individual to form an enduring romantic union that is mutually satisfying to both partners" (Donnellan, Larsen-Rife, & Conger, 2005, p. 563) and considered Neuroticism the most important threat to these behaviors. The authors concluded that neurotics' predisposition to easily experience anger, distress, and anxiety is "relatively destructive for relationships" (Donnellan, Larsen-Rife, & Conger, p. 572). Evidence for the role of other personality variables is lacking.

Studies have also examined whether being together in a marital relationship increases similarity between partners' personalities; that is, whether couples tend to

FOCUS POINT 3.3   THE RELATIONSHIP BETWEEN DIMENSIONS OF LOVE, PERSONALITY, AND RELATIONSHIP LENGTH

What is love? Love is one of those abstract nouns that we hear in fairytales and poetry and even see depicted in paintings. It is often taken to represent a complex range of human emotions, extending from simple feelings of pleasure to an overwhelming attraction toward another person. Although love is said to be largely ineffable, given its role in human society psychologists have tried to study it scientifically, especially in the past decade.

In one study, Ahmetoglu, Swami, and Chamorro-Premuzic (2010) set out to examine the associations between love, personality, and relationship length. They measured love using Robert Sternberg's triangular theory of love, which outlined three dimensions: intimacy, passion, and commitment. These dimensions form different types of loving experiences, either on their own (intimacy alone: liking; passion alone: infatuation; commitment alone: empty love) or in combination (intimacy and passion: romantic love; intimacy and commitment: compassionate love; passion and commitment: fatuous love; and all three dimensions in combination: consummate love). The authors formulated several hypotheses: that Conscientiousness would have a positive relationship with intimacy and commitment; that Agreeableness would have a positive relation with all three love dimensions; that Neuroticism would have a negative association with all three dimensions. Finally, the authors predicted that all three love dimensions would be positively associated with relationship length.

METHOD

Participants:
- In all, 16 030 participants took part in this study, ranging from "under 20" to "over 70" (*M* = 31–40 years).

- 61% were women (*n* = 9827) and 39% men (*n* = 6203).

Measures:
- Adapted Triangular Love Scale: a nine-item scale assessing the three dimensions of love; namely, intimacy, commitment and passion.
- The Big Five-Short Inventory.
- Relationship Length was assessed via a single item with the following options: 1 = not applicable; 2 = less than one month; 3 = 1–6 months; 4 = 7–11 months; 5 = 1–3 years; 6 = 4–9 years; 7 = 10 years or over; 8 = 20 years or over; 9 = 30 years or over.

RESULTS AND DISCUSSION

Agreeableness was found to be positively correlated with all three love dimensions. This is not surprising, as agreeable people are more likely to engage positively with others as well as perceive them more positively. They are also more likely to adopt constructive tactics when dealing with conflict. Thus higher Agreeableness confers an advantage for romantic relationships.

Conscientiousness was found to associate positively with intimacy and commitment. This may be explained in terms of the high-achievement tendencies of Conscientious people, who tend to be more motivated "workers" in their relationships. They are also more reliable and persistent individuals, which would translate into greater commitment.

Extraverts were found to be more passionate. This fits with the idea that they are more likely than introverts to communicate love outwardly.

Some interesting results that appeared in this study related to age. Age appeared to affect love dimensions even when personality traits were accounted for. Specifically, the older participants were, the less passionate they were and the more committed (regardless of their personalities).

These findings only begin to scratch the surface of the "personality of love." Indeed, in order to gain a deeper understanding of this subject, other measures such as attractiveness and emotional intelligence should also be included.

That said, the data from this study highlight many significant links between personality and love, as well as some important effects of age. Such results may have important implications for marriage or couple counselling services, as well as being relevant for the study of relationship initiation, maintenance and dissolution.

Source: Ahmetoglu, G., Swami, V., & Chamorro-Premuzic, T. (2010) The relationship between dimensions of love, personality, and relationship length, *Archives of Sexual Behaviour*, 39(5), 1181–90.

become more similar as they spend more time together. Interestingly, and consistent with theories of personality traits and behavior-genetic evidence, the data show little longitudinal variability in partners' personalities, suggesting that couples tend to maintain the same degree of similarity across time (Caspi & Herbener, 1992; Tambs & Moum, 1992).

3.5 PERSONALITY AND PERFORMANCE

Performance correlates of personality have long been hypothesized across a variety of settings. In fact, human performance constitutes a major domain of research within experimental psychology (Matthews *et al.*, 2000). In one of the first attempts to conceptualize the relationship between personality and broad performance, Eysenck hypothesized that individual differences in cerebral arousability may explain both personality traits and performance. The basic three assumptions were:

(a) Extravert and introvert, and neurotic and stable, individuals differ in their levels of arousal.

(b) Performance is best at an intermediate level of arousal.

(c) Individuals are motivated to seek an intermediate level of arousal (see Chapter 9).

Studies have generally supported all three assumptions. Introverts and neurotics tend to be more aroused than extraverted and stable individuals, people perform best when they are moderately aroused, and there is a general tendency to revert to these levels of moderate arousal when higher or lower levels are reached. However, the prediction of specific performance outcomes requires a much more refined account of the processes and variables involved. Two aspects of performance that received salient attention in the context of individual differences and personality traits are educational and occupational attainment.

3.5.1   *Personality and Educational Performance*

Personality traits have been increasingly explored in relation to educational performance. Typically, studies of this sort have examined correlations between personality inventories and measures of school or university achievement, such as final exam or continuous assessment (e.g., essays, participation in class, attendance) grades (see Figure 3.6).

As early as 1915, Webb conceptualized *persistence of motives* as an important personality trait for the prediction of academic outcomes, and a similar concept was later put forward by Alexander (1935) under the label *factor X*. However, the emergence of ability and IQ tests (see Chapter 5) meant that differential psychologists were largely focused on cognitive performance factors when it came to predicting individual differences in learning and educational attainment. Whereas IQ tests are still the best and most widely used individual difference predictor of academic performance (Deary *et al.*, 2004; Gottfredson, 2002), the idea that the amount of energy or effort students put in does not fully depend on their actual ability (Stanger, 1933) has been backed up systematically since the consolidation of the Big Five as the major personality dimensions, no doubt because of the improved reliability of such measures.

The most consistent personality correlate of exam and continuous assessment performance is Conscientiousness. This is not surprising, as conscientious individuals are more organized, motivated, responsible, and proactive than their less

PHOTO 3.5 *Even at an early age, children differ in their personalities and these differences explain differences in learning-related behaviors, such as school performance.*

Image courtesy of Nadia Bettega, reproduced with permission.

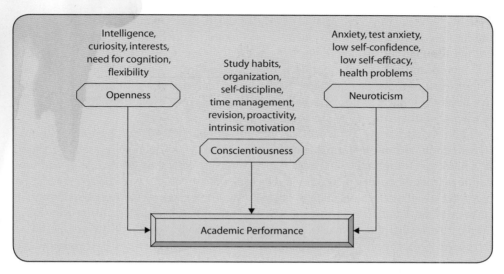

FIGURE 3.6 *Personality and academic performance*

conscientious counterparts. Thus several behaviors that may lead to improved academic performance, such as attending class, doing homework, and revising for exams, may be a natural consequence of higher Conscientiousness. Likewise, less conscientious individuals may be more likely to miss or be late for class, forget to complete assignments, and be more careless about revision and preparation for exams (Chamorro-Premuzic & Furnham, 2003a, 2003b, 2005).

There is also evidence for the idea that Neuroticism is detrimental for academic performance, particularly when assessed via exams. It is likely that the relationship between Neuroticism and exam performance is mediated by state anxiety (Spielberger, 1972a), such that higher Neuroticism (trait anxiety) increases the chances of experiencing stress and anxiety under test conditions (see also Zeidner, 1998). The tendency to worry is an inherent characteristic of high Neuroticism and interacts with external stressors (e.g., exams, deadlines, presentations) to enhance the subjective component of stress, affecting the individual's perception of the stressor and their ability to copy with it (Lazarus & Folkman, 1984; Matthews *et al.*, 2000). Accordingly, Neuroticism may tap into individual differences in **self-efficacy** or the extent to which an individual believes that they can successfully master goals. For example, neurotic students will be more likely to have fears of failing an exam, which may in turn increase their experience of stress, which in turn would lead to poor exam performance (Halamandaris & Power, 1999). It is also quite common for neurotic students to divert their attention from the actual test, which may lead to difficulties in understanding test instructions.

self-efficacy
individuals' belief about the extent to which they can successfully carry out the appropriate behaviors to control and influence important life events.

A third factor that has been identified as relevant with regard to educational outcomes is Openness to Experience. It seems that Openness would enable individuals to have a wider use of strategies and learning techniques, for example critical evaluation, in-depth analysis, flexibility, and so on. In addition, meta-analytic studies (notably Ackerman & Heggestad, 1997) revealed that Openness to Experience is moderately correlated with *crystallized intelligence* (see Chapter 5), which is a well-known correlate of academic performance. However, several studies have failed to find significant associations between Openness and exam grades (for a review see Chamorro-Premuzic & Furnham, 2005), and even more failed to control for cognitive ability, so that it is not clear whether Openness may explain unique variance in academic performance (beyond cognitive ability).

There is also some evidence for the link between academic performance and Extraversion, although findings have been variable. It has been suggested (Furnham & Chamorro-Premuzic, 2005) that the relationship between Extraversion and academic performance may be moderated by type of assessment. For example, tasks that highlight social interaction, such as oral or viva voce exams, as well as participation in class, may be easier for extraverts. On the other hand, tasks requiring long-term intellectual investment – that is, revising for long hours – may be advantageous to introverts. Other moderating variables in the relationship between Extraversion and academic performance may include age and level of education. Thus extraverts may have an advantage over introverts in primary school and the early years of secondary school, but introverts may outperform extraverts thereafter (Entwistle & Entwistle, 1970; Eysenck & Cookson, 1969; Sanchez-Marin, Rejano-Infante, & Rodriguez-Troyano, 2001). The link between age and Extraversion is intriguing, and there have been suggestions that academically more able students tend to become more introverted over time, whereas their counterparts become more extraverted (preferring social activities to studying or reading).

3.5.2   *Personality and Job Performance*

The validity of personality traits as predictors of job performance has been increasingly explored in the past 20 years, since an early meta-analysis by Schmitt *et al.* (1984) reported correlations between personality traits and job performance in the region of $r = .20$.

Consensus on the Five Factor personality traits has enabled researchers to explore the avenues between personality and job performance in a more organized and systematic fashion. Thus six meta-analyses in just over a decade (Barrick & Mount, 1991; Judge, Heller, & Mount, 2002; Judge & Illies, 2002; Salgado, 1997; Schmidt & Hunter, 1998; Tett *et al.*, 1999) provided robust data to assess the importance of personality traits in the workplace. These studies indicate that Conscientiousness is the strongest and most consistent personality correlate of job performance, whereas the relationship of other traits with job performance seems weaker and moderated by various factors, in particular characteristics of the job.

Schmidt and Hunter (1998) reported job performance to be correlated with Conscientiousness in the vicinity of $r = .31$ (see Table 3.1), which suggests that personality inventories are not as useful at predicting job performance as are work samples, IQ tests, or structured interviews, but are better than references (letters of recommendation) and a wide range of other factors (e.g., age, graphology, interests, years of education, and job experience) that are often used as predictors. It is

PHOTO 3.6 *How good you are at your job is partly determined by your personality. In this picture, a group of (probably highly conscientious) people walk to work . . . at 6 a.m.!*

Image courtesy of Tomas Chamorro-Premuzic.

Table 3.1 *The prediction of job performance (JP)*

Predictor	Correlation with JP
Work sample test	*r* = .54
Intelligence tests	*r* = .51
Interview (structured)	*r* = .51
Integrity tests	*r* = .41
Interview (unstructured)	*r* = .38
Conscientiousness	**r = .31**
References	*r* = .26

Source: Adapted from Schmidt & Hunter (1998); bold added.

Table 3.2 *Personality and job performance*

Personality trait	Number of studies	Sample size	True validity
Neuroticism	37	5671	−.13
Extraversion	39	6453	.10
Openness	35	5525	.08
Agreeableness	40	6447	.11
Conscientiousness	45	8083	.20

Source: Adapted from Hurtz & Donovan (2000).

unsurprising to find Conscientiousness to be significantly associated with job performance, as conscientious individuals are described as being competent, organized, dutiful, achievement striving, and self-disciplined (Costa & McCrae, 1992). Judge *et al.* (1999) found that Conscientiousness is also significantly correlated with job satisfaction, which emphasizes the important motivational aspects of this trait: people who are more satisfied with their jobs can be expected to perform better, which would in turn increase their satisfaction with the job.

Another personality trait that has been quite consistently, albeit not as strongly, correlated with job performance is Neuroticism. In general, studies have found that Emotional Stability (low Neuroticism) is beneficial for performance in most job settings, a finding that has been attributed to the self-confidence, resilience, and calmness of emotionally stable individuals as well as the higher anxiety, angry hostility, and vulnerability of neurotic individuals (Costa & McCrae, 1992). Indeed, some studies suggested that the effects of Emotional Stability on job performance may be as general as those of Conscientiousness (Hough *et al.*, 1990; Salgado, 1997).

However, other studies reported lower correlations between Neuroticism and job performance and suggest that, when one looks at the wider picture, the Big Five seem to have modest predictive validity in the workplace (Hurtz & Donovan, 2000). The question remains as to whether these correlations (see Table 3.2) are indicative of the true importance of personality traits in the workplace or whether the reliability of both personality and job performance measures is insufficient to reflect their importance at work.

3.6   PERSONALITY AND HEALTH

Differential psychology has also examined the validity of personality traits as predictors of different indicators of psychological and physical health (see also Chapter 4).

PHOTO 3.7 *Make space for the runner. A healthy jogger enjoying his daily run. How healthy people are is partly determined by their personality traits.*

Image courtesy of Nadia Bettega, reproduced with permission.

An interesting historical connection is that between personality and blood pressure. As seen in Section 2.4 in Chapter 2, the notion of temperament has been associated with individual differences in physiological factors since the time of Hippocrates and is represented by **somatogenic** approaches, which regard physical factors as the cause of psychological differences in personality (Shontz, 1975). Along these lines, studies have found that injuries that lead to cerebral vascular changes can directly cause behavioral changes (Elias & Elias, 1993). On the other hand, **psychogenic** or psychosomatic approaches view the association between personality and physical factors as indicative of the influence of the former on the latter (Alexander, 1939). For instance, hypertension, which is the diagnostic label for elevated blood pressure of unknown origins, can be understood as a direct cause of individual differences, such as particular reactions to conflicts, frustration, and repression (Shontz, 1975). Thus, Jorgensen *et al.* (1996, p. 294) note that "persons with [hypertension] have been described as passive, unassertive, submissive, and prone to suppress anger and hostility" (see also Johnson & Spielberger, 1992). Studies on subjective evaluations also suggest that low self-efficacy can induce physiological activation and psychological distress (Bandura, 1986). However, the relationship between personality and blood pressure is likely to represent a reciprocal causality between psychological and physiological factors and to confound a variety of moderating variables such as age, gender, and socioeconomic status (Jorgensen *et al.*, 1996).

somatogenic an approach that views physical factors as the cause of psychological differences in personality.

psychogenic of psychological (rather than physiological) origin.

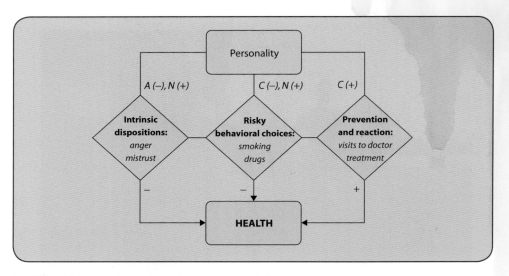

FIGURE 3.7 *Personality and health: three types of influence*

Key: A = Agreeableness, N = Neuroticism, C = Conscientiousness, + = positive influence, – = negative influence.

Personality traits have also been reported to predict broad indicators of physical health, such as absence of illness and longevity (Caspi, Roberts, & Shiner, 2005). Contrada, Cather, and O'Leary (1999; see Figure 3.7) conceptualized three ways by which personality may influence health outcomes:

(a) *Intrinsic characteristics* of personality traits may be associated with psychological processes that have negative physical outcomes. For example, low Agreeableness, in particular its minor dimensions of anger and mistrust, may lead to higher activation of the sympathetic nervous system and in turn enhance the chances of coronary artery disease (Smith & Spiro, 2002).

(b) *Risky behavioral choices*, such as smoking, unhealthy diet, and substance abuse (see Photo 3.8), which may threaten individuals' health. Unhealthy behaviors are more typical in individuals with low Conscientiousness scores.

(c) *Prevention of and reaction to health problems*. For example, conscientious individuals will be more likely to visit the doctor if they sense health problems and take a more proactive approach to treatment of illness (e.g., take all prescribed medication, adopt beneficial behaviors).

After "invading" the world of occupational and educational psychology, the Big Five personality traits seem to be increasingly explored in connection with clinical settings. The overarching question here is whether normal personality dimensions have predictive validity in regard to mental health problems. In contrast to psychiatric or psychopathological scales – which are designed specifically to predict mental illness – personality inventories such as the NEO-PI-R (Costa & McCrae, 1992) assess general individual differences. However, since most forms of mental disorders develop from healthy personalities, general trait models like the Five Factor framework may be important to anticipate psychopathological vulnerability or *diathesis*. For example, Meehl's (1962, 1989) diathesis-stress model (see Chapter 4) of schizophrenia postulates that anxiousness, submissiveness, introversion, and eccentricity are pre-morbid personality factors. There is also support for the idea that high Neuroticism and low Extraversion combine in a variety of psychiatric populations (Zuckerman, 1999). Furthermore, traits may predict mental illness prognosis, including individuals' responses to treatment (American Psychiatric Association, 1994; Quirk *et al.*, 2003). Thus psychological disorders may eclipse individual difference factors that, if considered, facilitate personalized interventions.

PHOTO 3.8 *Fancy a pint? Personality predicts unhealthy behaviors, such as drinking. For instance, high-conscientious individuals are less likely to binge drink than their low-conscientious counterparts.*

Source: Olaf Speier/Shutterstock.com.

An interesting question is whether the relationship between normal personality traits and psychological disorders is indicative of common etiological factors. For instance, interaction between biological dispositions and environmental constraints may cause both introversion (social withdrawal) and clinical depression, and could be manifested in terms of both depressive symptoms and "changes" in responses to general personality questionnaire items such as "I make friends easily" or "I enjoy being part of a crowd" (Schelde, 1998). This is also consistent with some findings (e.g., Ruchkin *et al.*, 2005) of the common genetic basis (specifically, activity of the MAO enzyme on neurotransmitters) for novelty-seeking and externalizing psychopathology.

Quirk *et al.* (2003) reported high correlations between the Big Five personality traits and several indicators of psychopathology as measured by the Minnesota Personality Inventory (Butcher *et al.*, 1989). As shown in Table 3.3, Neuroticism was found to be a consistent predictor of psychopathological factors, whereas the other four main personality dimensions were negatively related to these scales. Indeed, the authors concluded that although the NEO-PI-R was not designed to explain mental illness (and does not include assessment of delusions or hallucinations), it "holds promise for providing information relevant to clinical concerns such as self-perception, interpersonal functioning, treatment response, and outcome prediction" (Quirk *et al.*, 2003, p. 323).

Table 3.3 *Big Five correlates of MMPI-2 scales*

Indicators of psychopathology	Neuroticism	Extraversion	Openness	Agreeableness	Conscientiousness
Depression	.64	−.57	−.23	−.18	−.51
Paranoia	.38	−.32	−.02	−.29	−.39
Schizophrenia	.70	−.44	−.11	−.39	−.51
Obsessiveness	.68	−.35	−.12	−.29	−.48
Antisocial	.41	−.15	−.08	−.48	−.34
Addiction	.42	−.16	−.02	−.30	−.33
Negative treatment	.67	−.54	−.27	−.38	−.56
Family problems	.61	−.30	−.06	−.43	−.41

Note: N = 1342. MMPI-2 = Minnesota Multiphasic Personality Inventory.

Source: Adapted from Quirk *et al.* (2003).

3.7 PERSONALITY AND HAPPINESS

The final section on personality correlates concerns what is arguably the most valuable outcome variable of all; namely, happiness. Although it seems unnecessary to explain the importance of happiness, it has been shown to have benefits for marital quality, income, productivity, sociability, and creativity, among other things (Lyubomirsky, Tucker, & Kasri, 2001). There is consistent evidence for the idea that Extraversion and Emotional Stability (low Neuroticism) predispose individuals toward happiness (Furnham & Cheng, 1997, 1999). Furthermore, happiness is generally associated with a higher level of self-esteem, which is also a function of high Extraversion and low Neuroticism. As one would expect, there are also strong cultural influences on happiness that moderate its relationship with personality traits (see Figure 3.8).

People will suffer many losses (e.g., death of relatives, friends, and partners) and experience a number of other adverse life events (e.g., unemployment, divorce, stress, health problems). At the same time, they will experience important positive events, such as graduation, engagement, marriage, promotion, and children. These events may represent objective causes of happiness or upset, yet the subjective component of happiness is equally important and, over longer periods, personality traits are pervasive indicators of happiness.

positive psychology studies constructs such as happiness, fulfillment, and life satisfaction in contrast to "negative" emotions such as fear, anger, or sadness.

In the past decades, there has been a renewed interest in the relationship between personality and *subjective wellbeing*, which refers not only to happiness but also to fulfillment and life satisfaction. This triad (group of three) represents the key aspect of intrapersonal or **positive psychology** and shows a significant overlap with internal dispositions such as high Extraversion and low Neuroticism. On the other hand, the "wider picture" is completed by economic and social wellbeing, which, together with subjective wellbeing, are indicative of quality of life (see Figure 3.9).

The stability of subjective wellbeing over time is testimony to its dependence on dispositional or trait variables. Thus Diener, Oishi, and Lucas (2003) argue that health, income, educational background, and marital status account for only a small amount of the variance in wellbeing measures. They claim that research instead shows that subjective wellbeing "is fairly stable over time, that it rebounds after major life events, and that it is often strongly correlated with stable personality traits" (Diener, Oishi, & Lucas, 2003, p. 406). Three different avenues by which dispositions influence happiness are:

(a) *Baseline affect*: levels of positive affect are generally higher in extraverted than introverted, and stable than neurotic, individuals (see also Chapter 9 on mood).

(b) *Emotional reactivity*: individual differences affect the degree to which people react to specific life events; that is, whether and to what extent they are emotionally affected by positive and negative life episodes.

PHOTO 3.9 *We all experience happy and sad moments, but individual differences in personality explain why some people are generally happier than others (even in the face of the same circumstances). Indeed, personality even explains why some people smile much more frequently than others.*

Image courtesy of Nadia Bettega, reproduced with permission.

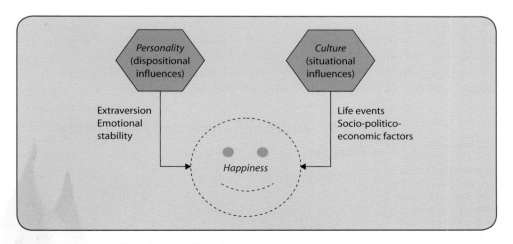

FIGURE 3.8 *Personality, culture, and happiness*

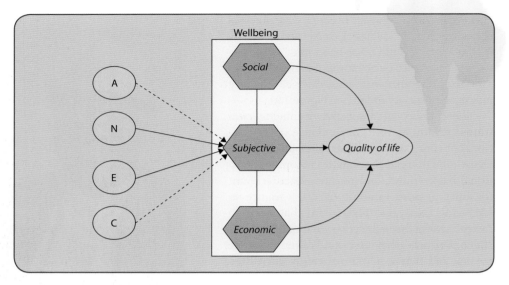

FIGURE 3.9 *Personality and subjective wellbeing: the "bigger picture"*

Key: A = Agreeableness, N = Neuroticism, E = Extraversion, C = Conscientiousness.

(c) *Information processing*: individual difference factors predict people's interpretation of events, in particular whether they regard events as negative or positive. Thus there are positive or negative *biases* (the former are self-serving, whereas the latter are self-handicapping).

3.8 CURRENT DEVELOPMENTS OUTSIDE THE DISPOSITIONAL PARADIGM

Most of this book is concerned with the dispositional or trait approach to personality. Although traits are no doubt the "global currency" in personality research, other approaches exist and should not be neglected. Thus the forthcoming sections will examine the current status of nondispositional approaches, including some of the "grand theories" of personality that have dominated the field in the past.

3.8.1 *Psychoanalysis and Personality Theory*

psychoanalysis a therapeutic method and theory, developed by Freud, based on the idea that unconscious motivations and needs influence behavior.

Despite drifting away from the scientific approach to personality more than 50 years ago, **psychoanalysis** is still one of the most popular and arguably *the* most famous personality theory, no doubt thanks to the fame of its inventor, Sigmund

Freud (1856–1939). Psychoanalytic theories are often called **psychodynamic** because they conceptualize personality as the result of a dynamic conflict between unconscious and conscious psychological forces (dynamic because they are in permanent struggle). This conflict gives rise to a variety of behavioral and psychological outcomes, such as symptoms, dreams, and fantasies.

> **psychodynamic theories** these deal with the processes underlying dynamic conflicts between unconscious and conscious psychological forces.

Although psychoanalysis had a substantial influence on social and human sciences during the 20th century, its impact on modern personality psychology has been marginal, particularly outside psychopathology. Today, most personality researchers regard psychoanalysis as an obscure, outdated, and pseudoscientific branch of psychology, preferring to exclude it from the individual difference curricula. But what are the fundamental claims of psychoanalytic theory?

Psychoanalysis is both a *theory* and a therapeutic *method* (some information on the clinical applications of psychoanalysis can be found in Section 4.4.1 in Chapter 4). In fact, rather than a single theory, psychoanalysis is represented by a group of related theories that are sometimes incompatible, though they more or less adhere to the same core principles. Thus, regardless of the specific psychoanalytic "school" (e.g., Freudian, Lacanian, Jungian), psychoanalysts tend to accept the following propositions:

PHOTO 3.10 *Sigmund Freud (around 1920)*

Image from http://en.wikipedia.org/wiki/Freud.
© Max Halberstadt (1822–1940)

- Most of the thoughts, feelings, and motives underlying behavior are *unconscious* or unknown to the individual. This means that people are rarely aware of the true reasons they choose to behave as they do, and that there is often no choice at all. Instead, people are "fooled" by apparent motives.

- Unconscious and conscious motives operate *in parallel*, so that, in the same situation, an individual can be consciously motivated to do *x* (e.g., hate, hit, remember) but unconsciously motivated to do *y* (e.g., love, kiss, forget).

- *Nurture*, in particular the child's experience with their parents, has a fundamental and long-lasting impact on the development of their personality. Thus personality is largely acquired: "The child is father to the man."

- An individual's *representations* of others – i.e., how friends, family members, and colleagues are regarded – affects that person's relations with them as well as psychopathological reactions (e.g., symptom formation). Thus psychoanalysis seeks to show how unconscious factors determine interpersonal relations, which in turn determine mental health.

- The normative *development* of personality requires the progressive transition from instinctual (i.e., aggressive and sexual) to social behavioral motives. Thus psychological disorders are indicative of maturational deficits or a "regression" to infantile sexuality.

The major problem with the above propositions is that they cannot easily be tested, at least not by the empirical methods that have constituted the mainstream approach in scientific psychology since the 1930s, particularly after the rise of the behaviorist paradigm in the United States (see Section 3.8.2). On the other hand, the validity of psychometric self-reports quickly undermined the importance of core psychoanalytic notions such as the unconscious. If people's self-descriptions can accurately reflect individual differences in actual behavior (which is what this chapter has shown), the idea that these differences have unconscious motives seems of little importance. Thus scientific and psychoanalytic approaches to personality were quickly regarded as antonymous.

Whereas few personality researchers today explain individual differences in terms of psychoanalytic principles, these are often compatible with empirical findings. For example, the idea that consciousness and behavior are the result of a constant trade-off between different autonomous subsystems of the mind is widely accepted and explains how individuals may learn implicitly or without awareness of the underpinning cognitive and affective psychological processes.

Like psychoanalysis, dispositional approaches posit that personality is largely developed during childhood and that traits remain relatively unchanged after adolescence or early adulthood. Thus, in a mainstream personality review, Triandis and Suh (2002) argue:

> when parents accept their children (there is much hugging, comforting), the children become sociable, emotionally stable, have high self-esteem, feel self-adequate, and have a positive world view. When parents are rejecting (hitting, using sarcastic language, humiliating, neglecting), their children become adults who are hostile, unresponsive, unstable, immaturely dependent, and have impaired self-esteem and a negative world view. (Triandis & Suh, 2002, p. 135; see also Rohner, 1999)

There has been a clear increase in psychoanalytic articles submitted to leading empirical journals, such as the *Journal of Personality* (e.g., Cramer & Davidson, 1998; Norem, 1998) and *Psychological Bulletin* (Westen, 1998).

behaviorism the study of observable behavior that explains human behavior not in terms of internal psychological processes but as a result of conditioning, or learning how to respond in specific ways to appropriate stimuli.

3.8.2   *Behaviorism and Personality Theory*

Behaviorism as an approach to personality has a longstanding history and, like psychoanalysis, applies to a variety of areas beyond personality theory. In fact, when the behaviorist approach was founded in the United States by John Watson (1878–1958), the aim was not the development of a theoretical framework that would account for individual differences in personality but the creation of an entirely novel

FOCUS POINT 3.4   SIGMUND FREUD

Sigmund Schlomo Freud was born on 6 May 1856 in the Marovian town of Příbor, which is now part of the Czech Republic, but was then part of the Austro-Hungarian Empire. His father Jakob, a wool merchant, married his third wife and mother of Freud, Amalié, at the age of 21.

Sigmund was the first of eight children from this marriage and, owing to his high intellect, his parents scraped together some money to invest in his education. Freud went to the highly prestigious school of Leopoldstädter Kommunal-Realgymnasium and graduated in 1873 with honours. In the same year, he joined the medical faculty at the University of Vienna where he studied under the Darwinist professor Karl Claus. Here Freud spent some time trying to find the male sex organs of eels; this was at a time when not much was known about this fascinating topic! It was in the following year that Freud was exposed to the concept of "psychodynamics" when German physiologist Ernst von Brücke and physicist Hermann von Helmholtz proposed in a lecture that all living organisms are governed by a principle similar to that of thermodynamics.

Freud's famous theory of the psyche was founded by the idea that humans have a fixed amount of energy that is channeled into the three parts of the psyche: id, ego, and super-ego. The id operates on the "pleasure principle" and is driven by primal urges such as sex and hunger; it wants what it wants and disregards all consequences. The super-ego is the opposite, and is constrained by socially constructed morals and culture; this is the last part of the psyche to develop, as the child has to learn what moral boundaries exist. Finally, the ego is the "referee" of the psyche: it negotiates a balance between the hedonistic urges of the id and the over-moralistic super-ego.

The amount of psychic energy is fixed and limited, but exerted in different quantities to the different parts of the psyche. Thus if more energy is being expended on the id there will be an imbalance, and the person's hedonistic urges might lead them to behave in socially inappropriate ways. To balance this, one must *redirect* this energy, as no more can be "created" as such. This is what psychoanalysis attempts to do: it channels this psychic energy into the necessary parts of the psyche in order to create a balance and thus a "healthy" mind. Freud is the founder of the psychoanalytic school of psychology.

Freud is also famous for his theories of the unconscious mind and the notion of repression, whereby thoughts are buried out of conscious thought in order to protect the individual from being harmed by these unacceptable ideas. Through psychotherapy, one uncovers these repressed memories from the unconscious

PHOTO 3.11 *Sigmund Freud (1856–1939)*

© Mary Evans Picture Library/Alamy.

and releases this trapped energy, relieving the patient of their symptoms.

In his lifetime, Freud also developed the therapeutic techniques of free association, where one says the first thing that comes to one's mind in order to unveil unconscious thoughts to the therapist; his theory of transference, which is where the patient transfers their emotions toward their parents, or other figures toward which emotions are needed to be expressed, onto the therapist; and also the interpretation of dreams as the road par excellence to the unconscious.

Being an avid cigar smoker, Freud underwent over 30 surgeries for his oral cancer. In the end he asked his friend Dr. Max Schur to assist him in suicide. So Schur injected Freud with doses of morphine until he died on 23 September 1939 at his London home.

Check out this link to the Freud Museum: www.freud .org.uk

PHOTO 3.12 *John Watson (1878–1958)*

© Underwood & Underwood/CORBIS.

form of psychology, one that could distance itself from speculation and concerns about unobservable "mental processes" and replace subjective evaluation with objective experimentalism. In the words of Watson (1913, p. 158):

> Psychology as the behaviorist views it is a purely objective experimental branch of natural science. Its theoretical goal is the prediction and control of behavior. Introspection forms no essential part of its methods, nor is the scientific value of its data dependent upon the readiness with which they lend themselves to interpretation in terms of consciousness. The behaviorist, in his efforts to get a unitary scheme of animal response, recognizes no dividing line between man and brute. The behavior of man, with all of its refinement and complexity, forms only a part of the behaviorist's total scheme of investigation.

Thus behaviorism attempted to replace the construct of mind with observable variables such as behavior, and assumed that behavior was entirely caused by external stimuli rather than internal psychological processes. Behaviorists were also more concerned with producing behavioral *change* than with understanding behavior per se. In doing so, they focused on the role of learned associations as determinants of behavioral outcomes and attempted both to identify existing associations and to create novel ones. Hence the label "learning theories" is often applied to behaviorist approaches.

According to behavioral theories, personality could be explained simply as the sum of all learned associations, though strictly speaking a behaviorist would never employ the term "personality" as it is a latent and theoretical abstraction.

John Watson carried out what is now considered one of the most unethical experiments in psychology: the so called "Little Albert" study. Watson was trying to determine whether fear was innate or a conditioned response. So, he sat 9-month-old Little Albert in a room and exposed him to several neutral stimuli, including a white rat and a rabbit, and the child displayed no anxiety toward them. For two months he was exposed to such stimuli without any conditioning. Then, Little Albert was placed in the room with the rat again, but this time when he touched it, Watson would make a loud noise in the background such as a hammer striking a steel bar. This would shock Albert and he would start crying. Watson continued to do this until Little Albert was distressed at the sight of the rat without the loud bang; but not only that, he associated anything white or fluffy with the loud noise and became phobic of several such items, even cotton wool! Watson did not have enough time to desensitize him to the now conditioned stimuli, and these phobias probably would have remained with him until later life. Little Albert's real identity has been unveiled by a recent article and apparently he died in 1925 (Beck *et al.*, 2009).

The evolution of behaviorism followed different paths. On the one hand, B.F. Skinner (1904–90) developed *radical behaviorism*, expanding the theory into a philosophical and political system. This line of behaviorism proposed that "everything important in psychology . . . can be investigated in essence through the continued experimental and theoretical analysis of the determiners of rat behavior

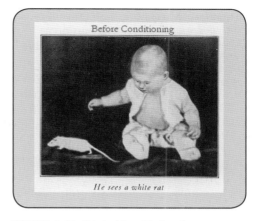

PHOTO 3.13 *"Little Albert" before he was conditioned to fear rats*

Image provided courtesy of www.all-about-psychology.com.

PHOTO 3.14 *B.F. Skinner (around 1950)*

Source: http://en.wikipedia.org/wiki/B_f_skinner

at a choice point in a maze" (Tolman, 1939, p. 34), and that "the variables of which human behavior is a function lie in the environment" (Skinner, 1977, p. 1). On the other hand, less radical versions of behaviorism proposed that "in order to characterize behavioral patterns, propensities, or capacities, we need not only a suitable behavioristic vocabulary, but psychological terms as well" (Hempel, 1966, p. 110). Thus moderate behaviorist approaches aimed at resurrecting unobservable variables such as memories, emotions, and perceptions to expand the theoretical and explanatory scope of behaviorism.

cognitive psychology
the study of unobservable mental constructs such as perception, thinking, memory, and language.

Ironically, a large part of the behaviorist movement evolved into the paradigm of **cognitive psychology**, which focused on the study of unobservable, internal, mental constructs. Furthermore, cognitive psychologists would seek to revindicate subjectivity to emphasize the importance of beliefs and establish a clear-cut differentiation between human and nonhuman learning. Although associations between environmental stimuli and behavioral responses may provide a basic explanation of how organisms learn, human learning is much more dependent on individuals' beliefs about behavioral reinforcements than on the reinforcements themselves. This idea was emphatically conceptualized in Bandura's (1986) theory of *self-efficacy*, which refers to an individual's beliefs about their capacities to influence specific outcomes, and about the self-fulfilling prophecies of such beliefs.

Even from a strict behaviorist perspective, there are valid epistemological arguments that apply to our understanding of personality traits. For example, the idea that mental states are empirically validated only insofar as they relate to observable behavioral outcomes is very much applicable to the psychometric assessment of personality. Thus the psychometric method of *inferring* individual differences in thought and emotionality from observable behavior may be considered a reminiscence of the behaviorist paradigm. In fact, psychometric approaches to personality are much closer to behaviorist than to psychoanalytic theories, though early trait taxonomies have also been influenced by clinical observations.

3.8.3   *Phenomenological Personality Theories*

phenomenology the study of things (phenomena) as they are perceived or represented.

Phenomenological approaches to personality, also known as *humanistic* or *existential*, are a theoretical hybrid between psychology and philosophy. Indeed, the term **phenomenology** refers to a philosophical paradigm, which explains why phenomenological approaches to personality have been more influenced by philosophical than psychological theories.

Phenomenology is not only a rich and comprehensive theoretical framework but also a type of epistemology (philosophy of science), in that it defines and conceptualizes the relationship between subject and object of knowledge; that is, how the world is perceived or represented. To the extent that life is experienced and interpreted in a unique and subjective manner, it argues, emphasis should be placed on *individuality*, and no two individuals have the same perception of the world. Thus Kohler (1947, p. 3) argued:

> There seems to be a single starting point for psychology, exactly as for all the other sciences: The world as we find it, naively and uncritically.

In fact – and you may have realized this even before studying phenomenology – two different people will experience the same event in different ways. Philosophically, this leads to the position of *subjectivity*. Psychologically, it is the maximal expression of individual differences, which is arguably why phenomenology deserves to be seriously considered in any book on the subject. Indeed, phenomenology takes the concept of personality to a different level because it equates personality with individuality.

Two other concepts that constitute the theoretical skeleton of phenomenological approaches to personality are *freedom* and *self-determination*. Thus phenomenology posits that all human beings are free to choose and create their lives, making life a self-determined enterprise. This idea was highly influential in determining the theoretical layout of personality approaches in the 1960s and 1970s, and represented the central message of humanistic psychology largely associated with Carl Rogers (1902–87), Abraham Maslow (1908–70), and George Kelly (1905–66). In brief, humanistic personality theories argued that:

- Individuals, just like an opening flower, have a natural tendency toward personal improvement and self-perfection. Thus every person has the potential for *self-actualization* or self-realization.

- *Actualization* is the capacity to enhance the organism, gain autonomy, and be self-sufficient (Rogers, 1959). In simple terms, to actualize oneself means to *grow*.

- If individuals are unaware of their potential for self-actualization or find obstacles that stop them from unleashing this potential, (humanistic) psychologists can guide them and help them overcome obstacles.

- Self-actualized people tend to enjoy life and be happy, whereas failure to unleash one's potential for growth can lead to mental health problems (Kasser & Ryan, 1993; Ryan, Rigby, & King, 1993).

- Failure to self-actualize may also lead to a state of *reactance* (Brehm & Brehm, 1981), which is the feeling that our freedom of choice has been taken away.

- Self-actualization leads to congruence between one's *ideal* and *actual* self (Rogers, 1961). Conversely, incongruity between one's aspirations and reality causes anxiety.

Perhaps the most significant contribution of the humanistic paradigm has been the application of phenomenological/constructivist principles to the study of *cross-cultural* issues. Accordingly, reality is subjectively constructed within the range of social meanings available in each culture. This theoretical position emphasizes and praises individuality, positing that individuals can only be understood in terms of their own personal experiences (rather than by imposing a "universal" system of meaning; see Rogers, 1951; Kelly, 1955).

3.8.4   *Social-Cognitive Theories of Personality*

The *social-cognitive* paradigm (for a review of the literature see Cervone & Shoda, 1999) is itself a ramification of late behaviorist theories, though its emphasis is largely on subjective processes. For example, Higgins's (1999) research is concerned with *self-comparative* processes by which individuals contrast their aspirations (what or who they would like to become) with their self-views (who they think they are). The bigger the difference or contrast between individuals' self-views and aspirations, the higher the likelihood of experiencing anxiety and even depression.

schema a knowledge structure that guides individual expectations and beliefs, helps make sense of familiar situations, and provides a framework for processing and organizing new information.

In a similar vein, Baldwin (1999) referred to a *relational* **schema** as a representational form of self-image that arises from social interaction. Interestingly, these schemata are not only self-fulfilling (in that they may affect information processing and behavior), but may also fluctuate according to the situation, notably depending on the representation of other individuals. Thus you may behave like a "daughter" at home and in the company of your parents, but act like a "girlfriend" in the company of your boyfriend. The implications of this argument are that individuals may have several, and often plenty of, relational schemata, an idea that is in direct conflict with trait theories of personality (as representational schemata lead to inconsistencies not only in behavior but also in self-perception). However, some social-cognitive theorists have raised concerns and formulated direct criticisms of such fragmented notions of the self, positing that "there is only one self that can visualize different futures and select courses of action" (Bandura, 1999, p. 194).

Social-cognitive theories have also focused on self-perceptions with regard to intellectual competence, in particular whether individuals believe intelligence to be a fixed *entity* (innate, and thus unaffected by efforts and hard work) or *incremental* in nature (and thus dependent on one's level of intellectual investment and effort to succeed; see Dweck, 1997; Grant & Dweck, 1999). Individuals who hold incremental beliefs about intelligence tend to set higher goals and work much harder to accomplish them, regardless of their actual level of intelligence. Conversely, people who think that intelligence is a fixed entity tend to have self-defeating cognitions and strive less for success. Furthermore, while entity beliefs are usually associated with performance goals, incremental beliefs tend to emphasize learning goals, hence they are of an intrinsic rather than extrinsic nature (see also Chapter 9).

Although research has only also begun to examine the relationship between entity / incremental beliefs and well-established personality traits (Furnham, Chamorro-Premuzic, & McDougall, 2003), Dweck's theory represents a promising prospect for unifying trait and social-cognitive theories as well as shedding light on the developmental effects of personality on intellectual competence (Chamorro-Premuzic & Furnham, 2006). Although some social-cognitive psychologists have explicitly rejected the prospect of integrating their theories with trait approaches, believing both paradigms to be not only incompatible but also in direct theoretical opposition (Cervone, 1999; Cervone & Shoda, 1999), others have emphasized the complementary potential of these two paradigms. Thus Mischel (1999, pp. 55–6) notes:

> Personality psychology has been committed since its beginnings to characterizing individuals in terms of their stable and distinctive qualities. Other personality theorists and researchers have focused instead on the processes that underlie these coherences and that influence how people function. These two goals . . . have been pursued in two increasingly separated (and warring) sub-disciplines with different agendas that seem to be in conflict with each other . . . [but] both goals may be pursued in concert with no necessary conflict or incompatibility because . . . dispositions and processing dynamics are two complementary facets of the same phenomena and the same unitary personality system.

3.8.5   *Biological Approaches to Personality Theory*

Biological approaches aim to identify observable links between physical (anatomical and physiological) and psychological variables. Thus biological theories of personality are concerned with the relationship between psychometrically assessed personality traits and the nervous system. This means that trait and biological approaches are not mutually exclusive but complementary. Insofar as psychometrically obtained scores (e.g., on Neuroticism or Extraversion) correlate with measures of anatomical or physiological variables, one may assume that personality traits are simultaneously expressed in physical and psychological ways.

There has been much scientific progress in identifying biological correlates of personality traits. For instance, anatomical studies have shown that general areas in the brain such as the *frontal lobes* are associated with the execution of planning and behavioral guidance (Damasio, 1994), while the *amygdala* seems to play a role in determining levels of aggression and emotionality (Buck, 1999). On the other hand, physiological studies have indicated that the hormone testosterone is relevant in regard to social interaction – for instance, determining whether someone will behave in an agreeable or aggressive manner – and sexual behavior (Dabbs, Alford, & Fielden, 1998; Dabbs, Strong, & Milun, 1997). Not only hormones but also neurotransmitters such as serotonin and dopamine seem to have solid links with emotion regulation and sociability (Zuckerman, 1999). This is consistent with the finding that recreational drugs, such as MDMA, tend to alter levels of serotonin and dopamine.

3.8.6   *Behavioral Genetics*

> Studies of heritability, limited parental influence, structural invariance across cultures and species, and temporal stability all point to the notion that personality traits are more expressions of human biology than products of life experience.
>
> (McCrae *et al.*, 2000, p. 177)

Another approach to personality research and theory is represented by the so-called *behavior-genetic* movement (discussed extensively in Chapter 7). This area of research assesses the impact of genetic (inherited) and nongenetic (environmental) factors, not only on personality traits but also on intellectual abilities. Here, I shall only summarize the implications of behavior-genetic findings on personality theory and research.

Behavior-genetic research has provided compelling evidence in support of the hypothesis that those general dispositions used to describe, classify, and compare individuals we refer to as personality traits are, to a great and observable extent, biologically transmitted and inherited (Plomin, Chipuer, & Loehlin, 1990). There are two important similarities between behavior-genetic and biological approaches discussed above. First, both attempt to explain psychological outcomes in terms of physical causes. Second, both rely on psychometrically assessed traits (therefore complementing the dispositional approach to personality). This emphasizes once again the importance of trait approaches to personality as a ubiquitous method and framework at the center of personality theory. Given that personality traits are latent constructs, we can only test hypotheses regarding the causes of personality traits in an indirect manner; that is, once we have inferred traits from psychometric sources. In fact, this has been often highlighted as a weakness of behavioral genetics, if only because the field would be more accurately labeled "trait genetics" (Funder, 2001).

As you will note from Chapter 7, there is evidence for the heritability of both personality and intelligence. However, estimating the extent to which individual differences may be affected by genes is only a first step toward addressing psychologically more important questions. A fundamental issue for psychologists and educators is what happens with the nongenetic or environmental causes of individual differences. For instance, studies suggest with quite remarkable consistency that even the *shared environment* (e.g., family, parenting, early experiences at home) has little impact on an individual's personality (Harris, 1995; Rowe, 1997; Scarr, 1992). However, critics have argued that specific behavioral outcomes are substantially more influenced than broad personality traits by shared environment (Turkheimer, 1998). In any case, the most fertile area of behavior-genetic research seems to involve the identification of interactive effects between environmental and genetic variables, notably the question of how personality-related choices that affect the environment may be genetically predetermined.

3.8.7   Evolutionary and Cultural Approaches to the Study of Personality

The *evolutionary* approach to the study of personality, also known as *sociobiology*, is based on the identification of the biological variables underlying personality and behavior and how these evolved from other species. As such, evolutionary approaches are more concerned with similarities than differences between individuals and should not, accordingly, be considered part of individual differences. It is clear, however, that identification of the most basic aspects underlying human behavior, thought, and emotionality will also provide information on individual differences. Evolutionary theories are therefore useful to mark the boundaries of individual differences and, more importantly, to scrutinize the biological roots of the major psychological aspects of human behavior.

In the same way as evolutionary theory explains an animal's (human or nonhuman) attempt to defend its territory, protect its offspring, and compete against others for available resources, sociobiologists posit that a number of behaviors often regarded as cultural or social, such as women's tendency to prefer wealthy men and men's tendency to prefer faithful women, are influenced by biological instincts rather than learned cultural norms (Buss, 1989). Furthermore, studies (e.g., Gosling & John, 1999) have shown that "human" personality dimensions such as Extraversion and the minor trait of dominance can be accurately used to describe and predict individual differences in animals too.

Evolutionary theories are also useful to explain findings derived from other types of designs, such as consequential or genetic studies. For instance, research into the personality correlates of interpersonal relationships and marital status suggests that there are mediating gender differences underlying the relationship between personality and propensity to marry. These differences can be interpreted in evolutionary or sociobiological terms, such that for men marriage desire would be an expression of dominance, while for women it would be an attempt to obtain affiliation and protection (Buss, 1987; Johnson *et al.*, 2004).

It is important to bear in mind that, at the other end of the line from evolutionary studies, *cultural* approaches to personality traits argue quite emphatically for cross-cultural differences in personality. These differences would affect not only the distribution of scores at levels of each trait, but also the very validity of dispositional and situational frameworks. Thus, according to Triandis and Suh (2002, p. 137):

> traits exist in all cultures, but account for behavior less in collectivist than in individualist cultures. Situational determinants of behavior are important universally, but more so in collectivist than in individualist cultures.

At the same time, cultures may prescribe and set the parameters in which personality may be expressed. Collectivistic cultures tend to be more *homogeneous*, which is itself in contradiction with the expression of individual differences. Conversely, individualistic cultures (as the name clearly suggests) praise individuality and are therefore more *heterogeneous*. These cross-cultural differences are even noticeable during the developmental stage of adolescence, which is commonly associated with rebellious attitudes and defiance of authority. In homogeneous countries such as Singapore, adolescents tend to conform to cultural norms, rejecting the use of alcohol, cigarettes, or drugs and maintaining a moral sexual practice (Ball & Moselle, 1995).

Evolutionary and cultural approaches are not always incompatible. Cultural effects can be understood as the result of evolutionary changes. For example, it is likely that homogeneous/collectivistic societies may have evolved from *farming* cultures, while heterogeneous/individualistic societies may have evolved from *hunting* cultures (Berry, 1976). Evolution may therefore play a key role in shaping socialization patterns, which in turn affect the expression of individual differences (Maccoby, 2000). However, the distinction between farmers and hunters is out of date, at least when it comes to characterizing today's modern world. Developed countries represent information rather than hunting or farming societies, and this implies a higher order of complexity in the expression of values, attitudes, and individual differences such as personality traits.

3.9 SUMMARY AND CONCLUSIONS

This chapter has covered three main topics: methodological approaches to the study of personality, validation of personality traits as predictors of real-life outcomes, and alternative approaches to the psychometric/dispositional approach to personality (notably, grand theories of personality). As has been seen:

- A great deal in the evolution of personality research has been achieved by the incorporation of correlational designs and similar statistical methods introduced by Pearson. Most dispositional studies are done on large datasets and use sophisticated procedures for data analyses, such as regressions, tests of mediation and moderation, and structural equation modeling (SEM), which enable researchers to test personality theories against a variety of real-life outcomes.

- Personality traits, such as the Big Five, have been found to be valid predictors of academic and occupational performance, psychological and physical health, and even happiness. Each of these outcomes has been the focus of different personality researchers and will probably one day represent an entire area of research. Reviewers such as Ozer and Benet-Martinez (2006) illustrate the importance of personality across different settings, indicating that the Big Five have behavioral consequences in every aspect of our lives. In simple terms, personality matters.

- Personality research has not been confined solely to the study of traits or validation of the Big Five. Indeed, it is only in the last two decades or so that dispositional approaches started to dominate the field of personality. Until then, personality was largely associated with "grand theories" of psychology, such as psychoanalytic, behaviorist, and evolutionary paradigms. Unlike trait approaches, grand theories tend to highlight similarities rather than differences between individuals and are concerned with universal aspects of human behavior.

The theories of personality covered in Chapters 1 and 2 have focused on normal behaviors, or what may be considered general aspects of individual differences. However, individuals also differ in regard to psychological health. The causes and consequences of such differences will be examined in Chapter 4.

TEXTS FOR FURTHER READING

Chamorro-Premuzic, T. & Furnham, A. (2006). Intellectual competence and the intelligent personality: A third way in differential psychology. *Review of General Psychology*, 10(3), 251–67.

Funder, D.C. (2001). Personality. *Annual Review of Psychology*, 52, 197–221.

Grant, H. & Dweck, C.S. (1999). A goal analysis of personality and personality coherence. In D. Cervone & Y. Shoda (Eds.), *Social-Cognitive Approaches to Personality Coherence* (pp. 345–71). New York: Guilford Press.

Matthews, G., Davies, D.R., Westerman, S.J., & Stammers, R.B. (2000). *Human Performance: Cognition, Stress, and Individual Differences*. London: Psychology Press.

Mischel, W. (1999). Personality coherence and dispositions in a cognitive-affective personality system (CAPS) approach. In D. Cervone & Y. Shoda (Eds.), *Coherence in Personality* (pp. 37–60). New York: Guilford Press.

Salgado, J.F. (1997). The five factor model of personality and job performance in the European Community. *Journal of Applied Psychology*, 82, 30–43.

Watson, J. (1913). Psychology as a behaviorist views it. *Psychological Review*, 20, 158–77.

Westen, D. (1998). The scientific legacy of Sigmund Freud: Toward a psychodynamically informed psychological science. *Psychological Bulletin*, 124, 333–71.

4   Psychopathology

LEARNING OUTCOMES

BY THE END OF THIS CHAPTER, YOU SHOULD BE ABLE TO ANSWER THE FOLLOWING FIVE KEY QUESTIONS:

1. How can we judge whether someone is normal?
2. What are the main approaches to psychopathology?
3. What is schizophrenia?
4. What are anxiety disorders?
5. What is the dimensional or continuum view of psychopathology?

KEY WORDS

Biopsychosocial Approach • Concordance Rate • Diathesis-Stress Model • Expressed Emotion • Maladaptiveness • Mental Illness Approach • Negative Symptoms • Obsessive-Compulsive Disorder • Personality Disorder • Positive Symptoms • Psychopathology • Psychotic Symptoms • Social Norm • Statistical Deviance

CHAPTER OUTLINE

4.1   INTRODUCTION

psychopathology (also called **abnormal psychology**) studies the causes, treatment, and consequences of psychological disorders or mental illnesses such as depression, anxiety, and psychoses.

This chapter is concerned with **psychopathology** or the study of abnormal behavior. Before we start, it is important to notice that this is a major area of psychology, with links to wider clinical practices such as psychiatry, psychiatric nursing, social work, and the medical sciences in general. Thus even a summary of psychopathology would exceed the scope of this book. However, the contribution of psychopathology to our understanding of individual differences cannot be neglected.

Differential psychology attempts to explain differences between individuals, and such differences can often be explained in terms of mental illness or psychological disorders. Although this may suggest an overlap between personality and psychopathology, there is a distinction between the two. Whereas personality refers to individual differences in general or normal behavior, psychopathology focuses exclusively on abnormality (see Figure 4.1). In the past decade there has been increased interest in the relationship between personality and psychopathology as conceptualized in terms of a continuum between normality and abnormality.

I present the topic of psychopathology in this chapter by beginning with a look at definitions of abnormality and the historical development of this discipline. Then I examine the dominant approaches and systems of classification in psychopathology, which are widely used to define, describe, and categorize specific psychological disorders. Next I look at the salient diagnostic categories for the major psychological disorders, with a particular focus on personality disorders. Applied implications and criticisms, as well as links to other individual differences, are discussed at the end of the chapter.

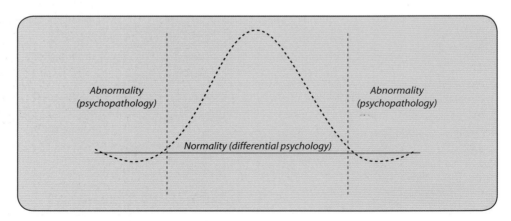

FIGURE 4.1 *Differential psychology and psychopathology*

4.2 DEFINING ABNORMALITY

It would be impossible to understand the meaning and object of study of psycho-pathology without first defining abnormality. Unfortunately, this is one of the most contentious issues in psychology, which makes for a complicated start! However, the difficulties of this task are also a sign of the variety of approaches to the study of abnormal behavior. There are several conventional criteria for defining abnormality, such as statistical deviance, social and moral norms, personal distress, and maladaptiveness associated with behavior, as well as the mainstream clinical approach of mental illness diagnosis (Davison & Neale, 1998).

> **statistical deviance** an approach that conceptualizes abnormality in terms of behaviors that are extreme, rare, or unique, as opposed to typical.

The **statistical deviance** approach conceptualizes abnormality in terms of behaviors that are extreme, rare, or unique, as opposed to typical. Looking back at Figure 4.1, we can think of normal behaviors as those that fall within the central range of the bell curve, while abnormal behaviors would be found at the two ends or extremes. One problem, however, is that, even if we had a clear cut-off point to distinguish between frequent and infrequent behaviors (which is not the case anyway), there are many examples of statistical outliers (observations or measurements that are unusually large or small relative to the other values in a dataset) that would rarely be described as "abnormal." For instance, few people can play

> **social norm** a rule or guideline, determined by cultural factors, for what kind of behavior is considered appropriate in social contexts, e.g., whether burping after a meal is seen as a compliment or a sign of rudeness.

the piano like Mozart or football like Diego Maradona, and there are probably even fewer people with Einstein's ability to discover the hidden laws of physics. We could in fact compile an extensive list of unusual behaviors that would often be considered eccentric, original, or creative, but rarely abnormal. Thus the statistical deviance approach refers to behaviors that are not merely infrequent, but also undesirable or negative, which suggests an implicit moral code.

There is arguably no better way to understand the underlying morals of judging abnormality than by examining the **social norm** approach, which considers the various cultural factors determining the perceived normality of a wide range of human behaviors (Scheff, 1966). For example, in some countries burping after a meal is seen as socially acceptable and complimentary to the chef, whereas in others it would simply be interpreted as rude or uneducated behavior. Some governments condemn the consumption of alcoholic

PHOTO 4.1 *Einstein (pictured in 1921) was a genius, a statistical outlier ... but would you say he was abnormal?*

Image courtesy of http://commons.wikimedia.org/wiki/File:Albert_Einstein_%28Nobel%29.png.

drinks, whereas others have very relaxed attitudes toward drugs. Some countries strive to promote an equal gender ratio in the workplace, whereas others encourage female circumcision. All these norms are dependent not only on geographical or cross-cultural factors, but also on chronological ones. Thus homosexuality was commonly regarded as abnormal in the past and, bearing in mind the fast advances in biogenetics, it would not be surprising if in a few decades' time sexual intercourse were no longer regarded as normal. People's perceptions of normality, then, are determined by cultural rules, which explains the moral discomfort in people's reactions to behaviors that are culturally condemned or unacceptable.

A more important form of discomfort, and a third criterion for defining abnormality, is the notion of personal *distress*, which takes into consideration individuals' level of suffering and whether they want to get rid of that suffering (Davison & Neale, 1998). Although this approach overcomes the disadvantages of statistical and social criteria, it has other weaknesses, notably the fact that abnormality is not always associated with subjective suffering or the experience of discomfort.

Just as individuals may be diagnosed with cancer, HIV, or diabetes, and nonetheless fail to experience any unpleasant symptoms until the very advanced stages of their illness, anorexic individuals (see Section 4.7.4 on eating disorders) may happily starve themselves for several days before experiencing any distress, whereas manic individuals (see Section 4.7.2) will experience exaggerated feelings of wellbeing even in negative circumstances. Everyday behaviors, such as smoking and drinking, may also be considered dangerous from a medical perspective and yet be associated with pleasure rather than pain in the short term. Conversely, it would be inaccurate to regard an individual as abnormal if she is suffering from the loss of a close relative or loved friend, or because she has just been made redundant. That said, the notion of personal distress is important, because most forms of physical and psychological illness are at least at some point associated with some subjective discomfort or personal distress, and it is this experience of suffering that often prompts individuals to seek help.

maladaptiveness the extent to which behavior interferes with a person's capacity to carry out everyday tasks such as studying or relating to others.

Another reason individuals may seek help is the **maladaptiveness** of their behavior; that is, the extent to which behavior interferes with their capacity to carry out everyday tasks (notably study, work, and relate to others). In fact, some consider this the most important criterion for defining abnormality (Davison & Neale, 1998). A common example of maladaptive or disruptive behaviors are those related to anxiety disorders, such as phobias, panic attack, and obsessive-compulsive disorder, all of which *inhibit* the individual in the action and completion of what would normally be regarded as very simple, mundane tasks. Thus fear of driving, flying, or enclosed spaces may stop individuals from working, going on holiday, or studying alone.

Despite their specific weaknesses, it would be harsh to deny that the above approaches (summarized in Figure 4.2) represent useful criteria for defining the boundaries between normal and abnormal behavior. Indeed, most people tend to rely, albeit intuitively, on these approaches when it comes to interpreting their own and others' behavior. Although it is usually more complicated to diagnose psychological than physical illness, both share an element of statistical deviance, social norms, personal distress, and maladaptiveness. Thus no matter how tempting it may seem

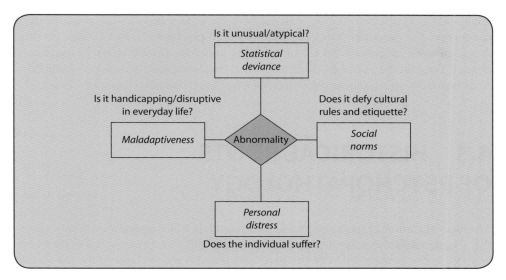

FIGURE 4.2 *Criteria for defining abnormality*

from a theoretical perspective to ignore these criteria (by claiming, for instance, that abnormality is simply a socially constructed, and therefore unreal, notion), the practical implications of doing so would be unfortunate. Just imagine a psychiatrist who, faced with a screaming individual who is pressing a knife against his own wrist, simply interprets that behavior as a sign of "individuality."

Although the four approaches described above represent important criteria for defining abnormality, professional practitioners tend to follow a more formal procedure in judging the abnormality of behavior. Thus clinical psychologists and psychiatrists focus on specific *symptoms* that meet the criteria for a predefined diagnosis (Davison & Neale, 1998). This approach, known as the **mental illness approach**, will be described throughout the rest of this chapter and attempts to integrate physical and psychological variables in order to account for a broad understanding of the processes underlying abnormal behavior. Most of the time, however, it works at a *descriptive* rather than a theoretical level. Based on clinical evidence derived from the therapist's observations, interviews, and assessments, and a compiled classification of psychological disorders, it establishes the normality or abnormality of behavior in terms of predefined pathologies (these are described and explained in Section 4.6).

mental illness approach an approach to psychological disorder that integrates physical and psychological variables in order to understand the processes underlying abnormal behavior.

As will be seen, there are few well-established psychophysical mechanisms in understanding mental disorders. Even when there is agreement on the taxonomy or system of classification that ought to be used, such as the DSM-IV or ICD-10 (explained in Section 4.5), these are simply descriptive and have little scope beyond the labeling of symptoms. "Obsessive-compulsive disorder," for instance, does not refer to a physically based disease but to obsessive and compulsive symptoms. The same can be said about eating disorders and other anxieties: they are self-explanatory but predominantly descriptive. On the other hand, psychological and psychiatric classifications for diagnoses are still influenced by cultural norms and may (fortunately) be subject to change. For example, until 1973 the American Psychological Association (APA) listed homosexuality among the most serious psychological disorders (Spitzer, 1981).

4.3 HISTORICAL ROOTS OF PSYCHOPATHOLOGY

The historical roots of psychopathology are relatively well documented. Hippocrates, the Greek philosopher and physician credited with the invention of medicine, believed in the connection between psychological and physical disorders, the former being caused by the latter. As seen in Section 2.4 in Chapter 2, this idea was present in his conceptualization of the major temperament types, though Hippocrates also attempted to explain pathologies such as melancholia, mania, and phrenitis, which were common disorders in ancient Greek society. Accordingly, psychological illness was attributed to a physiological dysfunction.

Conversely, Plato (428–348 BC) argued that disorders should be understood in terms of *intrapsychical* conflicts. Rather than looking for physical causes, Plato was convinced that mental disorders were, to put it simply, "all in the mind." Both approaches would be further developed by modern theorists and still coexist in contemporary views of psychopathology. Hippocrates' idea that psychological symptoms have physiological causes is represented by the *somatogenic* approaches to psychopathology, whereas Plato's interpretation of mental disorders in terms of intrapsychical conflicts is deeply embedded in some of the salient *psychogenic* theories of abnormal psychology. While both approaches focus on different causes, we will see that most psychological disorders can be best understood in terms of both psychological *and* biological determinants.

Although psychopathology did not develop as a major area of psychology until the beginnings of the 20th century, mental

PHOTO 4.2 *An Alaskan Shaman, known as a Yup'ik, in the 1890s. He is practicing an exorcism on the young boy.*

Image courtesy of http://en.wikipedia.org/wiki/Shaman.

disorders have a longstanding history and have been documented in every continent and form of society, from ancient China (as early as 2674 BC!) to ancient Greece, Rome, the Incan empire, and notably Egypt. In most cases, symptoms were regarded as the expression of supernatural forces that controlled the individual's mind and body, and mental disorders were treated through obscure rituals such as exorcisms and shamanism – a tribal form of medicine based on magical and spiritual intervention. Ancient Egyptians seemed particularly preoccupied with maintaining a healthy balance in the mind or "soul." They had special temples for the mentally ill and performed rituals that included the use of opium to reduce pain. Archeological discoveries of prehistoric perforated skulls suggest that ancient societies already implemented psychophysical treatments on mentally ill individuals, in many cases successfully. Until modern times, however, behavioral abnormalities were mostly treated with violence and mentally ill individuals were typically marginalized rather than looked after. This was particularly common in the Middle Ages, where "loss of reason" was believed to be caused by witches or demons. Thus in 1484 the Pope ordered "possessed" individuals to be burned alive (Nolen-Hoeksema, 2001).

An early exception to this reactive and aggressive approach to mental disorders was the small English housing facility of St. Mary of Bethlehem. Known as Bedlam and established in 1243, it is widely regarded as the first formal attempt at psychopathological hospitalization. However, and in spite of remaining open until the early 1800s, treatment was virtually nonexistent at Bedlam, making it more of a tourist attraction than a psychiatric institution.

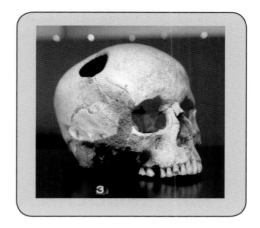

PHOTO 4.3 *A perforated skull from the Iron Age*

The process of cutting out a hole in the skull is known as trepanation. The new growth of bony tissue around the hole suggests that this person lived through the operation!

Image courtesy of Natural History Museum, Lausanne: http://en.wikipedia.org/wiki/Trepanation.

PHOTO 4.4 *Philippe Pinel, who proposed moral treatment of those who were classified as mentally ill.*

Image courtesy of http://en.wikipedia.org/wiki/Pinel.

The first attempt to treat and help the mentally ill dates back to the 1700s, when Philippe Pinel (1745–1826), anticipating the spirit of the French Revolution, proposed the *moral treatment* of those affected by mental disorders. Pinel's methods introduced friendlier policies for hospitalized patients, such as eliminating chains, preventing physical abuse, improving living conditions, and even offering advice or moral guidance (for a different account, see Section 4.8). Another major contribution by Pinel was his attempt to categorize symptoms, which led to the broad differentiation between melancholia, mania, dementia, and idiocy (diagnostic categories are discussed in Section 4.7). Inspired by Pinel, William Tuke founded the York Retreat in 1796. Despite the unsurprisingly limited efficacy of moral treatment for the cure of serious mental disorders, this deliberate attempt to help mentally ill individuals inspired the creation of several English and American institutions in order to both understand and treat mental disorders.

4.4   MODERN APPROACHES TO PSYCHOPATHOLOGY

Modern approaches to psychopathology tend to posit that mental illness has a physical origin and are thus consistent with early somatogenic theories, such as that of Hippocrates/Galen (see Section 2.4 in Chapter 2 and Section 4.3). One of the first representative figures of the modern somatogenic paradigm was Wilhelm Griesinger (1817–68), a German psychiatrist who argued that brain pathology was the cause of all mental disorders. Around the same time, Emil Kraepelin (1856–1926) and Eugen Bleuler (1898–1927) developed similar theories, no doubt due to the rapid developments in anatomy, physiology, neurology, and chemistry that were then taking place. Kraepelin's main contribution was the first modern classification of symptoms, labeling and describing different psychological disorders. An important distinction was made between manic depressive disorders and dementia praecox, later referred to as schizophrenia (see Section 4.7.1).

One particularly clear and famous example of how structural changes in the brain may impair normal psychological functioning is the Phineas Gage case. Gage was a 25-year-old railworker who suffered a spectacular injury when an iron bar penetrated his head (see Figure 4.3). Although Gage was lucky enough to survive the accident, he showed radical transformations in behavior after suffering the injury. Having been responsible, agreeable, ambitious, and hardworking all his life, after the injury he became irreverent and capricious, showing no respect toward social norms or other individuals. Surprisingly, and despite his losing every form of emotional and social control over his behavior, Gage's intellectual skills remained intact (Damasio *et al.*, 1994).

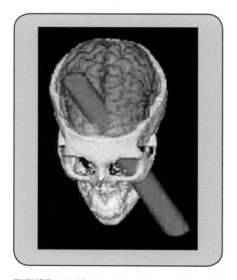

FIGURE 4.3 *Phineas Gage's Brain Injury*

Source: © Dana and David Dornsife Cognitive Neuroscience Imaging Center at the University of California.

On the other hand, the Austrian physician Franz Anton Mesmer (1734–1815), in the tradition of Plato and the psychogenic paradigm (see Section 4.3), believed psychological disorders to be the expression of psychical rather than physical factors. Mesmer's initial and no doubt obscure theory assumed mental illness to be caused by "magnetic fluids," a sort of astrological energy force inside people's bodies. Furthermore, Mesmer believed himself to be in possession of a healing touch that could positively influence ill individuals and cure them! He also developed a hypnotic method called *mesmerism* (which gave birth to the expression *mesmerized*) that he applied on patients, sometimes in sessions lasting for several hours.

Jean Martin Charcot (1825–93), a prestigious French neurologist who was initially skeptical of Mesmer's theory and believed that psychological disorders were caused by a degeneration of the brain, nonetheless experimented with mesmerism and found that patients experienced substantial relief after being able to talk about their symptoms under hypnosis. This process was called

PHOTO 4.5 *Freud's master, Jean Martin Charcot (1825–1893)*

Image courtesy of http://en.wikipedia.org/wiki/Jean-Martin_Charcot.

catharsis, alluding to the ancient Greek idea of tragic theater as a method of coexperiencing negative emotions with the actors, and would have a major influence on one of Charcot's students, Sigmund Freud (1856–1939).

4.4.1 Psychoanalysis and Psychodynamic Theories

Freud's studies of the so-called hysterical disorder, a bizarre illness that caused mostly well-off Victorian women to lose the functioning of or feeling in specific parts of the body, led him to conclude that there was an *unconscious* intrapsychical origin to mental illness. Evidence for this claim was derived from the fact that, under hypnosis – when patients are not conscious – hysterical symptoms could be induced.

Subsequent clinical observations led Freud to the theoretical development of psychoanalysis, a therapeutic method and theory based on the exploration of the unconscious. Psychoanalytic theories are often referred to as psychodynamic, for they deal with the processes underlying dynamic conflicts between unconscious and conscious psychological forces. Although psychodynamic theories developed in the context of abnormal behavior and mental disorders, they posit that *all* behaviors (normal and abnormal) are influenced by unconscious processes. Thus psychoanalysis has been used to understand human behavior in general and applied to a wide range of areas such as philosophy, literature, and sociology, making Freud the most famous psychologist of all times (Haggbloom *et al.*, 2002). Although even a summary of Freud's theory would exceed the space available for this book (he wrote more than 25 books and there are many more by other authors attempting to explain or reinterpret his theory), it is certainly important to summarize some of the basic ideas of the psychoanalytic approach to psychopathology.

Freud understood psychopathological symptoms as a compromise between unconscious and conscious forces that represents a symbolic expression of traumatic or repressed events. According to Freud, the sexual and aggressive drives are the two universal forces underlying human behavior. If social and cultural constraints did not exist, our instinctive reaction would be to release both our sexual and aggressive tensions in order to minimize pain and maximize pleasure. Freud called this "operating by the pleasure principle" or "primary process thinking." However, because every form of society is based on some form of prohibition, we are obliged to trade off immediate pleasures for long-term rewards and conform to the "principle of reality."

Drives not released through actual behavior are directed onto various symbolic formations that allow part of them to be expressed while conforming to the principle of reality. Examples of these formations are fantasies, dreams, and, as anticipated, psychological symptoms. In order to untangle the etiology of symptoms and psychological disorders, it is necessary to account for the unique and complex history of every individual. More importantly, there can only be hope of overcoming mental illness if the patient can elaborate on their own unconscious wishes – usually repressed childhood fantasies – to overcome the psychological conflict.

One possibility is to *transfer* unconscious desires onto the therapist, "pretending," say, that he or she is our father or mother, to allow unconscious desires (of hate or love) to be expressed in behavior rather than symptoms. This, however, is a long and tedious process that would prove ineffective with most serious, biologically based mental illnesses. Some treatments may last for 10 or 20 years, at a rate of more than one meeting per week! Besides, Freud's theory is based on few case studies and is largely untestable. Most claims are based on circular interpretations and speculative theories rather than robust and representative empirical evidence.

4.4.2 Behaviorism

In the first half of the 20th century, while psychoanalysis was gaining momentum in Europe, a very different psychological explanation for mental disorders developed within the behaviorist movement. Unlike psychoanalysis, behaviorism was concerned with the study of empirically observable behavior and was uninterested in hypothetical psychodynamic conflicts. Furthermore, behaviorism in its purest and more radical form denied the existence of any internal mental processes and explained human behavior, including psychological disorders, in terms of *conditioning*. Accordingly, symptoms would merely be a consequence of reinforcing or punishing specific behaviors, and psychology would cease to be the science of the mind and become the science of behavior. Figure 4.4 compares behavioral therapy with the two other main types of psychotherapy.

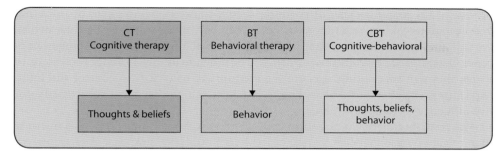

FIGURE 4.4 *Three main types of psychotherapy*

All types lead to the identification of personalized, time-limited therapy goals and strategies.

The roots of behaviorism are deeply experimental and attempted to replicate the robust research methodology of the hard sciences (e.g., biology, physics, and chemistry). Lightner Witmer (1867–1956) imported to the United States the techniques he learned in Germany from Wilhelm Wundt (1832–1920), one of the fathers of experimental psychology. Witmer inaugurated the first "experimental clinic" in the University of Pennsylvania, dedicated to the study of mental deficiencies in children. Meanwhile, Ivan Pavlov (1849–1936) in Russia and John Watson (1878–1958) in America applied the principles of classic conditioning to the study of phobias.

In what is arguably one of the most representative quotes of the radical behaviorist spirit of the early 20th century, Watson (1930, p. 104) famously claimed:

> Give me a dozen healthy infants, well-formed, and my own specified work to bring them up in, and I'll guarantee to take any one at random and train him to be any specialist I might select – doctor, lawyer, artist, merchant-chief, and yes, even beggar-man and thief, regardless of his talents, penchants, tendencies, abilities, vocations, and the race of his ancestors.

A variation of classical behaviorism was later introduced by Thorndike (1874–1949) and Skinner (1904–90), who noticed that rewarding desirable behaviors was more effective than punishing undesirable ones. This effect/method was referred to as *operant conditioning*. Despite the controversial ethical implications associated with behaviorism, it has been shown to be effective with regard to the treatment of anxiety disorders and phobias, and is still used widely today. Theoretically, however, behaviorism represents a reductionist explanation of behavior as it fails to account for a variety of mental processes, which, albeit hypothetical, are useful for understanding psychopathology and developing effective treatments for psychological disorders.

4.4.3 *Cognitive Revolution*

With the decay of behaviorism, a new wave of research emerged in the 1960s and 1970s that attempted to understand the internal mental processes so emphatically ignored and denied by behaviorists. These processes or *cognitions* were at the center of the cognitive revolution in psychology and represent another important contribution to our understanding of mental illness.

One of the major legacies of cognitive theory to psychopathology is the idea that people's subjective interpretations of events can have a direct impact on their behavior and emotion. Bandura (1986), a leading figure of the cognitive movement, conceptualized this idea in terms of *self-efficacy* or individuals' belief about the extent to which they can successfully execute the appropriate behaviors to control and influence important life events. According to Bandura, self-efficacy has a substantial positive influence on people's wellbeing.

The contribution of the cognitive approach to psychopathology has been not only theoretical but also clinical. A good example is Ellis's (1973) *rational emotive therapy*, which conceptualizes illness as the result of irrational negative beliefs about oneself and the world. These beliefs tend to be absolute, unrealistic, and self-defeating, even when they stem from apparently positive assumptions such as "everybody must love me all the time." The disparity between unrealistic ideals that are out of reach and the perceived reality is, according to Ellis, the main cause of mental illness. The role of the therapist is therefore to enable changes in the patient's beliefs, introducing a more realistic outlook on the world. This is often achieved through overt confrontation between the therapist and the client (Dryden & DiGiuseppe, 1990).

4.4.4 *Biological Approaches*

Technological advances in the past 50 years have caused an unprecedented increase in research into the *biological* causes of psychopathology. Broadly speaking, biological approaches can be divided into neuroanatomy or those dealing with the *structure* of the brain, and neurophysiology or those dealing with the *processes* or *functions* of the brain. In combination, neuroanatomy and neurophysiology represent the multidisciplinary field of neuroscience, which is rapidly developing within and outside psychopathology.

The most common biological studies in psychopathology investigate the biochemical correlates of mental illness, notably the role of *neurotransmitters*, which are chemical messengers that carry information between neurons and other cells. Imbalances in several of the at least 100 types of neurotransmitters are known to be associated with psychological disorders. For example, *serotonin* affects emotion and impulse regulation, such as levels of aggression, whereas *gamma-aminobutyric acid* (GABA) is a major inhibitor of behavior. Most notably, *dopamine* levels have been strongly linked to psychosis and schizophrenia, mainly since the effective introduction of the so-called phenothiazine drugs, which reduce psychotic symptoms through blocking dopamine receptors, and the identification of the increase of dopamine levels by amphetamines and cocaine (Valenstein, 1998).

Studies on the biological causes of psychopathology have also examined the potential role of the endocrine system, which is responsible for the production and release of *hormones* in the blood. Hormones are known to affect mood, levels of energy, and reactions to stress, all of which constitute important aspects of psychopathology. For instance, the *adrenocorticotrophic hormone* (ACTH) plays a substantial role in determining levels of stress, triggering the release of another 30 hormones.

In spite of technological advances in brain-measuring equipment, most biochemical variables can only be measured indirectly in living humans.

4.5   INTEGRATIVE APPROACHES TO PSYCHOPATHOLOGY: THE BIOPSYCHOSOCIAL MODEL

Although some (particularly psychiatrists) believe that the evolution of psychopathology is largely a function of replacing psychogenic approaches with somatogenic, much of the improvements in psychopathology in recent years have depended on the *integration* of the different approaches discussed above, though there are also other approaches such as humanistic and sociocultural theories of abnormal behavior. This multidisciplinary perspective is often referred to as the **biopsychosocial approach** to psychopathology, and its major exponent is the **diathesis-stress model**.

According to the diathesis-stress model (Cicchetti & Rogosch, 1996; Monroe & Simmons, 1991; Williams, 1985), psychopathological symptoms and diseases are caused by a combination of biological, psychological, and social factors. In simple terms, this model explains mental illness as a byproduct of inherited vulnerabilities (diatheses) and unbearable life experiences (stress) (see Figure 4.5). An individual's level of vulnerability or predisposition is biological and can be explained in terms of pathological brain structures or processes at the level of genes, neurotransmitters, and hormones. The life events or stressors that trigger that disposition, however, are environmental.

biopsychosocial approach a multidisciplinary approach to psychopathology based on the idea that mental illness results from a combination of biological, psychological, environmental, and social factors.

diathesis-stress model this model suggests that some people possess an enduring, inherited vulnerability (diathesis) that is likely to result in psychological disorder (e.g., schizophrenia) when they experience an unbearable life event (stressor).

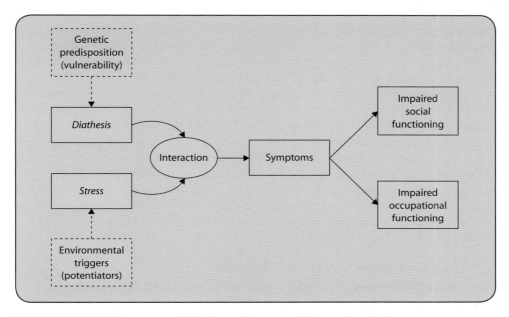

FIGURE 4.5 *Diathesis-stress model: An integrative approach to psychopathology*

For example, conflictive relationships with friends or other family members may cause dispositional factors to be manifested in the form of mental illnesses such as schizophrenia (see Meehl, 1962, and Section 4.7.1). Thus vulnerability is necessary but not sufficient in itself to cause the mental illness, as is the stressor.

The diathesis-stress model also explains physical illnesses such as hypertension, diabetes, or hyperlipidemia. For example, genetic factors alone may not lead to heart attack if there is sufficient exercise, balanced nutrition, and no smoking or alcohol abuse. Likewise, an unhealthy lifestyle may still lead to serious physical illness even if there is no history of previous illness in the family.

4.6   DIAGNOSIS: CLASSIFYING PSYCHOLOGICAL DISORDERS

Aside from the various theoretical approaches discussed above, there are two main frameworks for classifying psychological disorders; namely, idiographic and nomothetic. The *idiographic* framework, which is widely adopted by psychoanalytic and psychodynamic theories (see Section 4.4.1), emphasizes the singularity of mental illness and assumes psychological disorders to be manifested differently in every individual. Accordingly, it treats each case completely separately and establishes no comparisons with predefined norms or diagnostic classifications. Conversely, the *nomothetic* framework is based on preestablished categories and compares every case with previously defined, described, and classified psychological disorders. This framework, which will be the focus of the present chapter, represents the mainstream approach in psychopathology and is often referred to as the psychiatric model. As you may note, the distinction between idiographic and nomothetic frameworks in psychopathology is comparable to the distinction between situational and dispositional conceptualizations of personality (see Sections 2.2 and 2.5 in Chapter 2).

The two dominant taxonomies for diagnosing mental disorders are the *International Classification of Diseases, Injuries, and Causes of Death* (ICD) and the *Diagnostic and Statistical Manual of Mental Disorders* (DSM). The ICD, the latest version of which is ICD-10 (World Health Organization, 1992), covers both mental and physical disorders and is more widely used in Europe. The DSM, the latest revision of which is DSM-IV (American Psychiatric Association, 1994), represents the state-of-the-art classification system in the US and refers exclusively to mental disorders, though it is largely based on the ICD. Both systems have converged considerably in the past decades and there is large overlap between them today. Thus I shall focus only on DSM-IV.

Diagnostics are based on:

- some *core* symptoms that need to be present;
- prespecified periods of *time* for symptoms to be present; and sometimes
- symptoms that should *not* be present.

The DSM follows a *multiaxial format* comprising five different axes, though axes 1 and 2 alone may determine the diagnostic. *Axis 1* (shown in Table 4.1) describes the major types of disorders, for example affective disorders and anxiety disorders. *Axis 2* includes lifelong conditions such as mental handicap and personality disorders (e.g., paranoia, schizoid, antisocial behavior, narcissism; see Section 4.9) that lead to enduring maladaptive behavior. *Axis 3* refers to the medical or biological causes of mental dysfunctions. *Axis 5* focuses on daily adaptive functioning; that is, the extent to which illness interferes with everyday life.

Two major aspects to assess the usefulness of the DSM and ICD are *reliability* and *validity*. Reliability refers to the extent to which there is agreement about the diagnosis. Just as a reliable scale will signal the same weight for the same object every time it is weighed, different observers using the same criteria should arrive at the same diagnostic for the same individual, and different targets exhibiting similar symptoms should be diagnosed with the same illness. Although both DSM-IV and ICD-10 have shown improved reliability with regard to earlier versions, especially for schizophrenia, mood, and anxiety disorders (Sartorius *et al.*, 1993), the system is far from ideal and inter-agreement correlations are typically modest to moderate, but rarely high.

Table 4.1 *DSM-IV, Axis 1 (Major Types of Disorders)*

Infancy/childhood/adolescence disorders: e.g., learning and development disorders, attention deficit, hyperactivity, and autism.

Late adulthood disorders: serious and often irreversible impairments of cognition and mental functioning, e.g., delirium, dementia, amnesia.

Substance-related disorders: disorders that involve ingestion of drugs that bring change to mental functioning.

Detachment from reality: disorders that involve hallucinations, delusions, and thinking impairment, either intermittently or indefinitely (e.g., schizophrenia and other psychoses).

Affective disorders: disorders based on severe alterations of mood/affect (e.g., depression, mania, bipolar disorder).

Anxiety disorders: disorders characterized by anxiety and exacerbated worry (e.g., phobias, obsessive-compulsive disorder, post-traumatic disorder).

Somatoform or dissociative disorders: disorders characterized by physical symptoms that do not correspond to physical illness, i.e., have no apparent physical cause.

Sexual/gender disorders: deviations from normative sexual practices (e.g., paraphilias, fetishism, pedophilia, and sadomasochism).

Eating and sleeping disorders: e.g., anorexia nervosa, bulimia nervosa, insomnia, narcolepsy, and apnea.

Factitious disorder: a rare case whereby individuals self-induce physical or psychological symptoms to attract people's attention.

Adjustment disorder: emotional or behavioral disorders that follow stressful life events and do not fit into any other category.

Impulse control disorder: disorders characterized by impulsive behaviors that are out of control, e.g., kleptomania (compulsive stealing), pyromania (compulsive burning), and gambling (in its pathological form).

Validity, on the other hand, refers to the question of whether the system of classification can effectively distinguish one diagnosis from another. Thus two individuals with different symptoms should be diagnosed with different illnesses, just as two individuals who differ in weight should be given different weights. There are different types of validity. *Etiological validity* is based on the causes of the diseases: the same or similar causes should be identified for the same diagnoses. *Concurrent validity* refers to the idea that the same disorders should be expressed in terms of the same secondary symptoms. For instance, most schizophrenics suffer from memory impairment, though this is not a central symptom of schizophrenia (Stirling, Hellewell, & Hewitt, 1997). *Predictive validity* refers to the extent to which we can accurately anticipate the outcome and course of a disorder, as well as individuals' response to treatment. For instance, people suffering from bipolar disorders will typically respond well to lithium drug treatments. Again, the validity of diagnostic categories is far from perfect and has often been the focus of harsh criticism (see, e.g., Section 4.8).

4.7   MAJOR PSYCHOLOGICAL DISORDERS

Major psychological disorders are at least as likely to occur and be reported as are medical illnesses such as heart diseases and cancer. According to the National Alliance for the Mentally Ill, more than 20 percent of US adults will experience some kind of mental illness every year, and half of those will also experience maladaptive symptoms. Some of the most common groups of mental illness, which are briefly examined below, are schizophrenia, affective disorders, anxiety disorders, and eating disorders, though the overall lists of disorders today includes 374, up from only a dozen at the beginning of the 20th century and 192 in the early 1950s.

4.7.1   *Schizophrenia*

At the turn of the 20th century, a form of madness that came to be called schizophrenia was described and distinguished from mood disorders like mania and melancholia. [It] was observed in young people and persisted for years, working its way deeply and intimately into mind and behavior. People with the illness might hear the roars of Satan or the whispers of children. They might move armies with their thoughts and receive instructions from other worlds. They might feel penetrated by scheming parasites, stalked by enemies, or praised by guardian angels. People with schizophrenia might also speak nonsensically, their language at once intricate and impenetrable. And many would push, or be pushed, to the edge of the social landscape, overcome by solitude. (Heinrichs, 2005, p. 229)

Schizophrenia is one of the most severe and debilitating forms of mental illness. It is a psychotic disorder characterized by the patient's lack of insight and loss of contact with reality. It is *episodic*, which means that normal and abnormal functioning interact.

In the worst form of the illness, schizophrenic individuals are completely unable to distinguish between inner (mental) and external reality, suffering from severe thinking and perception impairment. Some of the salient syndromes or groups of symptoms of schizophrenia are:

- *Hallucinations* or fake perceptions, most commonly noises/voices, though other senses can be involved, too.
- *Delusions* or false beliefs, e.g., of persecution or power; they can often be part of complex conspiracy theories.
- *Disorganized speech*: speaking incoherently or abstractly.
- *Disorganized behavior*: acts that deviate from normative cultural parameters, such as dressing strangely, crying or laughing for no apparent reason, and so on.
- **Negative symptoms**: reduced or inappropriate emotional responses, lack of affect, reduced motivation and speech.
- *Passivity*: the experience that an external "evil" force is in control of the individual's thoughts and behavior (Liddle, 1987).
- *Neurocognitive deficits*: impairments in memory, attention, executive function, and social cognition (Heinrichs, 2005).

> **negative symptoms** in schizophrenia, symptoms that indicate the absence of something normal, e.g., reduced or inappropriate emotional responses, lack of affect, or reduced motivation.

Most patients will usually experience more than one of the above-listed syndromes throughout the course of illness. If two or more syndromes are present for at least one month, individuals will meet diagnostic criteria for schizophrenia, though the presence of auditory hallucinations (i.e., hearing voices) alone may be considered sufficient to diagnose schizophrenia. As emphasized by the maladaptive conception of abnormality (see Section 4.2), symptoms should also impair normal functioning in areas such as work or interpersonal relations. Besides the one-month rule for central syndromes, some kind of disturbance ought to persist for at least six months before a reliable diagnosis is made.

Schizophrenia was originally conceptualized by Kraepelin as dementia praecox or "early madness" because its symptoms appeared much earlier than in other mental illnesses. When Bleuler renamed the disorder "schizophrenia" (literally, "split mind"), he attempted to emphasize the dysfunctional nature of associative thinking and other basic cognitive functions such as attention, memory, and judgment. Despite popular belief and the etymology of the term, however, schizophrenia does not involve a split or double personality. It is also uncharacteristic of schizophrenic individuals to behave in an aggressive manner, though aggression may sometimes be a consequence of their reaction to intolerable symptoms, for instance responses to paranoid hallucinations and delusions.

Historically, different types of schizophrenia have been identified, notably *catatonic*, *hebephrenic*, and *paranoid*. More recent classifications, such as the DSM-IV, have included two further types; namely, *residual* and *undifferentiated*. Catatonic schizophrenia is characterized by kinetic abnormalities, such as abrupt or odd body movement. Disorganized schizophrenia (also known as hebephrenic) is manifested in terms of both thought disorder and decreased affect. Paranoid schizophrenia consists of vivid

positive symptoms in schizophrenia, symptoms that indicate the presence of something unusual, e.g., delusions, hallucinations, and thought disorder.

and horrifying hallucinations, but rarely manifests itself in terms of thought disorder or disorganized behavior. Residual schizophrenia is typified in terms of **positive symptoms** (e.g., delusions, hallucinations, and thought disorder) that are only present at a low intensity. Finally, undifferentiated schizophrenia comprises none of the above psychotic symptoms; that is, symptoms that are representative of any other type of schizophrenia. See Table 4.2.

Schizophrenia is rarely manifested before late adolescence. It may start with frequent states of low mood, high anxiety, and abrupt changes of affect, then gradually develop to hallucinations. The initial or *acute* phase of the illness is often characterized by positive symptoms, whereas the more advanced or *chronic* phase, which may take place several years later, shows reductions in activity, motivation, and emotional response as well as increasing hallucinations. The positive symptoms that characterize the acute phase make it difficult to diagnose schizophrenia before the disorder has advanced and developed to its chronic phase.

In statistical terms, schizophrenia is a rare disease. Traditionally estimates suggested that about 1 person in 100 will suffer from schizophrenia at some stage of their lives, though recent estimates are more conservative and report the number of cases to be in the region of 2 to 4 per 1000. This may seem like a low percentage rate, but if you multiply it by the overall population of a city or a country the number of affected patients will be substantial. There is generally little cross-cultural variability in the number of schizophrenic cases reported, a fact that has often been used to emphasize the biological basis of this disorder. Of those suffering from schizophrenia, 20 percent will typically experience only one acute episode, with about 30 percent experiencing more than one. In both cases, full or partial recovery will be the most frequent outcome, with only 10 percent of cases being permanently impaired after several incidents.

There are many factors that may help recovery, such as being married, having a good educational background, or having a good past employment record (Shepherd *et al.*, 1989). In addition, females tend to recover better and more frequently than males. It is also noteworthy that a progressive and early start of the illness is more likely to be associated with a slower and more difficult recovery, especially if there are no identifiable external stressors to which the disorder can be attributed. In all cases, symptoms need to be treated as soon as possible.

Schizophrenic patients are usually treated with *antipsychotic/neuroleptic* drugs, acting mostly on the dopamine and, to a lesser extent, serotonin and histamine neurotransmitters. These chemical messengers affect levels of mood and emotionality and

Table 4.2 *Main types of schizophrenia*

- *Paranoid*: preoccupation with delusions and hallucinations (but no disorganized speech or behavior, nor inappropriate affect). Has best prognosis.
- *Disorganized*: disorganized speech, behavior, inappropriate affect (but no catatonia).
- *Catatonic*: movement abnormalities, mutism.
- *Undifferentiated*: none of the above.

are overactive in schizophrenics (Seeman, 1980; Snyder, 1976). However, causal links at the neuropsychological level are yet to be investigated. Cognitive therapy, if combined with antipsychotic drugs, can help to reduce hallucinations and delusions, especially in the first stages of illness, and has long-term beneficial effects (Crow *et al.*, 1986; Kuipers *et al.*, 1998).

Little is known about the cause of schizophrenia. Somatogenic approaches focus on the role of brain structure and genes. Although these effects cannot be directly observed, family, adoption, and twin studies provide indirect evidence for the biological etiology of schizophrenia. It is estimated that there is a 10 percent risk of developing the disorder among first-degree relatives, 3 percent among second-degree relatives, and 2 percent among third-degree relatives (Kendler & Diehl, 1993; Slater & Cowie, 1971). Adoption studies suggest that the risk of developing schizophrenia is virtually the same if individuals have been adopted away than if they were raised by their natural parents (Heston, 1966; Rosenthal, 1971). Most impressively, twin data indicate that the **concordance rate** for monozygotic (MZ) or identical twins, who have 100 percent of genes in common, is 38 percent higher than for dizygotic (DZ) or nonidentical twins, who have 50 percent of genes in common, and first-degree relatives (Gottesman & Shields, 1972). Although this provides convincing evidence for the importance of genetic factors in the etiology of schizophrenia, it does not rule out environmental causes.

concordance rate the extent to which people show the same disorders.

Other attempts to identify the biological determinants of schizophrenia have included genetic mapping (Sherrington *et al.*, 1988), searching for deficient chromosomes, computed tomography (CT), magnetic resonance imaging (MRI), and measuring brain and cerebral ventricles (Raz & Raz, 1990). Cognitive neuroscientists have found that certain brain areas, such as the left frontal lobe, may fail to monitor plans and intentions, leading to lack of awareness and hallucinations (Frith, 1992; Spence *et al.*, 1997).

On the other hand, psychogenic theories have emphasized the impact of early childhood and family experiences on the development of schizophrenia. Freud (1966/1896) interpreted schizophrenia as the expression of an unconscious conflict between sexual impulses and sociocultural norms. Accordingly, schizophrenic symptoms would be a compromise between these two forces, though mediated by several complex defense mechanisms. As with most psychoanalytic hypotheses, there are not many ways to test this assumption empirically. However, the more general idea that stressful events or environmental demands may trigger schizophrenic symptoms has been accepted more widely (see Section 4.5).

Other psychoanalysts suggested that schizophrenia could be caused by chaotic family relations or abnormal parenting styles (Fromm-Reichmann, 1948; Laing, 1971). This view is consistent with the **expressed emotion** perspective, which points out that when families express their negative emotions to the schizophrenic individual, his or her illness will be likely to aggravate (Vaughn & Leff, 1976; Stirling *et al.*, 1993). Hence the importance of *family therapy* for the treatment of people with schizophrenia (Hogarty *et al.*, 1991).

expressed emotion the specific set of feelings and behaviors directed at people with schizophrenia by their family members.

4.7.2 *Affective Disorders*

Another major type of mental illness is represented by the so-called affective disorders, which are characterized by the exaggerated intensity of mood experiences throughout long periods. Crucially, such experiences seem either unrelated or disproportionate reactions to external real-life events.

Depression, as the everyday connotation of the word suggests, is characterized by a persistent low mood or *anhedonia*. It causes speech reduction, lack of joy, and pessimistic, often suicidal, feelings of guilt. Perceptual abnormalities and reductions in appetite and sex drive are also frequent. In addition, depression is often associated with lack of concentration and attention, and increased anxiety. Depressive symptoms are classified as *reactive* if they develop as a response, albeit disproportionate, to real-life stressors, or *endogenous* if they have no external cause at all. They are also classified on the basis of their gravity; namely, as neurotic if minor or psychotic if severe, though no clear-cut distinction exists (Paykel *et al.*, 1988).

Depression is one of the most common and disabling mental disorders, with approximately 20 percent of reported cases globally, including 6 percent with lifetime risks. It is more frequent in women, poor, and lonely people (Brown & Harris, 1978), suggesting cultural and social determinants. Depression can last from a mere few weeks up to several years (Angst, 1978), but most treated patients will tend to recover.

The most widely used and effective treatment for depression is antidepressant medication, though in urgent cases quicker methods such as electroconvulsive therapy (ECT) are often applied. ECT is a speedy but controversial technique by which electrical activity is induced on the brain. Specifically, it involves the introduction of a tonic seizure where the patient loses consciousness for at least one minute. Contrary to popular belief, long-term negative effects of ECT are rare (Zervas & Fink, 1992), especially when administered under anesthesia and muscle relaxants, as it normally is. Another alternative to psychopharmacological treatment is cognitive therapy (CT), which requires patients systematically to collect information about distorted self-beliefs and restructure them in an adaptive fashion (Beck *et al.*, 1979). It has recently been argued that CT is superior to psychopharmacological treatment because it prevents future relapses (Hollon, Stewart, & Strunk, 2006). The authors claimed that "prior CT has an enduring effect that is at least as large in magnitude as keeping patients on medications" (Hollon, Stewart, & Strunk, p. 11.6). However, it is not clear why such an effect would take place. One plausible explanation is that the newly introduced cognitions would persist over the original self-defeating beliefs, thus making the individual less vulnerable to future stressors (Hollon, Shelton, & Loosen, 1991; see also Figure 4.6).

Psychoanalytic theories explain depression in terms of lack of maternal affection and symbolic loss (Freud, 1957/1917; Klein, 1935), while psychosocial approaches similarly emphasize the etiological aspects of stressful life events (Brown & Harris, 1978), for instance the loss of a partner or family member. According to Seligman (1974), repeated exposure to negative and unpleasant events will lead to a state of *learned helplessness/hopelessness*, which predisposes individuals to negative expectations and feelings. Along these lines, cognitive psychologists have argued that depression

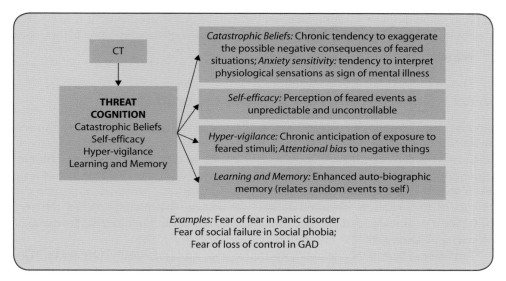

FIGURE 4.6 *CT and the view of mental illness as a thought disorder*

may be caused by low self-esteem and *negative attributional style* (Lewinsohn *et al.*, 1994), particularly in adolescence. These biased and self-defeating beliefs can often be changed through cognitive therapy (Beck, 1983).

The second major type of mood disorder is mania and is represented by the opposite extreme of affect than depression. Thus manic individuals experience exacerbated elevated mood and an inappropriate sense of wellbeing (e.g., optimism, overconfidence, and overexpression of positive emotions). These states can last for several weeks, though usually in alternation with normal mood states. Other symptoms may include abnormal thought and speech (e.g., rapid, uninterrupted, incoherent, inconsistent) as well as **psychotic symptoms**, notably delusions of grandeur. Manic behavior is characterized by overactivity and increased sexual and aggressive impulses.

psychotic symptoms symptoms such as hallucinations, incoherent speech, and delusions that indicate a distorted perception of reality.

About 1 percent of the population is estimated to suffer from mania, though manic symptoms are more frequent in the context of bipolar mood disorders, where manic and depressive symptoms alternate. Manic patients are treated with lithium and antipsychotics and require hospitalization, often against their will, no doubt because of their subjective feeling of wellbeing. If adequately treated, the most common prognosis for manic patients is recovery within six weeks.

Biological explanations point at *genetic* factors underlying affective disorders. Twin studies indicate that the concordance rate for MZ is very high (68 percent if reared together, 67 percent if reared apart), and much larger than in DZ (23 percent) (Shahuria, 2003). It is possible that genetic factors determine biochemical differences in neurotransmitters, particularly in the so-called *monoamine* group, involved in mood regulation (Sachar & Baron, 1979). In addition, endocrinal factors (hormones) seem particularly relevant with regard to depression, notably the underactivity of the thyroid gland. However, causal links are difficult to demonstrate and it is likely that psychological processes affect physiological states as much as physiological processes affect psychological states.

4.7.3 Anxiety Disorders and Obsessional States

Another main psychopathological category comprises anxiety disorders and obsessional states, both of which are characterized by the experience of high levels of anxiety. As noted elsewhere (Chapters 2, 3, and 9), anxiety is a fundamental human emotion and is therefore not exclusive of abnormal disorders. Further, it has long been observed that anxiety has several positive adaptational functions, preparing the individual for action by signaling danger in threatening situations. When chronic, however, it is unrealistic (disproportionate to any threat) and unbearable for the individual (see Figure 4.7).

Anxiety can be experienced both psychologically and somatically (physically). The most common psychological symptoms are unpleasant and dreadful feelings, though in severe cases they may include panic attacks and fear of death. Somatic symptoms include increased heart rate, accelerated breathing rate, muscular tension (e.g., scalp, back, shoulder), and, in general, increased arousal (e.g., inability to relax/settle, fall asleep, concentrate).

One of the most common anxiety disorders is phobias; that is, the experience of irrational or disproportionate fear of an object or *phobic stimulus* that leads the individual to avoid contact with that object. The object of phobias can be anything from spiders to darkness and social interaction, though usually it is represented by a group of related stimuli (e.g., insects, heights, people). Even when phobic individuals are aware of the irrationality of their fear, they are still unable to establish contact

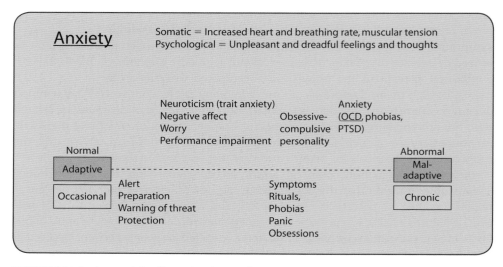

FIGURE 4.7 *Anxiety and the dimensional view of normality–abnormality*

with the phobic event or object, which impairs normal functioning. Women are more commonly affected by phobias than are men, except during childhood when there are no significant gender differences in phobias. Thus, adult phobias are often regarded as a continuation of normative childhood fears. A common treatment for phobias is *systematic desensitization*, which consists of progressive exposure to the phobic object. In recent years this technique has also been combined with computer technology, notably applying virtual reality experiences that simulate an encounter with the phobic object (useful if you fear crocodiles).

Grouped alongside phobias and anxieties is **obsessive-compulsive disorder** (OCD), which is defined by intense and repetitive obsessional experiences and compulsive acts. These acts are in fact rituals to relieve the individual from anxiety. However, they are often performed against the individual's will, becoming a problem in itself. OCD tends to start in early adulthood, and about 3 percent of the population is reported to suffer from it at some point.

There are several theoretical models for explaining the causes of phobias and other anxiety disorders. Psychodynamic theories have tended to follow the Freudian conception of symptoms as symbolic

obsessive-compulsive disorder a disorder characterized by intense and repetitive obsessions that generate anxiety, e.g., fear of contamination, and compulsive acts or ritualistic behaviors to reduce anxiety, e.g., hand washing.

PHOTO 4.6 *If you live in Chicago (pictured) you may have a problem, because such irrational fears would probably be maladaptive, turning into a phobia.*

Image courtesy of Tomas Chamorro-Premuzic.

formations representing the conflict between unconscious sexual or aggressive impulses and social/cultural norms (Freud, 1955/1909). Behaviorists, such as Watson and Rayner (1920), believed that phobias could be induced in humans as in animals through associationism and conditioning. More recent behaviorist approaches have postulated a *two-process theory*. The first phase would involve conditioning and inducement of fear, while a second phase, called operant conditioning, would involve avoidance of contact with the phobic stimulus (Eysenck, 1976). For example, if a child is attacked by a dog (stage 1), she may avoid contact with other – potentially *good* – dogs (stage 2). In turn, this avoidance would somehow perpetuate the child's fear of dogs.

Evolutionary explanations, on the other hand, have emphasized the fact that not just any object will be easily associated with fear and phobias. Rather, phobic stimuli possess a certain element of real threat, which explains why insects, snakes, heights, and dentists are common objects of phobias. In that sense, there would be a certain element of *preparedness* and adaptation underlying the causes and manifestations of phobias (Seligman, 1971).

Cognitive approaches have suggested that phobic individuals may be unusually sensitive or have more vulnerable *schemata* (knowledge structures) for interpreting events (Beck & Emery, 1985). Thus they would be more predisposed to develop phobias.

Biological approaches have emphasized the *evolutionary basis* of anxiety disorders. This emphasis derives from the fact that anxiety is not only a psychopathological symptom but also – and much more frequently – a ubiquitous human emotion. Twin studies suggest that there is a large inherited component of anxiety disorders, as the concordance rating for MZ (49 percent) is substantially larger than for DZ (4 percent) (Slater & Shields, 1969). This would indicate that genes are largely influential in determining the individual's *vulnerability* to anxiety disorders. Neuropsychological studies have shown that overactivity of the noradrenaline (norepinephrine) neurotransmitters

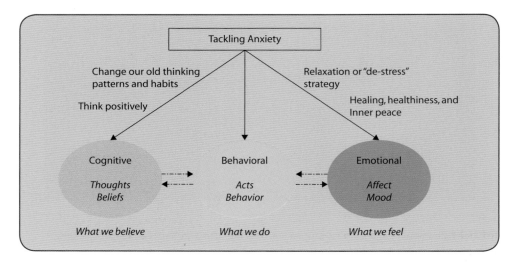

FIGURE 4.8 *Three ways of tackling anxiety via CBT*

is largely associated with anxiety attacks, while serotonin (another neurotransmitter and major regulator of emotionality) has sometimes been associated with the adaptational function of preparing the individual for danger and stress (Deakin & Graeff, 1991).

Ways of tackling anxiety disorders are outlined in Figure 4.8. In line with the diathesis-stress model (see Section 4.5), it should be noted that a combination of both psychological and biological theories can best help to understand the etiology of anxiety disorders. Thus genetic factors, which contribute to an individual's vulnerability, are likely to interact with environmental stressors, which *trigger* mental illness. A typical example is post-traumatic stress disorder (PTSD), which emerges as a reaction to stressful or traumatic events that exceed an individual's psychophysiological coping mechanisms.

4.7.4   *Eating Disorders*

Eating disorders, which include *anorexia* and *bulimia nervosa*, are a common psychological illness characterized by exacerbated worry about food, body shape, and weight, and related physical symptoms. More than any other mental illness, eating disorders are related to cultural, economic, and social factors, being much more common in Western industrialized countries than others. This is probably due to the current Western stereotype of beauty, which encourages women (and increasingly

PHOTO 4.7   *There is increasing pressure on the fashion industry to change their ideals of female beauty, which encourage women to be extremely slim. This trend has coincided with the growing cases of eating disorders.*

Image courtesy of Nadia Bettega, reproduced with permission.

also men) to stay thin – see Photo 4.7. Thus gender differences in eating disorders, a mental illness traditionally associated with women, have been reduced in the past 50 years or so.

Most anorexics start by dieting and can be objectively overweight initially, though their dieting efforts will persist after they have lost weight. Another common aspect is the experience of low self-esteem, for instance after being bullied at school or breaking up with a partner. In later phases of the illness, negative effects on relationships are typical, mostly driven by arguments about not eating. Thus psychotherapists have emphasized the importance of group/family therapy in treatment.

Like anxiety disorders, anorexia may be associated with the experience of anxiety, in particular when anorexic individuals fail to stop themselves from eating. Conversely, excessive concerns with food that successfully lead to a reduction of food intake will generate personal satisfaction and reduce anxiety. Anorexic individuals have often been described as quiet, unassertive, anxious, and sexually inexperienced. They also tend to be ambitious and achievement oriented, but have low self-esteem. In any case, this mere combination of personality attributes is not enough to predict illness.

Approximately 25 percent of individuals who suffer from anorexia will have long-term difficulties, while the rest normally recover after one year of treatment (Hsu, 1990). Long-term symptoms may range from menstrual disorders in women to infertility, starvation, and even suicide. It is also not uncommon for anorexic individuals to develop *bulimia nervosa* before fully recovering. Unlike anorexia, bulimia is not associated with actual weight loss and abnormal body weight, but bulimic individuals are significantly more likely than the average person to indulge in alcohol and drug consumption. Again, a combination of both psychotherapy and psychopharmacological drugs constitutes the best treatment for eating disorders (Agras *et al.*, 1992).

FOCUS POINT 4.1   EATING DISORDERS AND THE MEDIA

Jen Hunter, the winner of the 2006 "Make Me a Supermodel" competition, sparked a huge debate about the fashion industry's ideals relating to body shape when she won the contest ahead of the skeletal Marianne Berglund. Jen repeatedly got told she was too fat and had to lose weight when she was a healthy size 12, whereas Marianne received continual compliments about her great body despite her unhealthy BMI of 16. Soon thereafter, several big names in fashion stopped hiring size zero models after young Brazilian model Luisel Ramos died of self-starvation. This story highlights the dangers of anorexia and the role of the media in shaping people's self-perceptions of body ideals.

The three major characteristics of anorexia nervosa are:

- A serious and permanent concern about one's *body shape*, weight, and thinness.
- An active pursuit and maintenance (through vomiting, dieting, or laxatives) of low *body weight*.
- The absence of menstrual periods in females, indicating a disturbance of hormonal status.

There has been much speculation about the etiology of eating disorders, particularly in recent years. Unlike other disorders, there is little evidence for the vulnerability hypothesis, though there is some proof of genetic influence, as the concordance rate for relatives is 10 percent, compared to 2 percent in the general population (Theander, 1970). Twin studies have found higher concordance rates for MZ than DZ twins (Sullivan, Bulik, & Kendler, 1998). On the other hand, from a feminist perspective (Bemis, 1978), eating disorders have been explained as an attempt to conform to certain stereotypes (usually portrayed by the media), while the family interaction hypothesis focuses on the role of dysfunctional families (Minuchin, Rosman, & Baker, 1978), notably intrusive or overinvolved parents.

4.8 CRITICISMS OF THE DIAGNOSTIC APPROACH

Whereas the classification of syndromes into predefined diagnostic categories represents the dominant approach to mental illness in both psychiatry and psychopathology, there have been several opposing views, most notably criticisms by the antipsychiatry movement (Szasz, 1960).

In his famous book *Madness and Civilization*, French philosopher Michel Foucault (1926–84) presented a comprehensive historical analysis highlighting the subjectivity underlying the idea of mental illness and the fact that madness has always been associated with punishment. In the Middle Ages, lepers, the homeless, and "lunatics" were locked up or shipped away; in the 17th century, they were imprisoned alongside criminals. Even with the introduction of treatment by the likes of Pinel and Tuke (see Section 4.3), says Foucault, the aim was to *control* rather than help those suffering from mental illness. Tuke's method was largely based on punishment and intimidation of the mad until they were able to behave like most people, whereas Pinel's treatment included freezing showers and straitjackets. Likewise, preestablished definitions of mental illness may merely reflect a political maneuver to punish individuals who do not "fit" into desirable social models, and diagnostic manuals such as the ICD or DSM would be designed to justify medical and social action against individuals who, albeit not responsible for any crimes, deviate from the norm.

Critics of the diagnostic approach also include experimental psychologists, such as Bentall (1990), who questioned the scientific soundness of the notion of schizophrenia (see also Boyle, 1990). Evidence for the occurrence of hallucinations and other psychotic symptoms in normal populations has long suggested that there may be a "continuum" between mental illness and normality (Bentall, 1990; Galton, 1880; Laroi *et al.*, 2005). Indeed, Sarbin and Juhasz (1967, p. 353) argued:

Since the 1920s textbooks of general psychology have differentiated hallucinations from errors of perception by the simple expedient of locating them in separate chapters.

Even when hallucinations are indicative of mental illness, they are not exclusive of schizophrenia but can often be found in affective psychoses such as mania (Taylor & Abrams, 1975).

4.9   DIMENSIONAL VIEW OF PSYCHOPATHOLOGY AND PERSONALITY DISORDERS

In recent years, there has been an increasing shift toward a *dimensional* view of psychopathology; that is, the idea that mental illnesses merely represent quantitative (as opposed to qualitative) departures from normal behavior. This approach is epitomized by the notion of **personality disorders**, defined as an "enduring pattern of inner experience and behavior that deviates from the expectations of the individual's culture, is pervasive and inflexible, has an onset in adolescence or early adulthood, is stable over time, and leads to distress or impairment" (APA, 1994, p. 629). Less severe than major psychoses and famously conceptualized by Freud as "character neuroses," personality disorders affect an estimated 10–15 percent of the population (Zimmerman & Coryell, 1989). Although personality disorders may cause individuals to "feel at home in their own disordered condition" (O'Connor & Dyce, 2001, p. 1119), their disruptive nature is substantial and affects educational, occupational, and interpersonal functioning.

personality disorder a persistent pattern of thinking, feeling, and behaving that deviates from cultural expectations and impairs a person's educational, occupational, and interpersonal functioning. Such disorders begin at a relatively early age, are stable over time, and are pervasive and inflexible.

While personality disorders represent "either extreme or significant deviations from the way the average individual in a given culture perceives, thinks, and feels" (WHO, 1993), they have been traditionally classified in categorical terms. Thus *Axis 2* of the DSM (in its current as well as previous 1980 edition) lists the following clusters:

- Cluster A: *antisocial* (the most widely researched and oldest personality disorder, previously known as "psychopathic"), *borderline*, *narcissistic*, and *histrionic*, which are characterized by odd and eccentric behaviors as well as disregard for others.
- Cluster B: *schizotypal*, *schizoid*, and *paranoid*, which are characterized by dramatic, erratic, and emotional behaviors.
- Cluster C: *avoidant*, *obsessive-compulsive*, *dependent*, and *passive-aggressive*, which are characterized by anxious and fearful behaviors.

Despite widespread agreement on the above list, which is purely descriptive, mainstream personality researchers are hoping that the next revision of the DSM shifts to a dimensional model of personality disorders (McCrae, Loeckenhoff, & Costa, 2005). Indeed, a recent issue of the *European Journal of Personality* (2005) was entirely devoted to the cause of a model that integrates normal and abnormal classifications of personality along a continuum, with a focus on psychometric inventories (both self- and other-reports) rather than the currently dominant unstructured interviews (Westen, 1997). Thus Widiger and Samuel (2005, p. 279) argued that "few clinicians would attempt to diagnose mental retardation in the absence of a structured test, yet this is the norm for most other diagnoses."

Trull and Durrett (2005) proposed a dimensional model that conceptualizes abnormal and normal personality in terms of four common factors; namely, Neuroticism/negative affect/emotional dysregulation, Extraversion/positive affect, dissocial/antagonistic behavior, and Conscientiousness/constraint/compulsivity. This taxonomy is consistent with several previous studies (e.g., Austin & Deary, 2000; Livesley, Jang, & Vernon, 1998; O'Connor & Dyce, 2001) and suggests that, except for Openness to Experience, the same latent factors cause responses to both clinical and nonclinical personality inventories, which implies that they can be simultaneously used to describe normal and abnormal patterns of behavior. Accordingly, it should be possible to use specific levels and combinations of the Big Five personality traits to describe and predict personality disorders, but which ones?

In a recent meta-analysis of more than 15 studies (1967–2001), Saulsman and Page (2004) looked at the particular combination of the Big Five associated with each personality disorder, as well as the recurrent pattern of Big Five correlates of personality disorders. Table 4.3 summarizes these findings.

As can be seen, most personality disorders were positively correlated with Neuroticism (N), and negatively correlated with Agreeableness (A) and Conscientiousness (C). The Extraversion (E) and Openness (O) correlates of personality disorders are more variable in both direction and strength. For instance, people with histrionic personality disorder tend to be substantially higher on E, while those with avoidant personality disorder tend to be substantially lower on E. O, on the other hand, was negatively associated with schizoid but positively associated with histrionic personality disorders. The mean effects suggest that N (positively) is the most significant correlate of personality disorders, followed by A (negatively).

A clear advantage of incorporating a dimensional model in psychopathology would be the capacity to explain the stability of personality disorders, as these are extreme variations of genetically influenced traits (Cloninger, 1987; Zuckerman, 1991). Normal traits, such as the Big Five, are fairly stable throughout the lifespan, with typical reliabilities in the region of .50 over a 10-year period. Drastic changes are particularly odd for Neuroticism and Extraversion (the two classic dimensions of temperament) and after the age of 30 years.

Although the notion of stability seems incompatible with the idea of treatment – the success of psychotherapy, for instance, is largely based on the possibility of introducing change – this conflict is mainly apparent. Thus Costa and McCrae (1994, p. 35) explained that "behaviors, attitudes, skills, interests, roles, and relationships change over time, but in ways that are consistent with the individual's underlying personality."

Whereas personality traits are largely the product of genetic influences, "the personality pathology is found in the characteristic adaptations, not the basic tendencies" (McCrae et al., 2005, p. 273). In Figure 4.9 (adapted from McCrae & Costa, 1999), we can see how biologically based personality dimensions may affect an individual's

Table 4.3 *The Big Five and personality disorders*

DSM-IV personality disorders	Five Factor model personality dimensions				
	N	**E**	**O**	**A**	**C**
Paranoid	.28****	−.12****	−.04**	−.34****	−.07****
Schizoid	.13****	.23****	−.12****	−.17****	−.03*
Schizotypal	.36****	.28****	−.01	−.21****	−.13****
Antisocial	.09****	.04	.05**	−.35****	−.26****
Borderline	.49****	−.09****	.02	−.23****	−.23****
Histrionic	.02	.42****	.15****	−.06**	−.09***
Narcissistic	.04	.20****	.11****	−.27****	−.05*
Avoidant	.48****	−.44****	−.09****	−.11****	−.10****
Dependent	.41****	−.13****	−.11****	.05**	−.14****
Obsessive-compulsive	.08***	−.12****	−.07****	−.04	.23****
Mean	.24	−.07	−.01	−.17	−.09
Median	.20	−.12	−.02	−.19	−.09

Source: Saulsman & Page (2004), Table 5, p. 1068. Reproduced with permission from Elsevier.

adaptation and self-concept, which would in turn be affected by external influences (e.g., cultural and social norms, life events). Psychotherapy and other forms of treatment may be regarded as external influences, too.

4.10 SUMMARY AND CONCLUSIONS

This chapter has examined theories of psychopathology, an important area of psychology with historical roots dating back more than 2000 years. As has been seen:

- Throughout its history, the ongoing leitmotiv of psychopathology has been the study of abnormal behavior. Modern conceptualizations of normality are based primarily on the four conventional criteria of statistical frequency,

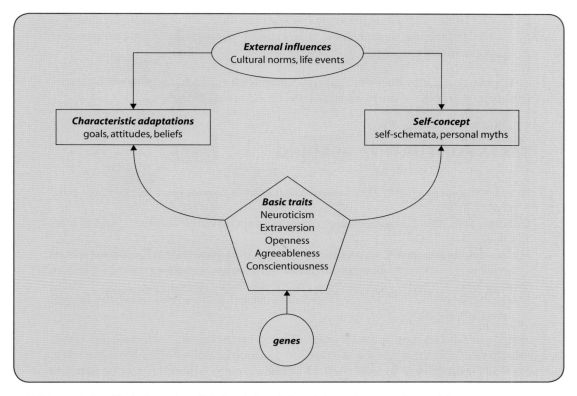

FIGURE 4.9 *A simplified adaptation of McCrae & Costa's (1999) dynamic personality model*

personal distress, social norms, and maladaptiveness, as well as the mental illness or diagnostic approach from mainstream clinical psychology and psychiatry. Despite their individual weaknesses and limitations, when combined these criteria represent an important tool for identifying psychopathological symptoms and are thus widely employed.

- There is broad consensus today on the idea that most psychological disorders are caused by a combination of genetic dispositions, known as diatheses, and situational demands, known as stress, that trigger the onset of psychopathological symptoms. Genetic influences on psychopathology are stronger in some mental illnesses, such as schizophrenia (the psychological disorder in which genes play the strongest role), than others, for instance eating disorders. This is clear from the effects of medication (i.e., psychoactive drugs) and recent studies in brain processes and structure.

- A great deal of the progress of differential psychology will depend on the extent to which personality theory and psychopathology can accurately define the boundaries between normality and abnormality. This may require a shift from qualitative to quantitative or dimensional conceptions of abnormality.

The latter has been increasingly advocated in the study of personality disorders and regards mental illness as an extreme and maladaptive manifestation of normal personality.

Chapter 5 will introduce the concept of intelligence, which, together with personality, represents one of the two major areas of individual differences.

TEXTS FOR FURTHER READING

Beck, A.T. & Emery, G. (1985). *Anxiety Disorders and Phobias: A Cognitive Perspective*. New York: Basic Books.

Heinrichs, R.W. (2005). The primacy of cognition in schizophrenia. *American Psychologist, 60,* 229–42.

McCrae, R.R., Loeckenhoff, C.E., & Costa, P.T. (2005). A step toward DSM-V: Cataloguing personality-related problems in living. *European Journal of Personality, 19,* 269–86.

Szasz, T. (1960). The myth of mental illness. *American Psychologist, 15,* 113–18.

Walker, E.F. & Diforio, D. (1997). Schizophrenia: A neural diathesis-stress model. *Psychological Review,* 104, 667–85.

5 Intelligence, Part I

LEARNING OUTCOMES

BY THE END OF THIS CHAPTER, YOU SHOULD BE ABLE
TO ANSWER THE FOLLOWING FIVE KEY QUESTIONS:

1. What is intelligence?
2. What is the history behind intelligence testing?
3. What does Cattell's model say about intelligence?
4. What do we know about the development of intellectual abilities?
5. Are there many intelligences, or is there just one?

KEY WORDS

Bell Curve • Crystallized Intelligence • Fluid Intelligence • *g* • Hereditary Genius • Intelligence Quotient (IQ) • Intelligence Testing • Mental Test • Socioeconomic Status (SES)

CHAPTER OUTLINE

5.1   INTRODUCTION

In earlier chapters I examined individual differences in personality (Chapters 2 and 3) and psychopathology (Chapter 4). As noted in Sections 1.4 in Chapter 1 and 4.1 in Chapter 4, personality encompasses individual differences in general, while psychopathology refers specifically to abnormal behavior and mental illness. Another major area of differential psychology is that concerned with the prediction of human performance (e.g., at school, work, and university). This area is commonly referred to as *intelligence* or *cognitive/intellectual ability*.

Given that performance is itself an aspect or type of behavior, intelligence, talent, or whichever construct is used to conceptualize individual differences in ability, ought to be considered a part of personality, too. However, personality and intelligence developed independently as the two major areas in differential psychology and, with the exception of Eysenck (see Sections 2.4 and 2.6 in Chapter 2) and Cattell (see Section 2.10 in Chapter 2), few researchers regarded intelligence as a component of personality. Thus textbooks and handbooks, whether edited or authored, have typically focused either on intelligence or on personality.

While there are sufficient methodological and theoretical reasons to justify the relative independence of personality and intelligence, there has been a recent marked increase of interest in the relationship between both constructs (Chamorro-Premuzic & Furnham, 2004, 2005). This book provides the *wider* picture of differential psychology, including both major areas: personality *and* intelligence. In this chapter, I review the historical aspects underlying the conceptualization and development of intelligence and salient issues concerning the structure of human abilities. In simple terms, this chapter addresses the question of *what intelligence is*. As personality, intelligence is also manifested in a number of real-life outcomes and is thus consequential. The consequences of intelligence are discussed in Chapter 6. In the same sense that Chapter 5 is to intelligence what Chapter 2 is to personality, then Chapter 6 is to intelligence what Chapter 3 is to personality (see Figure 5.1).

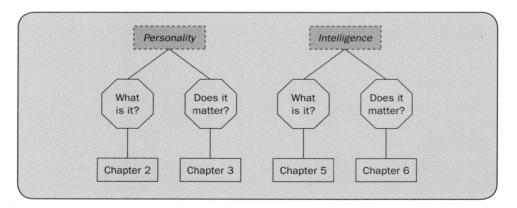

FIGURE 5.1 *Personality and intelligence chapters in context*

5.2   DEFINING INTELLIGENCE

To some extent, explaining the notion of intelligence may seem irrelevant since there is considerable overlap between lay and expert conceptions: both believe that certain mental or psychological processes account for differences in performance, and that these differences can be affected by biological as well as environmental factors. However, there is less agreement on how these differences can be measured, which abilities are more important, and whether people who score high on some ability may score low on others.

Despite these unresolved issues, the idea that some individuals are brighter than others has always been acknowledged in human society and is reflected in the number of language descriptors of ability. The *Oxford Thesaurus*, for instance, provides the following synonyms of intelligence: "clever, bright, sharp-witted, quick-witted, talented, gifted, smart, capable, able, competent, apt, knowledgeable, educated, sagacious, brainy, shrewd, astute, adroit, canny, cunning, ingenious, wily, inventive, skillful."

Contemporary uses of "intelligence" tend to be classified according to five different connotations, two of which are of psychological and three of military/organizational importance. The *Encarta Dictionary* provides the following definitions of intelligence:

(i) *Ability to think and learn*: the ability to learn facts and skills and apply them, especially when this ability is highly developed.

(ii) *Secret information*: information about secret plans or activities, especially those of foreign governments, the armed forces, business enemies, or criminals.

(iii) *Gathering of secret information*: the collection of secret military or political information.

(iv) *People gathering secret information*: an organization that gathers information about the secret plans or activities of an adversary or potential adversary and the people involved in gathering such information.

(v) *Intelligent spirit*: an entity capable of rational thought, especially one that does not have a physical form.

Only definitions (i) and (v) have a real psychological connotation, with definition (i)

PHOTO 5.1 *Greek commander of "great intelligence," who hid the Greek soldiers in a large wooden horse to attack the Trojans. This is one of the oldest uses of the word "intelligence" we know.*

Image courtesy of http://en.wikipedia.org/wiki/Odysseus

specifically reflecting the individual differences aspect of intelligence. Interestingly, though, definitions (ii), (iii), and (iv) are associated with military strategies and the concept of information, two aspects that are related to the development and conceptualization of the notion of intellectual ability in differential psychology. Indeed, intelligence has been associated with military strategy since ancient times. For example, in one of the oldest surviving literary works of European history, the Greek poet Homer (ca. eighth century BC) described Odysseus, the hero of the Trojan war, as "clever," "quick-witted," and of "great intelligence." Since the late 19th century, ability tests have been widely developed and used in the military for selection and recruitment (notably in the United States), and information is a key component of intelligence as it is linked to knowledge and learned facts (see Cattell's concept of *gc* in Section 5.4).

Table 5.1 provides several well-known definitions of intelligence by some of the most salient differential psychologists. Most of these definitions (1 to 11) appeared in a special issue of the *Journal of Educational Psychology* (1921) dedicated to "Intelligence and its measurement."

5.2.1 Conceptualizing Intelligence

Although the idea that some people are brighter than others predates scientific psychology, it was psychologists who contributed to *measuring* these differences in a systematic, robust, and unbiased way. The scientific notion of intelligence derives largely from the use of psychometric instruments to predict future performance in school, which explains why the concept of intelligence is closely related to scholastic achievement or the ability to excel academically. For many decades, however, intelligence was defined operationally rather than conceptually or theoretically (i.e., in terms of underlying psychological processes). For instance, one of the best-known definitions of intelligence has simply described it as what intelligence tests measure (Boring, 1923). Despite the circularity of this definition, often chosen by critics to accuse intelligence researchers of dealing with a meaningless construct, Boring also provided a much more descriptive (and empirically based) definition of intelligence, conceptualizing it as a "general ability" or "form of mental power that develops in the first five years of life to remain relatively stable after that."

Although intelligence is only an *inferred* notion – that is, a *latent construct* – it does refer to observable behavior. The extent to which intelligence is or is not a meaningful concept will therefore depend on empirical data or observable behavior. Typically, this behavior is measured in terms of individual differences in standardized performance on tests correlated with real-life outcomes, such as academic exam grades or job performance. Thus, the key issue is not whether we measure "intelligence" but whether we have found something worth measuring (Miles, 1957).

As shown in Figure 5.2, the notion of intelligence is directly inferred from the relationship between test scores (e.g., IQ points) and other criteria, such as performance in school or at work. If these are significantly correlated, we can assume that intelligence has similarly affected both test performance and school/job performance.

Any definition of intelligence will also have to conceptualize the underlying or latent processes that *cause* individual differences in test and school/job performance. Definitions of intelligence will be examined more closely throughout this chapter,

Table 5.1 *Some well-known definitions of intelligence*

Definition of intelligence	Author and year
1 The ability to carry out abstract thinking	Terman (1916)
2 The capacity for knowledge, and knowledge possessed	Henmon (1921)
3 The capacity to learn or to profit by experience	Dearborn (1921)
4 The capacity to acquire capacity	Woodrow (1921)
5 The power of good responses from the point of view of truth or facts	Thorndike (1920)
6 Sensory capacity, capacity for perceptual recognition, quickness, range or flexibility of association, facility and imagination, span of attention, quickness or alertness in response	Freeman (1921)
7 Ability to learn or, having learned, to adjust oneself to the environment	Calvin (1921)
8 Ability to adapt oneself adequately to relatively new situations in life	Pentler (1921)
9 A biological mechanism by which the effects of a complexity of stimuli are brought together and given a somewhat unified effect in behavior	Peterson (1921)
10 The capacity to inhibit an instinctive adjustment, the capacity to redefine the inhibited instinctive adjustment in light of imaginally experienced trial and error, and the capacity to realize the modified instinctive adjustment in overt behavior to the advantage of the individual as a social animal	Thurstone (1919)
11 Sensation, perception, association, memory, imagination, discrimination, judgment, and reasoning	Haggerty (1921)
12 Intelligence is what is measured by intelligence tests	Boring (1923)
13 A global concept that involves an individual's ability to act purposefully, think rationally, and deal effectively with the environment	Wechsler (1953)
14 The ability to use optimally limited resources – including time – to achieve goals	Kurzweil (1999)

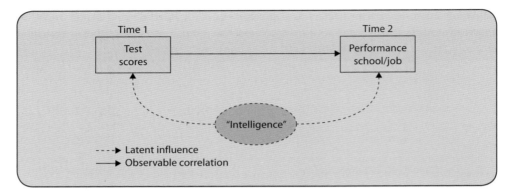

FIGURE 5.2 *The latent concept of intelligence in relation to both test scores and real-world performance*

but for an overview and preliminary understanding of the concept it should suffice to define it as a "general ability to reason, plan, solve problems, think abstractly, learn quickly, and learn from experience" (Gottfredson, 2000, p. 81). Intelligence, then, does not refer to specific abilities but to an "indivisible quality of mind that influences the execution of all consciously directed activities" (Robinson, 1999, p. 720).

5.3 HISTORY OF INTELLIGENCE TESTING

intelligence testing
the attempt to quantify and measure individual differences in cognitive ability by means of standardized tests that use words, numbers, or figures and are usually administered in written (paper or computer) or oral form.

A history of intelligence is largely a history of **intelligence testing**; that is, an account of psychology's attempt to quantify and measure individual differences underlying performance in an objective, scientific manner. In the words of René Descartes (1596–1650), a French philosopher and one of the most influential figures of modernity, "If something exists, it exists in some amount. If it exists in some amount, then it is capable of being measured." Accordingly, differential psychologists have dedicated themselves, in particular during the first half of the 20th century, to designing psychometric instruments to compare individuals on what they believed was the most important aspect of human intellect: intelligence.

5.3.1 Galton's Hereditary Genius

hereditary genius the idea that different levels of intelligence are determined by hereditary or genetic factors.

The first scientific attempt to conceptualize individual differences in cognitive ability is attributed to Francis Galton (1822–1911), who argued that **genius** was **hereditary** and normally distributed in the population. Both these ideas are still shared by most experts in the field. Galton's beliefs about talent and performance were heavily influenced by the work of his cousin Charles Darwin (1809–82), though autobio-graphical events played an equally important role (see Focus Point 5.1). Through the application of some of the statistical techniques developed by Quételet (1796–1874), Galton deduced that genetic forces determined different levels of intelligence, which in turn played a major role in selection and competition for survival. In some cases these assumptions led Galton to uphold some absurd conclusions, such as the belief that military leaders were usually short because taller men were more vulnerable shooting targets. With the same absurdity, Galton also believed in the intellectual superiority

FOCUS POINT 5.1   THE LIFE OF FRANCIS GALTON

Much has been said about the life of Francis Galton, often with admiration, but as often with dislike and disapproval. Regardless of any judgment, two things are probably beyond debate: (i) the fact that Galton can be counted among only a handful of highly influential figures in differential psychology (and, in light of the recent progress of behavioral genetics and the eloquent evidence for the causal nature of general intelligence, several experts would assess the impact of Galton's work as unmatchable in the field); and (ii) the fact that Galton's theory of eminent talent was closely related to (and probably

PHOTO 5.2: *Galton (1822–1911) in his later years.*

Image courtesy of http://en.wikipedia.org/wiki/ Francis_Galton

partly derived from) aspects of his personal life. It is this second fact that is most interesting, as interpretations differ as to how far and in which direction episodes in Galton's life led him to develop his theory of hereditary genius.

To some, the fact that Galton was born to a well-to-do aristocratic family (his ancestors included the founders of the Quaker religion and Barclay's bank, as well as Erasmus Darwin) inspired his ideas of inborn superiority and group differences in ability. However, Galton's emphasis on *nature* rather than *nurture* (the phrase is his) was not all determined by personal accomplishments. Although he was a prodigious child with an IQ once estimated at 200 points and compared only to the likes of Goethe, Leibniz, and John Stuart Mill (Boring, 1950; Terman, 1917), Galton's achievements were often below expectations, particularly in his adult academic career. Educated by his older sister Adele, he could read and write at the age of 2, read the clock and multiply by 2, 3, 4, 5, 6, 7, 8, and 10 at the age of 4, and was reportedly disappointed when, at the age of 5, he started school only to learn that none of his classmates had read the *Iliad* (which, by the way, he could partly quote by heart).

These signs of intelligence were, however, unmatched in subsequent years, most notably when he failed to excel in mathematics at Cambridge's Trinity College. This failure would have a profound impact on Galton's career, leading him to abandon the study of mathematics and explore other disciplines, notably geography (Galton is credited with the design of the first modern weather map, which appeared in *The Times* in 1875). By the time Darwin's *Origin of Species* was first published in 1859, Galton was already bitterly disappointed by his failure to become a leading mathematician, despite his enormous determination and hard work. In that sense, Darwin's ideas about evolution may have helped Galton to explain his own limitations rather than his extraordinary talent. Galton never denied the importance of effort and preparation, neither in theory nor in practice.

However, what attracted Galton's attention was the fact that, even after extensive training and preparation, differences in performance – and talent – still remained between individuals.

The eager boy [he said], when he first goes to school and confronts intellectual difficulties, is astonished at his progress. He glories in his newly developed mental grip, and [may believe] it to be within his reach to become one of the heroes who have left a mark upon the history of the world. The years go by, he competes in the examinations of school and college, over and over again with his fellows, and soon finds his place among them. He knows he can beat such and such of his competitors; that there are some with whom he runs on equal terms, and others whose intellectual feats he cannot even approach. (Galton, 1972/1869, p. 57)

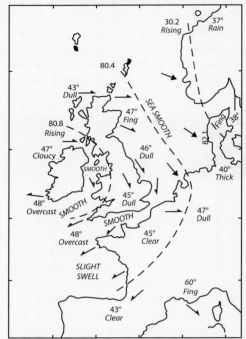

WEATHER CHART, MARCH 31, 1875.

The dotted lines indicate the gradations of barometric pressure
The variations of the temperature are marked by figures, the state
of the sea and sky by descriptive words, and the direction of the wind
by arrows–barbed and feathered according to its force. ⊙ denotes calm.

PHOTO 5.3 *The first ever weather map, by Galton, published in 1875 in* The Times.

Image courtesy of http://galton.org/meteorologist.html.

of some groups over others: he considered the ancient Greeks to be superior to his English counterparts, who were in turn superior to Africans and African Americans.

Galton also believed that the high correlation between the achievements of eminent judges and those of their ancestors signified the genetic source of genius, thus undermining the role of status and influence in determining those achievements. This was also true for his belief in women's intellectual inferiority:

> As a rule men have more delicate powers of discrimination than women, and the business experience of life seems to confirm this view. The tuners of pianofortes are men, and so I understand are the tasters of tea, and wine, the sorters of wool, and the like. (Galton, 1973/1883, p. 20)

Nonetheless, several of Galton's ideas and research methods are of major importance for modern differential psychology. His decision to look at indicators of academic performance and the distribution of university grades was undoubtedly groundbreaking, as was his idea to test the genetic basis of intelligence by comparing not only adopted and biological children with their parents but also MZ against DZ twins. In 1882, Galton set up an Anthropometric Laboratory in London's Science Museum, aimed at measuring individual differences in basic cognitive functions, which he considered proxy measures of human intellectual capacity. (Anthropometric literally means "measurement of man.") Both Galton and his student Karl Pearson were responsible for the invention of several important statistical methods and tests (notably correlations and regressions) that are still largely employed by psychologists and social scientists today (see Sections 3.2.1 and 3.2.2 in Chapter 3).

5.3.2   J.M. Cattell's Mental Test

Galton's statistical and methodological approach was emulated in the US by James McKeen Cattell (1860–1944), who studied in Germany under Wilhelm Wundt (1832–1920), one of the founders of experimental psychology. According to J.M. Cattell (not to be confused with R.B. Cattell, discussed in Section 2.10 in Chapter 2 and Section 5.4), intelligence could be conceptualized in terms of 10 basic psychological functions, such as tactile discrimination, hearing, weight discrimination, and so on. Furthermore, J.M. Cattell devised a psychometric instrument to measure individual differences in these basic processes, which for the first time received the name of **mental test**.

> **mental test** a series of psychometric tests originally devised by J.M. Cattell to measure individual differences in basic psychological functions such as tactile discrimination, hearing, and weight discrimination.

Rather than merely attempting to measure individual differences in cognitive ability, J.M. Cattell was concerned with the development of a scientific psychological discipline, one based on experimental and quantitative methods. Thus, most of the variables he measured were more "elemental" than "mental," and referred to very basic cognitive processes that are now known to be *related* to intelligence, although they certainly fail to define the concept in broad terms. Furthermore, although J.M. Cattell's (1890) mental tests represented reliable measures of individual differences in performance, later studies showed that these measures were neither intercorrelated nor related to academic performance indicators such as grades (Wissler, 1901).

Nonetheless, J.M. Cattell's contribution in providing the foundations of psychometric differential research (especially in the US) cannot be understated, as illustrated by the following quote:

> We do not at present wish to draw any definite conclusions from the results of the tests so far made. It is of some scientific interest to know that students entering college have heads on the average 19.3cm long . . . that they have an average reaction-time of 0.174 sec., that they can remember seven numbers heard once, and so on with other records and measurements. These are mere facts, but they are quantitative facts and the basis of science. Our own future work and that of others must proceed in two directions . . . (a) to what extent are the several traits of body, of the senses and of the mind interdependent? . . . what can we learn from the tests of elementary traits regarding the higher intellectual

and emotional life? (b) on the other hand we must use our own measurements to study the development of the individual and of the race, to disentangle the complex factors of heredity and environment. (Cattell & Farrand, 1896, p. 648)

The first goal outlined refers to the purer methodological and psychometric aspects of intelligence, which will be covered throughout this chapter and the beginning of the next. The second goal, attainable once individual differences in intelligence are conceptualized and measured, refers to the relationship between cognitive and other known variables, such as the causes and consequences of differences in ability (see Chapter 6).

5.3.3 Binet and the Origins of IQ Testing

By creating a more pragmatic measure of intelligence, accounting for basic cognitive processes and also for the more concrete abilities to perform mental operations and solve real-life problems, Alfred Binet (1857–1911) set the foundations of modern intelligence testing.

In 1904, the French Ministry of Public Instruction commissioned Binet to develop a method of identifying children with learning difficulties. Rather than relying on teachers' assessments, which were often biased against children with discipline problems, the French government wanted a method that effectively discerned capable pupils from less capable pupils. This implicit distinction between behavioral problems (such as absenteeism and disruptive behavior) and learning difficulties (such as lack of understanding of subjects) illustrates the differences between the realms of personality and intelligence. Binet (Binet & Simon 1961a/1905) believed that while personality describes and predicts individuals' behavior in and outside the classroom, intelligence would explain school performance based on the requirements to learn, understand, and relate concepts, theories, and methods acquired in the classroom.

Addressing the request of the French Ministry, and inspired by the readings of Galton (see Section 5.3.1), Binet and his student Theodore Simon (1873–1961) began to work on the creation of a standardized test to measure reasoning ability and the use of judgment. Up to 50 children representative of the average pupil of each year group were initially recruited to pilot tests. Individually, they responded to a total of 30 items in order of increasing difficulty, with every six items corresponding to a level relating to a year group. Level 3, corresponding to a 3-year-old, set the task of shaking hands with the examiner, following

PHOTO 5.4 *Alfred Binet (1857–1911)*

the movement of a lit match, and pointing to their eyes or nose; level 7, expected of a 7-year-old, set the task of describing a picture, repeating a series of digits, and completing a series of sentences. The most difficult tasks designed for older but also brighter children included rhymes and the repetition of up to seven random digits. The last level of difficulty answered correctly determined the level of reasoning and learning ability. This score was then computed in terms of years and months, so that answering correctly all questions of level 7 plus three in level 8 would indicate that the child's ability or mental age was that of someone aged 7.5 or 7½ years.

Binet's advances in psychological testing were undoubtedly a consequence of his pragmatic approach to individual differences in intelligence and school achievement. To Binet, intelligence was all about practical sense and adaptation to the real world. Instead of starting from a theoretical or experimental perspective accounting for intrapsychic processes and sensorial operations, like Galton and J.M. Cattell, Binet adopted a commonsense applied approach whose goal was specifically the design of an effective, robust tool to predict differences in school performance. Rather than observing people's reactions to meaningless stimuli, Binet gave his subjects real tasks such as reading the time or completing a sentence. More importantly, Binet's predictive tool allowed educators to compare learning potential at a very early age (i.e., 4 years), irrespective of previous instruction.

Binet was nonetheless very cautious about the usefulness of his measure and the meaning of what it assessed, as illustrated in his comprehensive definition of intelligence, which has stood the test of time:

> It seems to us that in intelligence there is a fundamental faculty, the alteration or the lack of which, is of the utmost importance for practical life. This faculty is judgment, otherwise called good sense, practical sense, initiative, the faculty of adapting one's self to circumstances. A person may be a moron or an imbecile if he is lacking in judgment; but with good judgment he can never be either. Indeed the rest of the intellectual faculties seem of little importance in comparison with judgment. (Binet & Simon, 1973/1916, pp. 42–3)

Aware of the limitations of his scale, Binet called for qualitative research on the developmental aspects of intelligence, a call later addressed by one of his students, Jean Piaget (see Section 5.6). In addition, Binet thought that his scale could only provide a *sample* of all intelligent behaviors, and that its use was limited to a few samples that shared a certain cultural background. Indeed, a shared cultural background was certainly necessary to provide individuals with the knowledge to solve most of Binet–Simon's tests.

As it was, then, such doubts discouraged Binet from claiming to have found a measure of any fundamental capacity:

> I have not sought in the above lines to sketch a method of measuring, in the physical sense of the word, but only a method of classification of individuals. The procedures which I have indicated will, if perfected, come to classify a person before or after such another person, or such another series of persons; but I do not believe that one may measure one of the intellectual aptitudes in the sense that one measures a length or a capacity. (Binet, quoted in Varon, 1936, p. 41)

While Binet's test is commonly recognized as the first psychometric intelligence test (and considered a milestone in the history of intelligence theory and research), it was the American adaptation of this test, introduced at Stanford by Terman (1916), that would have a greater impact on the psychometrics of intelligence (its revised versions still represent a state-of-the-art intelligence scale today). Henry Goddard (1866–1957), who studied with Binet and translated the scale into English, imported the test to the US, where it was quickly subject to larger and more robust validation studies. The popularity of the instrument in America was largely due to political and socioeconomic reasons. In a time of intense search (and hope) for a meritocratic society, Binet's scale seemed to provide a fair criterion for selection. The test went beyond being considered a mere predictor of children's performance in school to being hailed as an effective tool for "curtailing the reproduction of feeblemindedness and [eliminating] an enormous amount of crime, pauperism, and industrial inefficiency" (Terman, 1916, p. 7, cited in White, 2000, p. 38).

Terman's large-scale studies allowed him to test and improve the reliability of the scale and thus extend it to subtests and to a large age group from 3 to 14 years. Another modification from the Stanford/Binet version was the way in which the scores were calculated. A child's score would now be expressed as **intelligence quotient** or **IQ** (a term introduced by Stern, 1912); that is, the mental age divided by the chronological or real age, multiplied by 100. Thus, someone aged 10 who reached level 10 would have an IQ of 100 (average); someone aged 10 who reached level 8 would have an IQ of 80 (below average); and someone aged 10 who reached level 12 would have an IQ of 120 (above average).

> **intelligence quotient (IQ)** a score derived from standardized tests of intelligence, usually combining several subtests of different cognitive ability tests (e.g., verbal, mathematical, spatial).

In the 1960s these normative differences were standardized through a measure called *standard deviation* (SD), a comparative indicator of a person's score against the general population. The SD eventually replaced Terman's formula and is still used as a tool to compare individuals on intelligence (not just according to age but also according to specific population groups such as gender, ethnicity, and nationality). Today, the concept of IQ is almost synonymous with intelligence, used widely by both laypeople and academics and graphically represented by a normal distribution or **bell curve** of scores, with a mean of 100 and an SD of 15 (see Figure 5.3). On average, 50 percent of the population has an IQ of 90 to 100 points, 2.5 percent has an IQ of 130 or above, another 2.5 percent scores 70 or below, and only 0.5 percent – that is, 1 person in 200 – scores 140 or above.

> **bell curve** also known as normal distribution, referring to the graph that represents the frequency of scores or values of any variable. In psychology many variables, notably IQ scores, are normally distributed in the population.

One fundamental advantage of IQ tests is that they measure *stable* individual differences in intellectual ability. Accordingly, an individual's score on an IQ measure will not vary from day to day, month to month, or year to year. In fact, after the age of 6, individuals' IQ scores remain pretty much the same, though the development of adult intelligence takes place until the age of 15 (see Section 5.6).

Despite their usefulness in the prediction of school grades, early IQ tests were mainly an applied tool and did not refer to any theory or attempt to explain the mental processes underlying test performance. Even after Terman's (1916) American adaptation of Binet's scale into a reliable measure for the prediction of scholastic

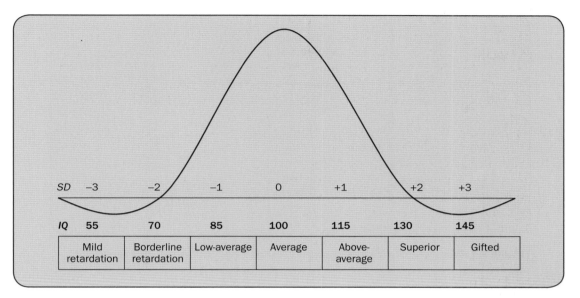

FIGURE 5.3 *The bell curve or normal distribution of IQ*

The "bell curve" figure above shows the normal distribution of IQ scores, which have a mean of 100 and a standard deviation (SD) of 15. Thus, if your IQ = 100 you have "average" intelligence, whereas an IQ of 130 shows superior intelligence, and an IQ of 70 signals borderline retardation.

achievement, one that was used for many decades and subsequently, though not substantially, revised in 1937, 1960, 1972, and 1986, there were few efforts to define intelligence or elaborate a theory for understanding individual differences in intellectual ability.

5.3.4   *Spearman's g Factor of General Intellectual Ability*

Meanwhile, in Britain, Charles Spearman (1863–1945), another student of Wundt's, applied factor analysis and data-reduction procedures (see Section 2.7 in Chapter 2) to show that different ability tests were significantly intercorrelated, and that the common variance could be statistically represented in terms of a single, general factor or *g* (see Figure 5.4). Like Galton and J.M. Cattell, Spearman (1904) started by examining individual differences in basic information processing, looking at elementary cognitive processes such as olfactory and visual-sensory discrimination. Like Binet, he compared these scores to academic performance indicators, creating a criterion to examine the validity of his measure in order to observe whether test scores could accurately distinguish between high and low levels of learning. Spearman therefore combined the strengths of both differential psychology and intelligence research. In the early German school he found the experimental methods to quantify cognitive processes, and in the early French tradition he found the criterion

g used to refer to the "general intelligence factor" underlying performance, which can be extracted statistically from scores on a range of ability tests.

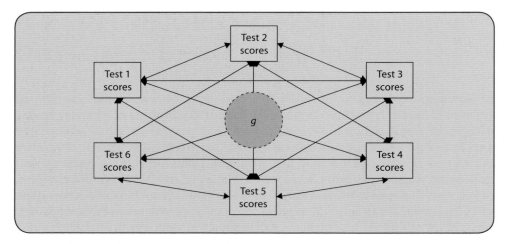

FIGURE 5.4 *The concept of* g *(general intelligence) as underlying common variance to different cognitive tests*

to validate his tests. The theory behind Spearman's research was also instrumental in continuing and consolidating the English paradigm (initiated by Galton) of intelligence as an inherited ability.

The main advantage of focusing on elementary processes to define individual differences in intellectual ability was the possibility of designing robust experiments in laboratory conditions. This opportunity led to a revival of cognitive research on intelligence in the 1970s and early 1980s, causing a paradigmatic revival of the early conceptualizations of Galton, J.M. Cattell, and Spearman. Rather than measuring intelligence through a series of abstract and unobservable mental operations (that are merely "assumed" to take place while participants complete an ability test), researchers defined intelligence in terms of *reaction time* (Jensen, 1982) or *inspection time* (Deary, 1986), which was more easily quantified and measured (see Chapter 6). Basic cognitive processes such as inspection time have been reported to account for up to 20 percent of the variance in IQ test scores (see Davidson & Downing, 2000).

Spearman, a skillful statistician, developed a series of tests that provided the empirical basis for his theory of intellectual ability as well as the foundation for future far-reaching research on individual differences. Indeed, even today, intelligence research is inspired by the application of similar statistical methods to the ones used by Spearman.

Spearman's first important finding was that different mental tests are significantly interrelated, so that performance on one type of test or exam is similar to that in others. Furthermore, because each test score reflects not merely the ability of the testee but also a certain level of error in measurement (rather than a "pure" measure of ability, tests can be "polluted" by several factors such as distractibility, stress, attention impairment, or fatigue), Spearman developed a formula to *attenuate* for these measurement errors and provide an estimate of the *true* relationship between two variables. This formula [r(true) = r(observed) × |(reliability of v1) (reliability of v2)] is still widely used. Taking into account the *reliability* (another concept introduced by Spearman) of a variable or measure, an accurate estimate of the true common or shared variance between two variables (v1 and v2 in the formula) is achieved, rather than the spurious correlation that may result from errors of measurement.

Another crucial statistical technique developed by Spearman and directly related to his concept of intelligence was *factor analysis* (see Section 2.7 in Chapter 2). This technique requires the researcher to obtain a series of measurements, which are then plotted into a correlation matrix to show the relationships between each pair of variables. Factor analysis can then be used to identify underlying patterns in the data, and co-variations between a group of variables are attributed to a latent factor. Thus, if individuals' scores on different tests are similar, one can assume that tests are measuring the same thing. This finding enabled Spearman (1927) to discover that, although there may be different aspects of cognitive performance, intelligence could be represented as a general underlying capability. Regrettably, much of the psychometric research after Spearman has focused on the statistical properties of standardized performance tests rather than on the nature of the processes underlying individual differences in intelligence.

5.3.5 Thurstone's "Primary" Mental Abilities

Louis Thurstone (1887–1955) questioned Spearman's general intelligence (*g*) factor and devised a competing statistical technique called *multiple factor analysis*. In direct contradiction to Spearman's procedure of data analysis, Thurstone's method was based on decomposition of the variance identification of multiple factor loadings and identification of an independent group of factors.

Thurstone regarded intelligence as an adaptational process by which individuals attained everyday life goals by planning ahead, imagining a specific goal/outcome, and inhibiting instinctive responses to prioritize rational, goal-oriented processes. While Thurstone accepted the hypothesis of a general underlying intelligence factor, he concluded that intelligence should also be conceptualized and measured at the "primary" level. To this end, he conceptualized seven "primary" abilities; namely, *verbal comprehension*, *word fluency*, *number facility*, *spatial visualization*, *associative memory*, *perceptual speed*, and *reasoning* (see Table 5.2).

Thurstone's seven primary abilities provide a more precise picture or profile of an individual's intellectual capability. However, Thurstone's claim that primary abilities are a more useful tool than the *g* factor to predict academic performance has obtained little empirical support. Despite their relatively low incremental validity (predicting performance over and above *g*), primary abilities do contribute to our understanding of individual differences in intelligence and may explain specific differences between individuals and different cognitive tasks.

Individual differences in the ability to solve this, and other similar problems, were attributed by Thurnstone (see Table 5.2) to an ability he called "number facility," which is basically equivalent to maths ability; that is, the ability to carry out mental

Table 5.2 *Thurstone's primary abilities*

1 *Verbal comprehension*	Vocabulary (knowledge of words), reading and comprehension skills, verbal analogies (capacity for conceptual association)
2 *Word fluency*	Ability to express ideas, generate large number of words, and use concepts (e.g., anagrams, rhymes, metaphors)
3 *Number facility*	Ability to carry out mental calculations with speed and accuracy
4 *Spatial visualization*	Ability to mentally rotate figures and orientate oneself in space
5 *Associative memory*	Rote memory
6 *Perceptual speed*	Ability to rapidly spot visual stimuli (similarities, differences, patterns)
7 *Reasoning*	Inductive, deductive, inferential, logical processes of thought

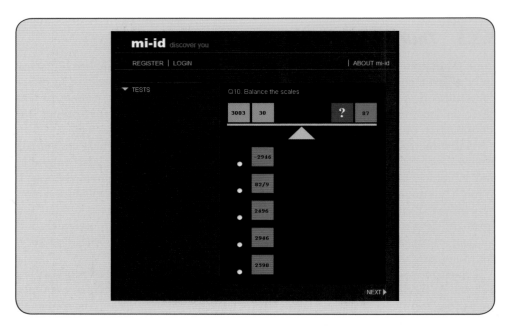

PHOTO 5.5 *An example of a numerical ability item – can you balance the scales?*

calculations with speed and accuracy. According to Spearman, however, this (and all other abilities) can largely be explained by general intelligence, implying that your score on these types of ability tests should predict how well you do in other ability tests (e.g., verbal or spatial).

Spearman's and Thurstone's rival theories and methods have since been successfully combined to establish a *hierarchical* model of abilities acknowledging both general and specific factors. This hierarchical structure is also consistent with Binet's scale and that of David Wechsler (1896–1981), a student of Spearman who would later come to design one of the most important intelligence measures to date. That intelligence can be conceptualized in terms of different hierarchical levels was largely supported by the intercorrelations between tests of different contents, such as understanding paragraphs, recalling words, interpreting pictures, and solving arithmetic problems. Spearman himself tested this idea on a small sample of 24 schoolchildren and found empirical support for his theory: although there are many specific abilities required to perform on different types of tests, there is a single underlying general intelligence factor that emerges when the (true) intercorrelations between specific abilities and tests are examined. The structure of human abilities can thus be conceptualized in terms of a two-tier hierarchical model comprising specific abilities (*gs*) on the one hand, and general intelligence (*g*) on the other.

Because *g* is a measure of general intellectual ability, it is less context and problem dependent than any specific ability test. Spearman argued that the common and essential element of abilities coincides with that of elementary functions. Thus *g* cannot be improved through practice but is, as Galton believed, largely biological.

FOCUS POINT 5.2   PERSONALITY CORRELATES OF THE FOUR-FACTOR MODEL OF CULTURAL INTELLIGENCE

INTRODUCTION

The world is fast becoming more and more globalized, with more people able to immerse themselves in a culture other than their own. What construct, if any, might one possess in order to find this process easier?

This phenomenon has been explored and researchers have come up with a four-factor model of cultural intelligence (CQ; see Table 5.3).

Metacognitive CQ highlights the processes that individuals use to gain and understand cultural knowledge, whereas cognitive CQ is the general knowledge that one possesses about different cultures. In a parallel fashion, motivational CQ is the effort and amount of energy one puts into learning about and functioning in a new culture, and behavioral CQ is the ability to exhibit the appropriate body language and verbal actions when interacting with those of a new culture.

CQ is a state-like individual difference; that is, it is malleable and we are able to change our behavior and mental processes in the appropriate situations. Thus in the broader nomological network of cultural intelligence, depending on what long-lasting personality traits one possesses, this construct may predict how culturally intelligent one is... and this is what this study by Ang *et al.* tried to uncover.

The hypotheses were:

1. *Conscientiousness will be positively correlated with metacognitive CQ:* those who are conscientious like to plan, are organized, and have a purposeful approach (especially in a work setting, those high in this trait tend to perform better academically and at work). So, before and during interaction with those from a different culture, they may devote time and attention to

planning and thinking about different cultures, considering cultural norms, and adjust their mental models appropriately.

2. *Agreeableness will be positively correlated with behavioral CQ:* Agreeable people are generally warm, courteous, cooperative, and flexible. Thus people high in agreeableness would be more flexible in performing appropriate verbal and nonverbal behaviors when interacting with people from different cultural backgrounds.

3. *Emotional stability will be positively correlated with behavioral CQ:* Emotionally stable individuals tend to be calm and even-tempered. They tend not to show much emotion, for instance they tend to get less anxious, depressed, angry, and insecure. Those who score highly on this trait should be better able to handle novel situations because they respond to uncertainty with greater patience and less heightened emotions. Thus, like agreeable people, stable individuals should be more flexible in their interpersonal skills, putting those from new cultures at ease.

4. *Extraversion will be positively correlated with motivational and behavioral CQ:* Extraverts are bold, forceful, and self-confident. They find it easy and purposefully seek to approach strangers, put themselves in novel situations, and ask questions. Thus they would be motivated to meet people from different cultures and would behave appropriately, as they enjoy the interpersonal aspect of being in the company of others.

5. *Openness to experience will be positively related to all the four factors of CQ:* This trait is linked to being creative, imaginative, open to new experiences (as the name implies!), broad-minded, and intelligent. Within work contexts, openness has hardly been related to any outcomes, thus people have questioned its utility as a personality trait. But within the context of being

immersed in a new culture, it should be related to all four constructs of CQ. They will seek out new experiences and be open to them, thus behave appropriately in (non)verbal manners, and they will learn and have broad knowledge of these cultures too as they are curious about these other aspects.

METHOD

PARTICIPANTS

In all, 338 business students at a university in Singapore took part in this experiment. Singapore is a multicultural nation with one fourth of its 1.2 million workforce being of foreign background (including workers from China, India, Southeast Asia, Europe, and North America). The university examined had more than 15 500 students, 23.1 percent of whom are foreign.

MATERIALS

The measures used in this study were the 20-item four-factor model of cultural intelligence displayed in Table 5.3 and personality, which was measured in terms of the Big Five.

RESULTS

Hypotheses 1, 2, 4, and 5 were all supported with reasonably strong positive correlations. However, Hypothesis 3, which stated that emotional stability would be positively correlated with behavioral CQ, was not supported. In fact, the authors found a negative correlation ($\beta = -.18, p < .01$) which is just the opposite of what they expected. The fact that openness was highly positively correlated with all aspects of CQ highlights the importance of this trait as a potential determinant of individual differences in CQ. It is advantageous to possess higher openness in order to be more efficient in socializing with

Table 5.3 *Measurement of cultural intelligence (CQ)*

Determinants of how able one is to immerse onself into a new cultural environment	
1 = Completely Disagree 2 = Strongly Disagree 3 = Disagree 4 = Neutral 5 = Agree 6 = Strongly Agree 7 = Completely Agree	
CQ Factor	**Questionnaire Items**
Metacognitive CQ	
MC1	I am conscious of the cultural knowledge I use when interacting with people of different cultural backgrounds.
MC2	I adjust my cultural knowledge as I interact with people from a different culture that is unfamiliar to me.
MC3	I am conscious of the cultural knowledge I apply to cross-cultural interactions.
MC4	I check the accuracy of my cultural knowledge as I interact with people from different cultures.
Congnitive CQ	
COG1	I know the legal and economic systems of other cultures.
COG2	I know the rules (e.g. vocabulary, grammar) of other languages.
COG3	I know the cultural values and religious beliefs of other cultures.
COG4	I know the marriage systems of other cultures.
COG5	I know the arts and crafts of other cultures.
COG6	I know the rules for expressing non-verbal behaviours in other in other cultures.
Motivational CQ	
MOT1	I enjoy interacting with people from other cultures.
MOT2	I am confident that I can socialise with locals in a culture that is unfamiliar to me.
MOT3	I am sure that I can deal with the stresses of adjusting to a culture that is new to me.
MOT4	I enjoy living in cultures that are unfamiliar to me.
MOT5	I am confident that I can get accustomed to the shopping conditions in a different culture.
Behavioural CQ	
BEH1	I change my verbal behaviour (e.g. accent, tone) when a cross-cultural interaction requires it.
BEH2	I use pause and silence differently to suit different cross-cultural situations.
BEH3	I vary the rate of my speaking when a cross-cultural situation requires it.
BEH4	I change my non-verbal behaviour when a cross-cultural situation requires it.
BEH5	I alter may facial expressions when a cross-cultural interaction requires it.

Source: Ang, S., Van Dyne, L., Koh, C., Ng, K.Y., Templer, K.J., Tay, C., & Chandrasekar, N.A. 2007. Cultural intelligence: Its measurements and effects on cultural judgement and decision making, cultural adaptation and task performance. *Management and Organisational Review*, 3(3), 335–71.

different cultures, especially today with several organizations being open to new cultures due to the boom in globalization.

DISCUSSION

Traditional notions of intelligence have always emphasized individual differences in the ability to adapt to the real world, though they rarely took into account how individuals may do this in unfamiliar environments. The concept of CQ presents an interesting avenue for research in this area.

Source: Ang, S., van Dyne, L., & Koh, C. (2005) Personality correlates of the four-factor model of cultural intelligence, *Group Organization Management* 31, 100–23.

5.4 CATTELL'S THEORY OF FLUID AND CRYSTALLIZED INTELLIGENCE

Spearman's (1904, 1927) findings had a crucial impact on one of his PhD students, Raymond Cattell (1905–98) (not related to J.M. Cattell), who went on to develop the well-known theory of crystallized and fluid intelligence. Cattell was actively involved in Spearman's development of factor analysis and, like Spearman, he was convinced of the advantages of applying multivariate statistical methods to behavioral research. Cattell's background in natural sciences led him to believe that with the help of statistical and mathematical techniques, psychology would soon be able to rival the objectivity of the hard sciences. Cattell's application of statistics was not limited to the study of intelligence but provided the empirical basis of his personality theory (see Section 2.10 in Chapter 2). Though his wider impact was in the major areas of personality and intelligence, throughout his 70-year academic career Cattell elaborated and tested a great number of theories and methods on virtually every salient aspect of differential psychology, publishing over 35 books and 500 chapters and papers.

fluid intelligence (*gf*) the ability to learn new things and solve novel problems, irrespective of previous knowledge, education, or experience.

crystallized intelligence (*gc*) the knowledge, information, and skills that can be used to solve problems related to what one has already learned.

Based on factor analyses of the structure of and relationship between different types of ability tests, Cattell distinguished between **fluid intelligence** (*gf*) – the ability to perform well on nonverbal tasks, which do not require previous knowledge but instead measure a rather pure, culture-free element of cognitive performance – and **crystallized intelligence** (*gc*) – the ability to do well on verbal tasks, which are substantially influenced by previous knowledge and acculturative learning.

Broadly speaking, *gf* represents information processing and reasoning ability; that is, inductive, conjunctive, and disjunctive reasoning capability used to understand relations and abstract propositions (Stankov, 2000). Conversely, *gc* is used to acquire, retain, organize, and conceptualize information. Whereas *gf* is dependent on the efficient functioning of the central nervous system, *gc* is dependent on experience and education within a culture. Therefore *gf* is biological and declines over the adult lifespan as the mind's efficiency diminishes, while *gc* may increase with cultural exposure and as experience makes individuals wiser and more knowledgeable. A useful metaphor to understand the relationship between *gf* and *gc* is that of a computer: *gf* represents the processor, memory, and other characteristics of the hardware, while *gc* represents the software as well as information and data stored. Hence *gf*, like the processor of a PC, refers to *processes* rather than content. Conversely, *gc*, like the data files and software saved onto a PC, refers to *content* (or information) rather than processes. Measuring both *gf* and *gc* is beneficial for estimating both a person's learning potential and their acquired knowledge (Stankov, Boyle, & Cattell, 1995).

In addition, Cattell (1987) added a third dimension of intelligence, *gsar*, to conceptualize performance on short-term memory and retrieval tasks; that is, tests that require manipulation and information retrieval in short-term memory. *Gsar* includes memory, visualization, and speed factors. Figure 5.5 depicts Cattell's three-component theory of intelligence, represented by *gf*, *gc*, and *gsar*.

Although there has been a longstanding tendency to employ tests of *gf* or nonverbal abilities rather than *gc* or verbal abilities, the last 15 years have been dominated by a vindication of measures of *gc* (see Ackerman, 1999; Ackerman & Heggestad, 1997). Studies have shown that intelligent individuals tend to do better on verbal rather than nonverbal measures, whereas the opposite is true for lower-IQ scorers (see Matarazzo, 1972). Measures of *gc* would therefore represent a better tool to distinguish between high and low intelligence. Moreover, one cannot fully understand adult human intelligence without reference to any conceptual knowledge (that is, individual differences in comprehension, use, and knowledge of concepts). Thus, verbal ability measures such as verbal comprehension, general knowledge, and vocabulary tests constitute an optimal route to the measurement of general intellectual ability.

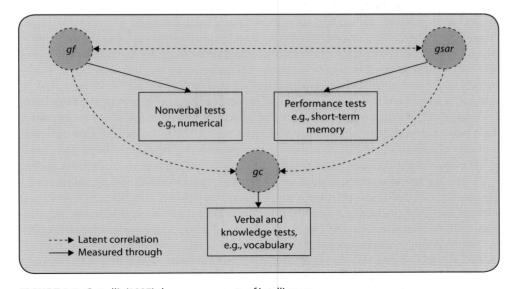

FIGURE 5.5 *Cattell's (1987) three components of intelligence*

5.5 GENETIC VS. ENVIRONMENTAL CAUSES OF INTELLIGENCE

The idea that intelligence may be inherited has powerful social implications and has therefore often escaped objective scientific scrutiny. Both Binet and Spearman, pioneers in the psychological study of intelligence, believed that there was a strong hereditary basis for individual differences in intellectual ability. Before them, Galton argued that not only talent but also character (now referred to as personality traits) were largely inherited. However, to a greater (Binet, Cattell) or lesser (Galton, Spearman) extent, these pioneers also acknowledged the influence of social and cultural (i.e., environmental) factors on the development of specific skills. Thus, while two individuals with similar educational backgrounds may differ in ability because of different genetic dispositions, two individuals with the same genetic history could also experience different intellectual developments if exposed to unequal training or environments.

socioeconomic status (SES) a measure of an individual's position within a social group based on various factors, including occupation, education, income, location of residence, membership in civic or social organizations, and certain amenities in the home (e.g., telephone, TV, books).

Environments and opportunities are often a function of social class or **socioeconomic status** (**SES**), long identified as a significant correlate of intelligence. However, as with most correlational studies, the causal direction underlying this relationship is difficult to identify. Further obstacles for empirical research have been caused by the lack of objectivity (and theoretical soundness) in the conceptualization and measurement of SES indicators. As there are several possible causal paths for interpreting the relationship between social class, education, and intelligence (see Figure 5.6), there has been a longstanding ideological debate as to whether SES determines intelligence or vice versa.

Few differential psychologists have developed such consistent and convincing arguments (and evidence) for understanding the relationship between SES and g as Linda Gottfredson (1997, 1998, 2004a, 2004b). Against the traditional sociological interpretation of SES as the key causal factor of social inequalities (e.g., in health, education, and income), Gottfredson shows how general intelligence may be identified as the fundamental cause not only of these inequalities but also of SES itself. This would explain disparities in educational level, health, and income among members of the same SES, leading to the conclusion that measures of g are better predictors of these outcomes than parental (or family) SES. Thus children with higher IQs than their parents will typically achieve higher SES. Similarly, g can explain the frequently large disparities in life opportunities among siblings who grow up in the same environment or home.

Because g remains stable from a very early age, influences of SES on an individual's intelligence seem unlikely. Even in closed and highly regulated political systems, such as hardcore socialism or communism, g is normally distributed in the population, with neither social nor economic regulation able to reduce individual differences in cognitive ability (Firkowska *et al.*, 1978; Jensen, 1998).

Of course, no one would argue that a simple measure of intelligence can map out an individual's future in all domains of life, or that key decisions determining life-changing events are the mere product of one's cognitive ability. However, "g's

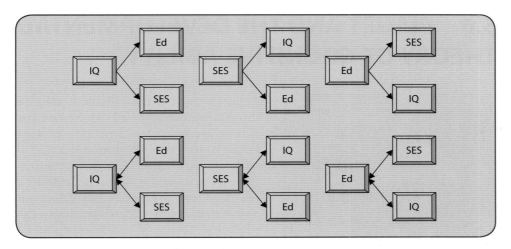

FIGURE 5.6 *Some possible combinations for the causal relationships underlying the significant correlations between intelligence, education, and socioeconomic status*

Key: IQ = intelligence, Ed = education, SES = socioeconomic status. Only unidirectional causations are presented.

effects are pervasive and consistent" (Gottfredson, 2004a, p. 180) and the aggregate performance of an individual in domains as diverse as school, work, health, and relationships is, to a substantial degree, affected by their level of intelligence. The consequences of intelligence in everyday life are examined in Chapter 6. Correlates of *g* range from physical fitness to alcoholism (negatively), and the notion that IQ measures at the age of 11 can predict a series of mental and physical illnesses at the age of 70 (Brand, 1987; Deary, 2000; Deary *et al.*, 2004).

Adoption and twin studies (see Chapter 7) have provided evidence in support of both genetic and environmental influences on intelligence, showing that individual differences in ability are determined by genes as well as the environment (though mostly by the former). Early evidence on the genetic basis of intelligence was reported by Newman, Freeman, and Holzinger (1937), who found that identical twins had a greater similarity in intelligence than nonidentical twins, even when the former were raised apart. Studies on adopted children confirmed these findings because they reported larger correlations in intelligence between natural parents and their children than between adoptive parents and children, even where children had virtually no contact with their natural parents. Most data showed that less than 20 percent of the variance in IQ could be accounted for by environmental (nongenetic) factors. However, several studies by Cyril Burt were found to report fake twin data that exaggerated the genetic basis of intelligence. In recent years twin studies have come to show that, although intelligence is largely inheritable, there are some environmental influences that cause siblings raised in the same family to have different levels of intelligence (Plomin & Petrill, 1997). Adoption studies, however, have yielded ambiguous results, with correlations ranging from *r* = .22 up to *r* = .77 (see Grigorenko, 2000; Sternberg & Grigorenko, 1997). The complexities of behavior-genetic studies will be examined in more detail throughout Chapter 7.

5.6 PIAGET AND THE DEVELOPMENTAL THEORY OF COGNITIVE ABILITY

PHOTO 5.6 *Jean Piaget (1896–1980), the most famous developmental psychologist and a pioneer of intelligence research*

© Bettmann/Corbis.

Although most of this chapter focuses on the *psychometric* approach to the concept of intelligence, the contribution of Jean Piaget (1896–1980), a famous developmental psychologist, deserves to be mentioned. Piaget was a student of Simon at Binet's research center in Paris. However, he soon abandoned psychometrics to investigate the qualitative aspects of intelligence. While working on the French standardization of Burt's intelligence scale, he noted that the crucial question to enable an understanding of intellectual ability was not how many correct or incorrect responses children could give, but why children of the same age tended to make exactly the same type of mistakes. This would come to be clarified not through standardized multiple-choice tests but through individual clinical interviews.

Piaget was therefore concerned with how individuals develop adult intellectual capacities, and he identified various developmental stages in the evolution of adult intellect. His theory of intellectual development is based on four universal stages – namely the *sensorimotor*, *preoperational*, *concrete operational*, and *formal operational* stages – which follow a baby's intellectual transition from a nonverbal, preconceptual, elementary stage in the early four years of life to the complex stages of language acquisition and conceptual reasoning in young adolescence (see Table 5.4).

Like Spearman, Piaget believed in a single, general intelligence factor but focused on the evolutionary or developmental aspects of intelligence, which he considered to be the result of a series of ubiquitous qualitative stages. More importantly, and unlike most early intelligence researchers, Piaget was more interested in elaborating a theoretical framework for understanding the development of the processes underlying adult intelligence than in individual differences in psychometric test performance. His theory was therefore more concerned with similarities than differences between individuals.

The essence of Piaget's (1952) theory is the universal interaction between biological and environmental variables. Biological (genetic) factors provide the raw materials required for the progressive construction, through active experiences and interactions with the environment, of adult intelligence. Each stage of development is therefore

Table 5.4 *Stages of intellectual development according to Piaget*

Development stage	Approximate age	Characteristics
Sensorimotor	0–2	No mental representations of objects outside child's immediate view; intelligence develops through motor interactions with environment
Preoperational	3–7	"Thought" emerges; child is able to make mental representations of unseen objects, but cannot use deductive reasoning yet
Concrete operations	8–12	Deductive reasoning, conservation of number, and distinction between own and others' perspectives
Formal operations	13–15	Ability to think abstractly

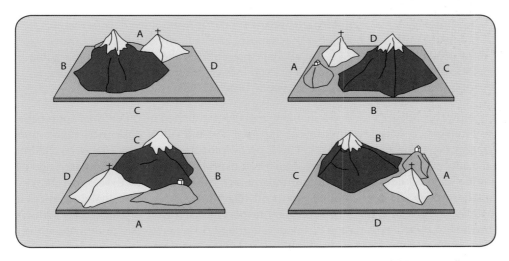

PHOTO 5.7 *These images are used in Piaget's mountain task to test whether children are still in the egocentric phase. Egocentric children are not able to take on the perspective of others, and will believe that other people have the same view of the three mountains as they do.*

Source: Piaget and Inhelder (1956).

genetically prescribed and inherent in human organisms, meaning that children cannot be "taught" the passage from one stage to another. At each evolutionary stage (i.e., sensorimotor, preoperational, concrete operational, and formal operational), there are certain cognitive operations an individual is able to perform and others she is not. Piaget's theory therefore explains the passage from basic sensorial and motor skills (at the age of 2 years) to very abstract (formal/logical) mental operations by processes of adaptation (assimilation and accommodation) and organization (linking mental structures and applying them to real-life problems), resulting in the progressive development of schemata; that is, groups of interrelated ideas or concepts.

Piaget is also responsible for some of the most comprehensive and detailed definitions of the concept of intelligence. Whereas such definitions do not necessarily emphasize aspects of individual differences, they have been accepted widely in all areas of psychology, including individual differences. Some of Piaget's definitions are presented below:

- "Intelligence is an adaptation . . . To say that intelligence is a particular instance of biological adaptation is thus to suppose that it is essentially an organization and that its function is to structure the universe just as the organism structures its immediate environment." (Piaget, 1963, pp. 3–4)
- "Intelligence is assimilation to the extent that it incorporates all the given data of experience within its framework . . . There can be no doubt either, that mental life is also accommodation to the environment. Assimilation can never be pure because by incorporating new elements into its earlier schemata the intelligence constantly modifies the latter in order to adjust them to new elements." (Piaget, 1963, pp. 6–7)
- "Intelligence does not by any means appear at once derived from mental development, like a higher mechanism, and radically distinct from those which have preceded it. Intelligence presents, on the contrary, a remarkable continuity with the acquired or even inborn processes on which it depends and at the same time makes use of." (Piaget, 1963, p. 21)

However, Piaget's theory remained virtually untouched by differential approaches to intelligence, with few attempts at applying it to individual differences taxonomies (for an exception see Kirk, 1977). This is predominantly because it applies to children and adolescents (with final stages of intellectual development at approximately age 15) rather than to adults. Despite its fundamental contribution to developmental psychology, then, the applied implications of Piaget's theory to individual differences in intellectual ability remain of secondary importance. However, since Piaget's theory provides a robust explanation of the development of the processes underlying universal cognitive functions that are ubiquitous to adult mental operations, it can be used to understand structural aspects of human intelligence. Once these are present, individual differences in intelligence can address why some are more intelligent than others.

5.7 THE GREAT DEBATE: *g* VS. MULTIPLE ABILITIES

Although the predictive validity of established IQ measures is well documented (see Chapter 6), critics have argued that the traditional conception of intelligence is not sufficiently comprehensive as it refers mainly to academic abilities or being "book smart" (Gardner, 1983; Goleman, 1995; Sternberg, 1985c, 1997). Instead, they propose that individual differences in intellectual ability should be defined in terms of *multiple intelligences* (see Chapter 8), as individuals may be good at some ability tests but bad at others.

The idea that human intellectual ability can be "broken down" into several unrelated components was most emphatically defended by Guilford (1959, 1967, 1977), who came to develop the most comprehensive catalogue of human abilities that extended to 150 different types based on a preliminary distinction between the three dimensions of *operations*, *products*, and *contents*. Accordingly, Guilford (1977) distinguished five types of operations (cognition, memory, divergent production, convergent production, and evaluation), five types of contents (auditory, visual, symbolic, semantic, behavioral), and six types of products (units, classes, relations, systems, transformations, implications) (see Figure 5.7). Guilford's (1981) revision of this model finally acknowledged the existence of a hierarchy comprising 85 second-order and 16 third-order factors. Evidence for this model is yet to be provided (Brody, 2000).

Although various theories have proposed an understanding of intelligence in terms of several unrelated abilities, the scientific study of intelligence has provided conclusive evidence for the existence of a general intelligence factor and its accurate predictive power with regard to academic outcomes. Thus, empirical evidence mainly refutes theories of multiple intelligence (Gottfredson, 2003; see also Chapter 8).

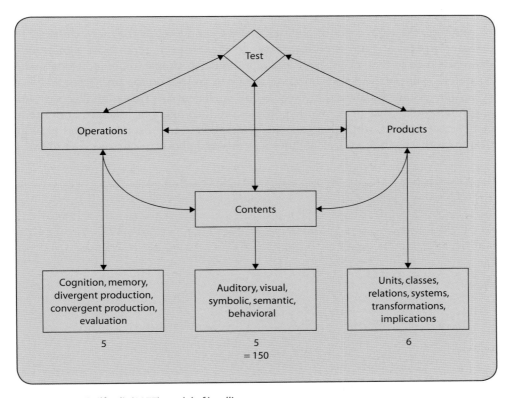

FIGURE 5.7 *Guilford's (1977) model of intelligence*

In a large US psychometric study involving nearly 2500 participants, all correlations between the 13 subtests of the Wechsler Adult Intelligence Scale (WAIS-III; see Section 6.2 in Chapter 6) were significant and positive (ranging from about $r = .30$ to $r = .80$; Wechsler, 1997). The pattern of correlations also supported Cattell's idea that some types of tests are more interrelated than others. However, the underlying general intelligence factor hypothesized to be the source of variations between individuals' cognitive performance was clearly identified in this large and representative dataset. Thus mental abilities, as tested by different ability tests, tend to be closely associated so that they cluster together in one common factor (see again Figure 5.4). This factor, which accounts for approximately 50 percent of the variance in IQ test performance, is the best existing measure of individual differences in human intelligence and a powerful predictor of a wide range of real-life outcomes.

The most compelling source of evidence for the existence of a general intelligence factor derives from Carroll's (1993) book on human intelligence, a great meta-analytic review of the salient 20th-century studies on intellectual abilities. After reanalyzing over 400 sets of data, results revealed that a single, general intelligence factor can account for a considerable amount of variance in ability test performance. This factor was identified at the highest hierarchical level of the pyramid and is the major determinant of different components of cognitive performance; namely fluid intelligence, crystallized intelligence, general memory and learning, processing speed, broad cognitive speediness, broad retrieval ability, broad auditory perception, and broad visual perception (see Figure 5.8).

Although the eight types of abilities at the second level of the hierarchy refer to different aspects of human performance, all these aspects tend to be significantly intercorrelated so that, in any large and representative sample, those individuals who do well in *some* tests will also show a tendency to do well on the *other* tests, and vice versa. The debate as to whether there is one intelligence or many intelligences supposes incorrectly that these two hypotheses are incompatible, whereas both are in fact correct. Indeed, while there are many identifiable and distinctive types of abilities, from the second level of abilities summarized above to narrower, third-order

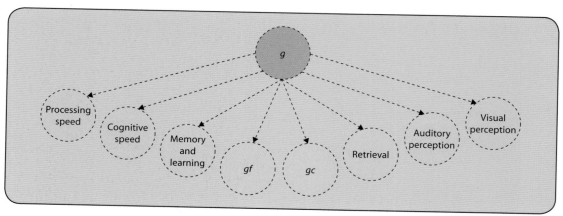

FIGURE 5.8 *Conceptual representation of Carroll's (1993) hierarchical structure of intelligence*

abilities that can be mapped onto the second level, there is also a general intelligence factor accounting for most of the variance in different ability test performance.

Accordingly, while data clearly show that the general intelligence factor does exist, there is no justification for arguments against it (Carroll, 1993; Deary, 2001; Wechsler, 1997). The real issue is whether the general intelligence factor can be useful by effectively predicting real-life outcomes, particularly beyond academic performance or school success. This issue is further discussed in Chapters 6 and 12.

5.8   SUMMARY AND CONCLUSIONS

In this chapter I have examined the concept of intelligence, which has a longstanding history in differential psychology and is closely linked to the development of psychometric tests. As has been seen:

- Intelligence is measured through standardized performance tests, which require participants to identify the correct solution to cognitive problems (e.g., mathematical, verbal, spatial). These tests were originally designed to predict school and military performance, but have shown to be valid predictors of a wide range of real-life outcomes as well. Indeed, the reliability and validity of well-established IQ tests is matched by few other psychological measures.

- There is some debate about the structure of intelligence, with some viewing it as a general factor and others seeing it as a set of largely independent, more specific abilities. Hierarchical models, on the other hand, recognize the existence of both general and specific factors, making better sense of the data. At the same time, there is wide consensus that there are two major aspects of intelligence; namely, fluid intelligence (gf), or the ability to learn new things and solve novel problems (irrespective of previous experience, knowledge, or education), and crystallized intelligence (gc), or the knowledge / information that can be used to solve problems related to what one has already learned.

- In 1996, leading intelligence researchers compiled a comprehensive dossier on the topic to clarify the knowns and unknowns about intelligence. This dossier shows that, contrary to popular belief, there is great consensus among experts on the nature of intellectual ability. Thus 52 eminent researchers in the field agreed:

Intelligence is a very general mental capability that, among other things, involves the ability to reason, plan, solve problems, think abstractly, comprehend complex ideas, learn quickly and learn from experience. It is not merely book learning, a narrow academic skill, or test-taking smarts. Rather, it reflects a broader and deeper capability for comprehending our surroundings – "catching on," "making sense" of things, or "figuring out" what to do. (Gottfredson, 1997, p. 13)

Now that I have introduced the concept and measurement of intelligence, it is time to understand the causes and consequences of intellectual ability; in other words, why some people are more intelligent than others, and what advantages this brings. This is the topic of Chapter 6.

TEXTS FOR FURTHER READING

Ackerman, P.L. (1999). Traits and knowledge as determinants of learning and individual differences: Putting it all together. In P.L. Ackerman, P.C. Kyllonen, & R.D. Roberts (Eds.), *Learning and Individual Differences: Process, Trait, and Content Determinants* (pp. 437–62). Atlanta: Georgia Institute of Technology.

Brody, N. (2000). History of theories and measurements of intelligence. In R.J. Sternberg (Ed.), *Handbook of Intelligence* (pp. 16–33). New York: Cambridge University Press.

Chamorro-Premuzic, T. & Furnham, A. (2004). A possible model to understand the personality–intelligence interface. *British Journal of Psychology*, 95, 249–64.

Deary, I.J. (2001). *Intelligence: A Very Short Introduction*. Oxford: Oxford University Press.

Gottfredson, L.S. (1997). Why *g* matters: The complexity of everyday life. *Intelligence*, 24, 79–132.

Plomin, R. & Petrill, S.A. (1997). Genetics and intelligence: What's new? *Intelligence*, 24, 53–77.

6 Intelligence, Part II – Validating Intelligence and Correlates of IQ (Causes and Consequences)

LEARNING OUTCOMES

BY THE END OF THIS CHAPTER, YOU SHOULD BE ABLE TO ANSWER THE FOLLOWING FIVE KEY QUESTIONS:

1. Are IQ tests valid predictors of educational success?
2. Are IQ tests valid predictors of occupational success?
3. How does intelligence affect health and longevity?
4. What are the main controversies regarding group differences in IQ?
5. What are the basic cognitive processes underlying individual differences in intelligence?

KEY WORDS

Event-Related Potential • Inspection Time • Job Analysis • Reaction Time • Wechsler Adult Intelligence Scale (WAIS)

CHAPTER OUTLINE

6.1   INTRODUCTION

Chapter 5 introduced the psychological concept of intelligence, starting with an examination of the historical development of early theories and measurement approaches, leading to salient structural issues such as the general intelligence factor (*g*), the distinction between fluid (*gf*) and crystallized (*gc*) intelligences, and the hierarchical structure of human abilities. The aim of this chapter is to follow up some of these themes by assessing the research evidence for the *validity* of ability tests, notably *g* and IQ. As with personality traits in Chapter 3, then, this chapter looks at whether ability tests are useful predictors of a wide range of behavioral outcomes, including occupational and academic performance, health, and longevity. Accordingly, it addresses the question of what it means to score high on ability tests; that is, what consequences this may have and whether, when, and where it matters to be more intelligent.

Whereas some correlates of IQ are usually interpreted in terms of outcomes, other correlates are often regarded as indicators of the causes of individual differences in cognitive ability. Among the latter are basic information-processing tasks and measures of brain efficiency, such as reaction time and electroencephalogram activity. Moreover, the study of biological differences in intelligence (also discussed in Chapter 7) has included what is arguably the most controversial research area in differential psychology; namely, group differences in cognitive ability – particularly sex and race. This chapter also deals with these issues.

6.2   WECHSLER'S IQ SCALE

Wechsler Adult Intelligence Scale (WAIS) a widely used measure of intelligence that has progressively replaced the Stanford/Binet test because of its suitability for measuring adult IQ; scores are calculated on the basis of between-subject comparisons rather than on the (mental age/chronological age) × 100 formula.

Before examining the salient correlates of intelligence, it is important to look at Wechsler's IQ scales, which have represented the most widely used measure of intelligence for decades. Introduced in 1939 as the Wechsler–Bellevue test, the scales progressively replaced the Stanford adaptation of Binet's test. One major reason for this was that, unlike Terman's scale, the Wechsler test could also be used to measure adult IQ (after the age of 14), and was validated on large and representative samples. For instance, the 1955 revision of this scale, relabeled the **Wechsler Adult Intelligence Scale (WAIS)**, was based on over 2000 individuals, aged 16–75. Moreover, Wechsler designed a specific version of his test for children (aged 5–16), called the *Wechsler Intelligence Scale for Children* (WISC).

Another advantage of Wechsler's scales was that scores could be calculated and interpreted on the basis of between-subject comparisons rather than the formula of (mental age/chronological age) × 100. Since mental age remains pretty much the same after the (chronological) age of 16, Wechsler's readjustment and standardization allowed him – and any test administrator – to compare testees' scores with an "expected" or "typical" score obtained by other testees. Sex, social class, nationality, and other group factors were carefully stratified so as to maximize accuracy in the interpretation of scores. Applied to the concept of normal distribution (see Figure 5.3 and Section 5.3.3 in Chapter 5), Wechsler's formula of (actual test score / expected score) × 100 could then be used to assign test takers a "relative" score with regard to the overall population or specific samples, representing differences in terms of standard deviation.

Although IQ is a quantification of standardized differences between individuals' performance, neither the formula nor the normal distribution or "bell curve" of scores refers to parametric data (see again Figure 5.3 in Chapter 5). In contrast, IQ scores and scales are *nonparametric* in nature, which means there is no absolute zero and the distance or interval between two data points is not homogeneous. Thus, an individual with an IQ score of 100 is not twice as clever as someone with an IQ score of 50, or half as bright as someone with an IQ score of 200 (if such a person existed). Further, the difference between an IQ of 120 and one of 130 is not the same as that between an IQ of 90 and one of 100, because scores are interpreted in terms of the relative position to others. If, then, most people tend to score between 85 and 115, scores outside this range are less frequent and every point difference outside this range represents more significant differences between individuals.

The construction of Wechsler's scale was influenced not only by Terman's (1916) American version of Binet's IQ scale but also by the army-oriented scale developed by Robert Yerkes in 1919; namely, the National Intelligence Test of the United States. This test comprised two different subscales, the Alpha and Beta scales, measuring verbal and nonverbal ability respectively. Likewise, the WAIS comprises different subscales of verbal and nonverbal (performance) scales (see Table 6.1). Verbal scales include *information*, *vocabulary*, *comprehension*, *arithmetic*, *similarities*, and *digit span*. Performance subtests comprise *picture completion*, *picture arrangement*, *block design*, *object assembly*, and *digit symbol*. The distinction between verbal and performance tests is based on empirical rather than conceptual grounds, specifically the use of factor analyses and other statistical techniques (i.e., some sections are correlated with each other, while others are not).

The inclusion of a wide range of subtests enabled Wechsler to measure intelligence in a global, comprehensive way, without however disregarding specific abilities. As will be noted (see Chapter 8), there has been extensive debate on whether intelligence should be conceptualized as a general, single mental capacity or as a large number of unrelated abilities. The WAIS seems to represent a third-way solution, a compromise between *splitters* (those who believe there are many distinct, independent abilities) and *lumpers* (those who believe that intelligence is a general, single psychological attribute), just as Carroll's (1993) hierarchical model prescribes. In the words of Wechsler (1958, p. 5):

> While intelligence may manifest itself in a variety of ways, one must assume that there is some commonality or basic similarity between those forms of behavior which one identifies as intelligent.

Thus researchers have largely focused on general cognitive ability or IQ when validating intelligence. Although this approach can be justified on both conceptual and

Table 6.1 *WAIS structure*

WAIS subtests (verbal and performance)	
Verbal	*Performance*
Information: Tests knowledge on various subjects (e.g., science, history, arts)	*Picture completion:* Presents illustrations of incomplete objects and requires testees to complete them
Vocabulary: Requires testees to provide definitions for words	*Picture arrangement:* Requires the person to put a disarranged sequence of pictures/cards in order, to recreate a story
Comprehension: Tests the individual's ability to understand sayings, rules, or proverbs	*Block design:* Tests the ability to form quick patterns with cubes of different colors
Arithmetic: Mental calculations (if 15 oranges cost $3, how much will 7 oranges cost?)	*Object assembly:* Similar to block design, involves disarranged objects which make up a jigsaw
Similarities: Asks people to relate two different concepts or objects (by identifying the underlying characteristic in common)	*Digit symbol:* Requires the person to memorize specific codes for different numbers and fill in a sequence with those symbols
Digit span: Requires the person to repeat a sequence of digits read out by the examiner (both in normal and reverse order)	

Note: Correlations between different subtests range from $r = .33$ (object assembly and digit span) to $r = .81$ (vocabulary and information).

psychometric grounds, it fails to provide a detailed account of the processes underlying the correlations between different test parts and why certain types of tasks are more intercorrelated than others. Accordingly, the choice of particular tests and, consequently, the identification of specific aspects of intellectual ability are matters of empirical evidence: if, in a large and representative sample, there is a general tendency for people who do well in some sections of the tests to do well in others, all sections can be justifiably included as part of the scale and considered partial measures of intellectual ability.

Conversely, if a section of the test does not distinguish between individuals' performance on other sections, it should neither be included in the scale nor be considered a measure of intelligence. In that sense, it could be argued (as critics have) that the only reason IQ tests seem to measure a single and general underlying intelligence is because the people who designed these tests have chosen to do so. Yet, the meaning and usefulness of any IQ test, as well as the very concept of intelligence, can only be judged against external indicators of validity, hence the importance of this chapter. The forthcoming sections deal with the validity of IQ and *g* as predictors of different performance and behavioral outcomes. As will be seen, intelligence is a highly pragmatic, functional variable with pervasive effects across a wide range of settings and outcomes, and individual differences in cognitive ability have clear implications in everyday life.

6.3 INTELLIGENCE AT SCHOOL AND UNIVERSITY: EDUCATIONAL OUTCOMES

To say that IQ tests predict school performance is almost tautological, because ability tests were specifically designed to predict individual differences in school and educational success (see Chapter 5). It is therefore unlikely that any ability test uncorrelated with school success (or learning outcomes in general) would meet the criteria for intelligence tests or be labeled "intelligence." Nonetheless, educational psychologists (and indeed some intelligence researchers) have often raised doubts about the predictive

PHOTO 6.1 *Can intelligence tests predict whether one will have a good or a bad result at university? Although intelligence is defined as learning ability, few universities employ IQ tests for student selection. Do you think they should? (I think I can guess the answer to that.)*

Photograph courtesy of Nadia Bettega, reproduced with permission.

power of ability tests in academic settings. Furthermore, academic assessment methods, particularly in higher education, are increasingly focused on continuous assessment or coursework assignments, which make academic performance more dependable on personality than cognitive ability (Chamorro-Premuzic & Furnham, 2005, 2006).

The finding that cognitive ability tests such as *g* or IQ are accurate predictors of student performance, particularly during primary and secondary school, has been replicated for over a century (e.g., Binet, 1903; Binet & Simon, 1961a/1905; Brody, 2000; Harris, 1940; Terman, 1916; Thurstone, 1919; Willingham, 1974). In fact, psychometric intelligence is by far the most robust and consistent predictor of academic performance (Elshout & Veenman, 1992; Gagne & St. Pere, 2001; Sternberg & Kaufman, 1998) and educational level in general (Brand, 1994). Some examples are summarized in Table 6.2.

Table 6.2 *Intelligence and academic performance*

Author (year of publication)	Key findings
Bright (1930)	High correlations between ability test and both academic and citizenship grades in public schools
Springsteen (1940)	Cognitive ability correlates with school performance in a sample of mentally handicapped school pupils
Tenopyr (1967)	Cognitive ability (SCAT) is a more powerful predictor of academic achievement than social intelligence (findings partly replicated by Riggio, Messamer, & Throckmorton, 1991)
Sharma & Rao (1983)	Hindu female school students' academic performance correlates with nonverbal intellectual ability (Raven's Progressive Matrices)
Bachman *et al.* (1986)	IQ test a better predictor of primary school grades than measures of abnormal behavior
Walberg, *et al.* (1984)	Meta-analysis of more than 3000 studies reported correlation in the order of $r = .70$ between the two constructs (replicated in Gagne & St. Pere, 2001)
Willingham (1974)	The graduate record examination (GRE) correlates substantially with cognitive ability and future performance at university
Kuncel, Hezlett, & Ones (2001)	A very large-scale meta-analysis ($N = 82\,659$) shows strong predictive power for GRE and undergraduate grade point average (UGPA) as predictors of postgraduate education level; yet these measures also confound noncognitive variables such as personality traits

Source: Based on Chamorro-Premuzic & Furnham (2005).

However, the predictive power of cognitive ability in educational settings seems to decrease as students progress to higher academic levels, probably because of restrictions of range in intelligence (i.e., brighter students are more likely to pursue further education, making ability levels more and more homogeneous). In fact, studies have often found weak or nonsignificant relationships between ability and academic performance measures beyond secondary school (see Mehta & Kumar, 1985; Sanders, Osborne, & Greene, 1955; Seth & Pratap, 1971; Singh & Varma, 1995; Thompson, 1934). Even such stalwart supporters of intelligence as Jensen (1980) reported a drop in correlations from $r = .70$ in elementary school to $r = .50$ in secondary school and $r = .40$ in college (see also Boekaerts, 1995). Likewise, Hunter (1986) argued that measures of g, as well as verbal and quantitative abilities, have only been found to be modest predictors of academic success for adults (see Figure 6.1).

The fact that ability tests may show weakened predictive validity at higher levels of education is also consistent with the increasing significance of personality or noncognitive traits at such academic stages (Chamorro-Premuzic & Furnham, 2005). Indeed, researchers have recently increased the search for additional predictors of educational outcomes in the hope of explaining further variance in student attainment levels (see Ackerman & Beier, 2003; Ackerman & Heggestad, 1997). Thus Ackerman and Rolfhus (1996, p. 176) argued:

> abilities are only one part of the complex causal framework that determines whether a student pursues the acquisition of knowledge and skills within a particular domain. Two other components of the equation are interests and personality traits.

See also Chapters 3, 9, and 12.

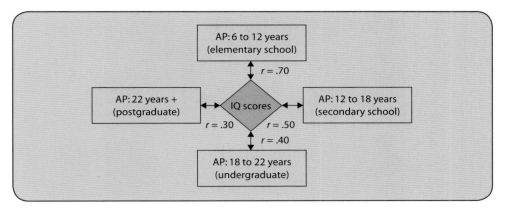

FIGURE 6.1 *Correlations between intelligence and academic performance (AP) at different levels of education.*

Note: All *r* values are approximate.

Source: Based on Ackerman (1994); Boekaerts (1995); Hunter (1986); Jensen (1980).

6.4   IN THE JOB: OCCUPATIONAL OUTCOMES OF INTELLIGENCE

Ability tests have been used as predictors of job or occupational performance for almost a century. In fact, some of the best-known tests were developed in the context of job performance, particularly in military settings. Thus Robert Yerkes developed a measure for the army (the National Intelligence Test, famous for its Alpha and Beta scales) as early as 1919, and ability tests were used to recruit and train fighter pilots in the Second World War (Matarazzo, 1972). Ever since, army data have represented an important source of information to assess the validity of ability tests, no doubt due to the large and representative samples they comprise. In more recent times, McHenry *et al.* (1990) published a large and comprehensive meta-analysis on the correlations between *g* (measured by the Armed Services Vocational Aptitude Battery test) and military performance. As seen in Table 6.3, *g* is substantially correlated with technical proficiency and general soldiering performance, and moderately correlated with effort and leadership as well as physical fitness and military bearing. Measures of personal discipline, on the other hand, are only modestly correlated with *g* (and are arguably more dependent on personality or noncognitive traits).

The most compelling evidence for the importance of *g* in military settings derives from a study by O'Toole and Stankov (1992), where the authors looked at the relationship between IQ scores (used in military selection) and noncombat deaths at the

PHOTO 6.2 *The first intelligence tests were designed to improve the selection of army personnel*

© domhnall dods/Shutterstock.

Table 6.3 *Correlations of g and military performance*

Technical proficiency	.63
General soldiering	.65
Effort and leadership	.31
Personal discipline	.16
Physical fitness and military bearing	.20

Source: Adapted from McHenry *et al.* (1990).

age of 40 in a sample that included over 2000 Australian veterans. Even after controlling for over 50 behavioral, psychological, and health variables, IQ scores predicted risks of death. In fact, with every additional IQ point, there was a 15 percent decrease in death risk (see also Section 6.5 on health and longevity).

It is a well-replicated finding that the more complex the job, the more important and stronger the effects of *g*. Thus the correlations between cognitive ability measures and job performance are moderated by job complexity. As one would expect, intellectually demanding jobs are substantially correlated with ability tests or *g-loaded*, whereas jobs that do not involve reasoning or intellectual tasks correlate lower with IQ.

In one of the first comprehensive meta-analyses of the relationship between intelligence and job performance, (Hunter 1983; Hunter & Hunter, 1984) showed that cognitive ability, as measured psychometrically through the US Employment Service General Aptitude Test Battery, was significantly correlated with a wide variety of jobs, including 515 occupations. Indeed, Hunter classified different jobs according to established norms and job complexity – a method called **job analysis** – and reported different correlations for each job family.

job analysis a method of classifying different jobs according to the nature and complexity of the work as well as the relationships of the job holder with other people

As shown in Figure 6.2, jobs were divided into *data* and *things*, according to whether individuals were more involved in manipulating information or physical objects, respectively. In turn, both groups were further divided according to complexity; namely, *high*, *medium*, and *low* in the case of data/information, and *precision* and *feeding* in the case of things/objects. Ability measures were correlated not only with job performance but also with training performance (which refers to an individual's ability to learn the required skills and tasks quickly and accurately). This distinction is important for at least two reasons. First, individuals may not always "replicate" their training performance on the actual job, because their motivation and incentives may decrease after they start working (see Chapter 9). Second, training may *mediate* the relationship between cognitive ability and job performance. This means that ability levels may not only have direct effects on job performance, but also influence how quickly and well individuals will learn and be trained, which, in turn, will further affect job performance levels (see Figure 6.3).

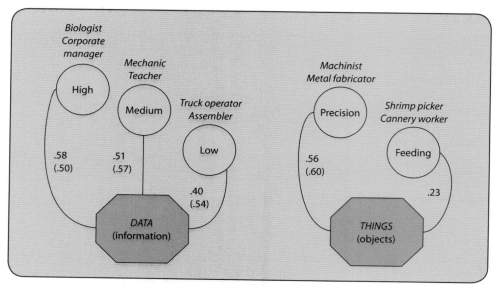

FIGURE 6.2 *Predictive validity of cognitive ability across different job types*

Note: All numbers are correlation coefficients; numbers in brackets refer to training performance; numbers outside brackets refer to job performance.

Source: Based on Hunter (1983); Hunter & Hunter (1984).

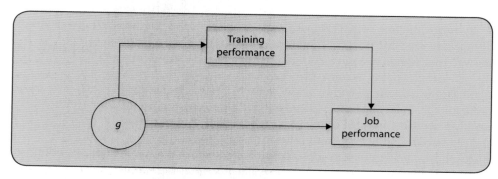

FIGURE 6.3 *Mediated and direct effects of g on job performance*

As seen in Figure 6.2, correlations between ability and both job performance and training increase with job complexity. For data jobs, the correlation between ability tests and job performance is .58 when the job complexity is high, .52 when it is medium, and .40 when it is low. This pattern of results is not manifested across measures of training performance. Yet, when we look at "things" (jobs involving manipulation of objects rather than information), there is a substantial difference in the size of correlations for high (precision) and low (feeding) job complexity. Thus, *g* is most important when the job is intellectually demanding and least important when the job is not intellectually demanding (as occurs in most physically demanding jobs

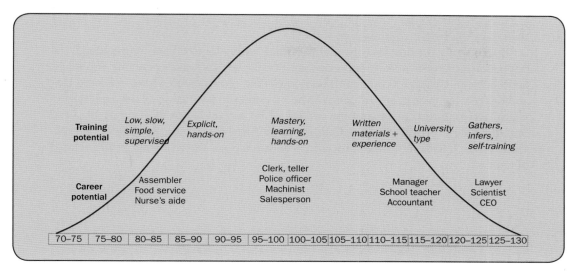

FIGURE 6.4 *Occupational consequences of IQ*

Source: Based on Gottfredson (2004b).

related to the manipulation of things). Experts have also emphasized that intellectually demanding jobs are not necessarily dependent on academic expertise or high educational attainment (Gottfredson, 1997). For example, the chief executive of a company may have few academic credentials and yet have one of the most intellectually demanding jobs, while dyslexic individuals may excel in the workforce despite failing in educational settings (see also Chapter 8). For example, Richard Branson is a British entrepreneur worth an estimated $3 billion; he is the fastest man to have crossed the Atlantic by boat and he has developed over 100 different enterprises for his *Virgin* empire – yet Branson is dyslexic and would probably do badly on an IQ test.

While it is important to understand that IQ is not destiny (even its highest correlation with job performance leaves unexplained variance), it would be fallacious to deny its importance in the workplace. In fact, cognitive ability provides a more accurate estimate of a person's potential for the job than other psychological or nonpsychological variables. More importantly, it is more objective and less exposed to bias than other methods. Figure 6.4 illustrates the typical distribution of IQ scores across a variety of occupations in terms of both training and career potential.

6.5   INTELLIGENCE, LONGEVITY, AND HEALTH

Intelligence researchers have also examined the validity of ability measures in regards to health outcomes and longevity. If intelligence represents an important adaptational tool, it should be significantly correlated with positive health outcomes as well as longevity, meaning that brighter people should be generally healthier and live longer than their less bright counterparts.

Traditionally, health and even differential psychologists have emphasized the importance of motivational and noncognitive factors such as personality traits (see Section 3.6 in Chapter 3) on health outcomes. Yet, recent studies have indicated that abilities may be even more influential when it comes to predicting health and longevity. In fact, longitudinal data on the validity of IQ as a predictor of a variety of social outcomes have provided compelling evidence for the importance of *g* in real life. Gottfredson (2004a) reported associations between *g* and the following health-related outcomes:

- Physical fitness
- Low-sugar diet
- Low-fat diet
- Longevity
- Alcoholism (negative)
- Infant mortality (negative)
- Smoking (negative)
- Obesity (negative)

PHOTO 6.3 *Are smarter people healthier? Your regular eating and drinking habits may influence how long you will live.*

Left © Julián Royagnati/Shutterstock; right © Quayside/Shutterstock.

While these behaviors are also associated with socioeconomic factors (such that poor or deprived groups tend to be more at risk than wealthy or educated individuals), Gottfredson emphasized the importance of cognitive ability over and above socioeconomic variables. In fact, it seems that the increase in availability of resources and improvements in socioeconomic conditions do little to reduce group differences between educated and less educated individuals. Rather, the more resources and information are available, the bigger the gap between lower- and higher-IQ individuals. Accordingly, measures of cognitive ability predict health outcomes even *within* the same socioeconomic groups, and individuals with higher intelligence seem to make more efficient and better use of the resources that are made available to prevent and improve health problems.

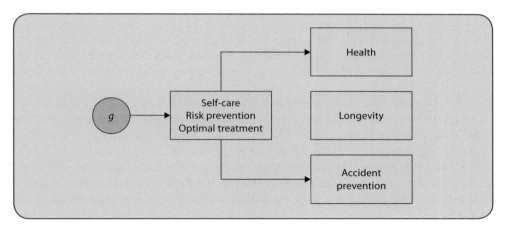

FIGURE 6.5 *Intelligence predicts health and longevity*

FIGURE 6.6 *The path from* g *to longevity*

The most impressive source of evidence derives from an almost nationwide study in Scotland, where measures of IQ obtained during childhood predicted individual differences in mortality (including cancer and cardiovascular illnesses) many decades later, even when socioeconomic factors were taken into account (Gottfredson & Deary, 2004). The Scottish survey examined IQ data for almost every 11-year-old Scottish citizen (*N* = 87 498) who attended school on June 1, 1932. Many decades later, Ian Deary and colleagues collected archival data and tracked medical as well as death records for thousands of participants. The results (reported in Deary, Whalley, & Starr, 2003) showed that IQ scores at the age of 11 predicted survival rate at the age of 76. Furthermore, participants who scored 1 standard deviation (15 points) lower in IQ had a 27 percent increase in cancer deaths if they were male, and 40 percent if they were female. For stomach and lung cancer deaths, the effects of IQ were found to be even stronger, no doubt due to the socioeconomic factors associated with these forms of cancer.

Similarly, Hart *et al.* (2003) reported that for every 15-point reduction in IQ scores there was a 17 percent increment in death risk (or 12 percent when socioeconomic factors were partialed out). The impact of cognitive ability on longevity is stronger in deprived or poor social groups, indicating that *g* moderates the correlation between socioeconomic status and mortality. Likewise, higher socioeconomic status may moderate the impact of IQ on longevity. Hart *et al.* (2003) also found that childhood IQ scores predicted the likelihood of dying from heart-related diseases and lung cancer. This is consistent with Gottfredson's (2004a) findings and the idea that brighter individuals are more likely to choose healthier diets and avoid or give up smoking.

Accordingly, cognitive ability seems to have pervasive effects on health outcomes. While there may be several mediating and moderating variables underlying the correlation between IQ and health factors, the mechanisms by which cognitive ability may lead to positive health are essentially no different than the ones affecting job or academic performance. Higher intelligence provides individuals with faster, better, and more efficient reasoning and learning ability; when this ability is applied to understanding the causes of good and bad health, IQ is no doubt advantageous for health-related decision making. Thus reviewers argued:

> Dealing with the novel, ever-changing, and complex is what health self-care demands. Preventive information proliferates, and new treatments often require regular self-monitoring and complicated self-medication. Good health depends as much on preventing as on ameliorating illness, injury, and disability. Preventing some aspects of chronic disease is arguably no less cognitive a process than preventing accidents, the fourth leading cause of death in the United States, behind cancer, heart disease, and stroke. (Gottfredson & Deary, 2004, p. 2)

One advantage of cognitive ability tests over personality and other latent psychological constructs that may be tested as predictors of health outcomes is that they provide an objective measure of individual differences. Thus they are not exposed to socially desirable responding or faking, as are self-reports. However, personality traits have also been shown to affect health outcomes (as seen in Section 3.6 in Chapter 3). In that sense, it would be important for studies to examine the joint impact of personality and intelligence factors on health-related behaviors as well as longevity. This would provide an indicator of the extent to which individuals' health may depend on their dispositions, preferences, interests, and abilities. For example, some individuals may choose to indulge in risky behaviors while being aware of the consequences of their acts, whereas others may avoid such behaviors without necessarily knowing that they have made the "right" choice. Likewise, health-advantageous and disadvantageous individual difference factors may combine in the same individuals, such that a person may score high on IQ as well as on Psychoticism or sensation seeking. Understanding such interactions would no doubt enhance our understanding of individual differences underlying health outcomes.

6.6   INTELLIGENCE AND SOCIAL CLASS

The idea that social class may in part be a consequence of individual differences in cognitive ability (rather than its cause) is no doubt controversial and has important political and sociological implications. Yet, evidence that:

(a) individual differences in intelligence *precede* and are more stable over time than socioeconomic status; and that

(b) both constructs are highly *intercorrelated*

has led mainstream intelligence research to emphasize the importance of both acknowledging and understanding the social consequences of *g* (see also Focus Point 6.1).

FOCUS POINT 6.1   THE BELL CURVE CONTROVERSY

Although genetic and group differences in IQ have concerned differential psychologists for over a century, much of the controversy surrounding these and related themes was sparked by the publication of *The Bell Curve* (Herrnstein & Murray, 1994), a bestselling book that takes its name from the normal distribution of IQ scores (see again Section 5.3.3 and Figure 5.3 in Chapter 5). In it, the authors assess the impact of intelligence in the United States, including a wide range of social, economic, and political consequences of differences in cognitive ability.

Fundamentally, Herrnstein and Murray argue that increases in socioeconomic status are the consequences of a "cognitive elite"; i.e., a group of individuals with a higher IQ. Thus success in life is not due to socioeconomic advantages but is the result merely of higher levels of cognitive ability. Accordingly, and most controversially, social deprivation is not a cause of lower IQ scores but its very consequence. Such claims led critics to accuse the authors of "scientific racism."

Whereas the book reports numerous statistics (particularly significant correlates of IQ), the

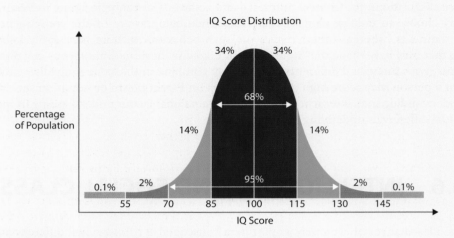

FIGURE 6.7 *The normal distribution or "bell curve" of IQ scores*

strength of its argument relies on the *heritability* estimates for cognitive ability – in the range of 40 to 80 percent (see Chapter 7) – that is, the fact that there are strong *genetic* influences on intelligence, notably psychometric *g*. Whereas this idea is not new (it had been anticipated by Arthur Jensen in the late 1960s), Herrnstein and Murray linked this argument with socioeconomic factors in an unprecedented manner. Furthermore, the authors "praise" the US economy as a model of meritocracy and highlight the importance of a society where wealth is distributed on the basis of intelligence rather than social class. However, this also implies that disadvantaged or unsuccessful individuals are responsible for their own misfortune and that little can be done to reverse inequalities.

The authors base their case on longitudinal evidence derived from analyzing archival data on the National Longitudinal Study of Youth. Information was available on the Armed Forces Qualifying Test (a sort of IQ test) and subsequent socioeconomic variables. Herrnstein and Murray found IQ scores to be a better predictor than socioeconomic status of most socioeconomic

outcomes than was social class background. In fact, after partialing out IQ scores, several race differences in socioeconomic outcomes seemed elusive.

Critics such as Leon Kamin regarded the book as "a disservice to and abuse of science," whereas Thomas Sowell criticized the authors for drawing partial conclusions in order to hold their argument. On the other hand, Jared Diamond argued that group differences in socioeconomic status are a result of geographic factors like terrain and natural resources. Yet *The Bell Curve* contains relatively moderate, and mostly implicit, views on the implications of genetic differences in cognitive ability, and even some of its critics have considered it a thorough and honest proposition.

More importantly, differential psychologists have been quite unanimous in their support for *The Bell Curve*. In fact, in the year the book was published, 52 eminent intelligence experts (not only from differential psychology) published a dossier entitled "Mainstream Science on Intelligence" in which they endorsed the core claims and data presented by Herrnstein and Murray.

Socioeconomic differences in cognitive ability are by no means a new finding. Many decades ago, Terman estimated a 14-point IQ gap between the "lowest-" and "highest-"class children tested. Likewise, early demographic studies found that suburban samples scored lower on IQ tests than urban ones, though this finding was attributed to the fact that "brighter" people were more likely to migrate to cities (Cattell, 1937; Terman & Merrill, 1937; Thomson, 1921). While ability differences between urban and suburban samples have tended to disappear over time, this may simply be a matter of migration and educational changes in demography, particularly in developed and industrialized countries.

There is evidence for both genetic and nongenetic or environmental causes of socioeconomic differences in IQ. For example, adoptive studies suggested that being adopted into a wealthier family tends to increase children's IQ (Mackintosh, 1998). However – as will be seen in Chapter 7 – genetic influences seem stronger and more pervasive than environmental ones, meaning that children tend to resemble their biological parents (in both personality and intelligence) more than their adoptive ones.

The average correlation between social class and IQ is approximately .55 and seems to persist generation after generation (Jencks, 1972; McCall, 1977). On the other hand, fathers and sons tend to differ more markedly in socioeconomic status (approximate $r = .35$) than in IQ (approximate $r = .50$). Crucially, generational decreases in IQ tend to be associated with decreases in socioeconomic status, whereas generational increases in IQ tend to be associated with increases in socioeconomic status (see Figure 6.8).

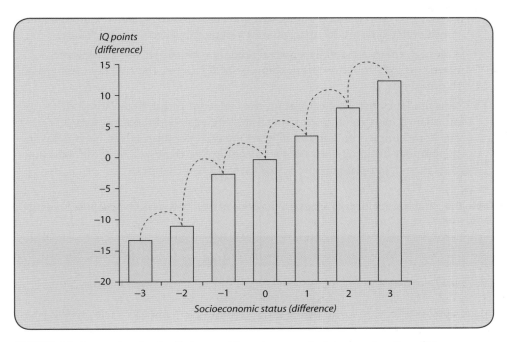

FIGURE 6.8 *Generational gains (father–son) in socioeconomic status as a function of IQ*

Source: Based on Mascie-Taylor & Gibson (1978).

Thus Mackintosh (1998, p. 147) argued:

> it is difficult to resist the conclusion that such an effect is partly responsible for the maintenance of the correlation between IQ and social class in each generation, and therefore that the direction of causality is partly that IQ differences cause social-class differences rather than simply imply that social-class differences cause IQ differences.

Few studies, however, simultaneously examined the direct effects of both environmental and genetic factors on the IQ–social status correlation. In one of the rare exceptions to this rule, Capron and Duyme (1989) managed to find four groups of children, two who were born to high social class parents and two who were born to low social class parents. In turn, each of these groups could be further divided on the basis of whether they were adopted by a low or high social class family. This 2 × 2 (high vs. low status of adoptive × high vs. low status of biological parents) factorial design showed that the social class of both adoptive and biological parents had similar effects on the child's IQ, though the sample size was small (i.e., each cell contained only 8–10 participants; see Table 6.4). Thus IQ scores were highest in children born to high social class parents and adopted by high social class parents (119.6), and lowest in children born to low social class parents and adopted by low social class parents (92.4).

Even if cognitive ability *causes* differences in socioeconomic status, it is important to bear in mind that:

- The correlation between socioeconomic status and IQ is not perfect and, at best, refers to an overlap of 30 percent between most measures.
- Even if this correlation is attenuated and corrected for reliability, there is still a considerable amount of unaccounted variance in socioeconomic status.
- Although there is certainly a *general* tendency for people in one socioeconomic group to obtain a particular type of IQ scores, the rule does not apply to everybody.
- This tendency has implications for the "relative" rather than "absolute" number of individuals from *x* social class that can be found among *y* IQ scorers. For example, the number of working-class people tends to exceed, by far, the number of upper-class people, meaning that there will be more working-class than upper-class people across most IQ score ranges.

Table 6.4 *Adopted children's IQ scores as a function of their biological and adoptive parents' social status*

	Adoptive parents	
Biological parents	High social status	Low social status
High social status	119.6	107.5
Low social status	103.6	92.4

Source: Based on Capron & Duyme (1989).

6.7   RACE AND SEX DIFFERENCES IN IQ: FACTS, CONTROVERSIES, AND IMPLICATIONS

No other topic in psychology has been as controversial as the issue of race differences in IQ, in particular the finding that white people tend to have higher IQ scores than black people. From the early 1920s up to the present day, studies have reported consistent differences of about 10–20 points between the IQ scores of black and white individuals, in favor of the latter (Mackintosh, 1998). This is a robust finding and has been replicated in many countries, though most studies examined US and UK data. Thus Mackintosh (1998, pp. 148–9) concluded:

> There can be no serious doubt that North American blacks have an average IQ score some 15 points below that of whites. This difference showed up in the early US Army data, was repeatedly confirmed in subsequent studies between the wars (Shuey, 1966), and has been maintained after the Second War (Loehlin *et al.*, 1975).

The fact that there are group differences in IQ test performance is a logical and arithmetic consequence of *individual* differences in such tests, one that applies to any

PHOTO 6.4 *Are there any meaningful race differences in intelligence? Although most differential psychologists prefer to discuss less controversial topics, several studies have been conducted to compare the IQs of different ethnic groups, particularly black people versus white people.*

Image courtesy of Nadia Bettega, reproduced with permission.

measured variable: if some people run faster than others, certain groups will run faster, too; if some people are taller than others, certain groups will be taller, too; if some people get higher IQ scores than others, certain groups will get higher IQ scores, too. It is not the differences but the *causes* and *implications* of such differences that ought to be assessed. However, lay and media reactions have generally preferred to distrust or deny these data, which is a common way of dealing with unpleasant news. It is therefore unsurprising that the media's position on any psychological study showing race or sex differences in IQ is one of skepticism and suspicion. Thus journalists have often questioned the reputation of psychologists reporting such differences, insinuating a hidden political agenda or accusing them of right-wing activism.

Such insinuations or accusations, however, would also imply that there is compelling evidence against the idea of sex or race differences in IQ, when such evidence may be elusive. As a matter of fact, this is misleading and reflects a lack of understanding of the processes underlying sound scientific research. The quality of scientific investigations is judged by experts on the basis of methodological, empirical, and theoretical rather than political grounds. As Mackintosh (1998, p. 149) has argued,

> however suspect the motives of many of those who use these data, and however strongly one may deplore their political aims, it is questionable to suppose that much will be gained by pretending that the data do not exist or by refusing to discuss them at all.

Ironically, media attempts to politicize the issue of sex or race differences in IQ have overemphasized the importance of such findings. Furthermore, the media's attempt to deny these differences introduces and consolidates the idea that such differences exist, increasing, reaffirming, and perpetuating the "war of the sexes" and racial prejudice when it supposedly wants to avoid it. The question, in short, is not whether group differences in IQ exist but how significant they are; that is, whether they help us explain real behavioral outcomes or not.

There can be no doubt that interpreting the effects of group differences in IQ (and, in fact, any individual difference variable) is not straightforward. This is where the real debate takes place, as psychologists have long been divided on the basis of whether they ignore, emphasize, or deny the importance or consequences of group differences in IQ. There have been three major theoretical positions when it comes to interpreting such differences; namely, attributing them to genetic, environmental, or measurement factors (see Figure 6.9). This applies not only to race differences but also to other group differences in IQ. Each of these positions has intrinsic consequences and implications for social policy.

Attributing IQ differences to genetic factors seems to imply that there is little to be done to reverse the social inequalities between different groups, and that certain people are just naturally disadvantaged in competing for resources and doing well in life. On the other hand, the opposite side of the argument is that environmental factors underlie the causes of group differences, such that socioeconomic status is the real cause of differences in cognitive ability. Thus changing the rules and increasing social justice and educational resources for deprived individuals may eventually lead to IQ gains. Last but not least, the argument that such differences are a mere artifact of psychometric tests – such that, say, the choice of questions or problems is unfair

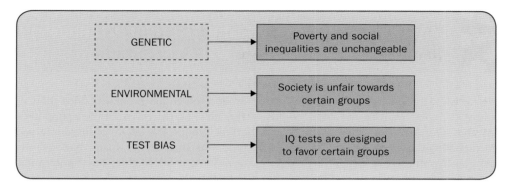

FIGURE 6.9 *Origin of race differences in IQ and implications*

toward certain groups of individuals – would oppose the use of IQ tests in applied or educational settings. Indeed, this argument posits that group differences are artificially created by test designers to justify excluding or favoring certain individuals or groups.

The fact is that even the most controversial reports on race differences in IQ have been careful to interpret the causes of these differences (see again Focus Point 6.1). Indeed, a recent issue of *Psychology, Public Policy, and Law* was entirely devoted to the topic of race differences in IQ. The most radical piece in this issue, written by Rushton and Jensen (2005) – two longstanding advocates of genetic and race differences in IQ – concluded that race differences in intelligence are mainly due to brain size and reflect 80 percent genetic to 20 percent environmental influences.

6.8   SEX DIFFERENCES IN IQ

Sex differences in IQ have sparked almost as much debate as race differences, no doubt due to their sociopolitical implications. Though not always admitted, there is some evidence for the fact that men tend to have an advantage over women on full-scale IQ tests. Most intelligence researchers accept, rather diplomatically, that men do better at some (spatial/mathematical) ability tests, whereas women do better at other (verbal) ability tests. Thus the choice of test may partly determine whether there are gender differences or not. Indeed, some have argued that IQ tests are specifically designed to cancel out rather than reflect differences in intelligence, meaning overinclusion of female-friendly ability problems. Thus Evans and Waites (1981, p. 168) argued that "the two sexes were *defined* to have equal intelligence rather than *discovered* to have equal intelligence" (emphasis in original; see also Garcia, 1981; Rose, Kamin, & Lewontin, 1984). On the other hand, implicit political censorship is likely to intimidate researchers who believe in sex differences and encourage those who deny them. The most notorious example is Chris Brand, who lost his academic position at the University of Edinburgh after publishing a book containing explicit views on group differences in IQ.

FOCUS POINT 6.2   WHAT IF THE HEREDITARIAN HYPOTHESIS WERE TRUE?

In this article, Linda Gottfredson reviews the bodies of evidence available to reveal the possibility that IQ differences between black and white individuals may be caused by genetic factors. This hypothesis has been a very contentious subject ever since it was first proposed in 1969. The possibility that the differences could be explained partially by genes raises many moral evaluations and critiques.

The hereditarian hypothesis states that differences in IQ can be explained by 50 percent environment and 50 percent genetics; the culture-only theory claims it is 0 percent genetics and 100 percent environment. The media paint a picture that agrees with most social scientists and is in line with the culture-only explanation. Also, the media usually argue that psychometric IQ tests are fundamentally flawed, but, as seen in this chapter, that is an invalid statement.

Hereditarian hypothesis (which is in line with *g* theory) predicts that differences in cognitive ability between any two particular races will be similar over time and place, regardless of cultural environments. On the other hand, culture-only theory predicts that IQ gaps will contract and expand depending on similarity of cultural environments, regardless of genetic basis.

The *g* theory receives a lot of support from several areas, which Gottfredson evaluates in some detail. For instance, IQ differences between black people, white people, and East Asian people seem to have remained constant over long periods, with black people having the lowest, white people intermediate, and East Asians the highest IQ scores. This is also in line with adoption studies, notably studies reporting above-average IQ scores in malnourished East Asian individuals adopted by white parents. Also, in 1969 several socioeducational interventions were introduced in schools, without succeeding at raising low IQs. There have been

other intervention programs since then, which also show no narrowing of the IQ gap between ethnic groups. The failure of these intervention programs thus shows that creating a similar environment for all does not significantly nor permanently reduce the IQ gap.

The evidence supporting the hereditarian theory is made even more compelling by the fact that many of the results in its support have been replicated. Moreover, this evidence also seems to contradict the culture-only explanation of group differences in IQ. Here are a few examples: worldwide differences in IQ, reaction time, and brain size (all of which are highly heritable) are consistent, with white people always scoring (on average) higher than black people and lower than East Asians. Also, within races, there is an evident rising heritability of IQ with age, and the virtual disappearance by adolescence of any shared environmental effects on IQ (e.g., parental income, education, etc.; see Chapter 7). There is also some more evidence showing small (.2) and moderate (.4) correlations of IQ, respectively, with skull size and in vivo brain volume, both highly heritable and different between races.

The *g* theory is consilient: a coherent theory formed by the concurrence of multiple inductions drawn in from different areas (genetic, physiological, psychometric, and socioeconomic). In contrast, the environmental theory has become increasingly tattered over time and trying to salvage itself with some disconnected ad hoc speculations.

At the psychometric level, the *g* theory manages not only to predict when differences between black and white people will remain the same in magnitude, but also when they will differ markedly. As mentioned before, there is the three-way uniformity of gaps between black, white, and East Asian people, with black individuals having the lowest IQ scores, and East Asians outscoring white individuals. Though, additionally, there seems to be growing evidence for there being four racial gaps in IQ, with Western black people (with an average 20 percent white admixture) outscoring black Africans. Regarding the differences in gaps for a given race, *g* theory successfully predicts that gaps will be larger in more *g*-loaded tests and in higher social classes. Thus, the gaps in IQ contract and expand *not* according to shifts in culture, but depending on the cognitive demands on the task and the individuals' genetic relatedness.

At the biological level, the three-way race pattern of IQ differences has been replicated with both reaction time and brain size, both of which are highly correlated with *g*. The *g* theory also extends out into the social realm: the most *g*-loaded tests predict school and job performance equally well in black and white people. This *g* prediction goes full circle, from the social back to the genetic, because major life outcomes such as earnings, occupation, and education are to some extent heritable, with half to two-thirds of their heritability being joint with *g*.

The culture-only theory does not seem to have this coherent flow; in fact, it has been known to retreat from its previous explanations to new-formed, less plausible ones. One of the main early claims that social scientists iterated was that mental tests were biased against black people. Indeed, some still maintain this and press more vigorously, claiming that any confirmed deficits in cognitive competencies among black people result from their having suffered more than white people from deleterious, IQ-depressing environments (e.g. poverty, socioeconomic status). However, adoption studies have refuted this, showing that once the IQ-depressing environment is rectified, no salient changes are evidenced (though only time will provide a compelling answer to this question).

Since socioeconomic status and parenting styles have failed to explain IQ gaps, the theory turned to more subtle race-specific psychological factors. These include racism-depressed motivation, racial stress, racial-based performance anxiety ("stereotype threat"), and low esteem. However, there is no evidence that any of these account for short- or long-term declines in actual cognitive ability; not all of them are lower for black people (e.g., low self-esteem); and they do not account for the other nonpsychological factors correlated with IQ, such as brain volume and reaction time. Also, there has been no narrowing in the gap between black and white people since the 1900s, and that is when there were difficult conditions for black people, but since then conditions have no longer been so hostile, thus the environment only seems an implausible explanation for the differences.

In summary, there is a compelling case to support the 50–50 percent hereditarian hypothesis in favor of the culture-only theory. To say that there is no genetic influence in the gap is implausible, as most "environments" themselves are partly genetic in origin, whereby different genotypes evoke different environments for themselves (see Chapter 7). That said, even if IQ tests are valid predictors of real-life outcomes, and even if a great deal of the variance shared between IQ and those outcomes can be explained in terms of genes, it is important to emphasize that social inequalities exist independently and represent a bigger obstacle to social mobility and career achievements than having a lower IQ.

Source: Gottfredson, Linda S. (2005). What if the hereditarian hypothesis were true? *Psychology, Public Policy and Law*, 11, 311–19.

PHOTO 6.5   *Is there a smarter sex?*

Men and women are physically different, but do they differ in their learning potential and thinking ability? Some psychologists have tried to answer these questions by looking at large sets of IQ data.

Image courtesy of Tomas Chamorro-Premuzic.

However, almost all pioneers in intelligence testing (e.g., Binet, Burt, Terman) believed that there were no sex differences in cognitive ability, and few would claim that these researchers were concerned at that time with "balancing" items to cancel out sex differences (for a review see Mackintosh, 1998). Thus Terman (1916, pp. 67–70) concluded:

> when the IQs of the boys and girls were treated separately there was found a small but fairly constant superiority of the girls up to the age of 13 years, at 14 however the curve for the girls dropped below that of boys . . . however the superiority of girls over boys is so slight . . . that for practical purposes it would seem negligible.

Subsequent reports yield somewhat ambiguous evidence. For example, Wechsler (1944, p. 106) admitted that in standardizing his IQ scale he had taken out items that were probably biased against women. Yet, he also argued that "we have more than a 'sneaking suspicion' that the female of the species is not only more deadly but also more intelligent than the male" (p. 107). Indeed, women seemed to outperform men on early versions of Wechsler's scales as well as the original Stanford/Binet scale.

In recent years, differential researchers – notably Richard Lynn – have launched a systematic series of studies into sex differences in IQ (see also Jensen & Reynolds, 1983; Reynolds *et al.*, 1987). Accordingly, there are differences in favor of men rather than women in the region of 3 to 5 points, though probably larger in IQ batteries that include spatial ability tests (Lynn, 1994). Indeed, there are no doubts about men's superior spatial intelligence, a finding that ties in with psychometric as well as biological evidence, as spatial ability is related to testosterone levels. Thus females overexposed to androgens (male sex hormones) tend to obtain significantly higher spatial intelligence scores than control groups, albeit not differing in overall IQ (Resnick *et al.*, 1986). Some have argued that sex differences in spatial intelligence are indicative of different evolutionary sex roles, particularly men's past as hunters or gatherers. Alternative (yet compatible) explanations point toward sex differences in *lateralization*, such that spatial abilities are more dependent on right hemispheric activity, though such claims remain contested. On the other hand, there is some evidence for the idea that women slightly outperform men on verbal ability tests (Feingold, 1988; Hyde & Linn, 1988; Mackintosh, 1998). Last but not least, when intelligence is measured in terms of nonverbal reasoning, such as through Raven's Matrices, results have sometimes shown female superiority, sometimes male, and sometimes no significant differences at all (Court, 1983).

Another famous argument (in favor of male intellectual superiority) is that the *distribution* of IQ points is different in women and men. Thus men are more often found among both lowest (below 70) and highest (above 140) scorers, whereas women tend to be more homogeneous and less frequently obtain very low or very high scores. In a similar vein, Lubinski and Humphreys (1990) looked at the sex distributions in IQ in a sample of approximately 100 000 teenagers and found the standard deviation for males to be 7 percent larger than for females. This led Lynn (1994) to the controversial assumption that IQ is the reason for the unequal sex ratio among eminent figures in the arts, sciences, and politics, who tend to be male rather than female, an assumption that is obviously controversial because it undermines a wide range of socioeconomic and political factors that have historically disadvantaged women in relation to men.

It has also been hypothesized that men's higher IQ scores may be a direct consequence of their larger brain sizes, a claim that has been backed up by consistent evidence of correlations in the region of .30 (though usually lower) between brain size and IQ scores (Rushton & Ackney, 1996). Controversially, correlations between brain size and IQ have also been used to support the idea of race differences in IQ, as white people tend to have larger brains than black people. Yet, these two assertions may be incompatible as (a) the average brain volume differences between black and white individuals is at least five times smaller than that between men and women, and (b) the average IQ difference between men and women is only one third of the average difference between white and black people. Furthermore, Asian groups (e.g., Chinese, Japanese) tend to score significantly higher on IQ tests than white people, despite not having significantly larger brains.

If publishing data showing gender differences in intelligence has been controversial and arguing otherwise may increase academics' popularity, attacking the concept of IQ has made many experts rich and famous. Ever since primary school exams, the mere idea of being tested or examined is bound to evoke anxiety and fear of failure.

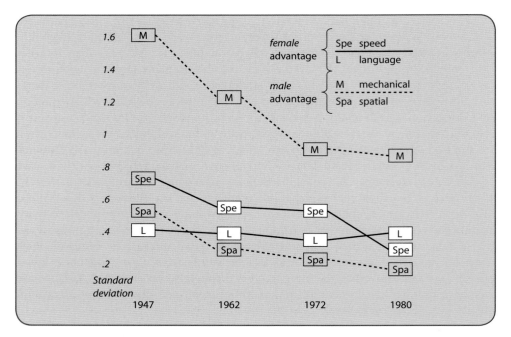

FIGURE 6.10 *In decline: Sex differences in abilities*

Source: Based on Feingold (1988).

It is therefore unsurprising that few individuals enjoy being tested and put under pressure by a psychometric test that may not only tell them how bright they are, but also decide on their future career. This may also explain the media and commercial success of the current crusade, led by the likes of Sternberg, Gardner, and Goleman (see Chapter 8), to destroy the reputation of IQ tests and attempt to replace the traditional notion of intelligence with other, more fashionable and "user-friendly" abilities, such as social, practical, and, in particular, emotional intelligence.

Although these "abilities" (which, by the way, are supposed to be higher in women than men) have met with wide lay enthusiasm, most academics remain unconvinced as to whether they provide any reliable, novel, or useful information. There are three major reasons underlying this skepticism:

(i) It is not possible to design objective tests of emotional, practical, or social intelligence, which means that these abilities can only be assessed through self-report inventories.

(ii) When assessed through self-reports, most novel abilities are substantially correlated with established personality traits, such that constructs like emotional or social intelligence may only be new names for known individual difference constructs (for instance, emotional intelligence may simply refer to a combination of low Neuroticism and high Extraversion).

(iii) Most novel intelligence theories are largely based on the assumption that traditional IQ tests are not a valid indicator of a person's real intelligence.

6.9   EVEN MORE BASIC: DECOMPOSING INTELLIGENCE

A number of researchers have also looked at "lower" correlates of *g*, with the idea of identifying the causes rather than the consequences of intellectual ability. These approaches have aimed at pinpointing the very basic component of *g* in the hope of obtaining a more biological, less cultural, "rawer" measure of brain efficiency. Intelligence researchers have for many decades speculated on the possibility of *g* being ultimately a measure of neural efficiency or neural speed (Anderson, 1992; Eysenck, 1982; Jensen, 1998; Spearman, 1904). In fact, as seen in Chapter 2, elementary cognitive processes represented an essential aspect in early experimental approaches to intelligence. The idea underlying these approaches is simple: more efficient brains should be capable of faster and more accurate processing, which in turn is advantageous for information acquisition. Thus "the 'intelligent' nervous system will respond accurately to incoming signals, and will therefore also be able to respond rapidly; the less intelligent will make errors and respond slowly" (Mackintosh, 1998, p. 233). Within this paradigm, two types of task have received widespread attention:

(i) Reaction time: this simply requires participants to "react" to a signal (sound or visual stimulus) by pressing a key; alternatively, *choice* reaction time experiments combine different signals, which participants need to discriminate between before reacting.

(ii) Inspection time: this requires participants to "inspect" characteristics of perceptual stimuli, such as comparing the length of two lines flashed briefly. The experimenter manipulates the time of exposure to affect individuals' response and error rate.

> **reaction time** a measure of the speed of intellectual processing in which a stimulus (e.g., a light) is seen until a decision is made by the participant and a response enacted.

> **inspection time** a measure of the speed of intellectual processing in which a stimulus (e.g., lines of different lengths) is presented and inspected for a very short time before being removed.

Both reaction and inspection time performance have been consistently correlated with measures of *g* and IQ. Furthermore, studies have also explored the relationship between these simple information-processing measures, IQ, and measures of brain functioning such as **event-related potentials** (ERPs) (see Figure 6.11). Correlations between ERP and IQ tests led Eysenck (1982, p. 6) to suggest that "we have come quite close to the physiological measurement of the genotype underlying the phenotypic IQ test results on which we have had to rely so far" (see also Section 6.7 on race differences in IQ). Yet, measures of reaction time, information processing, perceptual speed, or inspection time as measures of neurophysiological activity are poorer predictors of learning ability and educational/occupational outcomes than are cognitive ability tests.

> **event-related potential** a brain response to an internal or external stimulus, measured by a procedure known as electroencephalography (EEG), which measures electrical activity of the brain through electrodes placed on the scalp.

PHOTO 6.6 *Some differential psychologists argue that the "essence" of intelligence can be tested via simple reaction time experiments. If they are right, your IQ should predict how quickly you react to driving hazards.*

Image courtesy of Tomas Chamorro-Premuzic.

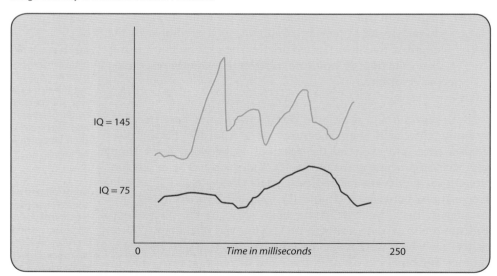

FIGURE 6.11 *Event-related potentials for low and high IQ subjects*

Source: Based loosely on Ertl & Schafer (1969).

In fact, recent findings by Ackerman and Heggestad (1997) show that crystallized abilities are more useful predictors of intellectual performance outcomes than are fluid or more "biological" markers of *g* (see also Chamorro-Premuzic & Furnham, 2005). For example, Rushton and Ackney (1996) report correlations between brain size and measures of academic and job performance in the region of .38. Yet, psychometric measures of *g* and IQ tend to have higher validities (as seen in Sections 6.3 and 6.4).

On the other hand, studies have examined measures of brain activity via electroencephalograph (EEG) records. EEG waves signal changes in mental states, for example engaged, drowsy, asleep, and there are clear individual differences in such patterns. The question, however, is whether such differences have any important relation to measures of cognitive ability (i.e., psychometric tests) and, if they do, what they mean. For example, studies have found that the difference in brain activation between states of rest and cognitive task performance is less marked in individuals with higher than lower IQs (Giannitrapani, 1985). This is consistent with the idea that individuals with higher IQs use their brain more efficiently and "tend to have a relatively lower rate of energy use (as measured by glucose metabolism)" (Gottfredson, 2004b, p. 38).

This does not tell us about the causes of cognitive ability but may, on the contrary, reflect the fact that higher intelligence may lead to reduced "brain consumption," to put it metaphorically. In fact, this type of interpretation applies to most correlational studies between brain (physiological) and behavioral (psychometric) outcomes, whereby cognitive ability may simply be a nexus or mediator between the two measures; that is, it influences both brain activity and cognitive performance (see Figure 6.12).

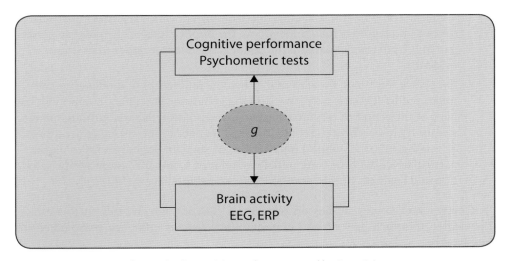

FIGURE 6.12 *g may influence both cognitive performance and brain activity measures*

6.10   SUMMARY AND CONCLUSIONS

This chapter has been concerned with the validity of intelligence; that is, the question of whether intelligence tests are useful predictors of real-life outcomes. In addition, this chapter reviewed some of the literature on the causes of group differences in IQ. As has been seen:

- There is little doubt today among academic psychologists that good IQ tests represent an excellent indicator of an individual's potential for achievement in the real world, in particular when adaptation to novel, complex environments is required.

- However, IQ tests are hardly the only indicator of an individual's ability to succeed in life. Even academic performance, which has been the validity criterion for IQ tests for more than a century, is dependent on factors other than IQ. Thus intelligence is necessary but not sufficient. Whereas a high IQ will never be a drawback per se, intermediate or low IQ levels will not necessarily preclude individuals from performing well on most everyday tasks. This will be the case even in the long run, provided that they are able and willing to compensate with other aspects of their personality, such as being stable, confident, motivated, organized, or hardworking. Likewise, if people lack confidence, stability, and motivation, and are unwilling to work hard, IQ scores will be a poor predictor of performance.

- Claims that gender differences in IQ are responsible for the achievement gap between women and men are exaggerated and show an incomplete picture of the multiple determinants of individual differences in achievement. Furthermore, failure to account for gender differences in self-assessed abilities, vocational interests, and motivational factors exposes the limitations of traditional ability measures, producing incongruent interpretations of findings. Until the combination of factors determining educational and occupational success and failure is fully understood, the implications of the possible gender gap in IQ will remain a matter of political speculation rather than scientific evidence.

- Ever since the 1960s, the idea that individual differences in intelligence, as measured by IQ tests, may have a strong genetic or hereditary component has been at the center of a heated academic and political debate. Although mainstream IQ researchers today are in agreement about the strong genetic basis of intelligence, the political implications of such findings are hard to digest, particularly as IQ tests were initially employed to enhance meritocratic selection and facilitate (rather than obstruct) social mobility.

Chapter 7 examines studies on behavioral genetics, which attempt to estimate the degree to which genetic and environmental factors influence personality and intelligence.

TEXTS FOR FURTHER READING

Ackerman, P.L. & Heggestad, E.D. (1997). Intelligence, personality, and interests: Evidence for overlapping traits. *Psychological Bulletin*, 121, 219–45.

Brody, N. (2000). History of theories and measurements of intelligence. In R.J. Sternberg (Ed.), *Handbook of Intelligence* (pp. 16–33). New York: Cambridge University Press.

Chamorro-Premuzic, T. & Furnham, A. (2006). Intellectual competence and the intelligent personality: A third way in differential psychology. *Review of General Psychology*, 10, 251–67.

Deary, I.J. (2001). *Intelligence: A Very Short Introduction*. Oxford: Oxford University Press.

Gottfredson, L.S. (2004). Intelligence: Is it the epidemiologists' elusive "fundamental cause" of social class inequalities in health? *Journal of Personality and Social Psychology*, 86, 174–99.

7 Behavioral Genetics

LEARNING OUTCOMES

BY THE END OF THIS CHAPTER, YOU SHOULD BE ABLE TO ANSWER THE FOLLOWING FIVE KEY QUESTIONS:

1. What are the early foundations of behavioural genetics?
2. What do we know about the heritability of individual differences?
3. How do nature and nurture interact?
4. Does nurture matter more than nature?
5. What is the significance of the Flynn effect?

KEY WORDS

Allele • Assortative Mating • Behavioral Genetics • Flynn Effect • Genome • Genotype • Heritability Estimate (HE) • Molecular Genetics • Multivariate Genetic Analysis • Phenotype

CHAPTER OUTLINE

7.1   INTRODUCTION

In Chapters 5 and 6, I examined theories and findings on intelligence or cognitive ability that attempt to describe, measure, and compare individuals on the basis of their ability to carry out mental operations, learn new things, and acquire knowledge. More than 100 years after Spearman's (1904) benchmark publication on the g factor of psychometric intelligence (see Section 5.3.4 in Chapter 5), intelligence is a consolidated psychological construct. There are now many reliable psychometric tools to predict academic and occupational achievement, as well as a wide range of other variables of psychological, economic, and political importance, which possess a great degree of accuracy.

However, the fact that some people score higher on IQ tests than others and that IQ tests are good predictors of performance does not really answer the fundamental question of *why some individuals are brighter than others*. Likewise, knowing whether someone is more or less Neurotic, Extraverted, or Open to Experience does not tell us about the causes of these differences; although, as has been seen, Eysenck and Gray hypothesized biological causes for such differences (see Sections 2.8 and 2.9 in Chapter 2 respectively).

PHOTO 7.1 *How much of our personality and intelligence is already determined before we arrive in this world? Research in the area of "behavioral genetics" suggests that individual differences in personality and intelligence are partly heritable or determined by genes. This chapter discusses these findings, which are quite controversial because they challenge our assumptions of free will.*

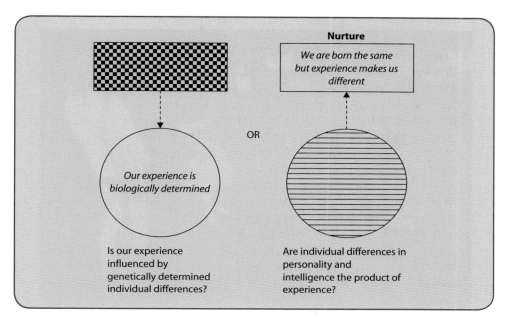

FIGURE 7.1   *Individual differences: Genetically or environmentally determined?*

In recent years, differential psychologists have invested considerable time and effort to assess the extent to which individual differences may be inherited. The most successful and influential of these approaches is represented by the field of **behavioral genetics**, which is concerned with the assessment of the *biological* (genetic) and *environmental* (nongenetic) causes of intellectual ability and personality traits. Behavioral genetics represents an area of overlap between genetics and behavioral sciences. Accordingly (see Figure 7.1), it attempts to provide an estimate of the extent to which individual differences, notably personality and intelligence, may be understood as the product of experience (e.g., learning, education, acquired values, nurture) or "genetically imprinted" information.

behavioral genetics
study of the biological basis of individual differences; it identifies genetic (biological) vs. nongenetic (e.g., environmental) causes of behavior, typically whether nature or nurture plays a larger role in determining individual differences in personality and intelligence.

7.2   EARLY FOUNDATIONS OF BEHAVIORAL GENETICS

Although the study of the genetic and environmental causes of intelligence has recently become a "fashionable" research area, it is by no means new. Since the very beginning of intelligence research, psychologists have attempted to assess the impact of *nature* and *nurture* on individual differences. Very often these attempts have been interpreted in a political rather than scientific light, such that ideological views have

PHOTO 7.2 *To what extent does parenting affect children's intellectual development?*

This is probably the million-dollar question. The reason the answer is not simple is that it is hard to separate upbringing from genetic heritage (and parents give us both). However, twin studies have long provided a "natural experiment" for separating the effects of genes and the environment on intelligence, though many questions remain about the exact impact of parenting on children's IQ.

Image courtesy of Nadia Bettega, reproduced with permission.

influenced several eminent IQ researchers either to embrace or to reject biological conceptions of intelligence.

However, a fair evaluation of early theories on personality and intelligence will indicate that, although most pioneers in this area believed that individual differences in intellectual ability and personality were largely inherited or *innate* (i.e., caused by biological factors), they were also aware of the effects of the environment (e.g., upbringing, rearing, education) on individuals' level of intelligence and personality traits. In most cases, though, it was the emphasis on the former that sparked controversies and debate.

Francis Galton was the first to speculate about the contribution of genetic and environmental factors to intelligence (see Section 5.3.1 and Focus Point 5.1 in Chapter 5). His conclusion that "nature prevails enormously over nurture" (Galton, 1973/1883, p. 241) set a paradigmatic trend in differential psychology, inspiring leading figures in the field even today. Although the first twin studies were not conducted until the mid-1920s (e.g., Theis, 1924), it was Galton (1876) who conceived of this type of research design. Twin studies are an extremely powerful tool to

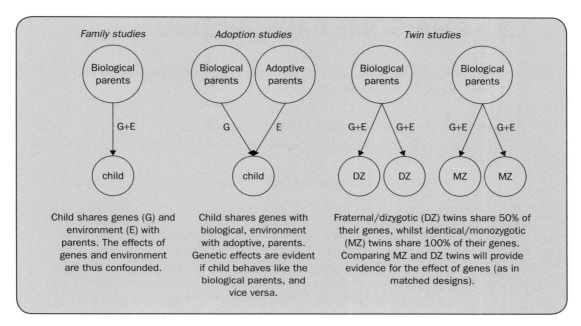

FIGURE 7.2   *Family, adoption, and twin designs*

reveal the genetic roots of a trait or **phenotype** in a specific population. Unlike family studies, which "confound" or mix environmental and genetic influences, twin studies, particularly those comparing identical or monozygotic (MZ) with nonidentical or dizygotic (DZ) twins, provide an accurate estimate of the variance accounted for by biological factors on the one hand and by environmental factors on the other (see Figure 7.2).

phenotype the expression of an individual's genes in behavioral traits that can be measured.

In statistical terms, indicators of genetic influences are represented by the so-called **heritability estimate** (HE). For instance, the HE of intellectual ability ranges from .50 to .70, which implies that 50 to 70 percent of the variance in IQ can be explained by genetic differences. Thus HEs indicate what proportion of the total variance can be attributed to genetic variation.

heritability estimate (HE) a statistical indicator of the influence of genetic factors on individual differences in behavioral traits, showing what proportion of the total variance is attributable to genetic variation.

In the early 1960s, a widely quoted article published in the prestigious journal *Science* reported the first systematic evidence, derived from twin and adoption studies, for the hereditary nature of intelligence (Erlenmeyer-Kimling & Jarvik, 1963). As differential psychologists had hypothesized for many years, genes were shown to have a strong influence on individual differences in cognitive ability. During this same period, unprecedented discoveries in biology, notably the structure of DNA, provided a robust scientific backup for psychology's new vision of differential psychology. But what is DNA, and what is its importance with regard to individual differences?

7.3   DNA: SOME BACKGROUND

DNA stands for *deoxyribonucleic acid* and represents a long formation or chain of acids called "nucleotides," which are in turn made of:

- *deoxyribose* (i.e., a pentose; that is, a 5-carbon sugar);
- *phosphoric acid* (i.e., a mineral acid represented by the chemical formula H_3PO_4);
- *organic/nitrogenous bases* (i.e., *purines* – "adenine" and "guanine," or *pyrimidines* – "cytosine" and "thymine").

The most important characteristic of DNA is that it remains unchanged throughout the lifespan and is transmitted intact to subsequent generations. In some cases genetic mutations may take place that may affect it, but only over millions of years. Whereas behavior may have an impact on neurotransmitters and cause physiological changes in the brain (for example, at this moment your brain is transcribing genes to create neurotransmitters and synthesize the information you are reading), DNA cannot be influenced by behavior. This has made DNA the most important correlate of behavioral outcomes, as it is always *causal* in nature. Thus individual differences at the DNA or **genotype** level can always be expected to cause individual differences at the trait or *phenotype* level, and not vice versa.

Almost half a century after the discovery of DNA (in 1953), scientists have been able to provide a "working map" of the genetic constitution of human beings, including a detailed description of DNA (see Figure 7.3 for a graphical depiction of DNA). These findings were unveiled by the Human Genome Project in 2001. Although there are far fewer human genes than we thought in the past (originally the number was estimated at 100 000, while the correct number is unlikely to exceed 30 000 by far), there are 3 billion DNA letters in the human **genome**!

genotype the genetic complement, coded in DNA, that individuals inherit from their parents. Only identical twins have identical genotypes.

genome the full complement of genetic information, including the set of chromosomes and the genes they carry, inherited by an individual organism from its parents.

One of the most significant scientific discoveries is that there are only minor structural differences between the DNA of human beings and that of other mammals. Thus very *subtle* variations in DNA are enough to determine the differences between one species and another (Brett *et al.*, 2002), even between men and mice! The implications for the study of individual differences cannot be underestimated. If there is only a marginal difference between the genetic makeup of humans and other species, such that, for example, humans and chimpanzees may share 98 percent of their genes, imagine how subtle genetic differences between two individuals would be, let alone if we compare their IQs.

Indeed, differences between two members of the same species are still unobservable at the level of the DNA. Most of the biological letters (*A*, *C*, *G*, *T*) composing the DNA sequence are the same for all humans, and many of them are even present in insects. Given the fast advances in genetic research, particularly in the area of molecular genetics, it is not unrealistic to expect that, sooner or later, behavior-genetic research *will* be able to map individual differences accurately onto specific DNA sequences, in order to compare one human genome with another.

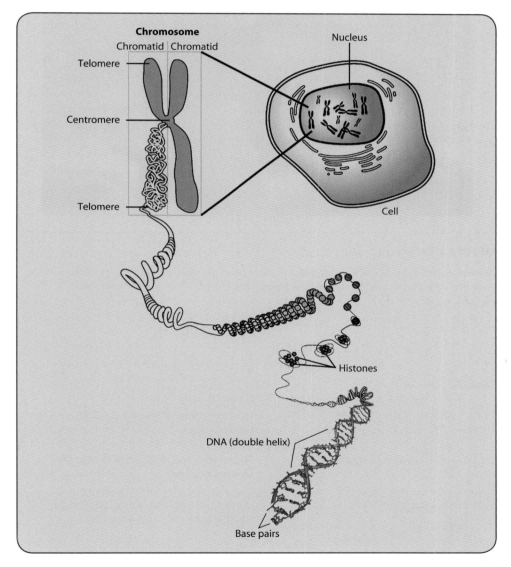

FIGURE 7.3 *Cell, chromosome, and DNA*

Source: National Human Genome Research Institute, Institutes of Health; www.accessexcellenceorg/AB/GG/chromosome.html.

PHOTO 7.3 *Our nearest ancestor*

Despite the few genetic differences between chimps and humans, we are much more evolved versions of them (the proof is that only humans – not chimps – can question this idea).

© Thomas Lersch

Table 7.1 *DNA at a glance*

DNA stands for *deoxyribonucleic acid*.	It is composed of *adenine, guanine, cytosine,* and *thymine*.
It is a long chain of acids (*nucleotides*).	There are 3 billion letters of DNA in the *human genome*.
It is shaped as a *double helix*.	These nucleotide bases are "steps" in the double helix staircase of the DNA.
It was discovered in 1953.	"Genes" are transformations of DNA into *ribonucleic acid* (RNA) and amino acids.
The genetic code was discovered in 1966.	Since 2001, the estimated number of human genes is approximately *30 000*.

7.4 THE POWER OF GENES: RECENT EVIDENCE FOR THE HERITABILITY OF INTELLIGENCE

Recent studies have provided compelling evidence for the biological roots of cognitive ability. Although most studies conceptualize cognitive ability in terms of the general intelligence factor g, thus undermining heritability differences at the level of specific abilities, the data indicate that about 50 percent of the total variance in g can be attributed to DNA differences between individuals. Although this percentage may suggest that "only" half of the variance in intelligence is of a genetic nature, implying that the "other half" must be due to environmental or nurture differences, the real impact of biological factors may be higher than 50 percent, especially because of confounded errors of measurement. Several nonability factors such as anxiety or motivation may slightly distort the accuracy of IQ tests as measures of cognitive ability, moderating the relationship between "actual" intelligence and IQ test performance. This means that correlations between ability measures and other criteria should be "corrected for attenuation" (see Section 5.3.4 in Chapter 5). When this is done, genes tend to account for more than half of the variance in intellectual ability.

Figure 7.4 summarizes the average IQ correlations between different family members, including both adoption and twin studies. As shown, the lowest IQ correlations are found between adoptive parents and their offspring, with an average r value close to .02. At the other end of the spectrum, we find correlations as high as $r = .85$ between MZ twins who grow up together. If you think that the "test–retest" correlation of (good) IQ tests is rarely higher than .90 (indicating that there is some variability within individuals' IQ test performance, such that they do not always obtain exactly the same score), the correlation between MZs' IQ scores is no doubt substantial.

In order to control for the confounding effects of both environment and genes, it is important to examine data from adopted-apart twins (i.e., twins who were separated shortly after birth and grew up in different families, thus lacking a shared environment) and adoptive children. In Figure 7.4, the IQ scores of adopted-apart MZ twins tend to be very similar (approximate average $r = .76$), while adopted-apart siblings (who share half the number of genes than MZ twins) are only vaguely similar in their IQs ($r = .24$). In fact, IQ correlations are much higher in adopted-apart MZ twins than in adoptive siblings ($r = .33$) and adoptive parent–offspring pairs ($r = .20$) growing up together. Another interesting finding refers to the differences in IQ correlations between DZ and MZ twins brought up together: the correlation for MZ twins is almost 30 percent higher than that for their DZ counterparts.

Overall, the pattern of results summarized in Plomin and Spinath's (2004) review illustrates quite clearly that there are strong genetic effects on intellectual ability, such that *the level of genetic relatedness is positively and significantly associated with the size of IQ correlation between family members*. At the same time, there are some environmental effects on IQ, too, such that shared environment (common upbringing) is also a positive predictor of similar IQ scores, though weaker than genes. This means that

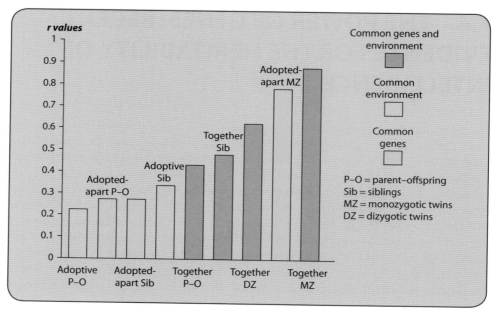

FIGURE 7.4 *IQ correlations for family, adoption, and twin designs*
Source: Adapted from Plomin & Spinath (2004).

people are more likely to have similar levels of intelligence if they have more genes in common (e.g., MZ twins share *all* genetic information as they develop from the same egg) and have been brought up in the same environment. It is no wonder, then, that both views on the causes of intellectual ability, namely environmentalist and biological, have found empirical support for their theories.

The debate around the determinants of intellectual ability has generated as much lay curiosity as academic research, and during the past 20 years intelligence has been the target of substantial behavior-genetic research. Thus, the results depicted in Figure 7.4 have been replicated cross-culturally, for instance in Russia, Germany, India, and Japan. Only personality traits have received comparable attention because of the relative straightforwardness of obtaining self-report data.

7.5   INTELLIGENCE AND ASSORTATIVE MATING

assortative mating the selection of a partner who possesses similar genetic characteristics, such as height, color of eyes, and cognitive ability.

One important aspect in determining the heritability of any trait (physical or psychological) is **assortative mating**, which consists in the nonrandom selection of a partner of similar genetic characteristics, such as height, color of eyes, and cognitive ability. If consistent, the procedure of assortative mating may result in the *evolution* of the species by "improving" the genes in a way that favors competition

PHOTO 7.4 *Do birds of a feather flock together?*

In behavioral genetics, this expression refers to *assortative mating* or the likelihood of choosing a sexual partner with similar characteristics to yours.

Image courtesy of Nadia Bettega, reproduced with permission.

and adaptation. For example, our eyes or our stomach may have developed into a more "efficient" or adaptable organ throughout time, and the same type of evolution may have affected the brain. Thus sociobiologists have long argued that the basic evolutionary goals are common to both human and nonhuman animals: finding and harvesting resources, avoiding predators and illness, and reproducing ("spreading the seeds" in the case of males, and looking for a male who can "protect their offspring" in the case of females) are universal instinctual objectives.

There is, therefore, an important evolutionary component underlying assortative mating, especially when it comes to intellectual ability, as the offspring of brighter parents will inherit more "intelligent" genes. Moreover, to the extent that partners with lower IQs tend to have significantly more children than their higher-IQ counterparts, assortative mating will affect the distribution of IQ scores (though this idea is inconsistent with evidence for the generational increases of IQ scores; see Section 7.12 on the "Flynn effect"). There is a substantial level of assortative mating with regard to intellectual ability, much larger (about twice as much) than for weight, height, and even personality traits. Thus the typical correlation between partners' IQ is $r = .40$, while for weight, color of skin, or personality variables it rarely exceeds $r = .20$.

Another reason for the importance of assortative mating in behavior-genetic research is that it *increases* the variance attributed to genetic factors, causing IQ correlations between family members to increase generation after generation. This leads to a growing longitudinal tendency for partners to become more homogeneous or alike and for genetic differences between them to be reduced. If this logic is applied to our interpretation of behavior-genetic studies (i.e., adoptive, family, and twin designs), we will realize that the effects of assortative mating are different for DZ than MZ twins, and that IQ correlations for the former are *inflated* by nonrandom processes of selection that take into account observable psychological traits such as intelligence. Thus, although DZ twins are not as closely related genetically as MZ twins (who share *all* genetic information), the genetic differences between the former have been progressively reduced through assortative mating.

7.6   THE IMPORTANCE OF THE ENVIRONMENT

Any objective and nonbiased reading of behavior-genetic research will lead to the conclusion that the debate between environmentalists and geneticists is fed by ideological rather than empirical motives. Within the scientific community, differential psychologists have long stopped arguing about the question of whether biological or educational factors lead to individual differences in intellectual ability, as there is longstanding evidence for the effects of both. The compelling evidence for the power of genes has not really undermined the environmentalist argument. Rather, the paramount achievements of genetic research to provide an accurate estimate of the impact of biological factors on individual differences in personality and intellectual ability have made an equally important contribution to demonstrating the effects of nongenetic factors.

As noted, twin studies provide indirect evidence for the effect of environmental or nongenetic factors on intelligence, because not all variance can be explained by genetic factors. That said, it may be exaggerated to conclude that because 50 or 60 percent of the variance in intelligence is explained by genes, the remaining 50 or 40 percent is due to "nurture variables" such as upbringing, education, and imitation. Instead, a more accurate estimate would include error

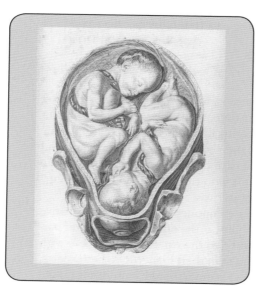

PHOTO 7.5 *Monozygotenous twin studies have been paramount in aiding psychologists in the genes vs. environment debate.*

Published in: Smellie, William. A set of anatomical tables, with explanations, and an abridgment, of the practice of midwifery. (London: [s.n.], 1754). http://www.nlm.nih.gov/exhibition/historicalanatomies/Images/1200_pixels/Smellie_10.jpg

variance in the equation and bear in mind that it would be unrealistic to explain 100 percent of the variance anyway, simply because our measures are not perfect. On the other hand, more direct evidence for the effects of environmental variables on individual difference traits can be obtained from studies on adoptive children and parents (see again Figure 7.4). Although there are nongenetic influences on personality and intelligence, these seem to be substantially smaller than genetic ones.

Plomin and Spinath (2004, p. 114) noticed that "because adoptive siblings are unrelated genetically, what makes them similar is shared rearing, suggesting that about a third of the total variance can be explained by shared environmental influences." However, differential psychologists have yet to identify the *specific* environmental factors that may cause individual differences (and similarities) between individuals. Apart from general environmental factors such as socioeconomic status or level of education, few influential factors have been specified.

On the other hand, while nurture has clear developmental effects on intellectual ability and skills acquisition, the importance of upbringing – as opposed to genes – declines after adolescence. Conversely, the effect of genes tends to *increase* over time, leading to higher IQ correlations between genetically related individuals after adulthood. Accordingly, and somewhat counterintuitively, genes have longstanding effects on behavior and are expressed longitudinally in a way that prevails over environmental factors.

However, it is difficult to "break down" the variance into biological and environmental factors, because genes play an active role in "selecting, modifying, and creating our own environments" (Plomin & Spinath, 2004, p. 114; see Sections 7.7 and 7.10 for a discussion of this point). Thus even adoption studies, which are supposedly aimed at testing the effects of nurture, may confound genetic sources of variability.

7.7 BIOLOGICAL EFFECTS ON INTELLIGENCE: WHY DO THEY INCREASE ACROSS THE LIFESPAN?

The consistent finding that genetic correlations for IQ tend to increase as individuals grow older is as surprising as it is enigmatic. Given that environmental influences on intelligence can only act on experience and would logically undermine the effect of genes, one would expect the opposite pattern of results to occur. How, then, can these findings be explained?

Two different methodologies have been employed to test the longitudinal effects of genes on intellectual ability. The first compares MZ and DZ twins across the lifespan and indicates that IQ correlations for DZ twins tend to *decrease* over time, notably after adolescence, while IQ correlations for MZ twins remain relatively stable until adolescence but continue to *rise* after that (up to $r = .86$ more or less). This pattern of results (shown in Figure 7.5) suggests that environmental influences

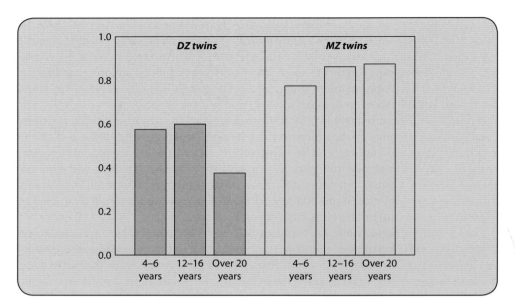

FIGURE 7.5 *DZ and MZ IQ correlations across age*

Source: Adapted from McGue, Bouchard, Iacono, & Lykken (1993).

on IQ do *not* undermine the effects of genes, especially when there is high genetic concordance between siblings, such as in the case of MZ twins.

A second type of design has aimed to identify changes across the lifespan in the correlation between IQ scores of biological parents and their children when the children have been given away for adoption. These correlations have also been compared with those between adoptive parents and children (that is, nongenetically related parent–offspring pairs), as well as control groups. These types of design can provide a relatively direct estimate of heritability, as they indicate that:

- IQ correlations between biological or "original" parents and their adopted-away or original children are similar in size to that of control groups; i.e., biological parents living with their children rather than giving them away for adoption. In simple terms, children's intelligence resembles that of their biological parents, regardless of whether they grew up together or not.

- IQ correlations were higher in control groups and biological-adopted-away pairs than in adoptive-adopted pairs. This means that the resemblance between the IQ scores of adopted-away children and that of their original parents was larger than the one between adoptive parents and their adoptive children.

- Adoptive parents show very little resemblance to their adopted children when it comes to IQ scores.

It seems that IQ-related genes may *activate* only in late childhood or adolescence, such that "relatively small genetic effects early in life snowball during development, creating larger and larger phenotypic effects as individuals select or create environments that foster their genetic propensities" (Plomin & Spinath, 2004, p. 114). Interestingly, this hypothesis is supported not only by the higher IQ correlations between biological parent–children pairs than adoptive parent–children pairs, but also in developmental studies that follow up adoptive siblings as they grow older.

Longitudinal adoption designs, such as McGue *et al.* (1993), indicate that correlations between adopted siblings tend to drop considerably after childhood, implying that, as individuals grow older, the effects of shared environment on IQ tend to decrease. This is consistent with the incremental effects of genes or biological factors on IQ scores: simply said, genes tend to matter more and more as one grows older, while the opposite is true for shared environment. One hypothesis to explain such a pattern of results is that genes "build up" novel cognitive functions, leading to higher-order, more sophisticated reasoning processes. On the other hand, the decreasing effects of environmental factors on IQ may be explained by *change* in environmental variables like socioeconomic status and education: until late adolescence, siblings are likely to have similar levels of income and education, but after that differences between them are likely to appear.

It is noteworthy that behavior-genetic studies have not always examined the same type of abilities or aspects of intelligence. In fact, most studies of this sort have conceptualized cognitive ability in terms of psychometric *g* (see Section 5.3.4 in Chapter 5 on Spearman). This has implications, because different abilities may develop at different stages and, moreover, be more or less affected by learning and education. For example, Cattell's distinction between *gf* (fluid intelligence) and *gc* (crystallized intelligence) (see Section 5.4 in Chapter 5) implies that certain aspects of cognitive ability have a strong biological component, whereas others are more exposed to environmental influences (e.g., education, learning, intellectual investment).

Like *gf*, the general intelligence factor is largely biological and "culture free," which means that there is little reason to expect nongenetic influences when intelligence is conceptualized in terms of psychometric *g*, a fact acknowledged by leading behavior-genetic researchers. For example, Plomin and Spinath (2004, p. 116) noted:

> attempts to find genes for specific cognitive abilities independently of general cognitive ability are unlikely to succeed because what is common among cognitive abilities is largely genetic and what is independent is largely environmental.

Even fluid abilities such as spatial intelligence and memory seem to have genetic loadings smaller than *g*. Thus *g* is the level at which genetic effects on intelligence are most clearly manifested. No wonder, then, that Spearman (1927, p. 403) concluded that only "the most profound and detailed direct study of the human brain in its purely physical and chemical aspects" will allow us to understand fully the meaning of *g*.

Recent advances have enabled researchers to examine the heritability of specific traits by carrying out **multivariate genetic analyses**, which compare the effects of genes on a pair of traits independently of their individual heritability levels. The statistical indicator known

multivariate genetic analysis analysis that compares the effects of genes on a pair of traits independently of their individual heritability levels, giving a statistical indicator known as the genetic correlation, which shows whether two specific traits are related.

as the *genetic correlation* thus tells us whether two specific traits are related, regardless of their level of genetic determination. So far, results suggest that the same genes are likely to affect different abilities, from spatial to verbal to more elementary cognitive processes. Moreover, consistent correlations between brain size, psychometric intelligence (*g*), and basic cognitive processes would be indicative of the general rather than specific effect of intelligence-related genes, manifested across different brain areas and functions. Interdisciplinary studies are rapidly facilitating the integration of different areas such as neuropsychology, cognitive psychology, behavioral genetics, and differential psychology, shedding light on the underlying causal paths that determine genetic and environmental relationships in IQ.

FOCUS POINT 7.1   AGE RELATED CHANGES IN HERITABILITY OF BEHAVIORAL PHENOTYPES OVER ADOLESCENCE AND YOUNG ADULTHOOD

One of the most counterintuitive findings in behavioral genetics is that throughout our lifespan genetic influences tend to increase. But why? Many studies have focused on the environmental and genetic variance at one point in time, but Bergen, Gardner, and Kendler's article uses a meta-analysis of longitudinal studies to explore this issue.

Genes and environment interact to form a phenotype, but this process is not necessarily additive, as people can be exposed to the same environmental conditions yet respond in different ways. This is termed the genotype–environment interaction. Genes can also mediate your exposure to the environment and this is known as the genotype–environment correlation. There are three types of genotype–environment correlation (*r*GE): passive *r*GE, whereby parents provide both genes and environment; active *r*GE, the tendency to seek out environments that reinforce their genotypic dispositions; and evocative/reactive *r*GE, which results from the elicitation of environmental responses by genetically influenced behaviors.

Heritability measures should increase if the growing active *r*GE influences exceed the declining rate of passive *r*GE influence in adolescence through to young adulthood. The timeframe of adolescence to young adulthood for measuring these differences in heritability was chosen because many life changes take place during this period.

If there is a change in heritability, then monozygotic twins (MZ) are more likely to select similar environments compared to dizygotic twins (DZ). This article explores this in a meta-analysis of studies researching heritability measures of a variety of phenotypic behaviors behaviorally expressed. These were IQ, depression, anxiety, externalizing behaviors (such as antisocial behavior, conduct disorder, and aggression), alcohol consumption, smoking initiation, social attitudes (religiousness and conservatism), and ADHD.

METHOD

A meta-analysis of studies including MZ and DZ twins with two or more points of heritability measures being used.

Participants were aged 13–25.

The phenotypic behaviors measured were IQ, depression, anxiety, externalizing behaviors, alcohol consumption, smoking initiation, social attitudes, and ADHD.

RESULTS

Results showed that IQ displayed a large significant heritability increase per year (t = .487, $p < .0001$). Not only IQ showed an increase in heritability, but also anxiety, depression, and externalizing behaviours. There were also modest significant increases in social attitudes (religiousness, conservatism) and, although nonsignificant, there was a slight increase in the heritability of smoking initiation and alcohol consumption behaviors. ADHD, however, showed almost a complete absence of change in heritability over the years.

With regard to sex differences, the only significant result was that women showed a higher heritability increase in relation to externalizing behavior, such as antisocial behavior, compared to males.

DISCUSSION

This meta-analysis shows a general trend of increasing heritability for various traits from adolescence through to young adulthood.

In relation to ADHD, a possible reason for the lack of change over the years could be that any change in heritability could have occurred antecedent to the study (i.e., in individuals younger than 13).

Reasons for low, nonsignificant increases in heritability for smoking initiation and alcohol consumption could be due to the low availability of these substances at younger ages. This could have attenuated heritability measures, since expression of these behaviors must follow exposure.

There have been several other studies that have supported the notion of heritability increase, but they have been studied too rarely to include in a meta-analysis. These behaviors include exercise, eating behaviors and attitudes, and vocabulary knowledge.

The active rGE theory is attractive, as it explains how someone will seek out a range of environmental options in order to provide greater opportunities to express their genetic dispositions. They will seek out environments that reinforce their genetic proclivities.

This meta-analysis looked at a young cohort in whom there are many biological developments taking place, which can affect the timing or the amount of change in heritability measures. In an older population, could it be that heritability measures continue to change throughout? IQ seems to decrease in heritability from 40 to 75 years of age. Maybe it is that environmental effects may accumulate at older ages and account for a larger proportion of the variance. This is clearly an area in which more research would be welcomed.

Source: Bergen, S.E., Gardner, C.O., & Kendler, K.S. (2007). Age related changes in heritability of behavioural phenotypes over adolescence and young adulthood: A meta-analysis. *Twin Research and Human Genetics*, 10, 423–33.

7.8   GENETIC CAUSES OF PERSONALITY TRAITS

Owing to space constraints and the uniformity of criteria to measure cognitive ability, I have chosen to focus on the behavioral genetics of intelligence rather than other traits throughout this chapter. However, behavior-genetic studies have not been confined to intellectual ability but have also investigated personality traits. In fact, some estimate that there are more studies looking at the biological causes of personality traits than intellectual abilities. Needless to say, people are usually more interested in the heritability of intelligence than that of personality, not least because of the controversies surrounding the concept and measurement of intelligence.

Whereas extreme IQ scores tend to have direct and obvious implications in everyday life, "extreme" personalities do not, with the exception of psychopathology, have major connotations. Thus the social implications of personality and intelligence are quite different. While intelligence may justify a job offer or promotion, individuals' score on personality dimensions may have little effect on their careers, even when used in occupational contexts. If, however, personality traits can significantly predict performance in educational and occupational settings, and affect a variety of real-world outcomes in general (as shown in Chapter 3), the implications of the heritability of personality should not be undermined.

In a state-of-the-art meta-analytic review of personality and behavioral genetics, Zuckerman (1991) concluded the following:

- There is a *substantial hereditary* aspect underlying most personality dimensions.
- *Genetic* correlations for personality tend to *persist* throughout the lifespan (just as for intellectual abilities).
- *Environmental* (shared environment) influences on personality traits are far *less* important than genetic ones.
- *Nonshared* environment has a greater *impact* than shared environment, but is less important than genes, in determining personality traits.

Overall results are summarized in Table 7.2. It is noteworthy that most of these results refer to studies on the Gigantic Three inventory (Eysenck's model) or comparable instruments. This is because, until 1992 (one year after Zuckerman's review), the Big Five had little significant impact on differential psychology studies and assessment was predominantly focused on Neuroticism, Extraversion, and, to a lesser extent, Psychoticism. In fact, these traits have not always been assessed with the same instrument, which may have partly contributed to the variability between studies that can be seen in Table 7.2.

It should also be noted that the samples reviewed by Zuckerman differed in age and, somewhat more, in size ($N = 151$ to 14 288). There is nonetheless a consistent pattern of results across samples, such that correlations between MZ twins are always larger than those between DZ twins. In some cases, such as Neuroticism in Tellegen *et al.*'s (1988) study, differences are relatively minor, but in most studies correlations for MZ twins are at least twice as large as those for DZ twins.

If personality traits were mostly "acquired" or "learned" – that is, determined by upbringing and rearing – we would not expect such differences between DZ and MZ twins. Furthermore, if strong environmental influences occurred we would certainly expect the correlations in Table 7.2 to decrease with age. It seems clear, however, that MZ twins tend to have more similar personality traits than do DZ twins, and that these similarities tend to "hold" clearly across the lifespan. For instance, for Extraversion, the correlation between MZ is $r = .61$ at the age of 18, and $r = .54$ at the age of 54 (Pedersen *et al.*, 1988). Thus studies on the Gigantic Three personality

Table 7.2 *A comparison between the personality of MZ and DZ (correlation coefficients)*

Researchers	Age	Neuroticism		Extraversion		Psychoticism	
		MZ	DZ	MZ	DZ	MZ	DZ
Loehlin & Nichols (1976)	18	.54	.22	.61	.25	.54	.32
Floderus-Myrhed *et al.* (1980)	17–49	.46	.21	.47	.20	–	–
	17–49	.54	.25	.54	.21	–	–
Eaves & Young (1981)	31	.47	.07	.55	.19	.47	.28
Tellegen *et al.* (1988)	21	.54	.41	.54	.06	.58	.25
Rose *et al.* (1988)	24–49	.33	.12	.46	.15	–	–
	24–49	.43	.18	.49	.14	–	–
	14–34	.41	.22	.60	.42	.70	.41
Pedersen *et al.* (1988)	59	.41	.24	.54	.06	–	–

Key: MZ = monozygotic (identical twins), DZ = dizygotic (fraternal twins).

Source: Adapted from Zuckerman (1991).

factors, notably the two longstanding traits of Neuroticism / Emotional Stability and Extraversion / Introversion, show that personality traits are largely inherited – that is, that there are strong biological influences on these individual differences – which, as has been said, are referred to the most general patterns of thought, behavior, and emotionality that make every individual unique and different from others.

Another important statistical value is that of the correlation between genetically *unrelated* siblings who were brought up in the same family (shared environment). Zuckerman's (1991) review of the literature concluded that, on average, the correlation for personality traits between these siblings is in the order of $r = .07$; that is, virtually *zero*. This is not just surprisingly low, it is also in direct opposition to the vast number of theories in developmental psychology that have long emphasized the importance of specific strategies for bringing up children. The behaviorgenetic evidence reviewed here suggests that psychological eminences as diverse as Freud, Skinner, and Bandura (to cite only a few) may have largely overestimated the importance of shared environment, and that the consequence of one or other educational strategy may be virtually meaningless, especially compared to the power of genes. Furthermore, most of the effects of nongenetic factors seem attributable to nonshared rather than shared environmental variables, meaning that people *other* than family members, for instance teachers and friends, would exert a bigger influence on individuals' personality development than parental rearing.

One of the most important studies about the genetic basis of personality traits was carried out by Loehlin (1992), who compared twin and adoption data on the Big Five personality traits (Costa & McCrae, 1992). This study showed that, on average, the HE for Neuroticism and Extraversion ranged from .30 to about .50 (the outbound figure is generally taken to be more reliable). These data are consistent with Eysenck's biological theory of personality, which hypothesized innate physiological differences (in cerebral arousability levels) underlying individual differences in Neuroticism and Extraversion.

molecular genetics an area of research that examines correlations between different genes and personality or intelligence scores and maps behavioral differences onto particular genes.

Recent research has achieved unprecedented progress in mapping behavioral differences onto particular genes, an area known as **molecular genetics**. Typically, this research examines correlations between different genes and personality or intelligence scores. For instance, Lesch *et al.* (1996) have identified a gene associated with individual differences in trait anxiety (Neuroticism/Emotional Stability). One of the most consistent associations (see Benjamin *et al.*, 1996) is that between the *neuroreceptor* gene, the D4 dopamine receptor (*DRD4*), and *sensation seeking*, a trait that shows considerable overlap with Openness to Experience from the Big Five model (see Section 2.11 in Chapter 2), as well as the Psychoticism trait from Eysenck's model (see Section 2.6 in Chapter 2). (Because of its wider use I have focused on Openness rather than novelty seeking or sensation seeking, but further references to this can be found in Zuckerman, 1994.)

allele one of two or more alternative forms of a gene that occupies the same position (locus) on paired chromosomes and controls the same characteristic.

Specifically, the length of the DNA marker for the DRD4 genes seems to be one of the causes of higher sensation seeking, such that longer **alleles** in the DNA structure are associated with higher sensation seeking and vice versa. Thus sensation seeking may be interpreted as an attempt to compensate for lower levels of dopamine (Plomin & Caspi, 1999).

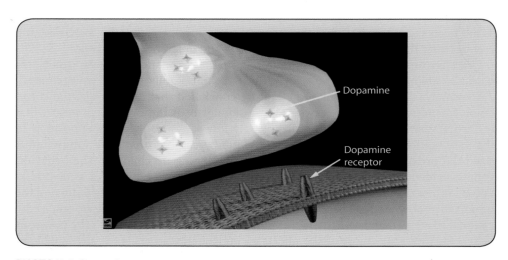

PHOTO 7.6 *Dopamine receptor.*

Source: http://www.drugabuse.gov/pubs/teaching/largegifs/slide-4.gif

7.9   GENETIC BASIS OF MALADAPTIVE BEHAVIORS

Recent studies in differential psychology and neuropsychology have attempted to shed light on the particular physiological processes underlying *addictive behaviors*, such as illegal substance use, smoking (which is increasingly banned in developed countries), and alcohol use and abuse. This wave of research has important clinical implications, as it could help early identification of vulnerability to addictions as well as improve treatment of patients, for example by preventing harmful habits and estimating the degree of risk associated with specific genetic imprints.

Blum *et al.* (2000) have argued that individuals may be genetically predisposed toward malfunctioning of the dopamine neurotransmitter, resulting in a structural "reward deficiency." Accordingly, they would experience higher levels of subjective relief/wellbeing and enhanced stress reduction following the act of drug ingestion.

Twin, family, and adoption studies (which have been reviewed by Ball & Collier, 2002) point toward salient genetic determinants of a variety of substance abuses. Typically, HE for use and abuse of alcohol, hallucinogens, stimulants, and cannabis range from .40 to .60, which is considered high. These figures have been replicated in studies looking at "initiation rates" or the likelihood of trying a substance or drug in adolescents (see Reich *et al.*, 1998; Uhl *et al.*, 2001). However, attempts to isolate or identify specific genes associated with addictive behaviors have so far been less successful, probably because, as with most individual difference variables, substance abuse is genetically *multidetermined*, which means that there are confounding genetic determinants underlying such behaviors, so that more than one gene contributes to their cause.

Aspects of personality significantly related to addictive/compulsive behaviors include broad traits such as Extraversion and Psychoticism, and more specific "primary traits" such as impulsivity and antisocial sensation seeking. At the neurotransmitter level, these facets of behavior and psychological dispositions seem linked through the dopamine chemical (for reviews see Depue & Collins, 1999; Pickering & Gray, 1999). For instance, Gray, Pickering, & Gray (1994) conducted an "emission tomography" study and found that the D2 receptor binding of the dopamine neurotransmitter is significantly related to impulsivity and antisocial behavior in healthy participants (see also Suhara *et al.*, 2001). It has been argued that the *incentive motivational systems* of the brain may be involved in determining levels of Extraversion and antisocial/maladaptive impulsivity, since these traits are positively, albeit modestly, intercorrelated (Depue & Collins, 1999; Pickering & Gray, 1999, 2001). This is consistent with the view of extraverts as more "reward sensitive" than their introverted counterparts.

The implications of the above associations with regard to substance abuse may not be as straightforward, however. Extraversion, for instance, is positively associated with constructs such as happiness, self-confidence, and life satisfaction (see Chapter 3). Thus the reward-deficiency hypothesis may lead us to expect extraverted individuals to have greater potential for drug and alcohol use, when personality taxonomies suggest that it is introverts who tend to experience lower self-esteem, lower levels of happiness, and lower levels of satisfaction with life. Accordingly, introverts should also be more vulnerable to addictions and represent an easier psychological "target" for addictive substances. When it comes to predicting substance abuse, it may therefore be more appropriate to look at antisocial behavior and impulsivity than the more general and seemingly "positive" trait of Extraversion (for a recent longitudinal study of this sort, see Sher, Bartholow, & Wood, 2000).

Another major personality trait associated with alcohol and drug use is Psychoticism (Newbury-Birch, White, & Kamali, 2000). This is perhaps unsurprising, as Psychoticism is a far better predictor of antisocial behavior and impulsivity than is Extraversion (Eysenck & Eysenck, 1985). Studies also report an interesting interaction between Psychoticism and *gender* differences, such that men tend to be more psychotic and abusive of alcohol and drugs than are women (O'Malley & Johnston, 2002), particularly among young populations. In addition, one would also expect *cultural* factors to play a significant moderating role in determining these differences.

7.10 PERSONALITY AND INTELLIGENCE: INTERPLAY BETWEEN ENVIRONMENT AND GENES?

Although both twin and adoption studies suggest that the environment has a minor influence on the development of individual differences in personality and intelligence compared to genes, some caution is needed to interpret the implications of these findings.

Most sociologists, anthropologists, and social psychologists tend to reject the idea that genes are more important than experience (e.g., formal and informal education) in shaping our personality and intelligence. Conversely, behavioral geneticists, and increasingly differential psychologists in general, seem inclined to believe that the "real" effect of genes on abilities and personality traits is underestimated by these data, mainly because of the unreliability or imperfection of the psychometric instruments used to assess individual differences. Furthermore, they point out that genes may not only exert an effect on traits, but also affect environmental choices, implying an *interplay* between genes and environment.

The idea of an interplay between genetic and environmental factors is conceptually complex and counterintuitive, as nurture and nature have always been conceptualized at opposite ends of the spectrum. Thus philosophers and scientists alike have examined whether nature *or* nurture is responsible for (i.e., the cause of) an event. Even when behavior-genetic studies estimate the degree to which one or other factor affects behavior, the assumption was that of an additive model, such that genetic + nongenetic factors = 100 percent of the variance in a phenotype. However, suggesting that genes may affect environmental choices, which in turn may affect individual differences (e.g., the development of personality traits or abilities), implies a *multiplicative* model; namely, genetic × nongenetic factors = 100 percent. Thus genetic factors are necessary not only to understand the outcome or phenotype, but also the type of environment or experience. For example, Plomin, Loehlin, and DeFries (1985) noticed that siblings' *shared* environment is influenced by genetic factors, such that activities and interests are shaped according to genetic predispositions. This hypothesis would explain why two siblings may not experience exactly the same environment even if they grow up together.

The multiplicative model of genetic–environmental influences is also important to examine possible developmental links between personality traits and cognitive abilities, an area that has been the focus of increasing research in recent times. Ever since Cattell's (1987) theory of intellectual investment, differential psychologists have considered the possibility of causal effects between intelligence and personality, such that traits may affect the development of crystallized abilities. Indeed, there are paths in the other direction, too. Chamorro-Premuzic and Furnham (2005, 2006) have argued that certain personality traits, such as Conscientiousness, may in part develop as a response to interactions between biologically based abilities and environmental demands.

For example, lower levels of fluid intelligence may be compensated by higher levels of Conscientiousness in order to accomplish challenging tasks (e.g., competitive university programs or jobs). If genes influence the level of intellectual investment, the effects of personality and intelligence would be confounded in environmental choices. Thus,

> the intelligent child will actively seek out intellectually stimulating environments – playing chess, asking parents for educational games, joining several clubs at school, reading educational magazines, and perhaps making friends who are also of above-average ability. (Cooper, 2002, p. 260)

Figure 7.6 presents a depiction of the premature effects of genes on shared and nonshared environments; that is, how biologically inherited factors can play an active role in shaping a child's experiences from a very early age until adulthood.

The model in Figure 7.6 may also be applied to personality traits, particularly to understand environmental choices. For example, extraverts' genetically determined

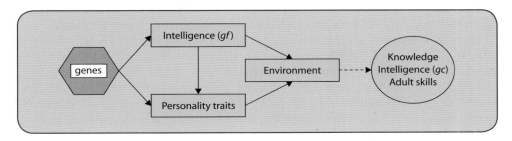

FIGURE 7.6 *Genetic interplay: Personality and intelligence*

lower levels of cortical arousal would lead them to *seek* stimulating or arousing environments, such as parties, social gatherings, and background music. Conversely, the genetic disposition toward introversion would be manifested in terms of higher levels of cortical arousal, which in turn would lead introverts to *avoid* similar stimulating or arousing environments. Thus introverts may be as aroused on their own as extraverts in the company of others (see again Section 2.6 in Chapter 2 on Eysenck's biological theory of personality).

7.11   IMPLICATIONS FOR UPBRINGING AND EDUCATION

The idea that intelligence and personality are largely inherited has important educational implications. Educational theories and practices have been traditionally based on the assumption that environmental factors (e.g., early family experiences, upbringing, formal schooling) are the major causal determinants of adult individual differences, and this applies to many areas of psychology (e.g., social, developmental, and clinical). As stated above, eminent psychologists as diverse as Skinner, Freud, and Bandura all seemed to agree on the importance of experience in shaping individuality. It is therefore quite astonishing that the effects of genetic factors on individual difference constructs have been replicated so widely.

While behavior-genetic findings may pose a big question mark against the environmentalist or social learning view of individual differences, the idea that experience has no effects on our lives is absurd. Behavior is rarely "completely genetic." A person with a genetic *predisposition* toward alcoholism will not become an alcoholic if they never take a sip of alcohol. If anything, behavior-genetic findings seem to question the importance of "shared" rather than "nonshared" environments, as the effects of the latter seem substantially more significant than the former.

Another key issue is that behavior-genetic research has mainly focused on *traits*, which, although encompassing a wide range of behavioral and psychological dispositions, are not perfect measures of individual differences. Even if psychometric inventories such as the Big Five personality questionnaire provide an adequate or good estimate of individuals' personalities, they are only *generalizations* of behavior, and therefore less focused on specific behaviors that may be less affected by genes and more affected by experience (just as specific abilities seem to be less affected by experience than *g*).

Heritability estimates (HEs) may also vary for extremely high or low scores on the same trait, and indeed differ for positive or negative manifestations of the same personality characteristics. For instance, Stevenson (1997) found that antisocial behavior (e.g., aggressiveness, destructive behavior, anger expression) had relatively low genetic causes, whereas the HEs for *prosocial behavior* (e.g., empathy, altruism, solidarity) were quite high. Thus "sociability" is a complex, multidetermined process that is influenced by an array of factors ranging from genes to shared and nonshared environments.

7.12 CONTRADICTING GENETICS: THE FLYNN EFFECT

Despite the robust and consistent evidence from behavior-genetic research that the major psychological differences underlying behavioral differences between individuals are of genetic origins, there are a few unsolved dilemmas that are almost in direct conflict with the findings from twin and adoptive designs presented above. The most salient inconsistency was highlighted in a series of studies conducted and reported by James **Flynn** (1987), a sociologist from New Zealand.

Flynn gathered large sets of cross-cultural and longitudinal data on psychometric intelligence from military databases, as several armies use IQ tests for selection. The list of countries included the Netherlands, Belgium, New Zealand, Norway, and Great Britain (see Figure 7.7). Because ability tests are usually "standardized" – that is, every newly introduced item or question is carefully balanced against old ones to prevent major changes in difficulty level and maintain similar standards – differences in scores on the *same test across time* may be interpreted as differences in "real" ability rather than in the instrument. Furthermore, two different versions of the same test (say, WISC 1978 vs. the 1998 version) may be administered to the same person to compare their performance on both versions, such that higher scores on the earlier version will indicate a generational increase in cognitive ability.

Flynn effect The finding by sociologist James Flynn that there are generational increases in IQ across nations.

PHOTO 7.7 *James R. Flynn in 2007*

Image courtesy of http://en.wikipedia.org/wiki/James_R._Flynn.

© Bryce Edwards

In Figure 7.7 it can be seen that there are generational increases in IQ across nations by about 15 points (1 SD) every 50 years (although four nations are graphically represented in this chart, Flynn's studies extended to a larger number of countries and have been reported elsewhere; i.e., Flynn, 1987, 1998, 1999). It is also noteworthy that most increments have been found in tests of fluid (*gf*) rather than crystallized (*gc*) intelligence, which means that increases in ability could not have been caused by improvements in educational factors, such that, say, current generations are more knowledgeable or educated than former ones. Rather, it is scores on so-called culture-free tests (e.g., nonverbal, logical, mathematical) that improved most over time, suggesting that current generations are mentally "quicker" and "faster" than older generations when it comes to learning new things.

The question of why IQ scores seem to have improved over time and why today's generations may be brighter than older ones is complex. Several hypotheses have been put forward, from technical assumptions on the structure of psychometric tests

FOCUS POINT 7.2   REQUIEM FOR NUTRITION AS THE CAUSE OF IQ GAINS

The 20th century has seen big gains in both IQ and height, leading many researchers to argue that improved nutrition may be a cause of both. However, since 1950, nutrition has not been an important factor in IQ gains, at least in developed countries. In this article, Flynn shows evidence for a three-level model as an alternative causal explanation for IQ gains in Britain.

Virtually everyone accepts that nutrition plays a vital role in developing nations (as it did in developed nations before 1950). Between the 19th and mid-20th century there were significant improvements in diets and child health. During the early stages of development, children's brains may have benefited from these improvements. However, looking at the history of nutrition, there is no evidence to suggest that Western societies' children have better diets today compared to 1950. Indeed, some food critics would even say that our current diets are worse than ever (just look at the current obesity epidemic in the US and the UK as an example). Yet, there have been large IQ gains post-1950. Let us look at an example: 1952 18-year-old male Dutch military boys were tested on a Raven's type test and these were compared with 1962 18-year-old Dutch military boys. Those in 1962 would have been in the womb or born in 1944. In that year, there was the great Dutch famine, where German troops monopolized food and brought sections of the population to near starvation. Yet, there was still an IQ gain prevalent in those 10 years. Thus, the lack of food had no effect on the pattern of IQ gains over the year.

Height and intelligence are modestly but significantly and constantly correlated. This has led to the assumption that improved nutrition is the principal cause. One hypothesis is that the more affluent had a better diet than the lower classes in 1950. Over the last 60 years, the nutritional gap between the upper and lower classes has diminished, therefore the IQ gap between the two classes would have diminished as well, and,

therefore, gains should be larger in the bottom half (lower classes) than in the top half (upper classes) of the IQ curve.

The correlation between height and intelligence may signal nutrition as a common cause: wherever height gains persist, nutritional gains might persist. Where nutritional gains persist, IQ gains should show a greater increase in the lower half. However, the evidence does not support this. In the Netherlands and France, there were height gains until the children born in 1965, but IQ gains were prevalent throughout the population. In Norway, height gains have been larger in the upper half of the distribution, but IQ gains were higher in the lower half, which together does not bode well for the nutritional hypothesis.

IN BRITAIN: NUTRITION AND INTELLIGENCE RESULTS

Flynn analyzed British IQ trends in detail and, in doing so, he showed that nutrition is an unlikely explanation for IQ gains. He analyzed British IQ trends on Raven's Progressive Matrices from 1938 to 2008. Progressive Matrices are an attempt to measure intelligence in a culturally free format. The data comes from three versions of the Standard Progressive Matrices (SPM). The Coloured Progressive Matrices (CPM) is designed for younger school children under 11. The SPM is very similar to the above, but with some harder questions, and the revised version of the SPM – the SPM PLUS – consists of new questions with even higher difficulty. All three measure on-the-spot problem solving and the ability to detach logic from the concrete.

CPM RESULTS

The CPM results show that from 1947 to 2007 children aged 5.5 to 11 years gained 15.59 IQ points. They gained at a much slower rate in the first period (1947–1982) with 0.170 points per year, than the second period (1982–2007) with 0.386 points per year. In both periods, the top half of the population showed greater IQ gains, directly contradicting the nutrition hypothesis, as according to it, IQ gains should be concentrated on the bottom half on the curve.

SPM RESULTS

The SPM results show that from 1938 to 2008 children aged 7.5 to 15.5 years gained 13.65 IQ points at a rate of 0.195 per year. Contrary to the CPM, gains are larger in the first half (1938–1979) at a rate of 0.229 per year compared to 0.147 per year in the second half (1979–2008). In both periods gains declined by age 12.

The above data would suggest that it is in concordance with the nutritional hypothesis; however, it is deceptive in the comparability of SPM with CPM. When rates of gain are calculated for the ages that all datasets have in common (7–11 years old), both CPM and SPM show higher rates in gain in recent years than in earlier years.

Looking at all the results for SPM shows that the top half have fewer gains than the bottom half, agreeing with the nutritional hypothesis. However, if we look at the dietary history of Britain, it is obvious that it is not due to nutritional improvements. Britain's nutritional history has many fluctuations, for example during the food shortages during the Great Depression and the Second World War; from 1964–1971 there was quite a large nutritional gap between the upper and lower half, then it diminished; and from 1977 until now there seems to be a growing nutritional inequality, just to mention some of the fluctuations. Yet, there is a constant trend in increase in IQ, so another explanation seems to be necessary.

AN ALTERNATIVE ANALYSIS

This alternative approach looks at a multifactor model. One of the most prominent exogenous causes was the radical industrialization that had been well underway since before 1900. How it serves to explain IQ gains over time are through advancements in health and nutrition (in the first half of the 20th century), more and different schooling, smaller family size, modern parenting, the rise of visual culture, more jobs requiring on-the-spot problem solving, and more leisure particularly devoted to cognitively demanding pursuits, such as radio, television, the Internet, and computers.

During the 20th century society evolved, and therefore set new problems that forced us to think differently than in the past. These new problems made us develop new habits of mind, using our minds in new ways to solve new issues, such as using logic to deal with abstract concepts. This fresh way of training the brain may be a partial explanation for this increase in IQ. For example, the brains of London taxi drivers have a larger hippocampus compared to nontaxi drivers, an area in the brain used for navigating three-dimensional spaces.

So Flynn's three facets on which he focuses to explain these IQ gains are the exogenous historical cause (technology); ultimate sociological causes (nutrition, family, schooling, work, leisure); and the proximate psychological causes (new habits of mind); and possibly also brain physiology.

Enhanced nutrition has made us taller people, but poor nutrition has made us obese. However, overall our diet does not make us very different from our ancestors as far as cognitive competence is concerned. We use our brains differently to how our grandparents did in relation to solving problems, and have thus ended up training our brains differently. The case of nutrition, at least the privation of it, is too weak an argument, and a broader, multifaceted approach is more suited.

Source: Flynn, J.R. (2009). Requiem for nutrition as the cause of IQ gains: Raven's gains in Britain 1938–2008. *Economics and Human Biology*, 7, 18–27. With permission from Elsevier.

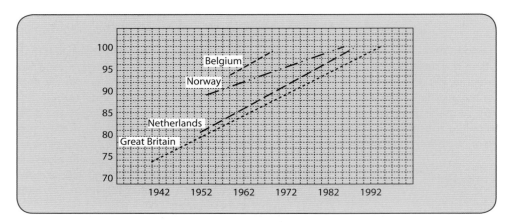

FIGURE 7.7 *On the rise: The Flynn effect in four nations (IQ increases across time)*

Source: Adapted from Flynn (1999).

PHOTO 7.8 *Nutrional advantage – can a healthier diet make us smarter?*

Image courtesy of Tomas Chamorro-Premuzic.

(notably, familiarity with questions or "type" of items) to more fundamental theories, including the role of nutritional advances (Lynn, 1990). For example, a better diet has a positive effect on physical health (a healthier body), which in turn translates into more efficient and effective brain functioning, including the cognitive processes that are required to excel on tests of fluid intelligence (however, see Focus Point 7.2).

7.13 SUMMARY AND CONCLUSIONS

This chapter has examined the role of genetic and nongenetic (i.e., shared vs. non-shared environment) influences on individual difference factors. As has been seen:

- Behavioral traits, such as intelligence and personality traits, are largely inherited, such that genetic resemblance is correlated with phenotypic resemblance (this is particularly noticeable in twin studies comparing nonidentical with identical twins). Although traits are also influenced by nongenetic factors, such that identical twins reared together are psychologically more similar than those separated after birth, genetic similarity is far more important than shared environment. Indeed, adoptive siblings are no more similar to each other than two people picked randomly from the streets (Pinker, 2002), and adopted children tend to resemble their biological rather than adoptive parents.
- Nonshared environment plays a larger role than shared environment in determining individual differences in such traits as personality and intelligence. Thus early childhood experiences are less influential than subsequent experiences outside the family home (e.g., primary and secondary school, childhood friends).
- Although the nurture vs. nature debate has a longstanding history in psychology, it assumes that genetic and nongenetic factors have additive or independent effects on behavior. However, genetic and environmental influences are multiplicative or interactive, such that the effects of nurture on behavior may be partly predetermined by nature. This idea is useful to integrate the traditionally opposite views of nurture and nature: genetic factors may influence environmental choices, which in turn may influence behavioral outcomes. Thus nurture may mediate or moderate the effects of nature on personality and intelligence.

Chapter 8 will examine alternative approaches to the study of intelligence. These approaches emphasize the role of emotional, interpersonal, and social factors as determinants of human achievement beyond IQ.

TEXTS FOR FURTHER READING

Eysenck, H.J. & Eysenck, M.W. (1985). *Personality and Individual Differences: A Natural Science Approach*. New York: Plenum.

Flynn, J.R. (1999). Searching for justice: The discovery of IQ gains over time. *American Psychologist*, 54, 5–20.

Plomin, R. & Spinath, F.M. (2004). Intelligence: Genetics, genes, and genomics. *Journal of Personality and Social Psychology*, 86, 112–29.

Zuckerman, M. (1991). *Psychobiology of Personality*. Cambridge: Cambridge University Press.

8 Beyond IQ – Theories of Hot Intelligence

LEARNING OUTCOMES

BY THE END OF THIS CHAPTER, YOU SHOULD BE ABLE TO ANSWER THE FOLLOWING FIVE KEY QUESTIONS:

1. Can you be streetwise without being book-smart?
2. How did Thorndike conceptualize social intelligence?
3. What are the problems relating the objective measurement of so-called "hot intelligences"?
4. What are the major claims of Goleman and Gardner?
5. Are self-report measures of emotional intelligence valid?

KEY WORDS

Emotional Intelligence • Hot Intelligences • Multiple Intelligences • Practical Intelligence • Social Intelligence • Trait Emotional Intelligence

CHAPTER OUTLINE

> There is nobody so irritating as somebody with less intelligence and more sense than we have.
>
> Don Herold (1889–1966)
>
> An intelligence test sometimes shows a man how smart he would have been not to have taken it.
>
> Laurence J. Peter (1919–1988)

8.1   INTRODUCTION

Despite the accuracy of cognitive ability measures in predicting school and work success (see Chapters 5 and 6), the importance of IQ scores has been repeatedly challenged in the last ten years. In turn, this has encouraged researchers to conceptualize alternative or novel abilities such as social, practical, and emotional intelligence. Thus some have argued that the ability to solve mathematical or logical problems, such as those included in traditional IQ tests, bears little relation to real-life success, and that IQ researchers have simply been "missing the point" when conceptualizing cognitive abilities. Because of the array of noncognitive (e.g., affective, interpersonal, dispositional)

PHOTO 8.1 *A gondolieri relaxes in Venice*

In a few hours he may be cashing in on naïve tourists (regardless of their IQ). If we could measure social intelligence or "street wisdom" objectively, *gondolieri* would surely score very highly, but can we?

Image courtesy of Tomas Chamorro-Premuzic.

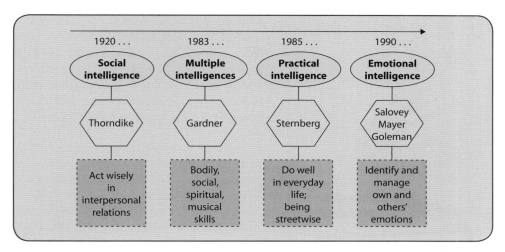

FIGURE 8.1 *Hot intelligences at a glance*

traits they encompass, these types of abilities are often referred to as **hot intelligences**, in contrast to the more analytical, logical, and perhaps "cold" characteristics of traditional cognitive abilities.

Throughout this chapter, I examine both claims and evidence associated with theories of hot intelligences. Although their contribution to individual differences theory and research has met with wide disapproval from the academic establishment, hot intelligences have attracted more popular interest than any other recent topic in individual differences and represent a growing area of research in differential psychology. What these abilities have in common is that they attempt to *expand* the traditional concept of intelligence and provide explanations for individual differences in performance *beyond IQ* in the real world.

Figure 8.1 summarizes basic labels, main authors, and quick definitions of the four most salient theories of hot intelligence; namely, Thorndike's original *social intelligence*, Gardner's *multiple intelligences* (which include traditional as well as novel abilities, the latter including bodily, social, spiritual, and musical intelligences), Sternberg's *practical intelligence*, and Salovey, Mayer, and Goleman's *emotional intelligence*. This chapter focuses mainly on social and emotional intelligence, though many of the conceptual and methodological problems underlying these abilities can be applied to any theory of hot intelligence.

> **hot intelligences** types of ability that encompass an array of noncognitive traits, e.g., the ability to interact with others in social situations, in contrast to the more analytical, "cold" characteristics of traditional cognitive abilities, e.g., the ability to solve abstract mathematical problems.

8.2 STREETWISE RATHER THAN BOOK SMART

Few arguments have been more effective in persuading people about the futility of IQ than the stereotypical example of the scientist who is practically handicapped when it comes to interacting with others. Likewise, IQ skeptics offer many examples of people

PHOTO 8.2 *Are high IQ people just "book smart"?*

© Svetlana Lukienko/Shutterstock.

who succeed in life despite their apparently low IQs, for example famous politicians who did poorly at school, rich businesspeople with no formal education, and so on. Being *street-wise*, it seems, is almost incompatible with, and more important than, being *book smart*. Consider, for instance, the following case:

> Paolo is 30 years old and has a PhD in physics, an IQ of 146, and the ability to solve mathematical problems most people would not even be able to read. Yet, the "power" of Paolo's brain is not as clearly manifested in apparently simple everyday life tasks. For example, he finds it difficult to make friends and has trouble communicating and, above all, establishing romantic or sexual relationships with others. It seems as though he is as incapable of understanding other people as he is capable of understanding the complex world of Black Holes, protons, and water molecules. Despite multiple academic awards, Paolo is single, unhappy, and has no close friends.

Most hot intelligence theorists have quoted similar examples to persuade people that traditional cognitive ability tests measure the wrong type of abilities. These tests, they say, may be useful to predict academic success, but the abilities they measure say little or nothing about a person's ability to do well in real life or where it really matters. For example, Figure 8.2 illustrates what employers assess during an interview; and Figure 8.3 gives an example of a scenario where situational judgment is required. Thus, regardless of their specific conceptual and empirical approaches, hot intelligence theories have more or less assumed that:

- *IQ is not everything*, i.e., it does not provide a full account of individual differences in the real world or everyday life success.
- *Interpersonal skills are independent of cognitive abilities*, i.e., people who score high on IQ tests are not necessarily "able" when it comes to dealing with others.
- *Interpersonal skills are more important in real life than academic abilities.*
- *Interpersonal skills should be conceptualized as a form of ability or intelligence*, i.e., it is better to be streetwise than book smart.

However, such assumptions require an array of scientific evidence that would largely disconfirm previous findings on intelligence (and by previous I mean 100 years of evidence for the validity of IQ tests, as reviewed in Chapters 5 and 6).

Why, how, and when, then, did psychologists begin the quest for novel abilities?

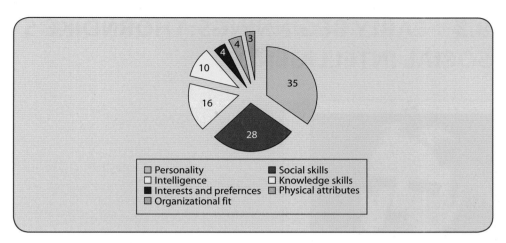

FIGURE 8.2 *What do employers assess during an interview?*

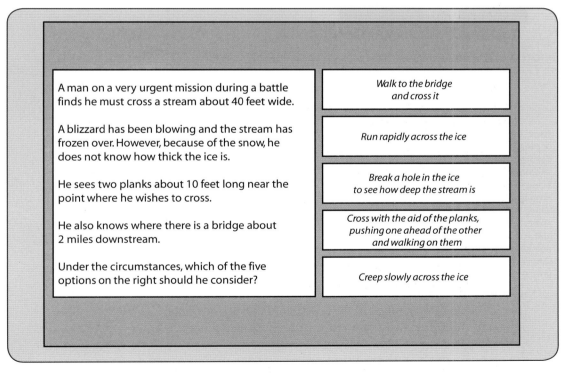

FIGURE 8.3 *Example of a situational judgment scenario*

Adapted from Chamorro-Premuzic & Furnham, 2010.

8.3   EARLY BEGINNINGS: THORNDIKE'S SOCIAL INTELLIGENCE

PHOTO 8.3 *Edward Thorndike (1874–1949)*

At a time when psychologists were largely concerned with the prediction of academic performance or military aptitude (see Chapter 5), Edward Thorndike (1874–1949), a student of J.M. Cattell (see Section 5.3.2 in Chapter 5), conceptualized individual differences in two domains that he hypothesized to be independent of the type of abilities that were normally regarded as determinants of educational and occupational success. These domains were the ability to *manage others* and *act wisely in relationships* and represented the essence of **social intelligence**. Although Thorndike was one of the pioneers of traditional intelligence test development, his distinction between "abstract" and "social" intelligence would many decades later inspire researchers to look beyond psychometric or traditional intelligence tests. In fact, several contemporary attempts to identify novel abilities were actually anticipated by Thorndike. For instance, Sternberg's theory of practical intelligence (see Section 8.11) is largely defined in terms of social competence, and the now famous concept of emotional intelligence (see Section 8.7) has its origins in Thorndike, too.

social intelligence one of three facets of intelligence hypothesized by Thorndike (the others being mechanical and abstract intelligence), which he defined as the ability to manage others and act wisely in relationships – put simply, the ability to get on with others.

8.3.1   Defining Social Intelligence

Thorndike (1920) saw intelligence as having three major facets: *mechanical intelligence* or the ability to manage concrete objects; *abstract intelligence* or the ability to manage ideas; and *social intelligence* or "the ability to understand and manage men and women, boys and girls – to act wisely in human relations" (Thorndike, 1920, p. 228; see Figure 8.4).

Soon thereafter, Moss and Hunt (1927) provided a simplified definition of social intelligence in terms of "the ability to get along with others" (p. 108), which is helpful to provide a quick and straightforward explanation of the construct.

Another classic, more comprehensive description of the construct of social intelligence was Vernon's (1933) definition as the "ability to get along with people in general, social technique or ease in society, knowledge of social matters, susceptibility to stimuli from other members of a group, as well as insight into the temporary moods or underlying personality traits of strangers" (p. 44). This definition points toward a

FOCUS POINT 8.1   EDWARD LEE THORNDIKE (1874–1949)

Edward Thorndike was born as son to a Methodist minister in Massachusetts. He became a prominent American psychologist who was very active in the fields of educational psychology (learning), intelligence, and psychometrics, designing several well-known tests and measures. One of his best-known theories is that of connectionism, and he is also known for designing intelligence tests for potential employees.

Thorndike began his studies in psychology at Wesleyan University, and went on to do a Master's at Harvard and a PhD at Columbia University under the supervision of James McKeen Cattell, one of the founding fathers of psychometrics. On graduation he spent almost his entire career as a psychology instructor at Teachers College in Columbia University, where he studied human learning, education, and psychometric testing. During his career, he became the second president of the Psychometric Society and the president of both the American Psychological Association and the American Association for the Advancement of Science.

One of Thorndike's most notable contributions to psychology was the Law of Effect, which states that a positive response to a stimulus is likely to strengthen the association between the two; conversely with an aversive response, the association with the stimulus is weakened. Most of Thorndike's studies in this area were carried out on hungry cats being placed in a puzzle box contraption from which they had to get out by pushing a button. The reward of the food would reinforce their desire to escape from the box. By plotting the time it took the cat to escape the box each time, Thorndike found that cats showed gradual learning, and not an "insight" technique to problem solving (which was the dominant explanation at the time). Put simply, the cats used trial and error and eventually learned.

Later, Thorndike developed his theory of connectionism, which stated that through experience, neural bonds are formed between perceived stimuli and emitted responses. In line, Thorndike argued that more intelligent people could form more of these connections more easily than their less intelligent counterparts. He also believed that the ability to form bonds is rooted in genetic influences over our brain, but that all intellect was ultimately explained by experience.

Thorndike is also known for designing exams to determine qualifications for enlistment in the US army during the First World War. These were the Alpha and Beta tests, with the Beta tests being administered to those who could not read very well. He later developed the CADV, an acronym for what it measures: one's abilities on completion, arithmetic, directions, and vocabulary. These tests provided some important foundations for modern psychometric testing.

Theorizing on his work on intelligence, Thorndike distinguished between three types of intelligence: abstract, mechanical, and social. He proposed four general dimensions for general intelligence: altitude – the complexity of the task one had to perform (and the most important dimension); width – the variety of tasks of a given difficulty; area – the function of altitude and width; and speed – the number of tasks one can do in a given time. Mechanical intelligence involved the ability to visualize relationships among objects and understanding how the physical world functions. Last, social intelligence entailed the ability to function well in interpersonal situations (see Section 8.3.1).

Thorndike died on August 9, 1949, aged 74, after publishing over 500 papers and many books. His work was very influential not only in individual differences but also in educational psychology and behaviorism, playing a key role in the development of Skinner's work.

WILLIAMS SYNDROME

Another source of evidence showing that social/emotional intelligence could have a separate function from IQ is not only the presence of autistic children, but, on the other side of the spectrum, children with Williams syndrome (WMS).

WMS is a rare genetic birth disorder affecting only 1 in 50 000 people. Sufferers tend to have mental retardation, with an abnormally low IQ in the region of the 60s; they also have heart problems, some pulmonary deficiencies, elfin faces, and characteristic dental malformations.

In spite of this, WMS children often have relative strengths in language and facial processing abilities, two vital skills when it comes to engaging with people. WMS sufferers are also very creative and have been described by researchers as friendly and loquacious individuals.

This is almost the complete opposite to the profiles of individuals with autism/Asperger's syndrome, who can be extremely proficient at spatial cognitive abilities (another domain in which WMS individuals score poorly) and have extreme skills in one area such as music or construction (Lego, etc.). This dichotomy in genetically based disorders provides some evidence in support of new or "hot" intelligence theories, which argue that interpersonal skills are independent of traditional abilities (*g* or IQ-related constructs).

PHOTO 8.4 *Hannah Gadlage (at age 6) displays WMS characteristic elfin facial features.*

Photos courtesy of Gadlage family, reproduced with permission.

PHOTO 8.5 *Streetwise kids in Istanbul chase a moving tranway – would a high IQ make this easier? Some psychologists have argued that social skills are independent of IQ.*

Image courtesy of Tomas Chamorro-Premuzic.

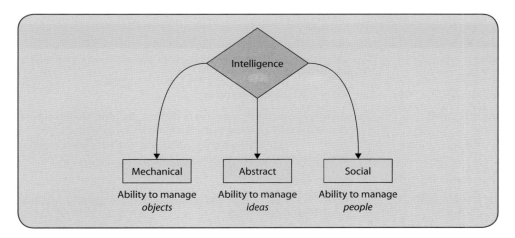

FIGURE 8.4 *Thorndike's three intelligences, mechanical, abstract, and social*

number of aspects or components of social intelligence: getting along; social technique; social knowledge; social sensitivity; social insight; and awareness of others' moods and personalities.

Last but not least, Gardner (1983, p. 243) argued that "the capacity to know oneself and to know others is an inalienable part of the human condition." Although he used the labels interpersonal (knowing others) and intrapersonal (knowing oneself), this definition has been largely applied to the notion of social intelligence.

multiple intelligences
Gardner's theory that there are many independent intelligences, including traditional as well as novel abilities such as bodily, social, spiritual, and musical intelligences.

Unlike most intelligence experts, Gardner rarely attempted to validate social intelligence or any of the other abilities that he conceptualizes psychometrically. Rather, Gardner based his theory of **multiple intelligences** on case studies and medical evidence for the idea that the isolation of specific brain injuries may impair some but not other abilities. For example, the Phineas Gage case (see Section 4.4 in Chapter 4) can be used to support the idea that the areas of the brain responsible for *cognitive* ("abstract" in Thorndike's words) operations are largely independent of those associated with *social* skills or personality traits. Likewise, Luria's (1972) case of Zazetsky, "the man with a shattered world," showed how Alzheimer's disease may progressively lead to the decay of cognitive but not social functions.

Finally, Wong *et al.*'s (1995) definition is representative of modern approaches to social intelligence, as it conceptualizes the construct as multifaceted or multidimensional. Thus the authors distinguish between the components of social perception, behavioral social intelligence, social insight, and social knowledge. More recent theoretical conceptualizations of social intelligence have emphasized its role in *solving life tasks* and managing *personal projects* (Cantor & Kihlstrom, 1987).

Table 8.1 presents a sample of well-known definitions of social intelligence in chronological order.

Table 8.1 *Some well-known definitions of social intelligence*

Reference	Definition
Thorndike (1920, p. 228)	"The ability to understand and manage men and women, boys and girls – to act wisely in human relations."
Moss & Hunt (1927, p. 108)	"The ability to get along with others."
Vernon (1933, p. 44)	"The ability to get along with people in general, social technique or ease in society, knowledge of social matters, susceptibility to stimuli from other members of a group, as well as insight into the temporary moods or underlying personality traits of strangers."
O'Sullivan *et al.* (1965, p. 5)	"[The] ability to judge people."
Gardner (1983, p. 243)	"The capacity to know oneself and to know others [which] is an inalienable part of the human condition."
Wong *et al.* (1995, p. 118)	"Social perception" or "a person's ability to understand or decode others' verbal and nonverbal behaviors."
	"Behavioral social intelligence" or "effectiveness in heterosexual interactions."
	"Social insight" or "the ability to comprehend observed behaviors in the social context in which they occur."
	"Social knowledge" or "knowing the rules of etiquette."

8.4 THEORETICAL IMPORTANCE OF SOCIAL INTELLIGENCE

There are several reasons why it may be important to study individual differences in social intelligence.

- Academic or cognitive abilities (such as those examined in Chapters 5, 6, and 7) are not perfect predictors of performance and do not provide a *full picture* of an individual's capacity to succeed in life.

- There is the related assumption that one may be clever in an academic sense but relatively incompetent in interpersonal relations (Sternberg *et al.*, 1981; Thorndike, 1920). Although this idea is in conflict with Spearman's (1927) *g* theory of intelligence (which predicts positive intercorrelations among *all* abilities; see Section 5.3.4 in Chapter 5), the idea of an independent social intelligence factor has occasionally been supported by psychometricians. For instance, Guilford's (1967) structure of intellect model (discussed in Section 5.7 in Chapter 5) conceptualized 30 facets of social intelligence that were largely independent of academic abilities. Moreover, Jensen (1998), one of the most stalwart supporters of *g*, admitted that social competence "show[s] remarkably low correlations with psychometric abilities, both verbal and quantitative" (p. 576).

- There is the notion that, in some situations, success is more dependent on our ability to relate to others or "manage people" than our ability to think abstractly or "manage ideas." Whereas such claims are yet to be supported by empirical evidence, the mere possibility of their being true would justify the study of individual differences in social intelligence.

- Last but not least, there is the idea that individual differences in social intelligence may help us understand psychological disorders, in particular where cognitive skills fail to distinguish between healthy and mentally ill individuals. Thus the DSM-IV's conceptualization of psychological impairment includes "communication, self-care, home living, social and interpersonal skills, use of community resources, self-direction, functional academic skills, work, leisure, health, and safety" (American Psychiatric Association, 1994, p. 46), which overlaps with some of the key elements of social intelligence. Studies on *autism*, an obscure neurodevelopmental disorder that consists of problems with social relatedness, communication, interest, and behavior, have also suggested that autistic and nonautistic individuals may merely differ in their ability to decode and understand *others'* intentions and behaviors. Whether this capacity is labeled "theory of mind" (Baron-Cohen, 1995; Premack & Woodruff, 1978) or "social intelligence," it is clear that interpersonal skills may be the key to understanding specific aspects of psychopathology.

Irrespective of scientific evidence, the above assumptions have met with wide approval and enthusiasm among laypeople. Indeed, this might add up to being a fifth argument to justify the study of social or hot abilities. For example, studies have shown that teachers, parents, and students consider the development of social abilities, such as having satisfying relationships, treating people respectfully, and communicating-well, to be of critical importance (Ford, 1986).

8.5   EARLY PROBLEMS

If defining social intelligence has been relatively straightforward, *measuring* it has almost been impossible. In fact, many of the problems underlying the assessment and measurement of individual differences in social intelligence had already been anticipated by Thorndike when he observed that "convenient tests of social intelligence are hard to devise," and that social intelligence could be found "in the nursery, on the playground, in barracks and factories and salesroom [*sic*], but [it] eludes the formal standardized conditions of the testing laboratory" (Thorndike, 1920, p. 231). Thus the theoretical idea that some individuals are simply more likely to do "the right thing at the right time" (O'Sullivan *et al.*, 1965, p. 5) may be difficult to demonstrate in practice, let alone under experimental laboratory conditions. Although early measures of social intelligence predicted social behavior (Chapin, 1942; Gough, 1968; Moss & Hunt, 1927; Moss *et al.*, 1927), these were also positively correlated with academic performance or personality scales (Feshbach & Feshbach, 1987; Green *et al.*, 1980).

One of the earliest measures of social intelligence was the George Washington Social Intelligence Test (GWSIT; Hunt, 1928) and included the facets of Judgment in Social Situations, Memory for Names and Faces, Observation of Human Behavior, Recognition of the Mental States Behind Words, Recognition of Mental States from Facial Expression, Social Information, and Sense of Humor. Hunt (1928) reported significant correlations between these facets and job status, extracurricular activities, and supervisor's ratings at work. Subsequent studies, however, found that GWSIT scores were substantially correlated with Extraversion and verbal intelligence tests. Thus Thorndike and Stein (1937, p. 282) concluded that GWSIT "is so heavily loaded with ability to work with words and ideas, that differences in social intelligence tend to be swamped by differences in abstract intelligence."

Despite the theoretical soundness and importance of the justifications for studying social intelligence (see Section 8.4), more often than not differential psychologists have expressed skepticism about the notion of autonomous or independent individual differences in the ability to manage and get along with others. Criticisms fall under different categories, but are almost always associated with the lack of *reliability* and *validity* of social intelligence measures. Thus there is a lack of empirical evidence in support of the construct of social intelligence.

The major problem with social intelligence measures is that they are often not distinguishable from traditional cognitive ability tests. Thus early measures of social intelligence were significantly and positively correlated with traditional intelligence measures (Gresvenor, 1927; Hoepener & O'Sullivan, 1968; Pintner & Upshall, 1928; Thorndike & Stein, 1937), the most evident overlap being found between measures of social and verbal intelligence (Thorndike & Stein, 1937; for a different view see Wong *et al.*, 1995).

Typically, validation studies (e.g., Keating, 1978) attempted to show that social intelligence is (a) *different* from academic intelligence (IQ) and (b) a more *accurate* predictor of social outcomes than are IQ scores. Studies have sometimes supported one hypothesis or the other (generally the former), but rarely both. Thus Keating (1978) argued that paper-and-pencil tests are too similar (in form and content) to standard IQ tests, and concluded that "the putative domain of social intelligence lacks empirical coherency, at least as it is represented by the measures used here" (Keating, 1978, p. 221).

Wechsler (1955), the creator of the Wechsler Adult Intelligence Scale (WAIS) and Wechsler Intelligence Scale for Children (WISC), two of the most widely used IQ measures (see Section 6.2 in Chapter 6), argued that social intelligence is merely a form of general intelligence that is used or applied to social situations. In line with this assertion, studies reported high intercorrelations between the Picture Arrangement subtest, which requires participants to put a sequence of randomly arranged pictures into chronological order to create a meaningful story, and other, more cognitive sections of the Wechsler IQ test. Thus the ability to comprehend social situations, which is reflected in high scores on the Picture Arrangement subtest, seems strongly associated with the ability to score high on other sections of the test.

Low intercorrelations between different measures of social intelligence (Walker & Foley, 1973) indicate that they are measuring different things. Accordingly, the "core" components of social competence may depend on a number of unrelated factors, which begs the question of *which* is the real social intelligence. (See Figure 8.5.)

A second major obstacle to the validation of social intelligence measures has been the difficulty of designing actual "tests" of social competence. Thus most scales have relied on self-report items, which resemble personality rather than intelligence measures. Unlike traditional cognitive ability tests, which rely on questions with one and

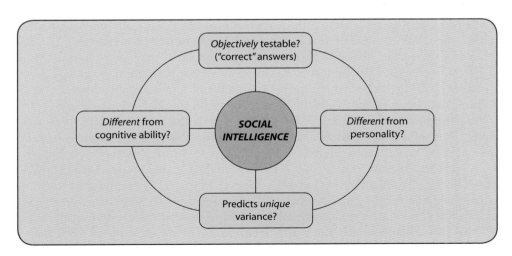

FIGURE 8.5 *Four related problems with the notion of social intelligence*

Table 8.2 *A comparison between sample items from traditional and social intelligence tests*

Item	Item example
Verbal intelligence	Foot is to shoe as head is to (a) brain, (b) pain, (c) hat, (d) hut
Numerical intelligence	$1000 \times 50 =$ (a) 500 000, (b) 5000, (c) 50 000, (d) 10 500
General knowledge	The capital of Brazil is (a) Buenos Aires, (b) Rio, (c) Brasilia, (d) São Paulo
Social intelligence (self-report)	I am generally very perceptive of other people's intentions YES/NO
Social intelligence (vignette)	You are driving back home after several drinks and are stopped by the police. Do you (a) apologize to the officer and confess to being drunk, (b) pretend you are sober, (c) tell the officer you've only had one drink, (d) try to run away?

only one correct answer, social intelligence measures tended to include self-descriptions (such as "I am very good at managing others") or *vignettes* ("If your boss does not like you it is best to (a) change jobs, (b) seduce him, (c) ignore him, or (d) none of the above") with uncertain or subjective answers. Indeed, this is a problem for most hot intelligences.

Table 8.2 presents sample items/questions for different types of intelligence. As can be seen, the first row provides an example for a verbal intelligence item, which requires participants to establish an analogy (association) on the basis of semantic relations (word meaning). Although the *only* correct solution to this problem is (c) hat, one may argue that, among the incorrect responses, some are more reasonable than others. For example, if you answered (d) hut, you were probably closer to the correct answer than if you answered (a) brain; and some may argue that (a) brain is more correct than (b) pain. It is, however, clear that the only objectively correct answer is (c). The second row features an example of a numerical intelligence item. Here it may even be more difficult to disagree with the fact that there is *only* one correct response, which is (c) 50 000. Then there is the third row, which contains an example of a general knowledge question; namely, what is the capital of Brazil. Again, there is *only* one correct answer, which is (c) Brasilia. Yet, one could again argue that choosing (b) Rio or (d) São Paulo would be "closer" to the correct answer than choosing (a) Buenos Aires (which is not even in Brazil). However, someone may argue that, like Brasilia, Buenos Aires is also a capital, while São Paulo and Rio are not. Yet all that would be irrelevant as the *only* objectively correct response is Brasilia.

Now, what happens when we attempt to assess or measure social intelligence? Rows four and five in Table 8.2 present two sample items for self-report and vignette, respectively. The self-report follows the same methodological approach as any personality inventory item. It requires participants to describe themselves by means of standardized, preselected statements that are supposedly related to essential aspects of the assessed latent construct – in this case social intelligence. Thus the same problems apply as with personality inventories; namely, people can lie, exaggerate, and fake responses or simply not know themselves well enough. Moreover, when Likert-type scales such as "1 2 3 4 5 6 7" are used, respondents may be more or less inclined to pick extreme answers.

The approach represented by the vignette item in the final row seems more innovative and appears to follow a similar logic to traditional ability tests (numerical and verbal intelligence or general knowledge). However, this similarity is only apparent, as there is *no* objectively correct response to the item. Vignettes attempt to encapsulate real-life scenarios or everyday problems that may, theoretically, require skills associated with the latent construct that one is trying to measure (here, social intelligence). In fact, it may not be too difficult to agree on the fact that individuals with a higher social intelligence should, in theory, be more likely to *choose the right behavior* or *make the correct decision* when it comes to solving real-life problems such as that described by the vignette in Table 8.2. The problem, however, is that any of the possible choices may be as successful as unsuccessful. Even if one thinks that some responses are "better" than others (in this case response (b) "pretend you are sober" seems like a good candidate), there is no *a priori justification* for any choice, and there are no ways of testing whether one response "would" have been better than others or not. In fact, we are not even sure that there are no *other* responses – not included in the vignette – that may work better than the ones listed, for instance (e) "bribe the officer," (f) "seduce the officer," or (g) "improvise."

Thus the difference between social and traditional intelligence items is that the former are based on *ill-defined* problems that have no clear-cut solutions and are very much context dependent and difficult to solve in theory. Conversely, traditional intelligences (as seen throughout Chapter 5) are based on well-defined problems that have objectively correct answers regardless of the context or situation.

Although the above examples may suggest that it is easier to *assess* social intelligence through self-reports than to *measure* it through vignettes or IQ-type items, self-reports of social intelligence are bound to have a substantial overlap with established personality dimensions. As seen in Section 2.10 in Chapter 2, the lexical approach to personality traits assumes that the Big Five factors are representative of all aspects of personality; thus any attempt to capture individual differences underlying behavior, thought, and emotionality will inevitably develop into a classification of a person's level of Neuroticism, Extraversion, Openness to Experience, Agreeableness, and Conscientiousness. While these traits are well established, social intelligence appears to "struggle" between the realms of intelligence (which demands objective performance measures such as IQ tests) and personality (which is largely based on self- and other-reports). Accordingly, using self-reports to assess social intelligence may lead one to conceptualize it as a personality trait, whereas using objective performance tests to measure social intelligence (if that were possible) would lead one to conceptualize it as an ability.

PHOTO 8.6 *Driving under the influence? What should you do if the police stop you? As there is no objectively correct answer to this question, it is problematic to include it in an intelligence test.*

Image courtesy of Tomas Chamorro-Premuzic.

8.6 RECENT APPROACHES: FROM MULTIDIMENSIONALITY TO IMPLICIT THEORIES

After decades of disappointing results for those attempting to find empirical support for the notion of social intelligence, Ford and Tisak (1983) succeeded in identifying a psychometrically coherent social intelligence factor in a sample of 600 high-school students. The authors attributed this success to their redefinition of the construct in terms of "behavioral effectiveness" and the use of *multiple* measures (self-, teacher, and peer ratings of social competence and behavioral observation). As they expected, academic and social intelligence loaded on different factors, and the ratings of social competence predicted observed social competence better than did academic intelligence measures.

The pattern of results found by Ford and Tisak (1983) was later replicated by Marlowe (1986). The author used a *multitrait–multimethod* design (Campbell & Fiske, 1959) consisting of five dimensions of social intelligence:

(i) Interest and concern for other people.

(ii) Social performance skills.

(iii) Empathic ability.

(iv) Emotional expressiveness and sensitivity to others' emotional expressions.

(v) Social anxiety and lack of social self-efficacy and self-esteem.

As predicted, these dimensions were largely unrelated to measures of verbal and abstract intelligence.

Barnes and Sternberg (1989) found that social intelligence had two distinguishable aspects, a cognitive component – that is, *decoding nonverbal cues* – and a behavioral aspect – that is, *self-reported social competence*. These components were positively and significantly correlated with each other but *not* with IQ.

In general, research has been much more successful in conceptualizing social intelligence in terms of multiple rather than single approaches. Thus Schneider, Ackerman, and Kanfer (1996) found seven dimensions of social competence: *extraversion*, *warmth*, *social influence*, *social insight*, *social openness*, *social appropriateness*, and *social maladjustment*. The authors concluded that "it is time to lay to rest any residual notions that social competence is a monolithic entity, or that it is just general intelligence" (Schneider, Ackerman, & Kanfer, p. 479).

Likewise, Wong *et al.* (1995) identified three dimensions of social intelligence; namely, social *perception*, social *knowledge*, and social *behavior* (see again Table 8.1). Although these components could be distinguished from academic or cognitive abilities, the sample consisted of high IQ individuals and was therefore unrepresentative of the wider population. In fact, the authors admitted that "academic and social intelligences may be discriminable only in young adults or in intellectually gifted populations" (Wong *et al.*, p. 131).

Despite recent progress and some encouraging findings, differential psychologists remain largely unconvinced about the existence and usefulness of a social intelligence factor within the wider realm of human abilities. Furthermore, in the past ten years differential psychologists attempting to expand the traditional notion of IQ have predominantly focused on emotional rather than social abilities, though often assessing social competence and interpersonal skills as well.

8.7   EMOTIONAL INTELLIGENCE

emotional intelligence (EQ) the capacity of individuals to identify and manage their own emotional state and accurately to interpret and deal with others' emotions.

The most famous exponent of hot intelligence is no doubt **emotional intelligence** (often referred to as EQ or EI). This construct owes much of its popularity to Daniel Goleman's (1995) bestselling book of the same name. Indeed, no other alternative conception of ability has even approached the impact of emotional intelligence in the field of differential psychology, and it has been argued that no other novel construct has had a comparable impact in so many areas of psychology (for a comprehensive review, see Roberts, Zeidner, & Matthews, 2001). But what is emotional intelligence?

Although definitions have varied, there is relative consensus (Sternberg & Kaufman, 1998) on the idea that emotional intelligence refers to individual differences in:

- The ability to *perceive*, *appraise*, and *express* emotions.
- The ability to *access* and/or *generate* emotions advantageous for thought.
- The ability to *understand* emotion and emotional knowledge.
- The ability to *regulate* emotions that enable emotional and intellectual growth.

The recurrent themes in these definitions (or components) are "ability" and "emotion," though some emphasize perception, regulation, or expression. While emotional intelligence may be part of many people's vocabulary these days, the notion is conceptually and psychologically counterintuitive, because it "bridges the gap" between the two worlds of thought and feeling, cognition and affect, reason and feeling.

Years before achieving international fame with Goleman's bestseller, the construct of emotional intelligence was introduced by Salovey and Mayer (1990). As with social intelligence, the two basic claims of EQ are that it is:

- *independent* from traditional cognitive ability (IQ);
- *more important* than IQ when it comes to determining performance in real-life settings.

FOCUS POINT 8.2   GENDER DIFFERENCES IN MEASURED AND SELF-ESTIMATED TRAIT EMOTIONAL INTELLIGENCE

A great deal of work in the past decade has investigated self-estimated IQ, especially in relation to gender differences. Petrides and Furnham's paper looks at gender differences in emotional intelligence (EI), a very fashionable individual difference construct.

Given the broad nature of EI (particularly in relation to the different measurement approaches use to assess it), researchers have distinguished between *trait EI* and *information-processing EI*. The former concerns behavioral dispositions, should be examined in relation to temperament (e.g. Extraversion and Neuroticism), and is measured through self-reports (e.g., "I know what others are doing just by looking at them"). Information-processing EI, on the other hand, is concerned with actual abilities and measured by means of maximum-performance tests (e.g., tests for measuring

emotion perception would require test takers to identify the emotional state of a target, shown in videos or photographs, and there is only one correct answer).

Previous research on gender and self-estimated IQ has focused on four themes. First, studies have examined gender differences in the overall estimate of their own IQ (*g*). Results revealed that males estimate their IQ significantly higher than females. Moreover, both males and females tend to rate their father as more intelligent than their mother and their grandfather as more intelligent than their grandmother. Parents were also found to give their male children higher IQ estimates than they did for their female children.

Second, a group of studies have looked at self-estimates of *multiple* intelligences (rather than overall intelligence, IQ or *g*). They found gender differences in mathematical, spatial, and body-kinesthetic intelligence (people with good motor skills), with females consistently rating themselves lower than did males. When parents were asked to rate their children, both parents rated their sons as having greater mathematical, spatial, and intrapersonal intelligence (ability to understand one's own moods and adapt to the environment).

Third, studies have examined the relationship between self-estimated and *psychometrically* measured or "actual" IQ. A correlation of $r = .3$ has been found, suggesting a weak yet positive relationship between the two.

Finally, there have been a few *cross-cultural* studies of gender differences in self-estimates of IQ. In one study, some British, Hawaiian, and Singaporean students were compared, and British students provided the highest self-estimates, with males' self-estimates of IQ exceeding those of females by three points on average. When American, British, and Japanese students were compared, there were consistent gender differences. Overall, Americans rated themselves the highest, followed by British and then Japanese students.

Petrides and Furnham's study investigates gender differences in actual and self-estimated scores on trait EI. They based their study largely on two conceptualizations of EI:

(i) The three-factor model encompassing appraisal and expression of emotions, regulation of emotions, and utilization of emotions.

(ii) The conceptualization of EI based on seven core elements: self-awareness, emotional management, self-motivation, empathy, handling relationships, interpersonal communications, and personal style.

The hypotheses for this study were that there would be a gender difference in the opposite direction from that observed for self-estimates of IQ, such that females would score and rate themselves higher than males; all correlations between self-estimated and measured EI scores would be positive and significant.

METHOD

PARTICIPANTS

There were 260 participants, mostly from British universities; 175 were female (67.3 percent) and 85 were male (32.7 percent). Their mean age was 23.4 years ($SD = 8.1$).

MATERIALS

A 33-item emotional intelligence questionnaire was used, including statements such as "I have control over my emotions," "I know why my emotions change," and "Other people find it easy to confide in me."

A second questionnaire was used to measure self-estimated EI and included 15 abilities and tendencies: "being able to accept responsibility," "effectiveness under pressure," and "really listening to others."

RESULTS

For the self-estimated EI scores, there were significant gender differences on three items: "ability to understand your own emotions" ($t_{(258)} = 2.62, p < .01$); "ability to handle conflict and settle disputes" ($t_{(258)} = 2.02, p < .01$); and "being positive and optimistic" ($t_{(258)} = 2.86, p = .01$). Each indicated that males thought they had higher EI.

When a factor analysis was carried out on the 15 facets of self-estimated EI, two clear factors emerged and were labeled "empathy" and "self-motivation." On analysis, it was found that males awarded themselves a higher score on self-motivation (mean = 659.7, $SD = 65.5$) than their counterparts (mean = 640.03, $SD = 55.06$). When their total self-estimated EI score was compared against their actual measured EI score, males' self-estimates of EI (adjusted mean = 1659.3) were significantly higher ($F_{(1,257)} = 4.94$, p , .05) than those of females (adjusted mean = 1624.4).

When researchers looked at gender differences in measured trait EI score, results revealed no significant gender differences in trait EI components, bar on one of the facets ("social skills," with females scoring higher than males).

With regard to the relationship between self-estimated and measured trait EI scores, with two exceptions, all correlations were higher for males. The correlation between "self-motivation" and "optimism" was higher in the female sample, whereas that between "empathy" and "optimism" was the same between the two samples. The correlation between total self-estimated EI scores with total measured scores was slightly higher in the male sample ($r = .48$) than the female sample ($r = .40$).

DISCUSSION

The findings of this study are in line with several other studies on gender differences in self-evaluations of performance, and IQ in particular. Men show a self-enhancing bias, and women show a self-derogatory bias in self-evaluations of EI. However, in contrast to findings in previous studies, there were no gender differences in actual or measured trait EI. There was, however, a significant gender difference on the "social skills" factor of the measured EI questionnaire, with females scoring higher than males. Yet men self-evaluated themselves as having more "social skills" than women, suggesting that the process of self-estimation is biased.

The correlations between self-estimated and measured EI scores suggest that people do have some insight into their own EI. This is, in itself, a sign of high EI, as it requires awareness of one's own temperament and abilities.

These studies have important implications for education, health, and psychotherapies. Positive self-perceptions (e.g., high EI) are related to healthy psychological adjustment and high self-esteem, whereas negative self-perceptions are related to depression. Moreover, low evaluations can lead to poor performance, thus adopting self-fulfilling strategies of a self-perpetuating behavioral pattern, leading to potentially lower esteem and greater depression. What is unusual about this study is that most elements of EI are considered "feminine" and have been found in other studies to be higher in females; thus to find that males estimate themselves to be higher is counterintuitive or further evidence of male hubris and female humility.

Source: Petrides, K.V. & Furnham, A. (2000) Gender differences in measured and self-estimated trait emotional intelligence. *Sex Roles*, 42(5/6), 449–61.

Unlike social intelligence, EQ emphasizes "emotions," though as will be seen the construct also conceptualizes individual differences in the ability to relate to others (interpersonal skills). Moreover, identifying and managing one's emotions may simply be a different name for intrapersonal competence (which, as has been seen, had already been conceptualized by Thorndike and Gardner).

If true, however, EQ's claims would have substantial implications for intelligence research and theory, which is why they have prompted a significant wave of research in the past ten years. In fact, the number of articles on EQ seems to multiply by two or three every year, particularly in individual difference journals such as *Personality and Individual Differences* and *Intelligence*, though the topic has also spread to nonspecialist publications. Inevitably, this means that a review of the topic is bound to be inconclusive and soon outdated. Insofar as the quantity of EQ studies has already justified many textbooks and handbooks, in the following sections I shall only introduce the central claims, findings, and, in particular, problems underlying the scientific conceptualization of individual differences in emotional intelligence.

8.8   DEBATE AND CONTROVERSY SURROUNDING EMOTIONAL INTELLIGENCE

With the inherent dialectic of any debate, emotional intelligence has divided laypeople and academics into believers and nonbelievers. To be precise, this division has occurred not only between laypeople and scientists but also within the respective communities, though popular support has clearly exceeded academic endorsement. Arguably, the reasons underlying the popularity of EQ among laypeople are no different from the ones explaining its unpopularity in academic settings, namely:

- The theory of emotional intelligence poses a challenge and theoretical threat to traditional or academic abilities such as IQ.
- The measurement of individual differences in emotional intelligence has been largely unsuccessful, particularly when judged by traditional psychometric criteria.

To put it simply, most people dislike IQ tests and the idea that it is more important to be in touch with one's own and others' emotions to succeed in life is far more appealing than having to solve mathematical or logical problems such as those contained in traditional cognitive ability tests. On the other hand, informed differential psychologists are aware of the predictive power of traditional cognitive ability tests (reviewed in Chapter 6): they know that IQ tests are both reliable and valid and very useful for predicting numerous aspects of individuals' performance in school, at university, and in the workplace. Furthermore, even when it is appealing to conceptualize a form of ability that takes into account individual differences in emotion, it is crucial to provide empirical evidence for the existence and usefulness of such individual differences.

Whereas laypeople may simply believe in emotional intelligence or not, the scientific study of individual differences in this – or any other – ability is only possible if we are able to measure the construct. This not only requires the development of specific psychometric tests but also adequate reliability and validity. In fact, the claims of emotional intelligence, and pretty much any other novel ability one wishes to put forward, have to address a number of questions (see Figure 8.6), namely:

- Does it *exist*?
- Can it be *measured*?
- Is it *important*?
- Is it an *ability*?
- Is it *more* important than IQ?

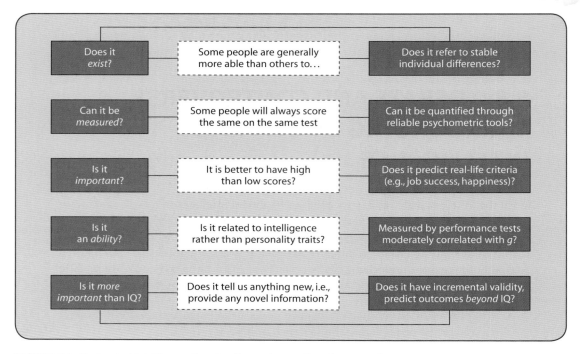

FIGURE 8.6 *Testing hot intelligence theories: five main questions for research*

There are also specific methods and procedures for addressing these questions. Thus if emotional or any other form of hot intelligence is to achieve recognition within the realm of established human abilities, it will have to be submitted to the same psychometric principles and validation techniques that are applied to other tests.

8.9   ORIGINS AND MEASUREMENT PROBLEMS OF EQ

The distant foundations of EQ can be attributed to Thorndike's (1920) notion of social intelligence (see Sections 8.3 and 8.3.1), whereas more recently Gardner (1983) has identified *intrapersonal* and *interpersonal* intelligences as part of his "multiple intelligence" framework. In essence, the constructs of Thorndike and Gardner refer to people's ability to relate to others, an ability that traditional conceptions of intelligence seemed to have overlooked. When Salovey and Mayer (1990) first defined and conceptualized EQ, they attempted to account for similar interpersonal and intrapersonal skills. Specifically, interpersonal and intrapersonal skills would be facilitated by the ability to recognize and control one's own emotions.

As shown by the initial example in this chapter (Paolo the physics nerd), the assumptions of EQ are:

- People who are extremely "bright" in the IQ sense of the word may often be unable to relate to others.

- People who do poorly at school or university may often succeed in the "real world" if they have great interpersonal skills.
- Success in the workplace may not be related to intellectual ability as measured by psychometric tests.

The difference between social and emotional intelligence is that the latter emphasizes the role of emotion identification and management in determining everyday life success. Indeed, this is the only novelty introduced by EQ theories.

Like social intelligence, EQ can be broken down into various dimensions, all of which are considered relatively independent of IQ but nonetheless essential for performance and real-life success in general. Thus emotionally intelligent individuals are *adaptable*, *flexible*, and able to *perceive*, *regulate*, and *express* emotions in efficient ways. They are composed rather than impulsive and able to relate to others. They have high self-esteem and self-motivation; they are socially competent and able to manage stress. In addition, emotionally intelligent people tend to be *happier*, more *empathic*, and more *optimistic* than others.

The problem with most EQ models is that they ignore the fundamental psychometric distinction (Cronbach, 1990/1949) between maximal and typical performance measures that applies to ability and personality constructs, respectively. As a consequence, emotional intelligence seems to represent a "no man's land" between personality and intelligence. Conceptually, it refers – or at least attempts to refer – to individual differences in *ability*. Methodologically and psychometrically, however, it assesses this ability in the same way as we assess personality traits or dispositions.

Just as we do not measure cognitive ability by asking someone whether they are intelligent, we should not measure emotional intelligence by asking people whether they are able to identify and manage their emotions. In that sense, emotional intelligence as assessed by self-report inventories is, at best, a self-report measure of individuals' ability. This limitation, however, should not stop us from trying to develop actual tests of emotional intelligence and examining the validity or usefulness of self-report measures of emotional intelligence. It is this latter approach that inspired Petrides and Furnham (2001) to redefine the concept in terms of *trait* emotional intelligence or emotional self-efficacy, a construct that they assessed through a self-report questionnaire (TEIQ).

8.10   TRAIT EMOTIONAL INTELLIGENCE: EMOTIONAL SELF-EFFICACY

trait emotional intelligence the theory of emotional intelligence as a personality trait, assessed by self-report inventories rather than performance tests and considered as a self-perceived construct rather than an ability.

Unlike other models of emotional intelligence, Petrides and Furnham's (2001) theory of **trait emotional intelligence** conceptualizes the construct as a personality trait. Thus they assess it through self-report inventories rather than performance tests and interpret it as a "self-perceived" construct. Whereas this approach may at first seem less appealing than the ambitious enterprise of developing an actual EQ test (of maximal performance and objectively scored), it represents a more realistic way of dealing with the concept and assessment of individual differences in emotional intelligence.

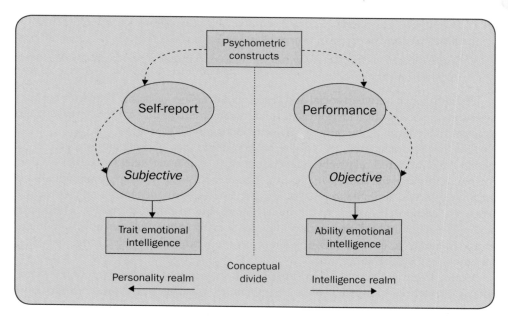

FIGURE 8.7 *Petrides and Furnham's (2001) distinction between ability and trait emotional intelligence*

Crucially, then, trait emotional intelligence and emotional intelligence are two different constructs, just as self-perceived and "actual" or psychometric intelligence are two different variables (see Figure 8.7). Measures of tested (psychometric) and self-assessed intelligence correlate in the region of $r = .30$, meaning an overlap of less than 10 percent (for a review, see Chamorro-Premuzic & Furnham, 2005). Likewise, studies reported low correlations between objective measures and self-reported measures of emotional intelligence (O'Connor & Little, 2003); even this comparison may be flawed because there are no reliable objective measures of emotional intelligence, since the scoring criteria differ substantially from those for cognitive ability tests. In fact, when there are objective measures of emotional individual differences, such as electrodermal activity, these are only meaningful if contrasted with self-report criteria (Watson, 2000).

Another advantage of trait emotional intelligence is that it is consistent with the *subjective* nature of emotional experience and does not attempt to challenge the psychometric importance of established cognitive ability measures. One cannot overestimate the importance of this advantage, and the fact that it is only when we have managed to measure or assess individual differences in emotional intelligence that we can start examining such differences with regard to other constructs or behavioral outcomes, which means validating the construct of emotional intelligence (just as we do with personality and cognitive ability, as shown in Chapters 3 and 6, respectively).

Thus, "ability" approaches to emotional intelligence may be as appealing as they are implausible, and seem to have rediscovered the psychometric limitations that have undermined the development of social intelligence tests for so many decades. Roberts, Zeidner, and Matthews (2001) have summarized the limitations concerning attempts to conceptualize emotional intelligence as an ability. As they concluded, the validity of performance measures of EQ seems elusive.

On the other hand, measures of self-report of trait emotional intelligence are sufficiently reliable to enable the exploration of the correlates and outcomes of this construct. Indeed, most studies looking at EQ in the context of clinical, educational, and occupational domains have used self-reports.

Arguably, the greatest progress has been achieved in academic settings, with increasing evidence for the idea that trait emotional intelligence is related to a number of positive behaviors at school. Specifically, Reiff *et al.* (2001) found that college students with learning disabilities had significantly lower trait emotional intelligence. Petrides, Frederickson, and Furnham (2004), on the other hand, reported an interaction between IQ and trait emotional intelligence, such that, among low IQ pupils, those with high trait emotional intelligence scores performed considerably better at school. Furthermore, their study showed that low trait emotional intelligence pupils had more unauthorized absences and exhibited more antisocial behavior.

Occupational research on trait emotional intelligence has been less robust. In fact, experts note that the amount of empirical data available is inversely proportional to the barrage of unsubstantiated claims. In one of the rare sound studies, however, Wong and Law (2002) provided evidence that trait emotional intelligence is related to job performance and job satisfaction. Furthermore, Jordan *et al.* (2002) reported that work teams comprising employees with high trait emotional intelligence generally perform better than those comprising employees with low trait emotional intelligence.

Petrides and colleagues also identified several components or facets of trait emotional intelligence (see Table 8.3). This means that trait emotional intelligence represents a constellation of different dispositions. However, research has yet to examine the validity of each of these components as predictors of educational, occupational, and clinical outcomes.

Figure 8.8 compares different EQ scales; and Figure 8.9 considers aspects of EQ in relation to work outcomes.

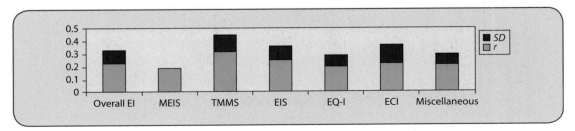

FIGURE 8.8 *Meta-analytic validities for different EQ scales (corrected correlations and their SDs)*

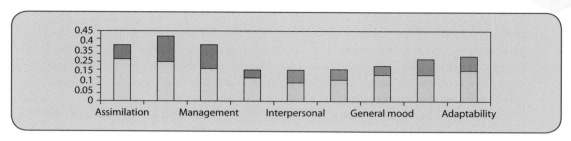

FIGURE 8.9 *Aspects of EQ that predict work outcomes*

Table 8.3 *Components of trait emotional intelligence*

Facets	High scorers perceive themselves as ...
Adaptability	...flexible and willing to adapt to new conditions.
Assertiveness	...forthright, frank, and willing to stand up for their rights.
Emotion perception (self and others)	...clear about their own and other people's feelings.
Emotion expression	...capable of communicating their feelings to others.
Emotion management (others)	...capable of influencing other people's feelings.
Emotion regulation	...capable of controlling their emotions.
Impulsiveness (low)	...reflective and less likely to give in to their urges.
Relationship skills	...capable of having fulfilling personal relationships.
Self-esteem	...successful and self-confident.
Self-motivation	...driven and unlikely to give up in the face of adversity.
Social competence	...accomplished networkers with excellent social skills.
Stress management	...capable of withstanding pressure and regulating stress.
Trait empathy	...capable of taking someone else's perspective.
Trait happiness	...cheerful and satisfied with their lives.
Trait optimism	...confident and likely to "look on the bright side" of life.

8.11   PRACTICAL INTELLIGENCE

practical intelligence
a component of Sternberg's theory of intelligence (also comprising analytical/academic and creative intelligence), referring to the ability to solve problems and apply ideas to real-life contexts independent of academic or traditional cognitive ability.

Another salient exponent of hot intelligences – namely, **practical intelligence** – can be found in Sternberg's (1985) triarchic theory of intelligence, which also includes *analytical/academic* and *creative* intelligences (see also Sternberg & O'Hara, 2000). Practical intelligence refers to one's ability to find effective solutions, solve problems, and apply ideas to real-life contexts. Thus it refers to tacit, practical, and everyday knowledge. Sternberg (1985a) argued that practical intelligence is independent from academic or traditional cognitive ability.

Sternberg and Wagner (1993) provided a detailed comparative distinction between academic/analytical and practical tasks, which would refer to the need to conceptualize an independent, more applied type of ability different from that defined in terms of traditional cognitive ability. As they argue, academic problems tend to be well defined, possess a single correct answer, and are of little intrinsic interest, whereas practical problems tend to be ill defined, have multiple correct responses, and require personal motivation to be solved.

Most evidence for practical intelligence has derived from lay beliefs about intelligence rather than objective psychometric measures. To some extent these theories are important on their own, as "subjective" beliefs about one's ability and performance need not be accurate to have a significant *impact* on one's intellectual performance. Thus differential psychologists have tended to focus on the academic aspects of intellectual ability, such as the prediction of school and university performance by psychometric tests requiring participants to solve mental problems, whereas laypeople seem solely to highlight the importance of practical abilities.

In one of the first sets of studies to examine implicit theories of intelligence, Sternberg *et al.* (1981; see also Sternberg, 1985a) found that lay beliefs about intelligence could be classified according to three major clusters; namely, *verbal ability* (which coincides with one of the abilities identified by most IQ researchers), *practical problem solving*, and *social competence*. This pattern of results was also replicated when teachers were asked to identify and evaluate the most important aspects of their students' abilities, in both primary and high school. There are also marked *cultural* differences in conceptions of intelligence, with Eastern cultures emphasizing spiritual, practical, and interpersonal skills more than their Western counterparts and those aspects of intelligence related to academic performance (typically measured through IQ tests). This probably illustrates the impact of Eastern philosophies and religions such as Hinduism and Buddhism, which value not only individual capacity, such as fluid intelligence, but also determination and effort as well as subjective beliefs such as confidence and moral strength.

Although these different aspects of ability were well mapped (factor analyzed) onto lay conceptions of intelligence (Sternberg *et al.*, 1981), there is little empirical evidence for the existence of testable individual differences in practical intelligence, particularly in terms of psychometric instruments. Furthermore, claims that individual differences in practical problem solving can be better explained in terms of practical rather than academic or general intelligence have yet to be supported empirically (for a close examination of this topic, see Gottfredson, 2002).

8.12 SUMMARY AND CONCLUSIONS

This chapter has looked at alternative theories of intelligence, such as social, multiple, emotional, and practical intelligence, which are often referred to as hot intelligences. As has been seen:

- Hot intelligences attempt to explain individual differences in real-life achievement beyond IQ. They emphasize interpersonal, emotional, and practical aspects of individual differences in order to broaden the traditional concept of intellectual ability, postulating that there is more to human performance than psychometric g. While theoretically appealing, there is more enthusiasm than evidence for the existence and usefulness of hot intelligences within the realm of human abilities.

- Psychometric tests of hot intelligences tend to lack sufficient reliability and validity. This is largely due to the difficulties associated with designing objective tests (including items with correct responses) for emotional, social, and practical abilities, and of ensuring that such tests are modestly correlated with general intelligence measures.

- Although the use of self-report inventories to assess hot intelligences has proven less problematic and generally achieves higher reliability, self-reports are often substantially correlated with established personality traits, suggesting that hot intelligences are neither novel nor have the characteristics of abilities, but are simply new names for known personality dimensions.

- Considering the vast amount of psychometric evidence in support of the g factor of cognitive ability, and the fact that it accounts for a substantial amount of variance across a wide range of real-life outcomes (as shown in Chapter 6), it has almost been de rigueur for IQ critics to turn a blind eye to the IQ literature. Hence, efforts to validate hot intelligences have often seemed to be prompted by commercial rather than academic interests.

It is, however, clear that our emotions play an important part in determining behavior. Affect is a powerful force that can often moderate the influence of cognitive abilities and impair performance. Theories of mood and motivation will be examined in Chapter 9.

TEXTS FOR FURTHER READING

Chamorro-Premuzic, T. & Furnham, A. (2005). *Personality and Intellectual Competence*. Mahwah, NJ: Lawrence Erlbaum.

Gardner, H. (1983). *Frames of Mind: The Theory of Multiple Intelligences*. New York: Basic Books.

Goleman, D. (1995). *Emotional Intelligence: Why It Can Matter more than IQ*. London: Bloomsbury.

Gottfredson, L.S. (2003). Dissecting practical intelligence theory: Its claims and evidence. *Intelligence*, 31, 343–97.

Matthews, G., Zeidner, M., & Roberts, R.D. (2002). *Emotional Intelligence: Science and Myth*. Cambridge, MA: MIT Press.

Petrides, K.V. & Furnham, A. (2001). Trait emotional intelligence: Psychometric investigation with reference to established trait taxonomies. *European Journal of Personality*, 15, 425–48.

Sternberg, R.J. & Kaufman, J.C. (1998). Human abilities. *Annual Review of Psychology*, 49, 479–502.

9 Mood and Motivation

LEARNING OUTCOMES

BY THE END OF THIS CHAPTER, YOU SHOULD BE ABLE TO ANSWER THE FOLLOWING FIVE KEY QUESTIONS:

1. What is the connection between personality and motivation?
2. How is motivation defined?
3. How do old biological theories of motivation differ from social-cognitive theories?
4. What are mood states and why do they vary?
5. What is the link between mood and motivation?

KEY WORDS

Acquired Needs Theory ● Arousal Theories ● ERG Theory ● Expectancy Theories ● Goal-Setting Theories ● Maslow's Hierarchy of Needs ● Mood States ● Motivation ● Two-Factor Theory ● Two-Process Theories

CHAPTER OUTLINE

9.1 INTRODUCTION

So far I have examined individual differences in relatively stable and invariable factors, such as personality traits and cognitive abilities. As seen in Chapter 7, there is strong evidence for the heritability of these factors. Even though environmental variables may influence the acquisition of crystallized abilities or the development of specific personality traits (e.g., Openness and Conscientiousness), variations *within* individuals tend to be less important when it comes to understanding individual differences in personality traits and intelligence. Individuals' IQ remains pretty much the same after the age of 15, and few individuals show drastic changes in their personality after the age of 30. Indeed, it would almost be impossible to establish any comparisons between people if everybody behaved differently all the time.

Equally, it would be foolish to think that individuals always behave in the same manner. If this were the case, measures of individual difference would be perfect predictors of everyday outcomes. Although ability and personality tests can predict a wide range of variables (e.g., academic achievement, life satisfaction, mental health) with relatively good accuracy, they rarely account for more than 50 percent of their variance. One reason for this is that trait measures encompass very general aspects of the individual and deliberately neglect situational influences on behavior (see Section 2.5 in Chapter 2 and Mischel, 1968). Thus personality inventories provide information on what a person usually does, whereas cognitive ability tests are aimed at measuring the best a person can do (Cronbach, 1990/1949; Hofstee, 2001). However, personality traits are only predictive of behavior insofar as they affect specific states. For example, if Neuroticism did not relate to state anxiety or the experience of anxiety at a specific point in time, it would not predict low performance in an exam (Spielberger, 1972b). Likewise, cognitive ability tests are only accurate to the extent that individuals are fully motivated to do their best when taking the test (Chamorro-Premuzic & Furnham, 2005).

Indeed, people do not always behave in the same way and it would thus be impossible to understand individual differences fully without taking into consideration two important sources of within-individual variability; namely, *mood* and *motivation*. Just as with other individual difference constructs, mood and motivation determine behavioral outcomes. The difference is that traits (including abilities) tend to be longitudinally stable, whereas mood and motivation tend to *fluctuate* and are largely dependent on situational circumstances, though they are also influenced by traits (Cooper, 2002).

The study of motivation and mood states attempts to shed light on individual differences from the perspective of situational factors; that is, taking into consideration the specific sets of processes that trigger behavior, regardless of a person's historical behavioral tendencies. As such, mood and motivation are more context dependent than traits and need not be reliable in traditional psychometric terms. An individual's score on an IQ test should be approximately the same every time they take the test (otherwise the test would be considered unreliable). However, a person's level of mood may vary within days or hours. In fact, we would probably expect individuals' mood to be higher on Fridays than on Mondays, and just before than after holidays. It is precisely this fluctuation of mood states and motivation that represents the essence of these constructs and this approach to individual differences.

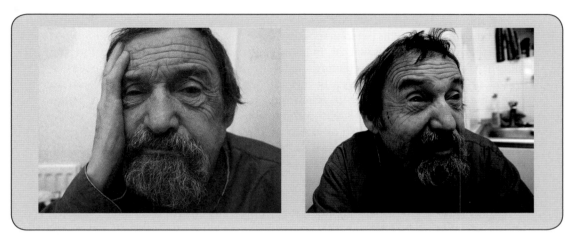

PHOTO 9.1 *Unlike personality, our mood state changes from situation to situation. In some cases, only a few minutes may separate depressed mood (left) from excitement (right).*

Source: Photos courtesy of Nadia Bettega, reproduced with permission.

9.2   BEYOND OR UNDERNEATH TRAITS

Although a plethora of psychometric studies has provided consistent evidence for the validity of personality traits in the prediction of a wide range of contexts (see again Chapter 3), traits do not always explain behavioral outcomes. In some situations it is necessary to look *beyond* or *underneath* traits to understand individual differences. For example:

> Mark is a cheerful, optimistic guy. He rarely worries about future or past events and has a positive outlook on life. Mark would score high on Extraversion and Agreeableness, and low on Neuroticism. He is thus a stable, friendly, easy-going individual.

Now, suppose Mark's wife is diagnosed with cancer. Do you think Mark would behave in a happy, cheerful manner? In other words, would it be useful, in that situation, to predict Mark's reaction on the basis of his personality scores or how he usually behaves?

Consider a second example:

> Roger is a lazy, unenthusiastic, and relaxed man. He rarely takes on challenges and prefers to sleep all day than go to work. He would score low on Conscientiousness and would rarely be described as proactive by his friends.

Suppose a friend of Roger's offered him £15 000 for a one-week job (stuffing envelopes), plus an extra £20 000 if he does the job properly. Do you think Roger would

not be motivated? In other words, would it be accurate to predict Roger's performance just by looking at his personality scores or typical behavioral patterns?

The above examples show that, in some circumstances, traits may have little significance when it comes to predicting – let alone understanding – an individual's likelihood of acting in certain ways. In fact, the above examples show that there are
many potential circumstances in which individuals would *not* be likely to behave
in their habitual manner. One reason for this is that both mood and motives can
influence behaviors irrespective of traits, and may depend on situational or external factors rather than on internal dispositions. Thus states may mediate the
relationship between traits and behavior, but situational factors may moderate
the relationship between traits and states (Rusting, 1998). This complex interaction is
illustrated in Figure 9.1.

In that sense, it is always more accurate to predict a person's behavior by measuring states rather than traits, at least theoretically. In practice, however, this would
involve collecting daily or hourly measures of mood and motivation, and even then
it would be difficult to account for all the possible situational changes that may
influence behavior. This is precisely why psychologists have devoted more time to
developing instruments for the assessment of general tendencies than for situational
factors (see Chapter 7).

Inevitably, emphasis on trait or dispositional approaches has generated a lack of
research on the psychology of mood and motivation within differential psychology.
There are nonetheless many theories that deal with the relationship of mood and
motivation with behavioral outcomes. Some of these theories will be examined
throughout this chapter.

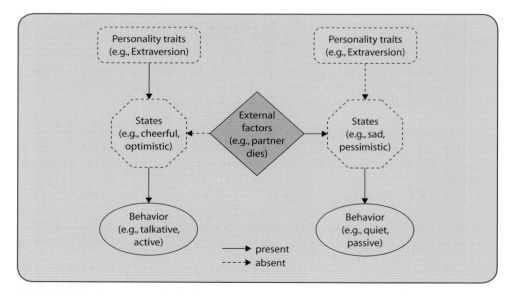

FIGURE 9.1   *Traits, states, and behavior*

PHOTO 9.2 *Lazy Sunday*

We all have lazy moments, but on average some people are much more proactive than others and this is partly explained by personality.

Image courtesy of Nadia Bettega, reproduced with permission.

9.3   DEFINING MOTIVATION

motivation an internal state, dynamic rather than static in nature, that propels action, directs behavior, and is oriented toward satisfying both instinctual and cultural needs and goals.

Although everybody knows what **motivation** is, most people would have trouble defining it, not least because motivation is a psychological notion; that is, a latent construct for explaining behavior. It is therefore impossible to observe motivation directly; we can only infer it through behavioral cues. So, what is motivation?

Motivation is an internal state that:

- *Drives* people into action.
- *Energizes*, *directs*, and *perpetuates* behavior.
- Is directed toward the *satisfaction of needs and drives*.
- If unsatisfied, will generate a state of physiological or psychological *arousal* (and sometimes both).
- Is a *general* rather than a specific psychological force.
- Is *dynamic* rather than static; i.e., a *process* rather than a trait.
- May encompass a wide range of goals, from instinctual (e.g., eating, sleeping, reproducing) to cultural (e.g., winning the Nobel Prize, composing a symphony, writing a book).

Motivation has been part of the psychological vocabulary for more than a century. Indeed, experts such as Furnham (2005, p. 277) have argued:

> one of the oldest, and most difficult, topics in psychology is the fundamental problem of why people are motivated to do anything at all, and if they do something, why that and not something else.

Yet, motivation was only established as an independent area of research in 1953, when the first symposium on the topic was held in Nebraska. A decade later, Cofer and Appley (1964) published the first textbook on the subject, and today there are several peer-reviewed journals (e.g., *Motivation and Emotion, Journal of Occupational Behavior, Journal of Applied Psychology*) and textbooks (e.g., Boggiano & Pittman, 1993; Chamorro-Premuzic & Furnham, 2010; Geen, 1995; Sorrentino & Higgins, 1986; Weiner, 1986; Wong, 2000) dedicated to the study of motivation.

Conceptions of motivation have varied over time. In the late 19th century motivation was simply regarded as the "spring of conduct" (Rommanes, 1881). In the late 1930s it was mainly conceptualized in terms of *needs* and *drives* (Hull, 1943; Murray, 1938). Later definitions (Buck, 1985) viewed motivation in terms of *potential* for the activation and direction of behavior within a specific system, in a similar way to mechanics and physics conceptualizing energy as a potential force (note that we never actually observe energy, only its effects). Kleinginna and Kleinginna (1981a, 1981b) compiled a list of definitions of motivation and noted that traditional approaches tended to emphasize *behavioral control* and distinguished between three components; namely, motives, goals, and behaviors. More recently, researchers have provided wider definitions of motivation. For example, Beck (1990) and Franken (1993) conceptualized motivation as "what makes people act the way they do." Thus motivation research asks two basic questions about behavior: why, and with what level of effort.

The distinction between physiological and psychological motives has marked a broad division in the study of motivation. In both cases, however, motivation is associated with the study of behavioral goals, which are central to distinguishing motivation from mood states (see Section 9.5), as the latter are not linked to the accomplishment of any goals.

FOCUS POINT 9.1   IS EMPATHIC EMOTION A SOURCE OF ALTRUISTIC MOTIVATION?

Altruistic motivation is the desire to help someone purely in order to reduce the stress or increase the benefit of the person in need. Although one can feel pleasant emotions from helping someone altruistically, the personal gain must be an unintended by-product. The concept of altruistic motivation therefore differs from egoistic accounts of prosocial behavior, which posit that we help others only to extract certain personal advantages (e.g., to increase the chances that they help us in the future, to make a favorable impression on others, to feel good about ourselves).

To infer whether motivation underlying behavior is altruistic or egoistic, the authors provide us with an empirical distinction. If a bystander's motivation is egoistic, in order to reduce their own distress, they could help or escape, removing contact with the cause of distress. The likelihood that the egoistically motivated bystander will help is directly related to the *costs* of choosing to escape. These costs may involve physical effort required to leave the situation or feelings of distress (guilt) anticipated for leaving the situation. Thus, increasing the cost of escaping, by making it difficult for the bystander to leave the situation and meaning that they have to continue watching the suffering of another, will increase the likelihood of helping. Conversely, decreasing the cost of leaving, such that it is easy, should decrease the likelihood of helping, so that they can leave and avoid thinking about the person suffering. If the bystander's motivation is altruistic, on the other hand, then this goal can only be achieved by helping, not escaping, independently of the cost of escaping, as that would be goal-irrelevant behavior (the goal being to reduce the other person's distress).

The empathy–altruism hypothesis therefore states that if individuals feel a high degree of empathy, they should help others regardless of associated costs (incurred by helping). On the other hand, if individuals feel little empathy, then they should help only when the cost of escaping or not helping is too taxing.

In Batson, Duncan, and Ackerman's research to test the hypothesis that empathic emotion leads to altruistic motivation to help, subjects observed a young woman, Elaine, receive (apparent!) electric shocks and were given an unanticipated chance to help her by volunteering to take her place and receive the remaining shocks themselves – instead of her. The cost of escaping without helping was manipulated by making escape difficult (they were told they would have to continue watching Elaine receiving shocks) or easy (they would not have to watch her receiving shocks). The level of empathy (low vs. high) was manipulated differently in

two experiments. Experiment 1 used similarity information to manipulate empathy, as previous research suggests that people tend to feel more affinity for those who are perceived to be similar to themselves. In experiment 2, empathy was more directly manipulated through the use of an emotion-specific misattribution to a placebo.

EXPERIMENT 1

METHOD

SUBJECTS

Subjects were 44 female students, out of which 11 participated in each of the four conditions (2 easy versus difficult escape $\times$ 2 similar versus dissimilar victim). All participants filled out a personal value and interest questionnaire, which formed the basis for the similarity manipulation.

PROCEDURE

Participants were deceived by being told that the experiment was about impression formation of a "worker" (the confederate) under aversive conditions (receiving electric shocks). The confederate, Elaine, sat in the other room attached to a chair with shock electrodes attached to her arms, while the participant sat in another room observing her from a screen monitor (which was actually a prerecorded tape of Elaine).

DIFFICULTY OF ESCAPE MANIPULATION

In order to manipulate the difficulty of escape without helping, participants were told varied numbers of trials that they were expected to observe in the last line of the written instructions they were given. In the easy-escape condition, subjects read: "Although the worker will be completing between two and ten trails, it will be necessary for you to observe only the first two" (p. 294). In the difficult-condition trial, participants read: "The worker will be completing between two and ten trials, all of which you have to observe." All participants were later told that Elaine chose to do ten trials, and were given the chance to help her by swapping places with her after the second trial.

SIMILARITY MANIPULATION

Participants were given a copy of the personal interests and values questionnaire that Elaine had filled out earlier. Elaine's questionnaire was prepared in advance so that it would either be similar or dissimilar to the one answered by the participant earlier on.

NEED SITUATION

After Elaine was apparently strapped into the chair, she asked about the level of pain, and was told that it was about two to three times more uncomfortable than static shocks. After Elaine had received two shocks, her reaction was so strong that the researcher asked if she was okay. Here Elaine asks for a glass of water. Later, she reveals that she has suffered severe trauma as a little girl because a horse threw her onto an electric fence, and in future she might react strongly even to mild shocks. Here is where the researcher then decides that it could be an idea to swap places with the observer (participant).

In the easy-escape situation, the participant is given the choice to swap places or leave, as they have seen the required minimum two trials. In the difficult-escape condition, they were again given the option to swap places, or finish watching the remaining trials. Later, participants were debriefed; all understood the nature of the deception, and were not upset by it.

RESULTS

On analysis, for the similar-victim condition, there was a highly significant main effect for similarity. Inspection of the proportion of helping in each condition revealed that the interaction

(Escape $\times$ Similarity) was of the form predicted by the empathy–altruism hypothesis; the proportion in the easy-escape–dissimilar-victim condition was much lower than in the other three conditions.

DISCUSSION

These results were quite consistent with the empathy–altruism hypothesis. Where the empathic emotional response to Elaine's distress was expected to be low (dissimilar-victim condition), motivation to help was expected to be egoistic, and the difficulty of escape had a dramatic effect on helping. When escape was difficult, participants were much more likely to help, presumably because receiving the remaining shocks was much less costly than watching them. In the similar-victim condition, however, where the empathic emotional response to Elaine's distress was expected to be high, the motivation to help should be at least in part altruistic; the difficulty to escape had no effect on participants' desire to help. This was presumably because they had a desire to relieve Elaine's distress, not just their own, even when escape was easy.

Overall, experiment 1 supports the empathy–altruism hypothesis. However, even though there is strong evidence to support the idea that a similarity manipulation *evoked* empathic emotion, the manipulation was indirect. Therefore a second experiment was conducted in which the same hypothesis was tested but manipulating empathic emotion more directly.

EXPERIMENT 2

When witnessing another person in distress, there are two qualitatively different emotional states that can be elicited: *empathic concern*, made up of emotions such as compassion and soft-heartedness; and *personal distress*, made up of emotions such as shame and guilt. In this experiment, by emotion-specific misattribution to a placebo, the participants would perceive their response to Elaine's distress to be predominated by the other. That is, if they attributed their feelings of empathic concern to the placebo, they should perceive their responses to Elaine as that of personal distress and vice versa.

So if empathic concern results in altruistic motivation to help, if they attribute that to Elaine, then regardless of the difficulty of escape (like the one used in experiment 1), participants should be altruistically motivated to help. If they attribute personal distress to Elaine, then they should be egoistically motivated to help, and will escape if it is easy, or help if it is a difficult-escape situation in order to decrease their own distress at witnessing her suffer.

METHOD

SUBJECTS

Subjects were 48 female students, 12 of which were placed in each of the four conditions (2 easy vs. difficult-escape × 2 personal-distress vs. empathic-concern as response to watching Elaine).

PROCEDURE

The procedure was the same as in experiment 1, except instead of using a similarity manipulation, the level of empathic response to Elaine's distress was manipulated by having participants misattribute either empathic concern or personal distress to a placebo pill that they would have to take.

EMOTIONAL RESPONSE MANIPULATION

Participants were asked to complete a memory task. Then they were given a capsule called Millentana, which was said to improve short-term memory recall and increase serotonin in the brain. They were told that it took up to 25 minutes to take effect, so during this time is when they watched Elaine receiving electrical shocks.

Before they took the capsule, they were informed that the pill has side-effects. Those in the personal-distress condition were told that these were a feeling of warmth and sensitivity, similar to that one might experience while reading a particularly touching novel. They were told the feelings should start 5 minutes after ingestion and will wear off after 25 minutes. Subjects in the empathic-concern condition were told that the side-effects were feelings of uneasiness and discomfort, similar to that while reading a particularly distressing novel. In the personal-distress condition, because participants should attribute feelings of empathy toward themselves, they should feel personal distress toward Elaine, and vice versa in the empathic-concern condition.

Participants were given the same options as in experiment 1 to take Elaine's place, and in the difficult-escape condition they had to stay and watch the remaining shocks being given if they did not take her place; in the easy-escape condition, they had a choice to leave.

RESULTS

Once the experiment was over, participants were asked to circle adjectives describing how they felt as a result of taking Millentana. If they circled more empathic-concern adjectives than personal-distress, they got a score of 1; if an equal amount, a score of 0; and if fewer, a score of −1. As intended, participants in the personal-distress condition reported experiencing a predominance of empathic concern as a result of taking the Millentana capsule ($M = .21$). Participants in the empathic-concern condition reported having experienced a predominance of personal-distress emotions ($M = −.46$). Participants in the personal-distress condition reported mainly feelings of uneasiness toward Elaine ($M = −1.50$); participants in the empathy condition reported more warmth and sensitivity ($M = .21$).

As with experiment 1, and predicted by the empathy–altruism hypothesis, helping was lowest in the easy-escape-distress condition than in the other three conditions. The results were consistent with the hypothesis that in the empathy conditions, where motivation was assumed to be at least in part altruistic, the rate of help remained high even when escape was easy; whereas in the distress condition, helping was significantly lower in the easy-escape condition than under the difficult-escape condition.

DISCUSSION

These two experiments seem to provide evidence that empathic emotion produces truly altruistic motivation, contradicting the egoistic assumptions of most theories of motivation. Indeed, the results of the two experiments were largely consistent; in each, conditions assumed to produce a relatively high empathic response to a person in distress led to helping regardless of whether escape without helping was easy

or difficult. In contrast, conditions assumed to produce a relatively low empathic response led to helping only when it was difficult to escape without helping.

The results of these studies were very influential in changing psychologists' explanations for prosocial behaviors and represent the strongest alternative view to the idea that humans are essentially motivated by selfish motives (even when they appear to help others). Importantly, these results highlight the role of empathy as a determinant of prosocial behavior, hence individual differences in empathy should predict people's tendency to help others (see Section 2.11 in Chapter 2 on Agreeableness and Section 8.7 in Chapter 8 on trait emotional intelligence).

Source: Batson, C.D., Duncan, B.D., & Ackerman, P. (1981) Is empathic emotion a source of altruistic motivation? *Journal of Personality and Social Psychology*, 40, 290–302.

© 1981 American Psychological Association. Reproduced with permission.

9.4   FROM BIOLOGICAL REFLEXES TO PSYCHOLOGICAL SELF-REALIZATION

As seen in Section 9.3, motivation is defined very widely. This makes it necessary to distinguish between different types of motives. One major distinction is that between impulses arising from within the organism and those resulting from external objects, including other individuals (Nuttin, 1984). Early developments in the field of motivation can be characterized by the transition from *biological* to *psychological* needs (Maslow, 1954; Murray, 1938).

9.4.1   Reflexes

One of the earliest scientific attempts to study motivation conceptualized behavior according to the *electromechanics* paradigm of physics. The concepts of *force*, *inertia*, and *energy* brought to psychology by the German physician and physicist Hermann Von Helmholz (1821–94) became very fashionable in the early 20th century, such that they even constituted a central feature in Freud's (1999/1900) early model of the *psychological apparatus*. This conception of behavior suggested that the mind and

PHOTO 9.3 *Professional athletes devote a great part of their lives to their sport, but what motivates them?*

Image courtesy of Tomas Chamorro-Premuzic.

the body are structured like a mechanical engine and operate according to the principle of energy discharge. Metaphorically, motivation was thought of as "gasoline," and some even attributed the causes of behavior to the type of food ingested (Holt, 1931).

A classic example of the mechanical approach to motivation was the notion of *reflexes* as fixed and unlearned motivational systems that react to specific external or internal stimuli. As such, they were regarded as the most basic determinants of human action (Cofer & Appley, 1964), representing automatic reactions such as salivating in the presence of food or closing your eyes when you are frightened. However, reflexes rarely explain individual differences. Instead, the apparatus model refers to what is constitutive of *all* human beings and, in fact, other mammals, too. Thus reflexes conceptualize similarities rather than differences between people. On the other hand, the gasoline metaphor is not an accurate reflection of human behavior: unlike cars, individuals tend to react when they "lack gasoline" rather than when the "tank is full" (Hull, 1952) (see Section 9.4.3).

9.4.2 Instincts

Instincts are psychophysiological entities that mobilize energy in specific directions to accomplish biologically predetermined goals. Like reflexes, they are largely innate and inherited, but, unlike reflexes, they pursue an action on the external world, affecting the environment. Examples of instinctual motives are the need for food, water, sex, and sleep. Such needs are generated by physiological imbalances and can be satisfied by a variety of stimuli or objects, though always through the same set of behaviors (eating, drinking, sleeping, etc.). Animal psychologists such as Konrad Lorenz (1903–89) showed that some behavioral patterns were predetermined for an entire species and thus referred to instincts in terms of "fixed-action patterns" (Hess, 1962; Lorenz, 1937). Like reflexes, instincts are useful to understand the causes of ubiquitous human behaviors, but cannot explain individual differences in social or cultural motives.

9.4.3   Drive Theories

Drive theories of motivation (Hull, 1952) were still based on the biological notion of instinct but emphasized the mediating role of internal *drives* as psychological forces. Indeed, Woodworth (1918) proposed the notion of drives as an alternative to instincts and conceptualized individuals' behavior as a consequence of their attempt to reduce drives. Thus drive-reduction theories account for the fact that behavior is often prompted in response to the absence rather than the presence of stimuli, such that absence produces the drive (see Section 9.4.2). For example, eating can be explained as an attempt to reduce the drive generated by hunger, whereas drinking would be an attempt to reduce the drive generated by thirst, and so on. The process of restoring physiological levels of balance was known as *homeostasis* and drives were seen as indicators or signals of homeostatic imbalance. Figure 9.2 represents motivation as the process by which biological needs push or drive individuals into action. As shown, behaviors that reduce the drive are preferred over those that do not (see also Section 9.4.5).

9.4.4   Psychodynamic Approaches to Motivation

On the other hand, psychodynamic approaches to motivation have used the term "instincts" to refer to quite different motivational processes. Freud quickly abandoned his mechanical model of the mind to develop an intrapsychic taxonomy of

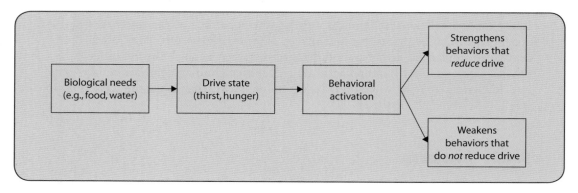

FIGURE 9.2 *Motivation as drive reduction*

behavior that conceptualized *sex* and *aggressiveness* as the two primary motivational forces. This idea was consistent with the philosophical *Zeitgeist* and represented a major step in the transition from biological to cultural or psychologically superior motives. Thus Nietzsche (1973/1886, Section XIII) famously argued:

> Physiologists should think before putting down the instinct of self-preservation as the cardinal instinct of an organic being. A living thing seeks above all to discharge its strength – life itself is will to power; self-preservation is only one of the indirect and most frequent results.

Although the psychological forces conceptualized by Freud were "instinctual," in the sense of being inborn and common to all humans, they were directed toward symbolic rather than biological objects. Thus we can feel hungry when reading the menu of a restaurant, or thirsty when seeing a Diet Coke ad on television. According to Freud, even artistic products could serve the expression of instincts. For example, Freud's concept of *sublimation* referred to the canalization of sexual impulses through socially rewarded behavior. Thus an artwork allows artists to channel their sexual energy in a subconscious manner. In a well-known psychoanalytical essay, Freud (1964) interpreted the prolific artistic and scientific activity of Leonardo da Vinci (1452–1519) as compensation for his sexual inactivity. Although Freud's ideas remained largely disputed, not only in regard to motivation, they were no doubt influential in increasing the focus on psychological motives.

9.4.5   *Reinforcement: Motivation as Learned Associations*

The motivational theory of reinforcement is essentially an application of the behaviorist paradigm to the study of motivation. As seen in Section 3.8.2 in Chapter 3 and Section 4.4.2 in Chapter 4, behaviorism is based on the idea that individuals' behaviors, as those of other animals, are modified or *conditioned* through rewards and punishments (Spencer, 1872). Accordingly, motivation was interpreted in terms of particular stimulus–response associations. For example, a stimulus (hunger) is initiator of a response (eating) that leads to another stimulus (food), which positively reinforces the association (hunger–eating–food). As seen in Section 9.4.3, a similar process was hypothesized by Hull's (1952) drive theory.

Skinner (1938) introduced important modifications to the behaviorist theory of motivation through the principle of *operant conditioning*, which conceptualized a variety of *reinforcement tools* for manipulating an individual's motivation and behavior. These were:

- Positive reinforcement (*reward*).
- Negative reinforcement (*punishment*).
- Avoidance learning (*removal of punishment*).
- Extinction (*removal of positive reward*).

More recent studies (e.g., Corr, Pickering, & Gray, 1995) have used the reinforcement paradigm to explore the relationship between personality states and traits, notably in the context of Gray's and Eysenck's personality models (see Sections 2.6 and 2.9 in Chapter 2). It seems that Neuroticism – trait anxiety – is associated with an oversensitive behavioral inhibition system (BIS), which compares expected versus actual events and consequently generates more intense responses to fear and novelty stimuli (Matthews & Gilliland, 1999). Thus physiological processes, at the level of the brain, underpin the expression of both traits and states (Eysenck & Eysenck, 1985).

Despite wide acceptance of the physiopsychological links outlined by Eysenck's and Gray's personality theories, the relationship between arousal, traits, and states may be more complex. To this end, Thayer (1989) differentiated between two dimensions of subjective arousal; namely *energetic* (vigor vs. tiredness) and *tense* (anxiety vs. calmness). The former reflects activity in the reticulo-cortical system and is associated with Extraversion/Introversion, while the latter reflects individual differences in the limbic arousal system and is associated with Neuroticism/Stability. Whereas high levels of energetic arousal (vigor) may improve performance (Matthews, 1992a, 1992b; Revelle, 1993), high levels of tense arousal (anxiety) are likely to cause negative emotionality. A third bipolar mood dimension – namely, *hedonic tone* – was incorporated by Matthews to account for the experience of feelings along the happiness–sadness continuum (see also Section 9.6).

9.4.6   Arousal Theories

motivational theories of arousal theories that account for individual differences in behavior in terms of differences in people's level of physical energy (arousal), which varies between as well as within individuals.

Motivational theories of arousal posit that individuals vary in their level of physical energy and that these differences are a major cause of individual differences in behavior. The simplest and arguably most elegant explanation of arousal defined it as the "inverse probability of falling asleep" (Corcoran, 1965). Arousal levels may vary between as well as within individuals. Accordingly, different people will have different average levels of energy (as seen in Sections 2.8 and 2.9 in Chapter 2), but the same individual may feel energetic at times and tired at others. For instance, most people feel tired after physical exercise, but not all people experience the same level of tiredness after the same exercise. On the other hand, some people may feel more energetic when they wake up than when they go to bed, whereas for others it may be the other way around.

There are two fundamental principles underlying the relationship between performance and arousal. The first is that this relationship is *curvilinear*, such that an intermediate level of arousal is optimal for performance (i.e., better than low and high arousal). This effect was first reported by Yerkes and Dodson (1908), who found that mice performed best after receiving moderate electro-shocks (a motivational factor!). The second principle posits that the optimal level of arousal will be negatively correlated with *task difficulty*, such that more complex tasks have lower optimal arousal level and vice versa (Duffy, 1962). When graphically represented, the relationship between arousal and performance resembles an inverted "U" curve (Hebb, 1949; see Figure 9.3).

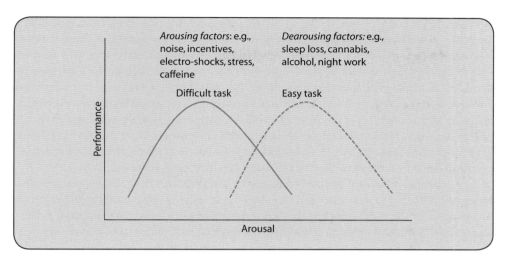

FIGURE 9.3 *Performance and arousal*

PHOTO 9.4 *Major competitions are the ultimate test for professional athletes and illustrate the psychological principle of arousal. If you see an athlete miss a shot they would not miss during training, it is probably because the occasion was too arousing for them.*

Image courtesy of Tomas Chamorro-Premuzic.

There are many everyday examples to illustrate the two laws of arousal. For example, professional athletes tend to perform better in competitions than in training sessions because they are underaroused during training. Conversely, they may be unlikely to perform at their best during major competitions, such as the Olympics or World Cup finals, which overarouse them. Likewise, one would expect students to perform better in real than in "mock" exams (dummy assessments), unless they were not prepared. In fact, if students know the subject perfectly, they will only perform well when their performance actually matters. Finally, experienced drivers may prefer to listen to the radio while driving long distances, whereas inexperienced drivers may prefer to drive in silence, as they will already be sufficiently aroused.

Conceptualizations of arousal have also been influenced by electrophysics and mechanics. Thus the concept of arousal is largely mirrored by Duffy's definition of *energy mobilization* as "the energy used in tensing the muscles in preparation for overt response as well as that used in the overt response itself. Figuratively speaking, it is the rate at which the bodily engine is running" (Duffy, 1951, p. 32). This rate can be measured in terms of:

- Major behavioral states (e.g., asleep vs. awake).
- Subjective alertness and perceived emotion.
- Peripheral nervous system activity (e.g., heart rate and skin conductance).
- Electroencephalogram (EEG) waveform patterns.

PHOTO 9.5 *Can we measure motivation via brain signals? EEG studies examine the physiological basis of individual differences in motivation.*

© Daniela Sachsenheimer/Shutterstock.

EEG measures are the most widely used indicator of activity in the central nervous system and have been described as the "standard measure of cortical arousal" (Eysenck, 1994, p. 167). They involve placing passive electrodes on the scalp of the participant and decoding the raw measure of electrical activity produced by the brain. Hence the obvious advantage of these studies, which provide an objective and quantitative measure of arousal and motivation. However, different measures of arousal (e.g., self-reports, neurotransmitter activity, and EEG) are not always significantly intercorrelated, implying that arousal may not be a unitary dimension (Lacey, 1967). Furthermore, arousal measures such as EEGs and indicators of peripheral nervous system activity are often complex to interpret, as they may confound sympathetic and para-sympathetic activity (e.g., the interaction of respiratory and cardiovascular systems; Matthews & Gilliland, 1999, p. 596). Arousal laws also fail to explain why higher levels of arousal would impair performance (Naatanen, 1973; Neiss, 1988). Indeed, excessive levels of arousal may lead not necessarily to quantitative differences in input (i.e., how much effort is applied to the task) but to qualitative ones (i.e., which other strategies should be used) (Sanders, 1983). Criticisms of the Yerkes–Dodson arousal laws have been extensively reviewed by Matthews and Amelang (1993).

9.4.7   Expectancy Theories

Another approach to motivation has been guided by **expectancy theories**, which posit that behavior is chosen, performed, and maintained according to the individual's evaluation or *expectation* of its consequences. Accordingly, subjective beliefs will not only predict but also motivate future behaviors (Bandura, 1977, 1989).

expectancy theories theories that explain motivation in terms of people's expectation of the consequences of a chosen behavior, emphasizing the role of not only individuals' predictions of the behavioral outcome but also their evaluation of its usefulness and importance.

Expectancy theories are particularly useful to explain people's behavior at work and have therefore been extensively tested in organizational or occupational psychology (Furnham, 1994, 2005). However, their scope goes beyond work environments and explains a wide range of everyday behaviors. For example, you may be unmotivated to train for a sports competition if you think the event is unimportant, and you may only be motivated to read this book if you think it is important to maximize your exam performance. Expectancy theories emphasize not only the role of an individual's prediction but also their valuation or *valence* of the behavioral outcome as well as the usefulness or *instrumentality* of the chosen behavior. Thus higher expectancy, instrumentality, and valence lead to higher effort, and in turn higher performance (see Figure 9.4).

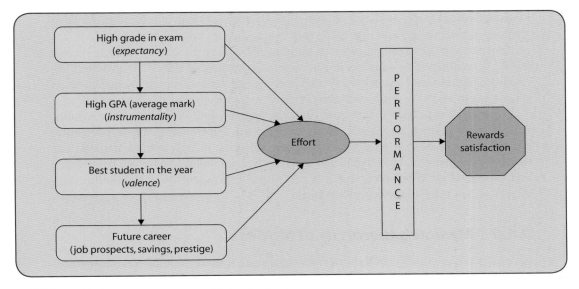

FIGURE 9.4 *Motivation as expectancy of behavioral outcomes*

9.4.8   Goal Setting

goal-setting theories
theories that conceptu-
alize motivation in terms
of the consequence of
behavior; behaviors that
are goal oriented or
motivated by their con-
sequences are extrinsic,
whereas behaviors that
are performed for the
sake of it are intrinsic.

Similarly to expectancy theories, **goal-setting theories** conceptualize motivation in terms of the consequences of behavior. However,
rather than assuming that behavior is always motivated by the
accomplishment of certain goals or rewards, they posit that it is often
executed without the prospect of accomplishing goals other than the
behavior itself. Behaviors that are goal oriented or motivated by their
consequences are called *extrinsic*, whereas behaviors that are simply
executed for the sake of it are called *intrinsic*. For example, you may be
attending lectures to keep a good attendance record (extrinsic motivation) or because you find them intellectually stimulating (intrinsic
motivation). Likewise, you may choose to go for a walk (intrinsic motivation) or to
walk to a meeting (extrinsic motivation). Finally, you may read this book because it
will help you revise for an exam (extrinsic motivation) or because you enjoy reading
it (intrinsic motivation). Thus extrinsic motives are "means to an end" and pursue
external rewards. Conversely, intrinsic behaviors are motives in themselves and are
performed with no other intentions (Deci, 1975; Deci & Ryan, 1985).

Although the distinction between extrinsic and intrinsic motivation is straightforward, it may be elusive at times. For example, a professional pianist may perform a
piano concerto as part of her job (extrinsic motivation) but still be intrinsically motivated; that is, feel thrilled and aroused when playing the piece. On the other hand,
intrinsic motives are difficult to conceptualize and may hide extrinsic motives. Even
prototypical intrinsic behaviors such as listening to music may have some extrinsic
components. If listening to music makes you feel good, the ultimate goal may be to feel
good rather than listen to music, and this logic can be applied to any intrinsic motives.

In addition, goal-setting theories (e.g., Wood & Locke, 1990) argue that goals must
be *specific*, *challenging*, and *attainable*. These principles are consistent with the Yerkes–
Dodson arousal laws, as they conceptualized a motivational equilibrium between
challenging (arousing) and attainable (not overarousing) tasks. Thus individuals are
motivated to perform complicated tasks, but only if they think they can accomplish
them. Very difficult or impossible tasks have demotivating effects, even when the
reward is high. Indeed, excessive rewards may overarouse individuals, increasing their
sense of responsibility and making them *choke under pressure* (Baumeister, 1984).

Integrating expectancy and goal theories, social-cognitive approaches to motivation, such as Dweck's (1986), have examined the self-fulfilling and self-defeating
effects of overconfident or underconfident cognitions in educational settings. For
example, believing that intelligence is fixed or an *entity* will lead to lower motivation
and efforts, whereas believing that it is malleable or *incremental* will have motivating
effects, and in turn improve performance.

9.4.9   Maslow's Hierarchy of Motives

An evolutionary classification of motives suggests that there are different hierarchical
levels of behavioral determinants. At the lowest level, one could conceptualize biological reflexes and instincts, which are simple, common to all individuals, and produce
relatively predefined and rigid responses to stimuli. At the highest level, one may

Maslow's hierarchy of needs Maslow's theory conceptualizing behavioral determinants in terms of a hierarchy or pyramid, with basic physiological needs at the base, followed by security needs, social needs, the need for esteem and recognition, and finally the need for self-fulfillment or self-actualization.

identify more complex psychological and cultural motives, which are more dependent on individual differences. In psychology, this idea was made famous by Abraham Maslow (1908–70), who developed a theory of the **hierarchy of needs**.

Maslow's (1954) theory is best illustrated by a pyramid, which summarizes the different hierarchical levels of human goals (see Figure 9.5). At the lowest level of the pyramid Maslow conceptualized *basic physiological needs*, such as the need for food, air, and water. The next level up comprised *safety needs*, which serve security and protection and attempt to reduce pain. One level up, Maslow conceptualized *social needs*, the need for friends, love, and relationships. Next he located *esteem needs*, the need for approval and recognition.

The top level of the pyramid comprised what Maslow referred to as *self-actualization* or *self-fulfillment needs*, which are the most intrinsic of all motives, such as art appreciation and intellectual curiosity. The bottom two levels of the pyramid refer to biological needs, whereas the top three levels refer to psychological needs.

Interestingly, Maslow argued that *all* needs are inborn and universal. This does not imply that all individuals should behave in the same way, but that they have goals in common. Thus different people may choose different behaviors to accomplish their safety needs, but all people will need to accomplish such goals. More importantly, Maslow emphasized that higher-order needs only emerge once individuals have satisfied lower-order needs.

PHOTO 9.6 *Abraham Maslow (1908–1970)*

Source: http://en.wikipedia.org/wiki/Abraham_Maslow.

However, critics have argued that it is often possible to choose behaviors that simultaneously satisfy different levels of the need hierarchy (Cofer & Appley, 1964). Indeed, the idea that individuals would progressively and systematically ascend the pyramid of needs seems oversimplistic. Human beings are immersed in a symbolic world that routinely confounds biological and psychological needs. For example, we can be thirsty for a specific brand of beer rather than a glass of water, and being in love does not imply that we have satisfied more basic needs such as sexual appetite.

9.4.10 *Alderfer's ERG Theory*

ERG theory theory of motivation based on **Maslow's hierarchy of needs**, but with three rather than five levels; namely, existence needs (E), relatedness needs (R), and growth needs (G).

Alderfer's (1969) theory of *existence*, *relatedness*, and *growth* (ERG) was based on Maslow's hierarchy of needs but introduced important modifications. In some ways **ERG theory** was a simplification of Maslow's theory, as it conceptualized three levels of motivational needs that could be mapped onto Maslow's pyramid (which had five). The lowest level of the hierarchy comprised *existence needs* and represented Maslow's physiological and safety needs, thus referring to

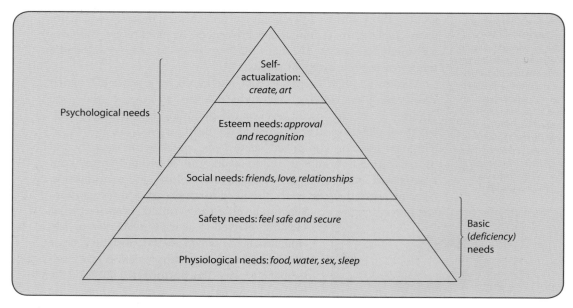

FIGURE 9.5 *Maslow's hierarchy of needs*

PHOTO 9.7 *Clayton Alderfer (1940–) introduced important modifications to Maslow's theory of motivation*

Image courtesy of Professor C. Alderfer.

Source: www.ClayAlderfer.com.

physical wellbeing. At the intermediate level, Alderfer conceptualized *relatedness needs*, which referred to the need to form social relationships (e.g., friends, partners) and were equivalent to Maslow's social needs. At the highest level, Alderfer located *growth needs*, such as the need to develop one's potential, satisfy one's intellectual curiosity, and increase one's competence. Hence growth needs represented Maslow's self-actualization goals.

Like Maslow, Alderfer believed that needs were prioritized counterhierarchically, such that individuals must satisfy basic needs before moving upward in the pyramid of goals. However, ERG theory also posited that failure to satisfy higher goals may lead individuals to focus on lower-order needs, a principle called *frustration regression*. In that sense Alderfer's theory is more flexible than Maslow's and suggests that satisfaction and dissatisfaction are two different processes, the former being represented by an escalation

FOCUS POINT 9.2   ABRAHAM MASLOW (1908–70)

Maslow was the son of uneducated Jews from Russia. He was born and raised in Brooklyn, New York, where he had an unhappy childhood due to being the only Jew in a non-Jewish neighborhood. These difficult years would influence much of his work. Maslow is considered the founder of humanistic psychology and his conceptualization of a "hierarchy of human needs" is probably the best-known theory of motivation.

Maslow studied psychology at the University of Wisconsin, focusing mainly on primate dominance behavior and sexuality. It was not until 1937, when he attended the faculty of Brooklyn College for 14 years, that he would form the basis of his lifelong work on human motivation. His inspiration came from his mentors at the college, Ruth Benedict and Max Wertheimer, whom he admired both professionally and personally. Maslow observed their behavior, took notes about them, and conceptualized concepts including the hierarchy of needs and self-actualization.

Against the dominant trend in psychology at the time to focus on mental illness and abnormal personality (see Chapter 4), Maslow focused on *healthy* individuals. His assumption that every person has a strong desire to realize their full potential led to his stressing the desire for self-actualization, which is represented at the top of the pyramid or the highest hierarchical order of human needs.

The five lower levels, which ought to be satisfied first, are (from bottom to top) "basic needs,"

"security and stability," "love and belonging," and "esteem" (see Section 9.4.9).

Maslow was particularly interested in understanding the motives of people who had clearly met the standard of self-actualization and was inspired by the writings of Albert Einstein. Maslow realized that all self-actualized persons had similar traits, which included being realistic, but preferring optimism to overpessimism; being problem centred (treating difficulties in life as problems that require solving); being comfortable on their own; and having healthy personal relationships.

Beyond the needs of fulfillment, Maslow believed that self-actualized people experience extraordinary moments, which he called *peak* experiences. These are profound moments of happiness, love, or understanding, a sort of epiphany but even stronger; during these moments, individuals feel complete, alive, and lose their sense of ego to become *one* with the world around them.

Maslow's work was influential and, as such, it was not without critics. Indeed, many argued that his work was unscientific and questioned the lack of empirical evidence in support of his theory. Yet Maslow inspired several therapies focused around the idea that people possess inner resources for growth and healing, which therapists can help unleash by removing the obstacles to self-actualization.

in the hierarchy of needs, the latter by a descent. This idea influenced the development of Herzberg's two-factor theory of motivation (see Section 9.4.11). Despite their popularity, particularly within humanistic psychology (a movement substantially indebted to Maslow), hierarchical theories of needs remain largely untested and have thus lost most of their appeal within differential psychology (Furnham, 1994, 2005).

9.4.11 Herzberg's Two-Factor Theory

two-factor theory
theory of motivation developed by Herzberg that conceptualizes satisfaction and dissatisfaction as two separate factors rather than two extremes of the same dimension. It argues that hygiene factors (e.g., good working conditions) determine individuals' level of dissatisfaction, while satisfaction is dependent on additional motivational factors such as high salary.

Frederick Herzberg (1923–2000) developed a **two-factor theory** of motivation that conceptualized *satisfaction* and *dissatisfaction* of needs as two separate factors rather than two extremes of the same dimension (Herzberg, 1966). Thus the opposite of satisfaction is not dissatisfaction but *no satisfaction*, while the opposite of dissatisfaction is not satisfaction but *no dissatisfaction*. This model is depicted in Figure 9.6.

Herzberg's theory has been extensively applied to occupational/organizational settings as it provides a useful model for identifying the causes of good job performance, as well as those conditions that need to be absent to ensure job satisfaction (Furnham, 2005). Specifically, Herzberg (1966) argued that *hygiene* factors, such as reasonable workload, friendly co-workers, and good working conditions, determined the level of dissatisfaction. If these needs are successfully addressed, employees will score low on dissatisfaction.

This alone, however, does not ensure employees' satisfaction. Rather, additional motivators are needed to enrich individuals' work experience and motivate them. Motivational factors may include extrinsic variables such as high salary, bonuses, and promotion, or intrinsic ones such as personal satisfaction with one's contribution to the organization. In some cases motivators can make up for low hygiene factors. For instance, soldiers' motivation to serve their country in war may compensate for the poor hygiene conditions of field combat, whereas highly paid professionals may be so motivated by their bonuses that they will happily sacrifice holidays. However, high hygiene can rarely compensate for low motivators. Thus employers should not only try to satisfy employees' basic needs but also ensure that they are motivated.

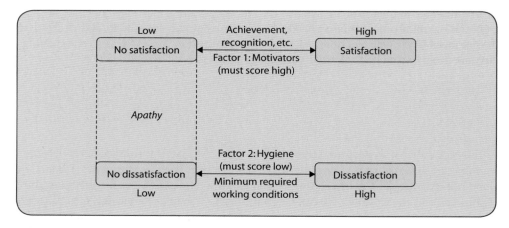

FIGURE 9.6 *Herzberg's two-factor theory*

9.4.12 McClelland's Acquired Needs Theory

Acquired needs theory, developed by David McClelland (1917–98), conceptualizes motivation as the acquisition of three basic needs; namely, *achievement*, *affiliation*, and *power* (McClelland *et al.*, 1953; McClelland & Steele, 1972; McClelland & Winter, 1969).

acquired needs theory according to McClelland, motivation is the acquisition of three basic needs: the need for achievement (desire to master skills), the need for affiliation (desire to be social), and the need for power (desire to influence others).

- Need for achievement can be defined as the desire to master skills and accomplish moderately difficult goals.

- Need for affiliation is described as the desire to form relationships and be social in general.

- Need for power can be understood in terms of the desire to influence and control others.

McClelland (1965) also provided a test, called the Thematic Apperception Test (TAT), to assess individual differences in these needs. TAT is a *projective* rather than a psychometric test and, as such, it differs substantially from most types of instrument described in this book. Whereas psychometric tests such as self-reports or ability tests involve multiple-choice questions and are scored objectively, projective tests such as TAT present individuals with open-ended stimuli and are based on the assumption that people "project" certain aspects of their personality in their responses (the most famous projective test is Rorschach's ink-blot test).

Crucially, projective measures are not scored or analyzed in comparison with other individuals but assess each response on its own. Thus they are *idiographic* rather than *nomothetic* (see Section 2.2 in Chapter 2), and individuals' responses are only meaningful in the context of a theory that the examiner uses to interpret them. According to McClelland, needs represent individual differences in acquired personality traits. For instance, individuals high in need for achievement are

PHOTO 9.8 *David McClelland (1917–98) conceptualized an important theory of motivation based on basic needs.*

Image courtesy of Harvard University Department of Psychology, reproduced with permission.

entrepreneurial, highly competitive, choose moderately difficult tasks, and tend to be rational in their assessment of the potential risks underlying their choice of behavior (McClelland *et al.*, 1953). McClelland argued that need for achievement is a ubiquitous human dimension that can be found in any form of society (McClelland & Winter, 1969). Thus a country's level of motivation may be used to predict its level of growth. Despite the commonsense idea underlying this argument, the projective

PHOTO 9.9 *An example of a TAT slide. From this the patient is asked to tell a story based on the picture they see.*

two-process theories theories of motivation widely used in organizational psychology that focus on the impact of extrinsic motivational factors and individuals' expectations of motivation and performance.

nature of TAT has made it difficult to test this hypothesis empirically, as there are no objective and reliable ways to quantify McClelland's trait with that instrument. However, dispositional approaches like the Big Five personality inventory (Costa & McCrae, 1992) have conceptualized and measured individual differences in achievement motivation as a subfacet of Conscientiousness (see Section 2.11 in Chapter 2). Figure 9.7 illustrates how the Big Five personality traits have been used as predictors of work-based motivation.

9.4.13 Two-Process Theories

Two-process theories of motivation apply economic principles to psychology (Adams, 1963, 1965) and tend to explain motivation in terms of social comparison; that is, the comparisons people make among themselves. These theories are widely used in management and organizational psychology, as they explain how employees select behaviors to meet their needs, and how they rate success (Furnham, 2005).

Adams's *equity theory* focuses on the role of extrinsic motivational factors or external rewards, and provides a formula to predict whether individuals will believe that they are treated fairly (compared to other employees) or not. As shown in Figure 9.8, equity results from the perception that the ratio between one's outcome (e.g., pay, fringe benefits, bonuses) and input (e.g., qualifications, effort, ability) is similar to others'. Thus, one's efforts and achievements need to be relatively in proportion to those of others; disproportions will lead to perceived inequity and, in turn, diminish one's motivation to perform. Adams hypothesized several consequences of inequity:

- Changing input (if an employee feels she is working more than others).
- Changing output (if an employee feels she is achieving more than others).
- Distorting one's perception (fooling oneself by "pretending" one works as hard/achieves as much as others).
- Leaving the job.

The second element of the two-process theory is, again, *expectancy*, in particular the impact of expectations on motivation and performance. Expectations can be influenced by self-perceived and actual abilities, and take into account the probability of performing at the expected level and the importance of achieving the specific outcome (see again Section 9.4.7).

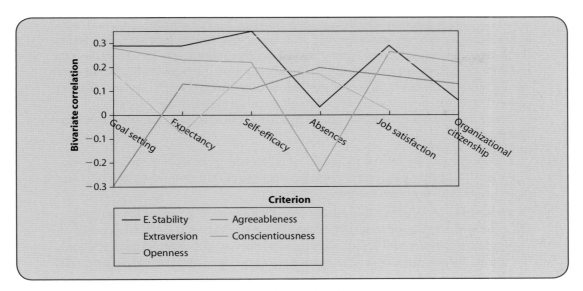

FIGURE 9.7 *Big Five personality traits as predictors of work-related motivation*

Based on Judge and Illies, 2002.

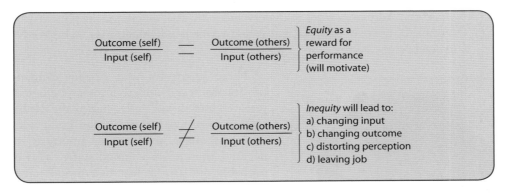

FIGURE 9.8 *Adams's equity theory*

9.5   MOOD STATES

Mood states have been defined as relatively sporadic emotional states, which tend to last for minutes or hours (Matthews *et al.*, 2000). Thus, they are indicative of human emotions, such as anger, happiness, and surprise, and are manifested physiologically (e.g., heart beat and perspiration) as well as behaviorally (e.g., smiling, crying, and shouting), though only the latter is intentional.

Although there is debate as to whether mood states and motivation are conceptually distinguishable (Cooper, 2002; Morris, 1989), motivation is traditionally associated with goals whereas mood states are

mood states sporadic emotional states, lasting for minutes or hours, that indicate emotions such as happiness or anger and are manifested through physiological signals, e.g., increased heart rate, and behavioral signals, e.g., smiling.

not. That said, it is conceivable to attribute behavioral consequences to certain mood states. For example, the experience of fear may cause you to seek help, and feeling displeasure may cause you to vomit. Yet, the same emotions may be felt without the presence of such or any other goals (for a different view see Buck, 1985). Mood states are also distinguishable from cognitive states, such as worry, though they are often correlated (e.g., anxiety and worry are often experienced together; Revelle, 1993).

There are several reasons for studying mood states in the context of individual differences:

- Mood states are related to individual differences in *personality*. In fact, personality traits may partly be regarded as aggregates of mood across different situations and moments in time.

- Mood states influence individuals' *behavior* irrespective of traits. For example, anxiety may impair people's performance in an exam or IQ test independent of their knowledge and ability; sadness may affect people's interpersonal relations (e.g., friends, work colleagues, partners) regardless of their charm or personality.

- Diagnostic classifications in psychopathology are often based on an examination of mood states in specific contexts. For example, feeling ecstatic after being fired, or depressed after getting married (assuming you had a choice!), may indicate departures from normal emotionality and anticipate mood disorders.

- Mood states are important to understand individual differences in *creativity*, specifically the psychological processes by which individuals may be inspired to create (see Chapter 10).

PHOTO 9.10 *Psychologists spend a great deal of time studying negative emotions like anxiety, depression, and stress; so what about positive emotions like happiness? What determines individual differences in positive affect?*

Photo courtesy of Nadia Bettega, reproduced with permission.

There seems to be a certain element of *Schadenfreude* underlying psychological research into mood states. Just as the media tend to prioritize bad news over good, psychologists have paid more attention to negative than positive mood states. This is probably due to the fact that mood states and emotions have been predominantly explored in the context of clinical psychology (see Chapter 4). As a consequence, there are more inventories to assess depression, anxiety, helplessness, and even suicidal tendencies than for happiness, excitement, enthusiasm, and satisfaction (Cooper, 2002).

One theoretical problem underlying the assessment of mood states is that there are no clear boundaries between one set of affects and others. Thus different researchers have used different labels for the same mood states, or the same names for different mood states. Either way, this has led to the development and use of numerous inventories, making it difficult to interpret results, compare findings, and integrate the literature. For instance, studies on negative affect, stress, anxiety, and negative self-efficacy may all refer to the same construct (Judge and Illies, 2002). There has also been a lack of conceptual clarity to distinguish between emotions at the state and trait level. Hence, anxiety may simultaneously refer to an emotion, a mood state, and a trait (Neuroticism). In order to overcome this problem, researchers have used data-reduction techniques such as factor analysis (see Section 2.7 in Chapter 2 and Section 9.6).

9.6   STRUCTURE OF MOOD

As with personality traits and abilities, differential psychologists have tried to identify the *structure* of mood; that is, to work out how many dimensions are needed to describe individuals' experiences of mood and whether they can be organized hierarchically. This requires researchers not only to compile an extensive list of mood adjectives but also to examine the degree of similarity and overlap between different words, which can be done via factor analysis (Cattell, 1973; Storm & Storm, 1987).

In a seminal review on the topic, Watson and Tellegen (1985) reanalyzed a number of studies of self-reported mood and concluded that the universal structure of mood comprised two robust factors; namely, *positive affect* and *negative affect*. These factors are orthogonal or uncorrelated, such that scores on one factor do not predict scores on the other (Diener, 1984). Watson and Tellegen (1985, p. 222) argued that the two-dimensional structure of mood "can be demonstrated across all the major lines of research on affective structure: Self-rated affect, studies of mood words, and analyses of facial expressions." Perhaps more importantly, the authors admitted that *minor dimensions* of mood may underlie these two factors and provided a detailed hierarchical taxonomy to integrate main and minor mood states (see Figure 9.9). For instance, negative affect may be represented in terms of the minor dimensions of sadness, fear, or anxiety, whereas positive affect may be indicative of activity, excitement, or happiness. Thus their bidimensional model "is complementary to, rather than competitive with, multi-factorial structures" (Watson & Tellegen, 1985, p. 220).

Some cognitive psychologists, such as Matthews, Jones, and Chamberlain (1990), have preferred to describe mood in terms of three dimensions; namely, *energy* vs. *fatigue* (which represents positive affect), *tension* vs. *relaxation* (which represents negative affect), and *happiness* vs. *unhappiness*. Unlike the first two dimensions, happiness–unhappiness is not significantly linked to autonomic arousal measures and is thus more psychological than physiological in nature. As seen in Figure 9.9, Watson and Tellegen (1985) conceptualized happiness at the crossroads of high positive and low negative affect rather than considering it a major dimension of mood.

Although studies on self-reported mood have been quite successful at replicating positive affect and negative affect as the basic dimensions of mood, there is some controversy about the universality of emotions. For example, Russell (1991) showed that some languages have no equivalent words for "fear" and "anger," though expression such as "I feel good" or "I feel bad" can be found in all languages (Wierzbicka, 1999).

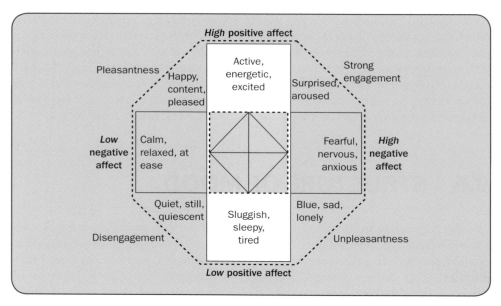

FIGURE 9.9 *The bidimensional structure of mood*

Source: Adapted from Watson & Tellegen (1985).

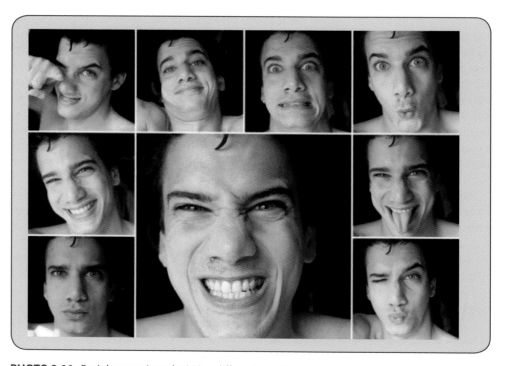

PHOTO 9.11 *Facial expressions depicting different moods*

Source: © Mazen Al-Ali, http://mazz1983.wordpress.com/2007/11/11/facial-expressions-a-mazen-al-ali-project/.

Ekman (1994) and Russell (1995) have disputed whether the expression of emotions (through facial cues) is a pan-cultural phenomenon or not, whereas Brebner's (2003) cross-cultural studies have revealed gender differences in the expression of some emotions in some countries but not others. Last but not least, Öhman (1999, p. 337) concluded that "different emotion systems have different evolutionary histories and are better viewed as independent than as parts of a general domain of emotion."

Despite considerable expectations generated by the consensual identification of the structure of mood, research into mood states vanished toward the early 1990s, a period which, nonincidentally, marked the beginning of the Big Five era and the dominance of dispositional approaches. Thus mood states became mere expressions of dispositions or personality traits (see Section 9.8).

9.7 SITUATIONAL DETERMINANTS OF MOOD

Like motivation, but unlike traits, mood states are largely a function of specific situational factors and are therefore subject to change over time. For instance, after winning the lottery or passing a difficult test, you will probably feel happiness, even if you are a negative person. Likewise, after failing an important exam or being fired you will probably feel miserable, even if you are an optimistic person.

Experimental studies provide evidence for the manipulation of mood states under laboratory conditions. This technique, known as the "Velten method" (Velten, 1968; Martin, 1990), requires participants to read a series of statements and *experience* the moods associated with these statements. Thus individuals' mood influences the way they perceive, encode, and retain information. In particular, inducing positive affect would bias individuals to interpret events in a positive vein, as though they "wore rose-coloured glasses" (Niedenthal, 1992). In contrast, individuals who have been primed to experience negative affect would exhibit a tendency to interpret events in a negative manner.

The problem with the Velten method is that participants can easily figure out whether they are expected to experience positive or negative affect, such that they may not be naïve to the experiment's aims. In fact, a meta-analysis of Venten studies found that mood induction was stronger when participants were told (explicitly) that the study intended to manipulate mood (see Rusting, 1998).

9.8 DISPOSITIONAL INFLUENCES ON MOOD STATES

The two dimensions of positive and negative affect (see Section 9.6) are often interpreted as personality traits. Thus they may reflect *dispositional influences* on mood states referring to individual differences in the experience of positive and negative affect (Watson, Clark, & Tellegen, 1988), which implies that individuals' mood experiences are relatively consistent over time (Diener & Larsen, 1984). Indeed, studies reported longitudinal stability of measures of mood up to a seven-year time period (Watson & Walker, 1996). Along these lines, various studies found substantial correlations between positive mood and Extraversion measures on one hand, and negative affect and Neuroticism on the other (Costa & McCrae, 1980; Gilboa & Revelle, 1994). This led Watson and Clark (1992, p. 468) to conclude that "individual differences in personality and emotionality ultimately reflect the same common, underlying constructs." However, McConville and Cooper (1999) concluded that a substantial percentage of mood variance cannot be explained by personality traits.

Dispositional approaches have also conceptualized individual differences in the stability of mood states experienced. Eysenck and Eysenck (1985) predicted that choleric individuals (those high in both Neuroticism and Extraversion; see Section 2.4 in Chapter 2) would display the most erratic mood states. In contrast, they expected phlegmatic individuals (those low in both Neuroticism and Extraversion) to show the least variable mood states. Because high Extraversion is associated with more frequent experiences of positive affect, and high Neuroticism is associated with more frequent experiences of negative affect, some have argued that in choleric individuals opposite average mood states would cancel each other out. Accordingly, one would expect a combination of high Neuroticism and *low* Extraversion to result in more variable mood experiences (Williams, 1990). Conciliating these two theoretical positions, recent studies (which used the Big Five rather than the Gigantic Three) have shown that high Neuroticism *alone* is the best predictor of mood variability (Murray, Allen, & Tinder, 2002).

Traditional approaches to mood regulation have also identified individual differences in the extent to which people focus on negative or threatening stimuli. These individual differences have been conceptualized in terms of *repression* and *sensitization*. Repressors tend to focus away from negative stimuli, whereas sensitizers tend to draw attention to such stimuli and are generally more prone to experience negative affect. In fact, Holmes (1974) reported correlations as high as .90 between anxiety and sensitization scales.

9.9 INTEGRATIVE AND RECENT APPROACHES TO MOOD STATES

The irony of mood states is that they were first used to refute (Mischel, 1968) and then to validate (Costa & McCrae, 1980) trait taxonomies. Although the latter caused a rapid slowdown of studies into mood states, there has been a recent increase of research in the topic.

These recent approaches to mood states have emphasized the importance of affect in regard to human performance (Matthews *et al.*, 2000; Revelle, 1993). While individual differences in ability and personality may predict various performance outcomes, individuals may underperform due to temporal mood states such as anxiety or fatigue (Matthews, Jones, & Chamberlain, 1990). If such mood states can be predicted by personality traits, there is reason to conceptualize an overlap between ability and personality, at least at the level of psychometric or measured constructs (Chamorro-Premuzic & Furnham, 2005). Similar implications derive from theories of emotional intelligence (see Section 8.7 in Chapter 8), which define individual differences in the ability to identify and manage one's own and others' emotions. However, there is heated debate as to whether such differences should be conceptualized within the ability or personality realm (Matthews, Zeidner, & Roberts, 2002; Petrides & Furnham, 2001; see also Section 8.10 in Chapter 8).

Rusting (1998) presented an integrative framework for understanding the link between personality traits and mood states. Mediational models posit a chain reaction or "domino effect" to explain causal paths between traits and states. For example, Spielberger's (1972a, 1972b) theory of anxiety indicated that trait anxiety or Neuroticism affects state anxiety or the experience of anxiety, which in turn impairs emotional information processing. On the other hand, moderational models predict that traits and states interact to affect emotional information processing and are therefore independent. Rusting (1998, p. 190) concluded:

> the mediation approach has not been directly tested; however, the personality and emotion literature suggests that a mediation framework may best capture the underlying processes responsible for emotion-congruent processing.

In a review of the literature, Russell (2003) attempted to provide a conceptual clarification of the different overlapping psychological concepts for emotion, such as affect, mood, emotion regulation, and empathy (see Table 9.1 for brief definitions). Furthermore, he conceptualized *core affect* as the most elementary or basic form of emotion:

> At the heart of emotion, mood and any other emotionally charged event are states experienced as simply feeling good or bad, energized or enervated. These states – called *core affect* – influence reflexes, perception, cognition, and behaviour and are influenced by many internal and external causes. (Russell, 2003, p. 145)

Table 9.1 *Core affect, mood, emotion regulation, and empathy: Short definitions*

Core affect	Neuropsychological state perceived as feeling; can be more or less hedonic (pleasure–displeasure) or arousing (sleepy–activated)
Mood	Extended affect with no reference to specific objects or events
Emotion regulation	Attempts to modify current emotional state
Empathy	Simulated experience of another individual's affect

Source: Adapted from Russell (2003).

These states are "primitive, universal, and simple (irreducible on mental plane). [Core affect] can exist without being labelled, interpreted, or attributed to any cause" (Russell, 2003, p. 148). Core affects, then, are comparable to corporal temperature: we always have them and extreme levels are particularly noticeable.

9.10 SUMMARY AND CONCLUSIONS

This chapter has examined theories of mood and motivation and their relevance in regard to individual differences. As has been seen:

- Theories of motivation have varied widely in their definitions, conceptualizations, and approaches to the topic, no doubt due to the scope of the concept. Biological theories are less useful than psychological ones for understanding individual differences because they refer to *common* instincts such as the need to sleep, eat, or drink. Thus they eliminate rather than emphasize individual differences, highlighting common goals. However, as we move from biological needs toward psychologically complex motives, it becomes more difficult to investigate motivation through objective or experimental means. For example, it is easy to obtain physiological measures of hunger, whereas the motivation to do well in a university exam may only be assessed through self-report inventories.

- Broad definitions of motivation, such as "what makes people act the way they do," are overly ambitious because they assume that one variable is sufficient to account for the complexity and diversity underlying human behavior. Yet, motivation continues to be understood as an overarching psychological phenomenon. Thus Revelle (1993, p. 346) concluded: "Motivation is the vital link between knowing and doing, between thinking and action, between competence and performance. [It] explains why rats solve mazes faster when hungry than well fed, why bricklayers lay more bricks when given harder goals than easier ones, why assistant professors write more articles just before tenure review than after, and why people choose to be fighter pilots rather than dentists."

- Mood states are an essential psychological component underlying behavior and individual differences, and it would be difficult to understand the meaning of major personality dimensions such as Neuroticism and Extraversion without reference to basic mood states such as positive and negative affect. Although emotions can often be predicted by stable personality dimensions, they are often independent and more influenced by situational variables. Crucially, mood states can influence cognitive processes and distort individuals' perceptions and interpretations of events.

- The link between mood and motivation represents one of the most promising areas for understanding the processes underlying individual differences. Although in this chapter I have treated them as separate, current progress in differential psychology is largely a function of integrating mood, motivation, and dispositional approaches with information-processing theories, which, in simple terms, involve investigating the (not so simple) link between cognition and emotion.

Chapter 10 will look at the construct of creativity, which has a longstanding history in individual differences despite only recently receiving sufficient attention in the field.

TEXTS FOR FURTHER READING

Bandura, A. (1977). Self-efficacy: Toward a unifying theory of behavioral change. *Psychological Review*, 84, 191–215.

Dweck, C. (1986). Motivational processes affecting learning. *American Psychologist*, 41, 1040–48.

Maslow, A.H. (1954). *Motivation and Personality*. New York: Harper.

Revelle, W. (1993). Individual differences in personality and motivation: Non-cognitive determinants of cognitive performance. In A. Baddeley & L. Weiskrantz (Eds.), *Attention: Selection, Awareness and Control. A Tribute to Donald Broadbent* (pp. 346–73). Oxford: Oxford University Press.

Russell, J.A. (2003). Core affect and the psychological construction of emotion. *Psychological Review*, 110, 145–72.

Rusting, C.L. (1998). Personality, mood, and cognitive processing of emotional information: Three conceptual frameworks. *Psychological Bulletin*, 124, 165–96.

Watson, D. & Tellegen, A. (1985). Toward a consensual structure of mood. *Psychological Bulletin*, 98, 219–35.

10   Creativity

LEARNING OUTCOMES

BY THE END OF THIS CHAPTER, YOU SHOULD BE ABLE TO ANSWER THE FOLLOWING FIVE KEY QUESTIONS:

1. How is creativity defined?
2. What are the major paradigms for creativity research?
3. What do we know about the relationship between intelligence and creativity?
4. How do personality traits relate to creativity?
5. Can we measure creativity scientifically?

KEY WORDS

Alternate Uses Test ● Brainstorming ● Convergent Thinking ● Divergent Thinking ● Investment Theory ● Overinclusive Thinking ● Remote Associations Test ● Three-Ring Theory of Giftedness ● Threshold Theory of Creativity and Intelligence ● Torrance Test of Creativity and Thinking

CHAPTER OUTLINE

10.1 INTRODUCTION

Some people are more able to surprise us with original thoughts and novel solutions that are simply unexpected. These people seem to stand out in the crowd and are capable of innovating – in fact, they seem to prefer innovation to imitation and may often choose to defy the crowd. What makes these people capable of generating new ideas and discovering unknown paths? The study of individual differences in creativity attempts to answer this question.

In this chapter I examine the concept of creativity. Although this topic has a long-standing history in differential psychology (dating back to the very beginnings of intelligence testing more than 100 years ago), creativity researchers have constituted a minority within individual differences and have often pointed out that more attention should be given to the field (Guilford, 1950; Sternberg & Lubart, 1996). Despite growing research in the area and explicit economic interests, creativity has indeed been absent from the individual differences curricula, though it has often been discussed, peripherally, with regard to personality and intelligence. Thus creativity is associated

PHOTO 10.1 *Humans perform a wide range of creative tasks and from a very young age. Individual differences research on creativity attempts to provide a scientific approach for assessing creativity and explaining why certain people are more creative than others, and what consequences these differences have.*

Image courtesy of Nadia Bettega, reproduced with permission.

with a wide range of concepts, such as motivation, imagination, meta-cognition, social influence, intuition, potential, leadership, humor, and mental illness (Runco, 2004).

In a sense, it would almost be impossible to introduce the concept of creativity without reference to either personality or intelligence theories; but, then again, this is true for virtually any topic in differential psychology. Accordingly, the core of this chapter will focus on the relationship of creativity with established personality and ability constructs. On the other hand, if creativity deserves its own chapter in this book (and, of course, I think it does), it is because it represents *something other* than individual differences in personality and intelligence. It should therefore be noted that comparisons between creativity and personality or intelligence are useful to *define away* creativity from established individual difference constructs. In fact, in many passages of this chapter it should become clear that creativity may differ from intelligence and that it cannot be explained merely in terms of known personality traits.

Figure 10.1 presents a conceptual map of the contents of this chapter, which begins by introducing definitions and approaches to creativity and follows this up by focusing on differential approaches, in particular the relationship of creativity with intelligence and personality traits. The final sections of the chapter discuss the role of creativity in different contexts of everyday life.

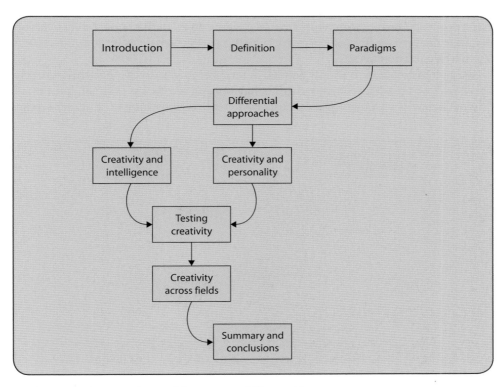

FIGURE 10.1 *Conceptual map of the contents of Chapter 10*

10.2   DEFINITIONS AND CONCEPTUALIZATIONS OF CREATIVITY

What is creativity? Like other individual difference constructs, creativity is part of everyday vocabulary and most people have a rather good idea of what creativity is about. In fact, one need not be an expert in the field to rate creativity in others, or even in oneself: for instance, I tend to think of myself as a highly creative individual but others tend to disagree!

That said, the term "creative" is used so widely that it is indispensable to define it and refine its meaning. There are creative and uncreative people, behaviors, and works. Moreover, there seem to be creative professions, such as writer, actor, or musician, and uncreative ones, such as police officer, accountant, and lawyer, though creativity may help police officers to capture a criminal, accountants to avoid taxes, and lawyers to win a legal case. Creativity, then, seems to be associated with a wide range of phenomena, from a football pass to a piano concerto, from a hairstyle to a mathematical theory, from a cooking recipe to a game of chess, hence it is used to characterize individuals, groups, and even societies.

One theoretical approach to overcome the multiplicity of meanings underlying the concept is to conceptualize creativity as a *syndrome* or complex rather than a single phenomenon. Accordingly, "creativity" can be used to refer to individuals, processes, products, and environments alike (see Figure 10.2). In this book, I shall focus on the individual perspective of creativity, which is particularly relevant for understanding individual differences.

Very often creativity is simply defined in terms of *originality*, though this is merely one aspect of creativity. Thus creative behaviors and works are original, but not all original behaviors and works are considered creative. For example, an exact replica

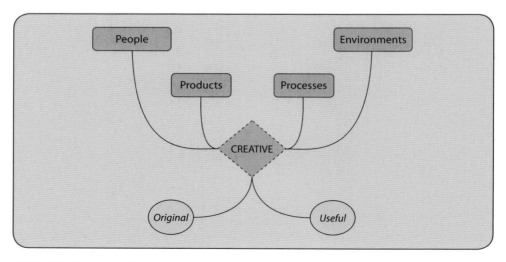

FIGURE 10.2 *Defining the creativity syndrome*

(if that were possible) of Leonardo da Vinci's *Mona Lisa* would not be considered creative, but my version of that painting would rarely be considered creative, even though it would not look like the original at all.

Critics of the conceptualization of creativity as originality have observed:

> creativity has finished up by being evaluated simply as an oddity or bizarreness of response relative to the population mean or as output of words per minute, etc. This indeed comes close to mistaking the shadow for the substance. (Cattell, 1971a, p. 409)

Creative products, then, should not only be original but also useful. Accordingly, a more accurate definition of creativity may be that of "the production of an idea or product that is both novel and useful" (Sternberg & O'Hara, 2000, p. 611).

Unfortunately, there are problems with this definition, too. First, few ideas are effectively "new." Even the most groundbreaking scientific discoveries tend to derive from previously considered ideas rather than appearing from out of the blue. Some philosophical systems, such as the dialectics of G.W.F. Hegel (1770–1831) and Karl Marx (1818–83), explained in great detail how new ideas tend to evolve from old ones. This would also apply to scientific discoveries. The philosopher of science Karl Popper (1902–94) argued that scientific knowledge can only advance through testing existing hypotheses, which is what we do in psychological research. This explains why it is rarely possible to publish research that is completely original in peer-reviewed scientific journals.

PHOTO 10.2 *How creative or useful is a pair of shoes?*

Do people agree on the creative merit of different designs, and are these related to usefulness? A robust theory of creativity should enable us to quantify creative products across different product categories.

Image courtesy of Nadia Bettega, reproduced with permission.

On the other hand, the "usefulness" of an idea may depend on a subjective or personal evaluation: useful for whom? For example, what is the usefulness of Picasso's *Guernica* painting? Is Beethoven's 9th Symphony more useful than Einstein's relativity theory? Is Einstein's relativity theory more useful than a pair of designer shoes? Is a pair of designer shoes more useful than a religious doctrine? Are creative things ever useful? In his introduction to *The Picture of Dorian Gray*, Oscar Wilde (1854–1900) famously claimed that "all art is quite useless."

Thus definitions of creativity will depend on whether one refers to socially valuable products or intrinsically creative processes, such as dreams, thoughts, and even naïve curiosity (Barron & Harrington, 1981). The latter conceptualization is less relevant in regard to performance, but still important for understanding individual differences in creative thinking.

Other definitions of creativity have focused on the level of difficulty, aesthetic value, or impact of creative products, or have taken a systems approach (Figure 10.3), but there are limitations to these approaches, too. Assessing the level of difficulty may be subjective and there are no objective parameters to establish interdisciplinary comparisons (for example, is it more difficult to compose a piano concerto or to create a sculpture?). Beauty is equally subjective and depends not only on individual taste but also on chronological factors. For instance, Van Gogh's paintings were only considered beautiful long after his death and many of Bach's compositions were equally unsuccessful during his lifetime. Thus creative impact may depend on factors other than creativity, such as networking, marketing, promotion, and politics.

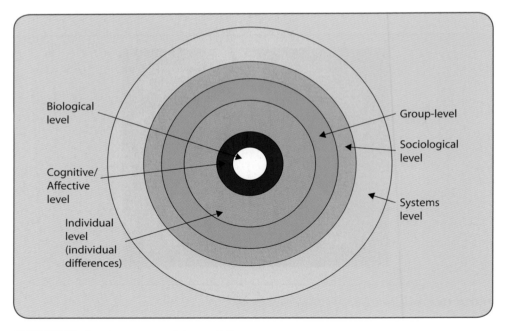

FIGURE 10.3 *A systems approach to creativity*

Adapted from Hennessey & Amabile, 2010.

10.3   CREATIVITY ACROSS DIFFERENT PSYCHOLOGICAL PARADIGMS

Approaches to creativity may be classified in terms of psychological paradigms, such as evolutionary, biological, cognitive, and differential, and are summarized in Figure 10.4. The differential approach is the focus of this chapter and is examined in more detail in Section 10.4.

The *behavioral* paradigm conceptualizes creativity in terms of novel associations and tries to identify the behavioral correlates of novel learning processes. One example is the concept of "insight," which has a longstanding history in psychology and refers to spontaneously synthesized learned associations. Behaviorists are especially interested in the effects of experience on insight and how these benefit creative thinking. However, the notion of creativity as a latent (not directly observable) variable is largely incompatible with the behavioral approach to creativity.

The *biological* paradigm, on the other hand, looks at the physiological correlates of creative thinking and how these processes may be manifested at the level of brain structure and neural processes. A central issue here is the extent to which creativity can be mapped onto either right or left hemispherical activity. Even though early research suggested that original ideas are caused by lower levels of cortical arousal, which enable defocused attention (Martindale & Hasenfus, 1978), more recent findings indicate that creativity requires both hemispheres to be involved (Katz, 1997). Thus creative thinking would involve rational as much as intuitive processes.

The *clinical* paradigm looks at the extent to which creativity is associated with abnormal behavior, either as a cause or a consequence of psychological disorders. A well-known idea that emerged from this area is the "mad genius" hypothesis (Becker, 1978), which prescribes a connection between insanity and artistic creativity. Established psychological theories, such as Eysenck's (1999), postulate a relationship between creativity and mental disorders. This link is examined in Section 10.6.1.

The *cognitive* paradigm (as you may have guessed!) emphasizes the role of cognitive processes, such as attention and memory, in regard to creativity. For instance, Wallach (1970) found that broader rather than focused attention is beneficial for creativity, as it enables individuals with a wider range of stimuli and memory traces to produce ideas

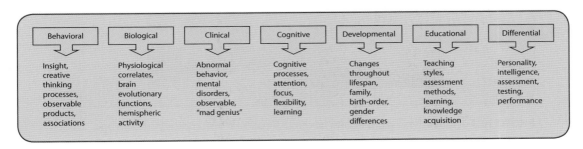

FIGURE 10.4 *Creativity across different paradigms*

(see also Martindale & Greenough, 1973). Studies have also reported that broader attention is more likely to occur in the absence of pressure (for example during evaluations or examinations), as it leads individuals to divide attentional resources between task-relevant and task-irrelevant stimuli (Smith, Michael, & Hocevar, 1990).

Other cognitive studies examined the link between creativity and previous knowledge and reported a negative correlation between these constructs (Hayes, 1978; Simon & Chase, 1973). Thus expertise is detrimental to creative thinking, probably because it reduces flexibility. This may explain why it is usually more difficult to convince experts to change their minds than novices (Frensch & Sternberg, 1989). Along these lines, the technique of **brainstorming**, which requires a group of individuals to say everything that comes to mind about a certain topic (without censoring any ideas), attempts to postpone judgment in order to increase fluency of responses and originality, although Rickards and deCock (1999) concluded that brainstorming is ineffective.

brainstorming a technique for generating ideas in a group setting that involves individuals saying everything that comes to mind about a topic, without self-censorship or inhibition.

The *developmental* approach attempts to identify changes in creativity throughout the lifespan and how certain characteristics of the family (e.g., size, age, birth-order) may affect levels of creativity. It has, for instance, been shown that middle-born children tend to be more rebellious than their siblings and are thus more likely to have creative personalities (Sulloway, 1996). Gender (as opposed to sex) is also associated with creativity, as androgynous individuals – that is, those low in both masculinity

PHOTO 10.3 *Is brainstorming an effective method to break free from constrained ideas and come up with new, innovative ones?*

© Corbis.

convergent thinking
the generation of a response to a problem that requires a single, "correct" answer, e.g., "Paris" for the question "What is the capital of France?" (compare with **divergent thinking**).

divergent thinking
widely regarded as an aspect of creativity, divergent thinking refers to the generation of multiple, "unique" answers to a problem, e.g., "Find as many uses as you can for a piece of string" (compare with **convergent thinking**).

and femininity – tend to be more flexible and more creative than stereotypically masculine or feminine people.

The *educational* paradigm looks at creativity in the context of formal education (e.g., primary school, secondary school, university) and attempts to assess how different teaching modalities may influence students' creativity. To the extent that educational methods may partly determine the development of creativity, the identification of the causes of high and low creativity would provide important information for policy and designing interventions. Traditionally, educational settings such as primary and secondary school tend to praise **convergent thinking** rather than **divergent thinking** or originality, requiring pupils to provide "correct" rather than "unique" answers. For example, school teachers are more likely to ask pupils what the capital of France is than what name *they* would give to the capital of France (if the answer were not Paris).

The *differential* or psychometric paradigm represents the leading approach to the study of creativity. Although the concept of creativity developed in the context of early intelligence theories and preliminary attempts to predict academic performance, it soon expanded to the field of personality traits and eventually became consolidated as an independent area of individual differences. There are four major perspectives by which differential psychologists conceptualize creativity (Rhodes, 1987/1961; see also Runco, 2004). These approaches are discussed below.

FOCUS POINT 10.1   EFFECTS OF PERSONALITY AND THREATS OF EVALUATION ON DIVERGENT AND CONVERGENT THINKING

Unlike intelligence, which involves the ability to find the correct solution to a problem, creativity is better understood as finding *numerous* solutions to a problem. In that sense, the former requires convergent thinking and the latter divergent thinking (though tests for creativity and intelligence suggest that convergent and divergent thinking are mildly correlated). However, there has been less research on the personality predictors of divergent thinking.

The most important correlate of creativity is Openness, so much so that researchers have often conceptualized Openness as a proxy for creativity. Indeed, there have been a number of studies reporting positive links between Openness and divergent thinking.

On the other hand, evidence on how other personality traits relate to creativity is more equivocal. For instance, Extraversion and Neuroticism have been reported to be both positively and negatively associated with creativity; Agreeableness and Conscientiousness have been found to be largely unrelated to divergent thinking.

Perhaps the above inconsistencies can be explained in terms of situational factors that moderate the effects of personality on creativity. Thus whereas Openness could relate to "actual" creativity (e.g., interests, abilities, attitudes), Neuroticism and Extraversion could relate to creativity primarily because they affect test performance on creativity tests – one candidate variable to explain these effects on test performance is arousal.

Although arousal has been found to affect performance negatively, the interactive effects of traits and arousal on divergent thinking have rarely been examined. In this paper, the authors explore the interactive effects of negative affect (unpleasant arousal) and personality on divergent and convergent thinking. Specifically, the authors set out to induce arousal by *threat of evaluation* and assess whether personality traits affect participants' performance differently under stressful and calm conditions.

METHOD

PARTICIPANTS

Participants were 82 UK psychology students – 23 males (age $M = 20.6$, $S.D. = 3.1$ years) and 59 females (age $M = 21.7$, $S.D. = 5.1$ years).

MEASURES

The authors used the Big Five Inventory; the Positive and Negative Affect Schedule, which asked participants how they felt "right now"; divergent thinking measures, which tested verbal fluency and creative problem solving; and a convergent thinking measure, the Baddeley Reasoning Test, administered under both calm and stressful conditions.

PROCEDURE

Participants were tested individually in 45-minute sessions. They were asked to fill out the tests in both calm and stressful conditions. The calm condition was in a quiet cubicle, whereas in the stressful condition participants were sat in front of a camera and were told that their performance was being filmed and compared to fellow students'.

RESULTS

The results revealed that threat of evaluation significantly affected divergent thinking ($t(82) = 2.96$, $p < .01$), and almost significantly affected convergent thinking, but not quite ($t(82) = 2.96$, $p < .06$). Extraversion and Openness were found to be significantly correlated with divergent thinking in both calm (Extraversion: $r = .33$, $p < .01$; Openness: $r = .53$, $p < .01$) and stressful (Extraversion: $r = .42$, $p < .01$; Openness: $r = .55$, $p < .01$) situations. Neuroticism significantly correlated negatively with divergent thinking under threat of evaluation ($r = -.21$, $p < .05$). Personality was a much stronger predictor for divergent (30 percent of variance) rather than convergent (6 percent of variance) thinking. In fact, there were no significant correlations with personality and convergent thinking in either direction. When Extraversion was taken into account for the effects of Neuroticism on divergent thinking, it fully accounted for the link between the two.

DISCUSSION

Openness and Extraversion were found to be significantly associated with divergent thinking under both threat of evaluation and no evaluation, suggesting that they facilitate divergent thinking and relate to "actual" rather than measured creativity. Openness conceptualizes many facets similar to creativity (as well as others, such as intellect, political attitudes, and aesthetic interests), thus it can be regarded as an investment trait and driving force underlying individual differences in "actual" creativity.

Extraverts outperformed their introverted counterparts in both conditions, especially under threat of evaluation. The larger effect of Extraversion on creativity under threat of evaluation is consistent with the idea that the arousing effects of evaluation should impair introverted individuals more so than extraverts (an old Eysenckian idea).

Neuroticism was found to relate to divergent thinking only under threat of evaluation, but when Extraversion was taken into account, this effect was fully explained. Thus Neurotic individuals are more impaired in their divergent thinking performance only because of their lower Extraversion scores. This is in concordance with the hypothesis that Neuroticism is only associated with "tested" rather than actual creativity, as their divergent thinking is only impaired under the stressful condition.

This study highlights the differential effects of personality on divergent and convergent thinking, and identifies a novel moderation–mediation effect between Neuroticism, threat of evaluation, divergent thinking, and Extraversion.

Source: Chamorro-Premuzic, T., & Reichenbacher, L. (2008). Effects of personality and threats of evaluation on divergent and convergent thinking. *Journal of Research in Personality*, 42, 1095–101. Reproduced with permission from Elsevier.

10.4 DIFFERENTIAL APPROACHES TO CREATIVITY

There are four main differential approaches to creativity, namely:

- The *person* approach, which attempts to identify the major characteristics of creative individuals, looking primarily at the personality traits and ability levels of creative people. As such, it is comparable to the *dispositional* approach to personality (which focuses on the individual rather than the situation or context), although it also deals with the relationship between creativity and established ability constructs.

- The *process* approach to creativity, on the other hand, aims at conceptualizing the cognitive mechanisms underlying the process of creative thinking, for example associative and divergent thinking. Unlike the person approach, process approaches to creativity are not aimed at distinguishing between creative and noncreative individuals, but try to explain the general process of creative thinking in all individuals alike. They are thus concerned with actual creativity rather than creative individuals and draw heavily from cognitive psychology. In fact, the process approach to creativity is best represented by the collaborative effort between cognitive and differential psychologists.

- The *product* approach to creativity studies the characteristics of creative outcomes or products, such as works of art (e.g., paintings, designs, sculptures) and scientific publications (e.g., theories, experiments, discoveries). The product approach is closely related to the study of *aesthetics*, which is a classic area of philosophy. Accordingly, it is largely concerned with productivity and achievement and focuses on individuals' creations rather than their personalities or the processes facilitating creative production (Simonton, 2004).

- Finally, the *press* approach to creativity looks at the relationship between individuals as creators and their environments. It therefore deals with the contextual determinants of creativity, resembling the *situational* rather than dispositional approach to personality. For example, "freedom, autonomy, good role models and resources (including time), encouragement specifically for originality, [and] freedom from criticism" (Runco, 2004, p. 662) are all contextual factors that can be expected to boost creative production and facilitate creative thinking.

Although I have examined several paradigms and approaches to creativity, such distinctions do not always hold in practice. Creativity is a multidisciplinary field and current progress is very much dependent on the integration of different paradigms and opportunities to exchange knowledge between different approaches. Thus there are several journals, such as *Intelligence, Journal of Creative Behavior, Gifted Child Quarterly, Journal of Mental Imagery*, and *Creativity Research Journal*, that encourage researchers to combine different methods and approaches to studying creativity. Those of you interested in the topic may also consult the comprehensive handbooks of creativity compiled by Sternberg (1999) and Runco (1998, 2003a, 2003b).

PHOTO 10.4 *How creative is this?*

Contemporary artists use installations that often require the public to interact with the art works. In the above picture, visitors to London's Tate Modern gallery enjoy – or try to enjoy – an installation that recreates a sunset. Many people (including those who pretend to enjoy such works at the gallery) question whether these forms of art have any creative merit. Can we judge this objectively?

Image courtesy of Tomas Chamorro-Premuzic.

10.5   CREATIVITY AND INTELLIGENCE

To repeat what others have said, requires education; to challenge it, requires brains.

Mary Pettibone Poole

As has been said, early studies on creativity were closely aligned with the study of intelligence (see Chapters 5 and 6). According to Gardner (1993), the reason for this was that creativity researchers had already established careers as intelligence psychometricians. The most salient example was no doubt Guilford (see Section 5.7 in Chapter 5), who quickly became the first leading figure in creativity research. In 1950, Guilford highlighted the importance of increasing creativity research after noting that only 186 of the 121 000 psychological studies in databases had dealt with creativity.

By the 1950s, differential psychologists had provided sufficient evidence in support of the validity and reliability of ability tests, consolidating intelligence as an important psychological construct (see Section 5.3.3 in Chapter 5). Thus any attempt to conceptualize, understand, and measure creativity would have to take into account established ability constructs. This led differential psychologists to explore the relationship between creativity and intelligence, which was the focus of much creativity research until the 1980s and progressively waned thereafter (Barron & Harrington, 1981; Runco, 2004), though there is still much to know about the link between intelligence and creativity.

In an attempt to instill some order in the literature, Sternberg and O'Hara (2000) considered five possible ways in which creativity and intelligence may be related:

- Theories conceptualizing creativity as part of intelligence.
- Theories conceptualizing intelligence as part of creativity.
- Theories conceptualizing creativity and intelligence as identical constructs.
- Theories conceptualizing creativity and intelligence as unrelated constructs.
- Theories conceptualizing creativity and intelligence as related constructs.

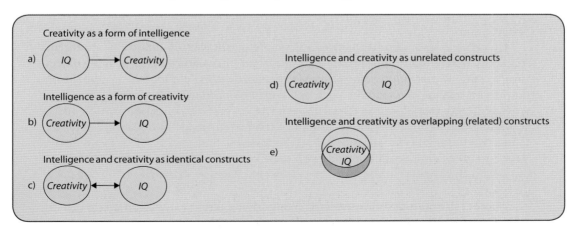

FIGURE 10.5 *Creativity and intelligence*

These hypotheses are summarized in Figure 10.5 and discussed in the forthcoming sections.

In addition, several researchers have conceptualized creativity as an aspect of personality rather than intelligence. Thus Torrance (1979, p. 360) pointed out that "educators and psychologists have tried to make an issue of whether creativity is essentially a personality syndrome that includes openness to experience, adventuresomeness, and self-confidence." The inclusion of creativity in the realm of personality traits is discussed in detail throughout Sections 10.6.1 and 10.6.2.

Despite the significant increase in studies investigating creativity since the 1950s, Guilford's plea for more creativity research has been echoed by experts on several recent occasions (e.g., Runco, 2004; Sternberg & Lubart, 1996).

10.5.1   *Creativity as a Form of Intelligence*

The idea that creativity may be a subset or form of intelligence is not new. Binet's early attempts to design an IQ test (see Brown, 1989) included open-ended items to measure children's imagination (see Section 5.3.3 in Chapter 5), though these were soon dropped because of unsatisfactory reliability.

Until the 1980s, many differential psychologists viewed creativity as an aspect of intelligence. For example, in Barron and Harrington's (1981) review of the literature, the authors still referred to creativity as "an *ability* manifested by performance in critical trials, such as tests, contests, etc." (p. 442, italics added). Moreover, insofar as creativity is associated not only with novel but also with *appropriate* responses, there is arguably a clear component of intelligence in creative thinking (Sternberg & Lubart, 1995).

The most explicit attempt to demonstrate that creativity is a component of intelligence was that of Guilford (1967), who proposed a comprehensive, multidimensional model of intelligence that encompassed more than 120 abilities (see Section 5.7 in Chapter 5). Crucially, one of the intellectual operations described in this model is *divergent production*, which refers to an individual's production of multiple solutions to problems rather than the identification of a single, correct response. If divergent production represents an aspect of intelligence, creativity would be a subset of intelligence, too.

Unfortunately, and unlike convergent thinking, the very definition of divergent thinking implies that it cannot be measured by multiple-choice items, making objective scoring almost impossible. However, Guilford (1975) did identify a number of important aspects of creativity such as *flexibility*, *problem identification*, *fluency*, and *originality* that would set the foundations for later creativity tests (see Section 10.7). Although Guilford is undoubtedly the most influential creativity researcher in differential psychology, his intelligence model (discussed in Section 5.7 in Chapter 5) had a relatively minor impact in the field, with most researchers favoring one-dimensional models such as Spearman's theory of general intelligence (discussed in Section 5.3.4 in Chapter 5).

Another theory that conceptualized creativity as a form of intelligence was that of R.B. Cattell (1971a). In particular, Cattell viewed creativity as a combination of primary skills, such as sensitivity, motor speed, musical rhythm, timing, and judgment, which he considered a subset of *fluid intelligence* (*gf*) (see again Section 5.4 in Chapter 5 for an overview of Cattell's intelligence theory). Interestingly, Cattell argued that personality traits were also important to determine and explain individual differences in creative performance, thus integrating personality and intelligence approaches to creativity (see also Chamorro-Premuzic & Furnham, 2005).

Finally, the view of creativity as an essential aspect of intelligence is also supported by Gardner's (1993) theory of *multiple intelligences* (see Section 8.3.1 in Chapter 8), which comprises eight independent abilities; namely *intrapersonal, logical-mathematical, spatial, bodily-kinesthetic, interpersonal, musical, naturalistic,* and *linguistic*. In a series of case studies, Gardner examined the lives of individuals who excelled at each of these intelligences and made exceptionally creative contributions to the fields of music (Igor Stravinsky), poetry (T.S. Eliot), psychology (Sigmund Freud), politics (Mohandas

PHOTO 10.5 *Mohandas Gandhi, a very influential politician*

© Bettmann/Corbis.

Gandhi), and others. According to Gardner, the creative achievement of these individuals can be explained as much by their unusually high levels of domain-relevant abilities as by their unusually low levels of other, domain-irrelevant abilities. For instance, Gardner notes that Freud had very high verbal ability but very low spatial and musical abilities. In any case, no combination of ability levels would be sufficient to explain creative achievement, because personality characteristics such as focus, persistence, and passion would play an equally important role in determining creativity levels.

10.5.2 Intelligence as a Form of Creativity

The conception of intelligence as a form or expression of creativity posits that one of the aspects of intelligence is the ability to shape one's environment (Ochse, 1990). A paradigmatic model that regards creativity as the precondition for intelligence is Sternberg and Lubart's (1995, 1996) **investment theory**, named after the idea that creative individuals have an extraordinary ability to invest in ideas, "buying low and selling high" (Sternberg & O'Hara, 2000). The authors also posit that creativity is an important determinant of intelligent thinking and intelligent behavior, because it enables individuals to "think differently" and "defy the crowd." For example, if a large number of individuals are buying property in a specific area or city, creative individuals may interpret this as a bad investment opportunity and avoid buying at already high prices, hence creativity would be beneficial for solving practical problems effectively.

investment theory
theory according to which creative individuals have an exceptional ability to invest in ideas; thus, creativity is seen as a precondition of intelligence and a determinant of intelligent thinking and behavior.

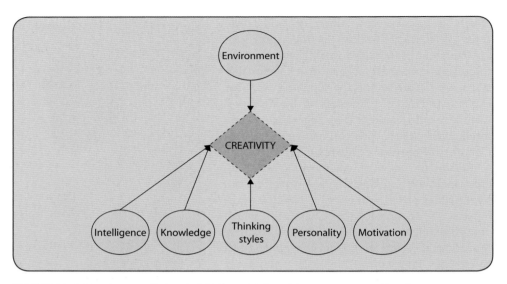

FIGURE 10.6 *Sternberg and Lubart's (1995) model: Creativity as a superset of intelligence*

Likewise, creativity may help individuals to "redefine" problems. As Sternberg and O'Hara (2000, p. 615) observed,

> Einstein redefined the way physicists and others understand physical laws and how they function in the universe. Darwin redefined the way we view the development of organisms over the aeons. Picasso redefined the way we perceive possibilities for artistic expression.

Thus creativity would enable individuals not just to solve problems, but to do so in new ways.

Figure 10.6 depicts Sternberg and Lubart's (1995) model in which six different factors converge to determine creativity; namely, *intelligence*, *knowledge*, *thinking styles*, *personality*, *motivation*, and the *environment*. When psychometrically assessed, each of these factors can be regarded as a proxy measure for creative thinking and creative behavior. Thus the arrows are pointed in the direction of the criterion variable – creativity – stemming from the predictors. Theoretically, this implies that the latent variable of creativity operates as a superset of the other factors.

Sternberg argued that three aspects of intelligence underlie individual differences in creativity; namely, *synthetic*, *analytical*, and *practical* intelligences. Synthetic intelligence is used to combine different cognitions and produce novel associations, such as in the case of insight. Analytical intelligence is important because it enables creative individuals to judge the value or appropriateness of an idea. Last but not least, practical intelligence would be advantageous for applying creative ideas in everyday life and "selling" them to others (for a review of Sternberg's creativity theory, see Sternberg & O'Hara, 2000).

10.5.3   Creativity and Intelligence as Identical Constructs

Some theorists have argued that creativity and intelligence are merely two different names for the same construct. This would require psychometric scores on creativity and intelligence measures to be highly intercorrelated, though since intelligence and creativity measures are not perfect, both types of tests may be tapping different but related aspects of the same underlying variable. Accordingly, Haensly and Reynolds (1989) conceptualized creativity and intelligence as a "unitary phenomenon" in which creativity would be regarded as the ultimate manifestation of intellectual ability.

Based on the theoretical similarities between the processes underlying creative and intelligent problem solving, Weisberg and Alba (1981; see also Perkins, 1981) argued that no qualitative differences exist between creativity and intelligence. Rather, the same cognitive mechanisms are employed when solving both creativity and intelligence problems.

The famous *nine-dot problem*, shown in Figure 10.7, is often used as an example of there being no real differences between creative and intelligent thinking, as the "correct" solution is also the "creative" solution. Intelligent people, then, would also be more able to "think outside the box." This is consistent with Barron's (1963, p. 219) idea that "[t]he very difficult and rarely solved problem requires by definition a solution that is original."

10.5.4   Creativity and Intelligence as Unrelated Constructs

A fourth interpretation of the relationship between creativity and intelligence is that they are completely unrelated constructs. As is often the case in psychology, two conflicting views can coexist on theoretical or empirical grounds, mainly due to ambiguous

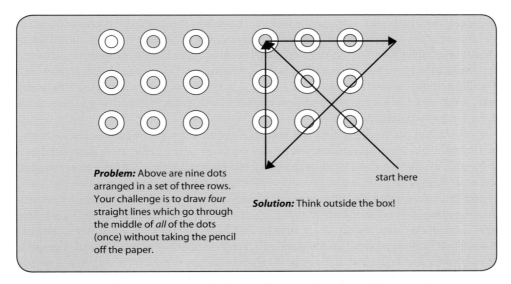

Problem: Above are nine dots arranged in a set of three rows. Your challenge is to draw *four* straight lines which go through the middle of *all* of the dots (once) without taking the pencil off the paper.

Solution: Think outside the box!

start here

FIGURE 10.7 *Thinking "outside the box": when intelligent and creative solutions are the same*

Source: Based on Weisberg & Alba (1981).

empirical evidence. The view of creativity and intelligence as unrelated variables is the complete opposite of the hypothesis examined in Section 10.5.3.

Conceptually, the independence of creativity from intelligence would be supported by the fact that, while intelligence refers to adaptation to existing environments, creativity involves *changing* existing environments to create new ones (Sternberg, 1985b). In that sense, creativity and intelligence would almost be mutually exclusive: if a response is intelligent, it cannot be creative, and if behavior is creative, it cannot be intelligent. Along these lines, Sternberg and O'Hara (2000, p. 611) noted:

> the ability to adapt to the environment – to change oneself to suit the environment – typically involves little or possibly no creativity and may even require one to suppress creativity. For example, adaptation to a school or job environment can in some instances mean keeping one's creative ideas to oneself or else risking a low grade or job evaluation.

Empirically, low or nonsignificant correlations between creativity and intelligence would be needed to support the idea that both constructs are unrelated. However, most findings reported significant and positive correlations between both measures. These are reviewed in the forthcoming sections.

10.5.5 Creativity and Intelligence as Overlapping (Related) Constructs

The most widely held view on the relationship between creativity and intelligence is that both constructs are related. In psychometric terms, this means that creativity and intelligence share a substantial amount of variance; in plain English, this means that creativity and intelligence have much in common. Whether the relationship between creativity and intelligence reflects the influence of the former on the latter or vice versa, or whether third-order variables (e.g., personality, motivation, educational level) may be affecting both constructs, are questions that cannot be answered by correlational studies. If, nonetheless, one is to support the claim that creativity and intelligence are related constructs, it is necessary to find positive correlations between measures of creativity and intelligence, and that is what differential psychologists have largely attempted to do.

Early attempts to document the relationship between intelligence and creativity were based on biographical measures of creativity and intelligence. A well-known series of studies by Cox (1926) retrospectively estimated the intelligence scores and creative impact level of a total of 301 eminences who lived between 1450 and 1850. Their level of impact was measured in terms of encyclopedic space (length of biographical article), while their IQ was estimated on the basis of biographical accounts; that is, information about their intellectual achievements. For instance, Francis Galton's IQ was estimated at 200 points because he could read books at the age of 2, speak Latin and French at the age of 4, and memorize pages of Shakespeare after a single read at the age of 7.

Although there are obvious limitations underlying this methodology, Cox's data provided interesting preliminary evidence for the relationship between creativity and intelligence. The correlation between eminence or level of creative impact and intelligence was significant but modest (in the region of $r = .16$), leading Cox to conclude that "high, but not the highest intelligence" was associated with achievement, and that personality variables such as persistence may play a more substantial role (the relationship between personality and creativity is discussed in Sections 10.6.1 and 10.6.2).

More direct evidence for the relationship between creativity and intelligence derived from Barron (1963), who administered divergent thinking and cognitive ability tests to students, army officers, writers, artists, and businessmen. Barron also asked "experts" on each domain to rate the creativity level of participants within that group in order to test whether creativity may manifest itself differently across domains.

Results showed correlations between creativity and intelligence measures in the region of $r = .40$. Although such correlations suggest that there is a significant overlap between creativity and intelligence, Barron noted that when participants' IQ was higher than 120, IQ scores were a poor predictor of creativity. For example, in a sample of army officers with an average IQ of 100, creativity and intelligence correlated in the vicinity of $r = .30$, but in a sample of architects with an average IQ of 130, the correlation between intelligence and creativity was only $r = -.08$.

Subsequent studies reported rather variable correlations between intelligence and creativity, ranging from as little as $r = -.05$ up to $r = .30$ (Barron & Harrington, 1981), though correlations between intelligence and divergent thinking tend to be higher, averaging $r = .30$ (Horn, 1976; Richards, 1976). At best, then, creativity and intelligence are related but *distinct* constructs. In an attempt to differentiate between creativity and intelligence, Shouksmith (1973) argued that intelligence is needed to provide "correct" responses to problems, while creativity would be required to provide "good" responses. If, however, good responses are also correct, creative responding is also intelligent and intelligence would be conceptualized as a prerequisite of creativity. This idea, often referred to as the **threshold theory of creativity and intelligence**, implies that a minimum level of intelligence is required to be creative (Guilford, 1967). For example, Guilford and Christensen (1973) found that students with lower intelligence scores rated significantly lower in creativity, but those with higher intelligence scores were neither significantly higher nor lower in creativity. Thus, intelligence is necessary but not sufficient for creative thinking (Schubert, 1973).

threshold theory of creativity and intelligence the idea that a minimum level of intelligence is required in order to be creative, but that intelligence does not of itself determine creative thinking.

In support of the threshold theory, studies indicated that the correlation between creativity and intelligence tends to drop when IQ scores are higher than 120 (Getzels & Jackson, 1962). Conversely, other studies reported that creative artists, scientists, mathematicians, and writers all tend to score higher than average on IQ tests (e.g., Bachtold & Werner, 1970; Barron, 1969; Cattell, 1971a; Helson, 1971; Helson & Crutchfield, 1970).

Part of the variability in these correlations may be explained by the different ability and creativity domains examined. For instance, fluid intelligence is likely to play a greater role in mathematics and physics than in music, fine arts, and humanities. Correlations between intelligence and creativity are also likely to vary depending on the type of creativity measure employed. For instance, Mednick and Andrews (1967) found correlations as high as $r = .55$ between the WISC (see Section 6.2 in Chapter 6) and a Remote Associations Test (Mednick & Mednick, 1967), which requires

three-ring theory of giftedness model that conceptualizes an overlap between creativity and intelligence, arguing that giftedness lies at the intersection between creativity, IQ, and task commitment (level of motivation, conscientiousness, determination, and passion).

participants to provide the correct answer for each problem (see Section 10.7).

A more conceptual approach to the possible overlap between creativity and IQ has been considered by Renzulli (1978, 1986). This model, often referred to as the **"three-ring" theory of giftedness**, is represented in Figure 10.8 and conceptualizes giftedness at the crossroads between creativity, IQ, and task commitment, which may be understood in terms of motivation, conscientiousness, determination, and passion.

It has also been noted that creativity may be related more to "perceived" than to "actual" intelligence, though higher correlations between other estimates of intelligence and creativity may simply result from the broader conception of intelligence held by nonexperts. Thus laypeople may confound the meaning of creativity and intelligence, thinking that they are the same. Accordingly, Sternberg (1985c) asked people to estimate both the intelligence and the creativity of imaginary targets and found a correlation of $r = .69$ between people's creativity and intelligence ratings.

Finally, it has also been argued (e.g., Simonton, 1994; Sternberg, 1999) that intellectual ability (as measured by IQ tests) may hinder rather than enhance creative performance. This hypothesis has been postulated on the basis of the lower incentives that higher IQ individuals may have to seek novel rather than correct responses. Furthermore, to the extent that higher IQ is associated with higher levels of knowledge, individuals with higher IQ would be less motivated and in addition likely to defy the status quo and come up with original solutions. Despite the theoretical soundness of this argument, negative correlations between creativity and intelligence have rarely been reported. On the contrary, most studies report a positive correlation between creativity and intelligence, leaving little room for the idea that intellectual ability is a disadvantage for creativity, though the threshold view of creativity and intelligence is not totally at odds with this idea.

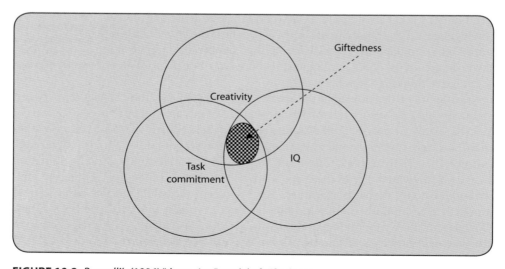

FIGURE 10.8 *Renzulli's (1986) "three-ring" model of giftedness*

10.6   CREATIVITY AND PERSONALITY TRAITS

> The creation of something new is not accomplished by the intellect but by the play instinct acting from inner necessity. The creative mind plays with the objects it loves.
>
> Carl Jung (1875–1961)

Soon after examining the link between intelligence and creativity, differential psychologists began to search for personality correlates of creativity in the hope of accounting for unique variance in creativity over and above intelligence. However, the lack of consensus on the identification of the main personality traits needed to describe individual differences (see Section 2.10 in Chapter 2) meant that early attempts to identify the personality correlates of creativity included a random and extensive list of personality adjectives comprising many overlapping dimensions.

PHOTO 10.6 *Conformist, me?*

Personality explains why some people are more motivated to stand out and do things differently, for instance dressing up eccentrically.

Image courtesy of Tomas Chamorro-Premuzic.

FOCUS POINT 10.2   CREATIVE PERSONALITY

In a seminal review of the literature, Barron and Harrington (1981) noted that creative individuals could be described in terms of their

> high valuation of aesthetic qualities in experience, broad interests, attraction to complexity, high energy, independence of judgment, autonomy, intuition, self-confidence, ability to resolve antinomies or to accommodate apparently opposite or conflicting traits in one's self-concept, and finally, a firm sense of self as 'creative.' (Barron & Harrington, 1981, p. 453)

Further adjectives included

> active, alert, ambitious, argumentative, artistic, assertive, capable, clear thinking, clever, complicated, confident, curious, cynical, demanding, egotistical, energetic, enthusiastic, hurried, idealistic, imaginative, impulsive, independent, individualistic, ingenious, insightful, intelligent, interested widely, inventive, original, practical, quick, rebellious, reflective, resourceful, self-confident, sensitive, sharp-witted, spontaneous, unconventional, versatile, and *not* conventional and *not* inhibited. (Barron & Harrington, 1981, p. 454)

PHOTO 10.7 *Two to tango*

Creative activities are intrinsically motivating, meaning that you enjoy the actual process and do not perform them as a means to an end. You should still tip the dancers, though!

Image courtesy of Nadia Bettega, reproduced with permission.

Barron (1963) was one of the first to emphasize the personality differences between creative and noncreative individuals, particularly those with higher and lower intellectual ability. While creative individuals with lower intellectual ability could be portrayed as "affected, aggressive, demanding, dependent, dominant, forceful, impatient, taking initiative, outspoken, sarcastic, strong, and suggestive," those with higher intelligence but lower creativity scores were better classified as "mild, optimistic, pleasant, quiet, unselfish" (Barron, 1963, p. 22). This description was later expanded (see Focus Point 10.2).

Creative individuals are also thought to be more *intrinsically* motivated (see Section 9.4.8 in Chapter 9) than their noncreative counterparts. This means that they tend to engage in activities and tasks because they enjoy doing them rather than because of the rewards for performing such tasks. Conversely, noncreative individuals tend to be involved in activities not necessarily for the tasks themselves but for their benefit, for instance high salary or social recognition, and are thus *extrinsically* motivated. Furthermore, extrinsic interests may hinder creative thinking because evaluations may constrain freedom of choice (Amabile, 1990).

10.6.1 Creativity in Abnormal Behavior (Psychopathology)

There is a thin line between genius and insanity.

The idea that creative behavior may be a consequence or the cause of psychopathology has been considered for several centuries (see Figure 10.9) and was emphatically expressed in the late work of Eysenck (1999), who believed that there is a substantial overlap between the processes underpinning creative and psychopathological thinking. Furthermore, Eysenck's Psychoticism trait (see Section 2.6 in Chapter 2) was thought of as a predictor of creativity, though that trait may refer to both normal and abnormal personalities.

Eysenck thought that most forms of psychoses – mental disorders distinguished by detachment from reality – were characterized by the same cognitive processes underlying creative thinking. The best example of such shared processes is **overinclusive thinking**, which is the tendency to use irrelevant information in problem solving (see Al-issa, 1972). Thus Barron and Harrington (1981, p. 462) noted that "the tendency to introduce complexity in perception goes both with creativity and with schizophrenia."

overinclusive thinking the tendency to use irrelevant information or to introduce complexity in solving problems, characteristic of both creative and psychopathological thinking.

Conversely, humanistic psychologists such as Maslow (1971) and Rogers (1980) have argued that creativity is associated with psychological health rather than mental disorders. Furthermore, they believed that creative individuals have a greater sense of *self-actualization* (see Section 9.4.9 in Chapter 9) and longevity, implying that creativity is also associated with good physical health. This assumption runs counter to several studies where creativity was positively correlated with alcoholism (Nobel, Runco, & Ozkaragoz, 1993), suicide (Lester, 1999), and stress (Carson & Runco, 1999).

FIGURE 10.9 *Creativity and mental illness*

From top left (clockwise): Schumann, Tchaikovsky, Van Gogh, Hemingway, Poe, and Newton. All experienced psychopathological symptoms.

Sources: POPPERFOTO/ Getty; INTERFOTO/Alamy; Library of Congress, Washington, DC, USA/The Bridgeman Art Library; Library of Congress, LC-USZ62-10610; akg-images/Nimatallah.

PHOTO 10.8 *The famous picture of Einstein that is often used to denote the thin line between genius and insanity.*

© Bettmann/Corbis.

Overall, the literature shows a relatively inconsistent pattern of results for the relationship between creativity measures and diverse indicators of abnormal behavior, though associations between creativity and mental disorders have been frequent. For example, Heston (1966) studied 47 children of American schizophrenic mothers who were raised by foster parents. Although half of them exhibited psychosocial disability, they possessed elevated artistic talents and demonstrated imaginative adaptations to life that were uncommon in a control group.

Other studies have looked at the link between creativity (or at least proxy measures of it) and Eysenck's Psychoticism trait (see Section 2.6 in Chapter 2). For example, Farmer (1974) found that Psychoticism was highly correlated with divergent thinking, whereas Woody and Claridge (1977) reported positive correlations between Psychoticism and self-reported creativity in a sample of 100 undergraduate students. In addition, *fluency* or quantity of ideas was positively correlated with Psychoticism (in the range of $r = .32$ to $r = .45$), and so was *originality* or quantity of unique ideas. Indeed, correlations between originality and Psychoticism were substantial, ranging from $r = .61$ to $r = .68$. Other personality variables were not found to be significantly correlated with any indicators of creativity.

Studies looking at the possible psychopathological aspects of creativity have analyzed not only student samples but also artists. In a well-cited study, Götz and Götz (1979a) showed that professional artists tended to have significantly higher scores on Psychoticism than a control group had. The authors conducted a follow-up study to compare the Psychoticism scores of successful versus unsuccessful professional artists and found that, as predicted, successful artists tended to be significantly more psychotic than their counterparts. No significant differences were found on other personality traits, such as Extraversion and Neuroticism (Götz & Götz, 1979b).

Several researchers failed to replicate the significant association between Psychoticism and creativity. For example, Kline and Cooper (1986) measured creativity through flexibility of closure, spontaneous flexibility, ideational fluency, word fluency, and originality, but found no significant correlations between any of these measures and Psychoticism (except for fluency in males). When Eysenck and Furnham (1993) tested the relationship between personality and creativity using the EPQ and the Barron-Welsh Art Scale (Barron & Welsh, 1952), they found no significant correlation between creativity and Psychoticism, though psychotic students were more likely to dislike art works than were their less psychotic counterparts. Thus Psychoticism may relate to aesthetic preference rather than creative output.

Researchers have also considered the possibility of a curvilinear relationship between creativity and psychopathology, whereby a moderate level of originality is indicative of normal creativity, whereas extremely high levels of originality may refer to Psychoticism or mental disorders such as schizophrenia (see Gough, 1976; Upmanyu, Bhardwaj, & Singh, 1996). In their study, Upmanyu, Bhardwaj, and Singh (1996) found that extremely unique word associations were related to Psychoticism and psychopathic deviation, while moderately unusual responses were indicators of creativity and verbal ability. Accordingly, Psychoticism contributes toward creativity in that it predisposes individuals to reject existing norms. This would explain the link of Psychoticism with antisocial behavior and lack of conformity.

More recent studies have often failed to replicate significant correlations between Psychoticism and creativity. For instance, Martindale and Dailey (1996) used several measures of personality (EPQ: Eysenck & Eysenck, 1975; NEO-PI: Costa & McCrae, 1985) and creativity (Fantasy story composition, Alternate Uses Test, and Remoteness of Association), but found low and nonsignificant correlations between these scales.

When creativity and personality are examined across different occupational domains, Psychoticism levels are significantly higher in "creative" professions. For example, Merten and Fischer (1999) compared actors, writers, and schizophrenics with a control group. They used a word association test requiring common and uncommon responses (Merten, 1995), two tests of verbal creativity (Schoppe, 1975), and two story-writing tasks as measures of creativity. Actors and writers scored higher on Psychoticism and original word associations than the control group. Artists (writers and actors) did not produce any response repetitions in the unusual response conditions, whereas schizophrenics did.

Despite the conceptual and psychometric associations between creativity and different forms of psychopathology, such as schizophrenia, there are no doubt salient features that differentiate creative from mentally ill individuals; such features should not be undermined. Perhaps the most important element to distinguish between creativity and psychopathology is the manifestation of *symptoms*. While creative products may – at least in a metaphorical sense – be regarded as the symptoms of creativity, the psychopathological conception of symptoms refers to the expression of unbearable, painful, and uncontrollable psychological or physical outcomes (see Sections 4.2 and 4.7 in Chapter 4).

Thus creative individuals may have every intention of producing original associations, while psychotic individuals may have little alternative or control over their original, unusual, or eccentric ideas. Accordingly, Barron interpreted creativity as a form of controlled weirdness. Mental patients, on the other hand, may not even be aware of the creative nature of their ideas (Merten & Fischer, 1999, p. 941).

FOCUS POINT 10.3   COULD CREATIVITY BE ASSOCIATED WITH INSOMNIA?

Creative people tend to be highly energetic. Time, personal investment, and commitment often characterize these young talents. It has therefore been suggested that task commitment, defined as the level of engagement with a given task, could be used as an indicator of giftedness; at very high levels, individuals would experience a sort of "binge" and get highly absorbed in their work.

At all ages, there seems to be a connection between creativity and time invested. For instance, in order to be creative, individuals may have to borrow time from their daily routine. This could involve staying up late, or even not sleeping, which could suggest a link between insomnia and creativity.

As anybody who has experienced it would know (and most people have), insomnia relates to difficulties in initiating or maintaining sleep.

Its most important determinant, in conjunction with sleep problems, is an overactive mind, including problem solving, reappraisal, planning, and rehearsal while trying to fall asleep. The processes involved in insomnia therefore mirror the ones underlying the process of creative cognition. Thus it is possible that a person deeply involved in creative processes could be at risk of developing insomnia.

Due to the lack of research into the sleep patterns of creative people, and the possible impact these can have on creative processes, Healey and Runco's study aims to examine empirically the relationship between sleep disturbance and creative potential. It was hypothesized that people with creative potential were expected to experience more insomnia than their less creative counterparts.

METHOD

PARTICIPANTS

In all, 60 children from New Zealand aged 10–12 years were recruited. They were divided into two groups: 30 (14 male, 16 female; mean age = 11.0, *S.D.* = 0.84) were identified as highly creative by scoring above the 90th percentile (mean percentile = 94.77, *S.D.* = 3.56) on the Torrance Tests of Creative Thinking (TTCT), Figural Form A; and the other 30 (13 male, 17 female; mean age = 11.10, *S.D.* = 0.89) were classified as controls with creativity scores below the 90th percentile (mean percentile = 45.97, *S.D.* = 23.37).

MEASURES

Creative potential was measured using the TTCT, Figural Form A. It consists of three tasks, all of which involve coming up with unusual drawings that have standard shapes as part of them (e.g., two parallel lines). Each drawing was scored on five subscales: originality, fluency, elaboration, abstractness of titles, and resistance to premature closure. The final percentile ranking was based on a combination of these five subscale scores as well as additional aspects such as humor, emotional expressiveness, and richness of imagery.

The sleep-related items on the Child Depression Inventory (CDI) and the Revised Child Manifest Anxiety Scale (RCMAS) were used to measure the presence or absence, as well as severity, of sleep disturbance.

The RCMAS involved children circling "yes" or "no" to statements depending whether they thought it was relevant to how they felt about themselves (statements pertaining to sleep were "It's hard for me to get to sleep at night" and "I worry when I go to bed").

The CDI involved children picking out one statement out of three that best described the way they were feeling about themselves in the past two weeks in relation to sleep (statements pertaining to sleep were "I have trouble sleeping every night," "I have trouble sleeping many nights,"" I sleep pretty well").

Participants were given a score ranging from 0 to 4, with 0 indicating no sleep disturbance and 4 indicating persistent sleep disturbances.

RESULTS

Of the 30 highly creative children, 17 (57 percent) showed signs of sleep disturbance (i.e., had a positive score on one or more of the sleep-related questions) compared to only 8 (27 percent) of the control children, indicating a significant difference: $X2(1,60) = 5.55, p < .05$.

Also, there was a significant, positive correlation between creativity and sleep disturbances, $r = .31, p < .05$. Further, the sleep disturbance between the two groups resulted in a large effect size (Cohen's $d = .98$).

DISCUSSION

The results support the hypothesis that creative children experience more sleep disturbance than noncreative children. They also lend support to the theory that due to the cognitive processing and level of mental activity associated with creativity (i.e., planning and problem solving), creative individuals may be at higher risk of developing insomnia.

The relationship between creativity and insomnia has implications for our understanding of the connection between creativity and psychopathology. Although the precise causal direction underlying this relationship is yet to be identified, it is plausible to suggest that higher creativity would lead to insomnia, which, in turn, could both foster certain creative processes but also impair individuals' creative performance (after a night of poor sleep).

One limitation of this study is that very elementary measures of sleep disturbance were used. Also, as is the case with several creativity studies, the creativity questionnaire used in the current study measures only one aspect of creativity – namely creative potential – rather than the broad domain of creativity. Despite these limitations, due to the lack of research into disturbed sleep patterns and creativity, this study makes for interesting preliminary findings in this area.

Source: Healey, D. & Runco, M.A. (2006). Could creativity be associated with insomnia? *Creativity Research Journal*, 18(1), 39–43. Reprinted by permission of Taylor & Francis Group.

10.6.2   Creativity in Normal Behavior (the Big Five)

Early studies on creativity and personality were characterized by the lack of convergence in the personality traits assessed. Since the acceptance of the Big Five model (see Section 2.11 in Chapter 2), psychologists have found a common language to report findings on the relationship between creativity and personality traits and assess the extent to which creativity may be explained in terms of individual differences in normal behavior. Moreover, the Big Five model also enables researchers to interpret the significant personality correlates of creativity retrospectively by translating different traits into the Big Five personality dimensions (see Table 10.1).

The most important personality correlate of creativity is Openness to Experience, a trait referring to individual differences in aesthetic preferences, values, fantasy, feeling, actions, and ideas related to novelty and intellectual experiences. Some have even argued that Openness should be interpreted as a self-reported measure of creativity, and consequently prefer the label of "Creativity" for this trait (Chamorro-Premuzic & Furnham, 2005; Matthews & Deary, 1998). Regardless of the labels we use, studies have found consistent positive links between Openness and different indicators of creativity.

Dollinger and Clancy (1993) reported a positive association between participants' Openness and their ability to improvise autobiographical story-essays on the basis of pictures. "Richness" of essays was mostly correlated with *aesthetic openness* in men and *ideas* in women. Furthermore, among females, richness was also positively correlated

Table 10.1 *The creative personality and the Big Five*

- **Originality:** Each response is compared with all other responses from all of the people to whom you gave the test. Responses that were given by only 5 percent of the sample are unusual (1 point), responses that were given by only 1 percent of your group are unique (2 points).
- **Fluency:** Quantity regardless of quality (the higher the fluency, the higher the originality; this "contamination" problem can be corrected by using the formula originality = originality/fluency).
- **Flexibility:** Use of different categories.
- **Elaboration:** Amount of detail, for example, "a doorstop" = 0 whereas "a doorstop to prevent a door slamming shut in a strong wind" = 2 (one for explanation of door slamming, two for further detail about the wind).
- **Appropriateness:** How useful (according to experts) the response is.

with Neuroticism. King, Walker, and Broyles (1996) found that verbal creativity was positively correlated with Extraversion and Openness to Experience, and negatively with Agreeableness. Multiple regression analysis revealed that Openness was the most significant predictor of creativity, a finding replicated by Furnham (1999).

Openness has also been found to be beneficial for creative performance in work settings (George & Zhou, 2001), particularly when there are many ways of performing a task or solving a problem. In that sense, Openness would have the reverse effect to Conscientiousness, which favors performance on structured, predefined tasks and is thus detrimental to creativity.

In what is usually regarded as the first comprehensive meta-analysis of the creativity literature, Feist (1998) investigated the role of creativity and personality in the arts and sciences. In order to analyze the disparate collection of personality data, data from 83 experiments were recoded into the Big Five taxonomy. Three main groups were compared, scientists vs. non-scientists; creative vs. less creative scientists; and artists vs. nonartists. Results indicated that Openness, Extraversion, and Conscientiousness could be used to distinguish accurately between scientists and nonscientists. The traits that most strongly distinguished the creative from the less creative scientists were Extraversion and Openness. Artists, on the other hand, were approximately one standard deviation lower on Conscientiousness and half a standard deviation higher on Openness than nonartists.

A year later, Feist (1999) summarized the findings on the link between personality and creative achievement in the arts and the sciences. He concluded that some personality traits are equally expressed in artists and scientists. For instance, both creative scientists and artists were found to be more open to new experiences, less conventional, less conscientious, more self-confident, more self-accepting, more driven, more ambitious, more dominant, more hostile, and more impulsive than their less creative counterparts. However, artists were found to be more affective, less emotionally stable, less socialized, and less accepting of group norms than the scientists, who tended to be more conscientious than the artists. If creativity is manifested in different personality traits across disciplines or academic domains, the idea of an overarching creative personality may be elusive.

Feist and Barron (2003) conducted a 55-year longitudinal study on personality and creativity on a sample of 80 male graduates from 14 different academic departments, looking at possible changes in the correlation between creativity and personality throughout adulthood. They hypothesized that personality would predict variance in creative achievement over and above the measures of ability and potential. Although complete personality data were only available for 43 participants, results indicated that personality traits at the age of 27 predicted originality and creative achievement until the age of 72, even when potential and ability were taken into account.

In a recent review of the literature, Chamorro-Premuzic and Furnham (2005) organized the Big Five personality traits according to whether they were positively or negatively related to creativity. They concluded that Neuroticism, Extraversion, and notably Openness to Experience are positively linked to creativity, whereas Agreeableness and Conscientiousness are negatively correlated with creativity (see again Table 10.1). However, the authors argued that a combination of both personality and intelligence is needed to explain and predict individual differences in creativity.

10.7   TESTING CREATIVITY

The first attempts at measuring creativity date back to the beginnings of IQ testing, when Binet developed open-ended tests such as sentence completion and interpretation of ink blots (Binet & Henri, 1896). Due to the difficulties associated with implementing an objective scoring system for these tests – an issue that continues to pose methodological challenges for creativity researchers today – open-ended problems were soon replaced by multiple-choice questions, which have since represented the common approach to intelligence testing. Whereas multiple-choice questions are useful to measure abilities, they are poor predictors of creativity as they require participants to provide a single, predefined correct response.

Alternate Uses Test a **divergent thinking** test that requires individuals to name all the things that can be done with a specified object, e.g., a chair.

However, several scoring mechanisms have been devised to increase the reliability of open-ended creativity measures. For example, the **Alternate Uses Test** requires individuals to "name all the things you can do with *x* object (e.g., hammer, brick, chair)" and can be scored in terms of *originality*, *fluency*, *flexibility*, and *elaboration*. Some have argued that it is also important to consider the *appropriateness* of responses, as creative ideas should not only be original but also useful (Runco & Charles, 1993). All scoring methods are explained in Table 10.2 (see also Figure 1.10 in Chapter 1).

Remote Associations Test psychometric test that requires participants to identify the correct associations between word groups; remote or unusual associations indicate individuals' capacity for generating novel or original ideas.

Another widely used measure of creativity is Mednick and Mednick's (1967) **Remote Associations Test**. This 30-item psychometric test is based on items with a single correct response rather than open-ended questions. Mednick's idea was that remote or unusual associations would be indicative of an individual's capacity for generating novel ideas, as remote combinations are generally more original. For example, participants may be asked to identify a fourth word that is associated with each of the following triads of words:

Table 10.2   *Scoring methods for the Alternate Uses test*

- **Consequences Test** (Guilford, 1954): "Imagine what might happen if all laws were suddenly abolished."
- **Remote Associations Test** (Mednick, 1962): Find a fourth word that is associated with each of these three words: (a) rat–blue–cottage; (b) wheel–electric–light; (c) surprise–line–birthday.
- **Unusual Uses Test** (Guilford, 1954): "Find as many uses as you can think of for (a) toothpick; (b) brick, (c) paperclip.
- **Word Association Test** (Getzels & Jackson, 1962): Write as many meanings as you can for the following (a) duck; (b) sack; (c) pitch.
- **Creative Test Battery:** *Torrance Test of Creative Thinking* (TTCT): Three picture-based exercises and six word-based exercises (figural and verbal). Does a good job of identifying gifted students.

(a) rat–blue–cottage–*???*

(b) railroad–girl–class–*???*

(c) surprise–line–birthday–*???*

(d) wheel–electric–high–*???*

(e) out–dog–call–*???*

Even if you guessed the answers (see p. 324), you may have noticed that there is still a degree of subjectivity in the choice of "correct" responses, more so than in standard IQ test items. Ultimately, the quality of creativity tests, and the extent to which we believe that such tests actually measure creativity, will depend on statistical indicators of validity and reliability.

Validation of creativity tests is no different than in ability or IQ measures. Thus *predictive* validity refers to the extent to which scores on creativity measures predict real-life indicators of creativity. *Incremental* validity refers to the extent to which creativity tests account for unique variance in selected outcomes beyond, say, personality and ability measures. *Discriminant* validity, on the other hand, refers to the extent to which creativity tests measure a unique construct, different from established personality and ability traits. Reliability is a more complex issue as it usually involves consensus between different judges, for instance on how "appropriate" a creative response may be. Reliability can be achieved through expert or majority consensus and is a necessary but not sufficient condition for validity.

Tests of divergent thinking represent the most widely employed measure of creativity and have been reported to be good predictors of creative achievement across a variety of settings (Barron & Harrington, 1981; Harrington, 1972) and at all levels of education (Anastasi & Schaefer, 1971; Torrance, 1974; Vernon, 1971). However, associations are often weak and "there is little reason to expect any randomly selected divergent thinking test to correlate with creative achievement in any randomly selected domain" (Barron & Harrington, 1981, p. 448). Besides, several factors, from time of day to type of instructions, may affect the correlation between creativity tests and indicators of creative achievement. For example, asking people to "be creative" will normally improve their performance on divergent thinking tests (Datta, 1963).

To this day, the best regarded test of creativity is the **Torrance Test of Creativity and Thinking** (TTCT; Torrance, 1974), which is based on the earlier version of Torrance's (1966) creativity test. The test measures divergent production of semantic units (e.g., "name all the things you can think of that are red and edible"); alternative relations (e.g., "in what different ways are dogs and cats related"); and production of systems (e.g., "write as many sentences you can using the words 'rain,' 'station,' and 'summer'").

Torrance Test of Creativity and Thinking test that measures creative thinking using picture-based and word-based exercises to assess fluency, flexibility (number of different categories of response), originality, and elaboration (amount of detail).

Torrance spent several decades conducting follow-up studies and reanalyzing datasets to validate his test. Longitudinal studies have shown that the aggregated creativity score provided by the different sections of the TTCT correlated in the region of $r = .51$ with creative achievement measures (Torrance, 1975). Torrance's review of creativity studies also led him to conclude that intelligence and creativity are only moderately associated: "No matter

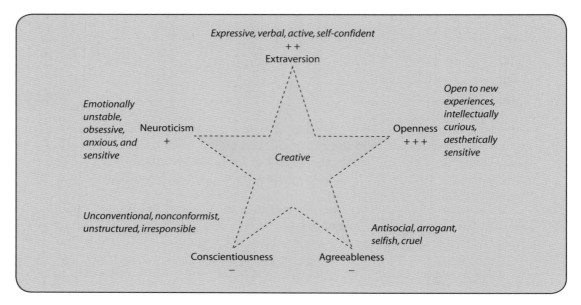

FIGURE 10.10 *Salient creativity measures*

what measure of IQ is chosen, we would exclude about 70% of our most creative children if IQ alone were used in identifying giftedness" (Torrance, 1963, p. 182). For an overview of traditional measures of creativity, see Figure 10.10.

In more recent years there have been some interesting innovations in creativity testing, notably by Sternberg and colleagues. For example, Sternberg's (1982) adaptation of the Goodman (1955) induction riddle requires participants to manipulate imaginary concepts such as "bleen" (blue until 2004, but green after that year), or "grue" (green until the year 2004, and blue after that). In a similar fashion, Sternberg and Gastel (1989) designed a test that requires individuals to evaluate logically valid but factually false statements, such as "lions can fly." Assuming that these items are useful to test individuals' flexibility, Sternberg's tests of induction are measuring an important component of creativity. Indeed, moderate correlations between these measures and fluid ability tests may be indicative of the discriminant validity of Sternberg's tests. Whether these tests measure creativity, flexibility, or something else is a matter of interpretation, however.

10.8   CREATIVITY IN DIFFERENT FIELDS (FROM ARTS TO SCIENCE)

Feist (1998) noticed that research into personality and creativity could be divided into two forms. The first attempts to identify significant personality differences *between groups*, such as artists versus scientists. The second is based on an analysis of *within-group* differences and aims at comparing the personality profiles of highly creative and non-creative individuals working in the same field. According to Feist, scientists show a larger variation in creativity ratings because they are frequently involved in "very routine, rote, and prescribed" tasks, in addition to the few scientists engaged in "revolutionary" work, whereas "anyone who makes a living at Art has to be more than one step above a technician" (Feist, 1998, p. 291). Thus within-group variance is markedly different for artists and scientists.

One of the biggest challenges to creativity researchers is to "bridge the gap" between "between-group" and "within-group" studies on creativity. This, however, would require the identification of the essential components of creativity, as well as appropriate measures to conceptualize and quantify individual differences in creativity within and across domains. Accordingly, the same measure would be used to distinguish between more and less creative professions or jobs, as well as more and less creative individuals within each profession or job, just as in ability research; that is, IQ.

10.9   SUMMARY AND CONCLUSIONS

This chapter has looked at the construct of creativity, which, despite its longstanding history, has only recently emerged as an important topic of differential psychology. As has been seen:

- Creativity is a complex and multidetermined psychological construct that has rarely been measured through objective means. Differential approaches to creativity comprise various, often conflicting, theories.

- Rapid technological advances are creating an increasingly complex world where adaptation to changing environments is crucial. This cultural evolution demands more flexibility from individuals than ever before. Given that creativity contributes to greater flexibility (Flach, 1990; Runco, 1986), creative individuals may be more prepared to adapt to the changes in everyday life and remain flexible in their responses to the environment. Thus "creativity is a useful and effective response to evolutionary changes [. . .] because older adults tend to rely on routines and, unless intentionally creative, become inflexible" (Runco, 2004, p. 658). This may explain why several studies found creativity indicators to be significantly correlated with late-life adaptation and growth (e.g., Dudek & Hall, 1991; Gott, 1992).

- Whereas personality and intelligence are important to explain some of the characteristics of creative and noncreative individuals, individual differences in creativity cannot be explained merely in terms of personality and ability factors but may also depend on individuals' interests, self-belief, and motivation. Even if these variables are considered, it may still be impossible to predict a person's level of creative achievement, because there are few objective criteria to determine such a thing.

Chapter 11 introduces another growing concept in the field of differential psychology; namely, leadership.

CHECK YOUR ANSWERS

The correct answers were (a) cheese, (b) working, (c) party, (d) chair or wire, (e) house. All items are taken from Sternberg and O'Hara (2000).

TEXTS FOR FURTHER READING

Amabile, T.M. (1990). Within you, without you: The social psychology of creativity, and beyond. In M.A. Runco & R.S. Alber (Eds.), *Theories of Creativity* (pp. 61–91). Newbury Park, CA: Sage.

Barron, F. & Harrington, D.M. (1981). Creativity, intelligence, and personality. *Annual Review of Psychology*, 32, 439–76.

Feist, G.J. (1998). A meta-analysis of personality in scientific and artistic creativity. *Personality and Social Psychology Bulletin*, 2, 290–309.

Runco, M.A. (2004). Creativity. *Annual Review of Psychology, 55*, 657–87.

Sternberg, R.J. & Lubart, T.I. (1996). Investing in creativity. *American Psychologist,* 51, 677–88.

Sternberg, R.J. & O'Hara, L.A. (2000). Intelligence and creativity. In R.J. Sternberg (Ed.), *Handbook of Intelligence* (pp. 611–30). New York: Cambridge University Press.

11 Leadership

KEY WORDS

Charismatic Leadership • Contingency Model • Identification • Implicit Theories of Leadership • Leadership Style • Presidential Leadership • Self-fulfilling Prophecy • Trait Approach • Transactional Leadership • Transformational Leadership

CHAPTER OUTLINE

11.1   INTRODUCTION

Before every political election, politicians focus on strategic policies, topics of controversy, and economic reforms in the hope of persuading voters of the benefits of electing their party. However, many if not all elections may largely be decided on the basis of one factor; namely, who will make the best leader. Likewise, children playing in a playground may differ in their potential for leading others, in school, university, or at work.

This chapter examines some of the salient psychological theories of leadership. What these theories have in common is their attempt to explain the emergence and effectiveness of leaders in terms of psychological variables, notably individual differences in certain aspects of personality, intelligence, and the capacity to influence others.

While the complex and multiple causes of leadership make it difficult to predict who will become a leader, psychology has provided valuable information to explain why certain individuals are better candidates to lead others and therefore more likely to become successful leaders than others.

Many scientific textbooks in the social sciences start by examining encyclopedic definitions of the constructs they will discuss. In the case of leadership, it seems more appropriate and interesting to examine *examples* than actual definitions (Figure 11.1). Let us consider some random (but relatively undisputed) cases: Winston Churchill (1874–1965), Mohandas Gandhi (1869–1948), Adolf Hitler (1889–1945), Martin Luther King, Jr. (1929–68), Nelson Mandela (b. 1918), Pope John Paul II (1920–2005), and Ronald Reagan (1911–2004). You may notice that most of these figures are associated with political leadership. However, several leaders outside the political arena have often been identified. For example, Pablo Picasso (1881–1973) and Salvador Dali (1904–89) were leading artists, Ludwig van Beethoven (1770–1827) and John Lennon (1940–80) were leading musicians, Isaac Newton (1642–1727) and Albert Einstein (1879–1955) were leading physicists, and Jean-Paul Sartre (1905–80) and James Joyce (1882–1941) were leading writers.

Interestingly, even when we compare individuals who excelled *within* the same domain (i.e., in the same field), it may be difficult to identify some overarching or common features that may help us describe and define the essence of leadership. There are nonetheless two aspects that are rarely disputed as the key elements of leadership:

- Excellence and outstanding *achievement* within one field or professional career. Thus leaders are people who excel at what they do and are recognized as competent by other people in the field.
- The capacity to *influence* others. This influence may involve direct leadership when there is personal interaction with the leader, or indirect leadership if the leader's impact is merely based on their ideas or products (Gardner, 1995).

Thus, if asked what Mohandas Gandhi and Pablo Picasso had in common, our answer may be that they were salient figures in their own fields (politics and art) and had a substantial influence in shaping some of the major ideas of the 21st century. If we wanted to provide a shorter answer, it would probably be sufficient to mention the word "leadership." However, what is leadership?

FIGURE 11.1 *Famous leaders – six examples*

Clockwise from left: Winston Churchill, Nelson Mandela, Albert Einstein, Ronald Reagan, Mohandas Gandhi, Che Guevara.

Sources: INTERFOTO Pressebildagentur/Alamy; POPPERFOTO/Getty; Library of Congress, LC-USZ62-13040; Topfoto/Dinodia; akg-images/ullstein bild.

PHOTO 11.1 *Picasso (left) and Hitler (right)*

Two very different men, but one thing in common – in their own ways and domains, they were both leaders.

© Bettmann/Corbis.

Most psychologists have regarded leadership as a *process* rather than as a static attribute or trait. In particular, advocates of the *contingency/situational* approach to leadership (see Focus Point 11.1) define it as "a process of social influence in which one person is able to enlist the aid and support of others in the accomplishment of a common task" (Chemers, 2000, p. 27).

From an organizational perspective, on the other hand, leadership has been defined as the ability to build, motivate, and maintain high-performing teams, groups, departments, and organizations. Accordingly, Hogan, Curphy, and Hogan (1994, p. 493) argued that "leadership involves persuading other people to set aside for a period of time their individual concerns and to pursue a common goal that is important for the responsibilities and welfare of a group."

As will be noted, the above definitions may apply to some (*charismatic* and *transformational*, see Sections 11.3.1 and 11.3.2, respectively) but not to other (*transactional*, see Section 11.3.4) forms of leadership. Very often, then, psychologists have used the word "leadership" to refer to quite different processes and psychological phenomena. This has marked different approaches to leadership, which ought to be examined in order to understand what leadership is about. Although psychological theories of leadership are often complex, they are generally aimed at answering three broad but simple questions, namely:

- *Who will lead?* (Leadership emergence)
- *Who should lead?* (Leadership effectiveness)
- *Are leaders born or made?* (Characteristics of leader)

11.2   APPROACHES TO LEADERSHIP

The concept of leadership has attracted popular and scientific interest alike and is examined not only in the context of differential psychology but also in areas such as psychoanalysis and social psychology. In fact, the inclusion of a chapter on leadership in this book may seem unusual and has been questioned by some reviewers who did not recognize leadership as a central topic in individual differences. While the leadership literature is far more eclectic and less empirical than other individual difference concepts, recent studies have provided valuable evidence for understanding individual differences in leadership. Thus the construct of leadership is not exclusive to individual differences, but should be included in any comprehensive textbook of individual differences, particularly because of its applied relevance.

Perhaps the most popular question regarding leadership (and this is one that has been asked with regard to most individual difference constructs) is the extent to which leadership can be explained by specific characteristics of leaders that would make them almost naturally different from the rest, or by certain situational events that bring leaders into effect. The two extreme alternative answers to this question have been reflected in the two principal approaches to leadership, the *trait* approach (see Sections 11.2.2 and 11.2.4) and the *situational* approach (see Focus Point 11.1).

FOCUS POINT 11.1 CONTINGENCY AND THE SITUATIONAL DETERMINANTS OF LEADERSHIP

After the 1950s, criticisms of and skepticism about the validity of trait approaches to leadership, notably the theory of the Great Man, increased substantially, no doubt influenced by the publication of Stogdill's (1948) review and the atrocities of the Second World War, which reminded both laypeople and scientists of the dark side of leadership.

Criticisms referred to three major problems:

- The list of traits used to distinguish between leaders and nonleaders was not *grouped*, *rank ordered*, or *parsimoniously described*, making it almost impossible to see how they did or did not relate to one another.
- The trait approach tended to be *retrospective*, raising questions about whether the identified traits were a cause or a consequence of leadership.
- It was uncertain whether all the traits on the list were *necessary* and *sufficient*. Thus, some attributes may not have been relevant while other relevant attributes may not have been listed.

Finally, it was clear that leadership could not be understood merely on the basis of personal characteristics, such as individual differences in personality and abilities, but was also determined by *situational factors*.

It was this final argument that inspired the development of the "contingency" approach to leadership, which received an important academic boost from the publication of Fiedler's studies in the 1960s and attracted increasing support during the 1970s (a period that, incidentally, was marked by growing skepticism toward the relevance and validity of stable personality traits; see Mischel, 1973, and Section 2.5 in Chapter 2).

Fiedler's (1967, 1993) contingency model is based on the distinction between task vs. emotional leadership roles (see also Bales, 1958, and Section 11.3 on behavioral approaches). Task-oriented leaders are believed to care about the appropriate execution of the task and are negatively predisposed toward low-performing individuals. On the other hand, emotionally oriented leaders emphasize the importance of good interpersonal relations and are therefore more likely to tolerate and accept poorly performing individuals.

There are specific conditions – Fiedler argues – under which task-oriented and emotionally oriented leaders may or may not be effective, and different individuals make better leaders under different circumstances. The extent to which the situation is favorable to the leader, in the sense of increasing their certainty, predictability, and control over the group, is reflected in the dimension of *situational favorableness* or situational control.

Thus different situations may require different styles:

When the task is clear and followers supportive, the leader should use more time-efficient, autocratic styles. If the task or information is unclear, using [the] consultative strategies increases the information yield and likelihood of a higher quality decision. When the leaders lack follower support, the participative strategy helps to ensure follower commitment to the decision and its implementation. (Chemers, 2000, p. 30)

Although Fiedler's theory remained more popular within social than differential psychology, today even trait advocates and psychometricians accept that context matters, often more than individual traits (Simonton, 1987).

Trait approaches to leadership assume that there are distinctive psychological characteristics accounting for the emergence and effectiveness of leadership, in much the same way that personality traits can account for the consistent patterns of thought, behavior, and emotion that make each individual different from others (see Sections 2.2 and 2.3 in Chapter 2). Consequently, specific individual differences in, say, personality or intelligence would explain why some people become leaders but not others, and why some people end up being "good" (successful) leaders but not others. Figure 11.2 shows the four essential attributes that are implicit in many views of leadership.

contingency model
theory of leadership that assumes that leadership is determined more by situational factors than by personal characteristics, positing that anyone has the potential to become a leader given a favorable context.

On the other hand, situational leadership theories, also known as **contingency models**, assume that leadership is determined more by situational factors than by the personal characteristics of the leader, in much the same way as situational approaches to personality conceptualized individual differences as a succession of volatile states that are dependent on the context more than on internal traits (see Section 2.5 in Chapter 2). Thus contingency theories of leaders posit that pretty much anybody has the potential to become a leader as long as they are "in the right place at the right time."

In recent decades, a third approach to leadership has been increasingly investigated and added to the trait and situational models; namely, the *behavioral* perspective on leadership (see Section 11.3). This approach posits that there are different behavioral patterns or *leadership styles* that may vary between, but also within, individuals. More importantly, different leadership styles can be expected to have different effects on people and involve different psychological processes and techniques.

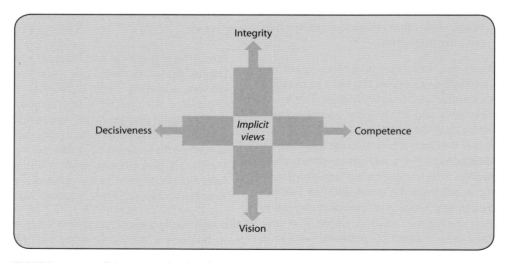

FIGURE 11.2 *Implicit views on leaders: four essential attributes*

Based on Kouzes & Posner, 2002.

Because of their relevance with regard to understanding individual differences, in this book we shall focus mainly on trait and behavioral theories of leadership, though situational approaches will be briefly examined.

11.2.1   Early Foundations of Leadership: Freud's Group Psychology

Whether acknowledged or not, Freud's work on group psychology (a relatively late development in his psychoanalytic theory, but one of the earliest psychological explanations of leadership) had a marked and longstanding impact on modern and contemporary leadership theories. It has even been argued (Goethals, 2005) that virtually all modern findings on leadership can be explained in terms of psychoanalytic theory, though this is probably an exaggeration, not uncommon in devoted psychoanalysts. It is, however, clear that Freud's ideas were unusually insightful and, albeit counterintuitive and surreal at times, they seem to explain some of the key processes underlying the relationship between leaders and followers with unmatchable elegance and surprising simplicity.

Freud's ideas on leadership were inspired by the French sociologist and early social psychologist Gustav Le Bon (1841–1931), who is extensively quoted in Freud's (1921) book on leadership entitled *Group Psychology and the Analysis of the Ego*. In this monograph, Freud's central thesis is that, in group situations, individuals are highly suggestible and easily influenced by others. In fact, so high is their level of susceptibility that they would seem to enter a trance-like state of mind, comparable to that of hypnotized individuals (see also Section 4.4.1 in Chapter 4). Furthermore, Freud argued that this state of mind would involve a "regression" to a lower intellectual level where individuals "are easily swayed by the words and actions of leaders toward a dramatic action and rapidly changing emotions" (Goethals, 2005, p. 546).

According to Freud, then, leadership emerges as the natural consequence of a group's "thirst for obedience" and willingness to "submit itself instinctively to anyone who appoints himself its master" (Freud, 1957/1921, p. 81). This almost instinctual "passion for authority" (p. 127) is consistent with Darwin's (1809–82) idea that "the primitive form of human society was that of a horde ruled over despotically by a powerful male," and Freud believed that "the fortunes of this horde have left indestructible traces upon the history of human descent" (p. 122; see Figure 11.3). Accordingly, individuals would experience a subconscious form of nostalgic desire to obey rules, which predisposes them – or shall I say "us" – to follow a leader. In that sense, leaders would be determined by the group rather than vice versa.

Freud's emphasis on groups as the very determinants of leadership would later be captured by contingency/situational leadership theories (see Focus Point 11.1), though theories focused on the characteristics of the leader – as opposed to the group – would receive most attention during the 20th century.

For Freud, the idea that leadership may be determined by the group's "hunger" for leadership is not incompatible with the notion of certain distinctive attributes that

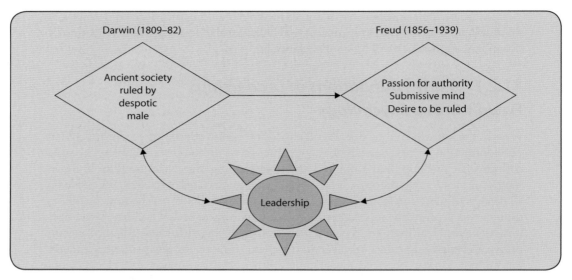

FIGURE 11.3 *Internalized authority (Darwin and Freud on leadership)*

leaders ought to possess to be elected or selected as such. Groups' craving for leaders may explain why leadership – as a general phenomenon – occurs, but the emergence or choice of a particular leader may be better explained by an individual's personal characteristics; specifically, whether they match the groups' instinctual leader figure: "People have an archaic memory of a despotic male leader who was feared and loved" (Goethals, 2005, p. 548). Freud (1957/1921) thought that leaders must be strong, well-spoken, and bright. More importantly, they must "possess the typical qualities of the [group] in a particularly clearly marked and pure form" (p. 129). Thus, leaders must be representative or prototypical of the group.

> **identification** process that refers to an individual's unconscious desire to be like someone else, involving an idealized perception of a role model.

Other aspects of Freud's psychoanalytic theory of leadership have been influential for understanding the processes underlying the relationship between leaders and groups, in particular the mechanisms by which leaders achieve their influence on subordinates; that is, **identification**. Used widely throughout psychoanalytic theory (not merely in regard to leadership), the concept of identification refers to the subconscious process by which the ego uses image to guide its action toward an object. In simple terms, it refers to an individual's unconscious desire to be like someone else. This desire is most strongly manifested during early childhood years, when individuals identify with their parents (most commonly boys with their father and girls with their mother). Identification involves an idealized perception of a role model.

An important aspect of the group's perception of a leader as role model is the "illusion" – in Freud's terms – that the leader loves each of the group members alike, almost like a son or daughter. Thus, individuals in a group would sacrifice their own selfish interests in order to devote themselves to the interests of a leader who, in return, will offer their unconditional love to the group. Figure 11.4 outlines the major ideas derived from Freud's theory of leadership.

PHOTO 11.2 *How did Hitler manage to connect with his audience? The Freudian answer: via the unconscious process of identification.*

© Bettmann/Corbis.

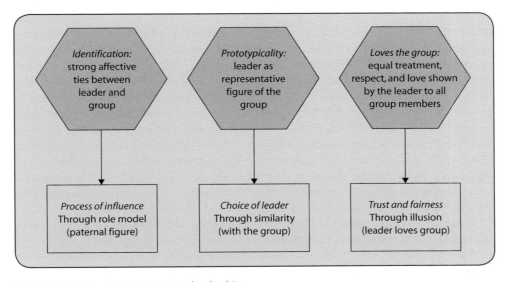

FIGURE 11.4 *Freud (1957/1921) on leadership*

11.2.2   Trait Approaches to Leadership: The Great Man Theory

The history of the world is but the biography of great men.

Thomas Carlyle (1907, p. 18)

trait approach theories of leadership that examine the psychological characteristics and personal attributes of leaders in an attempt to identify common traits and predict leadership potential.

There has been a great deal of speculation about the personality of leaders. Historians, political scientists, novelists, and business people as much as psychologists have long attempted to identify the characteristics of great, as well as failed and derailed, leaders. Psychological research and theories focusing on the personality of leaders are usually referred to as **trait approaches** to leadership and will be discussed throughout this section.

Trait approaches were characterized by Carlyle's (1907) *Great Man* or "Great Person" theory of leadership. Carlyle's theory is no doubt still popular and views leaders as essentially "different" from nonleaders in that they possess certain attributes or personal characteristics that are unique and absent in most individuals.

Three questions guided the research efforts of the trait theorist prior to the Second World War, namely:

- Which are the common traits underlying all great leaders?
- Can we predict people's leadership potential on the basis of these "appropriate" traits?
- Can people "learn" to become good (effective) leaders?

The Great Man theory assumed that a limited set of individual traits could be used to distinguish between leaders and nonleaders, and persuaded researchers to invest a considerable amount of effort into identifying these traits. Physical characteristics included height and energy, social variables comprised level of education and socioeconomic status, ability variables included IQ and verbal fluency, and personality traits comprised dominance, assertiveness, self-confidence, and stress tolerance. This mix of very different types of variables was problematic because of the lack of hierarchical or logical order to make sense of the literature. In a subsequent review of 30 years of leadership research, Stogdill (1948) concluded that only a handful of these traits could be used to distinguish effectively between leaders and followers, as well as between successful and unsuccessful leaders. Stogdill's list was topped by intelligence (see Focus Point 11.2), and also included dominance, sociability, responsibility, self-confidence, diplomacy, extraversion, ambition, integrity, emotional control, and cooperation. (Note that the writing of "Extraversion" with an upper-case E is usually reserved for the *Big Five* or *Gigantic Three* version of the trait; see Section 2.6 in Chapter 2.)

However, no single variable – not even intelligence – could predict leadership in all situations. Thus, there were no universal predictors of leadership that could be consistently identified in the literature. Stogdill's (1948) analysis went on to become an

FOCUS POINT 11.2 INTELLIGENCE AND LEADERSHIP

After Stogdill's (1948) review of 30 years of leadership research, several studies suggested, consistently with that review, that leadership could best be predicted on the basis of intelligence. This box presents a brief summary of the findings on the relationship between intelligence and leadership.

Lord, Foti, and De Vader (1984) found that intellectual ability was more prototypical of leaders than were honesty, charisma, and kindness. A meta-analysis published around the same time reported a correlation of $r = .50$ between leadership and intelligence (Lord, De Vader, & Alliger, 1986). Such findings are consistent with the more general assertion that "intelligence is the most important trait or construct in all of psychology, and the most 'successful' trait in applied psychology" (Schmidt & Hunter, 2000, p. 4).

However, other researchers have questioned the validity of intelligence measures as predictors of leadership, arguing that "intellectual abilities … do not predict leadership performance to any appreciable degree" (Fiedler, 2002, p. 92).

A recent meta-analysis by Judge, Colbert, and Illies (2004) examined the link between leadership and intelligence in a total of 151 samples. The authors estimated the true correlation

between intelligence and leadership to be in the region of $r = .27$. This correlation (based on an impressive sample of $N = 40\,652$) suggests that the link between leadership and intelligence is considerably lower than expected, and possibly even lower than the correlations of leadership with Extraversion ($r = .31$) and Conscientiousness ($r = .28$) (see Section 11.2.4, in particular Figure 11.5).

In their study, Judge, Colbert, and Illies (2004) emphasized the distinction between "objective" and "perceived" leadership, and the fact that these two constructs may be differentially related to intelligence.

While previous studies had examined the extent to which intelligence measures were correlated with perceived leaders (Lord, De Vader, & Alliger, 1986), more recent investigations found that intelligence is more related to perceived than "actual" leadership (the latter term is usually referred to as leadership effectiveness, while the former is associated with leadership emergence).

The distinction between objective and perceived leadership is useful to understand some of the inconsistencies across different studies on leadership and intellectual ability.

important determinant of the shift of paradigm from trait to situational approaches to leadership (see again Focus Point 11.1).

After the late 1950s, psychologists continued to search for the distinctive personality attributes that could effectively discriminate between leaders and nonleaders (Atkinson, 1958; McClelland & Winter, 1969). Toward the 1970s, leaders' personality was discussed in the light of Murray's (1938) basic motives (see Sections 9.3 and 9.4 in Chapter 9) and there was a growing consensus that effective leaders had a higher *need for power*, higher *activity inhibition*, and lower *need for affiliation* than ineffective leaders and nonleaders in general (McClelland, 1975; McClelland & Burham, 1976; see also Focus Point 11.3 on presidential leadership).

PHOTO 11.3 *These were the three main contestants for the UK election. What did the winner have that the others did not?*

© Toby Melville/Reuters/Corbis.

FOCUS POINT 11.3   PRESIDENTIAL LEADERSHIP AS A PARADIGM OF TRAIT APPROACHES

Some psychologists have addressed the study of leadership through a comparative examination of effective vs. noneffective presidents and presidential candidates, mostly in the United States. This small but growing area of research is referred to as **presidential leadership** and combines findings and theories from different disciplines, from psychology to political sciences, sociology, and economics.

presidential leadership area of leadership research that uses a multidisciplinary approach to examine the effectiveness of presidents and presidential candidates.

In a seminal book on the topic of presidential leadership, Simonton (1986) applied psychometric analysis to identify the attributes of successful American presidents and listed a total of 14; namely, moderation, friendliness, intellectual brilliance, Machiavellianism, poise and polish, achievement drive, forcefulness, wit, physical attractiveness, pettiness, tidiness, conservatism, inflexibility, and pacifism. Barber (1992, p. 153) provided a shorter, albeit largely overlapping, list of presidential attributes; namely, Machiavellian, forceful, moderate, poise and polish, and flexible.

In another retrospective analysis of the personality of effective vs. noneffective presidents, Spranger and House (1991) suggested that presidential performance may be largely explained by individual differences in the *need for power*, *affiliation*, and *achievement*.

A review article by Goethals (2005) concluded that successful American presidents could be characterized by their higher levels of *activity*, *intelligence*, *optimism*, and *flexibility*, though luck and opportunity play an important role, too.

As a consequence, leaders would exhibit significantly higher levels of concern when choosing actions that influence others' thoughts, emotions, and behaviors (Winter, 1973). This concern would be manifested in leaders' motivation to establish, maintain, and restore relationships with others (Heyns, Veroff, & Atkinson, 1958).

PHOTO 11.4 *Two very different presidents with different styles. Did their personalities influence their different political views and leadership styles?*

Source: Kennedy (left image) © Jason Grower/Shutterstock; Bush (right image) © Cecil Stoughton, White House.

11.2.3 From Attributes to Attributions: Leadership as a Perceived Construct

During the late 1970s and much of the 1980s, personality approaches to leadership were increasingly focused on the *perceived attributes* of leaders, which did not, however, differ substantially from the previously identified traits. Theoretically, however, attempts to identify followers' perceptions of leaders were inspired by the idea that leadership is largely determined by followers' choices. Hence there was "no way of measuring leadership apart from social perceptions, [and] leadership exists primarily as an *attribution* rather than a testable construct" (Chemers, 2000, p. 32, emphasis added).

Personal attributes, such as charisma, were "considered to be invested by followers and accorded or withdrawn by them" (Hollander, 1993, p. 41). This implied that leaders are ultimately *legitimated* or recognized as such by the group, an idea that had already been anticipated by Freud (1957/1921) (see Section 11.2.1). According to Hollander, the two main factors determining whether a group will legitimize a leader as such are perceived trustworthiness and task competence.

Accordingly, **implicit theories of leadership**, which study the nature of laypeople's beliefs about and perceptions of leaders,

implicit theories of leadership theories that study perceived attributes of leadership rather than leaders' personal characteristics, examining laypeople's beliefs about and attributions of personal qualities to leaders.

suggested that leaders are generally regarded as caring, outgoing, honest, competent, verbally skilled, decisive, educated, dedicated, aggressive, and elegant (Lord, De Vader, & Alliger, 1986). In a later study, Kenney, Blascovich, and Shaver (1994) identified four higher-order factors underlying people's conceptions of leaders; namely, the ability to learn the group's goals, taking charge (being in command), being a "nice person," and being emotionally stable (not being nervous).

Perhaps the most important legacy of attributional/implicit theories of leadership is the reminder that leadership effectiveness may only be judged in terms of followers' perception and performance. This is a crucial theoretical consideration because, while it may be relatively easy to agree on whether someone is a leader or not, it is often impossible to determine whether someone is a "good" (effective) leader or not (think, for instance, of Hitler and Stalin), except by judging their effects on others.

Thus leaders may consider themselves very effective but nonetheless have little or a negative impact on others. As Hogan *et al.* (1994, p. 496) argued, "there is a kind of manager who routinely over-evaluates his or her performance, and that tendency is associated with poor leadership." This is why implicit theories of leadership are generally better for explaining and predicting leadership emergence than leadership effectiveness, as people may often be "chosen" as leaders when they lack the necessary qualities to perform well (otherwise, all political elections would generate good results!).

11.2.4   Trait Approach: Survival and Revival

Although Great Man theories of leadership are part of the history – rather than the present – of leadership research, the trait approach has arguably survived the emergence of situational theories and began to be the focus of much leadership research during the 1990s. In fact, in recent years there has been a revival of the trait approach.

In a widely quoted article, Locke (1997) identified various leadership traits (see Table 11.1), which – unlike previous dispositional models – not only referred to 20th-century US leaders but were also *timeless* and *universal*. More importantly, higher-order factors could be identified to reduce the number of traits that characterize effective leaders:

> Would quantitative analysis support 12 distinct traits, or could they be grouped into a smaller number without loss of important information? My prediction is that they can be combined into a smaller number. Do the traits operate independently (e.g. in additive fashion) or are there interactions between them? I have one prediction here: I think dishonesty negates all a person's other virtues in that it divorces a person from reality in principle . . . A complicating factor, however, is that people are not always consistent in their honest and dishonesty. (Locke, 1997, p. 22)

Locke's (1997) paper is often referenced as an example of the reemergence or revival of the trait approach to leadership, and there are three reasons for this reemergence.

Table 11.1 *Locke's (1997) leadership traits*

Cognitive ability and thinking modes	Motivation, values, and action	Attitudes toward employees (subordinates)
1 *Reality focus*: Not susceptible to evasions and delusions, but facing reality however grim it may be	7 *Egoistic passion for work*: Intrinsic motivation, workaholic	11 *Respect for ability*: Hiring and developing people with drive, talent, and right attitudes
2 *Honesty*: Realistic assessment (accurate insight) of one's own and others' abilities and weaknesses	8 *Action commitment*: Doing (not just thinking)	12 *Commitment to justice*: Rewarding (and punishing) people appropriately
3 *Independence/self-confidence*: "Thinking outside the box,"* innovating, breaking new ground	9 *Ambition*: Personal drive and desire to achieve expertise and responsibility	
4 *Active mind*: Continually searching for new ideas and solutions	10 *Effort and tenacity*: Hard-working, resilient, not discouraged by failure	
5 *Intelligence* (IQ): Ability to reason, learn, and acquire knowledge		
6 *Vision*: Innovative, long-term plan, "thinking ahead"		

Note: * See Figure 10.7 in Chapter 10 for an explanation of the psychological conceptualization of "thinking outside the box."

Source: Adapted from Locke (1997) and Chamorro-Premuzic & Furnham (2005).

- As noted in Chapter 2 (in particular Section 2.11), there has been considerable consensus since the early 1990s around the idea that individual differences in personality are best described and predicted in terms of the Five Factor Model, allowing researchers – including leadership psychologists – to compare their findings and perform large-scale analyses (Goldberg, 1990; Matthews & Deary, 1998).
- Advances in measurement have helped to describe and understand some of the psychological mechanisms underlying differences in behavior.
- Robust, state-of-the-art, meta-analytical studies have demonstrated the predictive power of personality traits in applied settings, notably academic and job performance (for a review, see Chamorro-Premuzic & Furnham, 2005).

Furnham (1994) was among the first to speculate about the role of the Big Five personality traits at work. In contemporary organizations, he argued, leaders are likely to be open, conscientious, stable, agreeable, and extraverts (see Table 11.2). This combination of traits was replicated, the same year, in an often quoted review article by Hogan *et al.* (1994), where previously examined personality variables were "translated" into the Big Five language. In addition, Hogan *et al.* (1994) referred to the "dark side of personality" as a combination of traits likely to predict and explain derailed leadership; they named arrogance, hostility, passive aggressiveness, compulsiveness, and abrasiveness.

Cross-cultural studies have generally replicated the pattern of the Big Five correlates of leadership hypothesized by Furnham (1994) and Hogan *et al.* (1994). For instance, Silversthorne (2001) found that effective leaders tended to score significantly higher on Extraversion, Agreeableness, and Conscientiousness, and lower on Neuroticism, than noneffective leaders in US as well as Chinese samples. However, previous studies indicated that, while Conscientiousness and Emotional Stability (low Neuroticism) tend to represent sociably desirable traits in almost every culture, Extraversion (with its primary facets of assertiveness and dominance)

Table 11.2 *Probable relationships between personality and work variables*

Work variables	N	E	O	A	C
Absenteeism	+ + +	−			−
Accidents	+	−			
Creativity		+	+ + +		−
Derailment	+ + +		−		−
Leadership	−	+ +	+ + +	+	+ + +
Vocational choice	−	+ +	+		+ +
Sales		+ +		+	+ +
Job satisfaction	−	+ + +		+	+ +
Motivation	−	+ + +	+ +	+	+ + +
Productivity	−	+ +			+ + +

Key: N = Neuroticism, E = Extraversion, O = Openness to Experience, A = Agreeableness, C = Conscientiousness.

The "+" sign indicates a positive relation, while the "−" indicates a negative relation; the number of "+" and "−" signs indicates the strength of the correlation.

Source: Adapted from Chamorro-Premuzic & Furnham (2005).

is less likely to be regarded as a virtue in Eastern than in Western cultures (Redding & Wong, 1986).

Judge, Bono, *et al.* (2002) reviewed the extensive literature on personality and leadership. Ten writers, mainly from the 1990s, listed what they thought to be the essential traits of effective or emergent and effective leaders. Judge, Bono, *et al.* noticed considerable overlap, such that most writers included self-confidence, adjustment, sociability, and integrity, while a minority listed persistence and masculinity (see Table 11.3).

After this qualitative analysis of the literature, Judge, Bono, *et al.* (2002) performed a large-scale quantitative meta-analysis, which included 222 correlations from 73 studies. Results showed that Emotional Stability, Extraversion, Openness,

Table 11.3 *Traits of effective or emergent leaders as identified by past reviews*

Study	Traits
Stogdill (1948)	Dependability, sociability, initiative, persistence, self-confidence, alertness, cooperativeness, adaptability
Mann (1959)	Adjustment, extraversion, dominance, masculinity, conservatism
Bass (1990)	Adjustment, adaptability, aggressiveness, alertness, ascendance, dominance, emotional balance, control, independence, nonconformity, originality, creativity, integrity, self-confidence
Kirkpatrick & Locke (1991)	Drive (achievement, ambition, energy, tenacity, initiative), honesty/integrity, self-confidence (emotional stability)
Yukl & Van Fleet (1992)	Emotional maturity, integrity, self-confidence, high energy level, stress tolerance
Hogan *et al.* (1994)	Extraversion, Agreeableness, Conscientiousness, Emotional Stability
House & Aditya (1997)	Achievement motivation, prosocial influence motivation, adjustment, self-confidence
Northouse (1997)	Self-confidence, determination, integrity, sociability
Yukl (1998)	Energy level and stress tolerance, self-confidence, internal locus of control, emotional maturity, personal integrity, socialized power motivation, achievement orientation, low need for affiliation
Daft (1999)	Alertness, originality, creativity, personal integrity, self-confidence

Source: Adapted from Judge, Bono, *et al.* (2002).

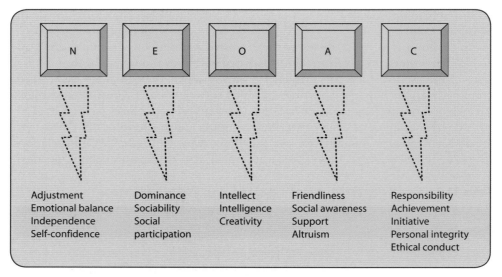

FIGURE 11.5 *Stogdill's (1974) leadership traits in big five language*

Key: N = Neuroticism, E = Extraversion, O = Openness, A = Agreeableness, C = Conscientiousness.
Source: Adapted from Hogan et al. (1994).

and Conscientiousness were all positively correlated with both leadership emergence (perceived leadership) and effectiveness (leadership performance). Judge, Bono, *et al.* (2002) concluded that Extraversion is the most consistent predictor of both leadership and emergence and effectiveness.

The estimated validities for the Big Five as predictors of leadership emergence and effectiveness are summarized in Figure 11.5.

Judge, Bono, *et al.*'s (2002) study showed strong support for the personality approach to leadership once the traits are organized according to the Big Five model. Extraversion was the most consistent correlate, no doubt because of the assertiveness, dominance, and sociability of extraverts (see Figure 11.6 and Focus Point 11.4). However, the authors accept that the research does not always explain why these traits related to leadership:

> Is Neuroticism negatively [related] because neurotic individuals are less likely to attempt leadership, because they are less inspirational, or because they have lower expectations of themselves or others? Similarly, Extraversion may be related to leadership because extraverts talk more, and talking is strongly related to emergent leadership. Alternatively, it may be that individuals implicitly expect leaders to be extraverted. Implicit views of leaders include aspects of both sociability ("outgoing") and assertiveness ("aggressive," "forceful"), or extraverts could be better leaders due to their expressive nature or the contagion of their positive emotionality. Open individuals may be better leaders because they are more creative and are divergent thinkers, because they are risk-takers, or because their tendencies for esoteric thinking and fantasy make them more likely to be

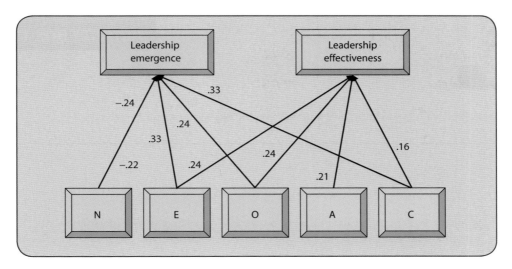

FIGURE 11.6 *Big Five correlates of leadership emergence and effectiveness: Meta-analytic findings by Judge, Bono,* et al. *(2002)*

Note: Estimated corrected correlation coefficients (number of correlations varied from 17 to 37).

Key: N = Neuroticism, E = Extraversion, O = Openness, A = Agreeableness, C = Conscientiousness.

FOCUS POINT 11.4   HELP!

How to interpret Figure 11.6. (*You should skip this section if you are confident of understanding Figure 11.6.*)

- Each arrow (connector) in Figure 11.6 represents a correlation between two variables. Variables (e.g., N, E, Leadership Emergence, etc.) are represented by boxes.
- The wider the arrow connecting two variables, the larger the size of the correlation (i.e., the stronger the association between two variables). However, correlations are based on a different number of studies, and tend to be all in the region of .15 to .35. Correlations can be negative or positive.
- A positive correlation implies that high scores on one variable are associated with high scores on the other variable, and vice versa. On the other hand, a negative correlation means that high scores on one

variable will be associated with low scores on the other variable, and vice versa.
- For example, we can see that the highest correlations in Figure 11.6 are between Extraversion (E) and leadership emergence (.33), as well as between Conscientiousness (C) and leadership emergence (.33).

Need some practice? Try answering the following questions.

(a) What correlation is larger, that between N and leadership emergence, or that between A and leadership effectiveness?

(b) Is Openness more highly correlated with leadership emergence or leadership effectiveness?

(c) What is the correlation between Conscientiousness and leadership effectiveness?

The answers are on page 358.

ACTIVITY BOX 11.1

Think of three leaders you know and rate them on the Big Five personality traits.

visionary leaders. Agreeableness may be weakly correlated with leadership because it is both a hindrance (agreeable individuals tend to be passive and compliant) and a help (agreeable individuals are likeable and empathetic) to leaders. Finally, is Conscientiousness related to leadership because conscientious individuals have integrity and engender trust because they excel at process aspects of leadership, such as setting goals, or because they are more likely to have initiative and persist in the face of obstacles? Our study cannot address these process oriented issues, but future research should attempt to explain the linkages between the Big Five traits and leadership. (Judge, Bono, *et al.*, 2002, p. 774)

11.2.5 *Criticism of the Trait Approach*

Despite its popularly unchallenged position at the center of the individual difference approach to leadership research and theory, there have been a number of criticisms of the trait approach to leadership.

Spangler, House, and Palrecha (2004) argued that, while the Five Factor Model had indeed helped our understanding of leadership, its various limitations should not be neglected. First, the Big Five fails to provide *causal* explanations for individual differences in thought, emotionality, and behavior, and this would also apply to work-related aspects of individual differences. Second, the Five Factor Model does not provide a theoretical explanation of individuals' *motivation* to become a leader, and how individual differences may operate in this respect. Third, there remains the debate as to the *comprehensiveness* of the Big Five in fully describing behavior at work (Block, 1995). Last but not least, the Five Factor Model does not explain the mechanisms by which traits interact with *situational* factors to produce leader behavior and outcomes.

However, in their review of the literature, Chamorro-Premuzic and Furnham (2005) concluded that the "bottom line" is that stable individual differences (i.e., traits) *do* predict who becomes, stays, and derails as a leader. Different datasets, from different countries and different perspectives and different historical periods, yield similar results. Great leaders tend to be bright, open to experience, conscientious, extraverted, and stable.

11.3   BEHAVIORAL APPROACHES: LEADERSHIP STYLES

Behavioral approaches to leadership attempt to conceptualize differ-ent **leadership styles** as well as their effects on subordinates. They are derived from an early tradition in social psychology that distin-guished between different strategies adopted by leaders and defined their relationship with others or with a group. Such a distinction was in turn derived from observational studies that were carried out in the form of laboratory experiments (rather than large correlational designs) and looked at the effects of different leadership styles on small groups (Lewin, Lippit, & White, 1939). However, the behavioral approach soon combined with psychometric techniques, specifically self- and other-reports, in order to identify leadership styles in real-life samples.

leadership style a stable pattern of behav-iors adopted by leaders that determines their relationship with and influence over group members.

One of the first consistent findings was that leaders differed on the basis of how "considerate" they were of their subordinates' feelings and needs. It is important here to emphasize the distinction between the identification of trait (discussed in Sections 11.2.2 and 11.2.4) and behavioral aspects of leadership. Although at first sight it may appear that showing consideration (a behavior) may be the natural consequence of being a considerate person (a trait), trait approaches would try to establish whether, *in general*, leaders tend to be considerate or not. On the other hand, behavioral approaches would posit that *some* leaders behave in a considerate manner, while *others* do not. This means that, from the perspective of trait theory, consideration may be a distinctive feature of leaders, while from a behavioral point of view some leaders may be considerate whereas others may not.

In the 1950s (e.g., Bales, 1950; Hemphill & Coons, 1957) researchers introduced another distinction, that between *task-oriented* and *interpersonally oriented* leadership styles (see Focus Point 11.1). Task-oriented leadership is characterized by the lead-er's concern with the completion of relevant tasks (in order to accomplish goals), whereas interpersonally oriented leadership is characterized by the leader's con-cern with maintaining good relationships with and between the group (followers/subordinates).

Another classification of leadership style was the distinction between *democratic* and *autocratic* leaders, also referred to as *participative* and *directive* leadership. Thus leaders differ in the extent to which they seek (democratic/participative) or avoid (autocratic/directive) participation of their followers/subordinates in key decision making and planning. Psychologists have also conceptualized the *laissez-faire* (literally "let do") style, which is characterized by a passive leader who tends to avoid decision making and escape responsibilities for group outcomes.

From the late 1970s onward, leadership research has tended to emphasize the effects of leaders on subordinates, with particular focus on leaders' effectiveness to *inspire* (motivate) and *empower* (give a sense of power to) their followers, enabling them to give of their best. Such attempts are best subsumed under the concepts of *charismatic* and *transformational* leadership (Burns, 1978) and are discussed in more detail in Sections 11.3.1 and 11.3.2.

Another salient classification for leadership style – often contrasted with the transformational/charismatic style – has been that of *transactional* leadership (Avolio, 1999; Bass, 1998), which is discussed in Section 11.3.4. Transactional leadership in part consists of merely the exchange of interests between the leader and subordinates. Thus transactional leaders focus on their followers' needs and establish a relationship with them based on the satisfaction of these needs. In many senses transactional leadership represents the prototypical relationship between manager and employees, as well as the inherent processes of rewards and punishment that underlie the accomplishment or failure to accomplish organizational goals, respectively.

11.3.1   *Charismatic Leadership*

charismatic leadership
a leadership style that is visionary, motivational, innovative, and capable of inspiring optimism in others, also characterized by exceptional communication skills.

In recent decades, differential psychologists have shown increased interest in the construct of **charismatic leadership** (Bass, 1997; Conger & Kanungo, 1987; House & Shamir, 1993). This leadership style is characterized by leaders who are visionary, who are capable of arousing motivation in their followers, and who project optimism, challenge the status quo, and represent excellent role models.

Experimental studies seem to indicate that charismatic leaders are also characterized by superior communication skills (more so than leaders with other leadership styles). In particular, charismatic leaders would "speak with a captivating voice tone; make direct eye contact; show animated facial expressions; and have a powerful, confident, and dynamic interactional style" (Kirkpatrick & Locke, 1996, p. 38). As seen in Section 11.2.1, the idea that leaders have superior communication skills was already present in Freud's leadership theory.

Unlike other leadership styles (notably autocratic or *laissez-faire*), charismatic leaders are particularly able and likely to *empower* their followers; that is, to raise followers' feelings of self-efficacy, motivation, and self-confidence (Bass, 1997). This is achieved through the leader's ability to describe "a better future for followers" (House & Shamir, 1993). Accordingly, followers would be more likely to emulate their leaders by taking risks, challenging the status quo, and searching for creative and innovative solutions.

Many psychologists have emphasized that charismatic leadership is mainly a "perceived" construct or leadership style, which depends almost exclusively on the image that the leader projects to others (see also Section 11.2.3). This is why charismatic leadership has been mainly assessed through *others' estimates* of charisma, such as the Transformational Scale of the Multifactor Leadership Questionnaire (Bass & Avolio, 1985, 1995). This scale comprises Likert-type items that assess inspirational motivation, attributed charisma, and idealized influence, such as "displays a strong sense of power and purpose" and "acts in ways to build your trust" (other sample items are shown in Table 11.4). In that sense, one may almost recognize charismatic leadership as the leadership style that is positively rated by others, in the sense of being associated with positive attitudes, perceptions, and performance of followers.

PHOTO 11.5 *Barack Obama, the current president of the US, is a very charismatic leader*

© Alan Freed/Shutterstock.

Table 11.4 *Leadership styles as defined by the Multifactor Leadership Questionnaire*

Scales and subscales	Description of leadership style
1 Transformational	
(a) *Idealized influence (attribute)*	Shows qualities that generate respect and pride from others associated with the leader
(b) *Idealized influence (behavior)*	Communicates the values, goals, and importance of organization's aims
(c) *Inspirational motivation*	Is optimistic and excited about goals and future plans
(d) *Intellectual stimulation*	Looks at new ways of solving problems and completing tasks
(e) *Individualized consideration*	Develops and mentors followers and attends to their needs
2 Transactional	
(a) *Contingent reward*	Rewards others for good performances
(b) *Management by exception (active)*	Attends to followers' mistakes and failure to meet standards
(c) *Management by exception (passive)*	Waits for problems to become serious before intervening
3 Laissez-faire	Frequently absent and not involved in critical decision-making processes/stages

Source: Adapted from Avolio, Bass, & Jung (1999) and Eagly, Johannesen-Schmidt, & van Engen (2003).

The concept of charismatic leadership is founded on the psychoanalytic notion of personal identification; that is, the process by which an individual's belief about someone becomes self-defining or self-referential. Simply explained, to identify with someone is to want to be like that person (see also Section 11.2.1 on Freud). Thus charismatic leaders would position themselves as *role models* for their subordinates, who would in turn imitate and adopt the beliefs, feelings, and behaviors of the leaders (Conger & Kanungo, 1998; Shamir, House, & Arthur, 1993). In that sense the leader is to a group what a father or mother is to a child.

Although there is wide consensus on the benefits of charismatic leadership for both the organization and the individual, identification with the leader and empowerment of subordinates also generate high *dependence* of subordinates on the leader. Conger and Kanungo (1988) pointed out that dependence is an intense form of identification and is the feature that distinguishes charismatic leadership from other leadership styles (except transformational leadership, which is itself a form of charismatic leadership; see Section 11.3.2). In simple terms, this implies that followers are dependent on the leaders' approval, by which I mean moral and psychological recognition rather than organizational reward. The consequences of dependency are manifested more clearly on the leader's departure, which "will result in a crisis, intense feelings of loss and severe orientation problems on the part of the followers" (Shamir, 1991, p. 96).

Charismatic leaders are influential in that they ensure and strengthen subordinates' level of *social identification* (Ashforth & Mael, 1989), the process by which individuals identify with the group or organization. Under social identification, individuals are happy to replace their own personal goals with those of the group, and tend to experience the group's success and failures as their own. Recent studies (see Bono & Judge, 2003) have shown that leaders who succeed at raising subordinates' level of social identification also increase subordinates' eagerness to engage with, and contribute to, group goals and projects.

transformational leadership a type of charismatic leadership style based on communicating and sharing the leader's vision in order to produce a change in followers' values, expectations, and motivations and inspire them to sacrifice personal interests for those of the group.

In recent years, the concept of charismatic leadership has been progressively replaced (and absorbed) by that of **transformational leadership** (discussed in Section 11.3.2). In fact you may have noticed that the subscale of the Multifactor Leadership Questionnaire shown in Table 11.4 is called "transformational" rather than "charismatic." It is therefore noteworthy that both notions have a clear overlap, and, moreover, some have interpreted transformational leadership as merely the effect of charismatic leadership.

For instance, House and Shamir (1993) argued that charismatic leadership produces transformational effects. Likewise, Bass (1997) conceptualized charisma as the overarching factor of transformational leadership, which includes the minor dimensions of motivation, inspiration, and consideration (see again Table 11.3).

Charismatic leadership has been recently linked with creativity (see Chapter 10; Bono & Judge, 2003; Sosik, Kahai, & Avolio, 1998). Such a link is hypothesized on the basis of the high degree of delegation of responsibility to subordinates by transformational leaders. Thus, rather than permanently giving orders or transmitting a specific set of instructions, transformational leaders allow their subordinates to come up with their own solutions and therefore encourage creative behaviors (Dvir *et al.*, 2002).

FOCUS POINT 11.5 CELEBRITY POLITICIANS: POPULAR CULTURE AND POLITICAL REPRESENTATION

In the past 20 years or so the world has seen an increase in "celebrity politicians," of which there are two major types: first, the elected politician or candidate who uses elements of "celebrityhood" to represent a group or cause; second, the celebrity – the star of popular culture – who uses their popularity to state their political opinions and make an entry into politics. This has been seen by critics to corrupt liberal democratic political representation. In this paper, Street challenges this critique, arguing that the celebrity politician is consistent with a coherent account of political representation today (at least in most cases).

CELEBRITY POLITICIANS

Celebrities are people who, via the mass media, enjoy a greater presence and are able to exert more impact and power than most of the population. *We* watch *them* move on the public stage. Here, Street focuses on two types of celebrity politicians.

The first is celebrity politician 1 (CP1): this represents the legitimately elected representative or candidate who uses popular culture in order to enhance or advance their pre-established political functions and goals. There are two types of CP1:

- An elected politician or candidate whose background is in entertainment and who uses this background to be elected, for example Arnold Schwarzenegger and Ronald Regan.
- A politician who uses associations with celebrities to enhance their image or communicate their message. They can do this

PHOTO 11.6 *Tony Blair "performs" on a new stage, kicking the football with former England Coach Sir Bobby Robson on his trip to China in September 2005.*

© AFP/Getty Images.

through photo opportunities with celebrities, such as Tony Blair with the English football coach (see Photo 11.6), or via the use of stars in advertisements. Another technique is to use nontraditional platforms to promote the image of the politician, such as Bill Clinton playing the saxophone on a famous American television show, or certain English MPs appearing on the satirical quiz show *Have I Got News For You?*.

The second kind of celebrity politician (CP2) is one that is becoming ever more evident nowadays. This is the entertainer who speaks out on their views of politics and claims the right to represent people and causes, but without seeking or acquiring elected office. The key features of CP2 are:

- Celebrities use their status and popularity and the medium within which they work to speak out on specific public policy domains with the aim of influencing political outcomes, such as the Hollywood A-listers who spoke out against the war on Iraq; another case is celebrities like Bono, who has had audiences with the likes of George Bush and Pope John Paul in his campaign to reduce third-world debt.
- They are taken seriously in respect of their political views in the sense that the media focuses on their political views (as opposed to their art); they receive political attention through politicians willing to discuss particular concerns with them; and through audience support beyond their duty as a fan, such as contributing to a cause such as Live Aid.

The main critique of celebrity politics is that of representativeness. Are these politicians representatives of the represented (the audience/public)? With regard to CP1, the main concern is that the relationship between the representatives (politicians) and represented (public) is being damaged, because the latter favor superficial appearances and irrelevant gestures over political substance. The represented are worried that politics is becoming personal, cosmetic, and shallow. Politicians are being constructed as "human" through the use of "intimate" television, such as close-ups, one-on-one interviews, and public appearances outside of a political framework. The worry is that candidates are being selected because of their "style" rather than based on who will make an effective leader, founded on who is a better negotiator or has more imaginative executive skills.

The critique in relation to CP2 is that such people are an unrepresentative sample of the population, and the fear is that they do not understand how the "rest of us" live, so how can they be representatives? They are ill-suited to the duties of statecraft because they lack knowledge of, or expertise in, public policy. Both types of celebrity politicians are argued to debase principles of representative democracy, either because they privilege style over political substance, or because they marginalize relevant expertise.

Street counters this critique by arguing that politicians are simply finding a new way to communicate in an ever more modernized world (especially with focus on the boom in mass media). With regard to CP1, the aesthetics they use in representing are symbols of what they represent rather than just superficial decoration. How they appear, and the fact they appear often on different media, allows the audience to scrutinize them on their authenticity, itself a measure of trustworthiness and integrity, both characteristics desired in a candidate.

Forms of popular culture can resonate more with the represented – the politicians speak and behave in a way that is more appealing to the public without using political jargon, so those previously intimidated by politics can feel closer to it. Many say that judging by appearances rather than on the quality of their policy proposals is an inappropriate basis for evaluating representatives. However, previous research, based on rational choice theory, has suggested that appearance has a place in the representative–represented relationship. Voting has to be seen as an expressive act, not as an instrumental act directed to specific policy outcomes. Thus as an expressive act the vote is understood as allowing the voter to identify with politicians and to see out what they (the voters) find "politically attractive," including appearance. Therefore it would be perfectly rational for a voter to base their vote on a candidate's appearance, or speaking voice, if that is what he or she identifies with.

Street argues in defense of CP2 first by mentioning their relationships. Celebrities and admirers are related – stars form an intimate relationship with distant others and can be seen as the basis on which to form a political representation. Celebrities have power to make political statements, but people have a choice of representativeness because they "elected" them to be there in the first place (not into office as they do not seek to run, but through being a fan and supporting their public policies, or through financially supporting such events as Live Aid).

Street also notes that the relationship between celebrities and politics is not really a new phenomenon. Musical movements, for example, such as punk rock, hip-hop, or the blues, were based on social movements at the time. In a way, they represented the "people's voice"; thus they are, arguably, valid representatives. Now, instead of just singing about it, they are being active about it.

Street's point is that the celebrity politician is not merely an exaggerated or exceptional form of all political representation, but is characteristic of the representation of politics generally. Indeed, political representation is a cultural act that seeks to realize a form of political attractiveness through the gestures and images of popular culture. Thus the aesthetics of politics are bound to include stylistic elements of our popular culture.

Source: Street, J. (2004). Celebrity politicians: Popular culture and political representation. *British Journal of Politics & International Relations*, 6, 435–52. With permission

Furthermore, leaders who motivate and inspire their subordinates – and this applies largely to charismatic leadership – are more likely to facilitate subordinates' creativity.

The link between creativity and leadership has been the topic of much recent debate in both academia and industry, because "managing creative talent" seems largely an unaccomplished goal (Hogan & Hogan, 2002).

11.3.2   *Transformational Leadership: Leaders as Mentors*

Burns (1978, 2003) and Bass (1985, 1998) distinguished between *transactional* (see Section 11.3.4) and *transformational* leadership styles. As noted above, transformational leadership is essentially a type of charismatic leadership style. Thus it is based on the communication to and sharing of the leader's vision with followers in order to inspire them to sacrifice personal interests for the interests of the group. This phenomenon was already conceptualized by Freud when he concluded that, in a group, "an individual readily sacrifices his personal interest to the collective interest"

(Freud, 1957/1921, p. 75, quoting Le Bon). However, Freud hypothesized this to be a process underlying any form of leadership and group psychology and did not distinguish between transformational and other forms of leadership, at least not explicitly.

With transformational leadership (which is defined by its effects on others/the group), followers tend to identify strongly with and are very dependent on their leader. In that sense they are transformed by the leader. This produces a change in the values, expectations, and motivations of both leaders and followers (Yukl, 1998). Thus transformational leadership occurs "when one or more persons *engage* with others in such a way that leaders and followers raise one another to higher levels of morality" (Burns, 1978, p. 20, italics in the original). Consequently, a recent study found that transformational leaders were perceived as having higher moral standards than transactional leaders (Turner *et al.*, 2002).

The construct of transformational leadership has attracted widespread attention from both academic and business settings because of consistent claims and accumulating evidence that it plays a substantial role in the processes that enhance employee motivation and performance (Barling *et al.*, 1996; Dvir *et al.*, 2002). Thus, several experts have indicated that in most contemporary organizational settings (at least in Western/industrialized economies), transformational leadership is highly effective and has benefits for the organization, the group, and the leader, and numerous studies reported that followers' commitment, loyalty, attachment, and satisfaction are all significantly related to transformational leadership (Becker & Billings, 1993; Conger & Kanungo, 1998).

Psychologists have also pointed out that transformational leaders (as with charismatic leaders) tend to be creative, innovative, and strive for changes and improvements. Accordingly, they

> state future goals and develop plans to achieve them. Skeptical of the status quo, they innovate, even when the organization that they lead is generally successful. By mentoring and empowering their followers, transformational leaders encourage them to develop their full potential and thereby to contribute more capably to their organization. (Eagly, Johannesen-Schmidt, & van Engen, 2003, p. 570)

Besides the benefits for the organization, transformational leadership may have a positive effect on the psychological aspects of the followers who experience growth, independence, and empowerment (Bass, 1990), although dependence on the leader may impose limitations on the subordinates (Howell, 1988). While empowerment increases the subordinates' independence and autonomy, dependence requires constant leader approval to maintain high self-esteem.

Several authors have therefore argued that dependence may be the most common disadvantage (for both individuals and organizations) of transformational leadership. Unlike empowerment, which boosts subordinates' self-efficacy, motivation, and performance, dependence creates submissive loyalty, conformity, and blind obedience in subordinates (Howell, 1988). However, future research is needed to clarify the extent to which dependence and empowerment interact in both charismatic and transformational leadership, and in which direction (Kark, Shamir, & Chen, 2003).

Traditionally, the concepts of empowerment and dependence have been treated as opposite, but in a recent study it was argued:

> in early stages of the relationship, some dependence on the leader is a necessary condition for the leader's empowering effects, whereas in later stages the empowerment effects would depend on the followers achieving independence from the leader and on their need for affirmation and recognition. (Kark *et al.*, 2003, p. 253)

Further, personality traits and the specificities of the task may contribute to an interaction between feelings of dependence and empowerment.

11.3.3   *Personality of Transformational Leaders*

Broadly speaking, leadership style could be defined in terms of "stable patterns of behaviors displayed by leaders" (Eagly, Johannesen-Schmidt, & van Engen, 2003, p. 569), which implies that there is a clear theoretical overlap between the concept of leadership style and personality traits. Accordingly, the question arises as to what specific personality dimensions are associated with each leadership style. In the past two decades several studies have aimed at answering this question by articulating or integrating established individual difference constructs (e.g., personality traits, intelligence, interests, and motivation) with different leadership styles. In particular, recent research has increasingly focused on the personality characteristics of transformational leaders, looking at empirical or psychometric links between measures of the Big Five and transformational leadership.

Recently, Judge and Bono (2000) looked at 14 samples of leaders in 200 organizations to see which of the Big Five traits predicted transformational leadership. They hypothesized that Emotional Stability (low Neuroticism), Extraversion, Openness to Experience, and Agreeableness would be positively related to ratings of effective leadership behaviors. Results were only partly supportive, as Extraversion ($r = .28$) and Agreeableness ($r = .32$), but not Emotional Stability and Conscientiousness, were related to leadership effectiveness.

Correlations between Extraversion and transformational leadership were mainly attributed to the "dominance" components of Extraversion, while correlations between transformational leadership and Agreeableness were interpreted in terms of the "empathy" components of Agreeableness. In addition, there was also a significant correlation between transformational leadership and Openness to Experience, though this correlation dropped to nonsignificant levels when Extraversion and Agreeableness were taken into account.

Hogan and Hogan (2002) argued that charismatic/transformational leaders tend to be more agreeable, open, and extraverted than transactional leaders. Transformational leaders need acceptance and status, which they would achieve by being generous and sensitive (agreeable). Transformational leaders also need to be expressive, dominant, and persuasive, for which their high Extraversion would be advantageous, while their high Openness score may be particularly beneficial in enabling them to "do things differently"; that is, to innovate and create through an imaginative vision of the future (see Figure 11.7).

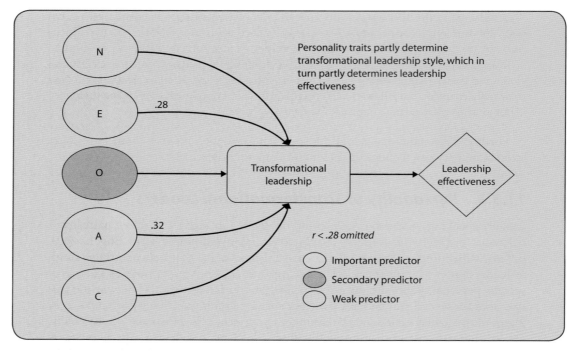

FIGURE 11.7 *Personality traits, transformational leadership, and leadership effectiveness*

Key: N = Neuroticism, E = Extraversion, O = Openness, A = Agreeableness, C = Conscientiousness.

11.3.4   Transactional Leadership: Controlling rather than Inspiring

transactional leadership a leadership style that is characterized by the leader's tendency to control followers' behaviors and to achieve influence by exchanging rewards (e.g., economic benefits) for compliance.

Transactional leadership is characterized by the leader's tendency to *control* followers' behaviors and apply corrective transactions (between leader and follower) that lead to the elimination of problems. Transactional leaders achieve influence over their subordinates by exchanging rewards (securing economic benefits) in return for compliance; that is, subordinates will grant authority to the leader.

The main difference between transformational (as well as charismatic) and transactional leadership is that empowerment of followers occurs only in the former. Thus, transformational and charismatic leaders may influence not only subordinates' behaviors but also their motivation, self-efficacy, and self-esteem, whereas transactional leaders will only affect subordinates' behaviors. More crucially, transformational and charismatic leaders manage to influence subordinates to think *beyond* their personal interests and act according to the interests of the whole group, whereas transactional leaders base their influence on the personal interests of the subordinates.

This theoretical distinction is manifested in the practicalities of everyday transactional leadership, which, unlike transformational leadership, does not include a high degree of delegation of responsibilities and decision making to subordinates (Dvir *et al.*, 2002). Rather, transactional leadership is based on a pragmatic exchange relationship between leader and follower that resembles a commercial/business agreement.

Think, for example, of the very basic relationship that arises between a boss and their employees. Employees will work in return for their salary/payment, and follow the boss's orders and rules as long as they are satisfied with what they get in return. Thus, if the salary is too low they may choose to "break" the agreement and finish their transactional relationship with their boss by moving to another company.

11.4   LEADERSHIP AND GENDER

The idea that there are observable gender differences in both leadership potential and effectiveness has been a topic of scientific, popular, and political debate. In simple terms, this debate can be explained by the unequal distribution of women and men in leadership positions across a variety of disciplines, professions, and fields (Eagly, Johannesen-Schmidt, & van Engen, 2003; Miller, Taylor, & Buck, 1991). For some this is an indicator of males' superior leadership potential, while for others it is simply a sign of the sexist society in which we live. It has, for instance, been reported that females constitute only 5 percent of top corporate positions and only 1 percent of chief executive officers among America's top 500 companies (Catalyst, 2002a, 2002b). In this section, we shall not concern ourselves with the ideological views that perpetuate this debate but with the scientific evidence that may help us shed light on the issue of gender differences underlying leadership.

PHOTO 11.7 *Women in power: from Cleopatra to Hillary*

Left © Konstantin Yolshin/Shutterstock; right © Alan Freed/Shutterstock.

Few careful studies of gender differences had been conducted prior to the 1970s. During the 1970s and 1980s, the most widely held psychological view in regard to gender differences in leadership maintained, with the support of experimental/laboratory evidence, that female and male leaders do *not* differ in their leadership potential and effectiveness (Bartol & Martin, 1986; Nieva & Gutek, 1981). For instance, in the second edition of the *Handbook of Leadership*, Bass (1981) concluded that there are no consistent gender differences in supervisory style. However, subsequent psychometric studies analyzed large sets of data and possible variations in leadership style between men and women, yielding conflicting results.

Theoretically, there are three major reasons to expect gender differences in leadership styles:

- Biologically, men and women are different.
- Culturally, men and women have different roles (these roles were more different in the past than they are now, but cultural differences still persist).
- Perceptions of men and women (by others) are different.

Thus, differences between men's and women's leadership styles can be directly enhanced – and even caused – by lay beliefs about gender differences in leadership (see Section 11.2.3, which looks at leadership as a perceived construct).

self-fulfilling prophecy the process by which expectations about other people or groups lead those people or groups to behave in ways that confirm those expectations.

These **self-fulfilling prophecies** (by which beliefs or expectations about an event cause the very event to occur) may explain stereotypical patterns of behavior that are particularly evident in regard to gender. Thus "internalized" gender roles would cause male leaders to behave in ways that are consistent with the "male-leader stereotype" and female leaders to act according to established "female-leader stereotypes" (Cross & Madson, 1997).

Given that, in most societies and cultures, women tend to be portrayed as more friendly, kind, and unselfish than men, the notion of leadership may be constructed on male-like attributes, such as dominant, masterful, and assertive (see also Section 11.2.1). Accordingly, Schein (2001, p. 676) concluded that, for most people, the "think manager, think male" rule is deeply internalized. In fact, we may have all come across situations in which successful female leaders have been more or less deliberately compared with males, or described as more masculine than other women. On the other hand, several popular books published during the 1980s claimed that "feminine traits, such as warmth, nurturance, and flexibility, made women better leaders and managers than power-oriented male leaders" (Chemers, 2000, p. 33).

Eagly and Johnson (1990) meta-analyzed 162 studies (in the period 1961–87), looking at gender differences in autocratic vs. democratic leadership styles. The overall pattern of results showed that women tended to be more democratic than men, while men tended to be more autocratic than women. This pattern of results was later replicated by another meta-analysis (van Engen, 2001) and contradicted early experimental evidence that had equated men and women in regard to their leadership style and effectiveness.

In a recent state-of-the-art meta-analytic comparison of gender differences in transformational, transactional, and *laissez-faire* leadership styles, Eagly, Johannesen-Schmidt, and van Engen (2003) analyzed data from 45 different studies (between 1985 and 2000) in order to test whether women and men differed in their *typical* leadership styles. Results showed that female leaders tended to be more transformational than their male counterparts, while male leaders were generally more likely to adopt transactional and *laissez-faire* leadership styles. Although overall gender differences were relatively minor, the authors concluded that "positive" features of leadership are manifested more clearly in female than in male leaders, so that, if anything, women would have an advantage – rather than a disadvantage – in regard to leadership effectiveness. This is consistent with several claims by other authors that female leaders tend to be less hierarchical, more cooperative, and more other oriented than their male counterparts (Helgesen, 1990; Loden, 1985). It has been noted, therefore, that in present-day organizations women's typical leadership styles would lead to greater effectiveness than those of males (Eagly, Johannesen-Schmidt, & van Engen, 2003; Sharpe, 2000), mainly because of their ability to display a transformational repertoire of leadership.

11.5 SUMMARY AND CONCLUSIONS

This chapter has looked at the construct of leadership, which is important in regard to individual differences because of the applied implications of understanding and predicting who will lead and, perhaps more importantly, who will make a successful leader. As has been seen:

- Traditional approaches to leadership, such as the Great Man theory, attempted to identify the key attributes or traits that distinguish between successful and unsuccessful leaders on the one hand, and leaders and nonleaders on the other. Although personality and intelligence were found to correlate with leadership emergence and effectiveness, they were insufficient to predict and understand leadership, partly because of their failure to account for important situational factors, which have been examined by contingency theories of leadership.

- In recent years increasing research has examined the behavioral or stylistic aspects of leadership. Three major types of leadership emerged; namely, transformational (previously referred to as charismatic), transactional, and *laissez-faire*. Transformational leaders are those who inspire and serve as role models for others. Transactional leaders are those who are pragmatic and task oriented (thus they may be obeyed but rarely admired). *Laissez-faire* leaders are those who adopt a passive approach and let the group take the initiative.

- Recent meta-analysis has reported several links between established personality traits and leadership styles, most notably the correlations of transformational leadership with Extraversion and Agreeableness. Thus there has been a reemergence of the trait approach to leadership, which simultaneously accounts for both behavioral and dispositional aspects of leadership.

- Meta-analytic comparison of gender differences in leadership styles has shown that female leaders tend to be more transformational than their male counterparts, while male leaders are generally more likely to adopt transactional and *laissez-faire* leadership styles. Overall gender differences were found to be relatively minor, although "positive" features of leadership are manifested more clearly in female than in male leaders.

Chapter 12 will look at individual differences in vocational interests; that is, the psychological factors that determine people's aspirations and career choices.

CHECK YOUR ANSWERS

Correct answers to the questions in Focus Point 11.4: (a) N and leadership emergence, (b) equally with both (.24), (c) .16.

TEXTS FOR FURTHER READING

Bass, B.M. (1997). Does the transactional-transformational leadership paradigm transcend organizational and national boundaries? *American Psychologist*, 52, 130–39.

Eagly, A.H. & Johnson, B.T. (1990). Gender and leadership style: A meta-analysis. *Psychological Bulletin*, 108, 233–56.

Hogan, J. & Hogan, R. (2002). Leadership and sociopolitical intelligence. In R.E. Riggio, S.E. Murphy, & F.J. Pirozzolo (Eds.), *Multiple Intelligences and Leadership* (pp. 75–88). Mahwah, NJ: Lawrence Erlbaum.

Judge, T.A., Bono, J.E., Illies, R., & Gerhardt, M.W. (2002). Personality and leadership: A qualitative and quantitative review. *Journal of Applied Psychology*, 87, 765–80.

Simonton, D.K. (1986). Presidential personality: Biographical use of the Gough adjective check list. *Journal of Personality and Social Psychology*, 51, 149–60.

12 Vocational Interests

LEARNING OUTCOMES

BY THE END OF THIS CHAPTER, YOU SHOULD BE ABLE TO ANSWER THE FOLLOWING FIVE KEY QUESTIONS:

1. What are vocational interests?
2. Do interests change much across the lifespan?
3. What is the person–environment fit?
4. What are the main factors of Holland's typology?
5. How do personality and intelligence relate to vocational interests?

KEY WORDS

Circumscription and Compromise Theory ● Person–Environment Fit ● Prediger's Three-Factor Model ● RIASEC Model ● Trait Complex Theory

CHAPTER OUTLINE

> The proof that the little prince existed is that he was charming, that he laughed, and that he was looking for a sheep. If anybody wants a sheep, that is a proof that he exists.
>
> Antoine de Saint-Exupéry, 1900–44
>
> It is the first of all problems for a man to find out what kind of work he is to do in this universe.
>
> Thomas Carlyle, 1795–1881

12.1   INTRODUCTION

The final chapter of this book is concerned with vocational interests. Despite their longstanding history in psychology and despite being considered the third "pillar" of individual differences (together with motivation; see Figure 12.1), vocational interests have received less attention than other individual difference constructs, although in recent years there has been an upsurge in research on this topic.

Definitions of interests have generally conceptualized the construct in terms of *preferences*. Owen and Taljaard (1995, p. 428) defined interests as "a spontaneous preference for certain activities as well as a spontaneous declination for other activities." Similarly, Greenhaus, Callanan, and Godshalk (2000) explained interests in terms of "likes" and "dislikes" attached to specific objects or activities. On the other hand, Carlson (2002) argued that interests could be understood as a form of desire, particu-

PHOTO 12.1 *Some people have interests in fetishism, while others may have more classical interests like ballet – it varies from person to person*

Left © Bruno Passigatti/Shutterstock; right © Ayakovlev.com/Shutterstock.

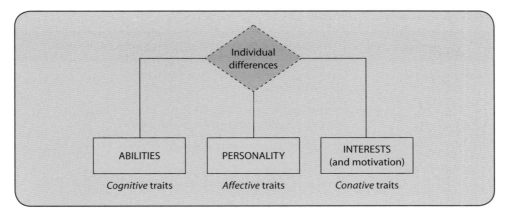

FIGURE 12.1 *The three pillars of differential psychology*

larly for what people wish to understand and do. Thus interests tell us what people enjoy and do not enjoy doing.

Clearly, definitions of interests overlap with both personality (see Chapter 2) and motivation (see Chapter 9). Indeed, interests may be regarded as constitutive of personality traits and motivation because they refer to individual differences in preferences, needs, and goals.

The importance of vocational interests, however, is that they explain variance in real-life outcomes where abilities and personality traits fail to do so. Thus individuals' choice of career, which affects their educational and occupational future, may not be predicted by personality or intelligence, though it may be affected by them (Ackerman & Heggestad, 1997; Gottfredson, 2005). For example, research has shown that vocational interests are often significantly related to the personality traits of Extraversion and Openness to Experience. Accordingly, vocational interests may be conceptualized as a link between personality and career choices. Furthermore, and as will be clear from this chapter, vocational interests can be predicted by individual differences in gender and intelligence (Chamorro-Premuzic, Furnham, & Ackerman, 2006).

12.2   APPROACHES TO VOCATIONAL INTERESTS

Although there are several theories of vocational interests, only few have been examined through rigorous empirical studies, and even fewer integrated with the broader individual difference literature. In a review of the literature, Furnham (1994) conceptualized six major types of theoretical approaches to the study of vocational interests (see Table 12.1).

The fact that Furnham's list of approaches did not include individual differences is unsurprising, because vocational psychology has largely avoided integrating other individual difference constructs into its theories, thus resulting in a more or less isolated paradigm. To some, this is a sign of the theoretical richness and diversity of the field. To

Table 12.1 *Approaches to the study of vocational interests*

Approach	Key focus
Developmental	• Examines *changes* in vocational interests throughout the lifespan and how these develop • Emphasizes the role of environmental factors, though individuals partly choose their career paths • A central role is given to the concept of "effort"
Psychodynamic	• Assesses the impact of *intrapsychic* conflicts (between unconscious and conscious processes) on vocational decisions • Such decisions are often irrational or based on unconscious motives • Interactions with "significant others" and role models play a major role in determining career choices and aspirations
Motivational (theories of needs)	• Takes into account the needs of the individual and how they can be satisfied in the context of organizational settings (see Chapter 9)
Sociological	• Highlights the importance of socioeconomic and political factors as determinants of vocational aspirations and possibilities • Stresses the importance of previous level of education and opportunities rather than personal attributes (e.g., personality and ability)
Decision making	• A relatively recent approach that examines the factors underpinning individuals' decision-making schemes (e.g., perceptions, attributions, valuations) and how these affect choices
Existential	• Derives from the humanistic approach to psychology and personality, with a focus on the self-actualization or self-realization of the individual through the accomplishment of vocational goals (e.g., comparing expected vs. actual career choices)

others, however, it is merely a testament to the area's conceptual fragmentation and, in turn, a reason for the relative lack of progress of vocational interests in comparison to personality or intelligence research. Admittedly, however, interests are as crucial to differential psychology as are personality and abilities, and any revision of the field that excluded interests would be truncated by definition. Thus a (very rough) description of the topic of differential psychology could be seen to conflate the following:

- Interests and motivation: *what* a person will do.
- Abilities: what a person *can* do.
- Personality: *how* a person will do it.

Although the above classification is oversimplistic, and the structure and contents of this book have shown that there are more than three or four constructs underpinning the study of individual differences, most if not all topics can be "accommodated" within the context of interests, abilities, and personality traits. Hence the importance of examining the conceptual and empirical links between these three areas of differential psychology.

In a special issue of the *Journal of Vocational Behavior* (the major publication in the area), Russell (2001) and Tinsley (2001) called for less isolation in vocational research, while Walsh (2001) concluded that one of the most important challenges for vocational psychologists is the incorporation of findings from other areas of differential psychology in order to pay more attention to individual differences (see also Kline, 1975).

12.3   LINKING THEORY AND PRACTICE

A key issue in vocational psychology is the link between theory and practice, and this makes vocational interests a more applied concept than personality and even intelligence. This means that, although personality traits, abilities, and interests may all influence individuals' lives, people pay explicit attention to their interests when making decisions in regard to their careers. Educational and occupational psychologists often apply theories of vocational interests to advise individuals on their career choices. Indeed, interests have been examined in a wide range of theoretical and applied contexts, including personnel selection, educational psychology, and motivation (see Table 12.2).

Lent (2001) proposed the following three goals for vocational theories:

- To explain individuals' career choices (causes and development) and how these affect entry, adjustment, progress, satisfaction, and change in both educational and occupational settings.

- To construct preventive and palliative vocational strategies that may help individuals identify the best choices and pursue them (put them into action).

- To include a wide range of clients, from primary and secondary school to university students, unemployed, workers, retirees, and even organizations (e.g., schools, businesses, institutions).

In an ideal world, clients would include not only Ivy League or Oxbridge students but also blue-collar workers (Fouad, 2001). Yet, it is clear that economic factors constrain freedom of vocational choices. Accordingly, individual differences in vocational interests may exist across socioeconomic classes but be expressed differently within the same salary range. Furthermore, socioeconomic factors, such as unemployment, will clearly limit individuals' choice of job and overshadow the importance of interests in determining their choices. One of the most consistent findings in cross-sectional and longitudinal data is that vocational interests and job expectations tend to adjust to socioeconomic circumstances from primary school to university (e.g., Borgen & Young, 1982; Taylor, 1985; Tremaine, Schau, & Busch, 1982).

Table 12.2 *Areas related to the study of interests (and key references in chronological order)*

Context (relation to)	Representative references/studies
Occupational success	Clark (1961)
Educational counseling	Walsh & Opisow (1983)
Job satisfaction	Assouline & Meir (1987)
Personnel selection	Hogan & Blake (1996)
Career development	Oleski & Subich (1996)
Vocational choice	Holland (1997)
Personality and intelligence	Ackerman & Heggestad (1997)
Job stress	Edwards & Rothbard (1999)

12.4 STABILITY OF INTERESTS: EVIDENCE FOR DISPOSITIONAL NATURE

One of the reasons for the importance of interests in differential psychology is their *stability* across the lifespan. In fact, reviewers have long noted that "extreme fluctuations in interest areas of young persons over a period of time would defeat any predictions based on them" (Herzberg, Bouton, & Steiner, 1954, p. 90). Moreover, appropriate psychometric tools for the assessment of interests (particularly in the context of career counseling and vocational guidance) would require evidence or test–retest reliability (little or no variation between an individual's score on the same inventory every time they complete it), which can only be ensured if inventories assess dispositional factors. Research has increasingly tested the possibility of within-individual variations in interests, hoping to find none (see Figure 12.2).

Early reviews relied primarily on qualitative accounts (Campbell, 1971; Strong, 1943; Swanson, 1999), which, albeit informative, are more exposed to inaccurate and subjective interpretations. However, a recent meta-analysis by Low *et al.*(2005) provided quantitative evidence for the stability of interests across the lifespan. This study examined longitudinal data from age 12 to age 40 and found compelling evidence for the *invariance* of interests across time. Figure 12.3 shows the correlations or reliability indicators for interests within each age gap. For instance, between the ages of 12 and 14, interests remained slightly unstable as two-year gap scores correlated in the region of .53 (see left bar). However, the chart shows that the stability of interests increased with time, peaking at the age of 25–30 years, and dropping thereafter,

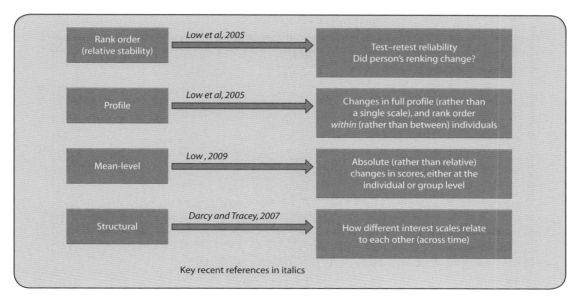

FIGURE 12.2 *Stability of vocational interests: four types*

Based on Armstrong, Su, & Rounds, 2011.

PHOTO 12.2 *Fashionably early*

A fashion graduate and a prospective students pose at Central St Martins. Some people pick their careers very young, while others never really decide what they want to do. What explains these individual differences?

Image courtesy of Tomas Chamorro-Premuzic.

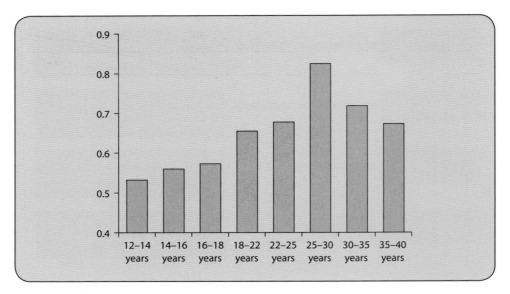

FIGURE 12.3 *Stability of interests across the lifespan*

Source: Based loosely on Low *et al.* (2005).

though only slightly under the .70 barrier. What these data show is that "interests stability remained unchanged during much of adolescence and increased dramatically during the college years (age 18–21.9), where it remained for the next 2 decades" (Low *et al.*, 2005). Indeed, the authors noted that the stability of interests is greater than that of personality traits. There can be no more compelling evidence, then, for the dispositional nature of vocational interests.

12.5 GENDER DIFFERENCES IN VOCATIONAL INTERESTS

Gender differences in vocational interests are important because of their potential to explain the distribution of sex differences in the workforce; specifically, why women or men may be over- or underrepresented in certain job types. In fact, this question has also been asked in regard to educational settings, as male–female ratios vary enormously from one faculty to another. Typically, female students represent the majority within arts and humanities, and in several social sciences including psychology. On the other hand, male students outnumber their female counterparts in hard sciences (e.g., maths, physics, engineering). For instance, Kirkcaldy (1988) reported women to have significantly lower interest levels than men in technical and scientific jobs, whereas the opposite was true for design and socioeducational jobs. In addition,

PHOTO 12.3 *Some jobs are more gender related than others, even if just in people's minds. Although modern society is defying these stereotypes, they still drive vocational interests. This photograph shows a female nurse taking a break. Would more males go into nursing if this weren't such a stereotypically female profession?*

Image courtesy of Nadia Bettega, reproduced with permission.

women preferred less structured, more creative, less task-oriented, and more permissive types of jobs, a description that fits well with artistically or emotionally involving jobs (Furnham, 2005).

Although this suggests that vocational interests may be the cause of gender differences in educational and occupational choices, a more complicated question is: What exactly explains or determines gender differences in vocational interests? This question is complicated because correlational designs rarely reveal the causal paths underlying the relationship between two or more variables. For example, one cannot be sure whether gender differences in vocational interests are influenced by cultural, personality, or ability factors (e.g., whether women prefer certain jobs because they suit their abilities, their personalities, or simply conform with social expectations; see Gottfredson, 2005, and Section 12.10). Furthermore, there is also the issue of whether gender differences are a consequence of sex or biological differences between men and women or simply the product of cultural factors.

It is obvious that expectations or beliefs about the job affect an individual's level of interests. This idea has been emphasized by schemata theories. For instance, Levy, Kaler, and Schall (1988) assessed participants' perceptions of 14 jobs and identified two main factors – namely, achievement vs. helping and low vs. high educational level – that represented people's schemata. In that sense, gender (or sex) difference in vocational interests may confound a mix of self-perceived and other-perceived attributes, including personality and ability factors. Thus women or men may choose some jobs rather than others because:

- They are genuinely better at them.
- They believe they are better at them.
- Others (e.g., individuals, parents, society) believe they are better at them.
- They simply enjoy them.
- They have few other alternatives.
- They believe they have few other alternatives.

And these are only *some* potential explanations for the gender divide in vocational interests, the educational system, and occupational settings. As if we needed yet another problem, the issue of gender differences (in respect to any individual difference variable) is hugely politicized. Thus some believe that gender differences in the workforce are a function of individual difference in ability (level and type), while others seem inclined to think that they result from sociopolitical factors or constraints. Somewhere along those lines (perhaps at the center) we can locate gender differences in vocational interests, which are affected by both personality dispositions (including abilities) and external factors.

FOCUS POINT 12.1   MASCULINITY, VOCATIONAL INTERESTS AND CAREER CHOICE TRADITIONALITY

Historically, women have tended to select jobs from a narrow range of traditionally female-oriented occupations (e.g., nursing and teaching), thus considerable research has gone into identifying personality and background variables that may contribute to this in order to facilitate and increase women's career options. Conversely, little research has gone into facilitators and barriers of men's career choices.

Researchers suggested that men and women approach career decision making differently, and that this is magnified when deciding on gender-nontraditional careers. For instance, women who choose male-typical careers are generally seen to be driven by status, while males would be

discouraged from pursuing female-typical careers because of their (perceived or actual) lower status and pay. Males would also be more at risk of being ridiculed for engaging in "gender-inappropriate" behavior.

What have often been theorized to influence men's choices of traditionally male-dominated careers are culturally prescribed gender roles and vocational interests. It has been posited, for instance, that early socialization experiences, notably gender-role orientation, shape interests that, in turn, circumscribe one's range of acceptable career alternatives. There are six widely accepted occupational/vocational categories (Realistic, Investigative, Artistic, Social,

Enterprising, and Conventional; see Section 12.7), and there are sex differences in these categories. It follows that men's endorsements of "masculine" vocational interests (e.g., Enterprising) should relate positively to their career choice, and inversely to "feminine" interests (e.g., Social). It has also been suggested that men may avoid seeking nontraditional careers for fear of being perceived as feminine or gay.

Men who opt for gender-traditional careers score highly on three masculinity-related constructs: masculine ideology, masculine gender-role conflict (rigid sexist roles resulting in personal restrictions), and homophobia. Yet there seems to be a lack of research into how vocational interests can influence men's career choices. In this paper, the authors explore the possible mediating effects of vocational interests in the relation between gender roles and career choice traditionality.

The authors thus hypothesized:

- Men's endorsements of the three masculinity-related constructs (aforementioned) would be positively related to their endorsement of traditionally masculine vocational interests (e.g. Realistic) and inversely to feminine interests (e.g. Conventional).
- Traditionally masculine interests would be associated with more traditional career choices, and less traditional interests would be related to less traditional career choices.
- Finally, vocational interests would *mediate* (account for or explain) the relation between masculine gender roles and career choice traditionality.

METHOD

PARTICIPANTS

Participants were 212 male university students from 51 different majors. Ages ranged from 17 to 54 years ($M = 24.1, S.D. = 7.0$).

MEASURES

MASCULINITY

The exogenous (i.e., independent) latent variable of masculinity was measured using three inventories: the Male Role Norms Scale (MRNS), the Gender Role Conflict Scale (GRCS), and the Index of Homophobia-Modified (IHP-M).

The MRNS was divided into three factors: Status, Toughness, and Antifemininity (men's expectation of avoiding stereotypically female behaviors).

VOCATIONAL INTERESTS

These were measured using the Self-Directed Search (SDS; see Section 12.7), consisting of six vocational interest types: Realistic, Investigative, Artistic, Social, Enterprising, and Conventional.

CAREER CHOICE TRADITIONALITY

Endogenous (i.e., dependent) latent variable of career choice traditionality was measured using indexes of traditionality of both current major at university (based on percentage of males currently enrolled in each major) and intended career choice (based on the Male Dominance Index, MDI).

PROCEDURE

Males completed instruments in classroom settings.

RESULTS

First, the six RIASEC interests were put into two dimensions for easier analysis: data–ideas (Enterprising and Conventional; male and female interests respectively) and things–people (Realistic and Social; male and female interests respectively).

The modeled paths being investigated are as follows: Status and Antifemininity to both data–ideas and things–people to career choice (see Figure 12.4).

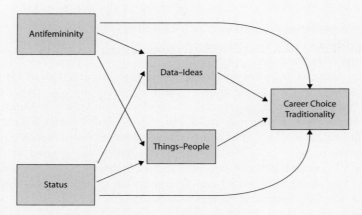

FIGURE 12.4 *Modeled paths*

Antifemininity was strongly positively related to things–people (ß = .57, t = 4.26, p < .001) but no significant relation to data–ideas. Conversely, status had a moderate positive relation to data–ideas (ß = .30, t = 2.15, p < .05) but did not predict things–people. Career choice traditionality was predicted positively by things–people (ß = .54, t = 7.81, p < .001) but not data–ideas. When assessing the total effects of Antifemininity on career choice traditionality, results were significant (ß = .37, t = 2.77, p < .01). After controlling for total indirect effects (things–people and data–ideas), the direct effect of antifemininity on career choice traditionality dropped to almost zero, whereas indirect effects were still significant (ß = .30, t =3.68, p < .01). Thus results indicated that 81 percent of antifemininity's total effect on career traditionality was mediated through a combination of data–ideas and things–people. Decomposing the total indirect effects to reveal which indirect path was most influential showed that approximately 100 percent of the meditational effect was through things–people.

DISCUSSION

The results revealed partial support for the model in which males' endorsement of masculine gender roles predicted their vocational interests and that in turn predicted their career choice tradi-tionality. The hypothesis for the meditational role of men's vocational interests in the relation between masculinity and traditionality of career choice was supported. However, contrary to predictions, results did not support the direct relation between masculinity and career choice traditionality. These findings suggest that both masculine gender roles and vocational interests are important as factors influencing men's career choices, and that career choice traditionality is indirect, through mediators such as interests.

This research sheds light on understanding how men limit their career options through antifemininity gender-role socialization, through its part in interest formation. To get a broader understanding, studying women's career choice formation would be relevant, as processes underlying this has been suggested to operate differently. Also, looking at a sample of already employed men could be useful, as the authors' career choice traditionality measure may not correspond to men's actual career choices on graduation. Finally, one must not forget that other factors, such as sexual orientation, can also play a mediating role in this model.

Source: Tokar, D. M., & LaRae, M. J. (1998). Masculinity, vocational interests and career choice traditional-ity: Evidence for a fully mediated model. *Journal of Counselling and Psychology*, 4, 424–35. With Permission from Elsevier.

12.6   PERSON–ENVIRONMENT FIT

One of the most prominent frameworks for investigating vocational interests is the so-called **person–environment** (P–E) **fit** theory, which posits that individuals' level of job satisfaction and performance is largely a function of *congruence* between their personal attributes (e.g., personality traits, abilities, expectations) and those of the environment (e.g., school, business). Indeed, interests have provided the ideal route to the study of congruence or match of individuals to appropriate and specific environments (Hogan & Blake, 1996). Thus, "the greater the match between the individual's needs and the environmental attributes, the greater will be the potential for the individual's satisfaction and performance" (Furnham, 2005, p. 116).

> **person–environment fit**   vocational theory that suggests that the congruence or match between a person's individual attributes (e.g., personality traits, abilities, expectations) and those of the environment (e.g., school, business) determines the level of job satisfaction and performance.

Numerous studies have reported evidence in support of the P–E fit model. For example, Furnham (1987) found that extraverted individuals preferred and worked better in open-plan offices, no doubt because of their interests in social interaction, while the opposite pattern was found for introverts. Thus "people tend to search for environments that will let them exercise their skills and abilities and express their personality. For instance, social types look for social environments" (Furnham, 2005, p. 122). As seen throughout Chapter 7, this idea is consistent with the finding that individuals' personality and ability influence the choice of their environment: individual differences (in personal or dispositional factors) thus affect the array of experiences with which an individual may be confronted, and individuals build *niches* according to their abilities, preferences, and interests.

12.7   HOLLAND'S RIASEC TYPOLOGY

The most famous theory of vocational interests is that of J.L. Holland (1973), which posits that there are six types of interests for classifying both individuals and environments: *realistic, investigative, artistic, social, enterprising,* and *conventional* (hence the acronym **RIASEC**). Holland's types are generally illustrated by a hexagon, such as in Figure 12.5.

> **RIASEC model**   Holland's typology of six interest types, classifying people and environments as realistic, investigative, artistic, social, enterprising, or conventional, which accounts for individual differences in interests in terms of the level of congruence or fit between the person's characteristics and those of the environment.

The beauty of Holland's theory is that it accounts for personality and environmental differences in interests at the same time and using the same factors. Accordingly, the central aspect underlying interests is not the environment or the individual's personality disposition, but the level of congruence between the two. In short, then, there are three components or levels of analysis characterizing Holland's theory, namely:

- *Person*: characteristics of the individual – dispositions, preferences, and interests grouped according to a typology of vocations.

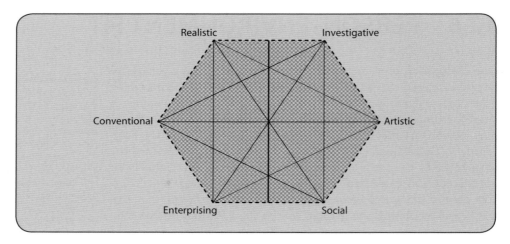

FIGURE 12.5 *Holland's RIASEC Model of Interests*

Source: Adapted from Cronbach (1990).

- *Environment*: characteristics of the environment – grouped according to the same typology of vocations.
- *Fit*: level of congruence between the characteristics of the person and the environment.

Realistic people are interested in "activities that entail . . . manipulation of objects, tools, machines, and animals" and fit occupations such as mechanic, carpenter, fisherman, and engineer. *Investigative* individuals tend to be interested in "investigation of physical, biological, and cultural phenomena in order to understand and control such phenomena." Examples of investigative professions are scientists, notably chemist, biologist, and physicist. *Artistic* people are interested in "verbal or human materials to create art forms or products" and are best tailored for artistic professions such as music, fine arts, and acting. *Social* individuals are interested in "activities that entail the manipulation of others to inform, train, develop, cure, or enlighten" and fit political, educational, or social jobs (e.g., minister, teacher, social worker). *Enterprising* types are interested in "the manipulation of others to attain organizational goals or economic gain." Accordingly, they are financially driven and business-minded and fit corporate jobs (e.g., lawyer, banker, salesperson). Finally, *conventional* types are interested in "keeping records, filling materials, organizing written and numerical data according to a prescribed plan, operating business machines and data processing machines." Examples of conventional jobs are file clerk, secretary, and accountant (Holland, 1997, pp. 19–23). See Table 12.3 for a more detailed description.

Graphical proximity between different types or points of the hexagon is a function of conceptual and empirical similarity. In the words of Holland (1997, p. 5), the RIASEC types are "inversely proportional to the theoretical relationships between them." For example, the investigative type is similar to artistic and realistic, but different from enterprising, social, and conventional types. Indeed, studies have reported precise correlations between different types of interests (see Table 12.4).

Table 12.3 Holland's Vocational Personality Types

	R REALISTIC	I INVESTIGATIVE	A ARTISTIC	S SOCIAL	E ENTERPRISING	C CONVENTIONAL
Traits	Hardheaded Unassuming Practical Dogmatic Uninsightful	Analytical Intellectual Curious Scholarly Broad interests	Open Non-conforming Imaginative Intuitive Sensitive Creative	Agreeable Friendly Understanding Sociable Persuasive Extraverted	Extraverted Dominant Adventurous Enthusiastic Power seeking Energetic	Conforming Conservative Unimaginative Inhibited Practical minded Methodical
Life goals	Invent apparatus or equipment	Invent valuable products	Artistic fame Write books	Help others Make sacrifices for others	Community leader	Expert in finance and commerce
	Become outstanding athlete	Theoretical contribution to science	Compose music Produce paintings	Teachers Therapist	Finance and commerce expert Dress well Be liked	Produce a lot of work
Values	Freedom Intellect Ambition Self-control Docility	Intellectual Logical Ambitious Wise	Equality Imaginative Courageous World of beauty	Equality Self-respect Helpful Forgiving	Freedom Ambitious (–) Forgiving (–) Helpful	(–) Imaginative (–) Forgiving
Models	Thomas Edison Admiral Byrd	Marie Curie Charles Darwin	T.S. Eliot Pablo Picasso	Jane Addams Albert Schweitzer	Henry Ford Andrew Carnegie	Bernard Baruch John Rockefeller
Aptitudes	Technical	Scientific	Artistic	Social and educational Interpersonal	Sales Leadership	Clerical ability Executive
Self-ratings	Mechanical ability	Math ability Research ability	Artistic ability		Business Clerical Interpersonal	
Suitable for	Mechanical engineering	Science and research	Arts	Human relations	Leadership	Business

Source: Adapted from Holland (1997).

PHOTO 12.4 *This photograph shows a nun at work. What type in Holland's RIASEC model do you think best predicts this vocational choice?*

Image courtesy of Nadia Bettega, reproduced with permission.

Table 12.4 *Intercorrelations between All RIASEC Types*

	I	A	S	E	C
R	.41	.15	.13	.26	.81
	.50	.13	.21	.02	.24
	.46	.16	.21	.16	.36
I		.42	.28	.47	.24
		.42	.33	.33	.02
		.34	.30	.16	.16
A			.45	.49	.15
			.42	.53	.19
			.42	.35	.11
S				.68	.39
				.61	.42
				.54	.38
E					.49
					.59
					.68

Note: All coefficients are Pearson's correlations: uppermost = Furnham & Schaeffer (1984); middle = Furnham & Walsh (1991); lowest = Holland (1973).

Key: R = Realistic, I = Investigative, A = Artistic, S = Social, E = Enterprising, C = Conventional.

FOCUS POINT 12.2   JOHN HOLLAND (1919–2008)

John Holland was one of the five most published scientists of the 20th century. A mild-mannered psychologist, he was mainly interested in designing psychometric tools for guiding people's lives. He was convinced that people can be better prepared for professional lives if they evaluate their strengths and weaknesses in relation to their interests.

Freud once said that the two biggest problems in life concern finding a mate and choosing an occupation (and that people never do either for rational reasons). Freud may have been right about the irrationality underlying the choice of a mate, but research has shown that it is perfectly possible to make rational career choices so long as a valid assessment and competent feedback are used. This is precisely what Holland created: the Self-Directed Search form (SDS) and the Vocational Preference Inventory (VPI). These are self-administered and self-marked tests that can help you find the job most suited to you by exploring the relationship between personality, hobbies, abilities, and dream careers.

Holland created what are called the "Holland Codes," which represent a set of personality types described in a theory of careers and vocational choice. These codes are represented by the "RIASEC" acronym. Each letter reflects an interaction of a personality and work environment in which Holland theorized that a person would have interests associated with each of the six types in a descending order of preference:

*R*EALISTIC	Hands on, manual, tool oriented
*I*NVESTIGATIVE	Analytical, scientific, explorative
*A*RTISTIC	Creative, independent, chaotic
*S*OCIAL	Supporting, healing, nurturing

PHOTO 12.5 *John Holland (1919–2008)*

*E*NTERPRISING	Persuading, leadership, sales
*C*ONVENTIONAL	Organizing, clerical, detailed

Holland's assessment is very popular and is employed for vocational guidance and personnel selection all over the world. His theory is simple, the test is easy to use, and the measurements are innovative.

As opposed to mainstream psychometrics, which is concerned with measuring entities (i.e., determining "true scores"), applied assessments are there to predict real-world outcomes; that is, things that really matter to people. Based on this approach, Holland successfully managed to create an integrative measure of personality and interests to predict one's more likely vocation, something no other researcher has accomplished so well.

Source: Based on an Obituary written by Robert Hogan.

Thus people with realistic interests may be happily adapted to investigative settings, people with artistic interests may adjust well to social contexts, and so forth. In some cases, though, correlations are not in tune with theoretical predictions. Further, studies often report different correlations for the same pair of types.

12.8   PREDIGER'S THREE-FACTOR MODEL

Prediger's three-factor model a reconceptualization of Holland's RIASEC model in terms of bipolar dimensions (ideas–data and people–things) rather than independent and unidimensional categories to describe people and environments.

Prediger (1976; Prediger & Vansickle, 1992a, 1992b) argued that Holland's RIASEC model could be reduced to a **three-factor model** incorporating two bipolar dimensions for work tasks – namely, *ideas–data* and *people–things* – and one general factor of response bias. Thus Prediger's model differs from Holland's not only in the number of factors but also in the type of variables conceptualized. Whereas Holland's theory is a circumplex model – each point defines the variable completely – Prediger's structure conceptualizes more than one level per variable.

Although this may sound complicated, the idea underlying Prediger's reclassification of the RIASEC is straightforward. One simply needs to fit a cross over Holland's hexagon to map the two dimensions of people vs. things and data vs. ideas (see Figure 12.6). At the midpoint between the enterprising–social–artistic triad, Prediger's "people" encompasses interests and tasks

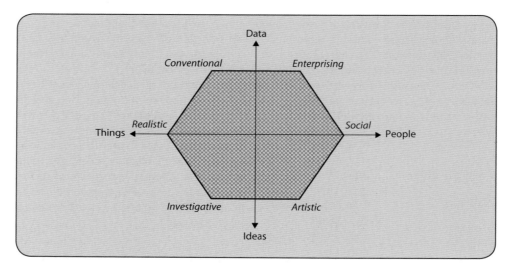

FIGURE 12.6 *Prediger on Holland*

characterized by high interpersonal contact, whereas at the opposite vertices – that is, the midpoint between the conventional–realistic–investigative triad – Prediger conceptualized "things," which refer to interests and jobs characterized by low interpersonal contact and typically impersonal in nature. Likewise, "data" represents both conventional and enterprising types and is defined by concreteness and practicality, while "ideas" represents both investigative and artistic and is best described in terms of thinking, creativity, and knowledge.

Prediger's dimensions have received wide empirical support (Prediger, 1982). The distinction between people and things has met with substantial support in the vocational literature. In fact, pioneers in differential psychology, such as Thorndike, pointed out almost a century ago that:

> the greatest difference between men and women [is] the relative strength of the interest in things and their mechanisms (stronger in men) and the interest in persons and their feelings (stronger in women). (Thorndike, 1911, p. 31)

Nonetheless, a large meta-analytic study by Rounds and Tracey (1993) provided little support for the compatibility between both models. After reviewing more than three decades of findings and synthesizing data from almost 80 RIASEC studies (published between 1965 and 1989), Rounds and Tracey concluded that the circumplex structure of the RIASEC is a unique and irreducible feature.

12.9   HOLLAND AND THE BIG FIVE

Studies have also examined the relationship of Holland's types with established personality traits, such as the Big Five. The two Big Five traits that seem most closely related to the RIASEC types are Extraversion and Openness to Experience. However, Holland's types seem more related to gender (masculinity–femininity) than to Big Five personality traits (Lippa, 1998).

Conceptually, one would expect the Big Five personality traits to "capture" variance in Holland's vocational types, because both frameworks encompass dispositional differences in interests. Furthermore, as both RIASEC and Big Five taxonomies are assessed through self-report inventories, there are also methodological or psychometric reasons to expect an overlap between both systems.

Gottfredson, Jones, and Holland (1993) examined correlations between the RIASEC and the Big Five and found that Openness related to artistic and investigative interests, whereas Extraversion related to social and enterprising interests. The authors also found associations between Conscientiousness and conventional interests, while Neuroticism was modestly but negatively correlated with all RIASEC types. However, the authors concluded that the degree of overlap was too small to substitute one measure with the other. In particular, Agreeableness, Conscientiousness, and Neuroticism seem largely unrepresented by RIASEC factors (though these personality traits are known to affect educational and occupational outcomes).

12.10   CIRCUMSCRIPTION AND COMPROMISE: GOTTFREDSON'S THEORY

circumscription and compromise theory
Gottfredson's vocational theory argues that career choices are determined by a complex interaction between individuals' self-perceptions and beliefs about jobs and their abilities, traits, and available opportunities (socioeconomic constraints).

In one of the most comprehensive and elaborate accounts of vocational interests, Gottfredson (2005) argued that vocational choices are determined by **circumscription and compromise** between an individual's self-concept and available choices. Thus interests are multidetermined and develop dynamically as a result of abilities and personalities (which have a substantial general component), specific skills and expectations (which are more determined by the environment), and socioeconomic constraints (see Figure 12.7).

Gottfredson's theory also enables one to make specific predictions about vocational choices, notably:

- Individuals will compromise jobs (and even fields) rather than move outside their circumscribed social status space.
- Individuals will compromise social status rather than move outside their circumscribed sexual space.

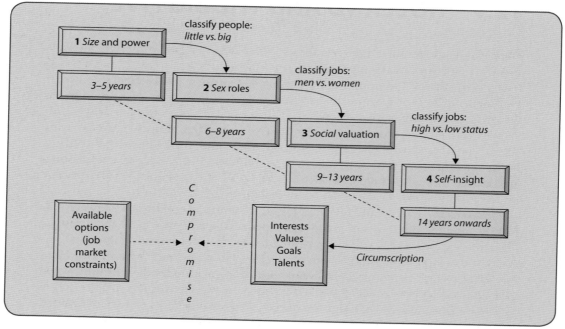

FIGURE 12.7 *Gottfredson's theory of circumscription and compromise*

Thus, Gottfredson (2005) conceptualizes a hierarchical and multidetermined vocational theory, where self-perceptions and perceptions about jobs interact with abilities, traits, and real-life opportunities (see also Holland, 1997). Perhaps more importantly, the theory allows for an integration of genetic and developmental aspects of individual difference factors, as well as integrating abilities, personality dispositions, interests, skills, socioeconomic factors, and self-concept.

12.11 TRAIT COMPLEXES AND INTERESTS

It is no coincidence that the final section of this chapter and book (before this chapter's summary) is devoted to the concept of **trait complexes**, as this idea represents the most promising research direction not only for vocational interests but also for individual differences in general.

> **trait complex theory**
> theory that attempts to integrate different constructs in differential psychology, such as personality, intelligence, and interests, in order to better understand and predict learning outcomes such as academic performance and knowledge acquisition.

In simple terms, trait complexes emphasize the importance of combining and integrating individual difference or trait factors to maximize our understanding and prediction of learning outcomes, such as academic performance and knowledge acquisition. The importance of trait complexes resides not only in the principle of *aggregation* (which enables us to include more than one type of trait or individual difference variable) but also, and especially, the *synergy* that may result from combining different traits. For example, individuals will learn better if they are bright (have a high IQ), work hard (high Conscientiousness score), and are intellectually curious (high Openness score). However, individuals who are high on all three traits may make better use of their intelligence (directing it toward relevant or interesting targets), work more efficiently, and be more effective in satisfying their intellectual curiosity.

Although this idea was put forward by Snow (1963) many years ago, it is only recently that differential psychologists have begun to focus on the integration of different constructs. Thus, established areas such as personality, intelligence, and interests were largely explored in isolation and mostly by different groups of researchers. This fragmentation of differential psychology – which, although not eliminated, has at least been reduced – was summarized by Cronbach (1957, p. 671) in the metaphor of the "Holy Roman Empire whose citizens identify mainly with their own principality."

Much of the revival of interest in trait complexes is due to Ackerman's recovery of Snow's work (Ackerman, 1996, 1999; Ackerman & Beier, 2003; Ackerman & Heggestad, 1997). In line with Snow's (1992, 1995) proposition, Ackerman and Heggestad's (1997) psychometric meta-analyses (see also Ackerman, 1999; Ackerman & Beier, 2003; Goff & Ackerman, 1992) identified four main trait complexes; namely, *social, clerical/conventional, science/mathematical*, and *intellectual/cultural* (see Figure 12.8).

The intellectual/cultural trait complex is dominated by crystallized abilities, creativity, Openness to Experience, and artistic interests. This trait complex overlaps slightly with the scientific/mathematical trait complex, which is characterized by realistic interests, mathematical reasoning, and visual perception ability. At the crossroads between intellectual/cultural and scientific/mathematical trait complexes we find investigative interests. Social trait complex represents a combination of Extraversion and both enterprising and social interests. Although it is not coupled with any traditional cognitive ability, it represents individual differences in interpersonal skills. The clerical/conventional trait complex includes Conscientiousness and high perceptual speed, as well as preference for traditional/conventional interests (in that sense it is pretty much the opposite of the intellectual/cultural trait complex).

Trait complex theory has important conceptual and applied implications. Conceptually, it provides a framework for the integration of individual differences. Personality, motivation, mood, abilities, creativity, and interests are, after all, characteristics of the same individual and what helps us distinguish between one individual and another. Just as we would not describe individuals' physical appearance only in terms of their height or weight or color of eyes, our psychological descriptions should include more than one aspect of individual differences. Furthermore, it is important that we learn to combine information about different traits, just as we combine information about different physical attributes. Whereas knowing that someone's weight is 95 kg would not be enough to get an accurate picture of that person's body shape, knowing their height as well just might.

Ackerman and Beier (2003) highlighted three advantages of the trait complex approach in regard to vocational interests:

- It abandons the "typological" representation of vocational interests (e.g., Holland's hexagon of six unidimensional interests).

- It capitalizes on the links between different individual difference constructs (notably synergetic links).

- It integrates career choices within the wider context of intellectual development.

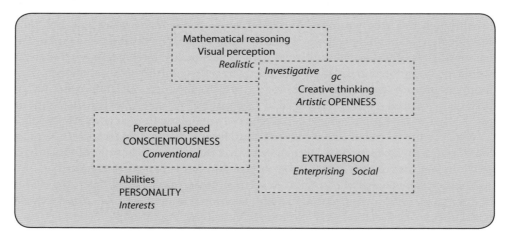

FIGURE 12.8 *Trait complexes*

Source: Based on Ackerman & Heggestad (1997).

12.12 SUMMARY AND CONCLUSIONS

This chapter has covered the construct of vocational interests, which is an important element in the study of individual differences because it complements the two other major constructs of differential psychology; namely, personality traits and intelligence. As has been seen:

- Vocational interests have received insufficient attention in differential psychology, and it is only in recent years that researchers (notably Ackerman and Gottfredson) have emphasized the importance of integrating this concept with other individual differences. Yet, interests have a longstanding tradition in psychology and are of practical importance, as career and vocational counselors tend to pay as much or even more attention to individuals' interests than to their personality and abilities.

- The most important individual difference approach to the study of vocational interests has been that of John Holland. Although his theory has often been referred to as a "personality model," it refers explicitly to interests and departs from typical personality taxonomies to assess not only the person but also the environment. Furthermore, Holland's model conceptualizes the interaction or "fit" between the person's and environment's characteristics to assess the degree of congruence between interests and what educational or occupational settings can offer. Although Holland's classification presents six independent interest types, such that people and environments can be described using one category, other theorists, such as Prediger, have postulated a dimensional model more akin to personality trait taxonomies (e.g., Eysenck, Big Five, Cattell).

- Thanks to the systematic and robust theoretical and empirical enterprises of Ackerman and Gottfredson, the field of vocational interests looks more promising than ever before. In fact, in recent years interests have been the focus of the most advanced conceptual frameworks for the integration of different individual difference factors.

Perhaps, in a decade, textbooks will no longer dedicate separate chapters to different individual difference constructs, but explain the causes, development, and consequences of their combined effects on behavior, in the hope of providing a less fragmented picture of individuality.

TEXTS FOR FURTHER READING

Ackerman, P.L. & Heggestad, E.D. (1997). Intelligence, personality, and interests: Evidence for overlapping traits. *Psychological Bulletin, 121*, 219–45.

Gottfredson, L.S. (2005). Using Gottfredson's theory of circumscription and compromise in career guidance and counseling. In S.D. Brown & R.W. Lent (Eds.), *Career Development and Counseling: Putting Theory and Research to Work* (pp. 71–100). New York: John Wiley & Sons Ltd.

Holland, J.L. (1996). Exploring careers with a typology: What we have learned and some new directions. *American Psychologist, 51,* 397–406.

Rounds, J. & Tracey, T.J. (1993). Prediger's dimensional representation of Holland's RIASEC circumplex. *Journal of Applied Psychology, 78,* 875–90.

Glossary

A

acquired needs theory According to McClelland, motivation is the acquisition of three basic needs: the need for achievement (desire to master skills), the need for affiliation (desire to be social), and the need for power (desire to influence others).

allele One of two or more alternative forms of a gene that occupies the same position (locus) on paired chromosomes and controls the same characteristic.

Alternate Uses Test A divergent thinking test that requires individuals to name all the things that can be done with a specified object, e.g., a chair.

assortative mating The selection of a partner who possesses similar genetic characteristics, such as height, color of eyes, and cognitive ability.

B

behavioral genetics Study of the biological basis of individual differences; it identifies genetic (biological) vs. nongenetic (e.g., environmental) causes of behavior, typically whether nature or nurture plays a larger role in determining individual differences in personality and intelligence.

behaviorism The study of observable behavior that explains human behavior not in terms of internal psychological processes but as a result of conditioning, or learning how to respond in specific ways to appropriate stimuli.

bell curve Also known as normal distribution, referring to the graph that represents the frequency of scores or values of any variable. In psychology many variables, notably IQ scores, are normally distributed in the population.

biopsychological Interaction between biological factors and psychological factors.

biopsychosocial approach A multidisciplinary approach to psychopathology based on the idea that mental illness results from a combination of biological, psychological, environmental, and social factors.

brainstorming A technique for generating ideas in a group setting that involves individuals saying everything that comes to mind about a topic, without self-censorship or inhibition.

C

central tendency Measures of the "average," which indicates what constitutes a typical value.

charismatic leadership A leadership style that is visionary, motivational, innovative, and capable of inspiring optimism in others, also characterized by exceptional communication skills.

circumscription and compromise theory Gottfredson's vocational theory argues that career choices are determined by a complex interaction between individuals' self-perceptions and beliefs about jobs and their abilities, traits, and available opportunities (socioeconomic constraints).

cognitive psychology The study of unobservable mental constructs such as perception, thinking, memory, and language.

concordance rate The extent to which people show the same disorders.

consistent patterns of behavior Those aspects of the individual that characterize the way they usually behave and make them different from others.

contingency model Theory of leadership that assumes that leadership is determined more by situational factors than by personal characteristics, positing that anyone has the potential to become a leader given a favorable context.

convergent thinking The generation of a response to a problem that requires a single, "correct" answer, e.g., "Paris" for the question "What is the capital of France?" (compare with divergent thinking).

correlation The extent to which two variables, e.g., traits and behavior, are related; a correlation of +1 indicates a perfect positive association, a correlation of −1 a perfect negative association.

crystallized intelligence (*gc*) The knowledge, information, and skills that can be used to solve problems related to what one has already learned.

D

diathesis-stress model This model suggests that some people possess an enduring, inherited vulnerability (diathesis) that is likely to result in psychological disorder (e.g., schizophrenia) when they experience an unbearable life event (stressor).

differential psychology The academic study of observable differences between individuals in terms of their underlying psychological determinants.

dispositional approach Views personality in terms of consistent and unchanging dispositions to act, think, and feel, regardless of context.

divergent thinking Widely regarded as an aspect of creativity, divergent thinking refers to the generation of multiple, "unique" answers to a problem, e.g., "Find as many uses as you can for a piece of string" (compare with convergent thinking).

E

emotional intelligence (EQ) The capacity of individuals to identify and manage their own emotional state and accurately to interpret and deal with others' emotions.

ERG theory Theory of motivation based on Maslow's hierarchy of needs, but with three rather than five levels; namely, existence needs (E), relatedness needs (R), and growth needs (G).

event-related potential A brain response to an internal or external stimulus, measured by a procedure known as electroencephalography (EEG), which measures electrical activity of the brain through electrodes placed on the scalp.

expectancy theories Theories that explain motivation in terms of people's expectation of the consequences of a chosen behavior, emphasizing the role of not only individuals' predictions of the behavioral outcome but also their evaluation of its usefulness and importance.

expressed emotion The specific set of feelings and behaviors directed at people with schizophrenia by their family members.

F

factor analysis Data-reduction technique where relationships between a large number of variables can be reduced to a relationship among fewer underlying factors.

Five Factor Model A trait theory of personality positing that there are five major and universal factors of personality; namely, Neuroticism, Extraversion, Openness, Agreeableness, and Conscientiousness (also known as the **Big Five**).

fluency The ability to produce a large quantity of creative ideas.

fluid intelligence (*gf*) The ability to learn new things and solve novel problems, irrespective of previous knowledge, education, or experience.

Flynn effect The finding by sociologist James Flynn that there are generational increases in IQ across nations.

G

g Used to refer to the "general intelligence factor" underlying performance, which can be extracted statistically from scores on a range of ability tests.

genome The full complement of genetic information, including the set of chromosomes and the genes they carry, inherited by an individual organism from its parents.

genotype The genetic complement, coded in DNA, that individuals inherit from their parents. Only identical twins have identical genotypes.

Gigantic Three Theory derived from Eysenck's investigations on personality and individual differences, which posits three major personality dimensions – Neuroticism, Extraversion, and Psychoticism – for classifying individuals.

goal-setting theories Theories that conceptualize motivation in terms of the consequence of behavior; behaviors that are goal oriented or motivated by their consequences are extrinsic, whereas behaviors that are performed for the sake of it are intrinsic.

H

hereditary genius The idea that different levels of intelligence are determined by hereditary or genetic factors.

heritability The extent to which differences between individuals are due to genetic factors.

heritability estimate (HE) A statistical indicator of the influence of genetic factors on individual differences in behavioral traits, showing what proportion of the total variance is attributable to genetic variation.

hot intelligences Types of ability that encompass an array of noncognitive traits, e.g., the ability to interact with others in social situations, in contrast to the more analytical, "cold" characteristics of traditional cognitive abilities, e.g., the ability to solve abstract mathematical problems.

I

identification Process that refers to an individual's unconscious desire to be like someone else, involving an idealized perception of a role model.

idiographic paradigm Assumes that individuals are unique and that two different people cannot be described using the same concepts or terms.

implicit theories of leadership Theories that study perceived attributes of leadership rather than leaders' personal characteristics, examining laypeople's beliefs about and attributions of personal qualities to leaders.

Inspection time A measure of the speed of intellectual processing in which a stimulus (e.g., lines of different lengths) is presented and inspected for a very short time before being removed.

intelligence The ability to solve mental problems that are related to performance in school, work, and most real-life settings.

intelligence quotient (IQ) A score derived from standardized tests of intelligence, usually combining several subtests of different cognitive ability tests (e.g., verbal, mathematical, spatial).

intelligence testing The attempt to quantify and measure individual differences in cognitive ability by means of standardized tests that use words, numbers, or figures and are usually administered in written (paper or computer) or oral form.

intelligence theory Describes, understands, and predicts individual differences related to competition and adaptation.

investment theory Theory according to which creative individuals have an exceptional ability to invest in ideas; thus, creativity is seen as a precondition of intelligence and a determinant of intelligent thinking and behavior.

J

job analysis A method of classifying different jobs according to the nature and complexity of the work as well as the relationships of the job holder with other people

L

leadership style A stable pattern of behaviors adopted by leaders that determines their relationship with and influence over group members.

lexical hypothesis The idea that the major dimensions of personality can be derived from the total number of descriptors in any language system.

longitudinal data Multiple measures of the same group of individuals, termed a cohort, across extended periods.

M

maladaptiveness The extent to which behavior interferes with a person's capacity to carry out everyday tasks such as studying or relating to others.

Maslow's hierarchy of needs Maslow's theory conceptualizing behavioral determinants in terms of a hierarchy or pyramid, with basic physiological needs at the base, followed by security needs, social needs, the need for esteem and recognition, and finally the need for self-fulfillment or self-actualization.

mean The average value, obtained by adding up all scores and dividing them by the number of cases.

mediation A correlation between two variables (e.g., gender and stress) that is caused by a third or latent variable (e.g., smoking).

mental illness approach An approach to psychological disorder that integrates physical and psychological variables in order to understand the processes underlying abnormal behavior.

mental test A series of psychometric tests originally devised by J.M. Cattell to measure individual differences in basic psychological functions such as tactile discrimination, hearing, and weight discrimination.

meta-analysis A review of previous research that involves statistical analyses combining the results of many studies.

moderation The independent effects of two or more variables on another variable.

molecular genetics An area of research that examines correlations between different genes and personality or intelligence scores and maps behavioral differences onto particular genes.

mood states Sporadic emotional states, lasting for minutes or hours, that indicate emotions such as happiness or anger and are manifested through physiological signals, e.g., increased heart rate, and behavioral signals, e.g., smiling.

motivation An internal state, dynamic rather than static in nature, that propels action, directs behavior, and is oriented toward satisfying both instinctual and cultural needs and goals.

motivational theories of arousal theories that account for individual differences in behavior in terms of differences in people's level of physical energy (arousal), which varies between as well as within individuals.

multiple intelligences Gardner's theory that there are many independent intelligences, including traditional as well as novel abilities such as bodily, social, spiritual, and musical intelligences.

multivariate genetic analysis Analysis that compares the effects of genes on a pair of traits independently of their individual heritability levels, giving a statistical indicator known as the genetic correlation, which shows whether two specific traits are related.

N

negative symptoms In schizophrenia, symptoms that indicate the absence of something normal, e.g., reduced or inappropriate emotional responses, lack of affect, or reduced motivation.

neuropsychology The area of psychology that studies how the brain relates to specific psychological processes.

nomothetic paradigm Assumes that individual differences can be described, explained, and predicted in terms of predefined attributes.

O

obsessive-compulsive disorder A disorder characterized by intense and repetitive obsessions that generate anxiety, e.g., fear of contamination, and compulsive acts or ritualistic behaviors to reduce anxiety, e.g., hand washing.

originality Whether an idea or response is unique.

overinclusive thinking The tendency to use irrelevant information or to introduce complexity in solving problems, characteristic of both creative and psychopathological thinking.

P

Pearson correlation Commonly used name for the Pearson Product-Moment Correlation Coefficient, represented by r, indicating the degree to which two variables are related.

personality disorder A persistent pattern of thinking, feeling, and behaving that deviates from cultural expectations and impairs a person's educational, occupational, and interpersonal functioning. Such disorders begin at a relatively early age, are stable over time, and are pervasive and inflexible.

person–environment fit Vocational theory that suggests that the congruence or match between a person's individual attributes (e.g., personality traits, abilities, expectations) and those of the environment (e.g., school, business) determines the level of job satisfaction and performance.

phenomenology The study of things (phenomena) as they are perceived or represented.

phenotype The expression of an individual's genes in behavioral traits that can be measured.

positive psychology Studies constructs such as happiness, fulfillment, and life satisfaction in contrast to "negative" emotions such as fear, anger, or sadness.

positive symptoms In schizophrenia, symptoms that indicate the presence of something unusual, e.g., delusions, hallucinations, and thought disorder.

practical intelligence A component of Sternberg's theory of intelligence (also comprising analytical/academic and creative intelligence), referring to the ability to solve problems and apply ideas to real-life contexts independent of academic or traditional cognitive ability.

Prediger's three-factor model A reconceptualization of Holland's RIASEC model in terms of bipolar dimensions (ideas–data and people–things) rather than independent and unidimensional categories to describe people and environments.

presidential leadership Area of leadership research that uses a multidisciplinary approach to examine the effectiveness of presidents and presidential candidates.

psychoanalysis A therapeutic method and theory, developed by Freud, based on the idea that unconscious motivations and needs influence behavior.

psychodynamic theories These deal with the processes underlying dynamic conflicts between unconscious and conscious psychological forces.

psychogenic Of psychological (rather than physiological) origin.

psychometrics Literally, measurement of the mind; the theory and measurement of psychological variables such as IQ (intelligence quotient) and personality via tests or questionnaires.

psychopathology (also called **abnormal psychology**) Studies the causes, treatment, and consequences of psychological disorders or mental illnesses such as depression, anxiety, and psychoses.

psychotic symptoms Symptoms such as hallucinations, incoherent speech, and delusions that indicate a distorted perception of reality.

R

reaction time A measure of the speed of intellectual processing in which a stimulus (e.g., a light) is seen until a decision is made by the participant and a response enacted.

regression analysis A statistical technique that enables one variable (the criterion) to be predicted by another set of variables (the predictors).

reliability The extent to which a given finding will be consistently reproduced on other occasions.

Remote Associations Test Psychometric test that requires participants to identify the correct associations between word groups; remote or unusual associations indicate individuals' capacity for generating novel or original ideas.

RIASEC model Holland's typology of six interest types, classifying people and environments as realistic, investigative, artistic, social, enterprising, or conventional, which accounts for individual differences in interests in terms of the level of congruence or fit between the person's characteristics and those of the environment.

S

schema A knowledge structure that guides individual expectations and beliefs, helps make sense of familiar situations, and provides a framework for processing and organizing new information.

self-efficacy Individuals' belief about the extent to which they can successfully carry out the appropriate behaviors to control and influence important life events.

self-fulfilling prophecy The process by which expectations about other people or groups lead those people or groups to behave in ways that confirm those expectations.

situational approach Views personality in terms of unrelated states or behaviors determined by situational factors.

social intelligence One of three facets of intelligence hypothesized by Thorndike (the others being mechanical and abstract intelligence), which he defined as the ability to manage others and act wisely in relationships – put simply, the ability to get on with others.

social norm A rule or guideline, determined by cultural factors, for what kind of behavior is considered appropriate in social contexts, e.g., whether burping after a meal is seen as a compliment or a sign of rudeness.

socioeconomic status (SES) A measure of an individual's position within a social group based on various factors, including occupation, education, income, location of residence, membership in civic or social organizations, and certain amenities in the home (e.g., telephone, TV, books).

somatogenic An approach that views physical factors as the cause of psychological differences in personality.

standard deviation A comparative indicator of a person's score against the general population.

statistical deviance An approach that conceptualizes abnormality in terms of behaviors that are extreme, rare, or unique, as opposed to typical.

T

taxonomy A system of classification; in differential psychology, taxonomies identify the major personality or ability factors by which people differ.

three-ring theory of giftedness Model that conceptualizes an overlap between creativity and intelligence, arguing that giftedness lies at the intersection between creativity, IQ, and task commitment (level of motivation, conscientiousness, determination, and passion).

threshold theory of creativity and intelligence The idea that a minimum level of intelligence is required in order to be creative, but that intelligence does not of itself determine creative thinking.

Torrance Test of Creativity and Thinking Test that measures creative thinking using picture-based and word-based exercises to assess fluency, flexibility (number of different categories of response), originality, and elaboration (amount of detail).

trait An internal psychological disposition that remains largely unchanged throughout the lifespan and determines differences between individuals. Examples of traits are extraversion, neuroticism, and agreeableness.

trait approach Theories of leadership that examine the psychological characteristics and personal attributes of leaders in an attempt to identify common traits and predict leadership potential.

trait complex theory Theory that attempts to integrate different constructs in differential psychology, such as personality, intelligence, and interests, in order to better understand and predict learning outcomes such as academic performance and knowledge acquisition.

trait emotional intelligence The theory of emotional intelligence as a personality trait, assessed by self-report inventories rather than performance tests and considered as a self-perceived construct rather than an ability.

transactional leadership A leadership style that is characterized by the leader's tendency to control followers' behaviors and to achieve influence by exchanging rewards (e.g., economic benefits) for compliance.

transformational leadership A type of charismatic leadership style based on communicating and sharing the leader's vision in order to produce a change in followers' values, expectations, and motivations and inspire them to sacrifice personal interests for those of the group.

two-factor theory Theory of motivation developed by Herzberg that conceptualizes satisfaction and dissatisfaction as two separate factors rather than two extremes of the same dimension. It argues that hygiene factors (e.g., good working conditions) determine individuals' level of dissatisfaction, while satisfaction is dependent on additional motivational factors such as high salary.

two-process theories Theories of motivation widely used in organizational psychology that focus on the impact of extrinsic motivational factors and individuals' expectations of motivation and performance.

V

validity (psychometric) The extent to which a test measures what it claims to measure.

W

Wechsler Adult Intelligence Scale (WAIS) A widely used measure of intelligence that has progressively replaced the Stanford/Binet test because of its suitability for measuring adult IQ; scores are calculated on the basis of between-subject comparisons rather than on the (mental age/chronological age) $\times$ 100 formula.

References

Ackerman, P.L. (1994). Intelligence, attention, and learning: Maximal and typical performance. In D.K. Detterman (Ed.), *Current Topics in Human Intelligence: Theories of Intelligence* (pp. 1–27). Norwood: Ablex.

Ackerman, P.L. (1996). A theory of adult intellectual development: Process, personality, interests, and knowledge. *Intelligence*, 22, 227–57.

Ackerman, P.L. (1999). Traits and knowledge as determinants of learning and individual differences: Putting it all together. In P.L. Ackerman & P. Kyllonen (Eds.), *Learning and Individual Differences: Process, Trait, and Content Determinants* (pp. 437–62). Atlanta: Georgia Institute of Technology.

Ackerman, P.L. & Beier, M.E. (2003). Intelligence, personality, and interests in the career choice process. *Journal of Career Assessment*, 11, 205–18.

Ackerman, P.L. & Heggestad, E.D. (1997). Intelligence, personality, and interests: Evidence for overlapping traits. *Psychological Bulletin*, 121, 219–45.

Ackerman, P.L. & Rolfhus, E.L. (1999). The locus of adult intelligence: Knowledge, abilities, and non-ability traits. *Psychology and Aging*, 14, 314–30.

Adams, J.S. (1963). Toward an understanding of inequity. *Journal of Abnormal and Social Psychology*, 67, 422–36.

Adams, J.S. (1965). Inequity in social exchange. In L. Berkowitz (Ed.), *Advances in Experimental Psychology* (Vol. 2, pp. 267–99). New York: Academic Press.

Adorno, T.W., Frenkel-Brunswick, E., Levinson, D.J., & Sanford, R.N. (1950). *The Authoritarian Personality*. New York: Harper & Row.

Agras, W.S., Rossiter, E.R., Arnow, B., Schneider, J.A., Telch, C.F. *et al.* (1992). Pharmacologic and cognitive-behavioral treatment for bulimia nervosa: A controlled comparison. *American Journal of Psychiatry*, 149, 82–7.

Ahmetoglu, G., Swami, V., & Chamorro-Premuzic, T. (2010). The relationship between dimensions of love, personality, and relationship length. *Archives of Sexual Behaviour*, 39(5), 1181–90.

Alderfer, C.P. (1969). An empirical test of a new theory of human needs. *Organizational Behavior and Human Performance*, 4, 142–75.

Alexander, F. (1939). Emotional factors in essential hypertension. *Psychosomatic Medicine*, 1, 175–9.

Alexander, W.P. (1935). Intelligence, concrete and abstract. *British Journal of Psychology*, 19.

Al-issa, I. (1972). Stimulus generalization and over-inclusion in normal and schizophrenic subjects. *Journal of Clinical Psychology*, 39, 182–6.

Allport, G.W. & Odbert, H.S. (1936). Trait names: A psycho-lexical study. *Psychological Monographs*, 47, 211.

Amabile, T.M. (1990). Within you, without you: The social psychology of creativity, and beyond. In M.A. Runco & R.S. Alber (Eds.), *Theories of Creativity* (pp. 61–91). Newbury Park, CA: Sage.

Amato, P.R. & Booth, A. (2001). The legacy of parents' marital discord: Consequences for children's marital quality. *Journal of Personality and Social Psychology*, 81, 627–38.

Amelang, M. & Steinmayr, R. (2006). Is there a validity increment for tests of emotional intelligence in explaining the variance of performance criteria? *Intelligence*, 34(5), 459–68.

American Psychiatric Association (APA) (1994). *Diagnostic and Statistical Manual of Mental Disorders* (4th ed.). Washington, DC: APA.

American Psychiatric Association (APA) (2000). *Diagnostic and Statistical Manual of Mental Disorders: DSM-IV-TR*. Washington, DC: APA.

Anastasi, A. & Schaefer, C. (1971). Note on the concepts of creativity and intelligence. *Journal of Creative Behavior*, 5, 113–16.

Anderson, M. (1992). *Intelligence and Development: A Cognitive Theory*. Oxford: Blackwell.

Ang, S., Van Dyne, L., & Koh, C. (2006). Personality correlates of the four-factor model of cultural intelligence. *Group Organization Management*, 31, 100–23.

Ang, S., Van Dyne, L., Koh, C., Ng, K.Y., Templer, K. J., Tay, C., & Chandrasekar, N.A. (2007). Cultural intelligence: Its measurements and effects on cultural judgement and decision making, cultural adaptation and task performance. *Management and Organisational Review*, 3, 335–71.

Angst, J. (1978). The course of affective disorders: II. Typology of bipolar manic-depressive illness. *Archiv für Psychiatrie und Nervenkrankheiten*, 226, 65–73.

Antonakis, J., Cianciolo, A.T., & Sternberg, R.J. (2004). Leadership: Past, present, and future. In J. Antonakis, A.T. Cianciolo & R.J. Sternberg (Eds.), *The Nature of Leadership* (pp. 3–15). Thousand Oaks, CA: Sage.

Armstrong, P.I. & Anthoney, S.F. (2009). Personality facets and RIASEC interests: An integrated model. *Journal of Vocational Behavior*, 75, 346–59.

Armstrong, P.I., Su, R., & Rounds, J. (2011). Vocational interests: The road less travelled. In T. Chamorro-Premuzic, S. von Stumm, & A. Furnham (Eds.). *Handbook of Individual Differences*. Oxford: Wiley-Blackwell.

Aronson, E., Wilson, T.D., & Akert, R.M. (2004). *Social Psychology* (5th ed.). Garden City, NJ: Prentice-Hall.

Ashforth, B.E. & Mael, F. (1989). Social identity theory and the organization. *Academy of Management Review*, 14, 20–39.

Assouline, M. & Meir, E.I. (1987). Meta-analysis of the relationship between congruence and well-being measures. *Journal of Vocational Behavior*, 31, 319–32.

Atkinson, J.W. (Ed.). (1958). *Motives in Fantasy, Action, and Society*. Princeton, NJ: Van Nostrand.

Austin, E.J. & Deary, I.J. (2000). The "four As": A common framework for normal and abnormal personality? *Personality and Individual Differences*, 28, 977–95.

Austin, E.J., Deary, I.J., Whiteman, M.C., Fowkes, F.-G.R., Pedersen, N.L. *et al.* (2002). Relationships between ability and personality: Does intelligence contribute positively to personal and social adjustment? *Personality and Individual Differences*, 32, 1391–411.

Avolio, B.J. (1999). *Full Leadership Development: Building the Vital Forces in Organizations*. Thousand Oaks, CA: Sage.

Avolio, B.J., Bass, B.M., & Jung, D.I. (1999). *Manual for the Multifactor Leadership Questionnaire (Form 5X)*. Redwood City, CA: Mind Garden.

Bachelard, G. (1996). *La formation de l'esprit scientifique*. Paris: Vrin. (Original work published 1938.)

Bachman, E.E., Sines, J.O., Watson, J.A., Lauer, R.M., & Clarke, W.R. (1986). The relations between Type A behavior, clinically relevant behavior, academic achievement, and IQ in children. *Journal of Personality Assessment*, 50, 186–92.

Bachman, J.G., Wadsworth, K.N., O'Malley, P.M., Johnson, L.D., & Schulenberg, J.E. (1997). *Smoking, Drinking, and Drug Abuse in Young Adulthood*. Mahwah, NJ: Lawrence Erlbaum.

Bachtold, L. & Werner, E. (1970). Personality profiles of gifted women: Psychologists. *American Psychologist*, 25, 234–43.

Baldwin, M.W. (1999). Activation and accessibility paradigms in relational schemas research. In D. Cervone & Y. Shoda (Eds.), *Coherence in Personality* (pp. 127–54). New York: Guilford Press.

Bales, R.F. (1950). *Interaction Process Analysis: A Method for the Study of Small Groups*. Cambridge, MA: Addison-Wesley.

Bales, R.F. (1958). Task roles and social roles in problem-solving groups. In E.E. Maccoby, T.M. Newcomb, & E.L. Hartley (Eds.), *Readings in Social Psychology*. New York: Holt, Rinehart, & Winston.

Ball, D. & Collier, D. (2002). Substance misuse. In P. McGuffin, M.J. Owen & I.I. Gottesman (Eds.), *Psychiatric Genetics and Genomics*. Oxford: Oxford University Press.

Ball, J. & Moselle, K. (1995). Health risk behaviors of adolescents in Singapore. *Asian Journal of Psychology*, 1, 54–62.

Bandura, A. (1977). Self-efficacy: Toward a unifying theory of behavioral change. *Psychological Review*, 84, 191–215.

Bandura, A. (1986). *Social Foundations of Thought and Action: A Social Cognitive Theory*. Englewood Cliffs, NJ: Prentice Hall.

Bandura, A. (1989). Human agency in social cognitive theory. *American Psychologist*, 44, 1175–84.

Bandura, A. (1999). A social cognitive theory of personality. In L. Pervin & O. John (Eds.), *Handbook of Personality* (2nd ed., pp. 154–96). New York: Guilford Press.

Bandura, A., Barbaranelli, C., Caprara, G.V., & Pastorelli, C. (2001). Self-efficacy beliefs as shapers of children's aspirations and career trajectories. *Child Development*, 72, 187–206.

Barber, J.D. (1992). *The Presidential Character: Predicting Performance in the White House*. Englewood Cliffs, NJ: Prentice Hall.

Barchard, K.A. (2003). Does emotional intelligence assist in the prediction of academic success? *Educational and Psychological Measurement*, 63, 840–58.

Barling, J., Weber, T., & Kelloway, E.K. (1996). Effects of transformational leadership training on attitudinal and financial outcomes: A field experiment. *Journal of Applied Psychology*, 81, 827–32.

Barnes, M.L. & Sternberg, R.J. (1989). Social intelligence and decoding of nonverbal cues. *Intelligence*, 13, 263–87.

Bar-On, R. (1997). *Bar-On Emotional Quotient Inventory: Technical Manual*. Toronto: Multihealth Systems.

Baron, R.M. & Kenny, D.A. (1986). The moderator–mediator variable distinction in social psychological research: Conceptual, strategic, and statistical considerations. *Journal of Personality and Social Psychology*, 51, 1173–82.

Baron-Cohen, S. (1995). *Mindblindness: An Essay on Autism and Theory of Mind*. Cambridge, MA: MIT Press.

Barraclough, J. & Gill, D. (1996). *Hughes' Outline of Modern Psychiatry* (4th ed.). London: John Wiley & Sons, Ltd.

Barrick, M.R. & Mount, M.K. (1991). The Big Five personality dimensions and job performance: A meta-analysis. *Personnel Psychology*, 44, 1–26.

Barron, F. (1963). The needs for order and disorder as motives in creative action. In C.W. Taylor & F. Barron (Eds.), *Scientific Creativity: Its Recognition and Development* (pp. 139–52). New York: John Wiley & Sons, Inc.

Barron, F. (1969). *Creative Person and Creative Process*. New York: Holt, Rinehart, & Winston.

Barron, F. & Harrington, D.M. (1981). Creativity, intelligence, and personality. *Annual Review of Psychology*, 32, 439–76.

Barron, F. & Welsh, G.S. (1952). Artistic perception as a possible factor in personality style: Its measurement by a Figure Preference Test. *Journal of Psychology*, 33, 199–203.

Bartol, K.M. & Martin, D.C. (1986). Women and men in task groups. In R.D. Ashmore & F.K. Del Boca (Eds.), *The Social Psychology of Female–Male Relations* (pp. 259–310). Orlando, FL: Academic Press.

Bass, B.M. (1981). From leaderless group discussions to the cross-national assessment of managers. *Journal of Management, 7*, 63–76.

Bass, B.M. (1985). *Leadership and Performance beyond Expectations*. New York: Free Press.

Bass, B.M. (1990). *Bass and Stogdill's Handbook of Leadership: Theory, Research, and Managerial Applications* (3rd ed.). New York: Free Press.

Bass, B.M. (1997). Does the transactional–transformational leadership paradigm transcend organizational and national boundaries? *American Psychologist, 52*, 130–39.

Bass, B.M. (1998). *Transformational Leadership: Industry, Military, and Educational Impact*. Mahwah, NJ: Lawrence Erlbaum.

Bass, B.M. & Avolio, B.J. (Eds.). (1985). *Leadership Performance beyond Expectations*. New York: Free Press.

Bass, B.M. & Avolio, B.J. (1995). *MLQ Multifactor Leadership Questionnaire for Research: Permission Set*. Palo Alto, CA: Mind Garden.

Batey, M., Chamorro-Premuzic, T., & Furnham, A. (2009). Intelligence and personality as predictors of divergent thinking: The role of general, fluid and crystallized intelligence. *Thinking Skills and Creativity, 4*, 60–69.

Batson, C.D., Duncan, B.D., & Ackerman, P. (1981). Is empathic emotion a source of altruistic motivation? *Journal of Personality and Social Psychology, 40*, 290–302.

Baumeister, R.F. (1984). Choking under pressure: Self-consciousness and paradoxical effects of incentives on skilful performance. *Journal of Personality and Social Psychology, 46*, 610–20.

Beck, A.T. (1983). Cognitive therapy of depression: New perspectives. In P.J. Clayton & J.E. Barrett (Eds.), *Treatment of Depression: Old Controversies and New Approaches* (pp. 265–90). New York: Raven Press.

Beck, A.T. & Emery, G. (1985). *Anxiety Disorders and Phobias: A Cognitive Perspective*. New York: Basic Books.

Beck, A.T., Rush A.J., Shaw B.F., & Emery, G. (1979) *Cognitive Therapy of Depression*. New York: Guilford Press.

Beck, H.P., Levinson, S., & Irons, G. (2009). Finding Little Albert. *American Psychologist, 64*(7), 605–14.

Beck, R.C. (1990). *Motivation: Theories and Principles* (2nd ed.). Englewood Cliffs, NJ: Prentice Hall.

Becker, G. (1978). *The Mad Genius Controversy*. Newbury Park, CA: Sage.

Becker, T.E. & Billings, R.S. (1993). Profiles of commitment: An empirical test. *Journal of Organizational Behavior, 14*, 177–90.

Bemis, K.M. (1978). Current approaches to the etiology and treatment of anorexia nervosa. *Psychological Bulletin, 85*, 3.

Benjamin, J., Li, L., Patterson, C., Greenberg, B.D., Murphy, D. L., & Hamer, D. H. (1996). Population and familial association between the D4 dopamine receptor gene and measures of novelty seeking. *Nature Genetics, 12*, 81–4.

Bentall, R.P. (Ed.). (1990). *Reconstructing Schizophrenia*. London: Routledge.

Bentler, P.M. (1995, 2002). *EQS Structural Equations Program Manual*. Los Angeles, CA: Multivariate Software.

Bergen, S.E., Gardner, C.O., & Kendler, K.S. (2007). Age related changes in heritability of behavioural phenotypes over adolescence and young adulthood: A meta-analysis. *Twin Research and Human Genetics, 10*, 423–33.

Berry, J.W. (1976). *Human Ecology and Cognitive Style: Comparative Studies in Cultural and Psychological Adaptation*. New York: Sage / Halsted.

Berscheid, E. (1999). The greening of relationship science. *American Psychologist*, 54, 260–66.

Binet, A. (1903). *L'étude expérimentale de l'intelligence* [Experimental study of intelligence]. Paris: Schleicher.

Binet, A. & Henri, V. (1896). La psychologie individuelle. *Année Psychologique*, 2, 411–65.

Binet, A. & Simon, T. (1961a). Méthodes nouvelles pour le diagnostique du niveau intellec-tuel des anormaux [New methods for the diagnosis of the intellectual level of subnormals] (E.S. Kite, Trans.). In J.J. Jenkins & D.G. Paterson (Eds.), *Studies in Individual Differences: The Search for Intelligence* (pp. 90–96). New York: Appleton-Century-Crofts. (Original work published 1905.)

Binet, A. & Simon, T. (1961b). The development of intelligence in the child (excerpts) (E.S. Kite, Trans.). In J.J. Jenkins & D.G. Paterson (Eds.), *Studies in Individual Differences: The Search for Intelligence* (pp. 96–111). New York: Appleton-Century-Crofts. (Original work published 1908.)

Binet, A. & Simon, T. (1961c). Upon the necessity of establishing a scientific diagnosis of interior states of intelligence. In J.J. Jenkins & D.G. Paterson (Eds.), *Studies in Individual Differences: The Search for Intelligence* (pp. 81–90). New York: Appleton-Century-Crofts.

Binet, A. & Simon, T. (1973). *The Development of Intelligence in Children*. Baltimore: Williams & Wilkins. (Original work published 1916.)

Block, J. (1971). *Lives through Time*. Berkeley, CA: Bancroft Books.

Block, J. (1995). A contrarian view of the five-factor approach to personality description. *Psychological Bulletin*, 117, 187–215.

Block, J. (2001). Millennial contrarianism. *Journal of Research in Personality*, 35, 98–107.

Blum, K., Braverman, E.R., Holder, M.M., Lubar, J.F., Monastra, V.J. *et al.* (2000). Reward deficiency syndrome: A biogenetic model for the diagnosis and treatment of impulsive, addictive, and compulsive behaviors. *Journal of Psychoactive Drugs*, 32, 1–112.

Boekaerts, M. (1995). Self-regulated learning: Bridging the gap between metacognitive and meta-motivation theories. *Educational Psychologist*, 30, 195–200.

Boggiano, A.K. & Pittman, T.S. (1993). *Achievement and Motivation*. New York: Cambridge University Press.

Bollen, K.A. (1989). *Structural Equations with Latent Variables*. New York: John Wiley & Sons, Inc.

Bono, J.E. & Judge, T.A. (2003). Self-concordance at work: Understanding the motivational effects of transformational leaders. *Academy of Management Journal*, 46, 554–71.

Borgen, W. & Young, R. (1982). Career perception of children and adolescents. *Journal of Vocational Behavior*, 21, 37–49.

Boring, E.G. (1923). Intelligence as the tests test it. *New Republic*, 34, 34–7.

Boring, E.G. (1950). *A History of Experimental Psychology* (2nd ed.). New York: Appleton-Century-Crofts.

Bouchard, G., Lussier, Y., & Sabourin, S. (1999). Personality and marital adjustment: Utility of the five-factor model of personality. *Journal of Marriage and the Family*, 61, 651–60.

Boyle, M. (1990). *Schizophrenia: A Scientific Delusion?* London: Routledge.

Brand, C.R. (1987). The importance of general intelligence. In S. Modgil & C. Modgil (Eds.), *Arthur Jensen: Consensus and Controversy* (pp. 251–65). New York: Falmer Press.

Brand, C.R. (1994). Open to experience, closed to intelligence: Why the "Big Five" are really the "Comprehensive Six." *European Journal of Personality*, 8, 299–310.

Brebner, K. (2003). Gender and emotions. *Personality and Individual Differences*, 34, 387–94.

Brehm, S. & Brehm, J. (1981). *Responses to Loss of Freedom: A Theory of Psychological Reactance*. Morristown, NJ: General Learning Press.

Brett, D., Pospisil, H., Valcarcel, J., Reich, J., & Bork, P. (2002). Alternative splicing and genome complexity. *Nature Genetics*, 30, 29–30.

Brewin, C.R. (1996). Theoretical foundations of cognitive-behavioral therapy for anxiety and depression. *Annual Review of Psychology*, 47, 33–57.

Bright, I.J. (1930). *A Study of the Correlation Obtaining between Academic and Citizenship Grades and between Academic Grades and Intelligence Quotients*. Oxford: Leavenworth Public Schools.

Brody, N. (1988). *Personality: In Search of Individuality*. New York: Academic Press.

Brody, N. (2000). History of theories and measurements of intelligence. In R.J. Sternberg (Ed.), *Handbook of Intelligence* (pp. 16–33). New York: Cambridge University Press.

Brown, G.W. & Harris, T. (1978). *Social Origins of Depression: A Study of Psychiatric Disorder in Women*. London: Tavistock.

Brown, P. & Hesketh, A. (2004). *The Mismanagement of Talent*. Oxford: Oxford University Press.

Brown, R.T. (1989). Creativity: What are we to measure? In J.A. Glover, P.R. Ronning, & C.R. Reynolds (Eds.), *Handbook of Creativity* (pp. 3–32). New York: Plenum Press.

Bryan, A. (1942). Grades, intelligence, and personality of art school freshmen. *Journal of Educational Psychology*, 33, 50–64.

Buck, R. (1985). Prime theory: An integrated view of motivation and emotion. *Psychological Review*, 92, 389–413.

Buck, R. (1999). The biological affects: A typology. *Psychological Review*, 106, 301–36.

Burns, J.M. (1978). *Leadership*. New York: Harper & Row.

Burns, J.M. (2003). *Transformational Leadership*. New York: Scribner.

Burtt, H.E. & Arps, G.F. (1943). Correlation of Army Alpha Intelligence Test with academic grades in high schools and military academies. *Journal of Applied Psychology*, 4, 289–93.

Buss, D.M. (1987). Mate selection criteria: An evolutionary perspective. In C. Crawford, M. Smith, & D. Krebs (Eds.), *Sociobiology and Psychology: Ideas, Issues, and Applications* (pp. 335–51). Hillsdale, NJ: Lawrence Erlbaum.

Buss, D.M. (1989). Conflict between the sexes: Strategic interference and the evocation of anger and upset. *Journal of Personality and Social Psychology*, 56, 735–47.

Butcher, J.N., Dahlstrom, W.G., Graham, J.R., Tellegen, A., & Kaemmer, B. (1989). *Minnesota Multiphasic Personality Inventory – 2: Manual for Administration and Scoring*. Minneapolis: University of Minnesota Press.

Butler, A.C., Chapman, J.E., Forman, E.M., & Beck, A.T. (2006). The empirical status of cognitive-behavioural therapy: A review of metaanalyses. *Clinical Psychology Review*, 26, 17–31.

Campbell, D.P. (1971). *Handbook for the Strong Vocational Interest Blank*. Stanford, CA: Stanford University Press.

Campbell, D.T. & Fiske, D.W. (1959). Convergent and discriminant validation by the multitrait-multimethod matrix. *Psychological Bulletin*, 56, 81–105.

Campbell, J. (1990). Modeling the performance prediction problem in industrial and organizational psychology. In M. Dunette & L. Hough (Eds.), *Handbook of Industrial and Organizational Psychology* (pp. 687–732). Palo Alto, CA: Consulting Psychologists Press.

Cantor, N. & Kihlstrom, J.F. (1987). *Personality and Social Intelligence*. Englewood Cliffs, NJ: Prentice Hall.

Capron, C. & Duyme, M. (1989). Assessment of effects of socioeconomic status on IQ in a full cross-fostering design. *Nature*, 340, 552–3.

Carlo, G., Okun, M.A., Knight, G.P., & de Guzman, M.R. (2005). The interplay of traits and motives on volunteering: Agreeableness, extraversion, and prosocial value motivation. *Personality and Individual Differences*, 38, 1293–305.

Carlson, A. (2002). *Interests* [Online]. Retrieved from vocationalpsychology.com/term-interests.htm.

Carlyle, T. (1907). *On Heroes, Hero-Worship, and the Heroic in History*. Boston, MA: Houghton Mifflin.

Carroll, J.B. (1993). *Human Cognitive Abilities: A Survey of Factor-Analytic Studies*. New York: Cambridge University Press.

Carson, D.K. & Runco, M.A. (1999). Creative problem solving and problem findings in young adults: Interconnections with stress, hassles, and coping abilities. *Journal of Creative Behavior*, 33, 167–90.

Carver, C.S. & Scheier, M.F. (2000). *Perspective on Personality* (4th ed.). Boston, MA: Allyn & Bacon.

Caspi, A. & Herbener, E.S. (1992). Shared experiences and the similarity of personalities: A longitudinal study of married couples. *Journal of Personality and Social Psychology*, 62, 281–91.

Caspi, A., Roberts, B.W., & Shiner, R.L. (2005). Personality development: Stability and change. *Annual Review of Psychology*, 56, 453–84.

Catalyst (2002a, November 19). *Catalyst census makes gains in number of women corporate officers in America's largest 500 companies* [Press release]. Retrieved February 20, 2003, from www.catalystwomen.org/press_room/factsheets/fact_women_ceos.htm.

Catalyst (2002b). *Fact sheet: Women CEOs*. Retrieved October 6, 2002, from www.catalystwomen.org/press_room/factsheets/fact_women_ceos.htm.

Cattell, J.M. (1890). Mental tests and measurements. *Mind*, 15, 373–80.

Cattell, J.M. & Farrand, L. (1896). Physical and mental measurement of the students of Columbia University. *Psychological Review*, 3, 618–48.

Cattell, R.B. (1937). *The Fight for our National Intelligence*. London: King & Sons.

Cattell, R.B. (1941). The measurement of adult intelligence. *Psychological Bulletin*, 40, 153–93.

Cattell, R.B. (1957). *Personality and Motivation Structure and Measurement*. New York: World Books.

Cattell, R.B. (1971a). The process of creative thought. In R. Cattell (Ed.), *Abilities: Their Structure, Growth, and Action* (pp. 407–17). Boston, MA: Houghton Mifflin.

Cattell, R.B. (1971b). *Abilities: Their Structure, Growth, and Action*. Amsterdam: North-Holland.

Cattell, R.B. (1973). *Personality and Mood by Questionnaire*. San Francisco, CA: Jossey-Bass.

Cattell, R.B. (1987). *Intelligence: Its Structure, Growth, and Action*. [Revised and reprinted version of *Abilities: Their Structure, Growth, and Action*]. New York: Springer.

Cattell, R.B., Eber, H.W., & Tatsuoka, M.M. (1970). *Handbook for the Sixteen Personality Factor Questionnaire (16PF)*. Champaign, IL: Institute for Personality and Ability Testing.

Caughlin, J.P., Huston, T.L., & Houts, R.M. (2000). How does personality matter in marriage? An examination of trait anxiety, interpersonal negativity, and marital satisfaction. *Journal of Personality and Social Psychology*, 78, 245–56.

Cervone, D. (1999). Bottom-up explanation in personality psychology: The case of cross-situational coherence. In D. Cervone & Y. Shoda (Eds.), *Coherence in Personality* (pp. 303–41). New York: Guilford Press.

Cervone, D. & Shoda, Y. (1999). Beyond traits in the study of personality coherence. *Current Directions in Psychological Science*, 8, 27–32.

Chamorro-Premuzic, T. & Furnham, A. (2003a). Personality predicts academic performance: Evidence from two longitudinal studies on British university students. *Journal of Research in Personality*, 37, 319–38.

Chamorro-Premuzic, T. & Furnham, A. (2003b). Personality traits and academic exam performance. *European Journal of Personality*, 17, 237–50.

Chamorro-Premuzic, T. & Furnham, A. (2004). A possible model to understand the personality–intelligence interface. *British Journal of Psychology*, 95, 249–64.

Chamorro-Premuzic, T. & Furnham, A. (2005). *Personality and Intellectual Competence*. Mahwah, NJ: Lawrence Erlbaum.

Chamorro-Premuzic, T. & Furnham, A. (2006). Intellectual competence and the intelligent personality: A third way in differential psychology. *Review of General Psychology*, 10, 251–67.

Chamorro-Premuzic, T. & Furnham, A. (2010). *The Psychology of Personnel Selection*. Cambridge: Cambridge University Press.

Chamorro-Premuzic, T., Furnham, A., & Ackerman, P.L. (2006). Ability and non-ability correlates of general knowledge. *Personality and Individual Differences*, 41, 419–29.

Chamorro-Premuzic, T. & Reichenbacher, L. (2008). Effects of personality and threats of evaluation on divergent and convergent thinking. *Journal of Research in Personality*, 42, 1095–101.

Chapin, F.S. (1942). Preliminary standardization of a social impact scale. *American Sociological Review*, 7, 214–25.

Chemers, M.M. (2000). Leadership research and theory: A functional integration. *Group Dynamics: Theory, Research, and Practice*, 4, 27–43.

Cicchetti, D. & Rogosch, F.A. (1996). Equifinality and multifinality in developmental psychopathology. *Development and Psychopathology*, 8, 597–600.

Clark, K.E. (1961). *Vocational Interest of Non-professional Men*. Minneapolis, MN: Universityof Minnesota Press.

Cloninger, C.R. (1987). A systemic method for clinical description and classification of personality variants. *Archives of General Psychiatry*, 44, 573–88.

Coan, R.W. (1974). *The Optimal Personality*. New York: Columbia University Press.

Cofer, C.N. & Appley, M.H. (1964). *Motivation: Theory and Research*. New York: John Wiley & Sons, Inc.

Conger, J.A. & Kanungo, R.N. (1987). Toward a behavioral theory of charismatic leadership in organizational settings. *Academy of Management Review*, 16, 262–90.

Conger, J.A. & Kanungo, R.N. (1988). Toward a behavioral theory of charismatic leadership. In J.A. Conger & R.N. Kanungo (Eds.), *Charismatic Leadership: The Elusive Factor in Organizational Effectiveness* (pp. 78–97). San Francisco, CA: Jossey-Bass.

Conger, J.A. & Kanungo, R.N. (1998). *Charismatic Leadership in Organizations*. Thousand Oaks, CA: Sage.

Conger, R.D., Cui, M., Bryant, C.M., & Elder, G.H. (2000). Competence in early adult romantic relationships: A developmental perspective on family influences. *Journal of Personality and Social Psychology*, 79, 224–37.

Contrada, R.J., Cather, C., & O'Leary, A. (1999). Personality and health: Dispositions and processes in disease susceptibility and adaptation to illness. In L.A. Pervin & O.P. John (Eds.), *Handbook of Personality: Theory and Research* (2nd ed., pp. 576–604). New York: Guilford Press.

Cooper, C. (1997). Mood processes. In C. Cooper & V. Varma (Eds.), *Processes in Individual Differences*. London: Routledge.

Cooper, C. (2002). *Individual Differences* (2nd ed.; 1st ed., 1998). London: Arnold.

Cooper, J.E., Kendell, R.E., Gurland, B.J. *et al.* (1972). Psychiatric Diagnosis in New York and London: A Comparative Study of Mental Hospital Admissions. London: Oxford University Press.

Corcoran, D.W. (1965). Personality and the inverted-U relation. *British Journal of Psychology*, 56, 267–73.

Corr, P.J., Pickering, A.D., & Gray, J.A. (1995). Personality and reinforcement in associative and instrumental learning. *Personality and Individual Differences*, 19, 47–72.

Costa, P.T., Jr. & McCrae, R.R. (1978). Objective personality assessment. In M. Storandt, I.C. Siegler, & M.F. Elias (Eds.), *The Clinical Psychology of Aging* (pp. 119–43). New York: Plenum Press.

Costa, P.T., Jr. & McCrae, R.R. (1980). Influence of extroversion and neuroticism on subjective well-being: Happy and unhappy people. *Journal of Personality and Social Psychology*, 38, 668–78.

Costa, P.T., Jr. & McCrae, R.R. (1985). *NEO Personality Inventory Manual*. Odessa, TX: Psychological Assessment Resources.

Costa, P.T., Jr. & McCrae, R.R. (1988). Personality in adulthood: A six-year longitudinal study of self-reports and spouse ratings on the NEO Personality Inventory. *Journal of Personality and Social Psychology, 54*, 853–63.

Costa, P.T., Jr. & McCrae, R.R. (1992). *Revised NEO Personality Inventory (NEO-PI-R) and NEO Five-Factor Inventory (NEO-FFI): Professional Manual*. Odessa, TX: Psychological Assessment Resources.

Costa, P.T., Jr. & McCrae, R.R. (1994). Set like plaster? Evidence for the stability of adult personality. In T.F. Heatherton & J.L. Weinberger (Eds.), *Can Personality Change?* (pp. 21–40). Washington, DC: American Psychological Association.

Costa, P.T., Jr., McCrae, R.R., & Arenberg, D. (1980). Enduring dispositions in adult males. *Journal of Personality and Social Psychology, 38*, 793–800.

Court, J.H. (1983). Sex differences in performance on Raven's Progressive Matrices: A review. *Alberta Journal of Educational Research, 29*, 54–74.

Cox, C.M. (1926). The early mental traits of three hundred geniuses. In L. Terman (Ed.), *Genetic Studies of Genius* (Vol. 2). Stanford, CA: Stanford University Press.

Cramer, P. & Davidson, K. (Eds.) (1998). Defense mechanisms in current personality research. *Journal of Personality: On Current Research and Theory on Defense Mechanisms, 66* (Special Issue), 879–1157.

Cronbach, L.J. (1957). The two disciplines of scientific psychology. *American Psychologist, 7*, 173–96.

Cronbach, L.J. (1989). Construct validation after thirty years. In L.L. Robert (Ed.), *Intelligence: Measurement, Theory, and Public Policy. Proceedings of a Symposium in Honor of Lloyd G. Humphreys* (pp. 147–71). Champaign, IL: University of Illinois Press.

Cronbach, L.J. (1990). *Essentials of Psychological Testing* (5th ed.; 1st ed., 1949). New York: Harper & Row.

Cross, S.E. & Madson, L. (1997). Models of the self: Self-construals and gender. *Psychological Bulletin, 122*, 5–37.

Crow, T.J., MacMillan, J.F., Johnson, A.L., & Johnstone, E.C. (1986). The Northwick Park study of first episodes of schizophrenia. II. A randomized controlled trial of prophylactic neuroleptic treatment. *British Journal of Psychiatry, 148*, 120–27.

Dabbs, J.M., Jr., Alford, E.C., & Fielden, J.A. (1998). Trial lawyers and testosterone: Blue-collar talent in a white-collar world. *Journal of Applied Social Psychology, 28*, 84–94.

Dabbs, J.M., Jr., Strong, R.K., & Milun, R. (1997). Exploring the mind of testosterone: A beeper study. *Journal of Research in Personality, 31*, 557–87.

Daft, R.L. (1999). *Leadership: Theory and Practice*. Orlando, FL: Dryden Press.

Damasio, A.R. (1994). *Descartes' Error: Emotion, Reason, and the Human Brain*. New York: Avon Books.

Damasio, H., Grabowski, T., Frank, R., Galaburda, A.M., & Damasio, A.R. (1994). The return of Phineas Gage: Clues about the brain from the skull of a famous patient. *Science, 264*(5162), 1102–5.

Darcy, M.U.A. & Tracey, T.J.G. (2007). Circumplex structure of Holland's RIASEC: Interests across gender and time. *Journal of Counseling Psychology, 54*, 17–31.

Darke, S. (1988). Anxiety and working memory capacity. *Cognition and Emotion, 2*, 145–54.

Datta, L.E. (1963). Test instructions and identification of creative scientific talent. *Psychological Reports, 13*, 495–500.

Davidson, J.E. & Downing, C.L. (2000). Contemporary models of intelligence. In R.J. Sternberg (Ed.), *Handbook of Intelligence* (pp. 34–49). New York: Cambridge University Press.

Davison, G.C. & Neale, J.M. (1998). *Abnormal Psychology* (7th ed.). New York: John Wiley & Sons, Inc.

Deakin, J.F.W. & Graeff, F.G. (1991). 5HT and mechanisms of defence. *Journal of Psychopharmacology*, 5, 305–15.

Deary, I.J. (1986). Inspection time: Discovery or rediscovery? *Personality and Individual Differences*, 7, 625–31.

Deary, I.J. (1994). Intelligence and auditory discrimination: Separating processing speed and fidelity of stimulus representation. *Intelligence*, 18, 189–213.

Deary, I.J. (2000). *Looking Down on Human Intelligence: From Psychometrics to the Brain*. Oxford: Oxford University Press.

Deary, I.J. (2001). *Intelligence: A Very Short Introduction*. Oxford: Oxford University Press.

Deary, I.J., Whalley, L.J., & Starr, J.M. (2003). IQ at age 11 and longevity: Results from a follow-up of the Scottish Mental Survey 1932. In C.E. Finch, J.-M. Robine, & Y. Christen (Eds.), *Brain and Longevity: Perspectives in Longevity* (pp. 153–64). Berlin: Springer.

Deary, I.J., Whiteman, M.C., Starr, J.M., Whalley, L.J., & Fox, H.C. (2004). The impact of childhood intelligence on later life: Following up the Scottish Mental Surveys of 1932 and 1947. *Journal of Personality and Social Psychology*, 86, 130–47.

Deci, E.L. (1975). *Intrinsic Motivation*. New York: Plenum Press.

Deci, E.L. & Ryan, R.M. (1985). *Intrinsic Motivation and Self-Determination in Human Behavior*. New York: Plenum Press.

Deci, E.L. & Ryan, R.M. (2000). The "what" and "why" of goal pursuits: Human needs and the self-determination of behavior. *Psychological Inquiry*, 11, 227–68.

Deffenbacher, K.A., Bornstein, B.H., Penrod. S.D. & McGorty, E.K. (2004). A Meta-Analytic Review of the Effects of High Stress on Eyewitness Memory. *Law and Human Behavior*, 28(6), 687–706.

Depue, R.A. & Collins, P.F. (1999). Neurobiology of the structure of personality: Dopamine, facilitation of incentive motivation, and extraversion. *Behavioral and Brain Sciences*, 22, 491–569.

DeYoung, C.G., Quilty, L.C., & Peterson, J.B. (2007). Between facets and domains: 10 Aspects of the Big Five, *Journal of Personality and Social Psychology*, 93, 880–96.

Diener, E. (1984). Subjective well-being. *Psychological Bulletin*, 93, 542–75.

Diener, E. & Larsen, R.J. (1984). Temporal stability and cross-situational consistency of affective, behavioral, and cognitive responses. *Journal of Personality and Social Psychology*, 47, 871–83.

Diener, E., Oishi, S., & Lucas, R.E. (2003). Personality, culture, and subjective well-being: Emotional and cognitive evaluations of life. *Annual Review of Psychology*, 54, 403–25.

Digman, J.M. (1986). Further specification of the five robust factors of personality. *Journal of Personality and Social Psychology*, 50, 116–23.

Digman, J.M. (1997). Higher-order factors of the Big Five. *Journal of Personality and Social Psychology*, 73, 1246–56.

Digman, J.M. & Inouye, J. (1986). Further specification of the five robust factors of personality. *Journal of Personality and Social Psychology*, 50, 116–23.

Dollinger, S.J. & Clancy, S.M. (1993). Identity, self, and personality: II. Glimpses through the auto-photographic eye. *Journal of Personality and Social Psychology*, 64, 1064–71.

Domino, S.J. (1974). Assessment of cinematographic creativity. *Journal of Personality and Social Psychology*, 30, 150–54.

Donnellan, M.B., Larsen-Rife, D., & Conger, R.D. (2005). Personality, family history, and competence in early adult relationships. *Journal of Personality and Social Psychology*, 88, 562–76.

Dryden, W. & DiGiuseppe, R. (1990). *A Primer on Rational-Emotive Therapy*. Champaign, IL: Research Press.

Dudek, S.Z. & Hall, W.B. (1991). Personality consistency: Eminent architects 25 years later. *Creativity Research Journal*, 4, 213–31.

Duffy, E. (1951). The concept of energy mobilization. *Psychological Review*, 58, 30–40.

Duffy, E. (1962). *Activation and Behavior*. New York: John Wiley & Sons, Inc.

Dvir, T., Eden, D., Avolio, B.J., & Shamir, B. (2002). Impact of transformational leadership on follower development and performance: A field experiment. *Academy of Management Journal*, 45, 735–44.

Dweck, C.S. (1986). Motivational processes affecting learning. *American Psychologist*, 41, 1040–48.

Dweck, C.S. (1997). The relations among children's social goals, implicit personality theories, and response to social failure. *Developmental Psychology*, 33, 263–72.

Eagly, A.H. & Johnson, B.T. (1990). Gender and leadership style: A meta-analysis. *Psychological Bulletin*, 108, 233–56.

Eagly, A.H., Johannesen-Schmidt, M.C., & van Engen, M. (2003). Transformational, transactional, and *laissez-faire* leadership styles: A meta-analysis comparing women and men. *Psychological Bulletin*, 129, 569–91.

Eaves, L. & Young, P.A. (1981). Genetical theory and personality differences. In D.E. Broadbent & R. Lynn (Eds.), *Dimensions of Personality* (pp. 129–79). New York: Pergamon Press.

Edwards, J.R. & Rothbard, N.P. (1999). Work and family stress and well-being: An examination of person–environment fit in the work and family domains. *Organizational Behavior and Human Decision Processes*, 77, 85–129.

Ekman, P. (1994). Strong evidence for universals in facial expressions: A reply to Russell's mistaken critique. *Psychological Bulletin*, 115, 268–87.

Elias, M.F. & Elias, P.K. (1993). Hypertension affects neurobehavioral functioning: So what's new? [Editorial comment]. *Psychosomatic Medicine*, 55, 51–4.

Ellis, A. (1973). *Humanistic Psychotherapy*. New York: McGraw-Hill.

Elshout, J. & Veenman, M. (1992). Relation between intellectual ability and working method as predictors of learning. *Journal of Educational Research*, 85, 134–43.

Engel, G.L. (1977) The need for a new medical model: A challenge for biomedicine. *Science*, 196, 129–36.

Entwistle, N. & Entwistle, D. (1970). The relationships between personality, study methods, and academic performance. *British Journal of Educational Psychology*, 40, 132–43.

Erlenmeyer-Kimling, L. & Jarvik, L.F. (1963). Genetics and intelligence: A review. *Science*, 142, 1477–9.

Ertl, J.P. & Schafer, E.W.P. (1969). Brain response correlates of psychometric intelligence. *Nature*, 223, 421–2.

Evans, B. & Waites, B. (1981). *IQ and Mental Testing: An Unnatural Science and its Social History*. London: Macmillan.

Eysenck, H.J. (1947). *Dimensions of Personality*. New York: Praeger.

Eysenck, H.J. (1957). *The Dynamics of Anxiety and Hysteria*. London: Routledge & Kegan Paul.

Eysenck, H.J. (1967). *The Biological Basis of Personality*. Springfield, IL: Charles C. Thomas.

Eysenck, H.J. (1976). The learning theory model of neurosis: A new approach. *Behaviour Research and Therapy*, 14, 251–67.

Eysenck, H.J. (Ed.). (1982). *A Model for Intelligence*. New York: Springer.

Eysenck, H.J. (1991). Dimensions of personality: 16, 5, or 3? Criteria for a taxonomic paradigm. *Personality and Individual Differences*, 12, 773–90.

Eysenck, H.J. (1992). Four ways five factors are not basic. *Personality and Individual Differences*, 13, 667–73.

Eysenck, H.J. (1994). Personality: Biological foundations. In P. A. Vernon (Ed.), *The Neuro-psychology of Individual Differences*. San Diego, CA: Academic Press.

Eysenck, H.J. (1995). Can we study intelligence using the experimental method? *Intelligence, 20*, 217–28.

Eysenck, H.J. (1999). Personality and creativity. In M.A. Runco (Ed.), *Creativity Research Handbook*. Cresskill, NJ: Hampton Press.

Eysenck, H.J. & Cookson, D. (1969). Personality in primary school children: Ability and achievement. *British Journal of Educational Psychology, 39*, 109–30.

Eysenck, H.J. & Eysenck, M.W. (1985). *Personality and Individual Differences: A Natural Science Approach*. New York: Plenum Press.

Eysenck, H.J. & Eysenck, S.B.G. (1975). *Manual of the Eysenck Questionnaire*. San Diego, CA: Edits.

Eysenck, H.J. & Eysenck, S.B.G. (1976). *Psychoticism as a Dimension of Personality*. London: University of London.

Eysenck, H.J. & Eysenck, S.B.G. (1991). *The EPQ-R*. Sevenoaks: Hodder & Stoughton.

Eysenck, H.J. & Furnham, A. (1993). Personality and the Barron-Welsh Art Scale. *Perceptual and Motor Skills, 76*, 838.

Fabricatore, A.N. & Wadden, T.N (2006). Obesity. *Annual Review of Clinical Psychology, 2*, 357–77.

Farmer, E.W. (1974). Psychoticism and Person-Orientation as General Personality Characteristics. BSc thesis, University of Glasgow, Scotland.

Feingold, A. (1988). Cognitive gender differences are disappearing. *American Psychologist, 43*, 95–103.

Feist, G.J. (1998). A meta-analysis of personality in scientific and artistic creativity. *Personality and Social Psychology Bulletin, 2*, 290–309.

Feist, G.J. (1999). The influence of personality on artistic and scientific creativity. In R.J. Sternberg (Ed.), *Handbook of Human Creativity* (pp. 273–96). New York: Cambridge University Press.

Feist, G.J. & Barron, F. (2003). Predicting creativity from early to late adulthood: Intellect, potential, and personality. *Journal of Research in Personality, 37*, 62–88.

Ferguson, E., Chamorro-Premuzic, T, Pickering, A., & Weiss, A. (2011). Five into one doesn't go: A critique of the general factor of personality. In T. Chamorro-Premuzic, S. von Stumm, & A. Furnham (Eds.). *Handbook of Individual Differences*. Oxford: Wiley-Blackwell.

Feshbach, N.D. & Feshbach, S. (1987). Affective processes and academic achievement. *Child Development, 58*, 1335–47.

Fiedler, F.E. (1967). *A Theory of Leadership Effectiveness*. New York: McGraw-Hill.

Fiedler, F.E. (1993). The leadership situation and the black box in contingency theories. In M.M. Chemers & R. Ayman (Eds.), *Leadership Theory and Research* (pp. 1–28). San Diego, CA: Academic Press.

Fiedler, F.E. (2002). The curious role of cognitive resources in leadership. In R.E. Riggio, S.E. Murphy, & F.J. Pirozzolo (Eds.), *Multiple Intelligences and Leadership* (pp. 91–104). Mahwah, NJ: Erlbaum.

Firkowska, A., Ostrowska, A., Sokolowska, M., Stein, Z., Susser, M., & Wald, I. (1978, June 23). Cognitive development and social policy. *Science, 200*, 1357–62.

Flach, F. (1990). Disorders of the pathways involved in the creative process. *Creativity Research Journal, 3*, 158–65.

Floderus-Myrhed, B., Pedersen, N.L., & Rasmuson, I. (1980). Assessment of heritability for personality, based on a short-form of the Eysenck Personality Inventory: A study of 12,898 twin pairs. *Behavior Genetics, 10*, 153–62.

Flynn, J.R. (1987). Massive IQ gains in 14 nations: What IQ tests really measure. *Psychological Bulletin, 101*, 171–91.

Flynn, J.R. (1998). Israeli military IQ tests: Gender differences small, IQ gains large. *Journal of Biosocial Science*, 30, 541–53.

Flynn, J.R. (1999). Searching for justice: The discovery of IQ gains over time. *American Psychologist*, 54, 5–20.

Flynn, J.R. (2009). Requiem for nutrition as the cause of IQ gains: Raven's gains in Britain 1938–2008. *Economics and Human Biology*, 7, 18–27.

Ford, M.E. (1986). For all practical purposes: Criteria for defining and evaluating practical intelligence. In R.J. Sternberg & R.K. Wagner (Eds.), *Practical Intelligence: Nature and Origins of Competence in the Everyday World* (pp. 183–200). Cambridge: Cambridge University Press.

Ford, M.E. & Tisak, M.S. (1983). A further search for social intelligence. *Journal of Educational Psychology*, 75, 197–206.

Fouad, N. (2001). The future of vocational psychology: Aiming high. *Journal of Vocational Behavior*, 59, 183–91.

Franken, R.E. (1993). *Human Motivation* (3rd ed.). Pacific Grove, CA: Brooks Cole.

Franken, I. & Muris, P. (2005). BIS/BAS personality constructs and college students' substance use. *Personality and Individual Differences*, 40, 1497–503.

Frensch, P.A. & Sternberg, R.J. (1989). Expertise and intelligent thinking: When is it worse to know better? In R.J. Sternberg (Ed.), *Advances in the Psychology of Human Intelligence* (Vol. 5, pp. 157–88). Hillsdale, NJ: Lawrence Erlbaum.

Freud, S. (1955). Analysis of a phobia in a five-year-old boy. In J. Strachey (Ed.), *The Standard Edition of the Complete Psychological Works of Sigmund Freud* (Vol. 10, pp. 1–147). London: Hogarth Press. (Original work published 1909.)

Freud, S. (1957). Mourning and melancholia. In J. Strachey (Ed. and Trans.), *The Standard Edition of the Complete Psychological Works of Sigmund Freud* (Vol. 14, pp. 239–58). London: Hogarth Press. (Original work published 1917.)

Freud, S. (1957). Group psychology and the analysis of the ego. In J. Strachey (Ed.), *The Standard Edition of the Complete Works of Sigmund Freud* (Vol. 18, pp. 65–143). London: Hogarth Press. (Original work published 1921.)

Freud, S. (1959). Character and anal eroticism. In J. Strachey (Ed.), *The Standard Edition of the Complete Psychological Works of Sigmund Freud* (Vol. 9, pp. 167–75). London: Hogarth Press. (Original work published 1908.)

Freud, S. (1964). *Leonardo Da Vinci and a Memory of His Childhood*. New York: Norton.

Freud, S. (1966). Heredity and the aetiology of the neuroses. In J. Strachey (Ed.), *The Standard Edition of the Complete Psychological Works of Sigmund Freud* (Vol. 3, pp. 143–56). London: Hogarth Press. (Original work published 1896.)

Freud, S. (1999). *The Interpretation of Dreams* (Joyce Crick, Trans.). Oxford: Oxford University Press. (Original work published 1900.)

Friedman, M. & Rosenman, R.H. (1974). *Type A Behavior and Your Heart*. New York: Knopf.

Frith, C.D. (1992). *The Cognitive Neuropsychology of Schizophrenia*. Hove: Lawrence Erlbaum.

Fromm-Reichmann, F. (1948). Notes on the development of treatment of schizophrenics by psychoanalytic psychotherapy. *Psychiatry*, 11, 263–73.

Funder, D.C. (1997). *The Personality Puzzle*. New York: Norton.

Funder, D.C. (2001). Personality. *Annual Review of Psychology*, 52, 197–221.

Furnham, A. (1987). The social psychology of working situations. In A. Gale & B. Christie (Eds.), *Psychophysiology and the Electronic Workplace* (pp. 89–111). Chichester: John Wiley & Sons, Ltd.

Furnham, A. (1994). *Personality at Work: The role of Individual Differences in the Workplace* (2nd ed.; 1st ed., 1992). London and New York: Routledge.

Furnham, A. (1999). Personality and creativity. *Perceptual and Motor Skills*, 88, 407–8.

Furnham, A. (2005). *The Psychology of Behaviour at Work* (2nd ed.; 1st ed., 1997). London: Psychology Press.

Furnham, A. & Chamorro-Premuzic, T. (2005). Individual differences and beliefs associated with preference for university assessment methods. *Journal of Applied Social Psychology*, 35, 1968–94.

Furnham, A. & Cheng, H. (1997). Personality and happiness. *Psychological Reports*, 83, 761–2.

Furnham, A. & Cheng, H. (1999). Personality as predictors of mental health and happiness in the East and West. *Personality and Individual Differences*, 27, 395–403.

Furnham, A. & Schaeffer, R. (1984). Person–environment fit, job satisfaction, and mental health. *Journal of Occupational Psychology*, 57, 295–307.

Furnham, A. & Walsh, T. (1991). The consequences of person–environment incongruence: Absenteeism, frustration, and stress. *Journal of Social Psychology*, 131, 187–204.

Furnham, A., Chamorro-Premuzic, T., & McDougall, F. (2003). Personality, cognitive ability, and beliefs about intelligence as predictors of academic performance. *Learning and Individual Differences*, 14, 47–64.

Gagne, F. & St. Pere, F. (2001). When IQ is controlled, does motivation still predict achievement? *Intelligence*, 30, 71–100.

Gale, A. (1973). The psychophysiology of individual differences: Studies of extraversion and the EEG. In P. Kline (Ed.), *New Approaches in Psychological Measurement* (pp. 211–56). London: John Wiley & Sons, Ltd.

Galton, F. (1876). The history of twins as a criterion of the relative powers of nature and nurture. *Journal of the Anthropological Institute*, 5, 391–406.

Galton, F. (1880). Psychometric experiments. *Brain*, 2, 149–62.

Galton, F. (1883). *Inquiries into Human Faculty, and its Laws and Consequences*. London: Macmillan.

Galton, F. (1972). *Hereditary Genius: An Inquiry into its Laws and Consequences*. Gloucester, MA: Peter Smith. (Original work published 1869.)

Galton, F. (1973/1883/1907). *Inquiries into Human Faculty and its Development*. New York: AMS Press.

Garcia, J. (1981). The logic and limits of mental aptitude testing. *American Psychologist*, 36, 1172–80.

Gardner, H. (1983). *Frames of Mind: The Theory of Multiple Intelligences*. New York: Basic Books.

Gardner, H. (1993). *Creative Minds*. New York: Basic Books.

Gardner, H. (1995). *Leading Minds: An Anatomy of Leadership*. New York: Basic Books.

Ge, X. & Conger, R.D. (1999). Early adolescent adjustment problems and emergence of late adolescent personality. *American Journal of Community Psychology*, 27, 429–59.

Geen, R.G. (1995). *Human Motivation: A Social Psychological Approach*. Pacific Grove, CA: Brooks Cole.

George, J. & Zhou, J. (2001). When openness to experience and conscientiousness are related to creative behavior: An interactional approach. *Journal of Applied Psychology*, 86, 513–24.

Getzels, J.M. & Jackson, P.W. (1962). *Creativity and Intelligence*. New York: John Wiley & Sons, Inc.

Giannitrapani, D. (1985). *The Electrophysiology of Intellectual Function*. Basel: Karger.

Gilboa, E. & Revelle, W. (1994). Personality and the structure of affective responses. In S.H.M. van Goozen, N.E. Van de Poll, & J.A. Sergeant (Eds.), *Emotions: Essays on Emotion Theory* (pp. 135–59). Hillsdale, NJ: Erlbaum.

Goethals, G.R. (2005). Presidential leadership. *Annual Review of Psychology*, 56, 545–70.

Goff, M. & Ackerman, P.L. (1992). Personality–intelligence relations: Assessment of typical intellectual engagement. *Journal of Educational Psychology*, 84, 537–53.

Goldberg, L.R. (1982). Facets of fascism. [Review of R.A. Altemeyer, Right-wing authoritarianism.] *Journal of Personality Assessment*, 46, 181–2.

Goldberg, L.R. (1990). An alternative "description of personality": The Big Five factor structure. *Journal of Personality and Social Psychology*, 59, 1216–29.

Goldberg, L.R. (1993). The structure of phenotypic personality traits. *American Psychologist*, 48, 26–34.

Goleman, D. (1995). *Emotional Intelligence: Why It Can Matter More than IQ*. London: Bloomsbury.

Goodman, N. (1955). *Fact, Fiction, and Forecast*. Cambridge, MA: Harvard University Press.

Gosling, S.D. & John, O.P. (1999). Personality dimensions in non-human animals: A cross-species review. *Current Directions in Psychological Science*, 8, 69–75.

Gosling, S.D., Rentfrow, P.J., & Swann, W.B., Jr. (2003). A very brief measure of the Big Five personality domains. *Journal of Research in Personality*, 37, 504–28.

Gott, K. (1992). Enhancing creativity in older adults. *Journal of Creative Behavior*, 26, 40–49.

Gottesman, I. & Shields, J. (1972). *Schizophrenia and Genetics: A Twin Study Vantage Point*. New York: Academic Press.

Gottfredson, G.D., Jones, E.M., & Holland, J.L. (1993). Personality and vocational interests: The relation of Holland's six interest dimensions to five robust dimensions of personality. *Journal of Counseling Psychology*, 40, 518–24.

Gottfredson, L.S. (1996, Winter). What do we know about intelligence? *American Scholar*, 15–30.

Gottfredson, L.S. (1997). Why g matters: The complexity of everyday life. *Intelligence*, 24, 79–132.

Gottfredson, L.S. (1998, Winter). The general intelligence factor. *Scientific American Presents*, 9, 24–9.

Gottfredson, L.S. (2000). Pretending that intelligence doesn't matter. *Cerebrum*, 2, 75–96.

Gottfredson, L.S. (2002). Where and why g matters: Not a mystery. *Human Performance*, 15, 25–46.

Gottfredson, L.S. (2003). Dissecting practical intelligence theory: Its claims and evidence. *Intelligence*, 31, 343–97.

Gottfredson, L.S. (2004a). Intelligence: Is it the epidemiologists' elusive "fundamental cause" of social class inequalities in health? *Journal of Personality and Social Psychology*, 86, 174–99.

Gottfredson, L.S. (2004b, Summer). Schools and the g factor. *Wilson Quarterly*, 35–45.

Gottfredson, L.S. (2005). Using Gottfredson's theory of circumscription and compromise in career guidance and counseling. In S.D. Brown & R.W. Lent (Eds.), *Career Development and Counseling: Putting Theory and Research to Work* (pp. 71–100). New York: John Wiley & Sons, Ltd.

Gottfredson, L.S. & Deary, I.J. (2004). Intelligence predicts health and longevity, but why? *Current Directions in Psychological Science*, 13, 1.

Gottman, J.M. (1998). Psychology and the study of the marital processes. *Annual Review of Psychology*, 49, 169–97.

Götz, K.O. & Götz, K. (1979a). Personality characteristics of professional artists. *Perceptual and Motor Skills*, 49, 327–34.

Götz, K.O. & Götz, K. (1979b). Personality characteristics of successful artists. *Perceptual and Motor Skills*, 49, 919–24.

Gough, H.G. (1968). *Chapin Social Insight Test Manual*. Palo Alto, CA: Consulting Psychologists Press.

Gough, H.G. (1976). Studying creativity by means of word association tests. *Journal of Applied Psychology*, 61, 348–53.

Grant, H. & Dweck, C.S. (1999). A goal analysis of personality and personality coherence. In D. Cervone & Y. Shoda (Eds.), *Social-Cognitive Approaches to Personality Coherence* (pp. 345–71). New York: Guilford Press.

Gray, J.A. (1981). A critique of Eysenck's theory of personality. In H.J. Eysenck (Ed.), *A Model for Personality* (pp. 246–77). Berlin: Springer.

Gray, J.A. (1982). *The Neuropsychology of Anxiety: An Enquiry into the Functions of the Septo-hippocampal System*. Oxford: Oxford University Press.

Gray, J.A. (1987). *The Psychology of Fear and Stress* (2nd ed.). Cambridge: Cambridge University Press.

Gray, J.A. (1991). Neural systems, emotion, and personality. In J. Madden IV (Ed.), *Neurobiology of Learning, Emotion, and Affect* (pp. 273–306). New York: Raven Press.

Gray, J.A. & Smith, P.T. (1969). An arousal-decision model for partial reinforcement and discrimination learning. In R.M. Gilbert & N.S. Sutherland (Eds.), *Animal Discrimination Learning* (pp. 243–72). London: Academic Press.

Gray, J.S. (1997). The fall in men's return to marriage. *Journal of Human Resources*, 32, 481–503.

Gray, N.S., Pickering, A.D., & Gray, J.A. (1994). Psychoticism and dopamine D2 binding in the basal ganglia using SPET. *Personality and Individual Differences*, 17, 431–4.

Green, K.D., Forehand, R., Beck, S., & Vosk, B. (1980). An assessment of the relationship among measures of children's social competence and children's academic achievement. *Child Development*, 51, 1149–56.

Greenberg, J. & Jonas, E. (2003). Psychological motives and political orientation: The left, the right, and the rigid: Comment on Jost *et al*. (2003). *Psychological Bulletin*, 129, 376–82.

Greenhaus, J.H., Callanan, G.A., & Godshalk, V.M. (2000). *Career Management* (3rd ed.). Fort Worth, TX: Dryden Press.

Gresvenor, E.L. (1927). A study of the social intelligence of high school pupils. *American Physical Education Review*, 32, 649–57.

Grigorenko, E.L. (2000). Heritability and intelligence. In R.J. Sternberg (Ed.), *Handbook of Intelligence* (pp. 53–91). New York: Cambridge University Press.

Guilford, J.P. (1950). Creativity. *American Psychologist*, 5, 444–54.

Guilford, J.P. (1954). *Psychometric Methods* (2nd ed.). New York: McGraw-Hill.

Guilford, J.P. (1959). Three faces of intellect. *American Psychologist*, 14, 469–79.

Guilford, J.P. (1967). *The Nature of Human Intelligence*. New York: McGraw-Hill.

Guilford, J.P. (1975). Creativity: A quarter century of progress. In I.A. Taylor & J.W. Getzels (Eds.), *Perspectives in Creativity* (pp. 37–59). Chicago: Aldine.

Guilford, J.P. (1977). *Way beyond the IQ*. Buffalo, NY: Bearly.

Guilford, J.P. (1981). Higher-order structure-of-intellect abilities. *Multivariate Behavioral Research*, 16, 411–35.

Guilford, J.P. & Christensen, P.R. (1973). The one-way relation between creative potential and IQ. *Journal of Creative Behavior*, 7, 247–52.

Haensly, P.A. & Reynolds, C.R. (1989). Creativity and intelligence. In J.A. Glover & C.R. Reynolds (Eds.), *Handbook of Creativity* (pp. 33–52). New York: Plenum Press.

Haggbloom, S.J., Warnick, R., Warnick, J.E., Jones, V.K., Yarbrough, G.L. *et al*. (2002). The 100 most eminent psychologists of the 20th Century. *Review of General Psychology*, 6, 153–65.

Halamandaris, K.F. & Power, K.G. (1999). Individual differences, social support and coping with examination stress: A study of the psychosocial and academic adjustment of first year home students. *Personality and Individual Differences*, 26, 665–85.

Harrington, D.M. (1972). Effects of instructions to "Be creative" on three tests of divergent thinking abilities. PhD thesis. University of California, Berkeley.

Harris, D. (1940). Factors affecting college grades: A review of the literature, 1930–1937. *Psychological Bulletin*, 37, 125–66.

Harris, J.R. (1995). Where is the child's environment? A group socialization theory of development. *Psychological Review*, 102, 458–89.

Hart, C.L., Taylor, M.D., Davey Smith, G., Whalley, L. J., Starr, J. M. *et al.* (2003). Childhood IQ, social class, deprivation, and their relationships with mortality and morbidity risk in later life. *Psychosomatic Medicine*, 65, 877–83.

Hart, W. & D. Albarrac'n (2009). The effects of chronic achievement motivation and achievement primes on the activation of achievement and fun goals. *Journal of Personality and Social Psychology*, 97(6), 1129–41.

Hayes, J.R. (1978). *Cognitive Psychology*. Homewood, IL: Dorsey.

Healey, D. & Runco, M.A. (2006). Could creativity be associated with insomnia? *Creativity Research Journal*, 18, 39–43.

Hebb, D.O. (1949). *The Organization of Behavior: A Neurophysiological Theory*. New York: John Wiley & Sons, Inc.

Heggestad, E.D. (2008). A really big picture of social intelligence. *Journal of Personality Assessment*, 90(1), 102–4.

Heinrichs, R.W. (2005). The primacy of cognition in schizophrenia. *American Psychologist*, 60, 229–42.

Helgesen, S. (1990). *The Female Advantage: Women's Ways of Leadership*. New York: Doubleday Currency.

Helson, R. (1970). Sex-specific patterns in creative literary fantasy. *Journal of Personality*, 38, 344–63.

Helson, R. (1971). Women mathematicians and the creative personality. *Journal of Consulting and Clinical Psychology*, 36, 210–20.

Helson, R. & Crutchfield, R.S. (1970). Mathematicians: The creative researcher and the average PhD. *Journal of Consulting and Clinical Psychology*, 34, 250–57.

Helson, R. & Moane, G. (1987). Personality changes in women from college to midlife. *Journal of Personality and Social Psychology*, 53, 176–86.

Hempel, C. (1966). *Philosophy and Natural Science*. Englewood Cliffs, NJ: Prentice Hall.

Hemphill, J.K. & Coons, A.E. (1957). Development of the Leader Behavior Description Questionnaire. In R.M. Stogdill & A.E. Coons (Eds.), *Leader Behavior: Its Description and Measurement* (pp. 6–38). Columbus, OH: Bureau of Business Research.

Hennessey, B.A. & Amabile, T.M. (2010). Creativity. *Annual Review of Psychology*, 61, 569–98.

Herrnstein, R.J. & Murray, C. (1994). *The Bell Curve: Intelligence and Class Structure in American Life*. New York: Free Press.

Herzberg, F. (1966). *Work and the Nature of Man*. Cleveland: World Publishing.

Herzberg, F., Bouton, A., & Steiner, B.J. (1954). Studies of the stability of the Kuder Preference Record. *Educational and Psychological Measurement*, 14, 90–100.

Hess, E.H. (1962). Ethology: An approach toward the complete analysis of behavior. In R. Brown, E. Galanter, E.H. Hess, & G. Mandler, *New Directions in Psychology* (pp. 157–266). New York: Holt, Rinehart, & Winston.

Heston, J.J. (1966). Psychiatric disorders in foster home-reared children of schizophrenic mothers. *British Journal of Psychiatry*, 112, 819–25.

Heyns, R.W., Veroff, J., & Atkinson, J.W. (1958). A scoring manual for the affiliation motive. In J.W. Atkinson (Ed.), *Motives in Fantasy, Action, and Society* (pp. 205–18). Princeton, NJ: Van Nostrand.

Higgins, E.T. (1999). Persons or situations: Unique explanatory principles or variability in general principles? In D. Cervone & Y. Shoda (Eds.), *The Coherence of Personality: Social-Cognitive Bases of Consistency, Variability, and Organization* (pp. 61–93). New York: Guilford Press.

Hoepener, R. & O'Sullivan, M. (1968). Social intelligence and IQ. *Educational and Psychological Measurement*, 28, 339–44.

Hofstee, W.K. (2001). Personality and intelligence: Do they mix? In M.J. Collis & S. Messick (Eds.), *Intelligence and Personality: Bridging the Gap in Theory and Measurement* (pp. 43–60). Mahwah, NJ: Lawrence Erlbaum.

Hogan, J. & Hogan, R. (2002). Leadership and sociopolitical intelligence. In R.E. Riggio, S.E. Murphy, & F.J. Pirozzolo (Eds.), *Multiple Intelligences and Leadership* (pp. 75–88). Mahwah, NJ: Lawrence Erlbaum.

Hogan, R. (2007). *Personality and the Fate of Organizations*. Mahwah, NJ: Lawrence Erlbaum.

Hogan, R. & Ahmad, G. (2011). Leadership. In T. Chamorro-Premuzic, S. von Stumm, & A. Furnham (Eds.). *Handbook of Individual Differences*. Oxford: Wiley-Blackwell.

Hogan, R. & Blake, R.J. (1996). Vocational interests: Matching selfconcept with the work environment. In K.R. Murphy (Ed.), *Individual Differences and Behavior in Organizations* (pp. 89–144). San Francisco, CA: Jossey-Bass.

Hogan, R., Curphy, G.J., & Hogan, J. (1994). What we know about leadership: Effectiveness and personality. *American Psychologist*, 49, 493–504.

Hogan, R., Johnson, J., & Briggs, S. (Eds.). (1997). *Handbook of Personality Psychology*. San Diego, CA: Academic Press.

Hogarty, G.E., Anderson, C.M., Reiss, D.J., Kornblith, S.J., Greenwald, D.P. *et al.* (1991). Family psychoeducation, social skills training, and maintenance chemotherapy in the aftercare treatment of schizophrenia II: Two-year effects of a controlled study on relapse and adjustment. *Archives of General Psychiatry*, 48, 340–41.

Holland, J.L. (1968). Explorations of a theory of vocational choice VI: A longitudinal study using a sample of typical college students. *Journal of Applied Psychology*, 52, Part 2.

Holland, J.L. (1973). *Making Vocational Choices: A Theory of Careers*. Englewood Cliffs, NJ: Prentice Hall.

Holland, J.L. (1977). *The Vocational Preference Inventory*. Palo Alto, CA: Consulting Psychologists Press.

Holland, J.L. (1996). Exploring careers with a typology: What we have learned and some new directions. *American Psychologist*, 51, 397–406.

Holland, J.L. (1997). *Making Vocational Choices: A Theory of Vocational Personalities and Work Environments* (3rd ed.; 1st ed., 1985; 2nd ed., 1992). Odessa, FL: Psychological Assessment Resources.

Hollander, E.P. (1993). Legitimacy, power, and influence: A perspective on relational features of leadership. In M.M. Chemers & R. Ayman (Eds.), *Leadership Theory and Research* (pp. 29–48). San Diego, CA: Academic Press.

Hollon, S.D., Shelton, R.C., & Loosen, P.T. (1991). Cognitive therapy and pharmacotherapy for depression. *Journal of Consulting and Clinical Psychology*, 59, 88–99.

Hollon, S.D., Stewart, M.O., & Strunk, D. (2006). Enduring effects for cognitive behavior therapy in the treatment of depression and anxiety. *Annual Review of Psychology*, 57, 285–315.

Holmes, D.S. (1974). Investigations of repression: Differential recall of material experimentally or naturally associates with ego threat. *Psychological Bulletin*, 81, 632–53.

Holmes, D.S. (1998). *The Essence of Abnormal Behavior*. London: Prentice-Hall Europe.

Holt, E.B. (1931). *Animal Drive and the Learning Process*. New York: Holt.

Hoover, R.N. (2000). Cancer: Nature, nurture, or both. *New England Journal of Medicine*, 343, 135–6.

Horn, J.L. (1976). Human abilities: A review of research and theory in the early 1970s. *Annual Review of Psychology*, 27, 437–85.

Horwitz, A.V., White, H.R., & Howell-White, S. (1996). Becoming married and mental health: A longitudinal study of a cohort of young adults. *Journal of Marriage and the Family*, 58, 895–907.

Hough, L.M., Eaton, N.K., Dunnette, M.D., Kamp, J.D., & McCloy, R.A. (1990). Criterion-related validities of personality constructs and the effects of response distortion on those validities. *Journal of Applied Psychology*, 75, 581–95.

House, R.J. & Aditya, R.N. (1997). The social scientific study of leadership: Quo vadis? *Journal of Management*, 23, 409–73.

House, R.J. & Shamir, B. (1993). Toward the integration of transformational, charismatic, and visionary theories. In M. Chemers & R. Ayman (Eds.), *Leadership Theory and Research: Perspectives and Directions* (pp. 81–107). New York: Academic Press.

Howell, J.M. (1988). Two facets of charisma: Socialized and personalized leadership in organizations. In J.A. Conger & R.N. Kanungo (Eds.), *Charismatic Leadership* (pp. 213–36). San Francisco, CA: Jossey-Bass.

Hsu, L.K.G. (1990). *Eating Disorders*. New York: Guilford Press.

Hu, Y. & Goldman, N. (1990). Mortality differentials by marital status: An international comparison. *Demography*, 27, 233–50.

Hull, C.L. (1943). *Principles of Behavior: An Introduction to Behavior Theory*. New York and London: Appleton-Century.

Hull, C.L. (1952). *A Behavior System: An Introduction to Behavior Theory Concerning the Individual Organism*. New Haven and London: Yale University Press and Oxford University Press.

Hunt, T. (1928). The measurement of social intelligence. *Journal of Applied Psychology*, 12, 317–34.

Hunter, J.E. (1983). *Test Validation for 12,000 jobs: An Application of Job Classification and Validity Generalization Analysis to the General Aptitude Test Battery (GATB)* (Test Research Rep. No. 45). Washington, DC: US Employment Service, US Department of Labor.

Hunter, J.E. (1986). Cognitive ability, cognitive aptitudes, job knowledge, and job performance. *Journal of Vocational Behavior*, 29, 340–62.

Hunter, J.E. & Hunter, R.F. (1984). Validity and utility of alternate predictors of job performance. *Psychological Bulletin*, 96, 72–98.

Hurtz, G.M. & Donovan, J.J. (2000). Personality and job performance: The Big Five revisited. *Journal of Applied Psychology*, 85, 869–79.

Hyde, J.S. & Linn, M.C. (1988). Gender differences in verbal ability: A meta-analysis. *Psychological Bulletin*, 104, 153–69.

Inness, M., Turner, N., Barling, J., & Stride, C.B. Transformational leadership and employee safety performance: A within-person, between-jobs design. *Journal of Occupational Health Psychology*, 15(3), 279–90.

Jackson, C., Furnham, A., Forde, L., & Cotter, T. (2000). The structure of the Eysenckian Personality Profiler. *British Journal of Psychology*, 91, 223–39.

Jencks, C. (1972). *Inequality: A Reassessment of the Effect of Family and Schooling in America*. New York: Basic Books.

Jensen, A.R. (1980). *Bias in Mental Testing*. New York: Free Press.

Jensen, A.R. (1982). Reaction time and psychometric g. In H.J. Eysenck (Ed.), *A Model for Intelligence* (pp. 93–132). Berlin: Springer.

Jensen, A.R. (1998). *The g Factor*. Westport, CT: Praeger.

Jensen, A.R. & Reynolds, C.R. (1983). Sex differences on the WISC-R. *Personality and Individual Differences*, 4, 223–6.

Johnson, E.H. & Spielberger, C.D. (1992). Assessment of the experience, expression, and control of anger in hypertension research. In E.H. Johnson, W.D. Gentry, & S. Julius (Eds.), *Personality, Elevated Blood Pressure, and Essential Hypertension* (pp. 5–25). Washington, DC: Hemisphere.

Johnson, W., McGue, M., Krueger, R.F., & Bouchard, T.J., Jr. (2004). Marriage and personality: A genetic analysis. *Journal of Personality and Social Psychology*, 86, 285–94.

Jordan, P.J., Ashkanasy, N., H‰ortel, M., & Hooper, G.S. (2002). Workgroup emotional intelligence: Scale development and relationship to team process effectiveness and goal focus. *Human Resources Management Review*, 12, 195–214.

Jˆreskog, K.G. (1978). Structural analysis of covariance and correlation matrices. *Psychometrika*, 43, 443–77.

Jorgensen, R.S., Blair, T.J., Kolodziej, M.E., & Schreer, G.E. (1996). Elevated blood pressure and personality: A meta-analytic review. *Psychological Bulletin*, 2, 293–320.

Jouanna, J. (1999). *Hippocrates*. Baltimore, MD: Johns Hopkins University Press.

Judge, T.A. & Bono, J.E. (2000). Five-factor model of personality and transformational leadership. *Journal of Applied Psychology*, 85, 751–65.

Judge, T.A. & Illies, R. (2002). Relationship of personality to performance motivation: A meta-analytic review. *Journal of Applied Psychology*, 87, 797–807.

Judge, T.A., Bono, J.E., Illies, R., & Gerhardt, M.W. (2002). Personality and leadership: A qualitative and quantitative review. *Journal of Applied Psychology*, 87, 765–80.

Judge, T.A., Colbert, A.E., & Illies, R. (2004). Intelligence and leadership: A quantitative review and test of theoretical propositions. *Journal of Applied Psychology*, 89, 542–52.

Judge, T.A., Erez, A., Bono, J.E., & Thoresen, C. (2002). Discriminant and incremental validity of four personality traits: Are measures of self-esteem, neuroticism, locus of control, and generalized self-efficacy indicators of a common core construct? *Journal of Personality and Social Psychology*, 83, 693–710.

Judge, T.A., Heller, D., & Mount, M.K. (2002). Five-factor model of personality and job satisfaction: A meta-analysis. *Journal of Applied Psychology*, 87, 530–41.

Judge, T.A., Higgins, C.A., Thoresen, C.J., & Barrick, M.R. (1999). The Big Five personality traits, general mental ability, and career success across the life span. *Personnel Psychology*, 52, 621–52.

Kaiser, R.B., Hogan, R., & Craig, S.B. (2008). Leadership and the fate of organizations. *American Psychologist*, 63(2), 96–110.

Kark, R., Shamir, B., & Chen, G. (2003). The two facets of transformational leadership: Empowerment and dependency. *Journal of Applied Psychology*, 88, 246–55.

Kasser, T. & Ryan, R.M. (1993). A dark side of the American dream: Correlates of financial success as a life aspiration. *Journal of Personality and Social Psychology*, 65, 410–22.

Katz, A. (1997). Creativity in the cerebral hemispheres. In M.A. Runco (Ed.), *Creativity Research Handbook* (pp. 203–26). Cresskill, NJ: Hampton Press.

Kaufman, J.C. (2011). Individual differences in creativity. In T. Chamorro-Premuzic, S. von Stumm, & A. Furnham (Eds.). *Handbook of Individual Differences*. Oxford: Wiley-Blackwell.

Kaufman, J.C. & Beghetto, R.A. (2009). Beyond big and little: The Four C model of creativity. *Review of General Psychology*, 13, 1–12.

Keating, D.K. (1978). A search for social intelligence. *Journal of Educational Psychology*, 70, 218–33.

Kelly, G.A. (1955). *The Psychology of Personal Constructs*. New York: Norton.

Kendler, K.S. & Diehl, S.R. (1993). The genetics of schizophrenia: A current genetic-epidemiologic perspective. *Schizophrenia Bulletin*, 19, 261–85.

Kenney, R.A., Blascovich, J., & Shaver, P.R. (1994). Implicit leadership theories: Prototypes for new leaders. *Basic Applied Social Psychology*, 15, 409–37.

King, L., Walker, L., & Broyles, S. (1996). Creativity and the five-factor model. *Journal of Research in Personality*, 30, 189–203.

Kirk, L. (1977). Maternal and subcultural correlates of cognitive growth rate: The GA pattern. In P.R. Dasen (Ed.), *Piagetian Psychology: Cross-Cultural Contributions*. New York: Gardner Press.

Kirkcaldy, B. (1988). Sex and personality differences in occupational interests. *Personality and Individual Differences*, 9, 7–13.

Kirkpatrick, S.A. & Locke, E.A. (1991). Leadership: Do traits matter? *Academy of Management Executive*, 5, 48–60.

Kirkpatrick, S.A. & Locke, E.A. (1996). Direct and indirect effects of three core charismatic leadership components on performance and attitudes. *Journal of Applied Psychology*, 81, 36–51.

Klein, M. (1935). A contribution to the psychogenesis of manic-depressive states. *International Journal of Psychoanalysis*, 16, 145–74.

Kleinginna, P., Jr. & Kleinginna, A. (1981a). A categorized list of motivation definitions, with suggestions for a consensual definition. *Motivation and Emotion*, 5, 263–91.

Kleinginna, P., Jr. & Kleinginna, A. (1981b). A categorized list of emotion definitions, with suggestions for a consensual definition. *Motivation and Emotion*, 5, 345–79.

Kline, P. (1975). *The Psychology of Vocational Guidance*. London: Batsford.

Kline, P. & Cooper, C. (1986). Psychoticism and creativity. *Journal of Genetic Psychology*, 147, 183–8.

Kohler, W. (1947). *Gestalt Psychology: An Introduction to New Concepts in Modern Psychology*. New York: Liveright.

Kotov, R., Gamez, W., Schmidt, F.L., & Watson, D. (2010). Linking "big" personality traits to anxiety, depressive, and substance use disorders: A meta-analysis. *Psychological Bulletin*, 136, 768–821.

Kouzes, J.M. & Posner, B.Z. (2002). *The Leadership Challenge* (3rd edn). San Francisco, CA: Jossey-Bass.

Krueger, R.F., Caspi, A., & Moffitt, T.E. (2000). Epidemiological personology: The unifying role of personality in population-based research on problem behaviors. *Journal of Personality*, 68, 967–98.

Krueger, R.F., Hicks, B.M., & McGue, M. (2001). Altruism and antisocial behavior: Independent tendencies, unique personality correlates, distinct etiologies. *Psychological Science*, 12, 397–402.

Kuipers, E., Fowler, D., Garety, P., Dunn, G., Bebbington, P., & Hadley, C. (1998). London-East Anglia randomized controlled trial of cognitive-behavioural therapy for psychosis, III. *British Journal of Psychiatry*, 173, 61–8.

Kuncel, N.R., Hezlett, S.A., & Ones, D.S. (2001). A comprehensive meta-analysis of the predictive validity of the graduate record examinations: Implications for graduate student selection and performance. *Psychological Bulletin*, 127, 162–81.

Kurzweil, R. (1999). *The Age of Spiritual Machines: When Computers Exceed Human Intelligence*. New York: Viking Press.

Lacey, J.I. (1967). Somatic response patterning and stress: Some revisions of activation theory. In M.H. Appley & R. Trumbull (Eds.), *Psychological Stress* (pp. 14–37). New York: Appleton-Century-Crofts.

Laing, R. (1971). *Self and Others*. Harmondsworth: Penguin.

Laroi, F., DeFruyt, F., Van Os, J., Aleman, A., & Van der Linden, M. (2005). Relations between hallucinations and personality structure in a non-clinical sample: Comparisons between young and elderly samples. *Personality and Individual Differences*, 39, 189–200.

Lazarus, R.S. & Folkman, S. (1984). Coping and adaptation. In W.D. Gentry (Ed.), *The Handbook of Behavioral Medicine* (pp. 282–325). New York: Guilford Press.

Lent, R. (2001). Vocational psychology and career counseling: Inventing the future. *Journal of Vocational Behavior*, 59, 213–25.

Lesch, K.P., Bengel, D., Heils, A., Sabol, S.Z., Greenberg, B.D. *et al.* (1996). Association of anxiety-related traits with a polymorphism in the serotonin transporter gene regulatory region. *Science*, 274, 1527–31.

Lester, D. (1999). Sylvia Plath. In M.A. Runco & S.R. Plitzker (Eds.), *Encyclopedia of Creativity*. San Diego, CA: Academic Press.

Levy, O., Kaler, S., & Schall, M. (1988). An empirical investigation of the role schemata: Occupations and personality characteristics. *Psychological Reports, 63*, 3–14.

Lewin, K., Lippit, R., & White, R.K. (1939). Patterns of aggressive behaviour in experimentally created social climates. *Journal of Social Psychology, 10*, 271–301.

Lewinsohn, P.M., Roberts, R.E., Seeley, J.R., Rohde, P., Gotlib, I.H., & Hops, H. (1994). Adolescent psychopathology II: Psychosocial risk factors for depression. *Journal of Abnormal Psychology, 103*, 302–15.

Liddle, P.F. (1987). The symptoms of chronic schizophrenia. A reexamination of the positive–negative dichotomy. *British Journal of Psychiatry, 151*, 145–51.

Ling, Y., Z. Simsek, Lubatkin, M.H., & Veiga, J.F. (2008). The impact of transformational CEOs on the performance of small- to medium-sized firms: Does organizational context matter? *Journal of Applied Psychology, 93*(4), 923–34.

Lippa, R. (1998). Gender-related individual differences and the structure of vocational interests. *Journal of Personality and Social Psychology, 74*, 996–1009.

Livesley, W.J., Jang, K.L., & Vernon, P.A. (1998). Phenotypic and genetic structure of traits delineating personality disorder. *Archives of General Psychiatry, 55*, 941–8.

Locke, E.A. (1997). The motivation to work: What we know. *Advances in Motivation and Achievement, 10*, 375–412.

Loden, M. (1985). *Feminine Leadership or How to Succeed in Business without Being One of the Boys*. New York: Times Books.

Loehlin, J.C. (1992). *Genes and Environment in Personality Development*. Newbury Park, CA: Sage.

Loehlin, J.C. & Nichols, R.C. (1976). *Heredity, Environment, and Personality: A Study of 850 Sets of Twins*. Austin, TX: University of Texas Press.

Loehlin, J.C., Lindzey, G., & Spuhler, J.M. (1975). *Race Differences in Intelligence*. San Francisco, CA: Freeman.

Lord, R.G., De Vader, C.L., & Alliger, G.M. (1986). A meta-analysis of the relation between personality traits and leadership perceptions: An application of validity generalization procedures. *Journal of Applied Psychology, 71*, 402–10.

Lord, R.G., Foti, R.J., & De Vader, C.L. (1984). A test of leadership categorization theory: Internal structure, information processing, and leadership perceptions. *Organizational Behavior and Human Performance, 34*, 343–78.

Lorenz, K. (1937). Uber den Begriff der Instinkthandlung. *Folia Biotheoretica, 2*, 18–50.

Low, K.S.D. (2009). Patterns of mean-level changes in vocational interests: A quantitative review of longitudinal studies. Unpublished doctoral dissertation, University of Illinois at Urbana-Champaign.

Low, K.S., Yoon, M., Roberts, B.W., & Rounds, J. (2005). The stability of vocational interests from early adolescence to middle adulthood: A quantitative review of longitudinal studies. *Psychological Bulletin, 131*, 713–37.

Lubinski, D. (2000). Scientific and social significance of assessing individual differences: "Sinking shaft at a few critical points." *Annual Review of Psychology, 51*, 405–44.

Lubinski, D. & Humphreys, L.G. (1990). A broadly based analysis of mathematical giftedness. *Intelligence, 14*, 327–55.

Luria, A.R. (1972). *The Man with a Shattered World: The History of a Brain Wound* (L. Solotaroff, Trans.). Cambridge, MA: Harvard University Press.

Lynn, R. (1990). The role of nutrition in secular increases in intelligence. *Personality and Individual Differences, 11*, 273–85.

Lynn, R. (1994). Sex differences in intelligence and brain size: A paradox resolved. *Personality and Individual Differences*, 17, 257–71.

Lyubomirsky, S., Tucker, K.L., & Kasri, F. (2001). Responses to hedonically-conflicting social comparisons: Comparing happy and unhappy people. *European Journal of Social Psychology*, 31, 1–25.

Maccoby, E.E. (2000). Parenting and its effects on children: On reading and misreading behavior genetics. *Annual Review of Psychology*, 51, 1–27.

Mackintosh, N.J. (1998). *IQ and Human Intelligence*. Oxford: Oxford University Press.

Mann, R.D. (1959). A review of the relationships between personality and performance in small groups. *Psychological Bulletin*, 56, 241–70.

Marks, I. & Cavanagh, K. (2009). Computer-aided psychological treatments: Evolving issues. *Annual Review of Clinical Psychology*, 5, 121–41.

Marlowe, H.A., Jr. (1986). Social intelligence: Evidence for multidimensionality and construct independence. *Journal of Educational Psychology*, 78, 52–8.

Martin, M. (1990). On the introduction of moods. *Clinical Psychology Review*, 10, 669–97.

Martindale, C. & Dailey, A. (1996). Creativity, primary process cognition, and personality. *Personality and Individual Differences*, 20, 409–14.

Martindale, C. & Greenough, J. (1973). The differential effect of increased arousal on creative and intellectual performance. *Journal of Genetic Psychology*, 123, 329–35.

Martindale, C. & Hasenfus, N. (1978). EEG differences as a function of creativity, stage of the creative process, and effort to be original. *Biological Psychology*, 6, 157–67.

Mascie-Taylor, C.G. & Gibson, J.B. (1978). Social mobility and IQ components. *Journal of Biosocial Science*, 10, 263–76.

Maslow, A.H. (1954). *Motivation and Personality*. New York: Harper.

Maslow, A.H. (1971). *The Farther Reaches of Human Nature*. New York: Viking Press.

Matarazzo, J.D. (1972). *Wechsler's Measurement and Appraisal of Adult Intelligence* (5th ed.). Baltimore: Williams & Wilkins.

Matthews, G. (1992a). Extraversion. In A.P. Smith & D.M. Jones (Eds.), *Handbook of Human Performance. Vol. 3: State and Trait* (pp. 95–126). London: Academic Press.

Matthews, G. (1992b). Mood. In A.P. Smith & D.M. Jones (Eds.), *Handbook of Human Performance. Vol. 3: State and Trait*. London: Academic Press.

Matthews, G. & Amelang, M. (1993). Extraversion: Arousal theory and performance. A study of individual differences in the EEG. *Personality and Individual Differences*, 14, 347–64.

Matthews, G. & Deary, I.J. (1998). *Personality Traits*. Cambridge: Cambridge University Press.

Matthews, G. & Gilliland, K. (1999). The personality theories of H.J. Eysenck and J.A. Gray: A comparative review. *Personality and Individual Differences*, 26, 583–626.

Matthews, G., Davies, D.R., Westerman, S.J., & Stammers, R.B. (2000). *Human Performance: Cognition, Stress, and Individual Differences*. London: Psychology Press.

Matthews, G., Jones, D., & Chamberlain, A. (1990). Refining the measurement of mood: The UWIST Mood Adjective Checklist. *British Journal of Psychology*, 81, 17–42.

Matthews, G., Zeidner, M., & Roberts, R.D. (2002). *Emotional Intelligence: Science and Myth*. Cambridge, MA: MIT Press.

Mayer, J.D., Roberts, R.D., & Barsade, S.G. (2008). Human abilities: Emotional intelligence. *Annual Review of Psychology*, 59, 507–36.

Mayer, J.D. & Salovey, P. (1997). What is emotional intelligence? In P. Salovey & D.J. Sluyter (Eds.), *Emotional Development and Emotional Intelligence: Educational Implications*. New York: Basic Books.

Mayer, J.D., Salovey, P., & Caruso, D. (1997). *Emotional IQ Test* (CD-ROM). Needham, MA: Virtual Knowledge.

Mayer, J.D., Salovey, P., & Caruso, D.R. (2002). *The Mayer–Salovey–Caruso Emotional Intelligence Test (MSCEIT): User's Manual.* Toronto: Multi-Health Systems.

McCall, R.B. (1977). Childhood IQs as predictors of adult educational and occupational status. *Science*, 197, 482–83.

McClelland, D.C. (1965). Toward a theory of motive acquisition. *American Psychologist*, 20, 321–33.

McClelland, D.C. (1975). *Power: The Inner Experience.* New York: Irvington.

McClelland, D.C. & Burham, D. (1976). Power is the great motivator. *Harvard Business Review*, 25, 159–66.

McClelland, D.C. & Steele, R.S. (1972). *Motivation Workshops.* New York: General Learning Press.

McClelland, D.C. & Winter, D.G. (1969). *Motivating Economic Achievement.* New York: Free Press.

McClelland, D.C., Atkinson, J.W., Clark, R.A., & Lowell, E.L. (1953). *The Achievement Motive.* Englewood Cliffs, NJ: Prentice Hall.

McConville, C. & Cooper, C. (1999). Personality correlates of variable moods. *Personality and Individual Differences*, 26, 65–78.

McCrae, R.R. (1987). Creativity, divergent thinking, and openness to experience. *Journal of Personality and Social Psychology*, 52, 1258–65.

McCrae, R.R. (1996). Social consequences of experiential openness. *Psychological Bulletin*, 120, 323–37.

McCrae, R.R. & Costa, P.T. (1997). Conceptions and correlates of openness to experience. In R. Hogan, J. Johnson, & S. Briggs (Eds.), *Handbook of Personality Psychology* (pp. 825–47). San Diego, CA: Academic Press.

McCrae, R.R. & Costa P.T., Jr. (1999). A Five-Factor theory of personality. In L.A. Pervin & O.P. John (Eds.), *Handbook of Personality Psychology* (pp. 139–53). New York: Guilford Press.

McCrae, R.R., Costa, P.T., Ostendorf, F., Angleitner, A., Hrebickova, M. *et al.* (2000). Nature over nurture: Temperament, personality, and life span development. *Journal of Personality and Social Psychology*, 78, 173–86.

McCrae, R.R., Loeckenhoff, C.E., & Costa, P.T. (2005). A step toward DSM-V: Cataloguing personality-related problems in living. *European Journal of Personality*, 19, 269–86.

McGue, M. (1993). From proteins to cognitions: The behavioral genetics of alcoholism. In R. Plomin & G.E. McClearn (Eds.), *Nature, Nurture, and Psychology* (pp. 245–68). Washington, DC: American Psychological Association.

McGue, M. & Lykken, D.T. (1992). Genetic influence on risk of divorce. *Psychological Science*, 3, 368–73.

McGue, M., Bouchard, T.J., Jr., Iacono, W.G., & Lykken, D.T. (1993). Behavioral genetics of cognitive ability: A life-span perspective. In R. Plomin & G.E. McClearn (Eds.), *Nature, Nurture, and Psychology* (pp. 59–76). Washington, DC: American Psychological Association.

McHenry, J., Hough, L., Toquam, J., Hanson, M., & Ashworth, S. (1990). Project A validity results: The relationship between predictor and criterion domains. *Personnel Psychology*, 43, 335–54.

McKenna, P.J. (1994). *Schizophrenia and Related Syndromes.* Oxford and New York: Oxford University Press.

McMillan, M. (2008). Phineas Gage: Unravelling the myth. *The Psychologists*, 21, 828–31. http://www.thepsychologist.org.uk/archive/archive_home.cfm/volumeID_21-editionID_164-ArticleID_1399-getfile_getPDF/thepsychologist\0908look.pdf, accessed December 2010.

Mednick, M.T. & Andrews, F.M. (1967). Creative thinking and level of intelligence. *Journal of Creative Behavior*, 1, 428–31.

Mednick, S.A. (1962). The associative basis of the creative process. *Psychological Review*, 69, 220–32.

Mednick, S.A. & Mednick, M.T. (1967). *Examiner's Manual, Remote Associates Test.* Boston, MA: Houghton Mifflin.

Meehl, P.E. (1962). Schizotaxia, schizotypy, schizophrenia. *American Psychologist*, 17, 827–38.

Meehl, P.E. (1989). Schizotaxia revisited. *Archives of General Psychiatry*, 46, 935–44.

Mehta, P. & Kumar, D. (1985). Relationships of academic achievement with intelligence, personality, adjustment, study habits, and academic motivation. *Journal of Personality and Clinical Studies*, 1, 57–68.

Merten, T. (1995). Factors influencing word association responses: A reanalysis. *Creativity Research Journal*, 8, 249–63.

Merten, T. & Fischer, I. (1999). Creativity, personality, and word association responses: Associative behavior in 40 supposedly creative persons. *Personality and Individual Differences*, 27, 933–42.

Miles, T.R. (1957). Contributions to intelligence testing and the theory of intelligence I: On defining intelligence. *British Journal of Educational Psychology*, 27, 153–65.

Milgram, S. (1963). Behavioral study of obedience. *Journal of Abnormal and Social Psychology*, 67, 371–8.

Miller, D.T., Taylor, B., & Buck, M.L. (1991). Gender gaps: Who needs to be explained? *Journal of Personality and Social Psychology*, 61, 5–12.

Minuchin, S. (1974). *Families and Family Therapy*. London: Tavistock.

Minuchin, S., Rosman, B., & Baker, L. (1978). *Psychosomatic Families: Anorexia Nervosa in Context*. Cambridge, MA: Harvard University Press.

Mischel, W. (1968). *Personality and Assessment*. New York: John Wiley & Sons, Inc.

Mischel, W. (1973). Toward a cognitive social learning reconceptualization of personality. *Psychological Review*, 80, 252–83.

Mischel, W. (1999). Personality coherence and dispositions in a cognitive-affective personality system (CAPS) approach. In D. Cervone & Y. Shoda (Eds.), *Coherence in Personality* (pp. 37–60). New York: Guilford Press.

Monroe, S.M. & Simmons, A.D. (1991). Diathesis-stress theories in the context of life stress research: Implications for the depressive disorders. *Psychological Bulletin*, 110, 406–25.

Morris, W.N. (1989). *Mood: The Frame of Mind*. New York: Springer Verlag.

Moss, F.A. & Hunt, T. (1927). Are you socially intelligent? *Scientific American*, 137, 108–10.

Moss, F.A., Hunt, T., Omwake, K.T., & Ronning, M.M. (1927). *Social Intelligence Test*. Washington, DC: Center for Psychological Services.

Murray, G., Allen, N.B., & Tinder, J. (2002). Longitudinal investigation of mood variability and the FFM: Neuroticism predicts variability in extended states of positive and negative affect. *Personality and Individual Differences*, 33, 1217–28.

Murray, H.A. (1938). *Explorations in Personality*. New York: Oxford University Press.

Naatanen, R. (1973). The inverted-U relationship between activation and performance: A critical review. In S. Kornblum (Ed.), *Attention and Performance* (Vol. 4, pp. 155–74). New York: Academic Press.

Neiss, R. (1988). Reconceptualizing arousal: Psychobiological states in motor performance. *Psychological Bulletin*, 103, 345–66.

Newbury-Birch, D., White, M., & Kamali, F. (2000). Factors influencing alcohol and illicit drug use amongst medical students. *Drug and Alcohol Dependence*, 59, 125–30.

Newman, D.L., Caspi, A., Moffitt, T.E., & Silva, P. (1997). Antecedents of adult interpersonal functioning: Effects of individual differences in Age 3 temperament. *Developmental Psychology*, 33, 206–17.

Newman, H., Freeman, F., & Holzinger, K. (1937). *Twins: A Study of Heredity and Environment*. Chicago, IL: University of Chicago Press.

Niedenthal, P.M. (1992). Affect and social perception: On the psychological validity of rose-colored glasses. In R. Bomstein & T. Pittman (Eds.), *Perception without Awareness* (pp. 211–35). New York: Guilford Press.

Nietzsche, F. (1973). *Beyond Good and Evil* (R.J. Hollingdale, Trans.). London: Penguin. (Original work published 1886.)

Nieva, V.F. & Gutek, B.A. (1981). *Women and Work: A Psychological Perspective*. New York: Praeger.

Nobel, E.P., Runco, M.A., & Ozkaragoz, T.Z. (1993). Creativity in alcoholic and nonalcoholic families. *Alcohol*, 10, 317–22.

Nolen-Hoeksema, S. (2001). *Abnormal Psychology* (2nd ed.). New York: McGraw-Hill.

Norem, J.K. (1998). Why should we lower our defenses about defense mechanisms? *Journal of Personality: On Current Research and Theory on Defense Mechanisms*, 66 (Special Issue), 895–917.

Norman, W.T. (1967). *2800 Personality Trait Descriptors: Normative Operating Characteristics for a University Population*. Ann Arbor, MI: University of Michigan, Department of Psychological Sciences.

Northouse, P.G. (1997). *Leadership: Theory and Practice*. Thousand Oaks, CA: Sage.

Nuttin, J. (1984). *Motivation, Planning, and Action*. Hillsdale, NJ: Lawrence Erlbaum.

Ochse, R. (1990). *Before the Gates of Excellence: The Determinants of Creative Genius*. Cambridge: Cambridge University Press.

O'Connor, B.P. (2005). Graphical analyses of personality disorders in five-factor model space. *European Journal of Personality*, 19, 287–305.

O'Connor, B.P. & Dyce, J.A. (2001). Rigid and extreme: A geometric representation of personality disorders in five-factor model space. *Journal of Personality and Social Psychology*, 81, 1119–30.

O'Connor, R.M. & Little, I.S. (2003). Revisiting the predictive validity of emotional intelligence: Self-report versus ability-based measures. *Personality and Individual Differences*, 35, 1893–902.

Öhman, A. (1999). Distinguishing unconscious from conscious emotional processes: Methodological considerations and theoretical implications. In T. Dalgleish & M.J. Power (Eds.), *Handbook of Cognition and Emotion* (pp. 321–52). Chichester: John Wiley & Sons, Ltd.

Oleski, D. & Subich, L.M. (1996). Congruence and career change in employed adults. *Journal of Vocational Behavior*, 49, 221–9.

O'Malley, P.M. & Johnston, L.D. (2002). Epidemiology of alcohol and other drug use among American college students. *Journal of Studies on Alcohol*, 14, 23–39.

Ones, D.S., Viswesvaran, C., & Schmidt, F.L. (1993). Comprehensive meta-analysis of integrity test validities: Findings and implications for personnel selection and theories of job performance. *Journal of Applied Psychology (Monograph)*, 78, 679–703.

O'Sullivan, M., Guilford, J.P., & deMille, R. (1965). *The Measurement of Social Intelligence* [Report from the Psychology Laboratory, No. 34]. Los Angeles, CA: University of Southern California.

O'Toole, B.J. & Stankov, L. (1992). Ultimate validity of psychological tests. *Personality and Individual Differences*, 13, 699–716.

Owen, K. & Taljaard, J.J. (1995). *Handleiding vir die gebruik van sielkundige en skolastiese toetse van die RGN*. Pretoria: Raad vir Geesteswetenskaplike Navorsing.

Ozer, D.J. & Benet-Martinez, V. (2006). Personality and the prediction of consequential outcomes. *Annual Review of Psychology*, 57, 8.1–8.21.

Ozer, D.J. & Reise, S.P. (1994). Personality assessment. *Annual Review of Psychology*, 45, 357–88.

Paykel, E.S. & Priest, R.G. (1992). Recognition and management of depression in general practice: A consensus statement. *British Medical Journal*, 305, 1198–202.

Paykel, E.S., Hollyman, J.A., Freeling, P., & Sedgwick, P. (1988). Predictors of therapeutic benefit from amitriptyline in mild depression: A general practice placebo-controlled trial. *Journal of Affective Disorders*, 14, 83–95.

Pedersen, N.L., Plomin, R., McClearn, G.E., & Friberg, L. (1988). Neuroticism, extraversion, and related traits in adult twins reared apart and reared together. *Journal of Personality and Social Psychology*, 55, 950–57.

Penner, L.A. (2002). Dispositional and organizational influences on sustained volunteerism: An interactional perspective. *Journal of Social Issues*, 58, 447–67.

Penner, L.A., Fritzsche, B.A., Craiger, J.P., & Freifeld, T.R. (1995). Measuring the prosocial personality. In J. Butcher & C.D. Spielberger (Eds.), *Advances in Personality Assessment* (Vol. 10). Hillsdale, NJ: Lawrence Erlbaum.

Pérez, J.C., Petrides, K.V., & Furnham, A. (2007). Measuring trait emotional intelligence. In R. Schulze & R.D. Roberts (Eds.), *International Handbook of Emotional Intelligence*. Cambridge, MA: Hogrefe & Huber.

Perkins, D.N. (1981). *The Mind's Best Work*. Cambridge, MA: Harvard University Press.

Perry, G.H., Yang, F., Marques-Bonet, T. *et al.* (2008). Copy number variation and evolution in humans and chimpanzees. *Genome Research*, 18(11), 1698–710.

Pervin, L.A. (1996). *The Science of Personality*. New York: John Wiley & Sons, Inc.

Petrides, K.V. & Furnham, A. (2000). On the dimensional structure of emotional intelligence. *Personality and Individual Differences*, 29, 313–20.

Petrides, K.V. & Furnham, A. (2001). Trait emotional intelligence: Psychometric investigation with reference to established trait taxonomies. *European Journal of Personality*, 15, 425–48.

Petrides, K.V. & Furnham, A. (2003). Trait emotional intelligence: Behavioral validation in two studies of emotion recognition and reactivity to mood induction. *European Journal of Personality*, 17, 39–57.

Petrides, K.V., Frederickson, N., & Furnham, A. (2004). The role of trait emotional intelligence in academic performance and deviant behavior at school. *Personality and Individual Differences*, 36, 277–93.

Piaget, J. (1952). *The Origins of Intelligence in Children*. New York: International Universities Press.

Piaget, J. (1963). *The Psychology of Intelligence*. New York: Routledge.

Piaget, J. & Inhelder, B. (1969). *The Psychology of the Child*. New York: Basic Books.

Pickering, A.D. & Gray, J.A. (1999). The neuroscience of personality. In L. Pervin & O. John (Eds.), *Handbook of Personality: Theory and Research* (2nd ed., pp. 277–99). New York: Guilford Press.

Pickering, A.D. & Gray, J.A. (2001). Dopamine, appetitive reinforcement, and the neuropsychology of human learning: An individual differences approach. In A. Eliasz & A. Angleitner (Eds.), *Advances in Individual Differences Research*. Lengerich, Germany: PABST Science Publishers.

Pinker, S.R. (2002). *The Blank Slate*. New York: Viking Press.

Pintner, R. & Upshall, C.C. (1928). Some results of social intelligence tests. *School and Society*, 27, 369–70.

Plomin, R. & Caspi, A. (1999). Behavioral genetics and personality. In L.A. Pervin & O.P. John (Eds.), *Handbook of Personality: Theory and Research* (2nd ed., pp. 251–76). New York: Guilford Press.

Plomin, R. & Petrill, S.A. (1997). Genetics and intelligence: What's new? *Intelligence*, 24, 53–77.

Plomin, R. & Spinath, F.M. (2004). Intelligence: Genetics, genes, and genomics. *Journal of Personality and Social Psychology*, 86, 112–29.

Plomin, R., Chipuer, H.M., & Loehlin, J.C. (1990). Behavioral genetics and personality. In L.A. Pervin (Ed.), *Handbook of Personality: Theory and Research* (pp. 225–43). New York: Guilford Press.

Plomin, R., Loehlin, J.C., & DeFries, J.C. (1985). Genetic and environmental components of "environmental" influences. *Developmental Psychology*, 21, 391–402.

Prediger, D.J. (1976). A world-of-work map for career exploration. *Vocational Guidance Quarterly*, 24, 198–208.

Prediger, D.J. (1982). Dimensions underlying Holland's hexagon: Missing link between interests and occupations? *Journal of Vocational Behavior*, 21, 259–87.

Prediger, D.J. & Vansickle, T.R. (1992a). Locating occupations on Holland's hexagon: Beyond RIASEC. *Journal of Vocational Behavior*, 40, 111–28.

Prediger, D.J. & Vansickle, T.R. (1992b). Who claims Holland's hexagon is perfect? *Journal of Vocational Behavior*, 40, 210–19.

Premack, D. & Woodruff, G. (1978). Does the chimpanzee have a theory of mind? *Behavioral and Brain Sciences*, 1, 515–26.

Quirk, S.W., Christiansen, N.D., Wagner, S.H., & McNulty, J. (2003). On the usefulness of measures of normal personality for clinical assessment: Evidence of the incremental validity of the NEO PI-R. *Psychological Assessment*, 15, 311–25.

Rachman, S. (1998). *Anxiety*. Hove: Psychology Press.

Rachman, S. (2009). Psychological treatment for anxiety: The evolution of behavioral therapy and cognitive-behavioral therapy. *Annual Review of Clinical Psychology*, 5, 97–119.

Raz, S. & Raz, N. (1990). Structural brain abnormalities in the major psychoses. *Schizophrenia Research*, 3, 295–301.

Redding, S.G. & Wong, G.Y.Y. (1986). The psychology of Chinese organization behavior. In M.H. Bond (Ed.), *The Psychology of Chinese People*. Hong Kong: Oxford University Press.

Reich, T., Edenberg, H.J., Goate, A., Williams, J.T., Rice, J.P. *et al.* (1998). Genome-wide search for genes affecting the risk for alcohol dependence. *American Journal of Medical Genetics*, 81, 207–15.

Reiff, H.B., Hatzes, N.M., Bramel, M.H., & Gibbon, T. (2001). The relation of LD and gender with emotional intelligence in college students. *Journal of Learning Disabilities*, 34, 66–78.

Renzulli, J.S. (1978). What makes giftedness? Reexamining a definition. *Phi Delta Kappan*, 60, 180–84.

Renzulli, J.S. (1986). The three-ring conception of giftedness: A developmental model for creative productivity. In R.J. Sternberg & J.E. Davidson (Eds.), *Conceptions of Giftedness* (pp. 53–92). New York: Cambridge University Press.

Resick, C.J., Whitman, D.S., Weingarden, S.M., & Hiller, N.J.(2009). The bright-side and the dark-side of CEO personality: Examining core self-evaluations, narcissism, transformational leadership, and strategic influence. *Journal of Applied Psychology*, 94(6), 1365–81.

Resnick, S.M., Berenbaum, S.A., Gottesman, I.I., & Bouchard, T.J., Jr. (1986). Early hormonal influences on cognitive functioning in congenital adrenal hyperplasia. *Developmental Psychology*, 22, 191–8.

Revelle, W. (1993). Individual differences in personality and motivation: Non-cognitive determinants of cognitive performance. In A. Baddeley & L. Weiskrantz (Eds.), *Attention: Selection, Awareness, and Control. A Tribute to Donald Broadbent* (pp. 346–73). Oxford: Oxford University Press.

Revelle, W. (2008). The contribution of reinforcement sensitivity theory to personality theory. In P.J. Corr (Ed.), *The Reinforcement Sensitivity Theory of Personality* (p. 508–27). Cambridge: Cambridge University Press.

Reynolds, C.R., Chastain, R.L., Kaufman, A.S., & McClean, J.E. (1987). Demographic characteristics and IQ among adults: Analysis of the WAIS-R standardization sample as a function of the stratification of variables. *Journal of Social Psychology*, 25, 323–42.

Rhodes, M. (1987). An analysis of creativity: The role of ability, cue consistency, and active processing. *Creativity Research Journal*, 9, 9–23. (Original work published 1961.)

Richards, R.L. (1976). A comparison of selected Guilford and Wallach-Kogan creative thinking tests in conjunction with measures of intelligence. *Journal of Creative Behavior*, 10, 151–64.

Richardson, M. & Abraham, C. (2009). Conscientiousness and achievement motivation predict performance. *European Journal of Personality*, 23(7), 589–605.

Rickards, T. & deCock, C. (1999). Understanding organizational creativity: Toward a multi-paradigmatic approach. In M.A. Runco (Ed.), *Creativity Research Handbook* (Vol. 2). Cresskill, NJ: Hampton Press.

Riemann, R., Grubich, C., Hempel, S., Mergl, S., & Richter, M. (1993). Personality attitudes toward current political topics. *Personality and Individual Differences*, 15, 313–21.

Riggio, R.E., Messamer, J., & Throckmorton, B. (1991). Social and academic intelligence: Conceptually distinct but overlapping constructs. *Personality and Individual Differences*, 12, 696–702.

Roberts, B.W. & Caspi, A. (2003). The cumulative continuity model of personality devleopment: Striking a balance between continuity and change in personality traits across the life course. In U. Staudinger & U. Lindenberger (Eds.), *Understanding Human Development: Lifespan Psychology in Exchange with Other Disciplines*. Dordrecht: Kluwer Academic.

Roberts, R.D., Zeidner, M., & Matthews, G. (2001). Does emotional intelligence meet traditional standards for an intelligence? Some new data and conclusions. *Emotion*, 1, 196–231.

Robins, R.W., Caspi, A., & Moffitt, T.E. (2002). Itís not just who you're with, it's who you are: Personality and relationship experiences across multiple relationships. *Journal of Personality*, 70, 925–64.

Robinson, D.L. (1996). *Brain, Mind, and Behavior: A New Perspective on Human Nature*. Westport, CT: Praeger.

Robinson, D.L. (1999). The "IQ" factor: Implications for intelligence theory and measurement. *Personality and Individual Differences*, 27, 715–35.

Rogers, C.R. (1951). *Client-Centered Therapy: Its Current Practice, Implications, and Theory*. Boston, MA: Houghton Mifflin.

Rogers, C.R. (1959). A theory of therapy, personality, and interpersonal relationships, as developed in the client-centered framework. In S. Koch (Ed.), *Psychology: A Study of a Science* (Vol. 3). New York: McGraw-Hill.

Rogers, C.R. (1961). *On Becoming a Person*. Boston, MA: Houghton Mifflin.

Rogers, C.R. (1980). *A Way of Being*. Boston, MA: Houghton Mifflin.

Rohner, R.P. (1999). *Handbook for the Study of Parental Acceptance and Rejection*. Storrs, CT: University of Connecticut, Center for the Study of Parental Acceptance and Rejection.

Rolfhus, E.L. & Ackerman, P.L. (1996). Self-report knowledge: At the crossroads of ability, interest, and personality. *Journal of Educational Psychology*, 88, 174–88.

Rommanes, G.J. (1881). *Animal Intelligence*. London: Kegan Paul.

Rose, R.J., Koskenvuo, M., Kaprio, J., Sarna, S., & Langinvainio, H. (1988). Shared genes, shared experiences, and similarity of personality: Data from 14,288 adult Finnish co-twins. *Journal of Personality and Social Psychology*, 54, 161–71.

Rose, S., Kamin, L.J., & Lewontin, R.C. (1984). *Not in our Genes*. London: Penguin.

Rosenbloom, J.L., Ash, R.A., Dupont, B. & Coder, L. (2008). Why are there so few women in information technology? Assessing the role of personality in career choices. *Journal of Economic Psychology*, 29(4), 543–54.

Rosenthal, D. (1971). *Genetics and Psychopathology*. New York: McGraw-Hill.

Rounds, J. & Tracey, T.J. (1993). Predigerís dimensional representation of Hollandís RIASEC circumplex. *Journal of Applied Psychology*, 78, 875–90.

Rowe, D.C. (1997). *The Limits of Family Influence: Genes, Experience, and Behavior*. New York: Guilford Press.

Ruchkin, V.V., Koposov, R.A., Klinteberg, B., Oreland, L., & Grigorenko, E.L. (2005). Platelet MAO-B, personality, and psychopathology. *Journal of Abnormal Psychology*, 114, 477–82.

Rummel, R. (1994). *Death by Government*. New Brunswick, NJ: Transaction Publishers.

Runco, M.A. (1986). Divergent thinking and creative performance in gifted and non-gifted children. *Educational and Psychological Measurement, 46*, 375–84.

Runco, M.A. (1998). *Creativity Research Handbook* (Vol. 1). Cresskill, NJ: Hampton Press.

Runco, M.A. (2003a). *Creativity Research Handbook* (Vol. 2). Cresskill, NJ: Hampton Press.

Runco, M.A. (2003b). *Creativity Research Handbook* (Vol. 3). Cresskill, NJ: Hampton Press.

Runco, M.A. (2004). Creativity. *Annual Review of Psychology, 55*, 657–87.

Runco, M.A. & Charles, R. (1993). Judgments of originality and appropriateness as predictors of creativity. *Personality and Individual Differences, 15*, 537–46.

Rushton, J.P. & Ackney, C.D. (1996). Brain size and cognitive ability: Correlations with age, sex, social class, and race. *Psychonomic Bulletin and Review, 3*, 21–36.

Rushton, J.P. & Irwing, P. (2011). The general factor of personality. In T. Chamorro-Premuzic, S. von Stumm, & A. Furnham (Eds.). *Handbook of Individual Differences*. Oxford: Wiley-Blackwell.

Rushton, J.P. & Jensen, A.R. (2005). Thirty years of research on race differences in cognitive ability. *Psychology, Public Policy, and Law, 11*, 235–94.

Russell, B. (1948). *Human Knowledge*. New York: Simon & Schuster.

Russell, J.A. (1991). Culture and the categorization of emotion. *Psychological Bulletin, 110*, 426–50.

Russell, J.A. (1995). Facial expressions of emotion: What lies beyond minimal universality? *Psychological Bulletin, 118*, 379–91.

Russell, J.A. (2003). Core affect and the psychological construction of emotion. *Psychological Review*, 145–172.

Russell, J.E. (2001). Vocational psychology: An analysis and directions for the future. *Journal of Vocational Behavior, 59*, 226–34.

Rusting, C.L. (1998). Personality, mood, and cognitive processing of emotional information: Three conceptual frameworks. *Psychological Bulletin, 124*, 165–96.

Ryan, R.M., Rigby, S., & King, K. (1993). Two types of religious internalization and their relations to religious orientations and mental health. *Journal of Personality and Social Psychology, 65*, 586–96.

Sachar, E.J. & Baron, M. (1979). Biology of affective disorders. *Annual Review of Neuroscience, 2*, 505–18.

Saklofske, D.H., Austin, E.J., & Minski, P.S. (2003). Factor structure and validity of a trait emotional intelligence measure. *Personality and Individual Differences, 34*, 707–21.

Sala, F. (2002). *Emotional Competence Inventory: Technical Manual*, Boston, MA: McClelland Center For Research.

Salgado, J.F. (1997). The five factor model of personality and job performance in the European Community. *Journal of Applied Psychology, 82*, 30–43.

Salovey, P. & Mayer, J.D. (1990). Emotional intelligence. *Imagination, Cognition, and Personality, 9*, 185–211.

Salovey, P., Mayer, J.D., Goldman, S.L., Turvey, C., & Palfai, T.P. (1995) Emotional attention, clarity, and repair: Exploring emotional intelligence using the Trait Meta-Mood Scale. In J.W. Pennebaker (Ed .), *Emotion, Disclosure, & Health* (pp. 125–51). Washington, DC: American Psychological Association.

Sanchez-Marin, M., Rejano-Infante, E., & Rodriguez-Troyano, Y. (2001). Personality and academic productivity in the university student. *Social Behavior and Personality, 29*, 299–305.

Sanders, A.F. (1983). Towards a model of stress and human performance. *Acta Psychologica, 53*, 61–97.

Sanders, W.B., Osborne, R.T., & Greene, J.E. (1955). Intelligence and academic performance of college students of urban, rural, and mixed backgrounds. *Journal of Educational Research*, 49, 185–93.

Sarbin, T.R. & Juhasz, J.B. (1967). The historical background of the concept of hallucination. *Journal of the History of the Behavioral Sciences*, 3, 339–58.

Sartorius, N., Ustun, T.B., Costa e Silva, J.A., Goldberg, D., & Lecrubier, Y. (1993). An international study of psychological problems in primary care. Preliminary report from the World Health Organization Collaborative Project on "Psychological Problems in General Health Care." *Archives of General Psychiatry*, 50, 819–24.

Saulsman, L.M. & Page, A.C. (2004). The five-factor model and personality disorder empirical literature: A meta-analytic review. *Clinical Psychology Review*, 23, 1055–85.

Scarr, S. (1992). Developmental theories for the 1990s: Development and individual differences. *Child Development*, 63, 1–19.

Scheff, T. (1966). *Being Mentally Ill*. Chicago, IL: Aldine.

Schein, V.E. (2001). A global look at psychological barriers to women's progress in management. *Journal of Social Issues*, 57, 675–88.

Schelde, J.T.M. (1998). Major depression: Behavioral markers of depression and recovery. *Journal of Nervous and Mental Disease*, 186, 133–40.

Schermer, J.A. & Vernon, P.A. (2008). A behavior genetic analysis of vocational interests using a modified version of the Jackson Vocational Interest Survey. *Personality and Individual Differences*, 45(1), 103–9.

Schmidt, F.L. & Hunter, J.E. (1998). The validity and utility of selection methods in personnel psychology: Practical and theoretical implications of 85 years of research findings. *Psychological Bulletin*, 124, 262–74.

Schmidt, F.L. & Hunter, J.E. (2000). Select on intelligence. In E. A. Locke (Ed.), *Handbook of Principles of Organizational Behaviour* (pp. 3–14). Oxford: Blackwell.

Schmitt, N., Gooding, R.Z., Noe, R.D., & Kirsch, M. (1984). Metaanalyses of validity studies published between 1964 and 1982 and the investigation of study characteristics. *Personnel Psychology*, 37, 407–22.

Schneider, R.J., Ackerman, P.L., & Kanfer, R. (1996). To "act wisely in human relations": Exploring the dimensions of social competence. *Personality and Individual Differences*, 21, 469–81.

Schoppe, K.J. (1975). *Verbaler Kreativitätstest. Ein Verfahren zur Erfassung verbal-produktiver Kreativitätsmerkmale*. Gˆttingen, Toronto, Z¸rich: Hogrefe.

Schubert, D.S. (1973). Intelligence as necessary but not sufficient for creativity. *Journal of Genetic Psychology*, 122, 45–7.

Schultz, D. & Schultz, S.E. (1994). *Theories of Personality* (5th ed.). Pacific Grove, CA: Brooks Cole.

Schutte, N.S., Malouff, J.M., Hall, L.E., Haggerty, D.J., Cooper, J.T. *et al.* (1998). Development and validation of a measure of emotional intelligence. *Personality and Individual Differences*, 25, 167–77.

Seeman, P. (1980). Brain dopamine receptors. *Pharmacological Review*, 32, 229–313.

Seligman, M.E.P. (1971). Phobias and preparedness. *Behavior Therapy*, 2, 307–20.

Seligman, M.E.P. (1974). Depression and learned helplessness. In R.J. Friedman & M.M. Katz (Eds.), *The Psychology of Depression: Contemporary Theory and Research*. New York: Winston-Wiley.

Seth, N.K. & Pratap, S. (1971). A study of the academic performance, intelligence, and aptitude of engineering students. *Education and Psychology Review*, 11, 3–10.

Shahuria, E. (2003). A review of genetic factors in depressive affects. *Social Behavior and Personality*, 31, 657–62.

Shamir, B. (1991). The charismatic relationship: Alternative explanations and predictions. *Leadership Quarterly*, 2, 81–104.

Shamir, B., House, R.J., & Arthur, M.B. (1993). The motivational effects of charismatic leadership: A self-concept-based theory. *Organizational Science*, 4, 577–94.

Sharma, S. & Rao, U. (1983). The effects of self-esteem, test anxiety, and intelligence on academic achievement of high school girls. *Personality Study and Group Behavior*, 3, 48–55.

Sharpe, R. (2000, November 20). As leaders, women rule: New studies find that female managers outshine their male counterparts in almost every measure. *Business Week*. Retrieved December 15, 2000, from www.businessweek.com/common_frames?ca.htm?/2000/00_47?b3708145.htm.

Shepherd, M., Watt, D., Falloon, I., & Smeeton, N. (1989). The natural history of schizophrenia: A five-year follow-up in a representative sample of schizophrenics. *Psychological Medicine*, Monograph Supplement 15.

Sher, K.J., Bartholow, B.D., & Wood, M.D. (2000). Personality and substance use disorders: A prospective study. *Journal of Consulting and Clinical Psychology*, 68, 818–29.

Sherrington, R., Brynjolfsson, J., Petursson, H., Potter, M., Dudleston, K. *et al.* (1988). Localization of a susceptibility locus for schizophrenia on chromosome 5. *Nature*, 336, 164–7.

Shontz, F.C. (1975). *The Psychological Aspects of Physical Illness and Disability*. New York: Macmillan.

Shouksmith, G. (1973). *Intelligence, Creativity, and Cognitive Style*. London: Angus & Robertson.

Shuey, A.M. (1966). *The Testing of Negro Intelligence* (2nd ed.). New York: Social Science Press.

Silversthorne, C. (2001). Leadership effectiveness and personality: A cross-cultural evaluation. *Personality and Individual Differences*, 30, 303–9.

Silvia, P.J. (2008a). Another look at creativity and intelligence: Exploring higher-order models and probable confounds. *Personality and Individual Differences*, 44, 1012–21.

Silvia, P.J. (2008b). Creativity and intelligence revisited: A latent variable analysis of Wallach and Kogan (1965). *Creativity Research Journal*, 20, 34–9.

Simon, H.A. & Chase, W. (1973). Skill in chess. *American Science*, 61, 394–403.

Simonton, D.K. (1986). Presidential personality: Biographical use of the Gough adjective check list. *Journal of Personality and Social Psychology*, 51, 149–60.

Simonton, D.K. (1987). *Why Presidents Succeed: A Political Psychology of Leadership*. New Haven, CT: Yale University Press.

Simonton, D.K. (1994). *Greatness: What Makes History and Why*. New York: Guilford Press.

Simonton, D.K. (2004). *Creativity in Science: Chance, Logic, Genius, and Zeitgeist*. New York: Cambridge University Press.

Singh, R. & Varma, S.K. (1995). The effect of academic aspiration and intelligence on scholastic success of XI graders. *Indian Journal of Psychometry and Education*, 26, 43–8.

Skinner, B.F. (1938). *The Behavior of Organisms*. New York: Appleton-Century-Crofts.

Skinner, B.F. (1977). Why I am not a cognitive psychologist. *Behaviorism*, 5, 1–10.

Slaski, M. & Cartwright, S. (2003). Emotional intelligence training and its implications for stress, health, and performance. *Stress and Health*, 19, 233–9.

Slater, E. & Cowie, V. (1971). *The Genetics of Mental Disorders*. London: Oxford University Press.

Slater, E. & Shields, J. (1969). Genetic aspects of anxiety. In M.H. Lader (Ed.), *Studies of Anxiety* (pp. 62–71). London: Headley Bros.

Smith, K.L., Michael, W.B., & Hocevar, D. (1990). Performance on creativity measures with examination-taking instructions intended to induce high or low levels of test anxiety. *Creativity Research Journal*, 3, 265–80.

Smith, T.W. & Spiro, A. III. (2002). Personality, health and aging: Prolegomenon for the next generation. *Journal of Research in Personality*, 36, 363–94.

Snow, R.E. (1963). Effects of learner characteristics in learning from instructional films. Unpublished doctoral thesis, Purdue University (University Microfilms No. 6404928).

Snow, R.E. (1992). Aptitude theory: Yesterday, today, and tomorrow. *Educational Psychologist*, 27, 5–32.

Snow, R.E. (1995). Foreword. In D. H. Saklofske & M. Zeidner (Eds.), *International Handbook of Personality and Intelligence* (pp. 11–15). New York: Plenum Press.

Snyder, M. (1987). *Public Appearances/Private Realities: The Psychology of Self-Monitoring*. New York: Freeman.

Snyder, S.H. (1976). The dopamine hypothesis of schizophrenia: Focus on dopamine receptor. *American Journal of Psychiatry*, 133, 197–202.

Sorrentino, R.M. & Higgins, E.T. (1986). *Handbook of Motivation and Cognition*. New York: Guilford Press.

Sosik, J.J., Kahai, S.S., & Avolio, B.J. (1998). Transformational leadership and dimensions of creativity: Motivating idea generation in computer-mediated groups. *Creativity Research Journal*, 11, 111–21.

Spangler, W., House, R., & Palrecha, R. (2004). Personality and leadership. In B. Schneider & D. Smith (Eds.), *Personality and Organization* (pp. 251–90). New York: Maliwah.

Spearman, C.E. (1904). "General intelligence," objectively determined and measured. *American Journal of Psychology*, 15, 201–93.

Spearman, C.E. (1927). *The Abilities of Man: Their Nature and Measurement*. New York: Macmillan.

Spence, S.A., Brooks, D.J., Hirsch, S.R., Liddle, P.F., Meehan, J., & Grasby, P.M. (1997). A PET study of voluntary movement in schizophrenic patients experiencing passivity phenomena (delusions of alien control). *Brain*, 120, 1997–2011.

Spencer, H. (1872). *Principles of Psychology* (3rd ed.). London: Longman, Brown, Green, & Longmans.

Spielberger, C. (1972a). Anxiety as an emotional state. In C. Spielberger (Ed.), *Anxiety: Current Trends in Theory and Research* (pp. 23–49). New York: Academic Press.

Spielberger, C. (1972b). Conceptual and methodological issues in anxiety research. In C. Spielberger (Ed.), *Anxiety: Current Trends in Theory and Research* (Vol. 2). New York: Academic Press.

Spinath, F. & Johnson, W. (2011). Behavior genetics. In T. Chamorro-Premuzic, S. von Stumm, & A. Furnham (Eds.). *Handbook of Individual Differences*. Oxford: Wiley-Blackwell.

Spitzer, R. (1981). The diagnostic status of homosexuality in DSM-III: A reformulation of the issues. *American Journal of Psychiatry*, 138, 210–15.

Spranger, W.D. & House, R.J. (1991). Presidential effectiveness and the leadership motive profile. *Journal of Personality and Social Psychology*, 60, 439–55.

Springsteen, T. (1940). A Wyoming State Training School survey on emotional stability, intelligence, and academic achievement. *Journal of Exceptional Children*, 7, 54–64.

Stanger, F. (1933). The relation of mental deficiency to crime. *Training School Bulletin*, 30, 22–7.

Stankov, L. (2000). Complexity, metacognition, and fluid intelligence. *Intelligence*, 28, 121–43.

Stankov, L., Boyle, G.J., & Cattell, R.B. (1995). Models and paradigms in personality and intelligence research. In D. Saklofske & M. Zeidner (Eds.), *International Handbook of Personality and Intelligence: Perspectives on Individual Differences* (pp. 15–43). New York: Plenum Press.

Stern, W. (1912). *Die Psychologische Methoden der Intelligenz-Pruifung*. Barth: Leipzig.

Sternberg, R.J. (1982). Reasoning, problem solving, and intelligence. In R.J. Sternberg (Ed.), *Handbook of Human Intelligence* (pp. 225–307). Cambridge: Cambridge University Press.

Sternberg, R.J. (1985a). *Beyond IQ: A Triarchic Theory of Human Intelligence*. Cambridge: Cambridge University Press.

Sternberg, R.J. (1985b). Implicit theories of intelligence, creativity, and wisdom. *Journal of Personality and Social Psychology*, 49, 607–27.

Sternberg, R.J. (1985c). Natural, unnatural, and supernatural concepts. *Cognitive Psychology*, 14, 451–88.

Sternberg, R.J. (1997). *Successful Intelligence*. New York: Plume.

Sternberg, R.J. (Ed.). (1999). *Handbook of Creativity*. New York: Cambridge University Press.

Sternberg, R.J. & Gastel, J. (1989). Coping with novelty in human intelligence: An empirical investigation. *Intelligence*, 13, 187–97.

Sternberg, R.J. & Grigorenko, E.L. (Eds.). (1997). *Intelligence, Heredity, and Environment*. New York: Cambridge University Press.

Sternberg, R.J. & Kaufman, J. (1998). Human abilities. *Annual Review of Psychology*, 49, 479–502.

Sternberg, R.J. & Lubart, T.I. (1995). *Defying the Crowd: Cultivating Creativity in a Culture of Conformity*. New York: Free Press.

Sternberg, R.J. & Lubart, T.I. (1996). Investing in creativity. *American Psychologist*, 51, 677–88.

Sternberg, R.J. & O'Hara, L.A. (2000). Intelligence and creativity. In R.J. Sternberg (Ed.), *Handbook of intelligence* (pp. 611–30). New York: Cambridge University Press.

Sternberg, R.J. & Wagner, R.K. (1993). The *g*-ocentric view of intelligence and job performance is wrong. *Current Directions in Psychological Science*, 2, 1–4.

Sternberg, R.J., Conway, B.C., Ketron, J.L., & Bernstein, M. (1981). People's conception of intelligence. *Journal of Personality and Social Psychology*, 41(3), 37–55.

Stevenson, J. (1997). The genetic basis of personality. In C. Cooper & V. Varma (Eds.), *Processes in Individual Differences*. London: Routledge.

Stewart, W.H., Jr. and Roth, P.L. (2007). A meta-analysis of achievement motivation differences between entrepreneurs and managers. *Journal of Small Business Management*, 45(4), 401–21.

Stirling, J., Tantam, D., Thomas, P., Newby, D., Montague, L., Ring, N., & Rowe, S. (1993). Expressed emotion and schizophrenia: The ontogeny of EE during an 18-month follow-up. *Psychological Medicine*, 23, 771–8.

Stirling, J.D., Hellewell, J.S.E., & Hewitt, J. (1997). Verbal memory impairment in schizophrenia: No sparing of short-term recall. *Schizophrenia Research*, 25, 85–95.

Stogdill, R.M. (1948). Personal factors associated with leadership: A survey of the literature. *Journal of Psychology*, 25, 35–71.

Stogdill, R.M. (1974). *Handbook of Leadership*. New York: Free Press.

Stone, W.F. & Smith, L.D. (1993). Authoritarianism: Left and right. In W. Stone, G. Lederer, & R. Christie (Eds.), *Strength and Weakness: The Authoritarian Personality Today* (pp. 144–56). New York: Springer Verlag.

Storm, C. & Storm, T. (1987). A taxonomic study of the vocabulary of emotions. *Journal of Personality and Social Psychology*, 53, 805–16.

Street, J. (2004). Celebrity politicians: Popular culture and political representation. *British Journal of Politics & International Relations*, 6, 435–52.

Strong, E.K., Jr. (1943). *The Vocational Interests of Men and Women*. Stanford, CA: Stanford University Press.

Su, R., Rounds, J., & Armstrong, P. I. (2009). Men and things, women and people: A meta-analysis of sex differences in interests. *Psychological Bulletin*, 135, 859–94.

Suhara, T., Yasuno, F., Sudo, Y., Yamamoto, M., Inoue, M. *et al.* (2001). Dopamine D2 receptors in the insular cortex and the personality trait of novelty seeking. *NeuroImage*, 13, 891–5.

Sullivan, P.F., Bulik, C.M., & Kendler, K.S. (1998). The epidemiology and classification of bulimia nervosa. *Psychological Medicine, 28,* 599–610.

Sulloway, F. (1996). *Born to Rebel.* New York: Pantheon.

Swanson, J.L. (1999). Stability and change in vocational interests. In M.L. Savickas & R.L. Spokane (Eds.), *Vocational Interests Meaning, Measurement, and Counseling use* (pp. 135–58). Palo Alto, CA: Davies-Black.

Swanson, J.L. & Hansen, J.C. (1988). Stability of vocational interests over 4-year, 8-year, and 12-year intervals. *Journal of Vocational Behavior, 33,* 185–202.

Szasz, T.S. (1958). Psychiatry, ethics, and the criminal law. *Columbia Law Review, 58,* 183–98.

Szasz, T. (1960). The myth of mental illness. *American Psychologist, 15,* 113–18.

Tambs, K. & Moum, T. (1992). No large convergence during marriage for health, lifestyle, and personality in a large sample of Norwegian spouses. *Journal of Marriage and the Family, 54,* 957–71.

Taylor, M. (1985). The roles of occupational knowledge and vocational self-concept crystallization in students' school-to-work transition. *Journal of Counselling Psychology, 32,* 539–50.

Taylor, M.A. & Abrams, R. (1975). Manic-depressive illness and good prognosis schizophrenia. *American Journal of Psychiatry, 132,* 741–2.

Tellegen, A., Lykken, D.T., Bouchard, T.J., Jr., Wilcox, K.J., Segal, N.L., & Rich, S. (1988). Personality similarity in twins reared apart and together. *Journal of Personality and Social Psychology, 54,* 1031–9.

Tenopyr, M.L. (1967). Social intelligence and academic success. *Educational and Psychological Measurement, 27,* 961–5.

Terman, L.M. (1916). *The Measurement of Intelligence: An explanation of and a complete guide for the use of the Stanford revision and extension of the Binet-Simon Intelligence Scale.* Boston, MA: Houghton Mifflin.

Terman, L.M. (1917). The intelligence quotient of Francis Galton in childhood. *American Journal of Psychology, 28,* 209–15.

Terman, L.M. & Merrill, M.A. (1937). *Measuring Intelligence.* Boston, MA: Houghton Mifflin.

Tett, R.P., Jackson, D.N., Rothstein, M., & Reddon, J.R. (1999). Meta-analysis of bidirectional relations in personality–job performance research. *Human Performance, 12,* 1–29.

Thayer, R.E. (1989). *The Biopsychology of Mood and Arousal.* Oxford: Oxford University Press.

Theander, S. (1970). Anorexia nervosa: A psychiatric investigation of 94 female patients. *Acta Psychiatrica Scandinavica,* Suppl. 214.

Theis, S.V. (1924). *How Foster Children Turn Out* (Vols. Publication No. 165). New York: State Charities Aid Association.

Thompson, D.M. (1934). On the detection of emphasis in spoken sentences by means of visual, tactual, and visual-tactual cues. *Journal of General Psychology, 11,* 160–72.

Thomson, G.H. (1921). The Northumberland Mental Tests. *British Journal of Psychology, 12,* 201–22.

Thorndike, E.L. (1911). *Animal Intelligence.* New York: Macmillan.

Thorndike, E.L. (1920). Intelligence and its uses. *Harper's Magazine, 140,* 227–35.

Thorndike, E.L., Terman, L.M., Freeman, F.N., Calvin, S.S., Pentler, R. *et al.* (1921). Intelligence and its measurement: A symposium. *Journal of Educational Psychology, 12,* 123–47.

Thorndike, R.L. & Stein, S. (1937). An evaluation of the attempts to measure social intelligence. *Psychological Bulletin, 34,* 275–85.

Thurstone, L.L. (1919). *Intelligence Tests for College Students.* Pittsburgh, PA: Carnegie Institute of Technology.

Tinsley, H.E. (2001). Marginalization of vocational psychology. *Journal of Vocational Behavior, 59,* 243–51.

Tokar, D.M. & LaRae, M.J. (1998). Masculinity, vocational interests and career choice traditionality: Evidence for a fully mediated model. *Journal of Counselling and Psychology*, 4, 424–35.

Tolman, E.C. (1939). The determiners of behavior at a choice point. *Psychological Review*, 45, 1–41.

Torrance, E.P. (1963). Creativity. In F.W. Hubbard (Ed.), *What Research Says to the Teacher* (No. 28). Washington, DC: Department of Classroom Teachers American Educational Research Association of the National Education Association.

Torrance, E.P. (1966). *Torrance Tests of Creative Thinking: Norms-Technical Manual*. Lexington, MA: Ginn.

Torrance, E.P. (1974). *Torrance Tests of Creative Thinking*. Lexington, MA: Ginn.

Torrance, E.P. (1975). Sociodrama as a creative problem solving approach to studying the future. *Journal of Creative Behavior*, 9, 182–95.

Torrance, E.P. (1979). *The Search for Satori and Creativity*. Buffalo, NY: Bearly.

Tracey, T.J.G. & Sodano, S.M. (2008). Issues of stability and change in interest development. *Career Development Quarterly*, 57(1), 51–62.

Trapnell, P.D. (1996). Openness versus intellect: A lexical left turn. *European Journal of Personality*, 8, 273–90.

Tremaine, L., Schau, C., & Busch, J. (1982). Children's occupational sex-typing. *Sex Roles*, 8, 691–710.

Triandis, H.C. & Suh, E.M. (2002). Cultural influences on personality. *Annual Review of Personality*, 53, 133–60.

Trull, T.J. & Durrett, C.A. (2005). Categorical and dimensional models of personality disorder. *Annual Review of Clinical Psychology*, 1, 355–80.

Tupes, E.C. & Christal, R.E. (1992). Recurrent personality factors based on trait ratings. *Journal of Personality*, 60, 225–51. (Reprinted from USAF ASD Tech. Report No. 61–97, 1961, Lackland Air Force Base, TX: US Air Force.)

Turkheimer, E. (1998). Heritability and biological explanation. *Psychological Review*, 105, 782–91.

Turner, N., Barling, J., Epitropaki, O., Butcher, V., & Milner, C. (2002). Transformational leadership and moral reasoning. *Journal of Applied Psychology*, 87, 304–11.

Uhl, G.R., Liu, Q.R., Walther, D., Hess, J. & Naiman, D. (2001). Polysubstance abuse–vulnerability genes: Genome scans for association, using 1,004 subjects and 1,494 single-nucleotide polymorphisms. *American Journal of Human Genetics*, 69, 1290–300.

Upmanyu, V.V., Bhardwaj, S., & Singh, S. (1996). Word-association emotional indicators: Associations with anxiety, psychoticism, neuroticism, extraversion, and creativity. *Journal of Social Psychology*, 36, 521–9.

Valenstein, E.S. (1998). *Blaming the Brain: The Truth about Drugs and Mental Health*. New York: Free Press.

Van Engen, M.L. (2001). Gender and leadership: A contextual perspective. Doctoral dissertation, Tilburg University, Tilburg, The Netherlands.

Van Hiel, A. & Mervielde, I. (1996). The Five-Factor Model personality dimensions and current political beliefs: An empirical update in a non-student sample. Unpublished manuscript.

Varon, E.J. (1936). Alfred Binet's concept of intelligence. *Psychological Review*, 43, 32–49.

Vasquez, N.A. & Buehler, R. (2007). Seeing future success: Does imagery perspective influence achievement motivation? *Personality and Social Psychology Bulletin*, 33(10), 1392–405.

Vaughn, C. & Leff, J. (1976). The influence of family and social factors on the course of psychiatric illness: A comparison of schizophrenic and depressed neurotic patients. *British Journal of Psychiatry*, 129, 125–37.

Velten, E. (1968). A laboratory task for induction of mood states. *Behavior Research and Therapy*, 6, 473–82.

Vernon, P.E. (1933). Some characteristics of the good judge of personality. *Journal of Social Psychology*, 4, 42–57.

Vernon, P.E. (1971). Effects of administration and scoring on divergent thinking tests. *British Journal of Educational Psychology*, 41, 245–57.

Verona, E., Patrick, C.J., & Joiner, T.E., Jr. (2001). Psychopathy, antisocial personality, and suicide risk. *Journal of Abnormal Psychology*, 110, 462–70.

Wai, J., Lubinski, D., & Benbow, C.P. (2005). Creativity and occupational accomplishments among intellectually precocious youth: An age 13 to age 33 longitudinal study. *Journal of Educational Psychology*, 97, 484–92.

Walberg, H.J., Strykowski, B.F., Rovai, E., & Hung, S.S. (1984). Exceptional performance. *Review of Educational Research*, 54, 87–112.

Walker, E.F. & Diforio, D. (1997). Schizophrenia: A neural diathesis-stress model. *Psychological Review*, 104, 667–85.

Walker, R.E. & Foley, J.M. (1973). Social intelligence: Its history and measurement. *Psychological Reports*, 33, 839–64.

Wallach, M.A. (1970). Creativity. In P. Mussen (Ed.), *Carmichael's Handbook of Child Psychology* (pp. 1211–72). New York: John Wiley & Sons, Inc.

Walsh, B.W. & Opisow, S.H. (1983). *Handbook of Vocational Psychology*. Hillsdale, NJ: Lawrence Erlbaum.

Walsh, W. (2001). The changing nature of the sciences of vocational psychology. *Journal of Vocational Behavior*, 59, 262–74.

Walton, K.E. & Roberts, B.W. (2004). On the relationship between substance use and personality traits: Abstainers are not maladjusted. *Journal of Research in Personality*, 38, 515–35.

Watson, D. (2000). *Mood and Temperament*. New York: Guilford Press.

Watson, D. & Clark, L.A. (1992). On traits and temperament: General and specific factors of emotional experience and their relation to the five-factor model. *Journal of Personality*, 60, 441–76.

Watson, D. & Tellegen, A. (1985). Toward a consensual structure of mood. *Psychological Bulletin*, 98, 219–35.

Watson, D. & Walker, L.M. (1996). The long-term stability and predictive validity of trait measures of affect. *Journal of Personality and Social Psychology*, 70, 567–77.

Watson, D., Clark, L.A., & Tellegen, A. (1988). Development and validation of brief measures of positive and negative affect: The PANAS scales. *Journal of Personality and Social Psychology*, 54, 1063–70.

Watson, J.B. (1913). Psychology as a behaviorist views it. *Psychological Review*, 20, 158–77.

Watson, J.B. (1930). *Behaviorism* (rev. ed.). Chicago, IL: University of Chicago Press.

Watson, J.B. & Rayner, R. (1920). Conditioned emotional reactions. *Journal of Experimental Psychology*, 3, 1–14.

Webb, E. (1915). Character and intelligence. *British Journal of Psychological Monographs*. Ser. 1(3).

Wechsler, D. (1944). *Measurement of Adult Intelligence* (3rd ed.). Baltimore, MD: Williams & Wilkins.

Wechsler, D. (1953). *Wechsler Adult Intelligence Scale Manual*. San Antonio, TX: Psychological Corporation.

Wechsler, D. (1955). *Manual for the Wechsler Adult Intelligence Scale*. New York: Psychological Corporation.

Wechsler, D. (1958). *The Measurement and Appraisal of Adult Intelligence* (4th ed.). Baltimore, MD: Williams & Wilkins.

Wechsler, D. (1997). *Weschsler Adult Intelligence Scale-III*. San Antonio, TX: Psychological Corporation.

Weiner, B. (1986). *Motivation*. New York: Holt, Rinehart, & Winston.

Weis, S. & Süß, H.-M. (2007). Reviving the search for social intelligence – A multitrait-multimethod study of its structure and construct validity. *Personality and Individual Differences*, 42(1), 3–14.

Weisberg, R.W. & Alba, J.W. (1981). An examination of the alleged role of "fixation" in the solution of several "insight" problems. *Journal of Experimental Psychology: General*, 110, 169–92.

Westen, D. (1997). Divergences between clinical and research methods for assessing personality disorders: Implications for research and the evolution of Axis II. *American Journal of Psychiatry*, 154, 895–903.

Westen, D. (1998). The scientific legacy of Sigmund Freud: Toward a psychodynamically informed psychological science. *Psychological Bulletin*, 124, 333–71.

White, S. (2000). Conceptual foundations of IQ testing. *Psychology, Public Policy, and Law*, 6, 33–43.

Widiger, T.A. & Samuel, D.B. (2005). Evidence-based assessment of personality disorders. *Psychological Assessment*, 17, 278–87.

Wiebe, R.P. (2004). Delinquent behavior and the five factor model: Hiding in the adaptive landscape. *Individual Difference Research*, 2, 38–62.

Wierzbicka, A. (1999). *Emotions across Languages and Cultures*. New York: Cambridge University Press.

Williams, D.G. (1990). Effects of psychoticism, extraversion, and neuroticism in current mood: A statistical review of six studies. *Personality and Individual Differences*, 11, 615–30.

Williams, M.J. (1985). Attributional formulation of depression as a diathesis-stress model: Metalsky *et al.* reconsidered. *Journal of Personality and Social Psychology*, 48, 1572–5.

Willingham, W.W. (1974). Predicting success in graduate education. *Science*, 183, 273–8.

Wilson, G.D. (Ed.) (1973). *The Psychology of Conservatism*. London: Academic Press.

Winter, D.G. (1973). Leader appeal, leader performance, and the motive profiles of leaders and followers: A study of American presidents and elections. *Journal of Personality and Social Psychology*, 52, 196–202.

Wissler, C. (1901). The correlation of mental and physical tests. *Psychological Review*, Monograph, No. 3.

Wong, C.S. & Law, K.S. (2002). The effects of leader and follower emotional intelligence on performance and attitude: An exploratory study. *Leadership Quarterly*, 13, 243–74.

Wong, C.T., Day, J.D., Maxwell, S.E., & Meara, N.M. (1995). A multitrait–multimethod study of academic and social intelligence in college students. *Journal of Educational Psychology*, 87, 117–33.

Wong, R. (2000). *Motivation: A Behavioral Approach*. Cambridge: Cambridge University Press.

Wood, J.V., Heimpel, S.A., Manwell, L.A., & Whittington, E.J. (2009). This mood is familiar and I don't deserve to feel better anyway: Mechanisms underlying self-esteem differences in motivation to repair sad moods. *Journal of Personality and Social Psychology*, 96(2), 363–80.

Wood, R.E. & Locke, E.A. (1990). Goal setting and strategy effects on complex tasks. *Research in Organizational Behavior*, 12, 73–109.

Woodrow, H. (1921). Intelligence and its measurement: A symposium (XI). *Journal of Educational Psychology*, 19, 463–70.

Woodworth, R.S. (1918). *Dynamic Psychology*. New York: Columbia University Press.

Woody, C. & Claridge, G.S. (1977). Psychoticism and thinking. *British Journal of Social Clinical Psychology*, 16, 241–8.

World Health Organization (1992). *International Classification of Diseases, Injuries, and Causes of Death*. Geneva: WHO.

World Health Organization (1993). *International Statistical Classification of Diseases and Related Health Problems* (10th Rev.). Geneva: WHO.

Yerkes, R.M. & Dodson, J.D. (1908). The relation of strength of stimulus to rapidity of habit-formation. *Journal of Comparative Neurology and Psychology*, 18, 459–82.

Yukl, G. (1998). *Leadership in Organizations*. Upper Saddle River, NJ: Prentice Hall.

Yukl, G. & Van Fleet, D.D. (1992). Theory and research on leadership in organizations. In M.D. Dunnette & L.M. Hough (Eds.), *Handbook of Industrial and Organizational Psychology* (Vol. 3, pp. 147–97). Palo Alto, CA: Consulting Psychologists Press.

Zeidner, M. (1998). *Test Anxiety: The State of the Art*. New York: Plenum Press.

Zervas, I.M. & Fink, M. (1992). ECT and delirium in Parkinson's disease. *American Journal of Psychiatry*, 149, 1758.

Zimmerman, M. & Coryell, W. (1989). The reliability of personality disorder diagnoses in a non-patient sample. *Journal of Personality Disorders*, 3, 53–7.

Zuckerman, M. (1991). *Psychobiology of Personality*. Cambridge: Cambridge University Press.

Zuckerman, M. (1994). *Behavioral Expressions and Biosocial Bases of Sensation Seeking*. New York: Cambridge University Press.

Zuckerman, M. (1999). *Vulnerability to Psychopathology: A Biosocial Model*. Washington, DC: American Psychological Association.

Index